Loving Men, Respecting Women:

The Future of Gender Politics

By Tim Goldich

Anima-Animus Publishing / Chicago

Copyright © 2011 by Tim Goldich
This is the revised edition, 2016

All rights reserved,
including the right of reproduction in whole or in part in any form.

Published by Anima-Animus Publishing / Chicago, IL

* * * *

About the cover:

The emphasis is on loving men, respecting women because, historically, men have been more respected but less loved and women have been more loved but less respected.

The scales are all about Balance: the balance that was, the balance that is, the balance that ought to be—the balance between love and respect, female and male.

The reflection is all about my belief that gender reality is mirrored.

Cover designed by Tim Goldich
Cover rendered by Price Thomas and Stephanie Lizabeta.

Text edited by David Shackleton and proofread by Len Nowakowski

ISBN 978-0-9827948-0-7

Table of Contents

Preface v
Foreword viii

Mirror Opposites 1
"Arrows" #1: "The War Against Women" 5
Mirror Opposites 9
Value vs. Validity 17
A Brief First Look at Masculism 19
The Love/Respect Dynamic 25
Blame vs. Accountability 29

The Duality Principle 33
"Just the Facts, Ma'am" 35
The Duality Principle Revisited 43
Female Power 44
"Arrows" #2: The Newsstand 50
Ideological Dictatorship 53
The Shoe Store Analogy 62
Issues Download 67
Issues Download #1 – Health 67
Issues Download #2 – Education 78
Issues Download #3 – Antipathy/Disposability 89
Issues Download #4 – The "Wage Gap" 97
Issues Download #5 – Misandry and "Male Bashing" 119
Issues Download #6 – Reproduction/Parenting: Glass Wall 135
Issues Download #7 – The "Sexual Harassment Industry" 149
Issues Download #8 – Sexual Inequities 158
"Arrows" #3: The Erotic Arena 180
Reality Check: 182
"Arrows" #4: The Donner Party 186
The Battle of Rhetoric 190
Deeper Into the Duality Principal 197
The Global Victim 202

Male Mea Culpa **215**
    Generally Speaking 220
    Nature/Nurture 221
  The Female Shadow: From Gray to Black 227
    Women's Gray Side 230
      Domination vs. Manipulation 230
    The Domestic Realm 237
      Woman Right/Man Wrong 239
      Domestic Sexual Power 242
      "Arrows" #5: Tiger Woods – The Endless Grovel 251
    Investment in Illusion 263
      The Matrisensus 273
    Women's Dark Side 285
      Domestic Violence 285
      Lady Madonna 296
  Protected Innocence 311
    Publicized Crime 312
      Presumed Innocence 318
    "Good Cop/Bad Cop" 322
  Man Demonized - The *Human* Cost 331
    Men, Women, and War 332
      Women in the Military 345
    Balanced Equality 358
      Taxing the "Criminal Gender" 367
      The Honorable Man 371
      "Arrows" #6: "Dumb and Dumber": Glib and More Glib 374
  Conclusion 384
    Afterword 406

Notes **407**
  Index 448

Preface

By Warren Farrell, Ph.D.

If there is a single word that will define a sane future, it is balance. If there is a single word that will describe a method toward achieving balance, it is "listening." In *Loving Men, Respecting Women,* Tim Goldich describes how that listening would work if both men and women listened to each other. And how the balance might look once both men and women have completed the process.

On the surface, it will appear that Goldich spends more time helping us understand men. But once we have completed *Loving Men, Respecting Women* we understand how much better a job we have done understanding women than men. This is counterintuitive because it seems readily apparent that men have had the power and told us what they want and need even as women have adapted and served men's wants and needs.

Goldich guides us to respect that truth for women even as we discover with him the human paradox of gender roles of boys and men's equal-and-opposite truth that to this day is buried. That is, it is also true that virtually every society that survived did so by training its boys to become men by becoming disposable.

Yes, disposable. Disposable in war, or disposable in coal mines in Chile or West Virginia; or as lumberjacks and fishermen risking the perfect storm; or on BP oil rigs run more profitably when corners are cut at the risk of male disposability. How do boys learn to think of it as being powerful by being disposable? From the rewards (the "bribes") of parents, culture, and sex. Think of ice hockey, football, X games... Lots of concussions; lots of applause and sex; lots of heroes.

Boys who did this became men who were respected, and therefore men who earned love. But they earned love by learning that when the going gets tough, the tough get going, not when the going gets tough, the tough go to a therapist. They learned that a prerequisite to thinking of themselves as having power was to repress feelings, not express feelings.

In *Loving Men, Respecting Women,* Goldich tells us about how, as men repressed their feelings, we came to respect men, but not love them. And what is life without love?

Boys learned the only way we could get love is to first gain respect. And we couldn't get that respect reading *Loving Men, Respecting Women* in the unemployment line. So to get love we read business books. We had to become human doings, not human beings. No one encouraged us to discover ourselves. And how much power is there in *not* discovering ourselves?

In the process, boys learn to become men by feeling obligated to earn money someone else spends while they die sooner. A definition very few women are pressured to accept.

The problem is not just in how this hurt men—it is also in how it hurts women who love men. In families with traditional roles, the dad experienced the "fathers' catch-22"—he learned to love his wife and children by being away from the love of his wife and children—by spending long hours at work, traveling, commuting.

Moreover, the very process it took to succeed at work often led to failure in love. For example, he might learn to succeed by self-listening—by listening to himself solving problems in his mind while others presented their problems. Yet when his wife and children presented their problems and sensed their husband or dad was just solving them, they didn't feel heard; they didn't feel compassion; they didn't feel loved. And therefore they tended to respect their dad or husband, but feel less depth of love for him.

In the traditional family, this division of labor led to the division of interests, *Mad Men* style. But as the traditional family has morphed into a family being defined as "anyone who parents and those they parent," a different male-female divide has followed.

Prior to the women's movement, women learned to row the family boat only from the right side (raise children); men, only from the left (raise money). The women's movement helped girls become women who could row from both sides; but without a parallel force for boys, boys became men who had still learned to row only from the left—to only raise money. The problem? If our daughters try to exercise their newfound ability to row from the left, and our sons also row only from the left, the boat goes in circles.

A family boat that goes only in circles is more likely to be sunk by the rocks of recessions. In the past, a man was a family's breadwinner and he might be with one company for life. In the future, advanced technologies make economic change the only constant, increasing the need for a family boat with flexibility—with our sons eventually able to raise children as comfortably as our daughters now raise money.

This is why *Loving Men, Respecting Women* is informed by different paradigms: an understanding that when only one sex wins, both sexes lose; and an understanding that the future is not about a women's movement blaming men, or a men's movement blaming women, but a gender transition movement helping us make a transition from the rigid roles of the past to flexible roles for the future. Goldich's *Loving Men, Respecting Women* will allow us to be a captain of a boat that doesn't go in circles, but that takes us toward a more mutually loving and respectful future.

Warren Farrell, Ph.D.
Author, *The Myth of Male Power*
and *Why Men Are the Way They Are*
Mill Valley, California
October 17, 2010
www.warrenfarrell.com

Foreword

I have a truth to share with you, a truth at once radical and moderate. It is a truth intuitively known but ideologically obscured. It is, I believe, the *one* gender truth to be raised above all others—the one truth that promises to deescalate the Battle of the Sexes replacing resentment, vengeance, and victim with accountability, compassion, and fairness. It is a truth just at the edge of awareness.

And it all begins with love and respect.

As is commonly the case, I grew up respecting and obeying my Dad more than my Mom while loving and appreciating my Mom more than my Dad. When Mom cooked our favorites she received our compliments and our gratitude. We came to the dinner table *hungry!* And she gave us sustenance we could not live without. Mom served us our meals, one of life's fundamentals at the very heart of family as well as religious, holiday, and other social gatherings.

When Dad did his giving, he did so in an office somewhere miles away where we could neither see nor fully appreciate it. I directly experienced what Mom was giving, but it often seemed as though Dad gave nothing. Growing up loving our mothers and resenting our fathers is more than just a matter of cultural cliché. It is, I think, the murky origin of a gender bias *deeply* internalized.

Have you ever considered a true and deep empathy toward fathers? What's at risk in directing culture-wide *love* toward men in general and fathers in particular? And why will so many of us react with derision at the very thought?

Did you know that on Mother's Day, more phone calls are made than on any other holiday, more than on Christmas Day and far more than on Father's Day. Father's Day, in contrast, is the day on which we make the largest number of *collect* calls.[a] If we love Mom and Dad equally then why do we buy and send half again as many Mother's Day cards as Father's Day cards?[b]

---

[a] See http://www.snopes.com/holidays/fathersday/collect.asp, "We Love You - Call Collect," May 21, 2006, "While Mother's Day is the biggest holiday for phone calls . . . Historically, more collect calls are made on Father's Day than on any other day of the year."

[b] See Mary Batten, "The Psychology of Fatherhood," Time.com, June 07, 2007, http://www.time.com/time/magazine/article/0,9171,1630551,00.html, "The folks at Hallmark are going to have a very good day on June 17. That's when more than 100 million of the company's ubiquitous cards will be given to the 66 million dads across the U.S. in observation of Father's Day. Such a blizzard of paper may be short of the more than 150 million cards sold for

It would seem that many of us grow up respecting our fathers, but not necessarily *loving* (empathizing with) our fathers. Likewise, many of us grow up loving our mothers, but not necessarily *respecting* our mothers. At least in part, this disparity in love and respect derive from the roles we play. Clearly, the husband role of protector/provider lends itself to being respected, while the wife role of lover/nurturer better lends itself to being loved. Now, of course, it doesn't *always* work this way—but, within the traditional model at least, it worked this way more often than not.

In serving our meals we could say that Mom was being "servile," *or* we could say that cooking and serving our meals was one of the ways in which Mom placed herself at the center of our affections. In "bringing home the bacon" we could say that Dad was being "dominant," *or* we could say that working long hours to earn his family's love was one of the ways in which Dad was separated from his family's love. Upon close examination, I believe we'll find that *every* gender reality has this same dual nature.

At home, Mom was as loving, giving, nurturing, and omnipresent as Dad was demanding, rule-enforcing, cranky, and absent. My emotional dependence on Mom was obvious and absolute. It was she who washed us, fed us, tended to our bruises, and taught us right from wrong. Within the mother/child glow we experienced a world of unconditional love. Yes, we were financially dependent upon Dad, but what does that mean to a child?

In our infancy did we experience Dad as he who suffered the slings and arrows, making it possible for mother and child to live within a nexus of love and safety? Or, did we experience Dad as he who competed for and often usurped our mother's love?

Every hour Dad devoted to earning his family's love left him with one fewer hour in which to *be* with his family's love. His work persona, so functional at work, was often *dys*functional at home. "I can't understand it," he said to me once. "I communicate so well with my young employees; why can't I communicate with you?" It's easy to get disgusted with Dad. "I'm your son, not your employee," I thought to myself. But how was Dad supposed to know about parenting?

Our dads didn't grow up playing with dolls, playing house, and babysitting. The male culture our dads grew up in did *nothing* to prepare them for the role of parenting.

I was born before 1970, which means that I was born at a time when fathers were not even *allowed* in the delivery room. Fathers got

---

Mother's Day, but it's still quite a tribute. What's less clear is whether dads—at least as a group—have done a good enough job to deserve the honor."

shut out right from the start. The anesthesiologist could be there. The family doctor could be there. A man with some *practical* value could be there. But, apparently, husbands/fathers, having no practical value in the delivery room, were only thought of as a nuisance with no value at all. Only wives/mothers were encouraged to think of their nurturing and empathy as valuable gifts to be shared.

Fathers have many such stories to tell: Father listens to the sounds of his child playing outside. The child slips and falls. Father hears crying sounds running for the front door. His heart goes out to his child. But the child runs past his father's open arms and into the arms of his mother instead. The child seeks comfort from the parent he loves most. In keeping with the male code, father does his best to keep his pain invisible, yet he is wounded nonetheless. It hurts to be loved second best. Is it any wonder if, from that day on, Dad begins to hide behind his newspaper? Is it any wonder if Dad begins spending more time at work, where he feels functional, and less time at home, where he feels dysfunctional?

Perhaps if we men better understood our father's inner experience, we'd have more empathy toward our fathers. And if we can have more empathy toward our fathers, then perhaps we can have more empathy toward ourselves.

Dad *did* give something. Among other things, my dad gave 40 years of long days that he counted down till retirement from a job that he *hated*. He might have taken a more enjoyable job that paid less; but that would not have been in keeping with his role as provider. Though he ended up spending more time at work than at home, there on his desk amid the folders and the memos were pictures of his family. There, under a sheet of glass covering his desk, was a poem I had written in the 4th grade.

What he did, he did for us. We might have thanked him more and blamed him less for not "being there for us." He was over there at work for us. Looking back on it, perhaps it was we who were not there for him—to lend an ear to his fears, to love and support him.

In some cases, a dark day of reckoning arrives in which such a man may come to see his life in pursuit of respect as having been "all for nothing." "Yes," he says to himself, "I was respected. I may have been obeyed, admired, and rewarded with authority, status, and titles, but I was never loved. Out of the blue, I awoke one day to be served divorce papers. I still love my wife, but she does not love me. And my children, to the extent they even know me, don't love me either. "Visitation" left me effectively shut out. I did it all for them, yet I lost them all. In desperation I turned to my brethren for solace and support, but following some perfunctory remarks ('Keep your chin up,' 'Hang in there, buddy'), there was nothing. Men don't love men. Father's Days come and go without a card or a call. I was never loved. It was all for nothing."

Similarly, a dark day may come when a woman comes to see her life in pursuit of love as having been "all for nothing." "Yes," she says to herself, "I was loved. I may have been adored, protected, financially supported, and showered with gifts, Mother's Day cards, and other affections, but even my women friends never really took me seriously. I took the central place in the emotional lives of our children, but I awoke one day to find my children grown and gone away. I never really achieved intellectually or creatively. I accomplished nothing with my life. I was never respected. It was all for nothing."

Historically, this love/respect dynamic has lived at the very core of gender polarity. And in our tendency to respect women less than men and love men less than women, it is also the primary basis of legitimate gender complaint. But here's the thing, the lack of love toward men begets a lack of empathy toward men. Society's challenge in all this is to concern itself with the issues afflicting men, at a time when society doesn't care to empathize with the men themselves.

Both love and respect are abundantly rewarding in some ways, yet each is lacking certain *essentials*. For their lives to be fulfilling, women need to be both loved *and* respected, and for *their* lives to be fulfilling, men need to be both respected *and* loved.

The gender system can be improved. The sexes can negotiate these improvements under a unified banner without resorting to resentment, vengeance or victimhood. *One* truth above all others leads the sexes down a golden path away from destructive battle and toward healthy negotiation, mutual understanding, and fairness.

So what is this wondrous truth that can do such wondrous things? Simply this:

It All Balances Out

Part One

Mirror Opposites
The LOVE/RESPECT Dynamic

Loving Men, Respecting Women
(The book in a nutshell)

The overarching principle that pervades and unifies every aspect of my book can be expressed in a single word: Balance. In defiance, the book's "radical" premise is simply this: in the benefits enjoyed and in the liabilities suffered, in the power and in the victimization, in the freedoms and the constraints, the good and the bad, It All Balances Out between Woman and Man—and it always has.

Historically, the gender system has certainly been less than perfect, inflicting injustices on both sexes alike. But these injustices have come out even. Ours has been an imperfect yet essentially balanced gender system, except for one thing—the highly *im*balanced gender *belief* system. If I could, I would shift our entire gender belief system away from feminism's MalePower/FemaleVictimization paradigm and toward a balanced gender paradigm.

As it stands, there's an assumption of imbalance—an "imbalance" of power enjoyed by men and an "imbalance" of victimization suffered by women. That's the story we make up, but that has *never* been more than half of the full story. The missing half can be found. It's contained within a shelf full of excellent but as yet rather obscure books. The female power/male victimization half of the story remains obscure because neither sex wants to hear it. Nevertheless, for every female complaint, there *is* a mirror-opposite male complaint. For every one CEO there've been many POWs.[1] Hard/hazardous labor, battlefields, prisons, mines, the streets, the sewers—men have always occupied both extremes, the most *and the least* enviable positions on earth—the latter in far greater numbers than the former.

Imagine, if you will, a gigantic scale with love on one end of the balance beam and respect on the other:

Mirror Opposites

This love/respect dynamic upon which gender balance pivots can be described in two brief statements:

Throughout history, both sexes have tended to respect men more than women.

Throughout history, both sexes have tended to love women more than men.

Feminism has rightly protested women's lesser status in all things along the respect axis. Both sexes have listened and both sexes have done much to change the cultural environment in ways that promote respect for women. That men are less loved, however, may ring true from the outset yet be met with cynicism just the same. Both sexes receive the female side with empathy and the male side without empathy exactly *because* both sexes love women more and men less.

Hostility, when directed at *women,* is given a pejorative label—"misogyny." We give it this very negative label because hostility toward *women* is forbidden. Arguably, our culture leans more toward misandry (hostility toward men). But few know this word misandry—a word that would *condemn* hostility toward men the same way the word misogyny condemns hostility toward women. Our lack of love toward men is so pervasive as to be invisible, and we concern ourselves with it so little that we don't even have a word for it.

Balance is revealed in the following four key statements:

One: At birth, members of both sexes are assigned roles, socialization, and conditioning that facilitate and ensure a world in which men are more respected/less loved and women are more loved/less respected.

Two: Historically, men have been no more empowered to escape their biology, role, socialization, conditioning, and concurrent fate than women have.

Three: The two sexes, equally powerless and equally powerful, have plied an equal overall force of influence in the molding of our world, and are thus equally responsible for outcomes.

Four: Throughout history, the enormous consequences and vast repercussions suffered by women for being less respected have been matched in full by the enormous consequences and vast repercussions suffered by men for being less loved.

These four statements are key, because taken together they lead inexorably to the one key truth: *It All Balances Out!*

Last year, while at a Christmas Eve party, I was asked what my book on gender was all about. "It All Balances Out between men and women," I said. "*What* balances out?" "Everything," I said: "the power, the victimization; the freedoms, the constraints; the joys, the sorrows; the good and the bad, the whole thing."

So, there I was, trapped in the kitchen with a half dozen women good naturedly ready to pounce. "I'm . . . going to go over there," I said, pointing to the dining room—a tactical retreat that drew a laugh. But, not long after, the hostess walked over, fixed me with a look and said, "You're probably right."

The truths of Balance stand in such direct contradiction to the *official* gender belief system that they may be taken for an "outrage." So it's telling I think that, *un*officially, these truths are so often met with a shrug—a shrug that says: "That sounds about right." In my experience, on a purely intuitive level, the truths of Balance ring true.

With sufficient courage, the case for Balance is convincingly made. Because these truths *are* true, as we'll see, these truths are well supported by the facts, which is why I can make my case well. Indeed, I intend to do so, because I firmly believe that a culture-wide understanding and perception of this Balance I speak of forms the *only* path leading to the full restoration and preservation of love and respect between the sexes.

Balancing out the "official" gender belief system, *that* is my goal; *that* is what this book is all about.

We've learned to take seriously the need to better respect women. But our lack of love for men *itself* blinds us to the need to be equally understanding and sympathetic when it comes to the issues and inequities of men. If average ordinary men were empowered enough, enlightened enough, and courageous enough to speak to what truly lives in their minds and in their hearts, doubtless a new gender ideology based on fairness, maturity, and sanity would soon replace the escalating "Battle of the Sexes" insanity wherein we now stand bewildered.

The goal ultimately is an equalist movement that would combine the concerns of men and women under one banner. But first, men must distract themselves from the business of rescuing women long enough to begin dealing with their own issues *and the issues of their less fortunate brethren*. Both sexes must forgo the illusion of "superman." Men must speak their vulnerable truth, and women must listen. Only then can the gender politics of the future be built upon an even foundation.

"Arrows" #1: "The War Against Women"

Now and then, throughout the book, we will dig deep into *emotion*. Now and then we'll stop and ponder "arrows."

"Arrows" come in many forms and fly in all directions. Everyone's a target. Some "arrows" irk and sting like pinpricks. Some enrage and embitter like spears through the heart. "Arrows" are insults heard in conversation, in jokes, and in the media; or seen in writing and cultural imagery; or experienced in the form of attitudes, laws, and policies. People in general and women in particular and feminists in the extreme seem well aware of every "sexist," "male-chauvinist," "misogynist" insult they encounter—so much so that a "patriarchal" world that denigrates, subjugates, and wages "war" upon women is, in many circles, accepted as gospel.

"I remain fully cognizant," says feminist author Phyllis Chesler, "of the continuing war against women."[2] Indeed, in my perusal of feminist literature, that sentiment echoes throughout. An author I admire concurs: "The assumption that women must defend themselves against an enemy who is waging an undeclared war against them," says Christina Hoff Sommers, "has by now achieved the status of conventional feminist wisdom."[3]

It is feminist, but is it wisdom? If Man, the one with *the* power, has been waging war and presumably pummeling powerless Woman, *the* victim, how is it then that, according to virtually every measure of wellbeing, women enjoy steady ascent while men endure steady decline? I have to wonder if what feminism perceives as a "war against women" is but a projection of feminism's war against men. What if Man and Woman are evenly matched? Might *Woman* sometimes be the competitive, ambitious aggressor?

The Battle of the Sexes has often been called "a battle in which only one side showed up." Given that there's feminism on the one hand, and on the other hand there's nothing, do I really need specify which sex did *not* show up? Masculinity, as I know and experience it internally, is invested in protecting women. When I receive the message that Man is waging war against Woman, I feel it like an "arrow" piercing my heart. What if it was the male sex that failed to "show up" for the Battle of the Sexes exactly because Man is at heart chivalrously *incapable* of inflicting battle upon Woman?

After more than 20 years of intensive study I still find the vagaries of gender extraordinarily enigmatic, perplexing, astonishing—and as yet, I think, poorly understood. Gender is indeed an endlessly fascinating subject to ponder and explore. But, can feminism be trusted to explore the subject fairly, evenly, and without bias? Are we exploring the territory in its *entirety,* or are we only exploring gender within the bounds that political correctness allows? Is our belief in a world comprised of male power/female victimization guided purely by fact and logic? Or, is our collective understanding of gender reality mostly an illusion sustained by ideological bias, sentiment, movie imagery, instinct, eroticism, narrow focus, and superficial differences in the physical appearance and vocal characteristics of men and women?

I see feminism's truths; of course I do. *And,* I see a whole other world of truth as seen from the politicized *male* perspective. In offering up the truths of female power and male victimization, masculism (a word not recognized by my Microsoft Word 2010) offers those truths most of us find rather disconcerting (if not downright repugnant)—which is why these are the truths that are *missing.*

Feminism works emotion; in this essay I will respond in kind. I imagine myself falling through the air, legs spread wide. I land on a two-by-four plank of wood. My testicles are crushed; my agony, indescribable. I now imagine an audience erupting with laughter. At times, that's how it *feels* to be male. That's how it *feels* looking up at the movie screen where a good swift kick in the balls is *guaranteed* to get a laugh. Aware women feel the sting of cultural "arrows" aimed at their femininity. Similarly aware men are few, but for those rare men not laughing along with everyone else, the sound of a packed theater laughing at this uniquely male pain can sting almost as much as the swift kick itself. Here's some more pure **emotion**:

Let's pretend. Let's free our minds to wild flights of fantasy. Let's imagine that we *love* men. Love *men?!* Did I hear you right, you ask? Isn't that like loving violent, selfish, ugly, crude, egoistic, baby-seal-clubbing, species-exterminating rapists of the earth? *Love* them? If loving men seems outrageous, don't worry—we're just *pretending.*

Take a moment to consider the WWI soldier boy who, upon witnessing mustard gas eating away the faces and genitals of his friends, runs away in horror only to be placed in front of a firing squad and shot dead for "cowardice."[4] Are the assumptions of a male paradise of patriarchal power and privilege truly unassailable? Spare a thought for Sam Legg. He refuses to live out the myth of the monstrous male killing other men on a WWII battlefield. To avoid the horrors of imprisonment, he jumps the grueling hurdles needed to achieve conscientious objector status. To assuage his uniquely male guilt and deflect taunts of "draft dodger" and "coward," he joins 200 other conscientious objectors for a starvation experiment that, six months in, torments him to such madness he takes an ax and chops off the middle three fingers of his left hand.[5] To avoid being branded a "quitter," he successfully begs to continue starving till the end. How might it deepen and enrich our understandings of gender if scenarios like *that* were studied in Women's Studies classrooms?

Consider the worker whose right arm is chewed off attending to heavy machinery (the only family-supporting wage he could find). Can we find no room in our hearts for hard/hazardous laborers? Consider the father laid waste by false accusation: his home, his family, his children taken from him, his reputation destroyed. What would it be like to *care* about that? Consider the prisoner, his bleeding rectum stretched open with a broom handle prior to gang rape. Can our compassion extend even to soldiers, workers, fathers, and prisoners? What if the pain and powerlessness of soldiers, workers, fathers, prisoners, miners, POWs, experimental test subjects, bums, laborers, et al., were re-understood as the pain and powerlessness of *men?*

Consider the 14-year-old boy raped by an adult woman—the court reacts by ordering the boy to pay his rapist child support.[6] Consider the man forced to exchange seats with a woman because the man (i.e., presumed pedophile) happens to have been seated next to an unattended child—according to airline policy the plane will *not* take off until he complies.[7] Focused as we are on the plight of girls and women, are we neglecting something? Rather than *assume* female powerless victimization, what if we were so un-chivalrous as to make an actual side-by-side *comparison?* What if the far greater cultural outpouring of stories and stats regarding female victimization is only indicative of our far greater *empathy* toward female suffering?

What if *male* pain mattered? What's at risk if we were to distract ourselves from the realities of female pain and powerlessness just long enough to take our first serious look at the *male* experience of pain and powerlessness? That is not a rhetorical question. Directing equal caring, concern, and compassion toward men changes *everything*. Is society prepared to deal with those changes?

Let's pretend. Let's free our minds to flights of fantasy. Let's imagine that we respect women. No, I mean *really* respect women, not as passive powerless pawns and perpetual victims, but as powerful participants, ultimately *equal partners* in the vast gender dance that molds our human world. What if power is not something Woman will have in the future, but something Woman possesses *now?* (Remember, it's OK, we're just pretending.)

If women are such powerless "chattel," why don't we send the chattel sex in for military slaughter, hazardous labor, and imprisonment by the millions? Unless, of course, that's exactly what we do. So, we're to believe that Woman being "powerless" plied *no* force of influence, no force of influence *of any kind,* in setting up and maintaining a gender system that helps to insulate her from the dark side of the world and human nature as well as most of the deepest dangers and horrors of this world?

In the U.S., women now comprise the majority of the workforce, including a slight majority of all management and professional positions.[8] Women claim 57.5 percent of bachelor's degrees and 61 percent of master's degrees, and control the majority of the nation's private wealth.[9] If women are truly powerless, how exactly did all these reversals come about? Beauty/sexual/intimacy power, moral authority power, motherhood power, majority-vote power, a power greater than that of men to inflict shame and elicit empathy; what would it be like to recognize female power as different from male power—generally more covert and subjective in nature—but no less *real* for that?

What if we acknowledged and *respected* women's power? What if we extricated women from a faction of humanity known collectively as "innocent women-and-children"? Can we allow ourselves to pretend that women are not innocent equals-of-children, but rather full-grown *adults* possessing, among other things, adult greed, aggression, and weaponry? What if feminism's effect in the world was not entirely righteous? Not entirely benevolent? What if feminism was subject to large-scale, *official* debate and critique?

What's at risk if we were to distract ourselves from the realities of male power and influence just long enough to take our first serious look at female power and influence? That is not a rhetorical question. Directing equal accountability, responsibility, and respect toward women changes *everything*. Is society prepared to deal with those changes?

If you believe as I do that truth and fairness are profoundly important for their own sake, and living a lie—no matter how seductive that lie may be—comes at too high a price; come along with me on this journey of discovery.

Come on, this is going to be fun!

I invite you to leave the flat earth of MalePower/FemaleVictimization on the shelf for a moment. Rise higher; rise enough to take in a more rounded view. In the lingo of *The Matrix*, I invite you to take the "red pill." Wake up from what you're *supposed* to believe . . . wake up to gender *reality*.

Mirror Opposites

> Because of the inner pressure to constantly affirm his dominance and masculinity, he continues to act as if he can stand up under, fulfill, and even enjoy all the expectations placed on him no matter how contradictory and devitalizing they are. It's time to remove the disguises of privilege and reveal the male condition for what it is. – Herb Goldberg[10]

> Fear of limiting the power of the sex with the greater spending power, the greater beauty power, the greater sexual power, the greater net worth among its heads of households, and the greater options in marriage, children, work, and life creates the corruptness of absolute power which will ultimately lead to a much bloodier battle between the sexes. – Warren Farrell[11]

Throughout this book we will be trekking through some unfamiliar territory, territory only recently opened by the likes of Herb Goldberg and Warren Farrell quoted above. For some, what these authors have to say may be so unlike, so contrary to what they've heard before as to seem unfathomable.

They are spokespersons for a field of thought known as masculism. For his deep psychological analysis and insight, I nominate Herb Goldberg for the title of father of modern masculism; and for his masterful research, cultural analysis, and politicized vision, I nominate Warren Farrell for the title of architect of modern masculism. They, along with many other important figures in this new field of thought, will become familiar as they are referred to throughout the course of this book. Perhaps one day, their names will be as well-known as those of their famous feminist counterparts. But for now, their names are as obscure as the realm they're exploring.

It's an upsetting, off-putting realm from which we all, male and female alike, tend to turn away. Yet, it is a realm we will be seeing and hearing more of in the years to come because the world has changed, and men, never quite the privileged sex they were made out to be, are experiencing an ever-diminishing place in this changing world.

But masculism, as I practice it, is not about placing men on the ever-growing list of victims. It is about taking women *off* that list—largely because self-identifying as victims is psychologically self-fulfilling. And, as we will see, in the Big Picture, women don't properly belong on the list of victims anyway. Not because women haven't been victims, but because, in the big picture, men and women have always been "victims" (if that's how you want to look at it) in equal measure. We generally don't know that yet, but it is my fervent hope that one day we will. Forever keeping women on the list of victims may serve a feminism determined to live forever, but I believe the feminist rhetoric that keeps women victims (in our cultural perception) is wreaking havoc with the constructive functioning of gender politics and the sexes' ability to love each other and remain united in their common humanity.

Nor is this about stifling women's issues. It is about replacing the one-sided sexual politics of *fem*inism with a new *two*-sex sexual politics. It is about placing women's issues within a sexual-political framework that includes men's issues—a framework which will ultimately be more effective at providing solutions to women's issues, as well as men's issues.

I believe that, within ordinary human experience, there is an essential duality. In all things there is light and shadow, gain and loss, gift and burden, positive and negative, yin and yang. If "There's no such thing as a free lunch," then there's no such thing as a positive without an accompanying negative. If "Every dark cloud has a silver lining," then every negative comes with an accompanying positive.

Feminism has eyes like an eagle when it comes to spotting the positives within the male experience and the negatives within the female experience. But it's blind as a bat when it comes to the opposite: the positives within the female experience and the negatives within the male experience.

Says feminist Natalie Angier, "Men in groups are said to 'reek of testosterone,' to be 'poisoned by testosterone,' to be 'cauldrons of testosterone.' It sounds cute, it sounds clever . . ."[12] Actually, it sounds just as biased and bigoted to me as would talk of reeking, poisoned cauldrons of estrogen. But a feminist sees no sexism inflicted upon men. A feminist sees Man's power, but not his victimization, and sees Woman's victimization, but not her power.

Beauty is "burden;" motherhood is "sacrifice." Read book after book of feminism and it can seem as if nothing in women's lot in life is positive—nothing at all.

What is feminism? Given that the "fem" in *fem*inism stands for female (or feminine); feminism is "female-ism" (or "feminine-ism"). When expanded to full length, the word may no longer seem so egalitarian, but in drawing it out, I have merely taken what was implicit in the word and made it explicit. On a fundamental level, feminism is, and has always been, female-ism.

Complexities abound, yet feminism is most accurately characterized as a political movement, an ideology, and a cultural force that advocates for females and females *only*. Clearly, an equity "female-ist" is a contradiction in terms. If there were such things as "black-ists" and "white-ists," the divisive nature of the labels would be self-evident. And no one would be taken in by someone who claimed to be an "equity" white-ist.

But, is it fair to characterize feminism as *one* thing? Aren't there many different *kinds* of feminist and feminism? Well, yes, of course, and . . . no. Feminism *is* one thing in the sense that it is one word. And it is that word itself that identifies the central problem.

Initially, as a *philosophy* of gender, feminism made vital contributions. It introduced us to the concept of gender-as-politics, and got us thinking about gender equality and "The personal is the political." But, as an ongoing *system* of gender politics, the divisive flaw in feminism is built into its very *name* and thus into its very *nature*. As compared with the far more inclusive, less biased term **equalism**, I consider *all* feminism-as-gender-politics to be fundamentally wrong-headed.

Of course, there are feminists who sincerely seek true equality. But until one has become versed in masculism—that is to say, until one has come to know the politicized perspectives of men as well as of women—one cannot know what *true* equality is.

There are certain individuals who call themselves feminists who have indeed come to know the politicized perspectives of *both* sexes and who *do* seek *true* gender equality. They are, of course, free to label themselves as they please. But to my mind, those who see and understand the issues of both sexes equally and advocate accordingly are better understood as *equalists*, not female-ists.

Who will deny that true gender equality is best sought under a gender-neutral banner (which female-ism most assuredly is not)? I advocate replacing feminism with what I'll call equalism, a sexual politics that would continue to address any and all female issues; it just wouldn't address female issues *exclusively*.

And what is "sexual politics"? Sexual politics (a.k.a. gender politics) may be simply defined as the politics of gender complaint. To whatever degree that men refuse to complain (especially on a political level), men will continue to have little presence in the realm of sexual *politics* (wherein there is feminism on the one hand and on the other hand there is nothing). It is widely assumed that men have the dominant voice. Well, in some realms they do; but, in gender politics they do not. Men, speaking out of their own politicized *male* point of view, have had almost no voice at all. Lacking a politicized perspective to call their own, men's issues have remained non-issues.

Isn't it time we had a sexual politics that gives voice to both sexes?

Feminism is generally regarded as the female perspective, but it is something more specific than that. It is the female perspective *politicized*. It is a *learned* perspective derived from "consciousness raising."

To be even more specific, feminism is the female perspective derived from focusing only on the positives for men—never the negatives for men—and focusing only on the negatives for women, never the positives for women. Women whose feminist perspective has them seeing only a male heaven and a female hell will, naturally, come to feel angry and victimized. This is a *politicized* perspective in that it maximizes discontent within its female constituency, thus maximizing the emotional fuel (anger) needed to sustain a political movement (the feminist movement).

From Marx to Mao, political movements begin in this manner. Anger, even rage is generated because complacent people don't take time out of their busy schedules to write books, march and rally, pamphleteer and protest. Only angry people find the time and motivation to write angry letters, campaign, and persuade their friends. By raising only female awareness, only female discontent was raised to the level needed to bring about the Women's Movement. Thus feminism has stood *alone* as a powerful instrument of gender-political change.

Inarguably, some of this change has been for the better. Men as well as women are relieved to have the constraints of strict gender roles relaxed. But "female-ism" cannot be expected to bring about change that is evenhanded to both sexes. While change wrought by a political movement may be for the good, the rage, negative outlook, victim mindset, and yearning for vengeance are not. Worse still is the standard practice of unifying a political constituency by identifying a common enemy. Where feminism is concerned, The Enemy (he who is waging "the war against women") is Man.

The primary justification for feminism in the absence of masculism lies in the false assumption that all inequities of any consequence that have been suffered in the world have been suffered by females. This is the faulty rationale that has us equating women with blacks and according women the same "victim" status and cultural reparations (affirmative action, Title IX, quota systems, etc.) accorded blacks. Again, because we believe that the female experience of victimization and powerlessness vastly exceeds the male experience of victimization and powerlessness, we believe that females have a special need for and special entitlement to their own special "ism"—female-ism.

But comparing conditions for blacks vs. whites in our culture against conditions for women vs. men in our culture is comparing apples with oranges. As compared to someone born white, someone born black is far more likely to be born into low socioeconomic conditions. As compared to someone born male, someone born female is not at all more likely to be born into low socioeconomic conditions. By infinite contrast with blacks—*and* as compared with *men*—women enjoy longer life expectancy, majority vote, higher rates of college graduation and consumer spending, lower rates of suicide and homelessness, plus relative immunity to hard/hazardous labor, imprisonment, and battlefields. As will become clear in due course, this comparison—which author Carol Iannone aptly labels "the unspeakably dishonest comparison of women with blacks"—is a *false* comparison.[13]

This book takes the position that Woman suffers nothing worse than her own particular version of the human condition. More shocking still, my next book will argue that Woman has *never* suffered anything worse than her own particular version of the human condition.

This book is the first in a four-book series. The next three books are: *Love and Respect in the Past, Love and Respect in the Present,* and *Love and Respect in the Future*. This book, book one, confines itself to the "modern" era. Book two explores Balance as manifested throughout history. Book three explores current gender issues in further detail and book four extrapolates upon current trends and predicts how the future may unfold *with* an understanding of Balance or, conversely, how the future may unfold with*out* an understanding of Balance.

But, if it does all balance out and always has, why then are we so insistent that women suffer more? The many and varied reasons why **MalePower/FemaleVictimization** looms large in our perception while FemalePower/MaleVictimization is something we must strain to see will occupy us throughout the entire series of books. For now, suffice it to say that it all comes down to the love/respect dynamic. Female pain is more prominent in our perceptions largely because female pain tugs at our hearts more. Thus, female pain expands within our hearts until it is perceived to eclipse male pain. For this reason, only female concerns have been raised to the level of major *societal* concerns. Only female pain elicits the requisite levels of caring and compassion.

In short, the assumption that Woman suffers all the worst of it is an assumption based on greater *empathy* toward women, which itself is based on our greater *love* of women.

We can choose to view each male and each female behavior under a light that is either sympathetic or unsympathetic. As we'll see, because we tend to love women more and men less, female attitudes and behaviors more often receive an *empathy interpretation* while male attitudes and behaviors more often receive an *antipathy interpretation*. One interpretation may contain as much truth as the other, but one is positive; the other is negative.

Loving women more and men less results in an anti-male bias that may be summed up in two rules we will encounter throughout the book: the Zero-Empathy-Toward-Men rule and the All-Fault-Is-Male rule. Taken together, these biases, among others, conjure up the MalePower/FemaleVictimization (MP/FV) and the ManBad/WomanGood (MB/WG) paradigms—one-sided and therefore false paradigms that underlie our sexual-political belief system.

This belief system—embraced by both sexes—is Man's greatest enemy. Indirectly, it is doing Woman great damage also. And because the sexes are so tightly interlinked, doing damage to one sex will do damage to both sexes in any case. Accordingly, this book is divided into three main sections. Section one (*Mirror* Opposites) lays the theoretical groundwork. Section two (The Duality Principle) takes on the MalePower/FemaleVictimization paradigm. Section three (Male Mea Culpa) takes on the ManBad/WomanGood paradigm.

The falseness of the MP/FV-MB/WG belief system can only be revealed through a clear and extensive presentation of its mirror-opposite: FemalePower/MaleVictimization (FP/MV) and WomanBad/ManGood (WB/MG). When the truths of FP/MV and WB/MG are fully revealed and understood, the higher realization—that It All Balances Out—becomes clear.

When we come to the realization that Man experiences his own particular version of powerless victimization (the human condition) in equal measure with Woman, we realize that Woman is not specially entitled to her own special "ism," nor is she entitled to her own special women-only liberation movement. When the falseness of the underlying assumptions is grasped, then the selfish self-righteousness inherent in female-ism is revealed.

I think it's important to say this bluntly because only then is Woman invited to "take it like a man," be accountable like a man, and take her *true* place, not as a powerless pawn *of* the system, but rather as powerful participant *in* the system. If Woman is ever to be as respected as Man, she must give up "victim" power.

If, as I believe, respect is what Woman lacks and desires most in our world, then equalism—with its emphasis on Woman as *equal partner*—is her ally, and feminism—with its emphasis on Woman as *the* powerless victim—is what stands in her way. An equal partner is someone we can respect; a self-proclaimed "victim" is not.

The realization of balance will serve *both* sexes. Since emotional reality is what we make of it, what Woman *most* needs liberating from is the one-sided image of herself as "uniquely" powerless and victimized—an emotionally self-fulfilling image fashioned and enforced by feminist ideology. Masculist ideology would show her all the ways in which Man experiences victimization thus freeing Woman from the internalized image of herself as *the* victim.

Likewise, masculism would enlighten Woman to all the ways in which Man experiences powerlessness and all the ways in which Man experiences Woman as power*ful*. Rather than suffer the feminist view of her heritage as "property" and "chattel," Woman's self-esteem can only benefit from the truer and more balanced view of herself as coequal cohort in the creation of our human world.

The positive outcome of feminism lies in its valid observations of MalePower/FemaleVictimization. The negative outcome of feminism lies in the false assumptions and conclusions drawn from those valid but one-sided observations. Feminism must be credited with adding vital information with regard to MP/FV to our culture's overall enlightenment. But our admiration for feminism's many achievements may be tempered when we realize that an equalist movement could have brought all that same information to our attention while simultaneously bringing to our attention the equal-opposite truths of FemalePower/MaleVictimization.

If, instead of a feminist movement, we had had a gender-transition movement, we would know all the truths we now know about MP/FV *and* we would also know all the truths of FP/MV we have yet to recognize. If we had come to know the politicized perspectives of both men and women *simultaneously*, we could have enlightened ourselves without making Woman *the* victim and without making Man *the* enemy.

A short-lived masculist movement could soon have us seeing gender reality in a balanced way. Then, having served its purpose, both masculism and feminism may best be phased out in favor of a gender-neutral equalist movement.

So long as feminists succeed in equating feminism with women, however, we will believe that to be anti-feminism is to be anti-woman, which is to be in the wrong, pure and simple. But women and feminism are *not* the same thing. Women are people; feminism is a political ideology. Moreover, I judge this political ideology to be power-hungry, victim-mongering, corrupt, slanderous toward men, female chauvinist and quite indifferent to truth and justice. For all these reasons, I proclaim myself anti-feminist. And I do so without apology.

Because I stand on such very thin ice of political *in*correctness, I want to be very clear about this. I have nothing against sexual politics. I have nothing against sexual politics from the female perspective. I have nothing against women seeking political fairness for themselves. I have nothing against an equalist movement in which women's issues (alongside men's issues) may be argued and redressed. I stand specifically against feminism, a political movement and ideology that has fallen deep into shadow.

If all that weren't enough, I believe that feminism often operates in a manner antithetical to its own stated goals. The day that feminism succeeds in fulfilling its goals is the day feminism loses its reason for being and feminists are left bereft of the fervent cause that sustains them. Therefore, on some hidden level, feminism knows that it must never *appear* to succeed. In my vast readings of feminist literature I've encountered no instances of a feminist anticipating a day when the feminist movement has accomplished its agenda and has, therefore, come to an *end*. It would seem that, to feminists, feminism is forever.

Incredible as it may seem, the truths of masculism, not feminism, hold the key to true gender justice. Not because the truths of masculism are greater than the truths of feminism, but because the truths of masculism are the truths that are *missing*.

MalePower/FemaleVictimization is the half of the story we all know. It's the story we've all been taught. It fits with emotion and instinct and chivalry and sentiment and Eros. It fits with the physiognomy (physical appearance) of the sexes and it resonates in the stories told in the media and in the mythos. But it fits only *half* of all human *reality*. It fits with the public world of CEOs and senators, but it fails in the private world of intimacy, vulnerable emotion, and parenting. It fits with our focus upon the tip of the success pyramid, but it falls apart when we refocus upon the vast *base* of the pyramid and the soldiers, POWs, convicts, laborers, and the homeless found therein.

FemalePower/MaleVictimization is and has always been the other, untold half of the story, the half that we don't know and don't *want* to know. Nevertheless, should we come to the realization that MP/FV is equaled by FP/MV, we will be knocking at the door of the single most important truth in the entire realm of sexual politics –

It All Balances Out.

Study the issues, the complaints, the stereotypes, the biases, the inequities of both sexes long enough and, eventually, you must come to only one conclusion. In the benefits enjoyed and in the liabilities suffered; in the gifts and in the burdens; in the advantages and in the disadvantages; in the power and in the victimization; in the joys and sorrows; the freedoms and constraints, it has all been split just about 50-50 between men and women. With that understanding, the lines on the sexual-political battlegrounds are, if not dissolved entirely, at least softened considerably.

Value vs. Validity

As a statement, It All Balances Out may be evaluated according to two factors, *value* and *validity*. The *value* derives from whatever beneficial influence a belief in Balance may effect in the world. The *validity* depends upon the quantity and quality of truth the statement contains.

This book is dedicated primarily to arguing the essential *validity*; even so, at this early juncture I'd like to make a case for the *value* of It All Balances Out. At the outset, I wish to express something of what I believe the world stands to gain out of shifting our gender belief system away from the MalePower/FemaleVictimization paradigm and toward a balanced gender paradigm.

It's funny but, I'm often asked: If it all balances out, then what's the *problem?* The assumption would seem to be that a balanced system is the same as a perfect system. But, as I see it, women suffer injustice along the respect axis, men suffer injustice along the love axis; these injustices may come out even (balanced), but they're injustices all the same. So, a balanced system is not *at all* the same as a perfect system. There are *many* problems. But the ***deepest*** problem lies in our failure to know and to acknowledge that It All Balances Out. This failure to *perceive* Balance results in the *one* overarching element in the gender system that is *im*balanced, the gender *belief* system. Believing that Man has *the* power and Woman is *the* victim is one-sided, which is why it is false, which is why it's poisonous. It is a belief system that maximizes victim, vindictiveness, and vengeance motives, which is why it's a belief system that escalates the Battle of the Sexes.

The Battle rages, inflicting damages on both sides. The damages may come out even, but they're *damages* all the same. So, again, a balanced system—especially when it is *not acknowledged to be* a balanced system—isn't the same as a perfect system and it certainly hasn't proven to be an entirely *peaceful* system. Understanding that It All Balances Out there remains much to be *passionate* about regarding gender issues and gender politics.

And, *crucially*, it's also true that the kind of immature emotional rage that both feminism and masculism can provoke finds no basis of support within an It All Balances Out belief system.

On what *legitimate* basis will we resent our opposite sex for the various powers, privileges, and exemptions it enjoys when we know our own sex enjoys powers, privileges, and exemptions in equal measure? When we come to the realization that the costs each sex pays for their respective privileges are costs that come out *even*, there remains no legitimate basis for inter-sex envy and bitterness.

But the only way to perceive this Balance I speak of is to come to an understanding of the politicized perspectives of *both* sexes. With that understanding, Balance is plain to see. At that point a whole new gender-political space opens up allowing for a whole new level of maturity, forgiveness and fairness. When we proceed from the understanding that It All Balances Out on the *global* level, then when we focus in on any specific instance of gender conflict on the *individual* level, we do so without the bias and emotional bile currently tending to poison love, respect, and healthy negotiation between the sexes.

The Battle of the Sexes is like any other battle in as much as it is fueled by rage and righteousness. But while other battles may be settled when one side defeats the other, because the sexes are so deeply intertwined, "when one sex 'wins,' both sexes lose." For the Battle of the *Sexes*, the only win position is a draw. The Battle will only deescalate when the warring factions become willing to accept a balanced perspective. We give up rancor and resentment when we admit that what "they" did to "us" is *balanced* by what "we" did to "them."

We acknowledge the wheel of complicity whereby Man exerts a force of influence upon Woman, and in turn, Woman exerts an equal force of influence upon Man. But we give up foolish blaming and take on accountability when we agree that—as is true of each of us as individuals—Man and Woman are really each *their own worst enemies* primarily responsible for creating their own predicaments. Finally, it's important to understand that while the predicaments of Woman and Man are different, they're equivalent. The two ends of the balance beam need not be identical to weigh the same.

Both sexes suffer gender injustice. A balanced system isn't the same as a perfect system. I don't go on about Balance to promote complacency. It All Balances Out is not an endpoint; it is a new beginning!

Moreover, a balanced system becomes a far more *workable* system from which to proceed when it is acknowledged to be what it truly is—*balanced*—(balanced that is **except** for the highly *im*balanced belief system). Believing that men have *the* power and women are *the* victims is the deep underlying problem. Proceeding from the understanding that It All Balances Out is the solution!

It All Balances Out can neither be proven nor disproven. It is a matter of discernment. Yet I believe that it is more than that. It is something that may be espoused even as a matter of *principle*. It's healthy. It's an "olive branch," a peace offering. It is a decision. *It is a leap of faith.* For both women and men, it is a constructive and magnanimous position from which to start anew. IABO doesn't lend itself to mischief. Balance is benign.

It is the one truly sustainable and inevitable future of gender politics, and the only mindset that leads to the full restoration/preservation of love/respect between the sexes because it is the *only* mindset that combines the perspectives of *both* sexes. It is, therefore, a gender-political structure offering real promise toward deescalating the Battle of the Sexes.

Perhaps the reader will bear in mind the *value* of It All Balances Out as we proceed to establish validity. The future "ceasefire" in the Battle of the Sexes in favor of a cooperative era of Peace, Love, and Understanding between the sexes is the reward; and it is attainable, but not without extending ourselves. To reach a perception of Balance we must embrace the truths that are rejected, the truths that are missing, the truths of FemalePower and the truths of MaleVictimization, the truths that go on the *other* end of the Balance beam.

A Brief First Look at Masculism

I have described masculism as something "new." In fact, formal critiques of feminism date back at least to *The Fraud of Feminism* (1913) by E. Belfort Bax. And masculism in its modern form can trace its roots at least as far back as 1976 with the publication of Herb Goldberg's *The Hazards of Being Male: Surviving the Myth of Masculine Privilege*. Yet masculism remains a word not found in the average dictionary, and unknown outside of its small domain.

"Defining masculism is made difficult by the fact that the term has been used by very few people, and by hardly any philosophers," states the massive *Oxford Companion to Philosophy*. Nevertheless, their definition is excellent: "the belief that women/men have been systematically discriminated against, and that that discrimination should be eliminated. Evidently, such a definition for 'feminism' is commonly understood, and among the few who apply the term 'masculist' to themselves, such is also their intent."[14] This is an excellent definition[a] in that it makes no distinction between feminism and masculism. They are essentially flip sides of the same coin.

The big difference between feminism and masculism is that feminism is omnipresent while masculism remains obscure. But this is unsurprising when you consider that feminism's message is in accord with paradigms that have ruled for thousands of years while masculism's ambition is to *overturn* those paradigms to which we are so very deeply, emotionally attached.

---

a   Though, I'd replace "discriminated against" with a phrase that more evenly describes the very different issues faced by Woman and Man.

The world has always recognized male power and it has always recognized female victimization. Humanity has always recognized the dark side of men and the light side of women. In presenting the truths of MalePower/FemaleVictimization (MP/FV) and the truths of ManBad/WomanGood (MB/WG), feminism presents truths in accord with those ancient and deeply internalized paradigms. By contrast, in presenting the truths of FemalePower/MaleVictimization (FP/MV) and the truths of WomanBad/ManGood (WB/MG), masculism asks us to examine truths that are not so readily embraced.

Because the truths of feminism are in accord with the MP/FV, MB/WG paradigms, these truths received attention even in the ancient world.[a] Yet, only 100 years ago, feminism was no more than it had always been—a cult, passionately advocated by a few but largely rejected by mainstream men, *and women*. Then, suddenly, technology (distributed by capitalism) radically changed our world.

In the world of women, reproductive and domestic technologies, together with the vast expansion of service industries, went a long way toward freeing women up. For the first time in history the traditional female role could be planned (through effective birth control) and eased (through the use of everything from dry cleaners and daycare to vacuum cleaners and microwave ovens), and suddenly motherhood and career were no longer such mutually exclusive endeavors.

Meanwhile, unions, paid medical coverage, paid vacations, plus workers' compensation, worker safety, and worker morale went a long way toward making the workaday world of men far more genteel and lucrative, cleaner, safer, less arduous, and therefore more suitable and far more *appealing* to women than it had ever been before. For the first time in history, machine power took the place of muscle power and women's strength disadvantage was rendered insignificant.

It was under all these unprecedented circumstances that women—not just a *few*, but women *in general*—began to support the feminist perspective and enter the newly improved world of men en masse.[b]

---

a See my upcoming book: *Love and Respect in the Past: The History of Gender Equality*.
b We may cut through the haze and see the *true* magnitude of female power when we consider how quickly change came the moment conditions were right, female solidarity was achieved, Woman chose to enter the workplace, *and* begin changing it to her liking (part-time work, flexible hours, paid maternity leave, extra safety measures, political correctness, onsite childcare). Women now obtain most of the advanced degrees, comprise the majority of the workforce, and young, never-married women now well out earn their male counterparts. Woman powerless? No coup in history ever encountered so little resistance nor effected a shift so dramatic, rapid, and bloodless.

By common agreement, feminism took modern form with the publication of Betty Freidan's *The Feminine Mystique* in 1963. Before that, mainstream women were nearly as oblivious of their politicized perspectives as men remain oblivious of theirs. Neither feminism nor masculism are ideologies that either men or women are born knowing. Because masculism is largely unknown, to learn it we must start from scratch. And because masculism is as diverse and comprehensive as feminism, there is a great deal of material to cover.

Masculism is the male perspective *politicized*. It's what a man sees when he becomes enlightened to the positives inherent in the female experience and the negatives inherent in his own. It is the world as he sees it while standing as resolutely in his own politicized perspective as a feminist stands in hers.

Both feminism and masculism are valid as far as they go and so, depending on circumstances, I regularly wear any one of three "hats"—one marked "feminist," one marked "masculist," and one marked "equalist"—my preferred gender-neutral hat.

There's nothing wrong with donning a masculist "hat" long enough to view the world as seen from a politicized male perspective. But, if I self-identify as a "male-ist," there is no inconsistency between that identity and a quest to make the world perfect for males with no regard for females. Likewise, there's nothing wrong with donning a feminist "hat." But, if I self-identify as a "female-ist," if I internalize that label, there is no inconsistency between that identity and a quest to make the world perfect for females with no regard for males.

If, on the other hand, I self-identify as an equalist, then, to be consistent with that label, I am honor bound to do my best to set personal bias aside and seek equality and justice for *both* sexes.

I'll define two kinds of masculism: *conscious* and *unconscious*. Unconscious masculism is the exact mirror-opposite of mainstream feminism. Unconscious masculism sees only a male hell and female heaven. It argues FP/MV as the only reality, and an end in itself.

Unconscious masculism is male-ism. As such, it is as selfish, one-sided, and divisive as female-ism. Over the Internet I have conversed with men who, having deeply internalized the politicized male perspective, see only positives, no negatives for women and see only negatives, no positives for men. Under those circumstances, I don my feminist hat and argue MP/FV with these men who have embraced the same "victim-dictum" (thank you, Warren Farrell, for this useful phrase) as their feminist counterparts. Sadly, however, such men often seem as intractable as their feminist opponents.

Thus far, such masculist men are few and their organizations too small, ill-funded, and weak to have large-scale cultural influence.

Masculism is now but a drop of water to feminism's ocean. But that appears to be changing. It is imperative that unconscious masculists and unconscious masculism become conscious before even more damage is done to male-female relations.

Conscious masculism is still the mirror opposite of feminism, but it is self-aware. It knows the political game it's playing. It knows it's engaged in what is essentially a battle of rhetoric. Conscious masculism doesn't try to tell you what the world *is*. It tells you what the world *looks* like *as seen from the politicized male perspective*—a distinction that feminism, being still unconscious, hasn't the humility to make.

Feminism tells us that society turns women into "sex objects." If feminism argued that position as a truth *as seen* from the *politicized female perspective*, I would have no problem with that—that stand is perfectly legitimate. The thing is, from a masculist perspective, those same "sex objects" look more like "sexual celebrities." But feminism doesn't recognize the existence or validity of masculism. "All women," says feminist Catharine MacKinnon, "live in sexual objectification the way fish live in water."[15] Feminism insists that *all* women are rendered "sex objects," *period*—everyone must see it that way—no alternate perspectives allowed. "But," comments Katie Roiphe, "I think it depends on where you learned to swim."[16] In other words, it depends on how you look at it.

Under an equalist gender-political system, the alternate perspectives of *both* sexes are embraced—debate, free exchange of ideas, and negotiation are stimulated, not suppressed.

Because masculism came into existence within a world and a belief system that embraces feminism, most masculism I've read is conscious masculism. Simply put, conscious masculism is conscious because it is conscious of the existence and validity of its own mirror-opposite ideology—feminism (Warren Farrell, for example, knows feminism well enough to have been elected three times to the New York board of NOW, the National Organization for Women). For this reason, a conscious masculist argues FP/MV not as an end in itself but as a means to an end—that end being the understanding that It All Balances Out.

David Thomas, author of *Not Guilty: The Case in Defense of Men*, has done his research. He writes eloquently of how poorly males fare in the realms of divorce, health, education, and social services. He knows the facts of male suicide, imprisonment, homelessness, and battlefield and work-related fatalities. He knows well the facts of male victimization. But he also knows female victimization so he doesn't internalize "victim" as part of his male identity. "The last thing that the world needs now," writes Thomas, "is another bunch of whining, self-proclaimed victims, and no one should close this book thinking that I spend my whole time feeling miserable about being male."[17] Like most masculists sophisticated enough to have authored and published books, Thomas is a *conscious* masculist. He doesn't stubbornly and irrationally reject the *facts* of male victimization, yet he avoids internalizing the victim-dictum that feminists seem to grasp with both hands.

Having read his book, I believe he knows, or at least would agree that, it all balances out. The funny thing is, though, he never comes right out and *says* it. Like other masculist authors, his focus is on countering feminism and that it all comes out even is never explicitly stated. That's unfortunate because It All Balances Out is the one gender-political truth to stress above all others.

If the masculist movement wishes to effect constructive change and peaceful resolutions, it would be wise to stand behind It All Balances Out as its first principle. To masculists everywhere I say, let It All Balances Out be the banner that unifies us and keeps us on a healthy and constructive path.

Because feminism came into existence within a world and a belief system wherein masculism had no acknowledged existence, feminism is rarely, if ever, conscious. (In fact, as previously argued, I believe that a feminism that becomes conscious ceases to be *femin*ism and becomes *equal*ism. Conscious masculism will transform into equalism also, but only *after* it has completed its essential task—adding the politicized male perspective onto the *other* end of the Balance beam.)

Feminist Joshua Goldstein begins his book *War and Gender* with some definitions:

> *Masculinism(ist)* refers to an ideology justifying, promoting, or advocating male domination. *Feminism*—my own ideological preference—opposes male superiority, and promotes women's interests and gender equality.[18]

Like other feminists, Goldstein is not conscious of the existence and validity of masculism. He sees only "masculinism."[a] In equating the mirror-opposite of feminism with "male domination," he and other feminists discredit the whole notion of gender politics from a male perspective. Thus, masculism, and the truths of FemalePower and MaleVictimization, get shut out of the equation.

---

a   Note: Feminists already plied the trick of expanding the word masculism to "masculinism"—to spotlight the male bias within—*before* I did the same with the word feminism (i.e., "feminine-ism" or "female-ism"). Also, though "MRA" (Men's Rights Activist) has become the preferred term, I still prefer "masculist" for the way it mirrors "feminist."

Feminism rarely recognizes the truths of masculism and therefore feminism is rarely conscious. Feminism opposes male superiority (promoting female moral/ethical/spiritual/parental superiority in its stead) and promotes women's interests (but never men's interests). How this all adds up to "gender equality" is something only a female-ist can fathom.

Despite the blatant gender bias built into it, our gender belief system is feminist, and so, to balance that out, I will be wearing my masculist hat throughout most of this book.

Some Particulars

Because women have spoken up and the mass media has so dedicated itself to it, female/feminist perspectives are firmly rooted within the realm of that which we already know. For this reason, although feminist perspectives will be referenced throughout, for the most part, this book does *not* present a balanced view. It presents a *masculist* view that, when combined with the already well-accepted feminist view, may hopefully *lead* to a balanced view.

Women seeking *true* equality needn't think of it as an opposing view. Throughout this book I quote *many* strong, high-integrity women who've grown weary of feminist flattery. They long for honest, frank expression from men, even if that expression isn't always easy to hear. These are women whom men can both love *and respect*. It is to such women that this book is dedicated.

One of the many complexities confounding discussions of gender is that gender issues are in flux. Female-male dynamics are changing day to day. But feminism makes its case based on the traditional model, so we too will float throughout the "modern" era. We proceed knowing that real change has taken place yet knowing also that "The more things change, the more they stay the same."

Another hurdle to leap is the notion that feminism has seen its day and is no longer a major force in our world. As we will see, while enjoying a relatively low profile, feminism continues to exert *enormous* influence within education, government, the legal system, and the belief system.

I'm not a detached "sociologist." I don't just study these matters, I also live them and *feel* them. I've chosen to give this book an honest human "voice." Who am I to be writing this book?

I'm president of the Chicago chapter of the National Coalition For Men (NCFM) and a board member of the ManKind Project, two organizations that variously support men politically and emotionally. I'm also an educator and mentor to boys on their way to becoming men. I facilitate the personal growth work of men on New Warrior Training Adventure weekends, and of men and women on personal growth weekends that we call Path To Spirit. And I'm currently supporting a nascent equalist movement (see, genderequalists.com).

I'm not among the men we typically hear from, the sort of men who have microphones placed before them. The elite male, living within an elite environment consisting of other elite males and their female secretaries, is a bit too easily convinced when feminists tell him that men have *the* power. The average guy, however, views the world from a different perspective. Once enlightened, he views the world from his *own* perspective (without losing empathy for female perspectives).

I can relate to how an early feminist must have felt because I'm her mirror opposite. Like she before me, I'm haunted by a vision of the truths that are *missing*. The many downsides to the Feminine Mystique have been expounded upon *ad nauseam* but few authors or commentators have wondered aloud if there might be any downsides to the *Masculine* Mystique. If men were to wake up and speak up, we'd soon discover that every gender issue is two-sided.

I have sought and found this more balanced view in the vast permutations surrounding love and respect.

The Love/Respect Dynamic

The Love/Respect dynamic will show up frequently throughout this book. We've already made note of it while comparing feelings toward mothers and fathers. Look for it, and the Love/Respect dynamic may be sussed out of any number of cultural artifacts. For example . . .

"Blonde jokes" reflect the degree to which beautiful women are loved but not respected; "lawyer jokes" reflect the degree to which successful men are respected but not loved. The blonde who is fired from the M&M factory for rejecting the "W"s is lovable but incompetent. The lawyer who wears a necktie to keep the foreskin from snapping over his head is competent but despicable. You may not respect the blonde, but she's lovable enough that you wouldn't wish her any harm. By contrast, if you're trapped in a room with a terrorist, a cannibal, and a lawyer, and all you've got is a gun with two bullets in it, what do you do? You shoot the lawyer twice.

In the *traditional* world, girls are raised within a cultural environment that encourages them to grow up to be women who are vulnerable, empathic, nurturing, and emotionally expressive—qualities that lead both sexes to love women more than men. Boys are raised within a cultural environment that encourages them to grow up to be men who are skillful, accountable, self-sufficient, and ambitious—qualities that lead both sexes to respect men more than they respect women. As women are made to feel inferior in terms of competence, so men are made to feel inferior in terms of goodness. *Both* sexes feel both superior and inferior to their opposite sex.

Girls are steered by their role and socialization into inhabiting the "light" side of the world and human nature (while denying their dark side). Kept relatively naïve, girls may grow into innocent women who are more lovable but less respected. Boys are steered by their role and socialization into inhabiting the "dark" side of the world and human nature (while denying their light side). Relatively worldly, boys may become cynical men who are more respected but less lovable.

In keeping with the ManBad/WomanGood paradigm, many believe that if men would just "disappear," the dark side of life would vanish as well. But the dark side is a part of *human* nature, not just *male* nature. Because men are relegated to it, the dark side is an area of life from which women are free to remain relatively detached. In this way, men act as partial insulation between women and the dark side of the world and human nature. This insulation has opened the way for women to experience themselves as morally superior to men. (Similarly, gifts that women give have opened the way for men to experience themselves as functionally superior to women.)

Because the dark side is considered masculine, men are inclined to occupy that realm as a point of pride. In fact, many a man's motto reads: "Yea, though I walk through the valley of the shadow of death, I shall fear no evil - because I am the meanest S.O.B. in the valley!" There's little masculist introspection over those aspects of the male role that cause so many "bad" boys to grow-up to be "bad-ass" men who fill battlefields, prison cells, and early graves. The *masculine* mystique has received little of the cultural scrutiny accorded the feminine mystique, and even less of the empathy.

When only women complain, the illusion is created that only women have anything to complain about.

When assembling a jigsaw puzzle, it doesn't help to be handed the *same* puzzle pieces over and over again. To complete the picture, we need those pieces of the puzzle we don't already have. So long as we maintain a cultural aversion toward truths from the politicized male perspective, we will not be working with a complete gender-political picture. When given a complete picture, the truth that It All Balances Out is plain to see. With a one-sided "female-ist" picture, however, this true balance is obscured and denied.

Our system of sexual politics has triumphed in its realization that men gain the greater share of respect through advantages facilitated by the culture, and that women earn being more loved, but only at the very high cost of being less respected. This same ideology has failed us however by steering clear of the realization that women also gain the greater share of being loved and lovable through advantages facilitated by the culture, and that men also *earn* being more respected, but only at the very high and poorly understood cost of being less loved.

All of the above are, of course, sweeping generalizations, but such is the stuff that gender politics is made on.[a]

Volatile Truths

When it comes to gender issues, there are no disinterested parties. We all have a deep vested interest in these matters. Aren't we *all* gender biased?

Volatile topics of conversation though they may be, religion and politics are but cool breezes in comparison to *gender* politics! *Oleanna* (1992), a play by David Mamet, delves into the conflicts between a male college professor and his female student. The gender politics involved have been known to provoke audience members into shouting at the stage!

It would seem that few issues can make us froth at the mouth quite like gender issues. But then, no other characteristic permeates our identity and defines who and what we are so deeply and *innately* as gender. From the moment we're born, half of us are wrapped in pink blankets half in blue blankets; and the twain never meet again. To keep a cool head while discussing gender issues, it may be helpful to think of male and female as *concepts*. And men and women may be thought of as immense populations . . . out there somewhere—detached from we individual men and women here in the room.

Seeing how gender issues are so very complex, I employ several devices for cutting through this complexity in an effort to get at essential truths.

One such device is to speak of *the world of men* and *the world of women*. In using these terms I am not necessarily advocating them, but merely acknowledging their traditional existence as a matter of expediency. I believe we all know what is meant by "world of men" and "world of women," and that common knowledge may be used to move an argument along with greater economy and efficiently.

---

a   For an in-depth exploration of generalizing, see "Generally Speaking" beginning on page 220 of this book.

Another device makes use of the terms *male equivalent* and *female equivalent*. For the purposes of this book, one's opposite-sex equivalent is an imaginary being whose equivalence allows for direct comparison. She and he have the same social, religious, political background—the same level of education, income, status, intelligence, wit, charm, physical attractiveness—everything about them is the same except which sex they belong to.

Yet another device is to speak of *Man* and *Woman* where Man may be thought of as all men everywhere, merged into a single entity, and Woman may be thought of as all women everywhere, merged into a single entity. Not only does speaking of Man and Woman help to simplify matters, it also helps us detach and not take these matters so personally. Man and Woman are obviously abstractions and, in using these terms, the fact that we are generalizing is plainly acknowledged.

The Matrisensus

If Patriarchy stands alone (aside from a token few female senators and CEOs) then it would seem only just that feminism should also stand alone. But, actually, there *is* an equal-opposite to patriarchy. If we don't recognize it, in part, it's because "matri*archy*" is the wrong word used to describe it.

Patriarchy is the male hier*archy* (patri-*archy*). There is no equivalent matri-*archy* because women do not generally compete and form clearly ranked status hierarchies as men do. Instead, Woman tends to work power through the strategies of solidarity. Banding together within a relatively unified collective, the sisterhood, Woman plies an equal overall force of influence. She does this *not* by wielding equal male (senator/CEO) power, but rather by wielding *more* than equal *Female-*Power through *female* channels. In large part, the *real* reason feminism stands alone is due to the solidarity of Sisterhood in the absence of an equivalent Brotherhood. (More on all this coming up.)

David Shackleton, author and editor of the journals *Everyman* and *G.R.I.P.: Gender Relations In Progress* (and also the editor of this book you're reading) has coined the term "matrisensus" to convey the true nature of this female con*sensus* (matri-sensus) and replace the deceptive misnomer that is "matriarchy." In many ways, matrisensus is synonymous with the world of women. Thus I envision two equally powerful worlds coexisting side by side.

Patriarchy is a valid word when understood in conjunction with the equal-opposite matrisensus. But, when "patriarchy" is feminist defined as a stand-alone power—*the* power that rules our human world—then I place the word in quotes to indicate its dubious validity.

Blame vs. Accountability

I take it as obvious that *both* sexes are fully indoctrinated as a result of immersion within the conditioning and socialization they've undergone since birth. By the time we are old enough to pronounce the word "socialization," it's too late by far to undo it. I'm not judging whether that's good or bad and I'm not setting myself apart. I grew up in this world and was acculturated along with everyone else.

I take it as equally obvious that both sexes are assigned their respective biologies at birth. This mysterious X-factor, the "nature" part of the nature/nurture debate, is something that orthodox feminism regards as irrelevant. Those of us whose thinking is not imprisoned by ideology will know better. But the point to be made here is that whatever we make of nature/nurture (to be discussed in more detail later in the book) it has little effect on accountability.

Speaking of Woman: "Instead of insisting on her innocence," says Patricia Pearson, "we might insist on the capacity of all women to bring their force of will to bear upon the world."[19] And we might insist that Woman be *held accountable* for this force she exerts in sculpting our world. For me, holding someone accountable is an *essential* aspect of respecting him, *or her*.

Although we all practice it from time to time, blame is a fool's game—hostile, accusatory, and judgmental. Blame is something one self-righteously places upon another. Accountability, though, is something that one more properly takes upon oneself.

There may be times when it becomes necessary to *hold* someone accountable, but there is still an essential difference. Accountability forgoes the judgment that would make the other person "wrong." When holding someone accountable for their actions, you judge that A B & C were the actions taken and you judge that X Y & Z were the consequences of those actions. But, because the *person* taking the action is not judged, there's a good chance that person will respond with "Yes, I did this and these were the consequences and I accept responsibility." This is the sort of interaction that is mature, productive, and necessary if there is to be constructive change.

The New Warriors, an organization I'm part of, stresses accountability as a first principle. As "Warriors" we don't take excuses. I'll illustrate with an example.

If one of us is late to a meeting, that man is held accountable. If that man is new to Warriors and not yet familiar with its principles, the following dialogue may ensue:

"Why were you late?" he's asked.

"Traffic was bad," he says.

"No," we say, "That's what *happened*; why were you late?"

"I couldn't find parking," he says.

"Wrong again," we tell him, "You know that traffic can be bad and you know that it can take time to find a place to park. Now, why were you late?"

This goes on until the man finally gets to his truth.

"The truth is I stopped on the way to the meeting to pick up some shirts from the cleaners. When I did that, I *chose* to make the completing of that errand a priority over giving myself enough time to ensure getting to the meeting on time regardless of ordinary traffic and parking delays."

There—now we're satisfied.

If the man was late because a bridge collapsed—an event outside his control and unpredictable—that would be different. But when a man makes controllable or predictable obstacles like "traffic" and "parking" responsible for the outcome he places the locus of control outside himself, when the truth is that his own choices are responsible for the outcome. Evading responsibility for his choices leads the man into disempowerment and victim mentality. In his own mind he becomes the "powerless" "victim" of "traffic" and "parking."

In the New Warrior ethos, however, "victim" is dismissed as nothing more than a *chosen* mindset.

Like medicine, accountability tastes bad, but it's good for you. Because it "tastes bad," both women and men develop lazy habits that lead them to evade accountability. But we're not *inflicting* accountability on a man to shame or blame him. We're offering him what we call the *gift* of accountability—not for *our* benefit but for his. We know that the more a man holds himself responsible for his own choices and his own life, the more empowered he will be in his life.

So, when feminism convinces Woman to lay the blame for all that's wrong in Woman's world on Man, it places the locus of control outside Woman's sphere and thus disempowers her. In this way, feminism denies Woman the gift of accountability. It leads Woman away from examining her own choices and leads instead to victim mentality. Hordes of angry, disempowered female "victims" may make for a driven and unified feminist constituency, but Woman herself is not served. Nevertheless, to justify itself and maximize its own political power, feminism *needs* women to feel angry, powerless, and victimized. (In due course I'll substantiate that claim with details and examples.)

Though at first accountability "tastes bad" to men as it does to women, as a group, men tend nevertheless to prioritize it. Becoming in effect an "acquired taste," men often come to *crave* accountability. That Warriors—a *men's* organization—stresses accountability above all else tells us something about Man's innate priorities and proclivities. Likewise, that this same men's organization adamantly, even dogmatically, rejects "victim" tells us something about why, when it comes to the politics of gender complaint, men are the silent sex.

The masculine impulse is to take Full Responsibility, but Man can*not* take *full* responsibility in our world. Man has only *half* the power. Woman has the other half of the power and with it, she bears the other half of the responsibility. When Man takes *Full* Responsibility, not only is he being grandiose, he is also enabling Woman's flight from accountability thus depriving her of the *gift* of accountability—and the personal empowerment that goes with it.

Note: accountability and compassion must go hand in hand.

Accountability without compassion is ruthless. It is what we more often direct at men. It is respecting men but not loving them. Compassion without accountability is infantilizing. It is what we more often direct at women. It is loving women but not respecting them.

Truths from the Mirror Opposite

The primary strategy for demonstrating the true and actual balance between women and men is to demonstrate that masculist rhetoric can do whatever feminist rhetoric can do (the "battle of rhetoric" mentioned earlier). Masculist rhetoric is certainly less present, less welcomed, more strenuously resisted; but that doesn't make it any less true or any less legitimate than feminist rhetoric.

To many, rhetoric has the negative connotation of being mere verbal trickery. But I'm using the term in the original Greek sense, meaning prose designed to persuade, or better yet, the *art* of argument. There is an appealing humility built into this definition. Being an art, argument is never finalized, never resolved, never fully proven. This acknowledges the elusive nature of truth—so subject to one's perspective—and allows one to remain open to further argument rather than settled into dogma.

Allow me to wax philosophic. Perhaps in God's world there is only one truth—The Truth. But in the world *we* live in, there are only *truths*—many truths from many perspectives.

When this book presents a truth opposite your own, rather than reject it as contrary to what you know, I invite you to think of it as new information that may place what you already know into a larger and more balanced context.

Everyone's truths should be received and treated with respect. But that doesn't mean that all truths are equal. One truth may vary from another in both quantity and quality of truth.

I'm reminded of a PBS show where various luminaries were asked whether they regarded the Beatles' statement, "All You Need Is Love," to be true or false. I would have a hard time with this question because it calls for a yes-or-no type of answer. Some who were asked deemed it a true statement; others deemed it false. But I felt they were being asked the wrong question. Clearly, the poverty-stricken will have a very different perspective on "All You Need Is Love" than the affluent. Can a difference in perspective transform a true statement into a false statement? A better question would have been, "How would you assess the statement 'All You Need Is Love' in terms of the quantity and quality of truth it contains?"

How do I figure it then? Well, seeing how it is a statement of only five words, I'd say "All You Need Is Love" holds a remarkable quantity of truth of very high quality indeed. It is high in quantity because its broad scope holds true over a wide variety of cultures and life circumstances. It is high in quality because it is positive, affirmative, and constructive. It is universal in nature, yet it would seem that for many it is not so apparent as to be dismissed as obvious.

The statement, It All Balances Out, may be similarly assessed.

Quantity and quality determine a truth's value, but the importance of a truth may also depend upon how prominent that truth is in the culture. The truths that are missing are often the more important truths to be stressed precisely because they are *missing*.

Part Two

The Duality Principle

Duality: A Brief Introduction

The I Ching teaches that there is an essential duality to all things. Every ordinary human reality contains both positives and negatives, gifts and burdens, benefits and liabilities. Thus good and bad come to us in bonded pairs. The I Ching divides all elemental opposites into Yin and Yang, and teaches that they are *inseparable*. It is, I think, a kind of law in the metaphysics of human reality, which is why I refer to it as the Duality *Principle*.

Gifts/burdens—it may not be possible to have one without the other, but you can choose to *focus* upon one and not the other. Whether you see the positive side for men and the negative side for women (the feminist perspective), or the negative side for men and the positive side for women (the masculist perspective), whichever way you see it, is a matter of which perception you *choose* (whether that choice is made consciously or unconsciously).

Moreover, it is this duality that allows a masculist to look at the same world and see the mirror opposite of what a feminist sees. In other words, the duality in all things allows the feminist worldview and its mirror opposite, the masculist worldview, to coexist simultaneously. These two worldviews (feminism and masculism) balance each other out, which is why It All Balances Out.

I will illustrate the Duality Principle in detail but first I want to substantiate the principle by showing how it plays out in the real world. I'll do that by painting a picture of the mirror-opposite world that the masculist sees. And I'll do that by looking first at the facts and then at the issues. In the process, this chapter will reveal the perceptual duality that has wreaked havoc in male/female relations, especially in recent decades.

"Just the Facts, Ma'am"

"The exact contrary of what is generally believed is often the truth."
Jean de la Bruyère (1645-1696)

Many of the facts and statistics substantiating the masculist worldview were first compiled by Warren Farrell. Building upon the pioneering work of psychologist and author Herb Goldberg, Farrell was first to assemble men's many issues into one coherent, politicized vision. Goldberg's books, including *The Hazards of Being Male* (1976), and Farrell's five books on the subject, *Why Men Are The Way They Are* (1991), *The Myth Of Male Power* (1993), *Women Can't Hear What Men Don't Say* (1999), *Father and Child Reunion* (2000), and *Why Men Earn More* (2005), compile a myriad of meticulously researched and documented conceptual and statistical eye-openers of the sort that can have one seeing the world in a new way.

Not Guilty: The Case in Defense of Men (1993) by David Thomas, *Who Stole Feminism?* (1994) and *The War Against Boys* (2000) by Christina Hoff Sommers, *The Masculine Mystique* (1995) by Andrew Kimbrell, *Ceasefire!: Why women and men must join forces to achieve true equality* (1999) by Cathy Young, *The Sex Change Society: Feminised Britain and the Neutered Male* (2001) by Melanie Phillips and *Save the Males: Why Men Matter, Why Women Should Care* (2008) by Kathleen Parker are a few other books which mine a similar territory. At the time of writing, there are *many* such books and more on the way.

Note that most of the facts introduced and summarized here will be revisited in more detail in subsequent chapters. The picture they paint may not be the world as you now know it, but consider how strange the feminist worldview appeared at first. And remember, "Just the Facts, Ma'am" lays no claim to being a balanced view. I'm here presenting material that, if combined with what feminism has taught us, would *lead* to a balanced view. I'm presenting masculism—the mirror opposite of feminism. If men were to observe, analyze and interpret the world with similar techniques, attitudes, and mindset as feminists, if the male perspective were *politicized*, what would men see? If men were to complain, what would they complain *about*?

The downsides of being male begin at birth. If you wrap a baby in a pink blanket, observers are inclined to interpret "her" cries as cries of fear and they will recommend picking "her" up and comforting "her." Wrap that same baby in a blue blanket and observers tend to interpret "his" cries as cries of anger and they will more often recommend that "he" be left to "stew in his juices".[20] The observers' biased responses speak to something real within us. Studies have also found that nurses in charge of infant care respond to the cries of girls measurably faster than they respond to the cries of boys.[21]

The school system is no better. "When both girls and boys are equally misbehaving, boys receive more frequent and severe penalties," asserts Aaron Kipnis, Ph.D.[22] In the average American classroom boys receive eight to ten times as many reprimands as girls.[23] Corporal punishment, often implicated as an underlying *cause* of delinquent attitudes and behaviors, remains an essentially male-only punishment. "Despite the evidence, the institutionalized practice of disciplining boys with paddles, belts, rulers, and other implements widely persists, both in school and at home."[24] Additionally, boys comprise "[t]he majority of children abused, neglected and murdered" and "[t]he bulk of children in foster care and juvenile institutions."[25] "Further, according to the U.S. Bureau of Justice Statistics, mothers are almost twice as likely to kill their sons as they are to kill their daughters"[26] and "[s]ons are more than twice as likely as daughters to be injured when their mothers hit them."[27]

The facts tell us that our nation's boys suffer comparison with girls on virtually every front. Eighth-grade girls, according to the U.S. Department of Education, are twice as likely as boys to aspire to a professional, business, or managerial career while eighth-grade boys, on the other hand, are 50 percent more likely to be held back a grade.[28] Among juveniles, boys receive 70 percent of the D's and F's. Boys are charged with 90 percent of all juvenile alcohol and drug violations and comprise 80 percent of those tried in a juvenile court, 66 percent of students labeled "learning disabled," 80 percent of those diagnosed with ADD, and 80 percent of high school dropouts.[29] Though college-age males currently outnumber females, just 43 percent—and dropping—of those enrolled in college are male.[30]

Every year thousands of boys are physically injured for the sake of sports. In the sport of football alone, "[a]nnually, over 300,000 high school boys are injured, 14,000 are hospitalized—many with permanent disabilities such as paralysis—and several are killed."[31] Add in injuries from basketball, boxing, wrestling, soccer, hockey, etc., and high school sports result in four million visits to hospital emergency rooms per year.[32] We hear a lot about anorexia, the human costs and what anorexia indicates regarding the psychological distress of girls but, feeling the exact same pressure to live up to a societal ideal, roughly one-half-million boys are regular users of highly dangerous "body enhancing" anabolic steroids and human growth hormone.[33]

If drugs play a part in maximizing masculinity out on the playing field, they also play a part in minimizing masculinity in the classroom. Despite warnings of potentially severe side effects, "[i]n 1996, 10 to 12 percent of all American schoolboys were taking the addictive Ritalin..."[34] The U.S. consumes 90 percent of all Ritalin production[35] and Ritalin is only one of a variety of "behavior modification drugs" used on our boys.

In the opinion of many, contemporary schools are an essentially female-centric system. The sedentary, stay-in-your-seat-and-be-quiet rules, the emphasis on book learning (begun in kindergarten before boys are developmentally prepared) and de-emphasis on learning by doing, the disappearing recess period—all are norms that favor girls over boys. The feminist rewrite of textbooks,[36] the average-90-percent-female teaching staff[37] and the internalized notion that, for boys, getting good grades is "gay," all tend to scholastically sabotage boys from the start. By middle school the message that girls are "good" and boys are "bad" has already become ingrained.[38]

By age ten, boys are twice as likely to commit suicide as girls the same age. By adolescence, boys are four times as likely to commit suicide and, among young adults (ages 20-24), the male rate of suicide has become over *six* times higher.[39] Yet the "crisis" of our nation's girls continues to receive most of the official hands-on attention. It's an example of what I call the Zero-Empathy-Toward-Men Rule—a rule that begins with blue blankets and lasts a lifetime.

Following boyhood, men's low sexual power, high financial obligations and deeply instilled obligations for toughness, strength, and courage can steer men into taking hard/hazardous labor jobs that pay a family-supporting wage (which for men is a kind of "minimum wage") but do so at the cost of exposing these men to filth, fire, explosives, guns, toxins, sewers, radioactivity, criminal activity, heavy machinery, deafening noise, extreme heat/cold, construction, corruption, trucking, mining, logging—in short, innumerable hazards and hardships of all kinds. All 10 of the 10 most hazardous jobs as well as the bottom 24 of the 25 worst jobs (as rated by *The Jobs Rated Almanac*) are 95 to 100 percent male-occupied.[40]

We readily sympathize with the low-status secretary, but her male equivalent may feel unable to pay the bills on what her safe, clean office-job pays. Having quit school to support his family, the young man without higher education or job skills and whose upbringing and/or aptitudes are "blue collar," may see no alternative but to take the kind of work that causes a man to be 16 times more likely to die on the job than a woman.[41] It is no longer politically correct to ask female office workers to make coffee, yet parallel stereotyping has us asking male office workers to move heavy filing cabinets or climb rickety ladders to change light bulbs.

We bemoan the "plight" of secretaries while ignoring, for example, that meat packers are induced to wield their carving knives so fast, these men disable themselves at an average rate of *40 percent* per year.[42] Meanwhile, on the basis of a mere *rumor*, we lavishly fund a large-scale investigation into the possibility that sitting in front of computer screens might increase the likelihood of miscarriage (not surprisingly, findings indicated that sitting all day in an ergonomic chair *decreased* the likelihood of miscarriage) even as we cut back on funding for the Occupational Safety and Health Administration.[43] "The United States has only *one* job safety inspector for every *six* fish and game inspectors," yet "[e]very workday *hour*, one construction worker in the United States loses his life."[44] We make it a point to set aside April 21 for "Secretaries' Day." Considering the death toll, we might also set aside a day for construction workers, miners, firefighters—perhaps something akin to Memorial Day. Instead, we pass laws that protect women from "sexist remarks" even as we fail to enforce laws that would protect men from "a 600 percent higher incidence of work-related accidents . . . including over two million disabling injuries and 14,000 deaths per year."[45]

We compare conditions for the secretary against conditions for The Boss, not the man (her husband, perhaps) outside her window dangling on scaffolding several hundred feet in the air in order to clean her window. We focus on the mostly male-occupied tip of the pyramid where the imbalance in power between the secretary and The Boss is plain to see. We ignore the vast *base* of the human pyramid, but it too is mostly male-occupied.

Men protecting women act not only as insulation between women and the dark side of the world and human nature, in addition, the "garbage" men occupying the true bottom rung of society serve as insulation between women and the vast majority of life-on-earth's most harsh and hazardous requirements.

Why should the above statistics surprise us? A man who is not "man enough" to get out of bed to face *alone* "things which go bump in the night" is a man not likely to share his bed with that woman again. We all know which sex is obligated to be tough and face danger bravely and we all know which sex is more often protected from danger. Take note of every wheelchair and prosthetic limb you see. I think you'll find, as I do, that better than 80 percent of the crippled, amputated, paralyzed, disfigured, and otherwise disabled people that you see are male. For women, success is gravy and courage is optional.

Only *men* who fail to show courage will be labeled "cowards," "gutless," and "spineless." Only *men* who do not succeed will be labeled "losers" and "failures." Only *men* who fail to pay are rejected as "cheapskates" and "tightwads."

The "pink ghetto" and "*fem*inization of poverty" make the six o'clock news. Here are some facts that don't make the news. Real (after inflation) wages for men have been steadily declining while real wages for women have been steadily rising.[46] Much of men's "blue-collar" manufacturing work has seen a mass exodus to other countries, while female-friendly computer and service-oriented work has generally increased.[47] Over a thousand female-centric organizations of all kinds[48] plus affirmative action and quota systems plus feminist-induced social pressures plus more women than men completing advanced academic degrees, results in young women in large urban areas receiving higher average wages than their male counterparts. If, *overall*, women don't yet earn as much as men, it is *not* for lack of opportunity, nor is it "discrimination." Fact: *Women's Figures: An Illustrated Guide to the Economic Progress of Women in America*, by Diana Furchtgott-Roth and Christine Stolba, is one of *many* books and articles offering proof that the feminist mantra, "Women are paid less simply for being women," is *false*.

It is said that men are obligated to pay women's way because men make more money, but isn't that putting the cart before the horse? It's more true to say that men make more money because they are obligated to pay. I'll have more to say about this "wage gap," but for now I'll say this: It is primarily men who will do just about *anything*, endure *any* hardship, take *any* risk, make *any* sacrifice for the acquisition of money, because only men are made to feel so socially, sexually, matrimonially, and parentally inadequate without it.

According to the Census Bureau, female heads of households average a 41 percent larger net worth than male heads of households.[49] Among the wealthiest 1.6 percent of the population, women's net worth is more than men's.[50] Women control most of the personal wealth in this country[51] and, by a wide margin, dominate consumer spending in nearly every category.[52] In fact, "Women control 88 percent of all purchases."[53]

Men *earn* more money, but women can marry these high-earning men and end up spending most of it. Or they end up with the money by divorcing or outliving them. Meanwhile, a great deal of men's higher average earnings gets siphoned off to pay men's higher average financial obligations (insurance, car payments, orthodontist's bills, mortgages, college tuitions). And much of what men earn is simply given to women, either officially (alimony and childpayments) or unofficially. Diamonds and automobiles represent two of the few consumer categories where male spending—just barely—exceeds female spending. We know the diamonds bought by men are mostly given to women, but how many of the automobiles bought by men are also given to women?

Simply put, women's earnings plus all the money spent on women is greater than men's earnings minus men's greater financial obligations. That, plus the fact that divorce more often leaves women owning the family home is how women end up with greater net worth as heads of households and greater spending power than men.

In addition, the Nielsen rating system tells us that average female viewership exceeds average male viewership in *every* television time slot;[54] so we can easily see why sponsors and indeed TV itself—the most powerful ideological force on earth—chooses to cater to women more than men. Add to that the fact that women hold the majority vote and we can see why the whole system, including the belief system, will want to cater to women more than men.

The fact that politicians are dependent upon their constituency to vote them into office, together with the fact that women command 56 percent of the vote, leads to the Democratic and Republican parties competing for those female-majority votes, which leads in turn to this ironic pair of facts: Hundreds of federal programs allocate billions of extra dollars to the medical, emotional, and financial support of females[55] while males die younger and in larger numbers from all 15 leading causes of death[56] and comprise 85 percent of the "street homeless" (those homeless without even a shelter to go to at night).[57]

The National Institute of Health (NIH) has an Office of Research on Women's Health, but no office of research on men's health. Ten percent of the NIH's budget is given over to female-specific research and prevention; but only five percent goes to male-specific research and prevention.[58] Breast cancer research and prevention receives enormous funding and is everywhere front-page news. Prostate cancer research and prevention receives one-fourth the federal funding, only a minute fraction of the private sector funding, and rarely makes the news at all. Did you know that prostate cancer now claims *20 percent more* lives than breast cancer?[59]

Despite cultural mythology, according to the U.S. Department of Justice, women over 65 comprise the category *least* likely to be the victims of violent crime. We only hear about violence against women; only violence against women rates its own "hotline," federally funded task force, and dedicated Violence Against Women Act. Just the same, men suffer nearly twice the levels of violent crime women suffer and more than three times the murder rate.[60] Every year men are raped in prison by the hundreds of thousands. Or is it over a million? We don't care enough about *men* being raped to find out.[61]

Males suffer a four to five times higher suicide rate, three times higher incidence of alcoholism, and a nearly 9 percent shorter life expectancy.[62] Men comprise 95 percent of the imprisoned[63] and nearly 100 percent of the battlefield and prisoner of war sufferers.

Of America's men, nearly one-third are veterans, 270,000 of whom are homeless.[64] "In Los Angeles alone, an estimated 20,000 homeless veterans walk the streets. The Veterans Administration Center has fewer than 300 beds in service for them."[65] The Vietnam War produced approximately three million veterans,[66] of which 50,000 are blind, 33,000 are paralyzed and 100,000 have committed suicide (almost twice as many as were killed in combat).[67] A decade after the war, "400,000 Vietnam veterans were either in prison, on parole, on probation, or awaiting trial."[68] To this day, Vietnam vets comprise 25 percent of the men in prison.[69] Although not quite one-third of men are veterans, veterans in general comprise over half the imprisoned—does this tell us something about the damage military service can do to the human psyche, a damage only men have been *compelled* to endure?

Says Andrew Kimbrell, "*The millions of American male veterans who have returned home from war with broken bodies or minds have been grossly neglected.*"[70] [Emphasis in the original] There's a simple explanation. The mirror reverse of love is hate. But the true *opposite* of love is *indifference*. Of the two, sheer indifference toward men has probably taken the larger toll. For men, the greatest cost of being less loved is that, as a society, we are relatively *indifferent* to the suffering of men.

An exhaustive search found a total of 54 English language surveys of domestic violence that questioned *both* women *and* men about their experience both as victim and as perpetrator of domestic violence. Unlike crime statistics, such surveys measure domestic violence both reported *and unreported*. All 54 surveys conclude that women initiate and perpetrate domestic violence, *at every level of violence*, at rates equal to or greater than men.[71] I know that's hard to believe but, when we have occasion to look at it in detail, I'll show you how it makes sense. For now it's enough to know that there exists a vast, seldom-revealed, body of literature by researchers both male *and female* telling us that domestic violence is a two-way street. "Violence against women" is *not* the only violence, even if it is the only violence that *concerns* us. In truth, men do far more to protect women than to harm them and generally test their prowess for violence on *each other*. Like "civilians," women are relatively exempt from violence.

Nationwide, men do more time for the same crime: 59 percent more cell time for aggravated assault, 70 percent more for burglary and 75 percent more for larceny.[72] "Being male contributes to a longer sentence more than race or any other factor—legal or extralegal."[73] "*For the same crime*, women are more likely to go free on probation; men are more likely to get prison sentences."[74] [Emphasis in the original] Men convicted of murder are 20 times more likely to receive the death penalty than women convicted of murder.[75] Although approximately 1,900 U.S. women commit homicide per year, as of 1994, "No woman who has killed only men has been executed in the United Sates since 1954 . . . When women commit homicide, almost 90 percent of their victims are men."[76] Typically, states devote greater funding (often twice as much) to the upkeep of female prisoners. For example, the state of Wisconsin spends about $1,000 per month on each male prisoner vs. $2,000 per month on each female prisoner.[77] Male prisoners are ten times more likely to die in prison (via suicide, homicide, or execution).[78]

Men may make and enforce the law but, as is true of the media, business, and politics, the courts and the legislature do most of their catering to women. The chivalric instinct to protect women runs deep. It is a primal force biasing both the creation and enforcement of legislation. The feminist female judge and the "patriarchal" male judge are both more inclined to protect women than prosecute them. As a result, women are indeed presumed innocent until proven guilty, while men labor under suspicion if not presumption of guilt.

When it comes to parenting—and what in life could be more fundamental?—men are clearly "the second sex." Here again, chivalrous laws and courts tend to protect women and punish men. Women automatically receive physical custody of the children 90 percent of the time and men who fight for custody are particularly vulnerable to false accusations.[79] Fathers face a long list of legal injustices: Anti-male custody bias, anti-male divorce courts, unenforced "visitation" rights, men ruined and deprived of their children on the basis of unsubstantiated female accusations, lack of due process, restraining order abuse, child support payments forced upon men even for children not their own, and men who are *unable* to pay child support incarcerated in what are, in effect, the last remaining debtors prisons (more on this later).

Finally, something of the sexes' relative emotional interdependency is revealed when we consider that, "husbands whose wives die commit suicide ten times more often than wives whose husbands die."[80]

You see, I told you this was going to be fun!

Feminists present a world of hell and massive injustice suffered by women. In response I have here presented, in sweeping terms, a world of hell and massive injustice suffered by men. The facts show that this mirror-opposite world of FemalePower/MaleVictimization is neither imaginary nor delusional. Like the feminist worldview, the masculist worldview is one-sided, but valid as far as it goes.

Whether it is men maimed by heavy machinery, traumatized by the battlefield, driven to criminal behavior by financial obligation, or driven to suicide for having their children taken from them—*whether they speak up and complain about it or not*—it is a world afflicting your brethren with pain and grief on a monumental scale. Given the above, one may fairly ask: where exactly is this patriarchal paradise of male power and privilege we've heard so much about? How can sexual politics be complete when it is comprised solely of female-ism?

Masculist rhetoric is incomplete and imperfect. The equal-opposite feminist rhetoric is also incomplete and imperfect. Feminists can counter-argue what masculists argue and in return masculists can counter-argue those feminist counterarguments. The result is stalemate. The final conclusion? It All Balances Out.

The Duality Principle Revisited

So, how can this be? How can a world that we *know* to be made up of MalePower/FemaleVictimization (MP/FV) get turned round into a world of FemalePower/MaleVictimization (FP/MV)? The answer is simple. MP/FV is not now, nor has it ever been, more than half of human reality. FP/MV is, and has always been, the *other* half.

The Battle-of-the-Sexes gender system is a balanced system, but that doesn't make it a perfect system. Coinciding with the rise of feminism, The Battle has escalated in recent decades owing to the one element in these matters that is *not* in balance—the belief system. So long as we operate within a female-ist belief system, our agenda, consciously or not, will be to eliminate all female negatives while all male negatives keep right on going, and eliminate all male positives while all female positives keep right on going. This is an agenda that can only wreak havoc with gender relations.

Nevertheless, everywhere a feminist looked at the traditional world she saw (and *still* sees) only MP/FV. Feminist ownership of sexual politics ensures that what feminists see informs our official belief system, which in turn informs how and what we perceive. Ironically, we are directed to see only MalePower, never FemalePower, according to the ideological dictates of feminism. In other words, the

MalePower manifesto is rigidly enforced by *Female*Power! The same can be said of our narrow focus upon FemaleVictimization, never MaleVictimization: it too is enforced by *Female Power* . . .

Female Power

What exactly *is* female power? At present I'll offer a cursory glance at this, the least understood element in sexual politics. In due course, I'll present the implications and ramifications in more detail.

As seen from the *politicized* male perspective, female power includes the following aspects:

1) Sexual Leverage Power: The power to turn men into sexual puppets: The power to confer or withhold a *vital* form of validation upon men: The power to "marry up." In her book *Ceasefire!*, Cathy Young recounts the oft-told tale of an ex-Ziegfeld girl who "made one of her five husbands slide a check for a million dollars under the bedroom door before she would admit him to the bridal bed"[81] Sexual power may not be the *kind* of power feminists *define* as power, but it is a power men must contend with, a power toward which men are extremely vulnerable, and a power that, in its own way, does much to shape our world (more on that coming up).

Moreover, sexual power is a conduit to an even greater power: Emotional Intimacy power. During sex a man's carefully constructed walls are breached and intimacy of a sort men cannot get from other men is experienced, perhaps for the first time. Once *true* emotional intimacy is experienced, a man often clings to this emotional lifeline as if his very life depended on it. Needless to say, the woman holding the other end of this lifeline gains great power.

2) Beauty Power: The power to profit, beguile, open doors, and dazzle through appearance alone. Beautiful women may be few in number (depending on how you look at it) but almost every man wants one (with a gnawing passion few women comprehend), and so almost all men know an inner drive to perform, achieve, and succeed their way into having what women in general, and beautiful women in particular, are empowered to demand. And beauty power is something *every* woman has to the extent that *every* woman has beauty power *as compared with her own male equivalent.*

When we hear about a beauty pageant, we don't wonder whether the beauty is female or male. Woman *owns* beauty. Woman rarely takes acknowledged ownership of this *power,* and prefers to frame it in the negative (i.e., "sex object"), but an increasing number of women are becoming more forthright about it.

Nancy Etcoff, a faculty member at Harvard Medical School and a practicing psychologist at Massachusetts General Hospital, has much to say about the power of feminine beauty.

> There is tremendous power in a young woman's beauty. In 1957, Brigitte Bardot was twenty-three years old and had starred in the film And God Created Woman. That year, the magazine *Cinemonde* reported that a million lines had been devoted to her in French dailies, and two million in the weeklies, and that this torrent of words was accompanied by 29,345 images of her. *Cinemonde* even reported that she was the subject of forty-seven percent of French conversation! In 1994, the model Claudia Schiffer spent four minutes modeling a black velvet dress on Rome's Spanish Steps. According to British journalists covering the "event" for the *Daily Telegraph,* four and a half million people watched and the city came to "a standstill."[82]

Meanwhile, about the only thing a man can get for showing a lot of skin is arrested. A naked woman seen through a window draws crowds; a naked man seen through a window draws curtains. Male beauty is, if not an oxymoron, certainly no match for female beauty.

3) Presumed Innocence/Moral Authority Power: In part, women are presumed innocent because they "look" innocent. That is, women's more childlike and angelic *appearance* has a profound effect upon the human psyche, an effect known as the "halo effect." This effect, combined with primal associations with motherhood, leads to the power that comes of being more trusted, less suspect in all walks of life, but especially in a court of law.

Presumed innocence can be a lifesaver under circumstances in which one needs help from strangers. Upon pounding on someone's door in desperate need at 3:00 in the morning, is it not true that the door is more apt to swing open for a woman than for a man?

Presumed Innocence power often yields a woman the greater power to elicit help, support, and protection for herself. In an otherwise fair fight the woman will often gain the upper hand when she who is presumed innocent is "protected" from he who is presumed guilty.

This dynamic leads also to Moral Authority power: The power to define morality and claim the moral high ground: The power a 110lb woman wields when she gets right up in the face of a 210lb man (something no 110lb *man* would dare to do) and chews him out for being "wrong."

4) Majority-Vote Power: The power to vote in or out of office every elected official in all 50 states. This is the power that has both major political parties competing for those votes, each vying to outdo the other in granting women their demands. This is one reason why masculists compare the men in government to chauffeurs, men with their hands on the wheel apparently driving the machine—but driving it wherever *women* tell them to go. When was the last time you heard a major politician speak of *men's* issues?

5) Net Worth Power: The greater power to demand alimony and child support payments and keep the family home. As previously noted, in this country, women-as-heads-of-households have an average net worth 40 percent higher than their male equivalents. How can that be so if women are "powerless"?

6) Spending Power: The power of priority in consumerism, advertising, television, and other media. On average, for every dollar a man spends a woman spends approximately a dollar and 40 cents. Female spending power is behind much of the misandry everywhere apparent in advertising and the consumer-driven media (books, magazines, newspapers, radio, TV, and movies).

"That's because advertisers and marketers are constantly seeking women, who hold the purse strings in our economy," says author Myrna Blyth. "Women make or influence 85 percent of all spending decisions, representing an enormous $6 trillion worth of annual purchasing power."[83]

7) Procreation Power: The power of choice: abortion, adoption, sue for child payments: Her choice is his fate. Unlike male modes of power, female powers, inclund to be distributed not merely among the elite, but among women *in general*.

Motherhood Power: the power to take social, emotional, and legal ownership of *her* children: The power to shape each successive generation: "The hand that rocks the cradle rules the world."

What influence do women in the form of mothers have on their children that later translates into an influence upon the world? Both sexes begin life absolutely dependent upon the guidance and nurturance of Mother. Both sexes' emotional lifeline is connected to the *female* parent. Both sexes will grow up and seek "girlfriends."

8) Domestic Power: The greater power to rule the roost, set the social calendar, and choose between fulltime arduous work, fulltime easy work, part-time work, or fulltime parenting.

A homemaker's sphere of control may be small but her autonomy in the home, especially while her husband is at work, is autonomy of a sort he is unlikely to experience anywhere in life. While the kids are in school or daycare, a homemaker can watch TV, take a nap, play cards with friends; she can do what she wants while "at work." Does her husband enjoy similar autonomy while at work?

9) The Greater Power to Elicit Empathy: The power that raises only female concerns to the level of major societal concerns: The power to focus cultural attention and reparations upon female issues exclusively.

Part of this power derives from greater latitude to express vulnerable emotions (including tears). Emotionally, women have a range, freedom, and facility of expression that can run rings around men. These two factors together with women's higher average verbal acuity (plus an entire library-full of feminist rhetoric to quote from) can leave the average male feeling profoundly powerless in almost any verbal conflict with almost any female. "At home, men routinely sit through harangues that demonstrate women's greater verbal skills and emotional agility," says author Daphne Patai. "The feeling of ineptness, of being no match for females at the verbal level, is the common inheritance of all but a few exceptional males."[84] The feeling is expressed in an oft-told joke: "If a man says something in the forest and there's no woman there to hear him, is he still wrong?"

10) The Power of Protection Under Chivalry: The power of a high degree of protection and exemption from corrupting influences, prison cells, corporal punishment, capital punishment, hard/hazardous labor, battlefields, POW camps, and much more. The degree to which women have been free of the obligation to obtain money is the degree to which women have been protected from "the root of all evil."

In days of old a "gentleman" wore a sword sometimes used to kill another man in defense of a woman's honor; the implication being that a man's life was worth less than a woman's honor. Today, women are routinely protected even from "sexist remarks." Women at work now have the legal right to feel "comfortable." If he suffers a "hostile workplace," it's tough luck. If *she* suffers a "hostile workplace," it's a lawsuit (more on this later).

11) The Power to Shame: If you were a *"real"* man you'd . . . do, be, and give whatever it is I want you to do, be, and give.

"One of the most effective ways I have seen women using to gain power over men is by shaming men," says Char Tosi (founder, president, and owner of Woman Within, Inc.), "using their tongue to put men down, to shame their sexuality, to shame their success."[85] Setting men up to be the "stronger" sex sets them up to be shamed. "Heroes" are set up to be used, exploited, and disposable in countless ways. The power to shame the would-be "hero" in a man is a key component in women's overall power to manipulate.

12) The Power of Accusation/Lawsuit: "He 'sexually harassed' me," "He 'discriminated' against me," "He tried to . . .": The power to keep men and employers fearful.

Feminists such as Susan Brownmiller and Marilyn French have said that not all men need to rape in order to keep all women fearful of rape. It is equally true that not all women need to falsely accuse men of rape in order to keep all men fearful of false accusations of rape, domestic violence, sexual harassment, and so on.

13) Academia Power: 90 percent of grade school teachers are female: The power of control over curricula, teaching methods, textbooks, and campus political correctness: The power to teach one-sided feminism (i.e., Women's Studies) even as a prerequisite to graduation: The power to procure an ever larger majority of academic degrees and achievements with all status and economic consequences that result.

14) The Power of Feminism Itself: The power to control the gender belief system, define the terms, define "political correctness," and focus cultural attention wherever feminism wants it focused: The power to control and use the media to defame, discredit, and disempower men with highly publicized officially circulated "Ms-information" (more on that coming up). The power of feminism is also Victim Power: The power to draw all empathy, demand and effect all manner of female-only "reparations" including over a thousand female-centric organizations of all kinds[86] plus Title IX, affirmative action, quotas and so on.

The unspoken goal of feminism is to secure for females all of the above *plus* "equality" (i.e., women retaining *better* than equal access to all female modes of power + *at least* equal access to all male modes of power = "equality"). The goal is for females to "have it all."

But then, what else would we expect of female-ism?

Power and Duality

Of course, the FemalePower described above can all be feminist-reframed to look like powerlessness. But, then again, what looks like MalePower as viewed from the *female* perspective politicized can be reframed to look like powerlessness when viewed from the *male* perspective politicized. Where feminists see male "power," masculists may see only male "obligation."

Later in the book, I'll delve into the dynamics between hero vs. victim, credit vs. blame, and domination vs. manipulation. But, for now, I'll say this: MalePower is the power we know. It is the power we choose to *define* as power. MP may be characterized as extrinsic, *very* unevenly distributed, objective, and overt in nature. MalePower may be visualized as three vast monolithic structures—business, government, and military—whose imposing presence makes them impossible to disregard or deny. MalePower is, however, largely contained within those three structures. Hierarchical in nature, MP is confined largely to the elite few and is *not* all it appears to be.

FemalePower is the power we do *not* define as power. FP may be characterized as intrinsic, subjective, and covert in nature. More evenly distributed, FP may be visualized as snow flurries whose very ubiquity and subjectivity allow FemalePower to go relatively unobserved, undefined, unmeasured, and all too easily denied.

Feminism's MP/FV paradigm is founded on pre-existing bias as old as the hills. In simplest terms, it is bias derived from directing most of our respect toward men and most of our love toward women. The attitudes, behaviors, personae, and obligations that go with being respected nudge us toward a biased perception that more readily equates respectability with power, not victim. The attitudes, behaviors, personae, and obligations that go with being loved nudge us toward a biased perception that more readily equates lovability with victim, not power.

Respecting someone and reveling vicariously in their power and prestige are congruent (they are sentiments aligned with one another). Respecting someone who self-identifies as a victim is non-congruent (those who complain and feel sorry for themselves don't tend to elicit much respect). Though victimized in many ways, the respected persona does not complain, creating the illusion that he has nothing to complain about. All this leads to a subtle but pervasive bias in our perception. We are biased *toward* perceiving the *power* inherent in the respected persona and biased *against* seeing the *victim* inherent in the respected persona.

Loving someone and perceiving their inner sadness, vulnerability, and victim are congruent sentiments. Moreover, it is easy to respect someone who is strictly logical, self-sufficient, invulnerable, and dominant, but not so easy to love them (As the song goes... "Workin' for *the man* ev'ry night and day": "The Man" may be spoken of with respect, but rarely is it a term of endearment). Our greater love for women urges us to focus on female victimization (we feel more empathy toward those we love more). But our greater love of women has us perceiving their *innocence*, not their *power*. Though powerful in many ways, the lovable persona works her power through covert manipulation. She pulls strings that cannot easily be traced back to her, reinforcing the illusion that she has no power. All this leads to a subtle but pervasive bias in our perception. We are biased *toward* perceiving the *victim* inherent in the lovable persona and biased *against* seeing the *power* inherent in the lovable persona.

Feminism is founded on something other than logic—something far more compelling. Being in alignment with sentiment, instinct, Eros chivalry, physiognomy, the myths and the mythos has thus far rendered feminism officially unassailable. However, if a masculist were to attempt to "fight fire with fire" and express himself emotionally, what might that look like?

"Arrows" #2: The Newsstand

It was one of countless such moments, but I remember it vividly. I was browsing an extensive newsstand when I heard it over the radio. It was close to Father's Day and as is so typically the case, an advertiser was using snide "humor" to sell gifts to "Dear old Dad." "He may not have been much of a father," the ad intoned, "but you know you have to get him *something*. So come and buy from us. We sell cheap goods at a discount, so it won't cost you much."

It was an-all-too-ordinary bit of misandry, but in the moment I was more than usually vulnerable to it. In fact, I was livid! It's not the particulars that stand out; it's the emotion, the burning in my gut that's etched in my memory. It was as if that ad had shot a flaming arrow into me. I felt, more acutely than usual, the impotent rage at the free and easy way my sex can be mocked, ridiculed, and denigrated at will.

And I felt the male brand of powerlessness that comes of having no avenue to express any part of that rage. It happens all the time and every time it does I feel myself immersed in a cultural mindset, a belief system, and even a tradition that has come to denigrate males *automatically*. And part of that tradition obligates males to "take it like a man," remain "strong and *silent*," and endure stoically.

With no masculist movement, no brotherhood to turn to, no forums to express *male* feelings of hurt and sadness and powerlessness, a man who allows himself to grasp the misandry that surrounds him will feel far more alone and unsupported than his female counterpart stung by an instance of cultural misogyny.

Men are not supposed to feel what I felt in that moment. And men are not supposed to express it if they do. But, in keeping our pain as absolutely invisible as possible, is that not the ultimate experience of powerlessness we men consign ourselves to? The world will not empathize with men's vulnerable feelings until men first prove they possess vulnerable feelings by expressing them. Women may not want their illusions of the Marlboro Man shattered. But much of what those vulnerable feelings generate inside men may be of particular interest to them.

In that moment, dark clouds took over my mind and women, marriage, parenting, were all rendered a hopeless farce to be avoided. What would be the point of immersing myself within a system wherein

I could never be thought of as anything more than a contemptible joke? Why give my life over to earning money for our home, family, and children when, inevitably, *our* home, family, and children would really be *her* home, family, and children/*my* mortgage and childpayments?

No man living alone in a studio apartment, fighting an uphill battle in the courts for unenforced "visitation" rights can have any doubt about whose home and family it was. Women initiate 70 percent of divorce actions.[87] Why make myself divorce fodder for a woman whose training in feminism has her seeing maleness only in the most negative terms? Children, the media assures me over and over again, grow up fine without fathers. Why inflict my worthless, ugly dirt male self upon a woman who needs me like a fish needs a bicycle?

Angry emotion generates angry thoughts and angry thoughts generate angry emotion. Men have such thoughts and feelings whether they are supposed to or not, whether they express them or not.

A woman standing next to me would probably not have felt that arrow's piercing. That arrow wasn't aimed at her. Other arrows—some I'm cognizant of and some I'm oblivious to—pierce *her* heart. The media and the culture in general send arrows flying in all directions; everyone's a target. I'm aware of *every* arrow for which *I'm* the target, but I can't be sure what percentage of all those other arrows flying in all directions enter my consciousness and what percentage escape me.

There was a time, not long ago, when the phrase "Women have no head for business" wasn't sexism; it was truth telling. Immersion in a feminist culture has raised male awareness and sensitized men and women to arrows aimed at women, but in the absence of masculist consciousness-raising, I can only wonder if women in general have *any* awareness of the arrows aimed at men. Will the phrase: "Children belong with their mothers" register as sexism, or truth telling?

I know arrows fly in all directions and women are the targets of some of those arrows, but I also know that *those* arrows have derogatory labels attached to them. Arrows that pierce women are labeled "sexist," "male-chauvinist," and "misogynist." Arrows that pierce women are officially *forbidden*. Men enjoy no such protection. Nevertheless, some arrows fly right through the protective barriers of political correctness and pierce their female targets just the same.

Some of those arrows are anachronisms now. When I was growing up, there was an ad for Geritol featuring a man listing his wife's many qualities and achievements, followed by the tag line "My wife . . . I think I'll keep her." Even as a child I knew that line was offensive. Those ads were widely protested and their like have been prohibited ever since.

Even so, in 1993, *decades* after it had been pulled from the airways, singer Mary Chapin Carpenter scored her first number-one single with a song deriding that commercial.

> Carpenter's song lyrics at first seem to echo the sentiments of the Geritol spot, describing the many duties and demands of a seemingly perfect wife. However, as the verses continue, and the litany of the wife's duties gets longer and longer, while the husband is away on business trips, it becomes clear that the husband's idea of perfection may not be what the wife views as a fulfilling life. Eventually, she "greets him at the door", and announces she is leaving, since she "doesn't love [him] anymore". The upbeat tempo of the chorus contrast with the slower lyrics, which detail the work of the wife, and the new reality she faces for leaving the "perfect" household: "For fifteen years she had a job / And not one raise in pay. / Now she's in the typing pool at / Minimum wage!"[88]

What burns my gut about this is not that a woman complains and protests, it is the one-sidedness and the *"righteousness"* that one-sidedness affords that has me seeing red.

Owing to female ownership of the gender belief system, Carpenter can count on falsehoods such as wives working harder than their "lazy" husbands, wives' work being "unpaid labor," and women's lesser employment opportunities being received as matters of common knowledge (all of which will be addressed in due course). And so, with the full weight of feminism backing her up, she gives Woman sole ownership of victimization within the standard marriage bargain, and in so doing gives her infinite righteousness in ridding herself of the dirt-worthless male. While it's true that women initiate divorce *far* more often than men do,[89] nevertheless it is usually the woman who keeps the home and the man who leaves, often because a restraining order *forces* him to leave.

While he's away on business trips earning his family's love, even as he is separated from his family's love, she takes her family's love as a matter of basic entitlement. She got a raise in pay every time her husband got a raise in pay and, as the spending gap makes clear, odds are she spent more of her husband's paycheck than he ever did. While she takes a safe, clean, easy, flexible job that pays accordingly, the ten most hazardous and the bottom 24 of the 25 worst jobs are all 95 to 100 percent male occupied. In part, that's because such jobs pay enough to allow a man to keep up with the alimony and childpayments, which keeps him from being locked up in debtors' prison. But such truths are kept hidden away in obscurity and not permitted to muddy the waters of Woman as *righteous* warrior in a *righteous* battle for a *righteous* cause.

It's all that righteous righteousness that is the single most enraging aspect of female-ism, especially for those men who've looked into it and begin to see feminism's many shadows, perpetrations, falsehoods, excesses, and hostilities. It's not easy being one of the few men whose knowledge of the politicized male perspective leaves him fully cognizant of the magnitude of the injustice that the belief system heaps upon men. How will the reader react when I admit that ubiquitous expressions of female flawlessness, Zero Empathy Toward Men and All Fault Is Male have left me feeling nauseous with rage and sadness and despair?

The song, *He Thinks He'll Keep Her*, was co-written with Don Schlitz and produced with Steve Buckingham and John Jennings, demonstrating the ease with which women can count on men to back them up in their expressions of self-righteousness. The video, in which Carpenter is accompanied by Emmylou Harris, Kathy Mattea, Patty Loveless, Trisha Yearwood, Suzy Bogguss, and Pam Tillis, demonstrates the sisterly solidarity (matrisensus) that stands resolutely behind this feminine self-righteousness.

Men are worse than useless, the song says, and women are better off without them. Before I took my leap of faith and concluded that It All Balances Out, propaganda such as this, together with the universal support given it, could quite literally make me want to die (the *same* emotional fuel feminists draw upon to write *their* books).

I do not vent simply to be self-indulgent. The point is, women in general and feminists in particular seem to believe that their inner experience of pain and suffering, their feelings of outrage in the face of sexist "arrows," their emotional experience of powerlessness and victimization, are unique to being female. In *truth*, it *all* balances out, but I can only verify that truth by revealing the equivalent feelings from within myself. I invite other men to do the same.

But this is not about competing for the title of most pain-soaked victim. This is about both sexes experiencing victimization, and for that very reason neither sex can fairly claim to be *the* victim. Bearing this in mind will help reduce the sense of "righteous" vengeance that is currently fueling feminism and dividing the sexes.

Ideological Dictatorship

Feminism is generic for sexual politics in the same way Kleenex is generic for facial tissues. And that makes *sexual* politics a one-party system, which, in turn, elevates feminism to a kind of ideological dictatorship immune to high-level, *official* critique or debate. Where dialog is desperately needed, we have instead only one vast "Vagina Monologue."[a] Feminism has maintained its monopoly on sexual politics largely because the truths of feminism are aligned with pre-existing love/respect bias. Therefore, the truths feminists speak are truths *both* sexes are predisposed to hear.

The particulars of Woman's sexual attraction to male power, together with her focus on being more loved leading to Woman's greater ego investment in holding the moral high ground, render her highly receptive to the truths of male power. In a world where women are powerless, women are innocent. Women will lose out on credit, but men will take the blame and women's aura of greater goodness and lovability will go unsullied. Women are receptive to hearing about female victimization because the message promises to elicit more sympathy, inspire further "reparations" (female-only organizations of all kinds, Title IX, affirmative action, etc.) more protective measures (sexual harassment laws, the Violence Against Women Act, violence against women task forces, etc.) and generally improve conditions for women all around.

Yes, victimhood *itself* is power. Author Nadine Strossen: "As writer Cathy Young has observed, from some perspectives it is considered strategically advantageous to depict women as victims: Victimhood is powerful."[90] Victimhood is particularly powerful for women because women being more loved elicit more empathy. Says Nancy Friday, author of *The Power of Beauty*, "Since the Anita Hill affair, matriarchal feminism has sucked more profit out of victimization than anyone would have imagined, and it still goes on."[91] For these and other more subtle reasons, many women are psychologically entrenched and emotionally invested in the image of themselves and their sex as "powerless" and "victimized." To suggest to women that they may currently be on the side that's "winning" is to elicit stares of disbelief that can quickly turn to outrage.

Ironically, feminism's message works similarly on men. Men, focused on being more respected, are receptive to hearing that they have the power because it is a message that flatters men and, quite naturally, has men feeling powerful. Since emotional reality is what you make of it, men tend to reject alternate truths that would contradict their perception of themselves as the powerful ones in charge, and contradict the fine feelings that go with that perception. The image of Man as victim is repulsive to men, but the image of Woman as victim appeals because

---

a   The name of a famous one-woman show authored by Eve Ensler and regularly performed by many different performers in theaters and on college campuses across the country.

it brings out the protector in him and helps reassure Man, deeply insecure of his *intrinsic* value to Woman (who needs him "like a fish needs a bicycle"?) that she still requires him. Men are even willing to absorb all fault and blame without much complaint because, again, it reinforces the image of men as being the ones in charge—the ones to be re-respected. Even in being blamed, men are declared the adults, the ones responsible—an image to which men have an equally deep emotional investment. To suggest to men that they may currently be on the side that's "losing" is to elicit stares of disbelief and laughter that can quickly turn defensive.

But why does feminism enforce the MP/FV paradigm in the first place? Because, only within a MalePower/FemaleVictimization belief system can feminism maintain its power or even justify its existence (in the absence of masculism). Only so long as men and women believe that women are powerless victims will they continue to support feminism through active protest. And, naturally enough, so long as men believe that only women are victimized and only men are powerful, men will *not* protest.

Feminists fight the perception of FP/MV because it weakens their bargaining position. Clearly, only in a world in which MalePower and FemaleVictimization are all that's *officially* acknowledged to exist can feminists come to the bargaining table saying: "You men have *everything*; we women have *nothing*—so *give* us half of what you've got because that would only be fair."

Efforts to disprove a world of MP/FV will *fail* because it *is* a world of MP/FV (as seen from the politicized female perspective). It is only when we understand that it is *also* a world of FP/MV (as seen from the politicized male perspective) that we can see how these two worlds mirror each other and we are left with a Big Picture in which It All Balances Out.

Still, though, how can these opposite worlds, a world of MP/FV and a world of FP/MV, coexist simultaneously?

The I Ching teaches that there is an essential duality to all things. To all things there is an upside and a downside. For every loss there is a gain and for every gain there is a loss. *Compton's Interactive Encyclopedia* states that "Together the yin and yang are depicted as a circle, one half dark and the other half light. Within the dark half there is a small light circle, and within the light half there is a small dark one. This suggests that, though opposites, there is a necessary relationship between the two. Neither exists in and of itself alone."

Acclaimed philosopher Eckhart Tolle calls it "the law of opposites. This simply means that you cannot have good without bad."[92]

And you cannot have bad without good. Light and shadow, gifts and burdens, good and bad—these fundamental opposites come to us in bonded pairs.

Not most, not the vast majority, but "*Every* dark cloud has a silver lining" is our culture's way of saying that *every* negative comes with a positive. "There's *no such thing* as a free lunch" is our culture's way of saying that there's *no such thing* as a positive that doesn't come with a negative.

This is not to say that positives cannot outweigh negatives or that negatives cannot outweigh positives but, given that every human reality is subject to reframing, it does make assessing a reality for good and for bad a trickier and more slippery business than is generally recognized. Look again at the symbol above and note how the yin and the yang appear to be swirling one into the other. This symbolizes the way one may beget the other.

Good may become bad and bad may become good. *The Lost Horse*, a Chinese folk tale often attributed to Taoist philosopher Liu An (179-122 B.C.), expresses this principle in a parable:

> A man who lived on the northern frontier of China was skilled in interpreting events. One day for no reason, his horse ran away to the nomads across the border. Everyone tried to console him, but his father said, "What makes you so sure this isn't a blessing?" Some months later his horse returned, bringing a splendid nomad stallion, everyone congratulated him, but his father said, "What makes you so sure this isn't a disaster?" Their household was richer by a fine horse, which the son loved to ride. One day he fell and broke his hip. Everyone tried to console him, but his father said, "What makes you so sure this isn't a blessing?" A year later the nomads came in force across the border, and every able-bodied man took his bow and went into battle. The Chinese frontiersmen lost nine of every ten men. Only because the son was lame did father and son survive to take care of each other. Truly, blessing turns to disaster, and disaster to blessing: the changes have no end, nor can the mystery be fathomed.[93]

How, with certainty, can we tell good from bad, bad from good, when one can so readily transform into the other?

When a feminist examines a female reality and declares it *all* bad, then examines a male reality and declares it *all* good, it is the product of self-serving thinking. Within ordinary human experience, every reality is like a magnet with two poles, one positive and the other negative. Because *every* human reality contains negatives, a feminist can look at *every* female reality and see negatives *everywhere* she looks. Because every human reality contains positives, she can look at every male reality and see positives *everywhere*.

Our MP/FV belief system is sustained through a narrow focus on the positive end of every male reality and the negative end of every female reality. Moreover, it is this duality that allows the MP/FV and the FP/MV worldviews to coexist simultaneously.

Feminism Is Pessimism

In short, it works like this: Feminism looks at female ownership of beauty, sifts through it, ignores the positives, gathers and compiles all the negatives, then declares the gift *nothing* but a burden. So, beauty equals "sex-object." Beauty means not being taken seriously. The seeking after and maintaining of beauty is framed as "the tyranny of beauty." In her best-selling book *The Beauty Myth: How Images of Beauty Are Used Against Women*, feminist author Naomi Wolf argues that beauty is nothing more than a patriarchal plot to subjugate women.

The feminist looks at beauty and sees negatives *everywhere*. And it's true. Woman's glass truly *is* half empty and beauty really *is* a curse (*truly*), *if* that's how Woman chooses to look at it. With his equal-opposite bias, the masculist looks at female beauty and sees positives *everywhere*. He sees the *powers* and the *privileges* of beauty that the feminist denies. And he sees the equal-opposite male financial burdens that she reframes as "male power."

Feminism takes a similar look at the gift of motherhood and declares it "sacrifice." Motherhood equals the "sacrifice" of career, the "sacrifice" of personal identity. It is the menial role of "slave" and nothing more. The *powers* and *privileges* of motherhood, the primacy in parenting, the ownership of the children that motherhood implies, are overlooked and denied. The equal-opposite male burdens of being loved second best and the very real possibility of having his children taken from him are either ignored or reframed. The Duality Principle guarantees that *every* negative experience can be reframed into a positive. Thus, even the cruelty of losing his connection to his children may be reframed as his being "relieved" of the "burden" of his children. This is how a feminist can look at the world and see *only* positives for men, no negatives; and see *only* negatives for women, no positives.

Feminism looks at women's power to "marry up," and sees only "financial dependence." It looks at women's exemption from the horrors of war and sees only "exclusion." For women, the glass is always half-empty, never half-full. Christina Hoff Sommers: "Sandra

Bartky, an expert on something she calls the 'phenomenology of feminist consciousness,' puts it succinctly. 'Feminist consciousness is consciousness of *victimization* . . . to come to see oneself as a victim' (her emphasis)."[94] Feminism willfully and methodically frames each and every female experience in the negative in order to maximize female discontent and thus maximize the emotional fuel (anger) needed to propel the active protest through which feminism maintains and maximizes its own political power.

Says Daphne Patai, author of *Professing Feminism*, "Women's Studies seems to need angry students in order to 'keep the momentum going,' as one feminist professor put it. . . . The perceived need to stir up feelings of outrage among students is also connected with the feminist sacralization of what is generally described as a 'click' experience."[95] Christina Hoff Sommers quoting *Ms.* Magazine: "The 'click' is a quantum leap in feminist awareness—'the sudden coming to critical consciousness about one's oppression'"[96] The "click" experience is a kind of semi-religious "epiphany" whereby a young woman suddenly "realizes" that women are and have always been the victims of a vast patriarchal conspiracy, which is to say, the victims of men.

> However, while religious conversion experiences are often followed by surges of euphoria and celebration, feminist epiphanies are more usually accompanied by strong waves of anger. . . . Hence, irascibility and ire have come to be seen as indicators of the depth of one's feminist insight and commitment, "a sign of one's authenticity," as Margaret [former Women's Studies program director] put it. From a feminist viewpoint, then, cultivating anger not only increases the likelihood that students will turn to activism but also serves as a precondition for equipping them with an authentic feminist conceptual framework. Those who are not full of rage, "just don't get it."[97]

Given such a feminist-induced mindset, women are apt to dismiss their gifts when they discover that these gifts come with burdens attached. Feminism identifies Man as the culprit to blame because every female positive is indeed plagued by a negative. But it is not patriarchy that imposes this toll; it is the basic physics of human reality.

No one can benefit from extra help without the liability of extra dependence. No one can enjoy extra sympathy without suffering extra condescension. No one can enjoy extra protection without suffering the infantilizing effects that come of being protected. Woman cannot own beauty without being an "object" of desire. Woman cannot take ownership of parenting and still have equal time and energy left over with which to climb all the way to the top of the "success" pyramid.

Woman cannot have a "free lunch." Why? Because there's no such thing. Not even Woman can have her cake and eat it too.

Masculism Is Pessimism

Beauty *could* be viewed as a bastion of female power, but feminism would have us view female beauty as emblematic only of female powerlessness. So, what if *masculism* was the dominant gender ideology? If, according to feminism, female beauty is female victimization, then how might masculism similarly redefine and reframe the officially perceived "reality" of, say, sports? Let's take a look . . .

For those boys who lack skill, sports may be experienced as endless harassment and misery: being picked last for the team, being picked on, being vilified for dropping the ball, and blamed for losing the game. Dodgeball?: 'nuff said. For many players, sports demand a de-emphasis on scholastics that may lead directly to "blue-collar," hard/hazardous labor or the military (some go directly from the football field to the battlefield). For the vast majority who are counting on it, sports lead to cruelly demoralizing failures; dead-ends that may lead to the streets or—with all that pent up aggression—imprisonment.

Sports reinforce a model of masculinity that is fraught with self-destruction. It produces a drive toward masculinity that can supersede reasonable considerations of health and safety. For example, boys in their early teens may use diuretics, laxatives, and other drugs in a reckless effort to make the lowest age-weight classification, thus maximizing their competitive edge. Herb Goldberg comments:

> One league commissioner reported, "I recall one incident where a kid was so weak from dieting that his father carried him to the scale. I refused to weigh him. Last year I saw one kid slumped on the floor and another who walked around in circles from losing so much weight. . . . I know of another case where the kid was so weak he contracted pneumonia." Reinforcement of the compulsion to prove is graphically demonstrated by the appreciative roar of the crowd when a football player is injured or knocked unconscious and returns soon thereafter to the game. It is as if the crowd were saying in unison, "What a man!"[98]

Imagine the agony of blowing out your knee and, in response, the doctor injects a painkiller directly into the wound. Now imagine how compelling it is to run back out on the field to the cheers of the crowd. And now consider how it feels knowing that the cheerleaders and cheering crowd don't give a second thought to how these actions may one day render you a cripple. Less fortunate still are those boys and men paralyzed, or even killed outright. Goldberg tells the story of a player who was on crutches owing to a badly injured ankle:

> It wouldn't function, so the team doctor injected it with Novocaine. He then had to have his ankle injected before and during each game for four weeks, because it never got a chance to heal. He now lives in

chronic pain from his problems with it. Another player reports teammates playing with tears streaming down their faces from pain in damaged knees.⁹⁹

It wouldn't "function"? Is a male a human being, or is he a machine? Given all the physical abuse it's no wonder that "A professional football player's average life span is merely fifty-four years."¹⁰⁰

Traditionally, "ex-athletes were like ex-soldiers who proudly displayed the wounds they received in battle," says Herb Goldberg. "To complain or to blame would have cast doubt on their masculinity. Each took it in silence 'like a man.'"¹⁰¹ They obey the dictum of "strong and silent." They keep their pain invisible and inaudible; thus their victimization is kept invisible and inaudible.

Now witness what a little male consciousness-raising can yield:

> I've come to realize that the real price of my education is the destruction of my beautiful, young black body for the amusement of my classmates who get their checks in the mail from Daddy. I keep my grades up, because one of these days I'm going to blow a knee or something and that'll be it.¹⁰²

With the right rhetoric at saturation levels (levels already achieved by feminism), masculism could have us seeing school sports as nothing more than arenas for mass male-only "child abuse"—a system designed to inure boys to fear and pain, setting them up to be "disposable" in war and labor; setting them up to absorb all the worst of it in life.

Both Susan Faludi's *Backlash: The undeclared war against American women* (1991) and Naomi Wolf's *The Beauty Myth* (1991) were massive bestsellers, widely regarded as feminist classics, and required reading in thousands of Women's Studies classrooms. If "classic" feminist tomes such as these can claim that female beauty is nothing more than a patriarchal conspiracy employed to trivialize and minimize women while men dominate the world of the elite, then masculism can claim male athleticism as nothing more than a matrisensus conspiracy employed to toughen and desensitize men toward dealing with the dark side of the world and human nature together with almost all of life's harshest and most hazardous requirements while women inhabit the world of love, innocence, nurturance, softness and safety.

Masculism thus concludes: "Sports is steroid poisoning!" "Sports is the exploitation of young men." "Sports is permanent injury, paralysis—even the death of men and boys witnessed merely for entertainment!" "Sports is misandry." "Sports is societal hatred toward males."

Likewise, male physical strength can be reframed from a gift to a curse that has, throughout history, turned males into mules. Man's relative ownership of toughness, courage, and heroism may be perceived as nothing more than that which renders him unprotected, manipulated, enslaved, brutalized, and disposable. This position, though extreme, is easily defended. For instance, about twenty-five *thousand* men, and no women, died building the Panama Canal[103] so that both men and women could enjoy the greatly improved travel safety and countless other accrued benefits that this singularly vital link between the Atlantic and Pacific Oceans provides. Further, it is estimated that 12,000 men (and no women) had previously died building the Panama Railway that provides safe transport to and from the Panama Canal.[104]

The point is, focusing on the negatives and ignoring the positives, human reality yields emotions, facts, truths, opinions, and statistics aplenty with which masculism can *catastrophize* the male condition.

Gazing into the mirror-opposite (and there's *always* a mirror-opposite), we see women enduring a lifelong "beauty contest" that begins at birth and does not end till death. It is an existential dilemma that afflicts women at *every* point along the beauty scale. Even the winner is a loser should her erotic radiance threaten to nullify everything else about her. Great beauty often draws toxic levels of envy. It fills a woman's plate. Both men *and women* tend to resent such women with the temerity to display *additional* gifts. So it's all too easy for the lovely young woman to grow increasingly dependent upon an asset that inevitably fades over time.

In *The Feminine Mystique* Betty Friedan disdained the "soul-killing" domestic routine, comparing stultified "housewives" to the "walking corpses" in Nazi concentration camps. *Many* women resonated. In granting men almost all the intellect, competence, and prestige, the "second sex" sacrificed far too much. And so it goes, on and on . . .

As is true of other men, feminism has reached me. I've really *tried* to understand. In fact, with what I know of women's issues, I could easily fill this book with readily embraced feminist truths, and reap the rewards that come of going with the flow.

But I could offer nothing new, nothing not already expressed within the vast feminist literature. And, besides, that's not why we're here. We're here to plead for the same understanding in reverse. We're here to fearlessly explore those gender truths *not* readily embraced—the truths of FemalePower and MaleVictimization.

"To even speak of males as victims, however, rubs against the dominant cultural grain," says gender specialist Aaron Kipnis.[105] He's right of course. Few hearts are open to receiving the case for *men* as victims. Indeed, I sense a *severe* drought of compassion toward men and masculinity which, in turn, leads to a profound imbalance in gender ideology—an imbalance in *perception*.

Shoe Store Analogy

When one's perspective is informed by an ideological agenda, one experiences the world accordingly. This is known as "perception leading reality" (in this case, perception leading *emotional* reality).

One woman confronted me thus: "If women *experience* themselves as victims and men do not, doesn't that speak for itself?" Let me tackle that question by examining the same scenario played out twice—first within the current worldview and then again within an imaginary world pervaded by masculism.

I) **Feminist Reality** – A man and a woman enter a shoe store. The man picks out some shoes, pleased by the simplicity and inexpense of his task. He is happy to get his shopping chore done as quickly and as easily as possible. But right away the woman starts complaining. "Just *look* at how much more I have to pay for these shoes than you pay for yours," she says. "You wear those comfortable shoes while I'm forced to wear these foot-killers a size too small and with three-inch heels. And why? To please *men*, that's why. I'm made to pay double and hobble about in these tight high heels, an ineffectual sex object, just so my feet look smaller and my behind is raised up for men to stare at. Women are the second sex. The world only values us for our bodies. I'm so angry! I'm going to devote myself to the feminist movement and do my part to overthrow male oppression."

If you would, take a moment to consider the above. Now . . .

II) **Masculist Reality** – A woman and a man enter a shoe store. The woman picks out several pairs of shoes, pleased to find a pair that match her dress. But right away the man starts complaining. "Just *look* at the wide variety of styles, colors, and textures you have to choose from," he says. "I'm limited to three styles and three colors—black, white, and brown. Of course my shoes are cheap. They're mass-produced for conformity. I can't augment my sex appeal with shoes. I don't get to have *sex* appeal, only *success* appeal. You wear those three-inch heels and grow those two-inch fingernails only suited to a 'princess' from whom *no work* is expected. Being a 'provider,' I remain drab and practical in shoes that are designed for nothing but *work*. And why? To please *women*, that's why. To make myself 'eligible,' I do the *really* stressful, arduous, hard/hazardous work that drives the industrial complex allowing women to fill their closets with forty pairs of shoes that some man somewhere, worked into an early grave, must pay for. Men are the disposable sex. The world only values us for our wallets. I'm so angry! I'd devote myself to the masculist movement except; of course, there *is* no masculist movement."

Like two observers, one at the front and one at the back of the proverbial "elephant," the feminist and the masculist are looking at the same world but seeing opposite realities. Yet each is convinced they are seeing and describing the "elephant" as it truly is. Their exasperation fueled by absolute certainty, each says to the other "Look, I *know* what I observe is true because *I'm looking right at it!*" Says one observer, "An elephant has a giant snake-like appendage." "What, are you *crazy?*" asks the other. "It's nothing more than a piece of rope."

Owing largely to the drought of compassion, masculist realities have little *official* existence in our culture. And so, masculist rants will appear outlandish, perhaps absurd. But having read it, try re-reading the feminist rant. Compare the two closely. Though more familiar, nonetheless, can't the complaints of the woman in the first scenario be considered equally flawed?

"Gender-Based Pricing"

Specifically, is the feminist claim that women are exploited by higher prices for certain gender-specific goods and services justified? Certainly there are valid feminist issues, but is this one of them? Bill Brady, of the *London Free Press*, describes the issue for us.

> Joanne Thomas Yaccato, who is a marketing expert, claims women are being grossly overcharged for hair-styling alone, to the tune of about $750 million. This debate now has expanded to include other services, such as dry-cleaning. I am told that some dry-cleaners charge $1.65 to clean and press a man's shirt, but $5.25 for a woman's blouse. . . . Liberal MPP Lorenzo Berardinetti is promoting the bill to outlaw "gender-based pricing." "I don't think it's fair that this price discrimination should exist," Berardinetti told CBC Television. "A dollar in my hand should be worth the same as a dollar in your hand or anyone's hand." The bill would impose a hefty $5,000 fine if a business is charging women more than men. I asked some hairstylists to predict what would happen if the legislation became law, and got the view that no one would be equalizing things by lowering prices and that it would mean higher prices for both genders. A Toronto dry-cleaner explains that women's blouses are more intricate and require more care in cleaning and ironing.[106]

If women were in fact being charged an artificially high price, then couldn't someone with a little business savvy simply lower that artificially high price, still make a profit, and force other vendors either to lower their prices or lose business? Apparently, we are to believe that no dry-cleaners or clothiers or hairstylists charge women a fair price because all conspire to exploit women because all hate women. I believe I can offer a more credible explanation.

If, on average, women's clothes cost more than men's, it is because, on average, women's clothes must meet higher standards for tailoring, detailing, and stylishness, which increase the cost of manufacture. If, on average, women's hair styling costs more than men's, it is because, on average, women have more hair to style and demand higher standards and more advanced techniques that require more time and expertise. If, on average, women pay more for dry cleaning it is because, on average, women's clothes "are more delicate and more intricate and require more care in cleaning and ironing."

And so, the only way to enforce "equality in pricing" is to enforce artificially high prices for men. Thus, a bill to outlaw "gender-based pricing" would actually create gender-politics-based pricing. "I'm not sure who would arbitrate the matter;" muses Brady, "it may mean a whole new department within consumer affairs, a few more bureaucrats, a bunch of blouse/shirt work-effort inspectors." No wonder "it would mean higher prices for *both* genders."

Could there yet be any validity to the feminist claim of "price discrimination"? Lorenzo Berardinetti (quoted above) thinks there is. "Berardinetti, who is an expert now that he recently married, said he didn't know how much more women paid until he went shopping for clothes with his wife. He noticed a man's suit cost about 30 percent less than a similar woman's outfit by the same designer."

Let's take a closer look at Berardinetti's claim. Are the "similar" suits by the same designer *truly* the same? Or, is the designer lavishing extra detailing, finer fabric, more elaborate tailoring, and smaller production runs for extra uniqueness upon garments marketed to the gender for whom fashion tends to be a higher priority?

Will Berardinetti enlist *true* experts and do some in-depth analysis before taking action? Or, having found a way to court the female-majority vote, will he get the bill to outlaw "gender-based pricing" passed without careful consideration of the validity of this "issue"? (Indeed, this looks suspiciously like a standard case of a man "in charge," his hands on the wheel, but, like a chauffeur, he steers wherever the female-majority vote demands.)

I further contend that there's only one circumstance under which relentless market pressures will fail to equalize pricing and that is when low price fails to be a selling point.

> There are shoes. There are heels. And then there are Manolo Blahniks. Women don't just buy Manolo Blahniks—they become Manolo addicts. They lust after them, guiltily hoard them by the dozens, build wardrobes around them and have traveling trunks made specifically for them. They bribe salespeople so they can be the first to own a certain heel in a particular shade.[107]

Clearly, where Manolo Blahniks are concerned, price is somewhat beside the point. In fact, if Manolo did lower his prices, it seems likely that his mystique would be compromised and sales would suffer.

The same goes for certain high-end audio brands. If you conducted a survey on what one must pay to get a "good" stereo amplifier, I'm confident that men would venture a considerably higher average figure than women. If you conducted a survey on what one must pay to get a "good" haircut, I'm equally confident that women would venture a considerably higher average figure than men.

Today, while perusing the magazine rack at the local Osco drugstore, I see *Short Hair, Hairstyling, Black Hair, 101 Hairstyles, Short Cuts, Hairdo Ideas, Cuts & Colors,* and *Celebrity Hairstyles*. Given such an obsession with hairstyling, cut-rate haircuts can have little appeal to most women. For those who wish to buy "the best," low price can be a turnoff. Perhaps male "lust" for electronic hardware is being "exploited." Perhaps female "lust" for fashion accessories is being "exploited." If so, *they have only themselves to blame*.

Currently, the Hair Cuttery, a chain that claims 1,000 locations, advertises unisex haircuts for $13. If women shopped around for the lowest-price haircut, merchants would soon see discount hairstylists getting an ever larger share of the business and they would adjust their prices (and services) accordingly.

Credibility for "gender-based pricing" as "exploitation of women" dissolves when you factor in women's own choices. Think about it: Are we seriously considering protecting women (a.k.a., "women-and-children"?) even from their *own chosen buying habits?*

There is one last point to make here. Note that no one asserts that women must pay more for a taxi or theater tickets or ice cream or any of thousands of other goods and services. The items on the short list of goods and services in which gender-based pricing is alleged all have two things in common. The items of clothing, the dry-cleaning of that clothing and the hairstyling, are 1) goods and services both sexes buy (thus allowing for price comparison); and 2) they are related to augmenting femininity.

Both sexes buy clothes and both sexes get their hair cut. But one sex more than the other pays extra for gossamer fabrics tailored to fit tight and accentuate curves. One sex more than the other pays extra for elaborate hairstyling to accentuate their facial beauty. Through the use of clothing, makeup, depilatories, skin creams, perfumes, and hairstyles, women make themselves look, feel, and smell as different from men as they possibly can. With awareness of the perks, powers, and privileges that go with femininity, it's easy to see why many women might *willingly* pay more for femininity enhancing goods and services that cost more to offer and are, therefore, more expensive to buy.

Are we having fun yet?

To sum up, there is no evil cabal of men dedicated to price gouging women. There is only the free market system.

I've delved into this "issue" of "gender-based pricing" because I believe, by example, it demonstrates feminism's power to raise even the *least* credible female concern to the level of a societal concern—a concern taken seriously enough to rate published articles, high-ranking pundits, class action suits,[108] and pending legislation.

By contrast, I believe the eight representative men's issues I'm about to present, are all of *vastly* deeper emotional and societal significance—their validity extremely well supported by a vast array of documented facts. Yet, for the most part, these men's issues remain non-issues within the major media.

The future "ceasefire" in the Battle of the Sexes is attainable, but only at a price. To gain a deep understanding and perception of the true Balance in gender power and victimization we must explore the *other* half of gender reality down at the other end of the balance beam. For both sexes, the truths of FemalePower/MaleVictimization go against the grain. FP/MV truths are the gender truths that cause us to squirm in our seats. They threaten cherished illusions. They are, therefore, the truths that are *missing*.

Issues Download

What you're about to read isn't pretty. It is negative and victim oriented—it is masculism, the mirror-opposite of feminism. Like a man reading feminism, a woman reading masculism may feel a little "beat up," judged, and accused. But, it is the MP/FV belief system that is the target of my ire, not women. If my personal anger should leak through from time to time, it is, at least, an honest vulnerable human male response to gross injustices resulting from our grossly imbalanced gender belief system. Let's shoulder on through the FP/MV rhetoric to reap the reward of a balanced belief system and a new era of gender justice that awaits us on the other side.

If men were to stand as resolutely in their own *politicized* perspective as feminists stand resolutely in theirs, what would men see? If men were to complain, what would they have to complain about?

Issues Download #1 – Health

If it seems that men have less to complain about, perhaps that's only because men do less complaining. If the "privileged" nature of men's lives is the reason men aren't complaining, why then are men four and a half times as likely as women to end their lives? If men were just 50 percent more likely to commit suicide, it would be highly significant. It would mean that for every two women that commit suicide, three men commit suicide. But men are not 50 percent more likely to end their lives than women are. Man will see one hundred percent of Woman's suicides and raise her an additional three *hundred and fifty percent*. For every *two* women that commit suicide, *nine* men commit suicide!

Yet we may *still* be understating the suicide gap.

When asked their preferred method of suicide, girls tend to talk about overdosing on pills or drugs. Boys talk about getting drunk and driving "off a cliff or into a telephone pole."[109] So, one mode of male suicide is surely hidden within male drunk-driving fatalities. Further, because men who've lost their jobs may feel they're worth more to their families dead than alive, and because many life insurance policies won't pay out when death is self-inflicted, doubtless, *some* of those suspiciously high numbers of men who die by "accident" following the loss of their careers died deliberately.[110] Also, notes Aaron Kipnis, "Suicide by police confrontation—in which desperate men intentionally force officers to shoot them—is now so frequent that forensic psychologists identify it as a syndrome."[111] Underlying all this self-inflicted death must lurk enormous human suffering.

Men do less complaining largely because *male* complaint is so often ill-received and dismissed as "whining." But, when women do all the complaining, it creates the *illusion* that only women have anything to complain about. Dan Bell: "According to Dan Kindlon, a Harvard lecturer, and co-author of *Raising Cain: Protecting the Emotional Life of Boys*, young men don't ask for help because we don't allow them to . . . 'In school a boy who shows a more effeminate side, or cries, or expresses his feelings, he's open to a lot of ridicule and teasing. Especially at these vulnerable ages when we see a lot of suicides.'"[112] What powerlessness can be more profound than a powerlessness you aren't even empowered to complain about?

"Young women between the ages of fifteen and nineteen are two and a half times more likely to attempt suicide than are young men," says Patricia Pearson. "But young men are *five* times more likely to actually kill themselves."[113] [Emphasis in original] In recent years that figure has been bumped up to six or even *seven* times.[114] However revealing of *true* pain and misery, perhaps some of those "*attempted* suicides" are really more like cries for help? What if males, expecting their complaints to be met with clichés such as "Be a man about it," "Pull yourself up by your bootstraps" and "Quit your 'bitching'" (i.e., stop complaining as women do), simply skip the cry for help and go directly to a bullet in the brain?

Have you ever seen the look on a baby's face when he's circumcised? Is the demand for male invulnerability related to our ongoing tolerance of circumcision—but only where *males* are concerned?

Now that more women are doing what men traditionally do, they are beginning to suffer what men have traditionally suffered, including taking on health problems more often associated with men. Author and *Esquire* columnist Harry Stein:

> [I]t is not for nothing that we have heard so much lately about the dramatic rise in stress-related illnesses among women. "It has now been clearly documented, as Dr. Paul J. Rosch, president of the American Institute of Stress, put it, noting the appalling increase in breast-cancer deaths among young and middle-aged white women during the past decade, "that emotional stress is associated in a decline in immune-system parameters responsible for defenses against cancer. Inability to express anger, frustration, loss of important emotional relationships and social isolation have been particularly incriminated, especially for breast malignancies."[115]

Stress is "incriminated, especially for breast malignancies," but stress is also responsible for cancers that kill *men* (younger and in larger numbers). "Each year over 55,000 more men than women develop cancer, and 30,000 more men than women die of cancer," says Andrew Kimbrell. "In every age group men's probability of developing invasive cancers is greater than women's."[116] In fact, at least until recently, "Men die[d] earlier than women from all *fifteen* of the leading causes of death."[117]

Note that each component of stress listed above is more closely associated with men and the male experience than with women and the female experience. Inability to express anger? "Contrary to stereotypes," writes researcher Richard Driscoll, Ph.D., "women are found to be freer and more open in expressing their anger than men."[118] Women are emotional; men are stoic. Frustration? Men endure more than their share of sex, success, and work related frustration. Loss of important emotional relationships? For men, fierce competition, homophobia, and working overtime are the norm. More often than married women, married men will tend to lose close contact with their peers. Social isolation? A "loner" is presumed male. Herb Goldberg:

> Thirty years ago men were twenty times as likely as women to get ulcers. Today the ratio is two to one. . . . Nancy Allen, a suicide prevention expert at UCLA's Neuropsychiatric Institute [says] . . . "In precisely those arenas where liberated women are making the most progress the male-female suicide ratios move toward equality." . . . women psychologists commit suicide at a rate nearly three times that of women in the general population. Likewise, the rate for female physicians is three times the rate of women in general. Perhaps these professional women are experiencing the stresses, conflicts and "payoffs" that many success-oriented men do, namely, isolation and loneliness, emotional overcontrol, and constant conflict between professional ambition, success demands, and the fulfillment of personal needs.[119]

Harry Stein expresses a truth held by many women with careers. "[T]here are vast numbers of women who, having pretty much gotten what they thought they were after, are now facing up to it; wondering, at long last, what it was that once, from the outside looking in, had seemed so terrific in the first place."[120] I think much of women's workplace anger derives out of the shock of discovery that being treated like men means being treated in a manner much more loveless and expendable than anything they were used to or had been led to expect—men *must* be hiding away all the "good stuff" somewhere . . . right?

The more women do what men do, the more women become what men are. An inability to express feelings, separation from loved ones, and emotional isolation are all frequent byproducts of "success"—the very thing that men are so motivated to strive for *at all costs*. Don't we hear a lot these days of women with high-earning husbands choosing motherhood over career? Is it any wonder?

The 1988 *Guinness Book of World Records* states: "The greatest *authenticated* age to which any human has ever lived is a unique 120 years 237 days."[121] The distinction went to Mr. Shigechiyo Izumi of Asan, Tokunoshima Island, Japan. At least, until very recently, the longest-lived human beings on record have been men as often as women. So why do we so easily accept the assumption that men's shorter life expectancy is *solely* biological?

Though biology may play a part, current ideological bias would have us believe that men die younger as a result of sheer biological inadequacy and nothing else. If that were so, then why in 1920 did the life expectancy of men and women differ by only one year?[122] It would seem that industrialization increases life expectancy roughly twice as much for women as it does for men.[123]

Warren Farrell:

> When women and men have approximately equal life expectancies, it seems to be because women die not only in childbirth (fewer than thought) but about equally from contagious, parasitic diseases; poor sanitation and water; inadequate health care; and diseases of malnutrition. In industrialized societies, early deaths are caused more by diseases triggered by stress, which breaks down the immune system.
>
> *It is since stress has become the key factor that men have died so much sooner than women.* . . . Why has the gap between women's and men's life span been *reduced* slightly (from eight to seven years) between 1975 and 1990? In part because men's health habits are becoming more constructive, women's more destructive. . . . But women are also working more away from home and suffering the stress-related diseases that go with the territory.[124] [Emphasis in original]

While masquerading as Ned Vincent, Norah Vincent, author of *Self-Made Man*, became one feminist whose incursions into the world of men turned her "women's studies" MP/FV expectations upside down. She, passing herself off as a he, infiltrated several all-male enclaves. In getting to know the "blue-collar" men on a bowling team, she discovered the old joke—Why do men die before women? . . . Because they want to—may contain some serious truth.

> Beer and cigarettes were their medicine, their primrose path to an early grave, which was about the best, aside from sex and a few good times with the guys, that they could hope for in life. The idea of telling one of these guys that smoking or drinking to excess was bad for his health was too ridiculously middle class to entertain. It bespoke a supreme ignorance of what their lives were really like—Hobbesian—not to put too fine a point on it. Nasty, brutish and short. The idea that you would try to prolong your grueling, dead-end life, and do it by taking away the few pleasures you had along the way, was just insulting.[125]

Supreme ignorance of what men's lives are really like lies at the heart of all female-ism. As the above makes clear, male suicide is hidden in *many* ways. In part, it would seem that men let go of life earlier than women do because men place less value on their lives.

So, if not purely due to biological inferiority, why *do* men suffer a lesser average life span? Extra long work hours under hazardous, stressful, tedious, repetitive, competitive, and emotionally stultifying working conditions—which include the separation of men from their families—are all probable factors. Hypertension due to job stress is a known cause of cancer as well as heart disease, the number one killer for both men and women. The pressure to appear strong and deny pain ("It's nothing, I'll be fine") causes too many men to delay seeking treatment for far too long. War and work related fatalities, higher rates of imprisonment, alcoholism, and substance abuse, death by murder and self-inflicted death are all statistically provable factors bringing about shorter average lives for men.

Clearly, none of this helps to paint a convincing picture of men as *the* primary beneficiaries of the gender system.

Owing to men's larger average tax bracket and the dearth of house-husbands as compared with housewives, "Men as a group pay *twice* what women pay into Social Security."[126] The stress involved in maintaining those higher tax brackets, however, contributes to men's average seven fewer years of life, and so, "women receive more than 150 percent of what men receive in total retirement benefits from Social Security."[127] No feminists have protested.

Because women live longer than men, female retirees will receive an average seven extra years of pension payments. And so, in an effort to make the *total* cash outlay in retirement benefits come out equal, there was a time when pension plans routinely paid lesser monthly amounts to women. The power of feminism soon stepped in, declared the practice unconstitutional and put a stop to it. Yet feminism has had no objection to insurance companies "charging men higher monthly premiums than women because men die sooner and thus make fewer payments during their lifetime."[128] Today I find in the mail a life insurance policy offer from Farmers Insurance and with it a reminder that these issues are more than merely theoretical. For a man my age, $400,000 in life insurance costs $71.52 per month. For my female equivalent the cost is $56.85 per month!

Clearly, *fem*inism advocates for *fem*ales and females *only*. Anyone who believes that *female*-ism is, or ever could be, egalitarian is allowing political correctness to cloud his or her reasoning. "Feminists acutely sensitive to bias against women show little concern for bias against men," says Cathy Young, "whether it's the informal leniency accorded female defendants in court or overtly discriminatory draft registration."[129] "The central mission of feminist activism is to put the needs of women first," say Daphne Patai and Noretta Koertge. "Its single criterion for appraising a political initiative is: Will it help women?"[130] I submit it is self-evident: sexual politics can be egalitarian; female-ism cannot.

In *principle* we can be pro-female without being anti-male, but in *practical* terms it doesn't work out that way. There are two sexes and limited funding and cultural attention to split between them. Pro-female bias that results in women getting *more* than their fair share leaves men suffering *less* than their fair share.

Warren Farrell comments:

> The belief that sexism has led to a focus on men's health at the expense of women's has led both the federal government and private industry to focus on women's health at the expense of men's.
>
> Thus the government . . . established an Office of Research on Women's Health but no Office of Research on Men's Health. It has also established an Office of Minority Health that defines women as a minority, but no Office of Minority Health that defines men as a minority (due to only men dying at a younger age from all fifteen of the major causes of death). The belief in women's neglect has led private hospitals and health-care companies to start women's health-care centers but almost no men's health-care centers.[131]

Feminists discovered that only 10 percent of the operating budget of the National Institute of Health (NIH) was set aside for female-specific research and prevention—and they raised hell about it. It was largely in response to their protests that the NIH created its Office of Women's Health. The fact is, only 5 percent of the NIH's budget was set aside for male-specific research (the remaining 85 percent being devoted to health issues common to both sexes). Because no one protested the NIH spending twice as much on women's vs. men's health, an Office of Men's Health has yet to be created.

Feminism makes mountains out of the fact that most of the medical research testing that has been done has been done on men. Here, according to Aaron Kipnis, are some facts left out:

> During the 1960s, 85 percent of all new pharmaceuticals were first tested on inmates before release to the public. The American prison system created a human subject experimental lab unparalleled since medical experiments were conducted on the inmates of Nazi death camps. Feminist activists rightly protested in the 1970s that a disproportionate number of medical studies were based upon males. There

was no similar outcry in the culture, however, that most of those male subjects were impoverished, coerced young prisoners.[132]

Social historian Todd Tucker: "In 1974, the Pharmaceutical Manufacturers Association of America estimated that about 70 percent of approved drugs had at some point been tested on prisoners."[133]

And not just prisoners but also soldiers have been used as "guinea pigs." For one of countless examples, a recently unearthed 1956 document confirms "24 Australian servicemen who were deliberately given excessive doses of radiation in so-called protective clothing experiments."[134]

> For the 1956 *Buffalo* tests, the British military established an "indoctrinee" force of 280 soldiers, including 175 from Britain, 100 from Australia and five from New Zealand, who were "indoctrinated" on the effects of atomic weapons. For one test, known as the *One Tree* explosion, they were stationed eight kilometers [five miles] from the blast, and then taken to the target point over the next two days, to be covered in dust. . . . Typical of the health consequences suffered by victims of the blasts is Rick Johnstone, a former air force mechanic and head of the Australian Nuclear Veterans Association. After spending 11 years in the courts, he became the only veteran to win a court case against the Australian government. He has heart disease, vascular disorders, leukemia, numerous carcinomas, calcified tendons and prematurely aged skin and sweat glands. His sons had birth defects—one did not develop any teeth and had chronic skin problems, while another had a harelip and an irregular palate.[135]

This sort of experimentation on men has gone on all over the world. As a result of such "experiments" we will obviously know more about the effects of radiation poisoning on men than we know about the effects of radiation poisoning on women. But for feminists to shamelessly cite this as an example of caring more about men's health than women's health takes a lot of hypocrisy.

If women have been such powerless, undervalued "chattel," why weren't women used to test the nightmarish effects of nuclear fallout? In many ways, women are and have always been *more* valued, not less. (For additional information regarding men used as "guinea pigs," see Issues Download # 3, "Antipathy/Disposability.") Why are men singled out for "testing" of this kind? Warren Farrell puts it bluntly: "We used men for experimental research for the same reason we use rats for experimental research."[136]

Women's health, however, has *not* been neglected. "In a search of more than three thousand medical journals listed in *Index Medicus,* *twenty-three* articles were on the subject of women's health for each *one* on men's."[137] [Emphasis in the original] As a rule, whenever the experimental research was deemed *safe* enough, the research has focused more on women than men.

Primal female bonding/solidarity against male physical strength and aggression, together with chivalry implanted deep within men's souls, have always led *both* sexes to protect women more than men.

For example, there were two overlapping studies done on the preventative effects of aspirin on heart attacks. The first from 1989 was conducted on 22,071 male physicians over a five-year period. The second from 1991 was conducted on 87,678 female nurses over a six-year period. "The press touted only the male study as sexism. Yet the women's study was longer in duration and there were four women studied for each man."[138] The myth that aspirin as stroke and heart attack preventative was tested solely on men is, to this day, used as a club with which feminists beat politicians over the head.

An article in the *New York Times*, in response to a report from the General Accounting Office on the status of women's health research at the NIH, decries the "neglect" of women in health care. Wendy McElroy, a research fellow for The Independent Institute in Oakland California, reads the same report and finds the opposite.

> For example, men constituted only 37% of participants in extramural research studies; 740 female-only studies were funded, but only 244 male-only ones. Nevertheless, the *Times* story — written by a medical reporter who should know how to read NIH studies — bore the headline "Research Neglects Women..." The slighting of men was not mentioned.[139]

Health issues are emblematic of the feminist tendency to take legitimate men's issues and co-opt them; thus transforming them into not so legitimate women's issues.

As a rule, where feminists complain of women being less *respected* (i.e., more pacified, dismissed, intellectually ignored; less obeyed, revered, and credited) the complaints are probably valid. Where feminists complain of women being less *loved* (i.e., more neglected, persecuted, and abused; less cared about, protected, or valued), however, they are probably turning a valid male complaint into a relatively bogus female complaint.

It is in this tendency that feminism sinks lowest. As a result, men are all the *more* marginalized with regard to public caring, concern, and compassion. Illegitimate feminist outcries of neglect toward women's health constitute a kind of strategic attack upon men—an attack that can, and sometimes does, cost men their lives. In this, and in many other ways, feminism may be justly labeled "militant."

For example: "A woman is 14 percent more likely to die from breast cancer than a man is from prostate cancer," said Warren Farrell back in 1993, "yet funding for breast cancer research is 660 percent greater than funding for prostate cancer research."[140] Here's Dr. Farrell writing on the subject again six years later:

> The chance of a man in the United States dying of prostate cancer is now about 20 percent greater than the chance of a woman dying of breast cancer. Yet the government spends almost four times as much money on breast cancer as it does on prostate cancer. This has, at least, improved from the almost 7 to 1 ratio I announced in 1993 in *The Myth of Male Power*. . . However, government spending creates only part of the prostate cancer/breast cancer gap. It is impossible to get a figure on the private spending gap, but I estimate it to be approximately 20: 1. And this does not include the "special efforts gap," such as the U.S. Post Office printing special 40-cent stamps to raise more than $25 million dollars for breast cancer research.[141]

Who could doubt that the vastly greater attention, effort, and funding directed at breast cancer research, as compared with prostate cancer research, accounts, at least in part, for this highly significant shift in death rates?

> In the 1920s, a new operation for an enlarged prostate replaced the old method. *For sixty years, no one studied the records to determine if the new operation was as beneficial.* When they did, it was found that the new operation resulted in a 45 percent *greater* chance of dying within five years of surgery. . . . If breast cancer researchers did not have funds to check for sixty years which form of surgery killed more women, the outcry would have been ferocious, and justifiably so.[142]
> [Emphasis in the original]

It would be great if there were unlimited funds for medical research, but funds are *limited* and when women receive *more* than their fair share men receive *less* than their fare share. Some of those men may justly be regarded "casualties" in the Battle of the Sexes.

Professor Tony Costello tells us, "Taxotere is the only effective chemotherapy for prostate cancer," but, at a cost of $3,000.00 per treatment and a requirement of up to 20 treatments, the drug is out of the financial reach of most men without health insurance. Yet "on the Pharmaceutical Benefits Scheme, women can access the drug for free."

How does Mr. Costello respond to an inequity that costs men their lives? His response is typical of those who discover an inequity suffered by men: "Men have been pretty poor advocates for their own cancer," he remarks.[143] True enough. Men have been pretty poor advocates for *all* their inequities. Men have been slow to cry "victim" and draw attention, social services, and funding away from women and children and toward themselves. But, then again, those men who do protest are routinely dismissed as "whiners." Perhaps it is society that has been a pretty poor advocate for men. Warren Farrell:

> What is the U.S. government doing about this disposability of almost half its population? It is identifying *women* as the at-risk group in its draft of "Healthy People 2010," the blueprint for legislation and funding for the first decade of the new millennium. It is treating women's *eating disorders* as more important than men's suicides, or men's heart disease, or men's occupational deaths, or men's seven-year-shorter lifespan. More precisely, it is virtually ignoring the causes of men dying. Overall, it specifies thirty-eight health objectives for women, two for men.[144]

Woman works the powers she has in compensation for the powers she lacks, same as Man. But, plying "victim" power is costly. In a world in which *both* sexes suffer, what is there to admire, revere and *respect* in Woman's self-proclaimed ownership of "victim"? If Man is less loved for being less lovable, mightn't Woman likewise be less respected for working power strategies that render her less respectable?

One neglected men's health issue involves an attack on masculinity itself. It comes in the form of excessive estrogenic chemicals in the environment and in the foods we eat. Many sources concur; estrogen and estrogen-related chemicals and even foodstuffs are ubiquitous at the local supermarket. And it could be that the attack on red meat and the tendency to replace it with soy products is a contributing factor.

In keeping with her wide-ranging study of the biological differences between men and women, gender scientist Anne Moir offers comprehensive scientific evidence that men have different dietary needs than women.[145] "It is time to take his needs into account," says Moir; "a healthy diet is not too healthy for him."[146] Moir claims that to get enough of the specific amino acids and proteins a man needs in the higher quantities he needs—to maintain healthy levels of iron and zinc—males need red meat in their diet. "Red meat has been demonized—health has been the excuse, but politics is the reason."[147] And, by politics, Moir means *gender* politics. If she's right, the oft-made claim that men are partly to blame for their own health issues, because men eat too much red meat, is turned on its ear.

More troubling is Moir's claim that the soy products replacing meat have estrogen-like properties that can feminize males. Apparently, soy is found in about 60 percent of all processed foods.[148] She also joins the chorus of scientists warning of the feminizing effect of various chemicals in the environment. A wide range of estrogenic chemicals, phthalates, dioxin, and other pollutants have been implicated. In nature, the feminizing effects on many species of fish, amphibians, and reptiles have been observed and documented for decades.

According to Janet Raloff of *Science News,* exposure in the womb, even to small amounts of certain plasticizers and solvents, may result in smaller-than-normal penis size, testes that do not descend into the scrotum properly, low testosterone levels, lower sperm production, and increased risk of testicular cancer. And, it is claimed, "more than one-quarter of U.S. women have phthalate concentrations in their bodies greater than those deemed in the new study to have genital-altering effects" on the boys they give birth to.[149] According to *Newsweek,* reduced sperm count in men is a "well-documented" trend, and "scientists wonder if endocrine disrupters in the water are partially responsible."[150]

Not only does estrogen pollution feminize males—both physically *and* behaviorally[151]—in sufficient quantities, it prevents males from being born at all. Reports are coming in worldwide:

> [S]everal recent studies point to the possible importance of ubiquitous hormonelike pollutants. For instance, a 1996 study reported the sex of children born to couples who had been exposed to large amounts of dioxin during a July 1976 industrial accident near Seveso, Italy. In the first 8 years after the accident, 12 daughters -- and no sons -- were born to the nine couples who had more than 100 parts per trillion (ppt) of dioxin in blood samples taken at the time of the accident.[152]

Apparently, in areas where dioxin and estrogen pollution is at its worst, the male birthrate has been cut in half!

The trend has not escaped the attention of documentarian Michael (*Stupid White Men*) Moore. "Guys! *Nature is trying to kill us off!* Why is Mother Nature doing this?" In answer to his own question: "If you were Nature . . . what would you do if you noticed that it was one particular gender of humans that was going out of its way to destroy you?"[153] Misandry, anyone? The evident delight with which Moore greets the news of declining male birthrates may offer a clue as to why this issue is so neglected.

Other neglected male health issues include:

A men's birth control pill

Suicide

Post traumatic stress disorder

Circumcision (as a possible trauma-producing experience)

Dyslexia

Autism

Nonspecific urethritis

Hemophilia

Lifespan

Depression (Rand Corporation finds 70 percent of male depression goes undetected)

Steroid abuse

Testicular cancer

Prostate cancer[154]

Health is a men's issue because it is primarily *men's* health that is being neglected. It is a men's issue because feminism twists the truth to make you believe that women's health is being neglected, which only intensifies attention paid to women's health at the further expense of men's health.

Issues Download #2 – Education

Schools all over the western world are adopting "zero tolerance" policies. Michael Crowley of *Reader's Digest* tells the tale:

> On a chilly December morning in Houston, Eddie Evans's 12-year-old son hurried out the door in shirt sleeves on his way to the bus stop. Feeling the cold, he ducked back into his house to quickly grab a jacket. It wasn't until he'd gotten inside the school building that he remembered his three-inch pocketknife was still in his coat. Why would a sixth-grader carry a knife? Because he was a Boy Scout and he'd brought it to his last Scout meeting. After asking a friend what he should do, the boy decided to keep quiet and hide the knife in his locker until the end of the day.
>
> But his friend mentioned the knife to a teacher, and school officials called the police. That afternoon, cops arrested the Evans child and took him to a juvenile detention center. "From that point on, my family's life was flipped on its head," the boy's father says. The boy was suspended from school for 45 days and enrolled in an alternative school for juvenile offenders. Evans says the place was like a boot camp, where his son—a good student, a youth leader in his church and a First Class Boy Scout—was so miserable he talked about suicide.[155]

Does "zero tolerance" apply equally to both genders, or does it, by its very nature, specifically target boys more than girls? Is the zero-tolerance-toward-boys rule an extension of the zero-empathy-toward-men rule? As seen from the politicized male perspective, we now turn our attention to the evidence suggesting that our current educational system is gynocentric, which is to say, biased in favor of female students and against male students.

In her book, *The Trouble with Boys* (2008), Peg Tyre describes recent dramatic shifts in preschool curricula—from an emphasis on building blocks and free play, to greater emphasis on reading and writing. As a result, a little boy "may encounter expectations that are so at odds with his natural development that they leave him bewildered and angry." Add to that all the hostility aimed his way for "refusing" to "keep still" and, "Instead of fostering a love of learning, his days in preschool may shake his confidence to the core."[156]

Scholastically sabotaged from the start, far too many boys are sent on an academic downward spiral from which they may *never* recover. Author and gender scientist Anne Moir:

> According to Dianne McGuinness, education is almost a conspiracy against the aptitudes and inclinations of the schoolboy: "In the early school years, children concentrate on reading and writing, skills that largely favor girls. As a result, boys fill remedial reading classes, don't learn to spell, and are classified as dyslexic or learning-disabled four times as often as girls. Had these punitive categories existed earlier they would have included Faraday, Edison and Einstein." Over 95 percent of children diagnosed as hyperactive are boys. . . . Given what we now know about the male brain and the female bias in education, the statistic of frustration is not surprising. Dr. Dianne McGuinness maintains that for too long this has been the guilty secret of educationalists: "Hiding the knowledge concerning sex-specific aptitudes in learning has done far more harm than good . . . it has caused a great deal of suffering in many boys who *normally* are slower to acquire reading skills when compared to girls. Even more pernicious is the spectacle of young boys on medication for a 'disease' that has no valid diagnosis."[157]

Newsweek columnist, George F. Will: "Consider the supposed epidemic of attention deficit/hyperactivity disorder (ADHD) that by 1996 had U.S. youngsters consuming 90 percent of the world's Ritalin."[158] Does this "epidemic" represent a change in *boys* or a change in our *attitude* toward boys? If "Jack Armstrong: The Aaaaaall-American Boy" (title of a popular radio adventure series, 1933-1951) was enrolled in the *current* American school system, would his boyish exuberance now be subdued with mega-doses of Ritalin?

Christina Hoff Sommers:

> Celeste Fremon, a Southern California writer and mother of boys, was stunned when she was informed that one of her sons had been punished for running during recess. On another occasion, he was almost suspended because he jumped over a bench. The principal told her, "He knows that jumping over benches is against the rules, so this constitutes defiance." Sad to say, normal youthful male exuberance is becoming unacceptable in more and more schools. . . . Recess—the

one time during the school day when boys can legitimately engage in rowdy play—is now under siege and may soon be a thing of the past. . . . The move to eliminate recess has aroused little notice and even less opposition. . . . school officials today would never act in a manner equally dismissive of girls' characteristic desires and needs, for they know they would immediately face a storm of justified protests from women advocates. Boys have no such protectors.[159]

Actually, *males* have no such protectors. Women and girls have both men *and* women primed to be their heroes. While I quote many exceptions in this book, in general, there is little reason to believe that either men or women possess a similarly chivalrous and/or protective impulse toward males.

Society remains largely focused on the girl "crisis." One of the leading proponents of the notion that American girls are in crisis, Carol Gilligan, author of *In a Different Voice: Psychological Theory and Women's Development* (1982) and professor of gender studies at the Harvard Graduate School of Education, has made quite a name for herself on the theory that girls "lose their voice" in adolescence. "Gilligan is the theorist who," says Sommers, "almost single-handedly, initiated the fashion of thinking about American girls as victimized, silenced Ophelias."[160] "Ophelia" refers to Hamlet's shrinking violet girlfriend, hence the book *Reviving Ophelia: Saving the Selves of Adolescent Girls* (2005) by Mary Pipher and Ruth Ross—required reading in any number of Women's Studies courses.

Gilligan's funding and power to dictate educational trends are clearly enormous, but is the validity of her theories and assumptions equal to her influence? Susan Harter, a psychologist at the University of Denver, set about trying to measure this "loss of voice."

> Using the common notion of voice as "having a say," "speaking one's mind," and "feeling listened to" and applying relatively objective measures, she and her colleagues recently tested the claims that adolescent girls have a lower "level of voice" than boys and that girls' level of voice drops sometime between the ages of eleven and seventeen. . . Harter concludes, "Findings revealed no gender differences nor any evidence that voice declines in female adolescents." In a second study . . . [t]heir conclusion is that "there is no evidence in our data for a loss of voice among female adolescents as a group." They could not even find a trend in that direction.[161]

Researchers have, however, found a trend in the *opposite* direction.

> In a 1990 U.S. Department of Education study of several thousand tenth-graders, 72 percent of girls "agreed" or "strongly agreed" with the statement "Teachers listen to what I have to say"; for boys the figure was 68 percent. Nor did Gilligan's portrait of adolescent girls

"losing their voice" agree with the findings of the AAUW self-esteem research that she herself helped to design. In that survey of children aged nine to fifteen, 57 percent said teachers call on girls more and 59 percent said that teachers pay more attention to girls. . . . Louis Harris Associates asked students to respond to the statement "I feel that teachers do not listen to what I have to say." Thirty-one percent of boys but only 19 percent of girls said the statement was "mostly true."[162]

In other words, at the very point in time at which girls had clearly and decisively pulled ahead of boys in virtually every measure of academic performance and self-confidence, Mary Pipher "calls American society a 'girl-poisoning' and 'girl-destroying culture.'"[163]

Again, if Woman truly desires respect, authentic well-earned respect, feminism's strategies seem like rather poor strategies for getting it. In an environment as girl-friendly and boy-hostile as the American school system, feminists sink mighty low to support their claims of MP/FV. That boys are about *nine* times more likely to be yelled at, reprimanded, and punished[164] has been used as evidence that teachers pay more attention to boys! I have seen girls' greater rate of *attempted* suicide presented as proof of a girl crisis while the fact that adolescent boys are *six* times as likely to *actually kill themselves*, was *literally* buried in a footnote! I don't know. Perhaps, on balance, feminists would rather women were *feared* than respected.

Statistical facts, and the negative picture for the performance and wellbeing of boys relative to girls that they paint, are growing ever harder to deny. So, after years of ignoring them, Gilligan finally turned her attentions to boys. But the approval, acceptance, empathy, and admiration shown girls are nowhere apparent in her outlook on boys.

Boys, Gilligan tells us, need saving from the malady that is masculinity. "Given Gilligan's extraordinary influence on American education, the doubts about her work become ever more pressing," says Sommers. "Do American boys need to be saved? And are thinkers like Gilligan and her followers equipped by knowledge and temperament to save them?"[165] When they came to the conclusion that the school system "short changes" girls, Gilligan and her followers endeavored to make schools more girl-friendly. Having now concluded that "patriarchy" (but not matrisensus) is crushing boys as well as girls, Gilligan and her followers endeavor to save boys from their own masculinity. But such efforts only make schools even more hostile toward boys and their naturally masculine energy.

> Does Gilligan really understand boys? She finds boys lacking in empathy, but does *she* empathize with *them?* Is she free of the tiresome misandry that infects so many gender theorists who never stop blaming

the "male culture" for all social and psychological ills? Nothing we have seen or heard offers the slightest reassurance that Gilligan and her colleagues are wise enough or objective enough to be trusted to lead the field in devising new ways of socializing boys.[166]

Socializing boys, that is, to behave more like girls.

Girls far outnumber boys in advanced placement classes and, with the exception of competitive sports; girls also dominate extracurricular activities including school newspapers, yearbook committees, student councils, and performing arts.[167] Meanwhile, according to one test, boys comprised four out of every five children with reading disorders such as dyslexia.[168] Boys, having *always* been perceived as essentially inferior to girls in terms of beauty, grace, goodness; home, family, and parenting, must *now* suffer a school experience in which they are clearly inferior to girls in virtually *every* parameter. Is it any wonder more boys than girls currently opt *out* of the school environment?

Ms. Sommers has also taken an in-depth look at how feminists have transformed textbooks. As a result of feminist rewrites, more high school students know of Harriet Tubman than either Winston Churchill or Joseph Stalin and know more about what Tubman did than they know, for example, of Abraham Lincoln's Emancipation Proclamation or that the U.S. Constitution divides powers between the states and the federal government.[169] This "padding" of women in history is something Sommers calls "filler feminism."

> Once Charles Lindbergh was a great role model for American boys; today, a textbook will make a point of informing students about Lindbergh's World War II isolationism. In the same text, Anne Morrow Lindbergh's very considerable achievements will be raised, but there will be no mention of her dalliance with fascism. . . . Filler feminism pads history with its own "facts" designed to drive home the lessons feminists wish to impart. . . [I]n some cases, feminist pressures determine what is excluded even more than they determine what is to be included. In an extensive survey of the new textbooks written under feminist guidelines, New York University psychologist Paul Vitz could find no positive portrayal of romance, marriage, or motherhood.[170]

"The problem of 'filler feminism' will get worse," warns Sommers. "Transformationists are well organized and their influence is growing apace. Because of transformationist pressures, the law in some states now actually mandates 'gender-fair' history."[171] Steven E. Rhoads, author of *Taking Sex Differences Seriously*, explains:

> In California the state education code demands that wherever reading presents achievements in science, history or other fields, "the achievements of women and men should be represented in approximately

equal numbers." As a result, one widely used history text gives more attention to Maria Mitchell, a nineteenth-century astronomer who discovered a comet, than to Albert Einstein; another has three pictures of Civil War nurses but none of General Sherman or General Grant.

During the 1980s, the most popular American history texts increase the representation of women important to the feminist movement on average from fewer than 10 to 35. . . . The same deficits occur as well in textbooks that teach students to read.[172]

Feminism influences not only textbooks,[173] but curricula as well. "While there is a vigorous national program to equalize male and female rates of success in science and math," says author/educator Lionel Tiger, "there is not a shred of equivalent attention to the far more central practical impact of the sharp deficit males face in reading and writing."[174] What effect has all this had on male students?

Columnist Melana Zyla Vickers:

> American colleges from Brown to Berkeley face a man shortage, and there's no end in sight. Yet few alarm bells are ringing. In the early 1970s, when the college demographics were roughly reversed [from what they are today] at 43 percent female and 57 percent male, federal education laws were reformed with the enactment in 1972 of Title IX, a provision that requires numerical parity for women in various areas of federally funded schooling. . . . The problem was structural, feminists never tired of repeating: A system built by men, for men, was blocking women's way. Today's shortage of men, by contrast, is largely ignored, denied, or covered up. Talk to university administrators, and few will admit that the imbalance is a problem, let alone that they're addressing it.
>
> Consider the view of Stephen Farmer, director of undergraduate admissions at the University of North Carolina, Chapel Hill, where this year's enrollment is only 41.6 percent male. "We really have made no attempt to balance the class. We are gender blind in applications, very scrupulously so." Why the blind devotion to gender-blindness? Because affirmative action for men is politically incorrect. And at universities receiving federal funding like UNC, it's also illegal. "My understanding of Title IX is that an admissions process that advantages men would be very difficult to defend," Farmer says.[175]

Like all feminist byproducts, Title IX serves females and females *only*.

In the opinion of many, the American university has become a sanctuary and stronghold for radical feminism and the misandry that goes with it. "At my university as at countless others," says Lionel Tiger, "one of the very first official greetings to students is a rape seminar predicated on the intrinsic danger which males carry with them."[176]

Emotions peak during ritual "Take Back the Night" rallies and marches. "At the end of the march, the victims are shuffled onto a stage and handed microphones and they're told that not only does their testimony have personal and therapeutic value for the listeners, but it has political value as well," explains Ruth Shalit, a reporter for *The New Republic* magazine. "By coming forward, they're helping to raise consciousness about male oppression."[177]

According to Shalit, the women getting up to speak "were encouraged by the campus Women's Center activists who ran the march to say, 'This happened to me, and it shows why all male-female interaction is just another structure of oppression.'"[178] Would it be surprising if hyped-up emotion, matrisensus solidarity to the cause, and competition for the coveted title of Most Victimized caused some of the student's stories of being raped to be embellished or even outright fabricated? Ms. Shalit reports on a case in point occurring at her alma mater, Princeton University. A woman got up to speak:

> She described a crime that was almost gothically brutal. She said that this guy dragged her to his room and tied her up. While raping her, he screamed things like, "My father buys me cheap girls like you to use up and throw away," and "public school bitch." He banged her head against the headboard until she was unconscious, and then dumped her at the entry to her dorm. . . . She said that after he raped her, she filed a complaint with the dean of students office, and the student agreed to withdraw for a year, but that he was now back on campus. She said he belonged to her eating club, so she saw him every day, and it was terribly disempowering for her to see this student and to know that no real action was taken against him.[179]

Thus far her story was much like the others and would have been accorded the same presumption of truth, but then . . .

> She got so caught up in her story that she submitted a written version to *The Daily Princetonian,* the student paper. The dean of students saw it and said, "Hey, wait a minute. This woman is maligning the dean of students office; she's saying that we failed to respond adequately to her complaint. I don't want women who are raped to be afraid to come and talk to us." So he wrote a letter explaining that if this had really happened, the male student would have been disciplined very severely. He would not have been allowed to remain in the community.[180]

When her story went from the general to the specific, it became vulnerable to fact checking and was discredited. But "rather than retract her story, she escalated it." Ms. Shalit continues:

> We can never know what was going through her head, but apparently her peers approached her and said, "Hey, what's going on? Dean Lowe said you never filed a complaint." She went on to name a particular student, spreading his name around campus. She had to escalate it into this huge conspiracy theory, and a web of deceit leading all the way up

to the university president's office. Later, she admitted she had never even met or spoken to the guy she accused. . . . Even after her retraction, she was supported by the Women's Center activists who said, "Listen, we cannot hope to find truth in all these stories. The goal is to reveal these women as 'lenses of oppression' through which the crimes of the patriarchy can be exposed."[181]

But how can the "oppressed" and the massively indulged be one and the same? How can the "oppressed" be the ones who have carte blanche to defame the character of their "oppressors"? And how can the supposedly "oppressed" be beyond accountability for truth?

"Her defense was, 'I was overcome by emotion.'"[182] Of course she was. "Take Back the Night" events are *designed* to ramp passions into overdrive. Aren't *all* participants overcome by emotion? And is this an excuse for outright lies that can destroy a man's life?

Author Kate O'Beirne tells us that at Vassar College:

> The female dean thought that men can benefit from being falsely accused. "They have a lot of pain, but it is not a pain that I would necessarily have spared them. I think it ideally initiates a process of self-exploration. 'How do I see women?' 'If I didn't violate her, could I have?' 'Do I have the potential to do to her what they say I did?' Those are good questions." I have a good question. How have we allowed women who think that falsely accusing our sons of rape is a helpful exercise in consciousness-raising to wield authority on our campuses?[183]

Avowed feminist Judith Grossman heartily approved of all things feminism; that is, until recent feminist "reforms" subjected her own son to a "nightmarish college tribunal":

> On today's college campuses, neither "beyond a reasonable doubt," nor even the lesser "by clear and convincing evidence" standard of proof is required to establish guilt of sexual misconduct. These safeguards of due process have, by order of the federal government, been replaced by what is known as "a preponderance of the evidence." What this means is that all my son's accuser needed to establish before a campus tribunal is that the allegations were "more likely than not" to have occurred by a margin of proof that can be as slim as 50.1% to 49.9%.[184]

Though well indicated, there was "no consideration," says Grossman "that jealousy or revenge might be motivating a spurned young ex-lover to lash out." Women *do* lash out sometimes:

> Women taking a class in feminist art at the University of Maryland publicly labeled male students whose names they picked from a campus phone book as "potential rapists" . . . on hundreds of posters put up around campus. . . . said every identifiable male name in the student directory was put on the list . . . Women involved in the project asked to remain anonymous fearing harassment.[185]

Who are the harassers and who are the harassed? Who are the oppressors and who are the ones running and ducking for cover? Wouldn't labeling every female student a "potential whore" be equally true—and equally inappropriate?

"William S. Pollack, a clinical psychologist at Harvard Medical School who heads the Center for Men and Young Men, calls schools 'some of the most boy-unfriendly places on Earth.'"[186] Not surprisingly, "[t]he number of boys who said they didn't like school rose 71 percent between 1980 and 2001"[187] All of which leads to the high dropout rate, which in turn, leaves fewer boys to apply for college. And does the American public understand what young men who make it to college may be facing? Author Nancy Friday asks:

> Have you spent time at a college lately? Are you aware of the matriarchal rule on these campuses where your sons as well as your daughters are being fed female-victim rhetoric that gains its fuel from the assumption that sleeping men will continue to back off from women's rage? Wake up, men! It baffles me why men continue to cave in at the slightest murmur of victimization of women.[188]

Indeed, men often seem *terrified* of offending women. In my experience the same does *not* hold true in reverse.

And, adds Friday, "there is another predicament a sexually unsure young man must face, which is how to respond to the new lesbian chic on college campuses. Today, The Power Bosom, clothed in the Wonderbra, is not flashed at him but at other girls."[189] Says Daphne Patai, "So much abuse is heaped on males that it becomes difficult for self-respecting women who consider themselves feminists to associate with them. This is epitomized in such expressions as 'sleeping with the enemy' and in the labeling of 'heterosexual feminist' as a 'paradoxical identity.'"[190] Sometimes, within the feminist realms of colleges and universities, efforts are made to reverse heterosexual women's sexual preferences and those who remain stubbornly hetero are said to be specially targeted for harassment.[191]

Apparently, highschool and college women who make a statement of turning away from men are common enough to have spawned the acronym, LUG (Lesbian Until Graduation).[192] So, males only become of interest *after* graduation (when a "wallet" will be needed)? That's some message these "LUGs" are sending. Given this level of hostility toward all things male it would be surprising if the percentage of men on campuses were *not* decreasing.

And it's not just male *students* who feel the wrath. Daphne Patai: "Tell a man such as Leroy Young, who lost his university position because of a barely investigated charge of sexual harassment, that feminists do not possess power."[193] Even before they become teachers, applicants are often required to present their "feminist credentials" as a prerequisite to getting hired.

The feminist legislation called Title IX dictates that female sports programs must equal male sports programs in size and funding. The problem? If there are 1,000 men but only 500 women within sports programs of equal size and funding, the individual male athlete will experience twice the competition to gain access to the program's resources and sports teams. Moreover, if universities can't interest female athletes in numbers that reasonably justify expanding their female athletic departments, then existing men's athletic departments must be downsized or cut entirely. Claire Yan writing in 2004 states that: "Since 2000, a total of 435 men's teams across America's college campuses have been eliminated."[194]

Yet Title IX has never successfully been employed to balance women's studies (often disguised as Gender Studies) with equal-opposite men's studies. Even worse, what "men's studies" there are only teach feminism to male students![a] [195]

This book and others like it prove that a *real* men's studies class, a *masculist* men's studies class, would have *plenty* to teach young men. (Though what we *really* need are equalist classes that teach both perspectives hand in hand and the "click" experience is the revelation that, in the big picture, It All Balances Out.) This book also makes clear that, contrary to feminist assertions, a history class is *nothing* like what a *real* men's studies class would be. Note that masculist perspectives are nowhere to be found within history books.

"Should it concern us that most teachers of women's studies think of knowledge as a 'patriarchal construction'?," asks Christina Hoff Sommers. "It should, because twenty years ago the nation's academies offered fewer than twenty courses in women's studies; today such courses number in the tens of thousands. Such rapid growth, which even now shows little signs of abating, is unprecedented in the annals of higher education."[196] Warren Farrell: "Nationwide, between a quarter and a third of universities now *require* women's studies courses for graduation. A study of college courses at fifty-five major universities found that every Ivy League school, with the exception of Princeton,

---

[a] Robert Connell is *the* authority, *the* architect of men's studies curricula, worldwide. Is this man who would teach young men gender politics empathic toward men and masculinity? In my opinion all there is to know about this man's attitude toward masculinity (and the current academic environment that would embrace and canonize him) is contained in the fact that he recently had himself castrated on the way to becoming a woman.

'now offers more courses in women's studies than economics, even though economics majors outnumber women's studies majors by roughly 10 to 1'"[197] [Emphasis in the original] In other words, astounding numbers of young women from all across the nation are being indoctrinated into victimhood and self-righteous contempt of men.

It doesn't take any great stretch of the imagination to see a connection between feminist-dominated anti-male bias at all levels of academia and the decline of male academic performance, attendance, and graduation. "Thirty years ago it was girls, not boys, who were lagging," writes Peg Tyre for *Newsweek*:

> The 1972 federal law Title IX forced schools to provide equal opportunities for girls in the classroom and on the playing field. Over the next two decades, billions of dollars were funneled into finding new ways to help girls achieve. . . . Boys, meanwhile, whose rates of achievement had begun to falter, were ignored and their problems allowed to fester.[198]

Now, when it is boys who are falling behind, the issue generates little empathy and less action. Yet the issue generates deeper *anxieties*. "This widening achievement gap, says Margaret Spellings, U.S. secretary of Education, 'has profound implications for the economy, society, families and democracy.'"[199] The situation was not so "profound" when it was girls suffering an achievement gap. What's the difference?

The difference is found within a politically incorrect yet *core* truth—a truth *shunned* by the media. The difference is this: low-achieving *females* still tend to be desired, cherished, loved, married, protected and provided for. Low-achieving *males* tend to be looked down upon, devalued, rejected, discarded and divorced.

Women—whether high-achieving or low-achieving—enjoy a kind of societally sanctioned "ownership" of beauty, grace, goodness; home, family, and parenting. In the past, high-achieving men "owned" intellect, competence, prestige; toughness, strength, and courage, but then as now low-achieving men are "bums," "losers," and "failures." When women fail to achieve they retain intrinsic value as lovers, nurturers, spouses, and mothers—through which they gain access to the earnings of men. When men fail to achieve they are granted far less *intrinsic* value (a theme I'll develop at length in the chapters to come).

It's a matter of degree, of course, but in general, women have far greater access to men's money than men have to women's money. I invite any man who doubts that to present himself as a potential "househusband" to every woman he meets so he can see for himself how little *intrinsic* value he is accorded. It's not so easy for men to gain access to the earnings of women, and those who do, will struggle to retain access over the long run (more on this later).

In an article with the title "Are Men Obsolete?" feminist author Jodie Allen catalogues all the ways in which women rising/men sinking is creating an ever-growing population of disenfranchised, jobless, family-less, and homeless men. She concludes: "All of which prompts the question: What shall we do with all the men?"[200] Indeed, we can't put them *all* in prison.

This is why *female* low achievement may pull heartstrings and demand action, but *male* low achievement has aware observers *worried*.

Education is a men's issue because men are experiencing ever diminishing levels of participation and success in all aspects of academia—a stronghold for feminism's anti-male bias. And education is a men's issue because men's declining academic performance leads to declining performance in every measure of economic status and success. This decline in male performance is particularly disturbing because *males* who fail to perform, achieve, and succeed are particularly vulnerable to becoming evermore societally, matrimonially, and parentally superfluous (even "obsolete").

Issues Download #3 – Antipathy/Disposability

Could it be true that we care less about men's pain and men's lives than we do about women's? Warren Farrell writes:

> I recently saw the movie *The River*. During the film Sissy Spacek has her arm punctured by a farm machine. The audience let out shouts of shock and revulsion. Several scenes later her husband – isolated from his family behind a picket line, living under conditions of squalor and low wages for weeks to earn enough to keep his family back in the warmth of their home – gets his face smashed in by the picketers. There was absolutely no reaction from the audience at the blood dripping out of the puncture wounds on his face."[201]

As is true in war, men may be butchered and slaughtered indiscriminately in "action/adventure" movies. As in war, men on the movie screen are disposable. But the camera need only follow a woman around ominously, and the mere *threat* of violence toward a *woman* is apt to get the movie re-categorized as a "horror film."[202]

If a filmmaker wants maximum impact from the death or mistreatment of a character that has had little or no screen time, a woman is a more likely choice to play the victim because strong feelings of heartrending pathos can be wrung from an audience toward even an unknown female victim. The cult classic TV show *Twin Peaks* spent one and a half seasons solving the mystery of who killed Laura Palmer, a character we meet only in flashbacks but whose death becomes the obsession of the entire town. Could such pathos have been wrung from the murder of *Larry* Palmer?

The movie *Saving Private Ryan* graphically illustrates the sheer *disposability* of men. We bear witness to men suffering the horrors of war, yet our deepest sympathies are directed elsewhere. It is for the sake of his *mother* that Private Ryan is saved. That is, the male (Private Ryan) is not removed from the fray in order to spare *him* further horror, hazards, and hardships; nor is he removed to spare him the death that has already taken his brothers. No, the male is saved in order to spare a *female* (Mrs. Ryan) further sorrow. *And,* in the effort to save Private Ryan—for the sake of Ryan's mother—five *more* men die.

Note how often hostage negotiators make special pleas for the release of female hostages. Worldwide outrage forced Saddam Hussein to release the women and children from among his hostages, but *only* the *women* and children.[203] Indeed, it's "women and children first" in every crisis situation. It is readily observable that 9 out of 10 pleas to help children in need feature the photograph of a girl.[204] Where danger is present, (e.g., the Titanic) men often act on culturally reinforced instinct to protect women. On a daily basis, men routinely act as "bodyguards" for women, even at the risk—or cost—of their lives.

U.S. Secretary of Defense, Casper Weinberger spoke for many when he said, "I think women are too valuable to be in combat."[205] As feminists observe that the *respected* male seems somehow more "important," so masculists observe that the *loved* female seems somehow more "valuable"—*intrinsically* valuable.

Author and men's rights activist Roy Schenk:

> "I've hauled around a lot of GIs who have been blown to hell in close combat. I wouldn't want to do that with women," was how Tech Sergeant Ron McCamish expressed it. . . . Obviously it is quite acceptable in our society to force men to risk and often lose their lives. But the overall attitude is that we cannot subject women to that threat. . . . In part, this is another aspect of men's training to protect women. But it clearly shows a value judgment that we men are somehow expendable.[206]

It is ironic that men who march off to war are vilified as the evil *cause* of war while men who refuse the battlefield are imprisoned for "draft evasion." Some have been placed before firing squads and shot dead for "cowardice." With such hostility directed against men who refuse the military role, is it any wonder that the guilt and shame internalized by conscientious objectors can goad such men into *volunteering* for even the most horrendous medical experiments?

In Minnesota, in 1944, Dr. Ancel Keys conducted an experiment to learn more about the effects of and recovery from starvation. More than two hundred conscientious objectors freely responded to Dr. Keys' initial call for volunteers. "It was amazing that so many men would volunteer to suffer for a full year, under constant supervision, at no small risk—for free."[207] Only those who fail to understand the extreme male vulnerability to shame will be amazed at what men will suffer to escape excruciating accusations of "weakness" and "cowardice"—and suffer they did.

Though little more than living skeletons, the men had to endure horrific ordeals on the treadmill. One man, mortified by his own physical deterioration, broke down emotionally. "It was an era when the sight of a man crying was still rare and terrible."[208] At *any* level of torment, historically, men have been obligated to endure stoically. But the starving men were not the only victims of emotional suppression. Utterly ill-equipped to cope with male tears and equally ill-equipped to offer a fellow male emotional support, the experimenters "just hurriedly completed their measurements and left the crying man alone as soon as possible."[209]

Men more "important"/women more "valuable," women intellectually suppressed/men emotionally suppressed: where feminists see only MP/FV, I see *mirror*-opposites everywhere I look.

Six months into the experiment, deranged with hunger, test subject #20 hatcheted off the middle three fingers of his left hand.[210] Was Sam Legg moved to become a masculist protesting the treatment of males? Did he come to understand his willingness to "volunteer" for torture as a form of "learned helplessness" and/or "internalized oppression"? Hardly. Despite loss of blood and risk of infection he refused food and successfully begged to remain in the experiment. "For the rest of my life," pleaded Sam to Doctor Keys, "people are going to ask me what I did during the war. This experiment is my chance to give an honorable answer to that question."[211] Do women *ever* experience psychological coercion ("learned helplessness," "internalized oppression") at *this* level?

"The Great Starvation Experiment" was only one of many dreadful experiments conducted on conscientious objectors under the supervision of the Civilian Public Service (CPS). "The suffering of the CPS guinea pigs was the stuff of legend.

> Forty eight CPS guinea pigs volunteered to wear lice-infested underwear in order to contract typhus. Other volunteers gargled the sputa from persons infected with pneumonia. Still another group strapped mosquito-filled boxes to their stomachs to contract malaria. The medical experiments satisfied some of the deep idealism held by these men;

it allowed them to take risks and suffer for the betterment of their fellow man, all the while remaining true to their pacifist convictions.[212]

Short of killing others, these men would endure *anything* to look themselves and others in the eye and say: "I might not have gone into battle, but I demonstrated my courage and paid the price for my country. I am a 'real' man." Feminism's power to define the terms has given "learned helplessness" and "internalized oppression" official credibility. In fact, these terms have been granted such *legal* credibility, they have been used successfully to defend women in courts of law—defend them even for the crime of killing their husbands.

Clearly, by any *rational* analysis of gender reality, these terms apply as well to men as to women, but what has reason to do with any of this? The terms are the exclusive property of females because only females have their own special "ism"—feminism.

While men who refused the battlefield searched their souls and agonized, their female counterparts were given a free pass. No such gnawing guilt trip was laid upon the souls of female "conscientious objectors." "Rosy the Riveter" encouraged women to take on the onerous and hazardous work that men left behind. But at no time was Woman ever coerced, or even *asked*, to share in the collective guilt, to get a little blood on her hands even indirectly by, say, working in a munitions plant.

If women are so undervalued and disposable relative to men, then why weren't women used to test the extremes of sleep deprivation, sensory deprivation, "g" forces, or the effects of LSD and many other dangerous drugs and medical procedures?

On the other hand, the lethal effects of radiation were well known when men were exposed to it in order to further medical knowledge on the subject. Just to satisfy military curiosity, U.S. soldiers were marched directly toward a mushroom cloud immediately following a nuclear test detonation (actual footage of this exists).[213] No masculist movement has raised awareness of male disposability. In general, we still believe that women are *the* victims specially entitled to virtually *all* cultural empathy.

Asking an audience to feel empathy toward men can result in dismaying levels of hostility. Christina Hoff Sommers describes the late *Playboy* columnist and men's advocate Asa Baber addressing an auditorium full of women.

> Baber opened his talk by observing that on Mother's Day, the phone lines throughout the United Sates are jammed because everyone is trying to call home to talk to their mothers. On Father's Day, the lines are free. "We have to ask why there is so much less interest in fathers" . . .

"It brought down the house," said Baber. "At first, I didn't get it. I thought my fly was open." But then he caught on and said, "If you think that is funny, you are going to think this is a laugh riot: I think the fact that our fathers are so much out of the loop is a major tragedy in our culture." ... An outraged audience hissed and booed him.[214]

In fact, the ensuing hostility actually drove him from the stage.

Nancy Friday has also attempted stir up some "Sympathy for the Devil" male. Says she, "It wasn't unusual at those college lectures for angry young women in the audience to stand and shake their fists at me for being sympathetic to men. 'We don't give a damn about men!' they would yell. 'Why are you talking about *their* freedom?'"[215] In her book, *Saving the Males: Why Men Matter, Why Women Should Care* (2008), Kathleen Parker allows that saving the males is an "unlikely vocation for a twenty-first-century woman."

> When I tell my women friends I want to save the males, they look at me as if noticing for the first time that I am insane. And then they say something like "Are you out of your mind? This is still a male-dominated world. It's women who need saving. Screw the men!" Actually, that's a direct quote. The reality is that men already have been screwed—and not in the way they prefer. For the past thirty years or so, males have been under siege by a culture that too often embraces the notion that men are to blame for all of life's ills.[216]

Indeed, I call it the all-fault-is-male rule.

Actually, saving the males is the *perfect* vocation for a twenty-first-century woman. Men have been acting as women's heroes for millennia. Now is the perfect time for women to step up, earn respect by holding womankind accountable for the damage the shadow side of feminism has done men and, at long last, *be* heroes. Heroes get respect; self-proclaimed victims, "damsels in distress" who insist that it is *they* who always and forever "need saving," do not. Too bad, then, that women who are concerned enough about men to have noticed the sufferings of men and who are *woman* enough to want to rise up in defense of men are so rare as to be stared at as if "insane."

Feeling and expressing empathy toward women is going with the flow. Express empathy toward men and you are apt to find yourself paddling upstream against the wind, a rather *icy* wind at that. We are still not prepared to love men enough to lend them empathy; nor are we prepared to respect women enough to hold them accountable.

In his book *The Myth of Male Power*, Dr. Farrell compares and contrasts the events surrounding a male oil tanker captain responsible for an oil spill, vs. the events surrounding a female air traffic controller responsible for the deaths of 34 airline passengers.

Captain Hazelwood was tried, convicted, fined, and imprisoned. The sudden, unexpected schedule change that forced this exhausted captain and crew back to sea was ignored. His name and person were publicized, reviled, and everywhere made the butt of jokes. That the Captain and his crew had been drinking the night before got massive press. That they had been drinking with the understanding that they were now *off-duty* got no press at all. By contrast, we don't know the air traffic controller's name because friends, colleagues and officials (many male, presumably) all rushed to protect her. They took her to a hotel room, comforted her there for days, furnished her with "humor therapy" and a counselor, shielded her from the press, and focused on *her* grief, not the grief of the injured or of the families of the dead.[217]

It may occur to the reader to wonder: If we respect men so much, then why are we so quick to heap contempt upon them? Paradoxically, the contempt toward Captain Hazelwood was born of high expectations toward him. Being a man and a ship's captain, we expect him to perform without lapse of judgment or attentiveness. When he failed, he fell from those high expectations. The ruthless public reaction also carries the expectation that, being a man, he ought to be able to take it like a man. We expect men to be competent and tough. Though disgraced, Hazelwood retained his high status as an adult man and as a ship's captain and was judged and treated accordingly.

But, when the female air traffic controller failed, she was let off the hook. She wasn't subjected to contempt because, in terms of competence, we expected less of her in the first place. She wasn't attacked in the media because we don't expect a woman to be tough enough to take it. Upon committing her fatal error, she immediately lost her professional status and even much of her adulthood, being transformed into a "damsel in distress" and protected accordingly.

It all comes down to a simple formula: Accountability without compassion is ruthless. It is what we more often direct at men. It is respecting men but not loving them. Compassion without accountability is infantilizing. It is what we more often direct at women. It is loving women but not respecting them.

When a man makes a fatal error he receives no empathy. When a woman makes a fatal error she receives nothing but empathy. Fault and blame are heaped upon him, while she is protected from fault and blame. Although women suffer all things along the respect axis, they are compensated with extra privilege in all things along the love axis.

Because we love women more than men, women have the greater *power* to elicit empathy. In fact, our disproportionate sympathies toward women provide the underlying emotional support for the women's movement. In reference to her early days in feminism, Nancy Friday writes, "There were men who were good feminists and who fought for women's rights."[218] Christina Hoff Sommers concurs: "It is worth remembering that Seneca Falls [feminist gathering] was organized by both men and women and that men actively participated in it and were welcomed."[219] Both sexes love women more, so *both* sexes have championed and raised women's concerns to the level of major societal concerns. But the zero-empathy-toward-men rule leaves men powerless to raise their concerns to an equal level. Thus, the conspicuous presence of feminism, together with the conspicuous absence of masculism, is *itself* a measure of how much more empathy women enjoy compared to men.

Arlie Hochschild's *The Second Shift* had quite an impact. In our extra empathy toward women/antipathy toward men, we were all too easily convinced that married women work their first shift on the job and a "second shift" at home, while married men put in their only shift at work—then come home and watch TV, beer in one hand, remote in the other. From time immemorial we've been told that "A man works from sun to sun, but a woman's work is never done." Studies into the question, however, indicate otherwise. Joel Waldfrogel for slate.com:

> Everyone from economists and sociologists to Oprah knows that women work more than men. Their longer combined hours, at the home and at the office, stop men from taking afternoon naps on the couch and cause fights that end with men spending nights on the couch. And yet according to new study, those longer hours are a myth, because it's just not true that women carry a heavier load. . . . In the United States and other rich countries, men average 5.2 hours of market work a day and 2.7 hours of homework each day, while women average 3.4 hours of market work and 4.5 hours of homework per day. Adding these up, men work an average of 7.9 hours per day, while women work an average of—drum roll, please—7.9 hours per day. This is the first major finding of the new study. Whatever you may have heard on *The View*, when these economists accounted for market work and homework, men and women spent about the same amount of time each day working.[220]

What ought to be understood as *A* View—namely, the feminist view—has shoved all other gender perspectives off the map until *A* View has become *The* View. Nevertheless, when contributions both inside *and outside* the home are accounted for, (including a man's longer average workweek and commute time), a University of Michigan study tells us that women average fifty-six hours per week fulfilling their role in marriage, while men average sixty-one hours per week fulfilling theirs.[221] Yet the disparity may be larger than that.

The Second Shift lists fifty tasks more often performed by wives than husbands and it is likely that the University of Michigan study took such tasks under consideration in compiling its figures. In his book, *Women Can't Hear What Men Don't Say,* Warren Farrell lists fifty-four tasks more often performed by husbands than wives, but it's doubtful the U. of M. researchers had similar masculist awareness.

Farrell's list includes: full-time bodyguard; driving the car when both he and she have had too much to drink or when driving conditions are particularly bad or when entering a city where neither she nor he has ever been; coaching Little League; raking and mowing and weeding and trimming and other yard work; remodeling jobs; painting; assembling/fixing things; lifting and moving heavy objects; car maintenance; taking out the garbage; shoveling snow; salting sidewalks; cleaning out the grill, the gutters, the fireplace, the basement, the attic, and so on. Perhaps it is because we so completely take for granted many of the tasks men perform, that they don't seem to fully register.

Shoveling snow off the roof to prevent roof collapse, painting atop a ladder, moving the piano, getting underneath the car to fix it—men's duties include all chores most likely to result in injury and/or heart attack; yet because these tasks don't come under the definition of "housework," studies ignore them. Here we have yet another example of feminism's power to define the terms. By defining housework to mean tasks done on a *daily* basis, not tasks done on an *as-needed* basis, feminism spotlights female efforts while male efforts remain under appreciated.

For every dollar a man spends, a woman spends about a dollar and forty cents—yet feminism gets considerable mileage out of the notion that women's work is "unpaid." On payday, many a husband comes home and hands his paycheck over to his wife. Rarely does a wife pay her husband. It is men's work around the home that tends to go unpaid *and unrecognized.* At any moment a husband is expected and obligated to protect and defend his wife at the risk of or cost to his own health and/or life. What is he paid for that?

"Typically, men are more active than women," asserts Anne Moir. To back the claim she cites a South Carolina study of over 2,000 adults, ages 30 to 60, concluding that "men were 43 percent more active than women."[222] So what perceptual biases would account for the common assumption that men are the "lazy" sex?

Consider: A man comes home from a hard day at work. His wife sleeping on the couch looks to him like an angel. Returning each day to this lovely sweet innocent makes all his toil, all his life worthwhile. He goes to the linen closet to drape her in a blanket, keep her warm and safe. He kisses his woman-child on the cheek filled with adoration.

A woman comes home from a hard day at work. Is the sight of her husband sleeping on the couch an equally warm experience for her? Does he appear an angel, or more like a lazy burden? I dare say that his laying there does not make her life worthwhile. She probably does *not* adore his passivity. However exaggerated this compare-and-contrast may be, nonetheless, I believe it contains an accurate snapshot of the male-female perceptual biases in these matters.

Because women are more often valued for what they *are* (intrinsic values) and men are more often valued for what they *do* (extrinsic values), a resting woman is not experienced in quite the same way a resting man is experienced. The image of the resting man takes on more weight and prominence in the mind because it is a relatively distasteful image. Words like "lazy," "indolent," and "burdensome" come to mind much more readily.

Media bias telling us that men are "lazy," make less effort, and suffer fewer sacrifices is a form of gender bigotry. Even worse, women who believe such assertions are invited to feel righteous, victimized, and enraged at men. Wives taught to see no fault in themselves but to see only laziness, slovenliness, insensitivity, oppression, and dominance in their husbands will be wives with one foot out the door. Women do in fact initiate about 70 percent of all divorce actions.[223] Men are relentlessly ridiculed for their fabled "fear of commitment." It would seem that, for many women, "commitment" is a sacred word indicative of adult maturity, but only up until the marriage contract has been signed. How many of those female-initiated divorces can be attributed to feminism's well-funded, systematic, and zealous dedication to poisoning the waters between women and men?

Disposable on the battlefield, disposable in hard/hazardous labor, disposable in divorce, disposable in parenting, disposable in prisons, disposable on the streets—Antipathy/Disposability is a men's issue because it is primarily men who are deprived of the support and concern that comes with gaining empathy, caring, and compassion. And it is primarily men who suffer the disposability that results.

Issues Download #4 – The "Wage Gap"

Warren Farrell tells a story that illustrates the modern issues of the "wage gap":

> A tall, silver-haired man . . . stepped forward cautiously. "Listen, I've got a problem. In the past few years, our company has been sued for sex discrimination three times. . . . [T]he lawsuits are wreaking havoc on the company and me. They're forcing us to put into legal fees what

we should be putting into products and into raises for people who are working, not suing." . . .

"Tell me, off the record. Are you paying women less than men?"

He thought about it long enough to make me assume the answer was "yes." Then he surprised me. "No. In reality, no. But sometimes it appears that we do . . . Sometimes we promote a woman faster than we would a man, giving her the same job title as a man, but she has fewer years with the company. . . . We'd pay anyone with fewer years less, but we move good women more quickly than we move good men, which is really discrimination against men, but it ends up looking like discrimination against women when we pay them less for seniority."

"Sort of ironic, huh?"

"Yeah. In fact, it's worse than that. Last year, I asked who was willing to relocate to bail out two of our problem branches: one in Alaska and one in Kansas. No one volunteered. So I offered extra pay. Then one of the men says, 'Maybe. I'll have to check with my family.' I ask if there are any women who want to go. The reaction is, 'Are you kidding? To Alaska?' . . . So I offered even more money to go to Alaska."

I laugh, "I can see it coming. She still says no, he says yes, but now you've got a guy with the same job title earning much more than his female colleague. . . . So you want to be fair—even acknowledged for bending over backwards to promote women—but when you're fair, the men get higher pay because they make more sacrifices, and even when you promote women faster, the men sometimes still get higher pay because they have more years of experience."

"Yes," he said. "And the HR people look at the raw data of men getting more pay and falsely conclude women are subject to discrimination. I feel this myself until I look more closely! Anyway, the result of no one understanding this is a lawsuit, an aggrieved woman, damaged morale, and even women managers who are afraid to hire women!"[224]

When these issues are viewed from a politicized male perspective, it requires only the most basic understanding of gender dynamics to see why women will tend to be less willing than men to chase a big paycheck all the way to Alaska.

The low-intrinsic-value male may endure several years of the harsh, hazardous, and isolated conditions involved in working on, say, the Alaskan oil pipeline, in order to return with sufficient extrinsic value (money) to place him on a "most eligible bachelors" list. What would similarly motivate his high-intrinsic-value female equivalent?

To the degree women experience less internal and external pressure to become "providers," it just stands to reason that they will be about that much less willing to accept high-risk, high-stress work involving odd hours, long hours, inflexible hours, long commutes, social isolation, demand for travel or relocation, commission-only wages, exposure to the elements, filthy, hazardous and/or arduous working conditions. Because more husbands than wives are truly, *lastingly* amenable to the role of financial provider, more wives than husbands are privileged with the option to take the kind of work that doesn't pay so well in order to avoid the kind of work that contributes to men's shorter life expectancy.

Nevertheless, it is officially accepted as fact that women are paid less than men for the exact same work for no other reason than oppression under "patriarchy." Actually, with or without passage of the Equal Rights Amendment, "Equality of opportunity now reigns," say Diana Furchtgott-Roth and Christine Stolba, authors of *Women's Figures: An Illustrated Guide to the Economic Progress of Women in America*. Ever since the Equal Pay Act of 1963, further reinforced by the Civil Rights Act of 1970, "Employers in the United States may not engage in sex discrimination involving unequal pay for equal work or in discriminatory hiring or promotion practices. Numerous court cases have upheld the statutes."[225] Roth and Stolba comment:

> Employment compensation is perhaps the bloodiest battleground in the wars between the sexes. It is also the area in which the most blatant distortion of statistics has occurred. . . . The statistics and arguments deployed as evidence for the existence of both the "wage gap" and "glass ceiling" do not . . . withstand close examination. . . . Although discrimination is frequently blamed for income differentials, a host of choices made by men and women—personal choices made *outside* the work environment—have important implications for men's and women's earnings. . . . For example, 80 percent of women bear children at some point in their lives, and approximately a quarter of employed women work part-time, so a higher percentage of women's work years are spent away from work. . . . Given those educational and career choices, comparing the *average* wages of men and women is a misuse of statistics and a grossly misleading comparison.[226] [Emphasis in the original]

If a man and a woman both started working for a company 20 years ago, yet he's paid more than she, political correctness points to discrimination and demands that they be paid the same. But further investigation, if there is any, may reveal that the woman had exercised her essentially female-only option and stayed home for four of those 20 years in order to take the central place in the emotional lives of *her* children. One day soon a woman's "entitlement" to "having it *all*" may be legally enforced. But, until then, the woman is paid less because companies are not in the feminism business; they pay and promote based on work performed on the *job*, not in the *home*.

Often, male/female wages are compared within a given field without taking into consideration the differing distribution of men and women among the various *sub*fields. Warren Farrell explains:

> When we see headlines proclaiming "Male Engineers Earn More Than Female Engineers" and don't ask whether they are working in the same subfields, we are ignoring, for example, that an aerospace engineer earns about $73,000 while a transmitter engineer earns about $32,000.

As a faculty member of the School of Medicine at the University of California, Farrell noticed that his female students were choosing subfields that had three characteristics in common:

> (1) contact with human life (for example, child psychiatry) rather than with human suffering and death (surgery); (2) the fewest round-the-clock emergency demands at unscheduled hours; (3) less specialization beyond the basic residency and internship. All three are low-pay formula choices, emphasizing fulfillment and flexibility. . . nationwide, men are 11 times more likely to become thoracic (chest) surgeons, 8 times more likely to be urological surgeons, and 9 times more likely to be orthopedic surgeons. The distinction is not just between surgery and nonsurgical choices, but between medicine that puts doctors in contact with life versus medicine that forces the doctor to deal with death.[227]

Because they must, jobs that deal in death pay more than jobs that deal in life. Both sexes know this at the outset when they choose their field of study. What if women are *privileged* to choose quality of life over paycheck? What if this is being powerful, not victimized? According to Dr. Farrell's research, when we compare wages within a specific subfield of medicine, men never out-earn women, but women sometimes out-earn men (e.g., general family practice, pediatrics, psychiatry, dermatology, neurology, radiation oncology, etc.)[228]

A woman goes home at the end of her 40-hour workweek, but a male coworker goes on to earn time-and-a-half for the last 20 hours of his 60-hour workweek. A feminist compares their *average* hourly pay and concludes that the man is being paid more just for being a man. Because feminism is so well protected from serious, high-profile challenge and critique, it is free to be just about as self-indulgent as it pleases. Nevertheless, on average, "When women and men work *less* than 40 hours a week, the *women* earn *more* than the men."[229]

Says Thomas Sowell, a renowned *econom*ist (not *femin*ist):

> The most important reason why women earn less than men is not that they are paid less for doing the very same work but that they are distributed differently among jobs and have fewer hours and less continuity in the labor force. Among college-educated, never-married individuals with no children who worked full-time and were from 40 to 64 years

old—that is, beyond the child-bearing years—men averaged $40,000 a year in income, while women averaged $47,000.[230]

It is a testament to Woman's power that when feminism speaks on her behalf, we forgo skepticism. *Think* about it: Jack and Jane sit side by side—same credentials, same output—they are identical in *every* way. And yet the Y chromosome is paid *26* percent more? You watch television, I ask you, is maleness really all *that* popular?

Companies will go to great lengths to protect their image and avoid controversy. Yet, even at the risk of enraged female employees, bad press, and potentially devastating Pay Gap lawsuits, **solely for being male**, Jack is paid $100,000 while Jane, **solely for being female**, is paid $74,000? To cut costs, companies will fire longtime employees just to avoid paying pensions. And yet a company will *not* simply fire Jack, hire Jill, save a whopping $26,000 a year, and lose *nothing?* Despite being irrational and illegal, we're told that this practice continues, all across America, undiminished, decade after decade . . . and we *believe* that.

Stating the obvious: "if women were paid only seventy-four cents on a man's dollar, then a firm could fire all its men, replace them with women, and have a cost advantage over rivals," say Roth and Stolba. But that never happens because: "both the *glass ceiling* and the *wage gap* are rhetorically powerful but factually bankrupt terms."[231]

And yet, where this feminist fable is concerned, there's no end in sight. "No matter how hard women work, or whatever they achieve in terms of advancement in their own professions and degrees, they will not be compensated equitably!" shouted Congressional Representative Rosa DeLauro at a "wage equity" rally in Washington, D.C.[232]

If we humans will choose *one* sex to stick it to, why on earth would we choose the sex that bands together, screams bloody murder, issues lawsuits, and raises hell over every inequity? Why not stick it to the sex that adamantly rejects victim, complaint, and protest? Why not stick it to the sex that never fights back? Unless, of course, that's exactly what we do.

By bringing us misleading wage discrepancy statistics, feminists promote hatred toward men and feelings of demoralization, hostility, rage, victim and vengeance in women. By not explaining *why* men earn more, feminists fail to empower women with a sense of what they could do about it. In his book, *Why Men Earn More: The Startling Truth Behind the Pay Gap—and What Women Can Do About It*, Warren Farrell—a masculist, not a feminist—explains in painstaking detail exactly how women, if they chose to endure everything men endure, could close the so-called "wage gap."

But feminists prefer an *easier* way. "I am proud," says President Obama, "that the first bill I signed into law was the Lilly Ledbetter Fair Pay Restoration Act."[233] When politicians like Rosa DeLauro, Bill Clinton (in his 1999 State of the Union Address), John Kerry (during his third debate with George W. Bush), Hillary Clinton, and Barack Obama pander to the "pay gap" myth, they set in motion laws, policies and pressures designed to *force* equal paychecks, *regardless*.

I'll distinguish between, and label, two overlapping forces operating here: *Reverse* Wage Gap, anti-male forces that reverse-discriminate against males, and what I'll call the Glass Escalators, pro-female forces that seek to propel women upward.

These forces include: a gynocentric educational system, affirmative action, feminist quotas, advantages created by myriad female-only organizations of all kinds (absent male equivalents), overcompensation for fear of "wage gap" lawsuits, plus feminist-induced "moral" pressures on employers (to reverse "centuries of discrimination"). Little wonder that women are rising and men are in decline.

The following is excerpted from an Op-Ed commentary by Gordon E. Finley in the *Washington Times*:

> A headline by Reuters on Nov. 7 [2008] was startling and certainly newsworthy: "Female U.S. corporate directors out-earn men: study." Yet, one full week later there was no newspaper coverage of this politically incorrect report, though the study was based on 25,000 corporate directors at 3,200 companies . . . Economist June O'Neill, the former director of the Congressional Budget Office, wrote an article titled "The gender gap in wages, circa 2000" in the May 2003 issue of the *American Economic Review*. By factoring in some of the many work-related differences between men and women such as hours worked per week, danger and travel requirements of the job, years of education, years in the field, and many other characteristics, she found the purported pay gap virtually vanished.[234]

The "pay gap" may vanish, but, narrow the focus a bit, and the *reverse* pay gap shows itself clearly: "Young women in New York, Chicago, and several of the nation's other largest cities who work full time have, according to an analysis of recent census data, forged ahead of men in wages. The shift has occurred in New York since 2000 and even earlier in Los Angeles and Dallas. . . . The analysis was prepared by Andrew Beveridge, a demographer at Queens College who first reported his findings in *Gotham Gazette*, published online by the Citizens Union Foundation. It shows that women from 21 to 30 living in New York City and working full time made 117 percent of men's wages, and even more in Dallas, 120 percent."[235]

Why is it particularly young women in large cities? Because "women have been graduating from college in larger numbers than men, and many of those women seem to gravitate toward urban areas."[236] Female advantages throughout the educational system lead to higher average female academic credentials (see Issues Download #2), and these Glass Escalators jumpstart women economically. And it is *also* true that young urban women are the women least likely to be married with children and are therefore the least likely to have shifted their priorities from money making to homemaking.

As the current recession heats up, the truth about men's economic woes becomes harder to hide and ignore. The *Boston Globe*, referring to the year 2008: "Some 1.1 million fewer men are working in the United States than there were a year ago, according to the Labor Department. By contrast, 12,000 more women are working."[237] As more men lose their jobs, more women are forced to get jobs. Where are women getting these jobs? In female-centric sectors like health care and the service industry—sectors that are booming. Meanwhile, male-centric sectors like manufacturing, construction, and technology industries are in decline. *The Globe* quotes Andrew Sum, director of the Center for Labor Market Studies at Northeastern University:

> During the same period, as jobs that allowed less-educated men to support a family have diminished, out-of-wedlock births to young women rose to 50 percent of births, from 20 percent in 1980. "We lost a lot of jobs that used to be an opportunity for these young guys," Sum said. "But we haven't figured out how to create good-paying, blue-collar jobs for men who don't have a college degree."[238]

Relatively less-educated/lower-wage men are not generally viewed as desirable "providers." As the numbers of such men increase, the numbers of such men rejected, divorced, and shut out of parenting also increase, leaving increasing numbers of single women to raise children.

Despite the reverse wage gap, men "keeping their noses to the grindstone," overall, still manage to earn a higher average wage. But the "wage gap," currently down to around 20 percent, is shrinking. And, in the next few decades, cultural trends promise to flip the traditional wage imbalance upside down. The reversal may even accelerate exponentially. If so, it would happen something like this: Should lesser achieving men resign themselves to permanent bachelorhood, they may give up on the quest for "success." With only their own modest needs to meet, they may be content to get by on low wages. But single mothers, with children to provide for, will be motivated to go after that big paycheck in order to pay those big childcare bills.

In an article for the *New York Post* entitled, "Men Worried They're Falling Behind in a 'He-cession'—They're Right," Maureen Callahan reminds us that 80 percent of recent job losses have hit men.

> But there's something else going on, a sort of free-floating anxiety about not just the current utility of men but what substantial role, if any, they will not have ceded to women in the future.... "The Decline of Men: How the American Male is Tuning Out, Giving Up, and Flipping Off His Culture," by the award-winning journalist Guy Garcia ... "Like an invisible epidemic with catastrophic implications, the decline of men cuts across all ages, races, and social-economic groups."[239]

If current trends continue and elite males become no longer prominent enough or numerous enough to steal focus, men's poor showing everywhere else *outside* the tip of the success pyramid must eventually shatter our illusions. We'll be *forced* into knowing what equalists already know—women rising and men sinking leads not toward, but *away* from *true* gender equality.

But, for the time being, we still have a lot of men paying the mortgage payments. We still have men working overtime to afford alimony and child-payments and we still have a lot of women receiving those payments who are relatively unmotivated to pursue long inflexible hours, harsh and/or hazardous, high-stress/high-wage work if that high-wage comes at too high a price (especially given their role as primary caregiver). And so, we still have a lot of men out earning women.

Owing to what may well be described as Paycheck Idolatry, the assumption is that life's meaning and quality depend solely upon the size of the paycheck. But what if women are relatively *privileged* to forgo 80-hour workweeks and have a life instead? From some perspectives, most careers and all jobs are akin to misery. They pay you to use you, not fulfill you. The more they pay you the more they use you up. Some women really do "sacrifice" their career for a husband, no small thing. But other women are "saved" from a miserable job by their husband. Moreover, for every man whose hard work, dedication, risk taking, and sacrifice lead to a higher wage, there is likely a woman attached to that man who is benefiting from that higher wage. Overall, women may earn less, but they spend more.

"In the U.S. alone, women account for $7 trillion in consumer and business spending and control more than $13 trillion in personal wealth, an amount that will almost double to $20 trillion in the next 15 years," says Fara Warner, author of *The Power of the Purse: How Smart Businesses Are Adapting to the World's Most Important Consumers—Women*. "Women make more than 80 percent of all consumer purchases around the world."[240]

"The serpent in the Garden of Eden knew it first," says Bernice Kanner, author of the nearly identically titled, *Pocketbook Power—How to Reach the Hearts and Minds of Today's Most Coveted Consumers—Women*. "Marketers caught on centuries later. Women are the ones to reach. Since Eve's time they've been the gatekeepers in the kingdom of consumer spending, the ultimate decision makers."[241] According to Kanner, "pocketbook power dominates the world of commerce. It decides not only what and who to buy (politically and entertainment-wise) but also when and where to buy it (online, boutiques, department stores, catalogs)." And, as we already learned with respect to "gender-based pricing," "Women are even dictating to retailers what they'll pay."[242]

> Statistics compiled by the Women's Entertainment Network, the sales promotion agency Frankel & Co., and others suggest that all told women make 88 percent of the retail purchases in America. . . . Four of every five homes in America have been selected by a woman, as have 7 of every 10 appliances. Women handle 75 percent of family finances . . . and write 80 percent of all checks. Demographers expect that by 2020, through inheritance, marriage, salary, or crook, women will control most of the money in America.[243]

Women controlling most of the money wouldn't be a problem if women were as generous with it as men. But they are not, and the biology (evolutionary psychology) of the matter suggests that they aren't going to be in anything like the foreseeable future.

Status—inextricably tied to wealth—is one of *the* primary cues eliciting the female sexual/romantic response. Women's "romance novels" are churned out by the millions. They account for a whopping 40 percent of paperback book sales.[244] These novels *always* feature a hero of *higher* status/wealth than the heroine. And because status is all relative, the higher women rise in status/wealth, the higher the bar is set for men to either rise even higher or suffer diminished marital attractiveness in women's eyes.

"I get the impression that if an African-American man can't produce economically, he's not considered good for much of anything," says interviewer Jack Kammer. "Is it common when a man loses his job for the woman to think he's no good anymore?" "Very common, I see it all the time," replies Doris Caldwell, psychiatric nurse and adviser to the national Black Men's Health Network. "It's a strong idea that the male should be the one who brings the funds in."[245]

As men in the black community have discovered, women earning more than men doesn't tend to put men on easy street as much as it just puts them out on the street. And yet, having observed black women's dramatic rise in educational and economic status leaving the black man in the dust, Ellis Cose makes the case for the "plight" of the black *woman:*

> Is this new black woman finally crashing through the double ceiling of race and gender? Or is she leaping into treacherous waters that will leave her stranded, unfulfilled, childless and alone? Can she thrive if her brother does not, if the black man succumbs, as hundreds of thousands already have, to the hopelessness of prison and the streets? Can she—dare she—thrive *without* the black man, finding happiness across the racial aisle? Or will she, out of compassion, loneliness or racial loyalty "settle" for men who—educationally, economically, professionally—are several steps beneath her?[246]

Owing to the relative low status of black men, black women tend to seek relatively high status men of other races or, conversely, single motherhood by choice, leaving the black *man* stranded, unfulfilled, childless, alone, and all too often homeless and/or imprisoned. Clearly, the black *man* has his own experience of a double ceiling of race *and gender*. But the zero-empathy-toward-men rule guarantees that it is the rising female, not the declining male who gets the empathy and victim status.

Newsweek cautions: "Even for women in 'mainstream' white America, says [sociologist Donna] Franklin, hard times may lie ahead. Black women may be the leaders in the trend of marrying less successful men, but white women are surely following."[247] Because the sexes are so tightly interwoven, doing harm to one sex does harm to both. Nevertheless, framing the economic decline of men (and the resultant rejection of men leading to increases in male homelessness/imprisonment) strictly in terms of its tending to render men inadequate in service to female purposes, thus making *women **the*** victims, is surely feminist sexism at its most *obscene*.

That aside, the question remains: could what's happening in the black community be a portent of things to come for society in general? Authors like Stephen Baskerville believe the future is now.

> The decline of the American family has reached critical and truly dangerous proportions. . . . Since the 1960s, we have been warned about a growing crisis of single-parent homes and fatherless children. Initially, this concerned mostly low-income communities in the inner cities. Four decades later, it has expanded to the affluent. The erosion of marriage, out-of-wedlock births, divorce, and fatherless children are now mainstream problems that threaten the general society.[248]

Currently, about 34 percent of children in general and 66 percent of African-American children are living in fatherless homes.[249] David Popenoe, author of *Life Without Father: Compelling new evidence that fatherhood and marriage are indispensable for the good of children and society*, notes that, back in 1960, the total number of years (15.1) the average black male spent living in households with children was about the same number of years (15.7) the average white male spent living in households with children back in 1980. Similar comparisons hold for out-of-wedlock births, teen pregnancies, and percentage of single-parent families.[250] Many believe that what you see in the black community now is what you'll see in families within the white community in about 20 years.

As the "wage gap" continues to close, will Man settle for being "settled for"? Or, will Man become ever more shut out of Woman's world altogether? Perhaps the above talk of prisons and the streets may begin to erode our confidence that the costs women pay for being shut out or rendered less-than in the world of men, necessarily exceeds the costs men pay for being shut out or rendered less-than in the world of women (more on that to come).

Women in general and feminists in particular would like to believe that the women's movement has been a purely righteous force with an influence purely for the good. But the Duality Principle (closely aligned with "the law of unintended consequences") guarantees positives and negatives, light and shadow in *all* human endeavors.

It is exactly because the women's movement has been so widely protected from official critique that its many shadows and destructive byproducts have been so freely indulged. Woman would greatly enhance her prestige by stepping up and owning her fair share of accountability for outcomes both good *and bad*.

Fara Warner, sums up "current reality":

> In the real world, at least 40 percent of marriages ended in divorce . . . and more people, especially women, were choosing to stay single as they gained more and more economic power. As author and professor Laura Kipnis wrote in an op-ed piece in The *New York Times* in January 2004: "The increasing economic self-sufficiency of women has certainly been a factor in declining marriage rates." . . . "While women control slightly more than half the wealth now, it will be a tsunami over the next 15 to 20 years," says Martha Barletta [author of the book *Marketing to Women: How to Understand, Reach, and Increase Your Share of the World's Largest Market Segment*].[251]

Indeed, the combined effect of "Fair" Pay Act legislation that tends to *force* equal (or better) pay to women for unequal work, together with over a thousand well-funded female-centric organizations, feminism in the absence of masculism, pervasive pro-female/anti-male sentiment, economic shifts that favor female-friendly job sectors, and a male-hostile educational environment resulting in women earning advanced degrees at increasingly superior rates, all add up to a portent of women leaving men in the economic dust. If heterosexual love, marriage, and parenting have taken a hit in recent decades, the situation promises to get much worse in the decades to come.

"When research finds that *wealthy* women worldwide marry up or don't marry at all," writes Warren Farrell, "she [feminist Natalie Angier] blames men for preventing women from making as much and claims women will *never* make as much [italics hers]. By missing the point that the wealthy woman has already made *more* than 99 percent of men she is able to dismiss wealthy women marrying for money or not marrying at all as men's fault."[252] [Emphasis in the original] All Fault Is Male?

A mere 15 percent of top female executives ever marry and almost all of them "marry up."[253] Every modern politician vows to put an end to the "wage gap." And yet, is the "wage gap"—meager as it is considering the extra financial pressures and the resultant extra efforts, risks, and sacrifices men make in order to make money—all that stands between men and an ever increasing matrimonial/parental irrelevance?

As usual, I'm skating on some very thin ice of political correctness here so let me be very clear about this. *Obviously* I don't object to equal *opportunity* in the form of equal pay for equal work. I do, however, object to efforts to *force* equal *results* without regard to fairness. I object to using reverse discrimination to undermine all of Man's extra efforts.

"To rise in the hierarchy," says gender scientist Anne Moir, "men are much more prepared than women to make sacrifices of their own time, pleasure, relaxation, health, safety or emotions."[254] If, in his fervent drive to achieve "success appeal," a man is willing to sign a contract allowing the company he works for to transfer him at will to any branch office, anywhere in the country, and his female equivalent is *not* willing to sign that contract, then *the man should be paid **more** than the woman.*

In suffering whatever it takes to earn more, men earn the *right* to earn more. And no Lilly Ledbetter "Fair" Pay Restoration Act should be fabricated to *force* employers to pay women the same, *regardless*. I object to achieving an end to the "wage gap" through the use of culture-wide anti-male bias at levels sufficient to sabotage and undermine male efforts to compensate for being male.

If cultural hostility toward all things male together with cultural forces that advantage women and disadvantage men socially, educationally, and economically should ever *force* the elimination of men's desperately achieved economic lead, then along with the disappearance of the "wage gap" I predict a concurrent diminishment of heterosexual love, heterosexual marriage, and heterosexual parenting.

Take a look around—look at the over 50 percent divorce rate, the 34 percent of children raised in fatherless homes[255]—it's in process even now. In fact, aged 18 and older, an entirely unprecedented 43 percent of adult Americans were single in 2007.[256] And, in the United States single mothers gave birth to an astonishing *40 percent* of the babies born in 2007.[257]

When it comes to women's right to equal pay for equal work, of course, no one would ever question it. Rightfully so. But, when it comes to women's obligation to be equally generous with the money earned, no one ever considers it. Such a concept is politically incorrect to the point of being unthinkable.

Any and all critique of the feminine may be labeled "sexism" and thus forbidden—but at what cost? Will feminism/chivalry *forever* circumscribe and stifle our search for truth? None of the above is an indictment of women. Both sexes seek love and romance, but the sexes are generally triggered into falling in love according to differing stimuli.

The average man's *first*-choice woman will probably be a woman possessing youth and beauty. The average woman's *first*-choice man will probably be a man possessing wealth and status. On that basis both sexes may be judged "shallow." But Man's attraction to youth and beauty is not purely carnal and Woman's attraction to wealth and status is not simply mercenary.

Youth and beauty are among the primary cues through which men ignite both sexually and *romantically*. Resources and status are among the primary cues through which women ignite *sexually* and romantically. Just as men respond to youth and beauty largely because they have no choice, so women respond to wealth and status largely because they have *no choice*. These responses are hard wired.

Why focus on gender generalizations, a practice many will find objectionable? There are, of course, any number of human qualities that both sexes find attractive. Male and female sexualities doubtless overlap more than they diverge. We focus on the divergence, however, because our understanding of gender dynamics comes of understanding not how the sexes are the *same*, but how the sexes are *different*. And the primary *difference* in male vs. female sexualities lies in the degree to which men tend to prioritize youth and beauty while women tend to prioritize wealth and status (more on this coming up).

Individual exceptions abound. There are women who'd be without two nickels to rub together so long as they're with the man they love.

Even so, these generalizations well describe the large scale human trends and tendencies in these matters. And it is the large scale trends and tendencies—not the exceptions—that drive the large scale societal machinery. Generalizations are employed in an effort to cut through overwhelming complexity and gain some measure of understanding of how things work in the Big Picture. Statistics, along with other cultural evidence, reveal that in the big picture heterosexual unions are diminishing significantly—in longevity, strength, and numbers. The costs to families, to children, and to society are inestimable. Keeping our focus on the large scale, we ask, what is going on here?

To express something complex in simplest terms: male wealth and status—primal cues that commonly, traditionally, instinctually draw women to men most intensely—are in decline. And Woman's sexual, romantic, and matrimonial desires toward Man have tended to decline in equal measure. By contrast, Man's sexual/romantic desires toward Woman haven't changed because Woman's desirable characteristics haven't changed. Man's emotional need for Woman remains as deep as always, but Woman has always gotten *her* emotional needs met primarily through children, family, and sisterhood. Meanwhile, Woman's material need for Man is a fraction of what it once was.

What must be said here is that much of what underlies this hetero-diminishment appears to lie within Woman's own biological *nature*. That doesn't make it Woman's *fault*, but to whatever extent that it is primarily *her* biological nature that is the limiting factor in all this, it is primarily Woman's *responsibility*.

If only focus could shift a bit from women's victimization to women's *power*, from Women's Rights to women's *responsibilities*, a whole new realm of gender politics might finally open up.

All Fault Is Male asserts that the problem isn't high status women turning away from low status men; the problem is low status men turning away from high status women owing to men feeling "threatened." There's truth in this assertion, but it's a truth applied ruthlessly without compassion. It is also a lesser truth often presented as the whole truth. I'll return to this subject, but, for now, I believe the *primary* truth is this: men have not the *least* problem attracting to and desiring marriage with women wealthier than themselves. But higher status women tend to see a lesser sexual/romantic value and *much* less marital value in lower status men; and the "problem" is, men know it.

Lower status men who back away from higher status women do so largely out of *legitimate* fears—fear of being judged and treated as inadequate; fear of eventual, inevitable rejection. The already high divorce rate increases by 50 percent when wives earn more income than their husbands.[258] And again, women initiate two-thirds to three-quarters of divorces.[a] Thus, the fears of lower status men are not without foundation.

In addition, as Man's status declines, many of his most attractive personal assets—confidence, competence, charisma, aggression, ambition—also decline. A woman may sidestep her attraction to male status by claiming, in all honesty, that it is these respect-inspiring qualities in a man that attract her, not his level of success. These driven qualities, however, serve as the best indicators either of a man's current level of success or a man's *potential* for success in the future. Attraction to a man's status or attraction to those personality characteristics that are the best predictors of a man's status, are pretty much one and the same attraction.

Deprived of the sense of purpose that goes with the role of protector/provider, insecure enervated men who may seem to lack even the *potential* for success are being rejected en masse. But I'm not angry because women tend to prioritize status. There's no sense heaping the judgments of blame upon either sex for being what two million years of human evolutionary psychology have made them. No, I'm frustrated because women, ego-invested in holding the moral highground, tend to deny their part in these gender dynamics. If we're to progress, *both* sexes must be accountable for who and what they are, their innate natures, their choices, and their effect in the world.

Evidence for the two sexes' biologically evolved divergent sexual preferences is overwhelming and examined extensively in book 2, *Love and Respect in the Past*. At this juncture, suffice it to say that men do not go ga-ga over breasts because it is the logical thing to do. Sex is not logical but biological.

While in other aspects men and women may differ only slightly, if there's one area in which the sexes could be expected to differ substantially, it would be the area of sex itself. I would not attempt to assign a number to so nebulous a measure. I would point out, however, that *if* the sexes' sexuality diverged by, say, 25 percent, that would leave a 75 percent overlap in which the sexes' sexuality works the same. Such a vast overlap could easily support those who take a stand in denial of biological difference. At the same time, when we consider how much

---

a It's worth noting that some sources claim *80* percent *or more*. See, for example: David C. Morrow, *How Women Manipulate: Essays Toward Gynology* (West Conshohocken, PA: Infinity Publishing, 2004) p.60. Also, Adryenn Ashley, *Every Single Girl's Guide to Her Future Husband's Last Divorce* (Petaluma, CA: ChickLit Media Group, 2008) p.65.: "In real life, women file for divorce 85% of the time."

is made of the 8 percent average divergence in height between men and women, a 25 percent divergence would be more than sufficient to yield *enormous* societal repercussions and consequences.

David M. Buss, avid researcher and author of *The Evolution of Desire,* has exhaustively studied the data and concludes: "In contemporary America, when women make more money than their husbands, they tend to leave them. One study found that the divorce rate among American couples in which the woman earns more than her husband is 50 percent higher than among couples in which the husband earns more than his wife . . . Men who do not fulfill women's primary preference for a mate who provides resources are jettisoned, especially when the woman can earn more than the man."[259]

"Perversely," comments Nancy Friday, "Buss's surveys seem to show that the most successful, educated women 'express an even stronger preference for high-earning men than do women who are less financially successful.'"[260] Indeed, according to Nancy Etcoff, author of *Survival of the Prettiest*, "Female medical students who expect to pull down large salaries say that they want to marry men whose incomes are equal to or higher than their own: not a single one reports wanting to marry a man who makes a lower income."[261]

So, if feminist dreams come true and we become a matriarchy comprised of female "doctors" and male "nurses," what happens to heterosexual love and marriage and parenting?

The crux of the issue is defined by the love/respect dynamic and obscured by a common phrase. Both sexes are said to "fall in love." Whether it is a man or a woman, the phrase is the same, but the *reality* is a bit different. Love truly is at the core of a man's romantic feelings toward a woman. But love is not *primarily* what a woman falls into. Traditionally, and still to this day, a kind of sexualized/romanticized *respect* lies at the heart of a woman's romantic feelings toward a man. I will substantiate that claim at length in book 3, *Love and Respect in the Present*. But, for now, suffice it to say that if a woman can't feel respect toward the man she's with, then she can't feel much of anything toward him—sexually/romantically.

Man continues to diminish and decline and, in so doing, Man continues to lose what he needs in order to gain Woman's respect, through which he gains Woman's love, through which he gains access to the world of women and the emotional sustenance therein. Certainly socialized factors enter into this dynamic, but biologically evolved sexual psychology is also a factor. And the biology of the matter sets limits on how far the traditional model can be stretched before the whole thing starts falling apart.

Anthropologist John Marshall Townsend has conducted studies in which photographs of men were rated for attractiveness and then these same photos were re-rated with the addition of describing the men in the photos as waiters, teachers, or doctors. Not surprisingly, "average-looking or even unattractive doctors received the same ratings as very attractive teachers."[262] Teachers are, of course, every bit as *lovable* as doctors, but teachers are not as *respected* as doctors, and in their romantic proclivities women tend to prioritize *respect*—so much so that, apparently, waiters need not apply.

Townsend went on to show that women were unanimously unwilling to date, have sex with, or marry men when those men are shown dressed in a Burger King outfit and baseball cap. Yet other women were willing to consider all three when shown pictures of *these same men* now shown wearing suits and Rolex watches.[263] By contrast, *Playboy* currently markets a DVD called "The Girls of McDonald's."

Toward men working behind a fast-food counter, women typically feel little. If a man is not sufficiently respect-worthy, a woman cannot fall in "love" with him. Toward women working behind a fast-food counter, men often feel sexual and romantic desire. A man can fall in love with a woman of *any* status, the only proviso being that he finds her lovable. The differences here are *not* subtle.

The evidence regarding gender and money is comprehensive and conclusive. Like other women's magazines, *Ms.* Magazine features many full-page ads for engagement rings and other gifts men are expected to give to women. Therefore, "I assumed *Ms.* would feature other gifts women could give to men," says Warren Farrell. "I checked the full-page ads of each issue from July 1983 through January 1985—nineteen months. Not one full-page ad for one gift a woman could give a man appeared in any *Ms.* Magazine for all nineteen issues—including two Christmas issues. Wait . . . there's one exception. One issue of *Ms.* Magazine does include an ad with a gift for a man: a subscription to *Ms.* Magazine."[264] Even the high-earning "liberated" women reading *Ms.* are neither expected nor invited to spend serious money on men.

"The generous man has higher value as a mate than the stingy man," says David Buss. "If, over evolutionary time, generosity in men provided these benefits repeatedly and the cues to a man's generosity were observable and reliable, then selection would favor the evolution of a preference for generosity in a mate."[265] The degree to which generous men are sexually favored determines the degree to which the genetic trait of generosity (toward women) gets passed down from fathers to sons. To a large extent, female sexual selection molds the male of the species (e.g., the peacock's tail).

On the issue of gender generosity, I'm not accusing Woman of a character flaw (monetarily/materially, women tend to be less generous than men, but in other ways women tend to be *more* generous than men); I'm saying that Woman is relatively unwilling to pay Man's mortgage because she feels a relatively lesser *internalized* need and/or obligation to do so. A man's ability and willingness to pay the mortgage is a key element in what makes the man romantically and matrimonially attractive and desirable. But it doesn't work that way in reverse. Male and female sexualities are *different*.

A woman wearing an Armani suit and Rolex watch may plunk her platinum American Express card down on the table of a fine French restaurant but, by itself, this action is *not* likely to give the man on the other side of that table an erection. By contrast, Katie Roiphe describes the "warm glow of security, as if everything in my life was suddenly going to be taken care of"[266] that sweeps over a woman when that same scenario is gender reversed. It is, in essence, the female "erection" she's describing.

Clearly, male and female sexualities *must* be different. If they were identical, there'd be no basis for *hetero*sexuality.

If women are the "fairer sex," what does that leave men as? Men feel such a need to compensate for being male they often *want* the role of sole provider. (Remember the 1950's stereotype—i.e., "Ralph Kramden"—*insisting* on being the sole provider?) What woman is so insecure of her intrinsic worth that she feels the need to "bring home the bacon" in order to be of value to her family?

In the gender dance men display relative financial generosity because only men *must*. It is one of the key ways men turn women on and it is the *only* way for men to compensate for being relatively less-than in sex, beauty, intimacy, domesticity, and parenting. It is this, not women's lack of money, that creates the Generosity Gap. As the Spending Gap makes plain, women have the money—they just don't feel the need to spend serious amounts of it on men. Why would they?

Both sexes spend more on the sex that both sexes love more.[267] When we consider not only all the money women spend but also all the money spent on women, it turns out that "Women influence two out of every three of the three trillion dollars spent in the United States each year!"[268] Yet we are to believe that women's labor is "unpaid." Surely, money is more fun to spend than to earn.

Given Woman's *true* economic situation and the reality of her feminine powers, we can see why, as compared to Man, she enters the work world freer to follow her heart/less pressured and therefore less inclined to sacrifice her time, comfort, safety, and social life in the single-minded pursuit of money. The so-called "pay gap" is the result.

It is clear to all college students that an engineering degree is bound to result in higher wages than an art history degree. So what does it tell us when more than 80 percent of the art history majors are women while more than 85 percent of the engineering majors are men?[269] All other things being equal, who wouldn't choose the emotionally enriching study of art over the sterile, numbers-driven study of engineering? But all other things are not equal. The "pay gap" derives out of women's freer choices, not "discrimination." Women's freer choices derive from power, not powerlessness.

Engineering firms are extra motivated to hire women especially to meet quotas—quotas that *must* be met if the firm will qualify to do business with the government (*the* source for many of the most lucrative contracts). With so few female engineering graduates to recruit from, competition for those female grads runs high. Little wonder, then, that despite lesser average initial qualifications, female engineers enjoy higher average starting wages than their male counterparts.[270]

Back in '99 when Carly Fiorina became CEO of Hewlett-Packard, the world's second-largest computer company, she told reporters, "I hope we are at a point that everyone has figured out that there is not a glass ceiling." Sally Pipes, President and CEO of *The Contrarian: News and Comments on Women's Issues,* concurs:

> Certainly no such obstacle prevented her rise to a position for which she was not ideally suited. Her bachelor's degree from Stanford, for example, was not in computer science or engineering but medieval history and philosophy. . . . She held important posts at Lucent Technologies for a decade but Carly Fiorina was the only candidate for the Hewlett-Packard job without direct experience in the computer business. She got the job anyway, confirming her belief that there is no glass ceiling.[271]

In fact, it sounds suspiciously like a Glass Escalator to me.

Being female certainly helped rather than hindered Fiorina's rise to the top of a "male dominated" arena. By all accounts Fiorina was confrontational, unpopular, reluctant to delegate authority, and with her at the helm, Hewlett-Packard stock dropped 18.2 percent. "The company's board opted to let her go, albeit with a severance package worth a reported $21.1 million."[272] With the news of Fiorina's departure HP stock prices immediately jumped 6.9 to 10.5 percent. "The stock is up a bit on the fact that nobody liked Carly's leadership all that much," said Robert Cihra, an analyst with Fulcrum Global Partners. "The Street had lost all faith in her and the market's hope is that anyone will be better."[273]

Even so, all too predictable cries of "sexism" and "glass ceiling" ensued. Sally Pipes:

By all appearances, the Fiorina case has caused the gender mavens to alter the very definition of the glass ceiling. It used to mean that women should have top jobs in proportion to their numbers in the population, a politically correct view that discounts personal differences, effort, and the choices that women make. In addition to the quota concept, the glass ceiling now apparently means that women are to be kept in top positions whatever their record as a leader, and regardless of whether, on their watch, the performance of the company suffers.[274]

"And as for Fiorina, despite a lack of experience in banking, she is now in the running to be the next president of the World Bank."[275] There's that Glass Escalator again. And, against incumbent Barbara Boxer, I see that Fiorina recently ran for a seat in the U.S. Senate.

Laura Ingraham, a lawyer on the advisory board of the Independent Women's Forum, writes, "True, there are still far fewer women than men in senior management positions, but feminists don't acknowledge that this disparity is at least partly the result of women's choices. . . . The idea that women are constantly thwarted by invisible barriers of sexism relegates women to permanent victim status . . . Instead of whining about an imaginary glass ceiling, why don't feminists celebrate the fact that women in the work force are at long last pushing against a wide open door?"[276] Why? Because the day feminists celebrate their victory is the day they become irrelevant.

As seen from the politicized male perspective, Man dominates, but Woman pulls the strings. Man disowns his gender truths accepting feminist truths as if they were his own.

Women are rising and men are in decline. Young, never-married women now well out earn their male counterparts. But it's all right feminism assures Man; we're just headed toward equality. The sexes are identical and interchangeable, we're told, so it will all just flip round. Women will be the breadwinners and men will be desired in the same way women have always been desired. Great, I hear men say; *let women bring home the bacon!* No need to climb success ladders. With the bar lowered so, men will be on easy street. So, what is there to worry about? It will all just flip around.

It needs saying that, to an extent—for some—feminist assurances have rung true. But, in the big picture: "To put it simply, the less a guy earns nowadays, the less likely they are to have ever been hitched."[277]

I see, especially in the poorer quarters, marriages plummeting both in numbers and in longevity. Recently, throughout the media, I see marriage described as being or becoming a "luxury good" reserved for the rich. I see fatherlessness accepted as the New Normal and I think . . . something here is not working.

In summation: the "wage gap," as commonly understood, is a myth, a myth used to justify anti-male discrimination and misandry—a myth created and sustained out of *female power* (female power to *choose* her level of involvement both in the homeplace and workplace, and female power to make us believe women are paid only 74 cents on the dollar). In actuality, what we think of as the "wage gap" is a measure of how much more intrinsically valued women are as lovers, spouses, and parents. To be as valued, men must present themselves as a package deal that includes themselves *plus* extrinsic values—resources, wages, status, and so on. David M. Buss comments:

> Women's desire for status shows up in everyday occurrences. A colleague overheard a conversation among four women at a restaurant. They were all complaining that there were no eligible men around. Yet these women were surrounded by male waiters, none of whom was wearing a wedding ring. Waiters, who do not have a high-status occupation, were apparently not even considered by these women.[278]

Which is why none of these waiters was wearing a wedding ring. If these men who surrounded them were not deemed "eligible," it's only because "eligible" is really a euphemism for successful—i.e., *at least* as successful as the women evaluating them. And so, *in general*, the higher women rise, the *higher* the bar is set.

No matter what beauty or brilliance he may bring to the table, a waiter could never hope to top a "most eligible bachelors" list. Such men must rise higher or risk either getting shut out of marriage altogether or only grudgingly "settled for" and treated accordingly.

Historically, and currently, men out-earn women as a direct result of extra sacrifices, efforts, and risk taking, fueled in large measure by female-imposed necessity. The *intrinsic-value gap*, born of women's relatively lesser sexual/matrimonial desires toward the *intrinsic* values of their opposite sex, is a driving force behind men's extra determination to perform, achieve, and succeed their way into having what women are empowered to demand of them.

Concurrently, women's "ownership" of the domestic realm rewards wives with options relatively unavailable to their husbands, i.e., fulltime, high wage demanding work (husbands will not experience this as an option as much they will experience it as an obligation); fulltime, low stress, low wage work; part-time work; volunteer work; fulltime parenting. To the degree that women still marry men and men still fulfill their role as Providers (of options), women are privileged to choose low wage options more often than men.

Men earning more out of a greater need to compensate/women earning less out of a lesser need to compensate—*that's* the wage gap *reality*. But, once again, feminism defines the terms. So the only "wage gap" commonly known is the Wage Gap *myth* in which women are paid 26% less simply for being women. It seems clear, however, that what little actually remains of the Wage Gap, it is rapidly being outdone by Glass Escalators and *Reverse* Wage Gap.

According to author Tom James, many men "measure their value in terms of how well they can provide for a woman and/or children. They may not show it, but inside they do not believe that they have any inherent value or worth in and of themselves."[279] According to author Jane Young, women are "very suspicious of men who want, say, to be househusbands or who end up that way because they're unemployed or underemployed."[280] Could it be that men's sense of self-worth is what Tom James says it is because many women measure men's value in terms of how well they can provide for a woman and/or children; and, they may not show it but, inside, women do not believe that men have inherent value or worth in and of themselves?

Socially, an unsuccessful man is a "bum," a "loser." Sexually, an unsuccessful man is, if not rejected outright, probably a temporary fling. Matrimonially, an unsuccessful man is a "barrel scraping." Parentally, an unsuccessful man is a "failure" who can't afford top-flight education and/or medical care for his children. And so, traditionally, it has primarily been men who would do just about *anything*, endure any hardship, take any risk, make any sacrifice for the acquisition of money, because only *men* are made to feel so socially, sexually, matrimonially, and parentally inadequate without it.

If women want to put an end to the "wage gap," they need only grant "waiters" the same sexual, matrimonial, and parental value men grant "waitresses." Ambition would equalize accordingly and the "wage gap" would be no more.

Feminism, however, proffers an alternate solution: Pay women *at least* as much as men *no matter what*. If women are generally less motivated to struggle and sacrifice all the way to the top, Glass Escalator them to the top. Up next, we'll examine cultural efforts to slander and disparage men as husbands and as fathers, driving a heterophobic wedge between men and women. Feminism watches as defamed men, deprived of their role, sink into emotional isolation/apathy, and then watches as flattered and supported ("you go, girl!"), educationally and economically advantaged, highly motivated single women/mothers out-earn men. Doubtless, if sufficiently indulged, feminism's strategy will soon put an end to the "wage gap;" but at what cost?

Is the "wage gap" all that stands against Man becoming Woman's *in*significant other? Is what's happening in the black community a portent of things to come for all races of men? These are questions I will explore at length in book 4, *Love and Respect in the Future*.

The so-called "wage gap" is a *men's* issue because: 1) The myth of it is used to apply societal pressures that result in a *true* reverse wage gap and 2) To the extent that men still feel the *need* to earn enough money to achieve "eligibility" in the eyes of women, the Wage Gap is really nothing more than the *Intrinsic-Value Gap* in disguise.

Issues Download #5 – Misandry: "Male Bashing"

Male bashing, driven by misandry (hatred/contempt toward men), is common and is just as commonly overlooked. Even authors whose books may flatter women at men's expense can be a bit taken aback by the magnitude of women's anger toward men. "For example, Dan Kiley, author of *The Peter Pan Syndrome* and *Wendy's Dilemma*, startled himself when, to an audience of several hundred Midwestern women, he was explaining research showing that men who are excessively self-involved are six times more likely to die of coronary heart disease than men who are not, *and four hundred women erupted into applause and cheers.*"[281] [Emphasis in the original]

Almost from the very beginning feminism has systematically, willfully and deliberately set about defaming the character of Man. In a book called *Who Stole Feminism?* (which Camille Paglia describes as using "ingenious detective work to unmask the shocking fraud and propaganda of establishment feminism"[282]), Christina Hoff Sommers debunks all-manner of spurious feminist claims.

Consider, for example, the extraordinary assertion that 150,000 women *die* from anorexia each year, an assertion that prompted Naomi Wolf to compare anorexia to the "Holocaust."

> In *Revolution from Within*, Gloria Steinem informs her readers that "in this country alone . . . about 150,000 females die of anorexia each year." That is more than three times the annual number of fatalities from car accidents for the total population. Steinem refers readers to another feminist best-seller, Naomi Wolf's *The Beauty Myth*. And in Ms. Wolf's book one again finds the statistic, along with the author's outrage. "How," she asks, "would America react to the mass self-immolation by hunger of its favorite sons?" Although "nothing justifies comparison with the Holocaust," she cannot refrain from making it anyway. "When confronted with a vast number of emaciated bodies starved not by nature but by men, one must notice a certain resemblance."[283]

Let's be clear about this. In asserting that men are inflicting a "Holocaust" upon women, Ms. Wolf is drawing a direct comparison between maleness and the evils of "Nazism."

It turns out that Wolf got her figures from *Fasting Girls: The Emergence of Anorexia Nervosa as a Modern Disease* by Joan Brumberg, former director of women's studies at Cornell University. Brumberg, who claims the American Anorexia and Bulimia Association as her source, "points out that the women who study eating problems 'seek to demonstrate that these disorders are an inevitable consequence of a misogynistic society that demeans women . . . by objectifying their bodies.'"[284] Owing to biases underlying its ideological agenda, in every gender reality, feminism *always* finds the Male-Power/Female Victimization that it seeks.

Sommers spoke with Dr. Diane Mickley, president of the American Anorexia and Bulimia Association:

> "We were misquoted," she said. In a 1985 newsletter the association had referred to 150,000 to 200,000 *sufferers* (*not* fatalities) of anorexia nervosa. What is the correct mortality rate? Most experts are reluctant to give exact figures. Reasonable estimates range from 100 to as many as 400 deaths per year. . . . such numbers are hardly evidence of a "holocaust." Yet now the false figure, supporting the view that our "sexist society" demeans women by objectifying their bodies, is widely accepted as true. . . . By now, the 150,000 figure has made it into college textbooks. A recent women's studies text, aptly titled *The Knowledge Explosion*, contains the erroneous figure in its preface.[285]

It seems clear to me that the most "anorexic" models appear in women's fashion magazines while the models who pose for men's magazines are better described as buxom, not anorexic. Studies show that when men and women are asked to draw the "ideal" female form, or choose the "ideal" female form from a set of drawings, the female figures women draw and choose are, on average, far thinner than the figures men draw and choose.

According to a survey published in *Cosmopolitan*,[286] when men were asked "What's your favorite female body type?" 61.6 percent of them checked the box marked "Curvy with an average rack." Only 11.6 percent checked the box marked "model-thin and small-chested." The comment chosen as most representative for this question read: "Bones aren't sexy, flesh is."

"It is not for men that we starve ourselves," says Nancy Friday, "but for the approving eyes of other women, who respond admiringly to the success of she who has managed to turn the lovely roundness of her body into sharp angles."[287] Other women agree. "Men don't mind a big behind," says writer Holy Millea, "Women do—both their own and every other large rump that goes by. And when we're not complaining,

'My ass is huge,' or pointing, 'Now *that's* a big ass,' we're thinking it so loudly we can hear each other."[288] "Dressing for women means you need to have a figure that looks good in clothes—meaning thin;" says writer Nigella Lawson, "whereas men, thank God, prefer women who look good naked, which translates into women who have curves."[289]

Perhaps the pressure Woman experiences to be without an ounce of fat is largely self-imposed? Is blaming men an example of the All-Fault-Is-Male rule? Could it be that feminist-fabricated statistics, the anti-male rhetoric that accompanies them, and the instant acceptance they receive are an inevitable consequence of a mis*andric* society that demeans men by blaming and defaming them?

Even as we extend empathy toward women for feeling the obligation to live up to the impossible standards of a supermodel, empathy toward men for feeling the same obligation to live up to the *even more* impossible standards of a superhero remains pretty much nil. If anorexic women think they look fat when they're actually thin, "Men with muscle dysmorphia think that they look small and weak, even if they are actually large and muscular."[290] If Barbie dolls and other cultural imagery instill an unrealistic expectation for thinness in girls and women, G.I. Joe dolls and other cultural imagery instill in males an expectation for bulk muscle that is *unachievable* without steroids. Accordingly, about one in ten adolescent males has taken some kind of "body enhancing" drug or supplement.[291] Potential side effects, sometimes permanent, include addiction, hyper-aggression, liver damage, breast and prostate enlargement, prostate cancer, shrunken testicles, infertility, loss of sex drive, and impotence.

Female and male issues like anorexia on the one hand and steroid abuse on the other, mirror each other all down the line. Logically, the issues are parallel, the consequences equivalent. Sentiment *alone* causes us to raise only female concerns to the level of major societal concerns—only female pain elicits sufficient societal empathy.

Consider the claim that: "Domestic violence (vs. pregnant women) is now responsible for more birth defects than all other causes combined."[292] Once again, Sommers did the fact checking that no one else did. She called Sarah Buel, a founder of the domestic violence advocacy project at Harvard Law School and the first to spread this Ms-information. Buel cited Caroline Whitehead, a maternal nurse and childcare specialist as her source. So Sommers talked with Ms. Whitehead.

> "It blows my mind. *It is not true*," she said. The whole mixup began, she explained, when she introduced Sarah Buel as a speaker at a 1989 conference for nurses and social workers. In presenting her, Ms. Whitehead mentioned that according to some March of Dimes research

she had seen, more women are screened for birth defects than are ever screened for domestic battery. . . . Ms. Whitehead had said nothing at all about battery *causing* birth defects."[293] [Emphasis in the original]

Nonetheless, the erroneous statistic proliferated unchecked throughout the media. The *Boston Globe* (09/02/91), *Time* magazine (01/18/93), *Dallas Morning News* (02/07/93), *Arizona Republic* (03/21/93), *Chicago Tribune* (04/18/93) among others all published this male-denigrating "fact."[294] Here again, FemalePower is revealed in the way that allegations of FemaleVictimization cause journalists to suddenly forgo the skepticism so fundamental to their trade.

> Battery responsible for more birth defects than all other causes combined? More than genetic disorders such as spina bifida, Down syndrome, Tay-Sachs, sickle-cell anemia? More than congenital heart disorders? More than alcohol, crack, or AIDS—more than all these things combined? Where were the fact-checkers, the editors, the skeptical journalists? Unfortunately, the anorexia statistic and the March of Dimes 'study' are typical of the quality of information we are getting on many women's issues from feminist researchers, women's advocates, and journalists.[295]

Dr. Richard T. Hise: "According to Jennifer Roback Morse, the press treats feminists with kid gloves, not asking them the tough questions leveled at other special interest groups like the tobacco industry or the National Rifle Association."[296] But then, the NRA and the tobacco industry are nowhere *near* as powerful as feminism.

Richard Hise quotes dissident feminist reporter Robyn Blumner of the *St. Petersburg Times* and a syndicated columnist for Tribune Media Services: "so many of the shibboleths about men being bad and women being good, women being victims and men being oppressors, are inaccurate. Even so, popular culture is full of such images, as in the television show, *Men Behaving Badly.*'"[297]

Media-driven discussions and depictions of "men behaving badly" go far beyond ridicule. When the media tells us that men beating on pregnant women account for more birth defects than *all other causes combined*, the media is telling us that men are *absolute scum*. This is defamation of character extreme enough to be a form of *violence*, a systematic, well organized, and well funded violence perpetrated by Woman upon Man. One consequence is *hetero*phobia. Says Ms. Sommers, "Many foundations and government agencies are involved in making it financially possible for a lot of resentful and angry women to spread their divisive philosophy and influence."[298] Yet, despite enormous political power, feminism is devoid of political accountability.

Countless anti-male falsehoods have become common knowledge. Take for example the myth of a 40 percent increase in violence toward women on "Super Bowl Sunday." When NBC prefaced the 1993 Super Bowl with "special pleas to men to stay calm," they accused men of being so worthless as to go about beating up women for no other impetus than a ballgame. Feminists called for "emergency preparations." "They also used the occasion to drive home the message that maleness and violence against women are synonymous. Nancy Isaac, a Harvard School of Public Health research associate who specializes in domestic violence, told the *Boston Globe*: 'It's a day for men to revel in their maleness and, unfortunately, for a lot of men that includes being violent toward women if they want to be.'"[299] Unfortunately, too many women believe that.

Upon investigation, *Washington Post* reporter Ken Ringle found the story was without basis in fact—not that it made any difference. All other journalists gullibly accepted the 40 percent figure and did their part in spreading the myth nationwide. "Millions of American women who heard about it are completely unaware that it is not true," laments Sommers. "What they do 'know' is that American males, especially the sports fans among them, are a dangerous and violent species."[300] What they know is feminist-induced heterophobia—an indoctrinated fear and hatred of men.

Little wonder then if women today are tending to avoid men and marriage. "But as women advance and men continue their downward slide," adds journalist and author Guy Garcia, "it's also true that more and more women are simply unable to find a man that they think is worth marrying."[301]

Feminism's false, anti-male aspersions comprise a devastatingly effective attack upon the masculine. In his book *The Decline of Men*, Guy Garcia catalogues the many signs and portents of Man's downward spiral. He quotes census statistics showing that the percentage of men reaching middle age (ages 40 to 44) without ever marrying has tripled in the last 25 years (from 6 to 18 percent). Not coincidentally, over the same period, the number of non-college-educated single men (ages 35 to 39) has nearly tripled (from 8 to 22 percent).[302]

Garcia goes on to make the connection between the increasing number of men without college degrees and men's decline in all other realms. "Experts agree," says Garcia, "that at least part of the reason is that men without college degrees have more difficulty finding women who will marry them."

> This trend of fewer male college graduates and the resulting decline in the number of married men is creating a vast pool of undereducated, lower-income bachelors for whom the economic, social, and emotional benefits of a stable family environment are permanently out of reach.

Even grimmer are the prospects for a generation of young men who will grow up without the example, support, and guidance of a loving father.... There is, in fact, a creeping sense that men are in some way an endangered species. From young boys who are slacking off and dropping out of school in record numbers, to grown guys who fritter away their time on video games and Internet porn.[303]

Google-search "men obsolete" and see for yourself the *astounding* outpouring of articles asking "Are Men Obsolete?" or proclaiming men already "obsolete."

Up to a point, the more devalued men are, the more fiercely competitive and driven they become in their need to compensate. Adversity, low intrinsic value, and low intrinsic power have always tempered men and driven men to perform their way to extrinsic value/power. Historically, these extra pressures have resulted in *both* a male elite at the tip of the "success" pyramid *and* vast throngs of "disposable" males occupying the pyramid's base.

In the past, Man coped with being relatively disposable by taking refuge in the one thing he could always count on. Man could always find meaning in being needed by Woman whom he adores and worships. Man could always draw vital emotional sustenance from gaining entrance to Woman's world of love, intimacy, home, family, and parenting. Of late, however, feminist-induced disadvantages in education and employment have been accompanied by Woman's increasing withdrawal of need, desire, and emotional support. The double whammy of increasing disadvantage together with female rejection has proved more demoralizing than motivating and has resulted in what Garcia describes as the current male malaise.

Even so, if there's one point upon which Garcia is adamant, it is this: "to blame the no-longer 'second' sex for the current male malaise is missing the point entirely. After all, what could possibly be less manly than seeking a scapegoat for our troubles?"[304] In his choice of the word "blame," Garcia forces our agreement. As we know, *blame* is indeed a fool's game. But what of *accountability*? Seeking a "scapegoat" is foolish, but what of Man taking a proactive stand to hold responsible cultural forces that do, *in fact*, seek to undermine him?

"The only thing that could possibly make things worse for men is if they made the mistake of blaming women for their predicament. The causes of the current male malaise are myriad," says Garcia declining to be more specific, "but one thing is clear: the solution certainly doesn't lie in shifting responsibility to the opposite sex. It would not just be wrong and false; it would be, well, unmanly."[305] Hmm, there's that word again. Could it be that holding Woman accountable would be neither wrong nor false; it would *only* be "unmanly"?

What *would* be "manly," of course, is for Man to take Full Responsibility. But, however much he may be inclined to do so, Man can*not* take Full Responsibility.[a] Garcia's entire book is a compendium of cultural indicators of political power shifting from Man to Woman, yet the idea of shifting responsibility accordingly is anathema. Don't power and responsibility go hand in hand?

Clearly, "unmanly" is synonymous with un-chivalrous. What we have here is a standard case of chivalry protecting women/feminism not just from the judgments of "blame" but also from adult *accountability*. The primal impulse is to maintain the status quo whereby the gift of compassion is directed exclusively to Woman and the gift of accountability is directed exclusively to Man.

But we've been all through this and we know that, as power and responsibility go hand in hand, so accountability and compassion must go hand in hand. Accountability without compassion is ruthless. It's what tradition would have us direct at men. It is respecting men but not loving men enough to allow for their human vulnerability. This ruthless accountability does not allow for "excuses" (i.e., "scapegoats") but extends further to disallow Man's vulnerability to powerful cultural forces that are damaging and diminishing him. Compassion without accountability is infantilizing. It's what tradition would have us direct at women. It is loving women but not respecting women enough to recognize women as powerful adults responsible for their effect upon the world—including their effect upon *men*.

Feminism is a creation of Woman and, being an autonomous adult, Woman must be held responsible for its byproducts—both good *and bad*. And not just card-carrying feminists but women *in general* are implicated in these matters.

In her role as media observer/analyst, Kathleen Parker notes: "men are variously portrayed as dolts, bullies, brutes, deadbeats, rapists, sexual predators, and wife beaters. Even otherwise easygoing family men in sitcoms are invariably cast as, at best, bumbling, dim-witted fools."[306] What lies behind this free-for-all of male bashing?

"If you follow the money and household spending, you find that women do most of the buying," says Parker, "including 59 percent of all automotive purchases. Women also watch TV more than men do.

---

[a] A distinction: on the personal level, we are, as individuals well served to take full responsibility for our own lives. On the political level, however, when Man takes Full Responsibility he is being grandiose to his own detriment. The world does not generally distinguish between responsibility and blame. When Man takes Full Responsibility, he draws Full Blame and suffers the Full Judgment and Full Hostility that go with it.

Apparently, women—who constitute four out of five sitcom viewers—are attracted to shows and ads that depict men as buffoons." Women's force of influence, includes inordinate control over TV, the most powerful ideological force on earth. In creating a demand for male-bashing imagery—a demand the media fulfills in response to FemalePower—what is the impact on men and masculinity? "What do these depictions telegraph to the children who also watch these shows?"[307]

Man would gladly enable Woman's flight from accountability and keep all the adult status for himself. That is indeed the "manly" thing to do, but it is false. Man has only half the power and can legitimately claim only *half* the responsibility. Woman owns the other half of the responsibility—whether she is *held* responsible or not.

We have already seen how feminist falsehoods together with strident feminist advocacy have resulted in over-allocating cultural attentions, efforts, and funding toward women/away from men in the crucial realms of health and education. We have seen that advocacy result also in a *reverse* pay gap. What more direct correlation between feminist influence and male decline could there be?

Up next we'll look at feminism's deleterious effect upon fathers' rights and follow that with a look at what effect the "Sexual Harassment Industry" is having on men in the workplace. But we are *now* examining feminist-induced and inspired heterophobia, misandry, and defamation of male character, everywhere apparent in both the political and the personal realms. In the political realm, misandry inspires anti-male laws and policies and media depictions that further male decline. In the personal realm, male decline is having the same result worldwide.

For example, in the Béarn region of France:

> Although the land no longer produced the impressive income it once had, the men felt obligated to tend it. Meanwhile, modern women shunned farm life, lured away by jobs and adventure in the city. They occasionally returned for the traditional balls, but the men who awaited them had lost their prestige and become unmarriageable.[308]

We *all* agree that a woman can't possibly be expected to marry some jobless man still living with his parents. That would be ridiculous . . . right? But wait—marrying someone without a job still living at home—hey, isn't that what men have been doing for millennia? In fact, at the very *sight* of her, haven't starry-eyed men felt a deep *need* to "go out and make something of themselves" so as to become *worthy* of such a woman? Haven't men gone into debt and gone down on their knees to present a diamond symbolizing their earnest intention to devote their lives to protect and provide for that jobless woman still living with her parents?

If "women are simply unable to find a man that they think is worth marrying," we can react with tacit agreement that men of lower prestige are "unmarriageable" and righteously shunned, *or,* we can hold women accountable for *their* sexist views that grant men such low intrinsic value in the first place.

In 1987 Marion L. Kranichfeld of Pennsylvania State University wrote: "Women occupy positions at the very center of the family, affectively and structurally, in contrast to men who seem to be becoming increasingly isolated from the family, and have virtually no substitute for this essential primary group form."[309] What is the effect of this increasing isolation from family—already evident in 1987 and overwhelming more than 20 years later? Shut out from this essential source of emotional sustenance, what damage is done men?

In my role as mentor to high school boys, I can *see* the damage misandry is doing. The boys I've worked with have "I'm of the sex that's bad, ugly, inadequate, at fault and to blame" written all over their faces. It's in their posture. It's in their listless attitude.

Out of their own *personal* experience, boys who've grown up fatherless *know* themselves to be parentally nonessential!

According to Katherine Hanson, director of the Women's Educational Equity Act (WEEA) Publishing Center, "Every year nearly four million women are beaten to death" and "Violence is the leading cause of death among women."[310] Who are the perpetrators of this annual "gendercide"? Who else but the scum of the earth, the heinous male.

"Hanson, [Nan] Stein, and other 'gender-fair' activists regularly whip themselves into an anti-male frenzy with their false statistics," says Christina Hoff Sommers.[311] How false? Per annum, in the U.S., the total number of women dying from *all causes combined* is about *one* million.[312] In 1996, according to the FBI, 3,631 women died by violence—at the hands of both men *and women*. To put that figure into perspective, approximately 6,000 women died by suicide. Meanwhile, in that same year, approximately 27,000 men (4.4 times as many) died by suicide.[313] Might some of the vastly greater number of male suicides rightly be considered casualties in feminism's war against men and masculinity? Author Howard Schwartz:

> I have no doubt that, someday, the distortion of the truth by the radical feminists of our time will be seen to have been the greatest intellectual crime of the second half of the twentieth century. At the present time, however, we still live under the aegis of that crime, and calling attention to it is an act of great moral courage. Of those who have stood up and told the story, none has done so more elegantly and effectively than Christina Hoff Sommers.[314]

Given that "History is written by the victors," I'm not so confident that feminism will *ever* be revealed. Too much of what Sommers calls "Ms-information" has already been unquestioningly accepted as fact, taught in schools, and circulated widely enough to become famous. The damage done gender relations along with male self-esteem, efficacy, and credibility, is incalculable.

I will leave it to other men to shield and shelter feminism from accountability. I for one see no sense in further protecting an already overprotected movement whose high ranking members will sink to any level to do me and my kind *every* damage they can inflict.

Little wonder we're getting books these days with titles like *The War Against Boys* (2000) by Christina Hoff Sommers and *The War Against Men* (2004), by Dr. Richard T. Hise:

> The radical feminist aims are pushed by a propaganda machine that is second to none and is bolstered by a supportive media which is controlled by women and biased toward their agenda. The amount of information touting the causes of women in general and radical feminism in particular is prodigious. A man can hardly go a day without being bombarded with their propaganda in some form or another—television, radio, magazines, newspapers, web sites, conferences, symposia, etc. and the number of women's organizations boggles the mind. . . . Pages 259-390 of *The Encyclopedia Of Women's Associations Worldwide* lists 1,027 different groups in the United States.[315]

Many of these female-centric organizations receive federal, which is to say taxpayer, which is to say primarily *male* funding.

Men are cowed by guilt and the omnipresent accusation of "male chauvinist pig" and women are cowed by the accusation of "traitor to the cause," leaving only a few "heretics" to play the vital role of skeptic. Men in the U.S. beating women to death at a rate of 4 *million* a year? Feminism has become so self-indulgent in its rhetoric, so corrupt, not because it is the product of women, but because it is a belief system so fiercely *protected* from high-level public critique. That protection *itself* has doomed feminism to ever-escalating hyperbole.

And that protection has also provided safe haven for the most aggressive, hate-filled minds to rise highest. Following a brush-up with such feminists, gender theorist Carol Iannone wrote, "I had glimpsed something of the ruthlessness of ideological commitment, at odds with its purportedly humane objectives. What good is it to insist that they were only the exceptions when 'exceptions' like that had muscled their way into power? Feminism of my type had no defense against aggression like that."[316] Even if one accepts the dubious notion of an "egalitarian" female-ism, such moderate feminism is marginalized under the thumb of a toxic "radical" feminism. What good is it to insist that the problem is restricted to "radical" feminism when "radical" feminism is the dominant feminism?

All products of the human mind (whether in art or science or ideology) *must* be subject to judgment and critique; it's the only way to promote high standards in quantity and quality of truth. In my judgment, *all* feminism is wrong-headed—moderate feminism is moderately wrong-headed; radical feminism is radically wrong-headed. The sooner we phase out female-ism and transition to equalism the sooner we'll move beyond this destructive era in gender politics with its matronizing attitude toward women and hostile attitude toward men.

We mustn't protect feminism for fear that it is all that stands between Woman's Liberation and some absurd notion of Woman "chained to the kitchen stove." It was technology, not ideology that freed women from biology-as-destiny. So long as reproductive and domestic technology continues to free women up and high tech keeps the workplace safe, suitable and appealing to women, gender roles will remain flexible. Besides, equalism would still address any and all women's issues; it just wouldn't address women's issues *exclusively*.

And what of skepticism toward Ms. Sommers' findings? In deciding whom to believe, one of the more important questions to ask ourselves is: Who stands to gain and who stands to lose? Richard Gelles and Suzanne Steinmetz are two of the *many* domestic violence researchers who conclude that DV is, in truth, a two-way street.

Christina Hoff Sommers:
> Richard Gelles claims that whenever male researchers question exaggerated findings on domestic battery, it is never long before rumors begin circulating that he is himself a batterer. For female skeptics, however, the situation appears to be equally intimidating. When Suzanne K. Steinmetz, a co-investigator in the First National Family Violence Survey, was being considered for promotion, the feminists launched a letter-writing campaign urging that it be denied. She also received calls threatening her and her family, and there was a bomb threat at a conference where she spoke. . . . However, in today's environment for feminist research, the higher your figures for abuse, the more likely you'll reap rewards, regardless of your methodology.
>
> You'll be mentioned in feminist encyclopedias, dictionaries, "fact sheets," and textbooks. Your research will be widely publicized; Ellen Goodman, Anna Quindlen, and Judy Mann will put you in their columns. Fashion magazines will reproduce your charts and graphs. You may be quoted by Pat Schroeder, Joseph Biden, and surgeon generals from both parties. Senator Kennedy's office will call. You should expect to be invited to give expert testimony before Congress. As for would-be critics, they're in for grief.[317]

Advocates of the MP/FV and the MB/WG paradigms not only enjoy ready acceptance, professional success, and prestige, they also enjoy material rewards as well. Clearly, a pro-female/feminist stance may be motivated by more than a simple desire to speak truth. What motivates those who would denounce pro-female/anti-male bias? Aside from the hate mail, hissing crowds, and death threats, speaking truth would seem to be a men's advocate's only motive.

Those who would challenge feminism, the world's most powerful ideology, have much to lose and little to gain.

Warren Farrell began his career as a feminist. As is typically the case with men who speak on behalf of women, Farrell thrived. His first publication, a feminist book (*The Liberated Man*), was a massive bestseller. He was applauded and flattered with remarks about what tremendous "internal security" he must have to speak from the feminist perspective. "How can we clone you?" feminists would ask.

It wasn't long, however, before Farrell discovered that "It took far more internal security to speak on behalf of men than to speak on behalf of women. Or, more accurately, to speak on behalf of both sexes rather than on behalf of only women."[318]

"For three years I served on the board of directors of the National Organization for Women in New York City. As I explained women's perspectives to men, I often noticed a woman 'elbow' the man she was with, as if to say, 'see, even an expert says what a jerk you are.' I slowly became good at saying what women wanted to hear. I enjoyed the standing ovations that followed." As Farrell became enlightened to *male* perspectives, he faced a dilemma. "Now when women asked, 'Why are men afraid of commitment?' or feminists said, 'Men have the power,' my answers incorporated both sexes' perspectives. Almost overnight my standing ovations disintegrated. After each speaking engagement, I was no longer receiving three or four new requests to speak. My financial security was drying up. I would not be honest if I denied that this tempted me to return to being a spokesperson only for women's perspectives."[319]

Consider also the case of Neil Lyndon, a British journalist who in 1992 wrote *No More Sex War: The Failures of Feminism*.[320] In a *Sunday Times* retrospective in December 2000, he recounts the wave of personal attacks that descended on him.

> Until December 1990, I was among the highest-paid and best-established feature writers in British journalism . . . After "Badmouthing" [the essay that preceded Lyndon's book], however, I became a pariah, a professional and social outcast. My income plummeted from many thousands of pounds a month to hundreds. In the whole year of 1993, I

earned less money in total than I had earned each month in 1989. . . . Many of the people who wrote about me had clearly not read the book. Their articles were almost entirely devoted to personal attacks on me. Most reviews declared - on the basis of no evidence - that the book emerged from personal disturbance in my life and was largely about me. Every literary editor gave my book to a feminist to review, which was like giving an anti-Catholic book to a cardinal. . . . The reason why they did not seek out the truth must be, I think, that the imaginary role in which I had been cast - as heretic, as moral derelict, as sexual inadequate, as maniac - was essential to the dismissal of my arguments."[321]

With what my long and varied studies have taught me about women's issues, I too could become a women's advocate and enjoy a far easier, more lucrative path. Like Warren Farrell and Neil Lyndon, I too have only *one* motive for taking on this arduous and thankless task. Why invite the feminist wrath of women, along with the "shoot-the-messenger" hostility of men, all for speaking on behalf of both sexes rather than speaking on behalf of women only? I do so out of the deep conviction that there is essential truth in what masculism has to offer and *both* sexes need to hear it. The MP/FV belief system is both false and poisonous and *must* be challenged.

Ever doubted and scrutinized, an unscrupulous masculist would be found out in a heartbeat, which is why *The Myth of Male Power* concludes with over fifty pages of documentation in support of its factual and statistical information. The extra effort masculists make toward accuracy doesn't render masculist facts infallible of course, but it does render them more credible than feminist advocacy stats that rarely stand up under scrutiny.

That said, it is worth repeating: when it comes to gender, there are no disinterested parties. Where gender is concerned bias is omnipresent. It is, therefore, wise to maintain healthy skepticism toward both feminist and masculist rhetoric. I can't know with certainty the accuracy of every fact and every assertion in this book; but I do know this: to demonstrate that It All Balances Out, masculist rhetoric need not be superior to feminist rhetoric, it need only be as good. And frankly, that's not setting the bar very high.

Sommers quotes feminists who express no regrets for *knowingly* fabricating and spreading false and misleading information, believing apparently that the feminist cause justifies *any* means. Men are slandered by a profusion of false statistics regarding rape, domestic violence, and "violence against women" in general.

It has become the stuff of legend that men are wont to drug women's drinks then rape them. But, "Doctors tested 75 women who claimed their drinks had been spiked by date rape drugs, not one tested positive. Women who claim to be victims of 'date-rape' drugs such as Rohypnol have in fact been rendered helpless by binge-drinking, says a study by doctors." The medical establishment has conducted an extensive investigation into the matter yet, "They found no evidence that any woman seeking help from emergency doctors because their drinks were allegedly spiked had actually been given these drugs."[322]

Not only does ubiquitous anti-male slander force the average man to work all that much harder to "prove himself" to the women he socializes with, but also, the more men are falsely depicted as dangerously brutal, the more women live with unnecessary fear. The result is ever escalating *hetero*phobia.

Having turned "Men are scum" into something like common knowledge, the culture feels justified in demeaning men. In their book, *Spreading Misandry: The teaching of contempt for men in popular culture*, authors Paul Nathanson and Katherine K. Young analyze a score of films and as many TV shows. In one category of misandric filmmaking they find that "The implication of many movies and television shows, for example, is that women do not or should not need men for any significant reason. Men are not necessarily evil, just superfluous. *Indifference* to men, not hostility, is encouraged."[323] [Emphasis in the original] Again, the true opposite of love is not hate; it is *indifference*.

Gloria Steinem's oft-quoted phrase, "A woman without a man is like a fish without a bicycle," would not have caught the public imagination so if there weren't at least some kernel of truth in how it sums up Woman's feelings (or lack of feelings) toward Man. I believe that there's truth *enough* in this worldview to lend support to my contention that *both* sexes love women more than men. In fact, as previously stated, I would go so far as to say that a woman doesn't fall in *love* with a man as much as she falls into a kind of sexualized and romanticized *respect* with a man.[a] Humanity's relative loveless indifference toward men equals humanity's relative lack of respect toward women, leading to an imperfect but *balanced* system.

A more virulent category of misandric films is summed up with:

> Almost any night of the week, viewers can watch innocent but vulnerable women go through the following cycle: caring diligently for their families and achieving their professional goals; worrying patiently over some danger sign; suffering patiently or screaming defiantly;

---

[a] For further explanation, please visit my website: http://www.anima-animus.com/wordpress/

fighting back with courage and intelligence; and finally, overcoming their evil or psychotic male adversaries."[324]

Clearly, we've moved now from indifference to *hatred*.

The Color Purple may be considered a trend setter in this regard. "Though not necessarily the first of its kind, this movie can now be seen as a kind of cinematic watershed. It was a sign of the times but also of things to come: what was still unusual in 1985 would become commonplace by 1990. Since then, movies based on this mentality have become pervasive."[325] For once, some men *actually protested!* Why? "In a nutshell, it was that every male character, without exception, is either a hopelessly stupid buffoon, a fiendishly evil tyrant, or both. And every female character, without exception, is a purely innocent victim, a quietly enduring hero, or both."[326]

ManBad/WomanGood: this film "consists ultimately of a battle between the forces of light represented by women and those of darkness represented by men." One of the men "eventually repents his evil ways. But the last scene finds him so crushed by guilt that he cannot bring himself even to ask for Celie's forgiveness. She, meanwhile, has successfully transcended the past and can thus move on into the future. Even in contrition, then, the men are worthless. At their *best*, in other words, they are irrelevant anachronisms"[327]

So, what are women to do about the obsolete male? "It proposes a very simple solution to the problem of hostility between the sexes. Women need to escape from suffering. Their suffering is due primarily or even solely to the evil of men. Ergo, women need to escape from men. Sure enough, four innocent and heroic women escape from four evil and stupid men."[328] Is there a connection between anti-male propaganda and women initiating 70 percent of all divorce actions?

Many have noticed the trend toward degrading men in the media. Dr Jim Macnamara, who works as a media researcher, has recently published his findings in a book, *Media and Male Identity: The Making and Remaking of Men*.

> [T]he study involved detailed analysis of over 2,000 media articles and program segments. Dr Macnamara found that, by volume, 69 per cent of mass media reporting and commentary on men was unfavourable, compared with just 12 per cent favourable and 19 per cent neutral or balanced. Some of the recurring themes in media content portrayed men as violent, sexually abusive, unable to be trusted with children, 'deadbeat dads', commitment phobic and in need of 're-construction'. "Men were predominantly reported or portrayed in mass media as villains, aggressors, perverts and philanderers, with more than 75 per cent of all mass media representations of men and male identity showing men in on one of these four ways," Dr Macnamara says. Further, in

somewhat of a back-handed compliment, when positive portrayals of men as sensitive, emotional or caring were presented, these were described as men's and boys' 'feminine side.'[329]

"As feminists are so fond of asking when confronted with what they consider patriarchal cultural productions, What is wrong with this picture? What is left out, and why?"[330] What is left out, of course, is the mirror opposite. We're not seeing nearly as much of kind, loving men being raked over the coals by cruel, loveless women. Why? Because women don't want to see that. What too many women *do* want to see are depictions of their own righteousness versus male guilt, stupidity, evil, and inadequacy. Says Cathy Young, "A poll in which 42 percent of women agree that 'men are basically selfish and self-centered' is presented as evidence of male rottenness, not female chauvinism. One could hardly imagine the reverse."[331]

It works like this: A negative said of women is sexism because a negative said of women can only be "false." A negative said of men is not sexism because a negative said of men can only be "true." So you see, negative stereotypes of men are not *sexism*, they're "truth telling." But then again, only fifty years ago the phrase "Women have no head for business" wasn't sexism; it was "truth telling." How long will it be before we realize that we've exchanged the old sexism for new?

The great irony is this: "manly," males absolutely *recoil* at "victim." In refusing to acknowledge his victimization, Man rejects *protesting* his victimization and, in so doing, he refuses to demand *justice* for himself. Instead, he rolls over, goes to sleep, and snarls at anyone who threatens to awaken him. While asleep, the "manly" man plays the unconscious role of feminist doormat (i.e., *victim*).

Even if grown men, armored knights every one, will deny the damage cultural misandry is doing them, what of all the young men and boys who can't even remember back to a time when the portrayal of men and masculinity was more generally favorable? Even if men will claim immunity to the pervasive denigration and ridicule, will we be so hardhearted as to deny the vulnerability of boys?

Misandry and male bashing are men's issues because they currently outweigh misogyny and female bashing. Every male, each in his own way, will internalize the generally male-negative cultural messages and every male, each in his own way, will be damaged by them. On a societal scale, misandry underlies the vastly higher rates of male suicide, incarceration, homelessness, battlefield and work-related death, as well as anti-male bias in social services, charities, courts of law, parenting, and, of course, the media. Just as importantly, misandry underlies our cultural *indifference* to all the above.

Issues Download #6 – Reproduction/Parenting: the Glass Wall

Herb Goldberg quotes a man who has encountered what we will dub the "Glass Wall": "Man's role—how has it affected my life? At thirty-five, I chose to emphasize family togetherness and neglect my profession if necessary. At fifty-seven, I see no reward for time spent with and for the family, in terms of love or appreciation. I see a thousand punishments for neglecting my profession."[332]

Should the husband/father prioritize family and decline to work more than 40 hours a week, he will lose out to other men willing to work 60+ hours a week. In truth, *most* fathers would choose to cut back on work in favor of family. But, in a world where a father may well be thought of more as "wallet" than parent, a man's efforts to emphasize parenting may cost him more than benefit him.

If men are to be true equals in parenting, if men are to break through the Glass Wall, we need to acknowledge, honor, and *support* fathers, not merely as "second parents," but as parents who contribute an important, uniquely different, masculine *style* of parenting.

As seen from the politicized male perspective, we now embark on an analysis of parenting in general and fatherhood in particular. Fatherhood, of course, begins at conception.

Because only girls and women can get pregnant, we preach that only females need be wary of sex. Isn't it true, however, that only males can be put to work paying off 18 to 21 years of legally enforced child support payments?

"Legally, women hold the cards," says Kathleen Parker.

> If a woman gets pregnant, she can abort—even without her husband's consent. If she chooses to have the child, she gets a baby and the man gets an invoice. Inarguably, a man should support his offspring, but by that same logic, shouldn't he have a say in whether his child is born or aborted?[333]

Even within wedlock a mother can abort a child with or without the father's consent. Yet fathers *not* married to the mothers of their children have even *fewer* parental rights. Given that 40 percent of children are born *out* of wedlock, father's rights suffer accordingly.

In the heat of the moment should he forgo the awkwardness of a pleasure deadening condom, only she has a birth control pill, and so only she has birth control. All he has is her word for it that she's taking the birth control, an assurance that's legally irrelevant in a court of law.

Upon pregnancy, the woman can choose between abortion, adoption, or suing for childpayments. About all the father can do is await the mother's decision, a decision in which the biological father has few legal rights, even though her decision will have a profound impact on all aspects of *his* future life—an impact that is not solely financial. While facilitating men's personal growth work I have seen many a man reduced to tears while telling the story of a woman he loved, the child they conceived, and the aborting of that child—*his* child—against his wishes.

Will the mother abort his child; will she give birth to his child? Will she include him in parenting or shut him out? Will she take the child and up and move away? Will he pay for a child he is not allowed to parent? Will he be deceived into paying for a child sired by another man? Will he refuse to pay and live life as a criminal ever at risk of imprisonment? Will she raise the child without his ever knowing he has a child? Will she then sue him for ten or more years of retroactive childpayments?

Sentimentality alone has us believing that women alone suffer vulnerability in sex. This gender sentimentality is powerful! There is great beauty and poetry in it. But if we are to strive for fairness in our gender analysis, we mustn't allow this sentimentality, driven by instinct, to derail our *thinking*.

We're told that it all comes down to "her body, her choice." How is the fetus part of a woman's body when, in fact, the fetus is a genetically unique individual? It's *his* body being used to work a job, *any* job, so long as it pays the bills. What makes her "labor" so much more important than his?

Anyway, if it all comes down to "her body, her choice," then how do we account for the low legal status granted surrogate mothers? How is it that a surrogate mother, having been paid to give birth to a child but who changes her mind and fights for the right to parent the child—*the child that came from **her** womb*—loses out in court to the woman who contributed an egg (genetic material) and payment? Does a father not contribute semen (genetic material) and pay for his child?

When parenting rights are contested between two women, a prior legal contract usurps giving birth. When parenting rights are contested between a woman and a man, generally, it's no contest. Given that physical custody is more or less automatically granted the woman, and abortion/adoption decisions are the woman's sole prerogative, perhaps it's not a matter of mother's vs. father's rights as much as it's a matter of the rights of women simply usurping the rights of men.

Warren Farrell describes the worst-case scenario as seen from the male point of view.

> [I]f a woman and man make love and she says she is using birth control but is not, she has the right to raise the child without his knowing he even has a child, and then to sue him for retroactive child support

even ten to twenty years later (depending on the state). This forces him to take a job with more pay and more stress and therefore earlier death. Although it's his body, he has no choice. He has the option of being a slave (working for another without pay or choice) or being a criminal. *Roe* vs. *Wade* gave women the vote over their bodies. Men still don't have the vote over theirs—whether in love or in war.[334]

It is said that only a man can conceive a child and walk away. But is a woman who has an abortion, or who gives a child up for adoption not a woman who conceived a child and walked away? In fact, most cities now have drop-off centers where mothers can free themselves of their infants anonymously, no questions asked.[335]

Even if a genetic test proves he is not the father, if she put his name on the birth certificate, he may still be required to pay should the judge rule that it is in "the best interest of the child." Often, there is a narrow window of opportunity for a man to contest paternity. If he misses the deadline, he's out of luck. Even if he is financially *unable* to pay, he risks imprisonment for failure to pay. Moreover, if the mother chooses to squander his childpayments on drugs, booze, fancy clothes, the father is legally powerless to do anything about it.

In the act of sex, men and women share equal risk. So what it comes down to is this: She is taught caution and prudent behavior and he is not. Whether in love or in war, framed as courageous, bold and brave, he is taught reckless behavior and suffers the consequences.

"Men are cold, calculating, unfeeling, inconsiderate, rude, selfish, those kinds of things," says Laurie Ingraham recounting the stereotypes about men that women are taught. "Basically, by the age of three, our parents, TV and movies have taught us not to trust you."[336] While women are socialized to assume that a man cannot be trusted until he has proven himself, men are more often socialized to assume that a woman can be trusted until proven otherwise. Perhaps, while he's out shopping for an engagement ring, she's on the Internet doing a background check?

In the act of intercourse a man quite literally puts his life in a woman's hands and, most likely, he's too ill informed of his own sexual-political perspectives to know it. Because most people are trustworthy, most women are trustworthy. But, because some people have low standards of conduct, some women have low standards of conduct.

His assumption that the woman can be trusted leaves a man more vulnerable to placing his trust where trust is not warranted. "[W]hen random DNA tests are taken of babies, about 10 percent turn out not to be the child of the father the mother declared. Since one father often has two or three children, this implies that about 15 to 20 percent of all fathers are spending their lives supporting at least one child they were deceived into thinking was theirs."[337] This is not just financial betrayal; it is *emotional* betrayal. And it can *only* happen to *men*.

Additionally, because women more often gain physical custody of the children, 86 percent of all stepparents are male.[338] And so, 86 percent of the special emotional strain and pain that goes with step parenting is also male.

Assuming the child is born and the father remains present in the child's life, what then? Says Nancy Friday:

> The competitive corporate world, as it exists, has no tolerance for parental leave programs, especially for men. "What [fathers] are hearing, from their bosses, from institutions, from the culture around them, even from their own wives," says the *Time* article on fatherhood, "very often comes down to a devastating message: We don't really trust men to be parents, and we don't really need them to be."[339]

Warren Farrell: "Almost 90 percent of men say that full-time involvement with their children would be their preference for between six months and a year if they knew they wouldn't be hurting their family economically and they knew their wife approved."[340]

So, why don't more men come right out and ask for what they want? Well, let's check out how it sounds: "Honey, would it be all right with you if I were to stay home fulltime? I'll take social, emotional, and legal possession of our children while you work overtime in order to earn your family's love by making money others will spend. OK?" Men don't venture to ask because:

1) Men's cultural conditioning leaves them feeling embarrassed even to want the role.

2) The severe beating men take in the media (i.e., "Mr. Mom") leaves them feeling deeply insecure with regard to their parental competence or even worthiness.

3) Men are in no way encouraged to feel needed, wanted or even *trusted* in the nursery. Who could doubt what Jane Young, professor of English at City University of New York, has observed: "The accepted wisdom these days is that, as long as children are loved, it doesn't matter whether they grow up without a father or even a stepfather, and that fathers often do more harm than good. [Fathers] are increasingly seen as verbally or sexually abusive, violent or physically and psychologically absent."[341]

4) Men often sense that the workplace is especially hostile toward men who make parenting a high priority.

5) Men don't ask for the role because they know they won't get it.

As for those men who don't want the role, many don't want it because they've never even thought about it. Many just don't know what they're missing. It could even be the case that men, consciously or unconsciously, fear developing deep emotional attachment to their children, knowing of the high statistical probability that divorce might one day take their children from them. Others, of course, are simply ill-suited to the role, but the same could be said of a higher percentage of women than we care to know.

Partly as a result of all the negative stereotyping, a man who would let it be known that he wants to become a househusband (a word only recently added to the dictionary) has little chance of attracting a woman who would want to marry him. Men who would "free" women of parental responsibilities are more often perceived as men who would encroach upon the woman's territory.

Nancy Friday:

> Overworked as women may be, they will not easily relinquish the nursery role. And though many deny it vehemently, on some level they know that she who bears and raises the human race plays the most powerful role in all of human life. The prospect of giving men parity in the nursery, of seeing some men doing "women's work" as well as they, is intolerable.[342]

Author Cathy Young has also observed women's reluctance to part with their parental primacy. This "Maternal Chauvinism," says Young, "is a dad's greatest obstacle to parental parity."

Women's determined efforts to maintain controlling interest in their children's lives is something Ms. Young refers to as "maternal gatekeeping." Historically, it is one of the principal mechanisms forming and maintaining the Glass Wall.

> In the 1994 book *Peer Marriage*, Pepper Schwartz, a sociologist at the University of Washington, reports that . . . for the most part, the resistance to fully shared childrearing came from mothers, not fathers. These women had been all for co-parenting in theory; once they actually became parents, Schwartz notes, they succumbed to "the siren call of motherhood" and started hogging the baby. In some cases, it was the men who rebelled against being shut out and pressured the women to curb their possessiveness. . . . In a 1985 survey, only one in four mothers strongly endorsed 50-50 parenting, while two out of three seemed "threatened" by the idea. . . . A few years ago, *Redbook* ran an article called "My Husband Is Too Good a Father" by Beth Levine. Levine's husband, a home-based freelance writer, was an active, nurturing father to their young son, which was exactly what she had always wanted. What she had not expected was to feel hurt every time the boy cried for Daddy, not Mommy.

"I'm ashamed, but I hate that I am not the center of my child's universe," she wrote. "When I am honest with myself, what I really want is for Bill to be an eager but charmingly inept father, a soldier to my general. . . ." "The man who's just trying the waters at being a parent and participating in the household feels very clumsy and unanointed, and then he gets defensive," says Braun-Levine. "We keep giving orders and saying, 'This is the way you do it, and if you can't do it my way, just stand here and hold the dirty clothes.'"[343]

To the degree that Man assumed authority in the workplace, Woman assumes authority in the homeplace. Woman's greater power in the domestic and parental realms may not be the *kind* of power feminists seek—who seeks that which they already have?—but the fact that women covet that power proves its worth. Says Dr. Roy Schenk:

> Even today, women are invested in continuing to be the primary socializers. For example, the National Organization for Women is fighting vigorously to block the increase of joint custody after divorce, even though greater involvement of divorced fathers in child rearing would be in women's best interests, first, because involved men have been repeatedly shown to pay child support and, second, because in joint custody the mother is relieved of the burden of total responsibility for child care. But these reasons don't stop NOW from fighting against joint custody, because the desire to maintain women's control of the socialization process is stronger than the desire to benefit women.[344]

Feminism's initial promise of deeper father involvement has only been fulfilled for some. Because, says men's activist Glenn Sacks, "whenever there's any kind of legislative attempt to try to make it so fathers can have more time with their children after divorce, or fathers could have shared parenting after divorce—the feminists, all the time, right down the line, they fight it like crazy! And, to me, that's just a total betrayal."[345] It was NOW's opposition to joint custody that precipitated Warren Farrell's split with feminism. And again the point is made that feminism's influence is often contrary to its stated goals.

These domestic/parental powers women possess are enviable. Without them, life can be an emotional wasteland. Herb Goldberg quotes a man who knows this truth all too well.

> I went through the wedding mechanically, devoid of any emotion. I simply figured I was following a road that was meant for me to follow. . . Our first baby was born. . . . Marie was ecstatic. I felt her joy. I really did. It would have been hard not to. But I did not feel my own joy. There was a glow coming out of her, but I had the feeling that it had nothing to do with me, that anyone could have stood in my place. It seems to me that there was a game plan laid out long before I got there and I merely was pushed from spot to spot, like some checker on a

board. Yes, I was happy I had a daughter, but I felt more of a numbness. Here I am. What am I doing here?[346]

Lacking his female equivalent's domestic/parental powers, a man often feels peripheral in his own home and suffers accordingly. The world of women is as vast, as deep, as essential, as rewarding, and at least as rich in the basic archetypes of life as is the world of men. To be disenfranchised and rendered inferior and subordinate in the world of women carries costs equal to being disenfranchised and rendered inferior and subordinate in the world of men.

Author Lauren Slater experienced the male brand of disenfranchisement firsthand when she took the role of "provider" while her husband took the role of "nurturer." Not surprisingly, their daughter Clara "started to like my husband more. This was the first problem, and it was piercing." Of course it was. And the situation grew more painful and increasingly competitive.

> "I'll go," I'd say, throwing off the covers. "No, I'll go" he'd say throwing off the covers. And then there was the night I heard it. "Papa!" she screamed. What happened next is obvious. Papa leaped up, ran to her room, and Mama lay alone, listening through the monitor to sounds of cooing and comforting, not mine. . . . I wanted to touch my daughter, my baby girl—it would not be too much to say I ached for it—but someone had usurped me, at my insistence. . . . I fully realized how the modern mother, freed from the burden of primary caretaking, gains a lot and loses a lot, in language, and in love. . . . I finally came to understand my father, and what must have been his inevitable feeling of "fringeness" as his wife ran the domestic show.
>
> To be loved second-best: How have men tolerated that all these years? How awful, how hurtful. It makes you want to withdraw. Now I see why fathers fade away. There is no way to compete with the devotion a child feels for her primary caretaker, and it's so easy to feel rebuffed when the little one shakes off your hand and runs for her obvious favorite. So you retreat, to your den, your desk, your TV, where there is always football.[347]

Sharing the workload is one thing, sharing the children equally is quite another thing. Naturally, a man will balk at equality in the childcare workload when he doesn't have equality in the actual parenting (including equal say in the big decisions). If, in some manner, he receives the message "These are *my* children;" she, in some manner, will most likely receive the message "Then *you* take care of them."

Men keep women "less than" in many ways and women keep men "less than" in many ways. But the most insidious part of "maternal gatekeeping" is the badmouthing. According to the kids themselves, "Moms are almost five times as likely to badmouth dads as dads are moms."[348] Moms wish to maintain primacy in the parental role. For economically empowered women the "male role" of protector/provider is available, but largely shunned. What does that tell us about what women *really* think of the male lot in life?

A woman looking through the Glass Ceiling can see the tip of the success pyramid but—owing to gender bias together with various sociopolitical structures—feels thwarted from inhabiting that same space in the same way. A man looking through the Glass Wall can see the mother/child nexus but—owing to gender bias together with various sociopolitical structures—feels thwarted from inhabiting that same space in the same way. Many women break through the Glass Ceiling. Lauren Slater's husband is a representative of the less common father who's managed to crack the Glass Wall.

Having gained power over men within the world of men, a female VP may experience herself struggling outside cultural norms and feeling extra-vulnerable. Having usurped power over a woman within the world of women, a "househusband" may experience himself struggling outside cultural norms and feeling extra-vulnerable. Some women in Lauren Slater's place might do just about anything to take back the parental primacy to which mothers feel specially entitled. To ensure their "rightful" place at the center of their children's emotional lives, some mothers might bad-mouth fathers. Some mothers might even divorce husbands who prove to be "too good" at parenting.

The book, *Divorced Dads,* by Sanford Braver (with Diane O'Connell), recounts three specific case studies of divorcing couples that, when combined together, "capture the essence of our findings." The first involves "Jeremy" and "Roxanne" and their son "Bradley." Jeremy enters fatherhood determined to be the very best dad he can be. But how does Roxanne *really* feel about that?

> She complained that he had bonded with Bradley even more than she had. She began to doubt her own femininity and maternal nurturance, he surmised. She now saw Jeremy as a threat, not an ally. That he had truly become a new-age father seemed a nightmare to her, not the dream-come-true he had assumed it would be. The hostility that emerged annihilated the foundation of their marriage. She secretly began interviewing divorce attorneys and eventually found a suitable one and served Jeremy with papers.[349]

Like other fathers faced with it, Jeremy was unprepared for the anti-male bias (misandry) he would soon encounter. He assumed such things only happened to *other* men, "bad" men who deserve it. Surely any judge *must* recognize and honor a father-son bond as profound as his, right? But "the judge just decided on the basis of traditional sex roles," says Jeremy. "She was the mother and I was 'only' the father, pretty much useless, like someone's appendix."[350] His attorney had warned Jeremy in advance that the mother would almost certainly win custody and she did. And now, "She's really trying to cut me out."

> I used to buy all the baby food because I knew what he liked and what he didn't like. I shopped for his clothes, I knew his favorite books, I knew his favorite Barney characters, I'd get on the floor and color with him. But now if she admits I have any role with him at all, it's as if that will undermine her role as the "primary parent," which the judge decreed she was. . . . She really would prefer that I just . . . pay my child support and disappear.[351]

In fact, to *guarantee* they will never again feel the piercing pain of being parentally "usurped," some divorcing mothers might even accuse the father of abuse and then, through the use of a restraining order, have the father removed from the picture *entirely*.

There is no masculist movement attempting to tear apart the matrisensus, or bring motherhood down from atop its pedestal. Motherhood power is secure. On the relatively rare occasion that a woman's parental primacy *is* threatened, however, we can see that the fragile male ego is matched by a fragile female ego. We can also see that such a woman, with the full backing of the legal system, is tremendously empowered to slap down the "usurping" male. Meanwhile, those women in vast numbers who penetrate the Glass Ceiling may *feel* extra vulnerable but, as we will soon explore in detail, there is reason to believe that such women—again with the full backing of the legal system—are *very* well protected indeed.

"To be loved second-best: How have men tolerated that all these years?" Men have endured being loved second-best just as women have endured being respected second-best. David Lindgren, therapist and cofounder of New Warriors, is wont to say, "We want respect, but we *need* love." ("All You *Need* Is Love"?) I suspect that being loved second-best is *so* painful, society in general and men in particular have felt the need to escape full cognizance of it through denial. Society knows full well that women are respected second best, but society has yet to come to grips with men being loved second best.

When women enter the male realm they encounter the male pain within. Only then, when *women* (like Lauren Slater) experience it, is this pain followed by complaint, complaint that gets published and circulated into public knowledge. And so, only now do we begin to hear about the downsides that come of *not* being the primary caregiver. Only fifty years ago, men were so disenfranchised within the world of women that a man who was both husband and father was not even *allowed* in the delivery room! Fathers did not penetrate that particular Glass Wall until the 1970s.

As viewed from a politicized male perspective, anthropologist Lionel Tiger describes the current legal environment many fathers face:

> And in family courts, the presumption of male behavioral malefaction has yielded heartbreakingly numerous cases in which men are charged with domestic violence to which courts overwhelmingly—often in brief hearings in which the male is not even present—issue temporary "restraining orders." These frequently segue into permanence, and award women the dwelling they've shared, financial support and the all-important privilege of custody—mothers gain custody in 66% of uncontested cases and 75% of contested ones. Less than a quarter of parents are awarded joint custody. Judges issue such orders based only on the word of the alleged victim. It is small wonder the overwhelming majority of such actions are sought and achieved by women. It has been legitimately argued that there is a merciless post-marital racket of therapists, lawyers, judges and governmental advocates who prosper because it is so easy to define males as guilty.[352]

If you doubt the ease with which women are granted restraining orders, consider the now famous case involving talk show host David Letterman. A New Mexico judge granted Colleen Nestler's request for a restraining order alleging that Letterman forced her to go bankrupt and caused her "mental cruelty" and "sleep deprivation."

> Nestler requested that Letterman, who tapes his show in New York, stay at least 3 yards away and not "think of me, and release me from his mental harassment and hammering." . . . Nestler's application for a restraining order was accompanied by a six-page typed letter in which she said Letterman used code words, gestures and "eye expressions" to convey his desires for her. . . . She said he asked her to be his wife during a televised "teaser" for his show by saying, "Marry me, Oprah." Her letter said Oprah was the first of many code names for her and that the coded vocabulary increased and changed with time.[353]

Before dismissing the above as nothing more than a bad "joke" that has nothing to do with *you*, consider this:

> Judge Daniel Sanchez issued a restraining order against Letterman based on those allegations. By doing so, it put Letterman on a national list of domestic abusers, gave him a criminal record, took away several of his constitutionally protected rights, and subjected him to criminal prosecution if he contacted Nestler directly or indirectly, or possessed a firearm. Letterman had never met Colleen Nestler, and this all happened without his knowledge. . . . Asked to explain why he had issued a restraining order on the basis of such an unusual complaint, Judge Sanchez answered that Nestler had filled out the restraining-order request form correctly.[354]

So, where then is the male protest?

It took national ridicule plus Letterman's team of high priced lawyers to *finally* convince Judge Sanchez to dismiss the case. Any woman, for *any* reason, can get a legally enforced restraining order against *you*. She need only fill out the request form correctly. If you should lack the clout that comes of wealth and fame, then *you* can expect repercussions both horrendous and long lasting. Over matters of infinitely less import, for vastly lesser powers men hold over women, *women* scream bloody murder!

And, if you doubt anti-male bias in divorce courts, consider the words of ex-judge Richard Huttner regarding divorced fathers:

> You have never seen a bigger pain in the ass than the father who wants to get involved; he can be repulsive. He wants to meet the kid after school at three o'clock, take the kid out to dinner during the week, have the kid on his own birthday, talk to the kid on the phone every evening, go to every open school night, take the kid away for a whole weekend so they can be alone together. This type of involved father is pathological.[355]

Can anyone be in doubt as to which parent was awarded custody in this man's court? And what of his influence as a member of the New York State Commission on Child Support? Obviously, not all judicial bias is as "pathological" as the bias displayed by this particular judge, but anti-male bias needn't reach *this* level to dash a whole lot of father's hopes of equality in parenting.

Along with accountability, we also need to empathy interpret the actions of fathers whose status as parents takes on meaning only when it comes time to pay. Like Lauren Slater, we need to realize that at least some of the men who fail to mail their support checks for the full 18 to 21 years do so because they care too *much*, not too little.

It is the pain of being reduced from father to "visitor," of having involvement with their children limited to the standard every-other-weekend "visitation rights"—a mere four days out of each month—or the pain of being shut out of their children's lives entirely that can make it all but unbearable to stay in their children's lives only to the extent of sending a check each month. It's not the money; it's everything the check represents and reminds him of that makes the monthly ritual of filling it out and sending it so painful for the ex-husband/father. Under the circumstances, a man may feel a deep need to make a clean break with this painful chapter of his life.

If all that weren't enough, he may *then* experience the conflict between his obligation to love and support children from his previous marriage vs. his *new* obligation to love and support the children of his *current* marriage (whether or not those children are biologically his own).

Phyllis Schlafly:

> In January, President George W. Bush signed the reauthorization of the Violence Against Women Act without public debate, even though evidence has surfaced that Congress should have examined it before the law was extended. The act, which costs nearly $1 billion per year, is one of the major ways former President Bill Clinton bought the support of radical feminists. . . . Passage of the Violence Against Women Act was a major priority of the American Bar Association for whose members it is a cash cow. . . . A recently issued ABA document called "Tool for Attorneys" provides lawyers with a list of suggestive questions to encourage their clients to make domestic-violence charges. Knowing that a woman can get a restraining order against the father of her children in an ex parte proceeding without any evidence, and that she will never be punished for lying, domestic-violence accusations have become a major tactic for securing sole child custody.[356]

Books like *Fathers' Rights* by Jeffery Leving (1997), *From Courtship to Courtroom* by Jed H. Abraham (1999), and *Taken Into Custody: The War Against Fathers, Marriage, and the Family* by Stephen Baskerville (2007) are filled cover-to-cover with the abuses of these ex parte proceedings wherein only the accuser need be present. The accused may have no knowledge of the legal machinery set in motion behind his back. So long as such cases are adjudicated under civil—as opposed to criminal—law, the accused is *not* assumed innocent and does *not* have to be convicted "beyond a reasonable doubt."

And then there's the purely emotional side of it all. In his book *A Man's World: How Real Is Male Privilege—and How High Is Its Price?*, Ellis Cose quotes Dr. Jean Bonhomme, president of the National Black Men's Health Network.

> I've found it easier to console people with cancer and AIDS than to console fathers who have lost all contact with their children. I mean, it is one of the most devastating things that can happen to anybody. . . . We think that men cannot love children. And I think that that's erroneous. I think that men have a huge capacity to love children. I think men love in a different way. I think they're protective. And they try to create a safe environment, but men can and have traded their lives to protect their children. They go to work in dangerous jobs. They'll face physical dangers and things of this nature. I mean, how can you say that a man can't love if he's willing to lay down his life for his child?[357]

Actor/musician Bob Geldof puts a human face on the matter. In an interview with TV host Daphne Barak, Geldof recounted how the discovery that the law was "skewed" in ex-wife Paula Yates's favor—just because she was a woman—plunged him into an "ocean of grief."

I could not live without my kids. I missed the sound of them turning in their sleep. I just wanted to go to some dark, grey corner of the world and howl into the void... The key in my pocket still fit in the door, but I was no longer allowed (to put) this key in the door and go into my home. It's very hard to get your head around that. I went to the door, and I was too humiliated to knock on my own front door. That's my house, my home, my children. I could hear them laughing in there. I was too scared of (knocking) and one of my kids opening the door and saying 'Hi Dad' and not being allowed to let me in. I didn't want to impose that on them. I didn't want it to happen to me. I didn't want her to come to the door and say, 'What are you doing here? You're not allowed to come here.' So, I went back out, and I sat in the car and I just cried. I just stayed and watched their bedroom lights go off, and I went home. That shouldn't happen to anyone. If you put impediments in the way of men seeing their children - making them jump through all sorts of humiliating hoops - the kids become a weapon, a sword and a shield simultaneously. You're suffering so much. Eventually, no person can take that and the kids lose a father. It is hurtful.[358]

If the Zero-Empathy rule were revoked, we'd know that many "deadbeat dads" are really "beat-dead" dads.

We'd find it in our hearts to do better than lump together, denigrate, and vilify disenfranchised fathers to the point of having what are, in essence, "debtors' prisons" (outlawed since the Debtors Act of 1869), reinstated solely to incarcerate them. And we'd be fair enough toward men to admit it if, for whatever reason, non-custodial fathers pay a larger portion (60 percent) of the child support they're ordered to pay than non-custodial mothers (46.8 percent).[359]

All men's issues are society's issues, but the issue of diminishing fatherhood especially so. "Fathers have a unique and irreplaceable role to play in child development," says David Popenoe, echoing so many in the field. "Fathers are not merely would-be mothers. The two sexes are different to the core, and each is necessary—culturally as well as biologically—for the optimal development of a human being."[360]

Father absence can be linked to almost every issue of delinquency in our world today. Stephen Baskerville:

> Virtually every major social pathology of our time: violent crime, drug and alcohol abuse, truancy and scholastic failure, unwed pregnancy, suicide, and other psychological disorders—all these correlate more strongly to fatherlessness than to any other single factor.... Children from affluent but separated families are much more likely to get into trouble than children from poor but intact ones, and white children from separated families are at higher risk than black children in intact families.... It is hardly an exaggeration to say that fatherless children are tearing down our civilization.[361]

Christina Hoff Sommers concurs:

> The boys who are most at risk for juvenile delinquency and violence are boys who are literally separated from their fathers. The U.S. Bureau of the Census reports that in 1960, 5.1 million children lived with only their mother; by 1996, the number was more than 16 million. As the phenomenon of fatherlessness has increased, so has violence.... In *Fatherless America,* the sociologist David Blankenhorn notes that "Despite the difficulty of proving causation in social sciences, the wealth of evidence increasingly supports the conclusion that fatherlessness is a primary generator of violence among young men." William Galston, a former domestic policy adviser to the Clinton administration (now at the University of Maryland), and Elaine Kamarck, a lecturer at Harvard's J. F. Kennedy School of Government, concur. Commenting on the relationship between crime and one-parent families, they say, "The relationship is so strong that controlling for family configuration erases the relationship between race and crime and between low income and crime. This conclusion shows up time and again in the literature."[362]

There's an equally strong correlation between lack of fathering and unwanted teen pregnancy. For example: "In a study of inner-city Baltimore women who were teenage mothers, one-third of their daughters also became teenage mothers," remarks Warren Farrell. "But not one daughter or son who had a good relationship with his/her biological father had a baby before the age of nineteen."[363]

Father energy is absolutely vital to a society's health and wellbeing. I don't mean to diminish single mothers or disparage their heroic efforts but, because women are equal partners in the sculpting of our world, the emphasis on Women's Rights must be accompanied by equal emphasis on women's *responsibilities*. Women's collective choices impact our world; therefore, like men's choices, women's choices must be held accountable to the greater good.

Unlike men's controlling interest in the work world, women's controlling interest in the domestic realm remains well protected and secure. The problem is that many women, perhaps unconsciously, want to "have it all." Some women mean to maintain advantage, privilege, superiority, and ownership in their traditional realms *plus* gain equality within men's traditional realms to boot. Such women apparently believe that the world will not be gender-equal until it has been made *perfect* for women—without regard for men.

Reproduction/Parenting issues are men's issues because it is in the profound and fundamental realm of reproduction/parenting that Man is most clearly seen as the "Second Sex."

Issues Download #7 – The "Sexual Harassment Industry"

The issue of Sexual Harassment has turned the corporate world into something of a litigious minefield. Granted, the vast majority of women are far too sensible to damage a man over trifles. But then there's the particular woman Jerold Mackenzie ran into.

> On the morning of March 19, 1993, [Jerold] Mackenzie was talking to coworker Patricia Best, the distributor services manager, about a *Seinfeld* episode that aired the night before. Mackenzie asked her if she saw it; she did not. He told Best that Seinfeld's date had a name that rhymed with a part of a woman's anatomy and asked her to guess what rhymed with Delores. Best could not. Mackenzie apparently did not want to use the term "clitoris," so he copied the page from the dictionary with the definition and showed it to Best.[364]

As a result, Jerold J. Mackenzie was fired from his $95,000-a-year job with Miller Brewing Co. for "poor managerial judgment" triggered by allegations that he had sexually harassed coworker Patricia Best. After two years and 71 attempts to find a new job, Mackenzie concluded that his colleague's charges had rendered him unemployable.[365] A jury awarded him $26 million, but then "The higher courts threw the entire award out."[366] Mackenzie went bankrupt.

Of all the volatile issues this book explores, none is more subject to perspective than the issue of Sexual Harassment. In presenting the politicized male perspective, it is not my intention to negate female perspectives. For some women, the issue of sexual harassment has had horrendous consequences in their lives.

But I will direct compassion toward *both* sexes and I will direct accountability toward *both* sexes. I will invite the female reader to cross the great gender divide and take in male reality as if she were visiting a foreign culture. What I present may not jibe with the world as you know it. A woman will probably want to say that I have it "wrong." But I only have it "wrong" as seen from a *woman's* perspective. What might a *man's* inner experience be in these matters?

In every seduction, a man's efforts to change a woman's nos into maybes and her maybes into yeses, have him walking a fine line between being forceful enough to be sexually exciting but not so forceful as to be prosecuted. The really scary part is that the difference between the two exists only in the mind of the woman he's pursuing.

Katie Roiphe:

> [A] Princeton pamphlet declares that "sexual harassment is unwanted sexual attention that makes a person feel uncomfortable or causes problems in school or at work, or in social settings." The word "uncomfortable" echoes through all the literature on sexual harassment.

The feminists concerned with this issue, then, propose the right to be comfortable as a feminist principle.[367]

Only she can decide whether or not she is "comfortable." And that decision will decide his fate. Will she melt and fall in love in his strong, forceful arms? Will she be flattered and excited by his refusal to take no for an answer, or will she damage or perhaps destroy him with an accusation of sexual harassment?

For men the bind is this: since only men are obligated to pursue and persist, only men can be judged to have done it "wrong." As Kate Fillion points out, "When sexual harassment is defined as anything that creates 'a hostile climate,' its meaning becomes highly subjective. A comment that fifty people consider innocuous may strike one person who has a highly developed sense of indignation as deeply offensive, and who can dispute her claim that she now feels her work environment is hostile?"[368]

But, is her work environment truly more hostile than his? Did Patricia Best experience a more hostile work environment than Jerold Mackenzie? In the end, who was in greater need of protection from the other's weaponry, he or she?

"Rules and laws based on the premise that all women need protection from all men, because they are so much weaker, serve only to reinforce the image of women as powerless," says Katie Roiphe.[369] She's right, of course, but you know those men who get destroyed for making a woman feel "uncomfortable"? They *also* suffer. Yet the infantilizing effects on women together with the fact that some *women* have been accused of sexual harassment have been the sole focus of nearly all critiques of sexual harassment legislation. So much so that Daphne Patai makes this extraordinary plea:

> Still—and I want to state this explicitly—the fact that women, too, are caught in the net should not be our sole reason for protesting against the Sexual Harassment Industry. We ought not to ignore that it is men who are the intended targets of feminists planning their brave new heterosex-free world.[370]

It's remarkable how an issue that can cost perfectly decent, ordinary men their livelihood, their families, defamation of character, and even jail time is still regarded as an issue only to the extent that it may adversely affect women in some way.

We are determined to protect women from suffering a "hostile workplace." We consider it her moral and legal right to feel "comfortable." But Camille Paglia is only right when she says, "The folly of this nomenclature is that *every* workplace is hostile, as any man who has worked his way up the cutthroat corporate ladder will testify."[371]

One of the fundamental problems with "femin-ism" is that, in its unabashed bias toward the feminine, it can never be satisfied with mere equality. Women are not to feel *as* comfortable or experience an *equally* hostile workplace, as men. No, women are to experience no hostility and no discomfort *at all*. Women are not to be *equally* protected; women are to be *extra* protected. Daphne Patai:

> The U.S. Court of Appeals for the Ninth Circuit established this view in *Ellison v. Brady* (1991) when it rejected a gender-neutral "reasonable person" standard. Such a standard, the court held, ignores women's particular experience of sexual harassment. We need to be very clear about the meaning of the new "reasonable woman" standard in relation to sexual harassment litigation. It means that what is actionable is not the *intent* to offend or discriminate, as determined by a hypothetical reasonable person, but rather whatever a "reasonable woman" *feels* to be offensive and discriminatory, that is, what she claims to spontaneously experience as offensive and discriminatory.... This set the stage for the elevation of women's word to the level of law—which was precisely the goal of feminist activists.[372] [Emphasis in the original]

A man's words or actions: "need not be intended as slights—and usually they are not. They need only be 'experienced' as such, at the time or *ex post facto*."[373] So, even if the "offense" didn't feel like an offense in the moment, it is a woman's legally established prerogative to change her mind and take "offense" at some future date! Perhaps she'll change her mind following a lecture by some Women's Studies graduates? Doubtless women so vigilant and sensitized may *feel* and *experience* "sexual harassment" at every moment.

Says Helen Fisher, Ph.D., an anthropologist at the American Museum of Natural History in New York:

> I think that women should recognize the incredible power of their sexuality. In fact this is one of the problems with sexual harassment. I feel very sorry for men. Women say, for example, "I have the right to wear anything I want to the office." ... But in the mating game they should know that there are consequences to wearing a blouse that is scooped down to your nipples and a skirt that is up to your fanny. Men respond to this. They respond naturally. We've got men absolutely terrified in the office. They don't know how to behave anymore.[374]

Women *do* have the right to wear what they choose, *and* rights *conflict*. Feminism would defend women's right to wear what they please but deny men the right to "respond naturally." If the goal is fairness, then female rights must come with female accountability, and make room for *male* rights.

One moment a woman leans over to give a man a good look at her behind. The next moment she is licking her lips suggestively and then pressing her breast into his arm but acting like she doesn't notice. If men were as well attuned to victimization, men could also *feel* and *experience* "sexual harassment" at every moment.

And what of rich men married by women who held the prior intention of divorcing the man and keeping his money? What of rich men plagued by false-accusation lawsuits, paternity suits, blackmail, and otherwise hounded for their money? If the sexually empowered female is experiencing "sexual harassment," might the economically empowered male be experiencing "economic harassment"?

Men are held *so* accountable for their effect on women that a "sexist remark," should it be thought to contribute to a "hostile work environment," could cost a man his career, his reputation, his marriage, his life. Yet, even women who *destroy* men with false accusations are not held legally accountable.[a] And there's reason to believe false accusations are common. Author Tom James:

> In a forensic study of 556 investigations of rape allegations, 33% were proven (by DNA and other evidence) to be false. In another 27% of the cases, the woman either failed a lie-detector test or admitted having lied when faced with the prospect of submitting to a lie-detector test. In other words, it was found that at least 60% of rape allegations are probably false. Even the liberal *Washington Post* has admitted that at least 30% of rape accusations are false. In a review of 350 criminal cases in which a person who had been convicted was later proven (by DNA evidence) to have been innocent, it was found that 23 had already been executed and 8 had already died in prison. 100% of them were male.[375]

Warren Farrell's research backs this up:

> With these admitted false accusations [Dr. Charles McDowell, formerly of the U.S. Air Force's Office of Special Investigations] was able to develop thirty-five criteria distinguishing false accusations and those known to be genuine. Three independent judges then examined the remainder of the cases. Only if all three reviewers independently concluded the original rape allegations were false did they rank them as "false." *The total of false allegations became 60 percent.* Rather than publicize the study as an antidote to the Tailhook scandal, the

---

a   Recently, there has been a shift toward prosecuting women who lodge *obviously* false charges of rape. Everything is in flux. But in all but rare instances, the only way a man can be cleared of a false charge lodged by a woman is for the woman to admit that she lied, and there is little chance of a woman admitting she lied if she knows it will mean jail time. For this reason—along with omnipresent chivalry—women are normally offered legal immunity in exchange for dropping false accusations.

study was buried. Dr. Charles McDowell was ostracized and moved—the Air Force equivalent of being sent to Siberia.[376] [Emphasis in the original]

Studies such as these don't really *prove* anything, but they do give one pause. Everybody's got their "studies that show" and their "data that indicates," but these studies place within the realm of credibility a disturbing possibility. With false accusations of rape, women may be "raping" men in *alarming* numbers. Carey Roberts:

> Experience reveals that rape is a red-meat accusation that triggers an aggressive prosecution. You may remember the 1989 rape of the Central Park jogger and the accusation that five "wilding" teenagers had perpetrated the attack. But when the DNA test results did not match, the prosecutor had to claim the semen came from a sixth "mystery" member of the gang. Despite that dubious explanation, the five were convicted. But 13 years later DNA evidence proved another man had committed the crime and the five were set free. Sorry about that, fellas.
>
> Twenty-five years ago civil rights attorneys Barry Scheck and Peter Neufeld established the Innocence Project, a group dedicated to protecting the innocent through post-conviction DNA testing. Earlier this month the group registered its 205th exoneration, most of the cases involving false convictions of rape.[377]

Given the assumption that women are vulnerable but men are not (or ought not to be), are women held *at all* accountable for their effect upon men? I'm told, "It's not fair that women should be held responsible for men's sexuality." If women are held so responsible, why do we so commonly say, "He got her pregnant" or "He knocked her up" as if she just happened to be walking by and he bore all, and she bore none, of the responsibility for the pregnancy?

When asked, "How does it feel to know that you can turn men into domestic pets with one look?" model Simona Krainova replied, "I don't see my modeling as a sexual thing. I'm not putting myself out sexually. It's a job"[378] I hear a woman choosing to see nothing sexual about being photographed in a highly eroticized manner and accepting no accountability for her effect on men or—in helping to generate "cheesecake" imagery—her effect on the world.

Is she (and other models) too young to be held so responsible? Perhaps, but boys no older are accepted or drafted into the armed forces, issued weapons, and made responsible for life and death. Should they be judged to have had a negative effect upon the world, boys in the form of soldiers are subject to the horrors of a general court-martial and military imprisonment.

Their female equivalents are called "girls" while the boys are called "men," but the extra respect comes at quite a cost.

Consider the contrast between that and this: "I think we must hold even teenaged girls responsible for the persona they choose," says Camille Paglia, "since for most of their lives it has brought them the rewards of attention and popularity."[379] Also the rewards of protection, and the kind of adoration that may lead to economic rewards. Women will be better respected when they hold themselves accountable for who and what they are and for their effect in the world. Obviously, Camille Paglia is such a woman. Laurie Ingraham is another:

> I've been in groups where women have owned it openly that they really get off on being hot. In a group in California an attractive young woman said, "I've done that to men millions of times; it feels good to know that they're panting after me, and I just have to go like this with my finger. That gives me great pleasure." One of the men in the group got up and screamed at her, "Goddamn you fucking bitch! I have been hurt by women like you so many goddamn times." And that's how women rape men.[380]

And some women rape men with false accusations of rape.

In telling the story of this young man's angry outburst, Ingraham could have taken the position that the young man was unfairly holding the young woman responsible for his own sexuality, but wouldn't that be blaming the victim? Instead, Ingraham models how women can aspire to higher levels of personal honor and accountability. By acknowledging this woman's power and holding *her* accountable for that power, and its effect upon men, Ingraham proves herself a woman whom men can both love *and respect.*

Speaking of the mismatch in sexual power, Nancy Friday tells us, "It is the girl who will teach him what *she* wants, which boy *she* feels weighs in opposite her beauty. Alas, she makes this decision blindly, without full awareness or even consideration of what the boy feels, of her effect on him; oh, she knows he looks at her, but she has no sympathy, no empathy."[381]

Only names of the accused are publicized so men don't even get to know the names of false accusers in order to avoid them. Even so, a man must take the risks involved in acting upon the knowledge that her "no" does *not* always mean no, otherwise, he'll surely lose out on much of the sex and much of the love in his life. Says Cathy Young:

> The human cost of this crusade also includes the incalculable: relationships that never got a chance to bloom in the chilly climate of the new workplace. The story of TV journalist Sam Donaldson's courtship of his wife, Jan Smith, twenty years ago—he was considerably higher in status, and pursued her despite her repeated objections—could be a classic story of sexual harassment. One article on electronic romance at

work tells the story of a woman who began receiving anonymous messages on her office computer: "Eventually she confronted her suspect . . . who immediately confessed. They were still dating at last report" this tale could have ended as easily with, "He was in sensitivity training at last report," a thought likely to discourage more cautious suitors, particularly since even a relationship that starts out as consensual can be re-imagined as sexual harassment later on.[382]

Like Sam Donaldson, despite receiving only the most resolute rejection, Richard Nixon pursued and persisted with his future wife, Patricia. Nixon was actually reduced to chauffeuring Pat to and from her dates with other boys. Incredibly, he would sit alone in the car for hours waiting until it was time to chauffeur her back home again!

> Nixon pursued Pat with the same dogged persistence he later used on Alger Hiss. Pat was one of the most popular young women in Whittier, and she dated all of the town's most eligible bachelors. As she remembered it, Nixon "would drive me to meet other beaux, and wait around to take me home." After 2 full years of this, Pat finally capitulated.[383]

If Nixon had pursued with anything less than intractable determination, he would not have won the love of his life (and she would not have won the man whose determination eventually transformed her into the First Lady). Moreover, their two daughters, Julie and Tricia, would never have been born.

A man knows he's treading on thin ice when he pursues too doggedly or persists for too long, but he also knows that, in reality, women often change their mind. In fact, a man has reason to believe that some women may *demand* that suitors take great risks, and overcome great obstacles as a test of their love and loyalty.

A woman who enacted the hundredth part of such extravagant overtures would be understood to have humiliated herself for having "thrown herself" at a man. Needless to say, men "throw themselves" at women as a matter of course, but every human reality is subject to reframe. So we *choose* to interpret the male reality in terms of "determination," "forcefulness," and "conquest." We do this out of a seeming *need* to view *all* human realities within a strict MP/FV framework. Kate Fillion, author of *Lip Service*, explains:

> Even if we detect that something unexpected is occurring—a woman is competing with others, say, or a powerful man is sleeping with a secretary who is trying to exploit their relationship for her own gains—we literally lack the language to discuss what is happening. Often, we try to reinterpret the situation to fit the script we've learned: the woman isn't competing, she's merely concerned; and the boss isn't being exploited, he's actually abusing his position of power.[384]

Men have *the* power; women are *the* victims. If we believe that strongly enough and internalize it deeply enough, that's what we'll "see" in every situation. It's what Fillion calls the "sexual script."

Consider Fillion's analysis of a typical office affair between "Bill," The Boss; and "Elaine," his subordinate. It all begins with an impetuous kiss.

> Beyond that first ill-advised kiss, Bill did not abuse his power, and in fact, Elaine does not believe that his initial advance was motivated by anything more sinister than sexual attraction. At any rate, she had options: forget the kiss altogether, or lodge a sexual harassment complaint as per their company policy. She was in no way intimidated out of laying charges, and did not fear that doing so would harm her career. Nor did Bill attempt to silence her, pressure her into bed, or even so much as hint that she would receive professional rewards if she had sex with him. As far as Elaine was concerned, Bill's kiss did not create a hostile climate but an exciting one, and he did not take advantage of his position of relative power. Rather, his power is precisely what attracted her. He made the initial advance, but she was the one who actively chose to escalate to a full-fledged, sexual affair. Her reasons—she was interested in him and deeply flattered by his interest in her, and she was bored, lonely, and in the market for romance—had nothing to do with coercion and everything to do with self-interest.[385]

Was even that first kiss either "ill-advised" or an "abuse of power"? What if, in the sexual arena, it was *he* who was "subordinate"? Perhaps it is exactly because the man has little power in the sexual arena that he's left with little choice but to stick his neck out, make the first move, and await her judgment.

If The Boss says "sleep with me and I'll promote you," his crime is clear and extremely punishable. If The Secretary says, "promote me and I'll sleep with you," it is a legal nonissue. The MP/FV perceptual distortions may make it all but impossible to see; yet in common occurrence the female "subordinate" may be the one with the power and The Boss may be the one exploited. Says Elaine:

> "When people look at it from the outside, they see his professional power but ignore the fact that I was holding the trump card: the threat of exposure. No matter how loving and real the relationship is, that threat is always there in the background, always. You have the ability to damage that man's marriage, his reputation, and his career . . . Bill was risking everything." . . . But Elaine, as it turns out, wasn't just risking less than he was. She also had more to gain . . . Elaine was privy to pillow talk that helped put her on the fast track; she also had the benefit of Bill's personal attention, advice, and guidance. She was able to perform at a higher level as a result, and he was in a position to ensure that her good work was recognized.[386]

The "sexual script," is feminism's one-sided MP/FV paradigm by another name: "In the sexual script, men are predators and women are defenseless prey, but real life is far more complex—and in real-life relationships, power shifts back and forth between partners all the time. Elaine felt sexually powerful, which she was, and professionally powerful, which she became, partly because Bill helped her."[387]

As seen from a *balanced* perspective, MalePower is matched by FemalePower:

> "Sexuality is a power tool for women," declares Laura, who is only thirty-four but already Bill's counterpart: a vice-president of a major advertising agency. Unlike Elaine, she has never had an office affair, but she readily confesses to using her sex appeal to get ahead: "I bluffed my way into advertising with no experience, and basically got my first job because the boss fancied me. He didn't do or say anything, it was just obvious.
>
> I wasn't the slightest bit interested in him, but the fact that he liked me meant that he went out of his way to help me. . . . He encouraged me and taught me how to do really advanced work, so by the time I got my next job, I was on my way. It makes me angry when any kind of flirtation is positioned as sexual harassment, because it makes women look so weak and spineless. If a man you work with is attracted to you, he's not abusing you or taking advantage of you - *you* can use *him,* get him in your corner professionally."[388] [Emphasis in the original]

Beyond a purely selfish stance, why isn't she equally "angry when any kind of flirtation is positioned as sexual harassment," because it's a position that can cause men to be ruined over nothing?

At any rate, Laura here demonstrates how femininity can be *so* powerful, it may ply a force of influence without a woman having to *do* anything. Obviously, power worked without action taken is power that will be difficult to measure and/or hold accountable. But that doesn't make such power any less *real*.

Sexual Harassment is also real. Some men *do* abuse power positions to coerce women sexually, and such men are indeed reprehensible and deserving of punishment. *And*, it's also true that our overall understandings and reactions are highly distorted by feminism's sole ideological ownership of this issue.

Under feminism, we begin the assessment of male/female conflict and/or issues under the global assumption that men have *the* power and women are *the* victims (MP/FV, MB/WG). Under equalism, we begin with the global assumption that It All Balances Out between women and men. Proceeding from this non-biased position, we focus in on the individual conflict and/or issue fully open and available to what*ever* truths present themselves.

The Sexual Harassment Industry is a men's issue because it is emblematic of the way women's issues receive such levels of attention, action, and priority as to shut the equal-opposite male perspective out entirely. As an *industry*, sexual harassment is a men's issue because it is an "industry" created out of feminist hostility toward men and a desire to punish and control men and male sexuality.

Issues Download #8 – Sexual Inequities

I have presented the world of sports as viewed from a politicized male perspective; witness now the politicized male perspective applied to the realms of sex, dating, and romance. By way of introduction to his techniques for bringing about *Intimate Connections* with the opposite sex, David Burns M.D. tells his story:

> Occasionally I'd sit for hours in the student union trying to strike up conversations with women. Whenever I saw an attractive woman I would greet her with lame comments such as: "Oh, what's your name? Do you go to school here? I'm a medical student," and so on. Within a minute or two she would inevitably excuse herself by saying, "I'm just waiting here for my boyfriend, who will be along any minute." This was discouraging, but I'd nevertheless try again. And again. And again. I probably became one of the most rejected men in Northern California, since I accumulated as many as fifty to sixty rejections per week. Despite a success rate of approximately zero, I continued to pursue the opposite sex, figuring that maybe *somehow* I might soon learn the ropes.[389]

If those same women had used those same lines to pick *him* up, would Burns still judge them "lame"? Is it just coincidence that David Burns' "luck" with women changed at the same time as he was making the transition from medical *student* to medical *doctor?* "Have women any idea," asks Nancy Friday, "how it feels to be rejected again and again?"[390] Who can doubt the connection between Man's drive for success and his desire to improve his "luck" with the ladies?

Certainly, technique and practice can improve one's success rate in *any* endeavor. With all due respect to Dr. Burns and his technique, however, what guy needs technique when he's got the letters "M.D." after his name? Further, why should a guy need "technique" in the first place? His female equivalent needs neither the technique, nor the M.D. If he were equally desired (for his *intrinsic* values), then he wouldn't need a technique or an M.D. either.

Last but not least among our eight representative men's issues is the issue of female sexual power which, from the politicized male perspective, appears vastly more effective and compelling than male sexual power. To complete our sexual-political picture, we need to understand this power: its magnitude, its effect on men, and its effect upon our world.

Any number of indicators might leave the male feeling doubtful as to the effectiveness of his masculine allure upon the fairer sex. For example, he may conclude that the combined flesh lust toward men of all the women in America is sufficient to sustain only *one* magazine, directed at women, featuring erotic images of men. Despite its fame, *Playgirl* is a small-scale publication boasting fewer subscribers than either *Mother Earth News* or *Workbench*. What's more, fully half its subscribers are men.[391]

The heterosexuality of women could not possibly be as socially suppressed as is the homosexuality of men; yet gay men find enough beauty in the flesh of men to allow gay erotica to flourish. And the heterosexual desires of men have made erotic imagery of women into a multi*billion*-dollar industry. But the hetero*sexual* desires of women would seem to be only *half* sufficient to keep one low-circulation magazine afloat. *Viva*, the only other magazine to attempt to sell imagery of male beauty to women, sank.[392] While women support over a dozen fashion magazines, featuring all the female skin the law will allow if they are to be sold in grocery stores, women do not spend enough money on erotic imagery of men to sustain a mere two women's magazines featuring *male* beauty as their selling point.

Are these not plain facts as viewed from where the male is standing?

To the average boy it appears obvious that the *enormous* degree to which pornography, prostitution, strip clubs, phone sex, and the sex trade in general sells more to men than to women could only reflect the degree to which male sexual desires toward women must vastly exceed female sexual desires toward men. In which direction does money more often flow as it changes hands between men and women? Women now make money of their own, but the direction in which money more often flows has not changed in equal measure.

Then as now: woman + nothing = man + family-supporting wage. Consider the two sides of this equation; don't they suggest a certain imbalance in sexual power based on gender? The basic courtship ritual (men pursue and persist, while women attract and resist) reflects this imbalance and would seem to indicate that only women have an allure that is powerful enough to affect and compel their opposite sex into *active* pursuit.

We see that when couples fight, the man is often banished from the woman's bed. His punishment is to suffer deprivation of her. We've no reason to believe she suffers deprivation of him. A man's erect penis is an unambiguous sign of his arousal. What can a man look to as an unambiguous sign of *her* arousal? The gifts he gives and money he spends, in exchange for "sexual favors," are also concrete unambiguous indicators of his desire Though they may *pay* for it, in receiving her "gift," men are to believe that they "get lucky."

According to lesbian author Pat Califia's observations of female heterosexuality, "The dynamic has to be: you do this awful thing to me that only you enjoy, so in return I expect summer vacations in Europe, diamond rings, and my own car."[393] If he lacks money and lacks even the *potential* to make money, a man may wonder if he is left with anything at all that a woman desires.

So long as money enters the equation—if he is paying for his date, or paying a prostitute, or even paying his wife's mortgage—a man has no way of knowing *for certain* whether he is truly *innately* desired or not. For *many* reasons, women's feelings toward men may appear rather, ambiguous.

Both sexes have sought to "sabotage" the other's confidence in an effort to keep the opposite sex out of "its territory." Remember *The Rules* (1995) by Ellen Fein and Sherrie Schneider? It was a massive #1 *New York Times* Bestseller. "The Rules" include "Don't meet him halfway or go Dutch on a date," "Don't talk to a man first and don't ask him to dance," "Don't call him and rarely return his calls." *The Rules* may be summed up: never give a man any reason to believe that he is desired and thus desirable. Keep him feeling as sexually insecure and inferior as possible. That way he'll feel maximally lucky, grateful, and indebted for any attention/affection he is given.

As *The Rules* clearly indicate, a woman will feel *humiliated* to have "thrown herself" at a man. Her "feminine pride" is wounded in making her desires known. And yet, as previously pointed out, in initiating contact, subjecting his "pickup line" to her judgment, pursuing and paying her way, men "throw themselves" at women as a matter of course. If *The Rules* dictate that women are to be neither "easy" nor "cheap," what else then can they be but difficult and expensive?

Isn't the word "cute"—women's universally preferred term for male attractiveness—a rather tepid adjective? "Cute" describes *nothing* a man aspires to be. If a man weren't so starving for *any* affirmation of desirability, his pride would have him reject "cute" as an insult. But men have little of the sexual confidence that sustains a woman's sexual pride. We hear that we're lousy in bed, we don't last long enough, women fake their orgasms with us, women are much better at cunnilingus than we are, and "Women need men like fish need bicycles." There's really not a whole lot for a man to base his sexual confidence and/or pride upon.

Taken all together, the perception that feminine sexual attractiveness is, at the very least, more commonplace, effective, and compelling than is masculine sexual attractiveness, appears self-evident to most males from the start. Author Thomas Ellis:

> The high school culture has been etched upon us forever. Guys have to try, girls do not. We have to approach them, they have to reject us. We have to impress them, and they have to remain unimpressed. Women are more desirable to men than men to women. They don't return our calls. They don't have time for us until next week. Then they cancel or don't show up. They can be late to meet us because their time is more valuable than ours. We have to pay. In a daily ritual we are called upon to sacrifice our own self-worth for theirs.[394]

Men, of course, seek after success partly for its intrinsic rewards. Nevertheless, the question remains: how much of this adolescent sexual powerlessness will later transform into the male drive to perform, achieve, and succeed motivated, in large part, by a desire to even out the sexual playing field and gain some measure of equality in the sexual/romantic arena?

Men generally have something boys don't have, a career. And with it, they add extrinsic value to themselves. *Clearly*, one of men's major motivators in seeking after money is to have something that women want as much as women have what men want. With *sufficient* extrinsic values (paycheck, job title, military rank) men will gain leverage out of granting or withholding "commitment" (i.e., financial security) sufficient to match the leverage women—perhaps even beautiful women—wield out of granting or withholding sex.

Gaining that leverage is a man's best, most surefire way to pursue relations with women from an equal position of strength that allows him to pursue, yet keep his pride.

When two women have dinner together, does the one who's making more money pickup the check? Men don't pay because they make more money; men make more money because they must pay. The boys' ability and willingness to support a woman's fantasies of "*Better Homes And Gardens*"—still far and away the largest selling woman's magazine in the world[395]—is symbolized in the act of paying her way. As mothers warn their daughters, "Why should a man buy the cow when he can have the milk for free?" so articles in *Cosmopolitan* speak for many women when they offer advice such as, "Make love the old-fashioned way. Make him *earn* it!"[396]

Warren Farrell has identified a list of nine conditions to be met before the average woman is willing to consent to sex with a man.[397] These are generalizations, of course, but see if they don't ring true.

1) He must be sexually attractive. He doesn't necessarily have to be "handsome," but he must have sex appeal.

2) He must be single. More often than men, women will cross a man off their list if he has a girlfriend, is engaged, or married.

3) He must be someone she can respect. If he wants to cross the street to avoid some young toughs, or if she regards his reaction to misplacing a twenty-dollar bill to be excessive ("I don't understand it. It was right here a moment ago. Where could it have gone?") her eyes roll, the silent buzzer sounds and, whether he knows it or not, he's "out." Should he be judged insecure, weak, lazy, cheap, timid . . . he is unlikely to wind up in her bed.

4) He must be someone with whom she feels some measure of intellectual connection. If she regards the gothic poems of Poe and Byron the height of romanticism and he regards them the height of indulgence, he'll probably spend the night alone. Should the dinner conversation reveal a fundamental conflict in their opinions, it is far more likely to be a sexual deal breaker for her than for him.

5) He must be someone with whom she feels some emotional connection. If she's an animal lover and he is not, or she worships Princess Diana and he doesn't get it . . . well, then he doesn't get it.

6.a) He must meet her standards for status and 6.b) He must meet her standards for successfulness. A man who makes a high wage might still fail this two-sided requirement. A plumber may be successful and well paid, but that may not help him if his date does not want to marry a "plumber."

7) He must initiate the first date. He must subject his "pick-up line" to her judgment. He must get her phone number and—assuming it's her *real* number—keep calling till he reaches her directly (The Rule is: "Don't call him and rarely return his calls"). He must present her with a date option she regards as adequate. He may satisfy all other requirements, but if he doesn't do what it takes to make the first date happen, what chance has he got?

8) He must pay her way. Women may deny it, but no matter what else he might have going for him, his failure to pick up the check is *very* apt to be a fatal error. As one 33-year-old female TV producer put it, "If you offer [to pay] and they accept, then it's over."[398]

9) He must initiate sexually. He must initiate the first kiss, the first handholding, etc. Even if he's met every condition up to this point, if, for any reason, he can't handle "putting the moves on her," he's history. As actress Lucy Liu put it, "I like to be the girl, you know?

I'm not going to make the first move, and if he's waiting around for that, then it's literally never going to happen."[399] In some cases (he'll never know which), his taking her "no" to mean "no" may also cost him sex and/or love.

Meanwhile, in the same manner of generalization as the above, her *first* requirement—sexual attractiveness—is his *only* requirement. When men complain that they can't get laid, they mean they can't get their one requirement met. When women complain that they can't get laid, they mean they can't get all nine of their requirements met.

I submit that the disparity between his one requirement and her nine is a fairly clear measure of the disparity in male vs. female sexual power.

A minority of men at the top do more than their fair share of the mating and marrying (leaving other males shut out). The same holds true in nature. "Almost all females mate and reproduce, but many fewer males do, the percentage varying with the species," asserts Marry Batten, author of *Sexual Strategies*. "Why don't more males mate? It isn't for lack of interest. Either they are killed off or prevented from mating by their rivals or they are rejected by females."[400]

A system of mating involving one male, multiple females, is known as polygyny. David M. Buss:

> Even in a mildly polygynous mating system like our own, where some men acquire multiple partners through serial marriage and affairs and others are left mateless, competition among men and selection by women of men who are high in status and resources are ultimately responsible for the evolution in males of risk-taking traits that lead to successful mating at the expense of a long life. Because the reproductive stakes are higher for men than for women, more men than women risk being shut out of mating entirely. Bachelors who are mateless for life are more numerous than spinsters in every society. In America in 1988, for example, 43 percent of men but only 29 percent of women had never been married by the age of twenty-nine. By the age of thirty-four, 25 percent of men but only 16 percent of women had never been married.[401]

Because fewer men possess the combination of looks, personality, and status that add up to sexual/matrimonial desirability, fewer men than women mate. And the discrepancy is not slight. If 25 percent of men but only 16 percent of women never marry, then rejected males outnumber rejected females by over 50 percent.

In fact, according to recent human DNA analysis, 67 percent of our human ancestors were female—only 33 percent were male.[402] In other words, "More men than women get squeezed out of the mating game," explains genetic researcher Jason Wilder of the University of Arizona. "As a result, twice as many women as men passed their genes to the next generation."[403] Historically, if about 80 percent of women managed to breed, then only about *40* percent—*less* than *half* of all men—were elite enough, or lucky enough, to do the same! If we opened our hearts to men, the predominantly male experience of being "squeezed out of the mating game," would surely rate the same societal empathy accorded any number of women's issues.

To have mate-appeal equal to that of his own female equivalent, a man must possess both *intrinsic* and *extrinsic* values. This truth is clearly observable in the fact that *every* male "sex symbol" is also a "*success* symbol." Though chased by hordes of female fans, even a beautiful Adonis like basketball superstar Magic Johnson knows what it's like to be rendered a "success object." Katie Roiphe: "As Magic describes it, these women wanted to talk about salaries as a kind of foreplay. 'I sometimes felt,' Magic wrote good-naturedly, 'that it was not me that they were excited by but my checkbook.'"[404] If men were not quite so "good-natured" regarding their inequities, if men spoke out, we'd have a better sense that It All Balances Out.

Could romance novel cover model Fabio be the sole exception? Could he be *so* beautiful that he is desired for his intrinsic values alone? Steven Rhoads:

> Fabio is a handsome male model with enormous shoulders and a rugged face. Men can see why women would find him attractive. What men don't understand is how his money and the power it brings can add to his *physical* attractiveness. But one columnist covering a Fabio appearance tells her female readers—"Lest the sex appeal of Fabio escape you, repeat 'multimillionaire' to yourself."[405] [Emphasis in the original]

Every romance novel features a handsome/powerful man known to romance novel publishers and naturalists alike as the "Alpha Male." And *every* male sex symbol is also a *success* symbol. A man's wealth/status adds to his physical/romantic attractiveness. Sex appeal and success appeal are inexorably linked within the female sexual psyche.

"Women's orgasm frequency increases with the income of their partner," states researcher Dr Thomas Pollet of Newcastle University.[406] To reach this conclusion one need only ask vast numbers of married women to self-report their frequency of orgasm during sex. The difference in the orgasmic level of one woman vs. another directly correlates with their husband's level of income. "There were of course, several factors involved in such differences but, said Pollet, money was one of the main ones."[407] No wonder Magic Johnson's bed partners used talk of salaries as a kind of foreplay.

Even decades later, I can *still* remember the names of all those Playboy "Playmates" I obsessed over. However much women may desire the celebrity male, men desire "Miss April" *every* bit as much. Yet she brings to the table only what she was born with. She doesn't bring wealth; she *spends* wealth. Beauty *alone* turns *any* woman into a celebrity.

Recently in the news, we had Natalie Dylan, a fairly ordinary looking 22-year-old Women's Studies student from San Diego selling her virginity to the highest bidder. According to various Internet sources, the highest bid reached was an absurd 3.7 *million* dollars![408] Along with myriad other cultural indicators, the sums top prostitutes command make it clear that female beauty/sexuality is far and away the most powerful and the most expensive drug on earth.

Most men will agree; making love to a beautiful woman is just about the greatest physical/emotional ecstasy this earthly reality has to offer. Men are embarrassed to admit to it but, for the promise of experiencing that ecstasy, a man can be made to do just about *anything*.

Take away every last bit of the beautiful celebrity female's celebrity status, and her sexual and marital appeal diminish only a little. Take away every last bit of the beautiful celebrity male's celebrity status, and his sexual appeal—and even more especially, his marital appeal—plummets. Put him in a Burger King uniform and regardless of his intrinsic values, his sexual/marital appeal is *gone*.

Knowing, for example, that only women's bodies can be "rented" for hundreds or even thousands of dollars an hour, how could women *not* assume that their bodies are worth more than men's? Men commonly overhear women speak of their sexual "*favors*" as something they *give* to a man. Only "Mr. Right" with both intrinsic *and* extrinsic values is "eligible" enough to meet her many conditions, receive her "gift"[a][409] and thus "get lucky."

Unlike his female equivalent, a man is in no position to expect someone to whom he feels attraction, who's single, and someone he respects and with whom he feels an intellectual and emotional compatibility and who meets his status/success requirements, to ask him out, pay his way, and keep initiating sexually until he gives in. Such expectations are quite literally beyond the imaginings of men, and yet a woman with no more than ordinary physical attractiveness will surely recognize these nine conditions as among the most *minimal* of her *requirements*. Men have all these same wants, but men are not empowered to turn such wants into *requirements*.

---

[a] For example, renowned "sexpert," Dr. Turndorf, aka, "Dr. Love" advises women to regard "sex as a loving *gift* to our men" [Emphasis in the original]

A woman may scope out some guy to whom she's attracted and hope to be "swept off her feet" and offered lifetime protection and financial support, but a man will have lesser hopes. When a man gazes upon a beautiful woman and desires sex with her, it's not that he "*only* wants to get laid." He only *aspires* to getting laid because that's as high as his low expectations take him.

In the sexual realm, men are *far* less than equal.

What is the source of female sexual power? How does it work and what force of influence does it ply in our world?

Women's greater average sexual power derives from a mix of biologically induced quantitative and qualitative differences in male vs. female sex drives, plus various cultural factors. The quantitative difference results in what Dr. Michael Bonaventura has dubbed the "libido gap."[410]

Simply put, we may each have a steaming bowl of soup to offer the other, but if you're starving and I'm only mildly hungry, then I'll operate from a stronger bargaining position. If men desire women's bodies more than women desire men's bodies . . . same thing.

Amid the many ambiguities two facts are asserted. One: "Perhaps the biggest difference between the male and female brain is that men have a sexual pursuit area that is 2.5 times larger than the one in the female brain."[411] Two: testosterone is largely responsible for fueling sex drives in both men and women, and men have, on average, about 10 to 15 times as much of the stuff coursing through their veins.

It will sway all but the most resistant that when women have that hormone administered to them, their sex drives soar accordingly. If a woman's low libido can be so effectively treated with a testosterone patch, how can her low libido be ascribed to sexual suppression under "patriarchy"? In discussing the perils of "testosterone replacement therapy," a *Newsweek* article states, "the surges of biochemical desire can leave patients reeling. One woman unwittingly doubled her dosage and had to excuse herself every few hours just to seek relief."[412] We men know the feeling.

Regarding the libidinous effects of testosterone treatments, Joan Sewell quotes Max Valerio, a transsexual born Anita Valerio:

> My sex drive went up after about a week and a half. And I thought I had a high sex drive before! And when people told me I would have a higher sex drive, I thought, "Well, how high could that be?" . . . It's like another world . . . Suddenly you understand why men tend to be more interested in pornography, why there's prostitution . . . of course![413]

Of course!

In her book *I'd Rather Eat Chocolate: Learning to Love My Low Libido*, Joan Sewell recounts her endless endeavors to bolster what everyone insists is her "psychologically induced" lack of sexual desire. She tries "sexpert" advice, sexual techniques and strategies, pornography, sexual meditation, "sensate focusing," sexual spirituality, whipped cream—none of it has any effect.

Even so, the "experts" keep telling her it's all in her head, yet the doctors transforming Anita Valerio into Max Valerio know perfectly well that testosterone is the key to libido. "They simply took it for granted," says Sewell, "that there was a direct correlation between high testosterone levels and higher libido."[414] Finally, Sewell must come to grips with reality. "Probably the most profound thing I've learned from my experiences and my research is that there is a very significant biological difference in the sex drives of men and women, and in my view, this natural limit to our sexual appetites should be acknowledged and respected."[415]

Every now and then, women's magazines run articles helping sexually disinterested women feel better by reminding them that their "disappointment in sex" is commonplace. Susan Jacoby, October 1996 issue of *Glamour* magazine:

> Nora, a medical student, doesn't like discussing her disappointment in sex. "I never mention it to the men I sleep with," she says. "What would they think if they knew that, on my list of enjoyable activities, sex ranks somewhere between eating yogurt and studying for exams? You have to understand: It's not that I hate sex, but if sex weren't so much a part of dating, and if I didn't want babies someday, I'd probably be perfectly happy not to do it." . . . Even today when sexual pleasure is assumed to be attainable by everyone—and when an unprecedented amount of sexual information is readily available—women like Nora are far more common than is generally recognized.

According to the book *Sex in America*, "women repeatedly claim in arenas like magazine articles that they find nude men unerotic, not particularly exciting."[416]

> Molly Haskell, writing in *Lear's* magazine, captured the woman's view of most male nudity when she explained that naked men in movies are curiously unstimulating to most women: "But the truth is that most of us women are not that eager to see male stars in the altogether. [William] Baldwin's brother Alec shows too much of his birthday suit in *Prelude to a Kiss* and Richard Gere's seminude thrashing and prancing in *Sommersby* are about as erotic as his self-consciously lusty smile." Holly Brubach, writing about mail-order catalogues in the *New York Times Magazine*, made a similar point. She spoke of International Male, for example, with its suggestively posed and scantily clothed models. "For me and for most of the women I know, an excursion

through this catalogue is uneventful: Here's a guy with a neck like a tree trunk; there's one with nice legs. So what?"[417]

"She's got *legs*, she knows how to use them," scream ZZ Top in a testosterone-fueled frenzy. In contrast, Jules Asner, the beautiful anchor of *E! News Daily*, comments: "We went to this nude beach, and there were all these naked men, the female body is a beautiful thing, but seeing 50 naked men was just . . . ugh."[418] In fact, says actress Shannon Elizabeth, "A man's naked body isn't always the prettiest thing to look at, even when he's in good shape."[419]

According to data collected and analyzed by online dating service OkCupid, men are "surprisingly charitable . . . the majority of women have been rated about 'medium.'" Nothing surprising about it, most people will, of course, be average. Yet, "women rate an incredible 80% of guys as worse-looking than medium."[420] If that's true, then it would seem that the vast majority of men are essentially "ugly" in the eyes of women. Perhaps we're in need of a second opinion?

"Several times a day I would retrieve a magazine and masturbate while fantasizing about those huge adult penises" recounts gay author Gary Griffin. Beheld by someone with a testosterone driven *sex* drive, the mere *image* of male beauty printed onto a piece of paper is enough to be intoxicating. Describing his sexual awakening: "I came to love, understand, and appreciate the beauty of the male body," says Griffin. "I had absolutely no attraction to the opposite sex."[421]

Men also have legs, longer and with better calf development, but I don't hear women screaming about them. Men are larger, stronger, more muscular, less bottom heavy. If beauty is in the eye of the beholder, then perhaps men don't lack beauty as much as men lack an opposite *sex* to fully appreciate, and *value* it?

To procreate, males *must* reach levels of sexual arousal sufficient to sustain erection and achieve orgasm/ejaculation. Because females can procreate whether they are libidinous or not, many are not. The "libido gap" shows itself clearly in any number of clinical studies.

One from 1994 concludes, "High school girls are less comfortable with their sexual experiences than are their male counterparts . . . while 81 percent of the sexually active boys said that 'sex is a pleasurable experience,' only 59 percent of the girls said they felt that way"[422] The *Janus Report on Sexual Behavior* by Sam S. Janus, Ph.D., and Cynthia L. Janus, M.D., offers the results of nearly 3,000 surveys. When asked "How much below maximum sexual potential are you?" not less than 24 percent of women answered *100 percent*.[423] And according to a massive survey published in the *Journal of the American Medical Association*, 32 percent of women "lacked interest in sex," 26 percent were "unable to achieve orgasm" and 23 percent reported "sex not pleasurable" (in men the results were 15%, 8%, 8%).[424] "One out of three women said they were uninterested in sex," report the authors of *Sex in America*.[425]

These same clinical findings also suggest that about a third of women have fully functional sex drives, which suggests that libidinous women are very commonplace. Add to that a certain characteristically feminine emotional/verbal effusiveness—together with her virtually unlimited *capacity* for sex—and, upon encountering such a woman, the "myth" of low female libido is apt to be replaced with an unshakable conviction: T*hey want it just as much as we do!* But women's lesser *average* sex drive is not a myth, it's a matter of degree.

Anita Valerio believed her sex drive was set at utmost but *Max* Valerio knows better. Woman's sex drive could average a *lot* less than Man's and still allow for a *lot* of female lust, enough to mislead men and women into believing that male and female lust are a match. Yet the culture-wide effect of such a mismatch in libido would certainly contribute to female sexual power.

At the risk of *way* oversimplifying, at this juncture, I'll offer a cursory glance at a few of the complex *qualitative* differences most commonly observed:

1) Female sexuality is not as "self-starting." The "Sleeping Beauty" parable derives from the observation of female sexuality being "asleep" until a man "awakens" it with a kiss. Evidence suggests that ejaculating into a woman's vagina transfers testosterone and increases her libido. Thus it is commonly observed that, deprived of sex, men become *in*creasingly desirous; women become *de*creasingly desirous. According to my research, supermodel Caprice spoke for many women when she said: "If you've been used to sleeping with someone regularly then it can be difficult, but it's dead easy to forget about it if you haven't had sex for a month or two."[426]

2) With women, there is desire *for* him, but, perhaps the greater desire is the desire to *be* desired *by* him. The desire to *be* desired is compelling to be sure, but is it as compelling as the desire itself? So long as her man remains in good standing, she *loves* fulfilling his sexual fantasies. The moment he falls out of favor, however, she may now take *no* interest in fulfilling *his* fantasies.

3) It seems clear that female sexuality includes an extra measure of ambivalence, reluctance, and reticence rarely found in male sexuality. The simple fact that females get pregnant and males do not has doubtless led to evolved differences in male vs. female sexual psychology.

Throughout human evolution, each copulation potentially used up one of her precious few pregnancies, each one fraught with potential hazard and vast investment in childcare. So it served Woman to be less sexually addicted and more sexually selective. For this reason, even if a woman has a strong libido, it may nevertheless be tempered by an equally strong capacity to say "no."

Dissident feminist and author of *Sexual Personae*, Camille Paglia knows full well that female sexual power is grounded in biology. Not one to mince words, says she: "If middle class feminists think they conduct their love lives perfectly rationally, without any instinctual influences from biology, they are imbeciles."[427]

> Films of the mating behavior of most other species—a staple of public television in America—demonstrate that the female chooses. Males pursue, show off, brawl, scuffle, and make general fools of themselves for love. A major failing of most feminist ideology is its dumb, ungenerous stereotyping of men as tyrants and abusers, when in fact—as I know full well from my own mortifying lesbian experience—men are tormented by women's flirtatiousness and hemming and hawing, their manipulations and changeableness, their humiliating rejections.
>
> Cock teasing is a universal reality. It is part of women's merciless testing and cold-eyed comparison shopping for potential mates. Men will do anything to win the favor of women. Women literally size up men—"What can you show me?"—in bed and out.[428]

"To some extent, males tend to be what females want them to be," asserts naturalist Mary Batten. "This means that enormous responsibility and power reside in the preferences of females. . . . Some scientists believe that female choice directs male behavior. 'Males are a breeding experiment run by females—a proving ground from which females can cull winning genes,' says evolutionary anthropologist John Hartung."[429]

In addition to Natural Selection, biologists recognize Sexual Selection as a powerful mechanism of evolution. Because females do indeed do the choosing (some "throw themselves" at the men they choose, others need only display a "green light" to compel the men they choose into active pursuit), in a very real sense females are empowered to literally breed the male of the species to their liking.

Known as secondary sexual characteristics (everything from the peacock's tail to humpback whale song), only males possess them because only males must compete for female sexual "favors." However burdensome it may be to its owner, a peacock either grows his excessively extravagant tail or peahens won't select him for breeding.

Is Man's financial generosity a secondary sexual characteristic in humans?

To all the above we now add the *socialized* repression of female sexuality. I will assert that it has been predominantly the matri*sensus*, not the patriarchy, that has suppressed women's sexuality, and it has done so purposefully. Nadine Strossen:

> In her book *Swept Away*, sex researcher Carol Cassell writes: "Sex has historically been a commodity. It's a valuable source of power . . . Sexual power is . . . the female commodity." In the same vein, author Nancy Friday has said that "women have always derived power from withholding sex." Former porn star Veronica Vera: "A dominant patriarchy? Wake up folks. . . . it never existed in the bedroom."[430]

From a masculist perspective, patriarchy is the male status hierarchy resulting from men everywhere set in fierce competition to rise high enough to have and to be what women in general, and beautiful women in particular, are sexually empowered to demand of them.

Historically, Woman has maximized her innate sexual power by taking her lesser, more ambivalent sex drive and suppressing it further through socialized sisterhood pressures. Like any commodity, the sexual commodity has value according to the laws of supply and demand. Decrease supply, intensify demand. Intensify demand and the value of the commodity increases accordingly. To function effectively, a large percentage of women (a con*sensus* of women) must play along with this "sexual cartel." So, women who would give their "sexual favors" away too freely are kept in line with taunts of "slut" and the omnipresent threat of being shut out of the tightly bonded female collective—the matri*sensus*.

"I could live without penetration, which loomed like Hell itself with its threat of ostracization from The Group," says Nancy Friday, recalling The Rules from before *The Rules* was written. "I applied my competitive spirit to outdistancing everyone in the Nice Girl Rules, which said No Competition and No Sex; try as I may, I cannot recall anyone ever saying The Rules out loud or suggesting that breaking the antisex rules would automatically eliminate you from The Group. But they existed more strictly than any perimeters I've known since."[431]

The Sexual Cartel is a prime example of matri*sensus* in action. The Rules applied to women but the consequences applied to both sexes and played a *very* significant role in sculpting our world.

All this begs the question, has the "sexual revolution" rendered this analysis an anachronism that no longer fits the world as it is now?

From cover to cover, the book *Sex in America: A Definitive Survey* affirms the old adage: The more things change, the more they stay the same. To my knowledge, *Sex in America* is far and away the most comprehensive, rigorous, and scientifically constructed sexual survey in history. Far from offering sensationalism guaranteed to sell books, the authors' findings seem quite *un*provocative.

As expected, it's true that the average American of today has had more sexual partners than the average American of 50 years ago. But why is that? The authors identify three factors: "earlier first intercourse, later marriage, and more frequent divorce" as the factors accounting for higher average numbers of sex partners.[432] Because we devote a larger percentage of our longer lives in search of a partner, we end up having more partners.

As for the "sexual revolution": "This period was not, we find, a sexual revolution, a time of frequent sex with many partners for all."[433] The authors' findings "give no support to the idea of a promiscuous society or of a dramatic sexual revolution reflected in huge numbers of people with multiple casual sex partners."[434] According to Midge Decter, the problem with the sexual revolution, "the problem of her having been left to the operations of her own lust is that young girls do not lust in any way that gives proper drive or guidance to action. . . . Her 'lust,' insofar as it is proper at all to use that term, is for an image of herself as erotically aroused."[435] Effective precautions against disease and pregnancy exist, but "Clearly, sex isn't what women really want," says Nancy Friday. "If so, they would be responsible and have more of it."[436] "The sexual revolution is largely built upon the misapprehension that each sex has an equal appetite and is equally receptive," says Anne Moir. "It will be seen as a mere blip of social fashion in the history of our evolutionary selves."[437]

According to *Sex in America*, in *action*, it was more myth than blip and we are left with no reason to believe that birth control has rendered the women of today significantly more "promiscuous" than women of the past.

> When we report that more than 80 percent of adult Americans age eighteen to fifty-nine had zero or one sexual partner in the past year, the figure might sound ludicrous to some young people who know that they and their friends have more than one partner in a year. But the figure really reflects the fact that most Americans in that broad age range are married and are faithful . . . We find only 3 percent of adults had five or more partners in the past year. Half of all adult Americans had three or fewer partners over their lifetimes . . . only one-third of Americans aged eighteen to fifty-nine have sex with a partner as often as twice a week. . . . a third have sex with a partner a few times a month, and the rest have sex with a partner a few times a year or have no sexual partners at all.[438]

Though men tend to brag and exaggerate their erotic effect upon women, sports writer Tony Kornheiser is refreshingly honest. "I'm between

45 and 49," says Kornheiser, "and the truth is that men my age, especially the married ones, can't even remember the last time they had sex. We'd have a better chance pinpointing the last time we took a chain saw and cut off the legs of the dining room table."[439] According to *Sex in America*, Kornheiser is about right.

By and large, sexual abundance is available only to the few and then, mostly, to the young. But, apparently, he's got one thing wrong. Though (from a male perspective) the rate of sex within marriage may be rather underwhelming, nevertheless, the authors of *Sex in America* insist that married people enjoy a far higher incidence of sexual intercourse than single people. Half the married engage in sex a few times a month, but only a quarter of singles do as well. Though 25 percent of single people are limited to sex a few times a year, the same is true of only 10 percent of married people.[440] So, Mr. Kornheiser, whatever your experience of sexual starvation may be, odds are you're still doing better than if you were single!

The authors of *Sex in America* say their results hold firm regardless of race or religion, or the region of this country they study, or other countries across the globe. Marriage is the great leveler. Marriage (i.e., Woman?) regulates sex.

> And marriage, we find, regulates sexual behavior with remarkable precision. No matter what they did before they wed, no matter how many partners they had, the sexual lives of married people are similar. Despite the popular myth that there is a great deal of adultery in marriage, our data and other reliable studies do not find it. Instead, a vast majority are faithful while the marriage is intact.[441]

Does this mean the standard characterization of men as unfaithful adulterers might be unfairly exaggerated?

"A large minority of males suffer reproductive oblivion, having no sex at all, or very little," author and sex researcher Steve Moxon confirms. This, Moxon believes, would extend to a majority of males if not for the custom of marriage. But, "A majority of males have no option of sex outside of marriage, and their marriages themselves may well be sexless."[442] If the situation is so bad for males, why then don't more males complain? "Unlike females, males cannot complain, however legitimately, without reducing both their social standing and appeal to females."[443] Confidence is one of the single most attractive features a man can have and a vital component of male sex appeal. Complaining men are not confident men. FemalePower compels men to remain "strong and *silent*."

From the masculist standpoint, if adult sex is largely limited to sex within the *matri*sensus institution of *matri*mony, then sex is largely limited to sex that's paid for by breadwinning husbands. The "sexual cartel," a system that fulfills female desires for protector/providers over male desires for sexual quantity and variety, is still in effect (bolstered by Woman's Moral Authority to define "promiscuity" and "adultery" in the worst way). This matrisensus prohibition against sexual quantity/variety is a prohibition that Woman will tend to profit from more and suffer less than Man.

A cursory glance through men's magazines will attest that the single greatest gnawing craving desire to be found within the average male psyche is frequent sex with multiple partners. Who could doubt that? Speaking of *Sex in America*: "the rates we find are so modest, at best, that they confound our expectations."[444] If sexual reality really is as paltry as the data indicates, it is *not* because that's how men want it.

To view a world of sex the way *men* want it, one need only look to the gay male community, where sexual partners commonly number in the hundreds (by contrast, within the lesbian community, there is talk of "lesbian bed death" referring to the frequency with which sex tends to die out in lesbian relationships). Joan Sewell:

> Gay men or straight men, it doesn't matter. Most want to get to the sex. Except gay men get more sex. Probably because they're with other men ... and ... ta-da! ... around people with similar sex drives—that is, not women. Oh, but we so like to minimize any differences. And it's not just a little difference between men's and women's sex drives. It's big.[445]

Within marriage, desires come closest to equalizing, but even within marriage, women act as the primary sexual limiters. David M. Buss:

> One of the most prominent changes within marriage over time occurs in the realm of sex. The study of newlywed couples showed that with each passing year, men increasingly complain that their wives withhold sex. Although only 14 percent of men complain that their newlywed brides have refused to have sex during the first year of marriage, 43 percent, or three times as many, of the men express this feeling four years later. Women's complaints that their husbands refuse to have sex with them increase from 4 percent in the first year to 18 percent in the fifth year. Both men and women increasingly charge their partners with refusing sex, although more than twice as many men as women voice this complaint.[446]

A friend of mine is wont to say: "Heaven is the place where you finally get all the sex you've always wanted. Otherwise, it just wouldn't be heaven." Truer words were never spoken. How do you get a young Palestinian male to strap on explosives with which to blow himself and anyone nearby to bits? Simple, "promise 72 houris—virginal beings with black eyes and alabaster skin—to attend the martyr's desires in paradise."[447] *Seventy-two* hot babes attending to my desires? Where's the ripcord? I'll pull it right now!

Are female suicide bombers promised 72 hot hunks? Of course not. Female suicide bombers are promised they'll "become the purest and most beautiful form of angel at the highest level possible in heaven."[448] To get a woman to do whatever you want her to do, you must reach her where *her* priorities are invested: beauty, grace, and goodness. You *could* promise 72 hot hunks, but for that, the average woman could hardly be induced to cross the street. As German author Esther Vilar puts it, "A woman would be bored to tears with an all-male harem. This has always been the case and will remain so."[449]

To men, *paradise* is a place in which sex happens the way men would want it to happen; but here on *earth,* sex happens only to the extent that women allow. If ours truly is a patriarchal paradise of male power and privilege, why then does the sexual world bear so little resemblance to being the way men would so fervently want it to be?

The *point* is: however subjective, covert, and indirect in nature it may be, with a little sussing out, FemalePower is *revealed*. Female-Power is *real.*

Let's take one last look at the mechanics of female sexual power. If, at any given moment, about *one*-third of the female population are lustfully and straightforwardly "on the make" while *two*-thirds of the male population are lustfully and straightforwardly "on the make," then the female out looking for sex is more apt to experience an economy of sexual plenty while the male out looking for sex is more apt to experience an economy of sexual scarcity. Under the circumstances, men are left with little choice but to initiate most social/sexual encounters with women. Men thus accept the strategic disadvantage that goes with initiating which, in turn, further increases female sexual power.

It's like this: you have a need to sell your watch and in so doing you get to choose between two scenarios. Will you choose: A) you approach someone saying: "Isn't this a great watch; how much will you give me for this watch?" Or will you choose: B) someone approaches *you* saying: "That's a great watch; how much will you take for that watch?" The strategic advantage inherent in option "B" is obvious. When you approach someone, you must take what you can get from someone who may or may not have any interest in what you've got. The potential for humiliation is clear. When someone approaches you their interest is plain to see and you bargain the price *up*, not down. Women generally choose option "B"—being approached—because it allows women to avoid the humiliation that comes of *direct* rejection and allows women to operate from a position of relative strength and strategic advantage. Men choose option "A" because option "B" is generally not available to them.

Historically, in choosing a rich man over a poor man, a woman had her children's future to consider. If she was born into a poor family, her beauty "sold" to a rich man may well have been her family's *only* way out of poverty. In withholding sexually, Woman did what she had to do. I'm not assigning blame; I'm trying to hold Woman *accountable*. I'm not saying what Woman did was "wrong." Arguably, in largely limiting sex to within the bounds of matrimony, Woman has acted as the driving force in forming families, the bedrock of human society. And, while a world of wall-to-wall sex is indeed the male's most fervent *craving*, the trick here is found in the old adage: Be careful what you wish for; you may get it. Just because sexual smorgasbord is the world as men *crave* it doesn't mean it is the world in which men are *happiest*. Men are equally romantic and equally as invested in the safety, security, and sacredness of monogamy as women are.

There's no need for judgment. In maximizing the powers she has in compensation for powers she lacked, Woman has done exactly what Man has done. But, as Man is accountable for his power, so Woman must be accountable for hers—a FemalePower we all *know* to be real even if we don't *officially* know it.

Joke: A little boy is taunting a little girl on the playground. He points to himself and says, "I have one of these and you don't." The little girl runs home crying. But the next day when the little boy taunts her again saying, "I have one of these and you don't," the little girl replies, "I asked my mother and she said that with one of *these*, I can get all of *those* I want." Note: No one needs to have this joke explained to them; no one believes the little boy can make the reverse claim.

So, why go to such lengths to "prove" Female Sexual Power (FSP) when this power is already *universally* recognized? Though widely recognized, FSP is as widely denied. The need to believe that men are *always* powerful and women are *always* powerless victims informs the official version of gender reality in *all* contexts. To maintain that fantasy, against an ocean of contrary evidence, we may even hear that women have a *stronger* sex drive, are *greater* users of pornography, and are *more* sexually frustrated than men. Within humans there is an irrational yet very powerful impulse to believe that women are *the* victims in *all* things.

So, *for what it's worth*, the effort to "prove" it is an effort to cut through denial and raise FSP to the level of the *officially* known. When Woman comes to the bargaining table saying, "I have *nothing*," Man will be emboldened to say: "That's wrong! Your powers are no less real than mine. I invite you to own your power and be accountable." If

Woman is officially offered the *gift* of accountability, perhaps she'll accept the gift: "Yes, I did A B & C, and X Y & Z were the outcomes. I'll step into my power and take responsibility for my equal part in the molding of our world." *Now* we have a gender system rendered more functional and more negotiable for being rendered more deeply honest, fair, fact-based, rational, and *true*.

Woman's sexual power is only one of *many* avenues by which Woman plied her influence. In fact, in many ways, FSP has only served as conduit for an even greater power—Emotional Intimacy power.

"Why are so many men so dependent on women?" asks author Marvin Allen.

> Perhaps the most obvious answer is sex. Nature has given men a bounty of testosterone, the hormone that creates physical desire. Men have from ten to fifteen times as much of this potent androgen as women, which is one of the reasons they have such a strong sex drive. Most men are willing to go to great lengths to satisfy that drive, especially in their teens, twenties, and thirties when their hormones are at peak levels. Said a friend of mine, "I don't think women realize what a strong force sex is in a man's life. When I was in my twenties, there was really nothing worth doing other than sex. If you had given me a choice between being a celibate millionaire and being poor with lots of sex, there would have been no contest. I would have chosen sex."[450]

Sex *is* the most *obvious* answer. Yet I believe that FSP leads into something of even greater leverage. Once in bed, a woman may introduce a man to a level of emotional intimacy the woman experiences with her girlfriends but the man experiences nowhere else.

To those deluded enough to believe men are the non-sentimental, non-romantic sex, the truth can be unsettling. Former President Ronald Reagan's "maudlin love letters reveal a little too much of his softer side," says *Chicago Sun-Times* columnist Paige Smoron.

> The letters are moving, tender---and *profoundly disturbing*. We're not just talking about the nicknames here, which are plenty creepy: Nancy Pants, Senator, Momie Poo, First Mommie, "peewee powerhouse." . . . One note in the book was scribbled on White House stationery. "I love you," he writes, *nine times*. He finishes, "And besides that---I love you." Yes, it's sweet. But this was written in the Oval Office? . . . He wrote this letter after a fight: "it is true that sometimes Mr. Reagan loses his temper and slams a door but that's because he can't cry, or stamp his foot—(he really isn't the type). But mad or glad, Mr. Reagan is head over heels in love with Mrs. Reagan and can't even imagine a world without her." I have heard that powerful men want to be dominated at home. But nobody told me how often they refer to themselves in the third person.[451]

A "real" man "can't cry" or get emotional needs met from other men.

Smoron is clearly shocked at what a mush-ball the "macho" man is on the inside. Well, the more "macho" the man the more dependent and "mushy" he's apt to be with regard to his one and *only* source of *deep* emotional intimacy, solace and support. The more dependent he is; the more power his one source of intimacy will have over him.

If the powerful man is dominated at home, perhaps he's not so powerful after all. For women whose primary parent is usually same-sex and whose deepest love and intimacy is usually same-sex, the extreme starry-eyed level of men's opposite-sex love/dependency may be hard to fathom. Within "patriarchy," this extreme need often brings elite males to their knees. Of course, Nancy also loved Ronald but, as always, it's a matter of degree. And, significantly, he was Governor of California and then President of the United States and, like it or not, much of her feeling toward him was surely based on that. Can you imagine "Madame President" having *this* level of goo-goo-eyed dependency on the "First Gentleman"? Neither can I.

It's always been this way. "Let's not forget about Edward, the duke of Windsor. The greatest romantic figure of the '30s, here's a guy who gives up the throne for a pinched looking American divorcee. In his abdication speech, he said eloquently, 'I have found it impossible to carry the heavy burden of responsibility and to discharge my duties as king as I would wish to do without the help and support of the woman I love.'" He too wrote gooey letters. "To his paramour, Wallis Simpson: 'Oh! 'Make ooh' to think you'll hold this piece of paper,' calling her 'Pooky demus' and" so on.[452]

He felt this way toward her not because she was either particularly young or particularly beautiful, but because she brought a vital depth of emotional intimacy to him, perhaps for the first time in his life. Once experienced, many men will cling to this intimacy, this emotional lifeline quite literally as if their life depended on it.

Psychologist Herb Goldberg describes only in the bleakest terms the inner lives of men who have no such female companionship. "Without a close relationship with a woman, most heterosexual men's personal lives are painfully empty and present an unknowing danger to their well-being. Intense hunger and deprivation of personal contact build in them, and they become prone to extreme and self-destructive behaviors and decisions in their pursuit of satisfaction and relief from their isolation and need for close contact."[453] Through relationship with a woman a man gains access to the world of women. Through marriage, men gain deeper, more permanent access.

It's called *matri*mony, not patrimony, because marriage is an essentially *matri*sensus realm. It is the world of women. If a man gets shut out, he will be deprived of any real depth of physical or emotional intimacy, companionship, love, home, family, and parenting. Many will experience this deprivation as akin to an emotional *death sentence*.

This is why "Males pursue, show off, brawl, scuffle, and make general fools of themselves for love." This is why men without a close relationship with a woman are "prone to extreme and self-destructive behaviors." This is why black men—doubly prejudiced against all their lives—prejudiced against for being black and prejudiced against for being *male*—are prone to extreme, illegal, and often *failed* efforts to achieve eligibility in the eyes of their sisterhood and why so many end up homeless and/or imprisoned. Overall, it seems to me that as financially dependent as women were in the 1950s, that's how sexually and emotionally dependent men *still are*.

If the men of the 1950s, in large numbers, had decided that relatively low status, low earning women were deserving of mass rejection, the societal uproar would have been unimaginable. The "shotgun marriage," together with prohibition against divorce, would have expanded as necessary to protect financially dependent women. In the new millennium women in large numbers have decided that relatively low status, low earning men have been rendered "unmarriageable." The societal uproar is nonexistent.

Along with her *far* greater Sexual Power and Emotional Intimacy power, Woman wields a *vastly* greater *power* to draw caring, concern, and compassion upon herself. When will we grasp that there are many *kinds* of power and while men may have more than their share of some modes of power, men have less than their share of other modes of power. When will we grasp the true *balance* of power?

Female sexual power is primal. It predates the patriarchal powers men have created for themselves in reaction to it. In fact it predates humanity itself.

During a Yale University conducted experiment in which monkeys were taught to use tokens to pay for grapes and other delectables, behavioral economist Keith Chen observed a male monkey using his tokens to pay a female monkey for sex.[454] *Science News* and *National Geographic* have recently reported on naturalists' observations of male chimpanzees in the wild offering meat they've hunted in exchange for sex. "Wild male chimps that share meat with females double their chances of having sex with those females."[455] The "world's oldest profession" is even older than we know.

"Despite our civilized and sophisticated veneer," says author John Moore, "we are still, like all other creatures, basically motivated by sexual energy."[456] Like Moore, I believe that the "urge to merge" is a fundamental driving force, in the natural world *and* in the human world. Women's control over breeding thus gives women enormous though officially unrecognized power. But Camille Paglia knows the truth of the matter: "[W]omen's sexual powers are enormous. All cultures have seen it. Men know it. Women know it. The only people who don't know it are feminists."[457]

One of my goals is to show that the male quest for power is, in large part, a reaction to unacknowledged female powers. Whether he knows it or not, Man's single-minded quest for success is a quest for *equality*. It is an effort to compensate for being male and gain confidence in his areas of greatest insecurity.

I know this because I feel it deep within myself.

"Arrows" #3: The Erotic Arena

"Arrows" come in many forms. A few days after a fight with the girl I lost my virginity to, I called trying to reconnect with her. Her mother answered the phone and told me she had moved in with some other guy. That's right; my girlfriend hadn't just begun dating some other guy. In the span of one week, she had *moved in* with another guy. This particular arrow pierced my head as well as my heart.

I guess I got my male naiveté busted. It had always been clear that boys experienced an absolute sexual craving desire for girls that was only ambiguously returned. Of course, any reasonably attractive female with a little nerve can walk into a bar and be desired, drink for free, dance with the guys, and go home with them as she pleases. But, like other boys, I'd been raised on imagery of Humphrey Bogart and Captain Kirk. I had internalized the assumption that, when push came to shove, as a man I would prevail. When my girlfriend's mother told me the news, however, I had to realize that in the sexual arena I was, shall we say, outmatched.

Not only did I feel the expected heartache of lost love, I also felt great pangs of amorphous fear. Being male, I had no idea what it meant to be "sexy." From my heterosexual male perspective, men's bodies seemed sexually *repulsive*. So it came as no surprise when, among the messages boys receive, there is the message that girls will merely "consent" or "submit" to sex—yet *I* found that message *devastating*. Sexually, in my *male*ness, I felt utterly power*less*.

For a male, sexual/emotional breakthrough with an attractive female is something rather extraordinary. It's no wonder males think of sex in terms of "conquest." But for girls, more often operating within a sexual economy of plenty, the social/sexual doors swing open. My girlfriend was a young beauty with a body worth a thousand dollars an hour. What male would stand in the way of that incredibly valued body moving in with him? Encountering little sexual ambivalence, resistance, or reticence; for her, access to moving in with a member of the opposite sex was never more than a phone call away.

What did I have to match that?

The truths of male vulnerability are profoundly rejected. I risk ridicule and dismissal revealing my own vulnerability in order to lead by example. I reveal these rejected truths because these male vulnerability truths are the *only* truths that allow for *empathy* interpretations of males, male attitudes and male behaviors.

Though it was way back in high school, I can still remember the phrase sewn onto the backpack of a girl with far more sexual confidence than I. The "arrow" read, "girls rule, boys drool." I was reminded of it recently when I saw a pretty girl flaunting the same slogan on her jean jacket. Then, as now, I resent women consciously wielding this power, without being responsible for it, and without even having to officially acknowledge its existence, let alone have it entered into the larger political equation. If sexual power could be measured as objectively as wages, then its imbalance could not be so easily denied and ignored. Further, if the personal were the political for men as it is for women, then men's personal experience feeling sexually inferior, dirty, inadequate, ugly, and rejected would rate the same credibility, high profile, and empathy accorded any number of women's issues.

In the exaggerated language of feminism, women are "sex objects." Women are "meat." In the exaggerated language of masculism, men are of the sex that's "ugly" and "shunned." If the masculist rhetoric is inflammatory self-pity, the feminist rhetoric is no better. If, on the other hand, the feminist rhetoric is judged true and valid from the female perspective politicized, then the equal/opposite masculist rhetoric must be judged true and valid from the male perspective politicized.

The point is that masculist rhetoric can do whatever feminist rhetoric can do. All that remains is for these equal/opposite perspectives to receive equal treatment in the halls of politics, legislature, academia, the courts, and the media.

Sexual inequities are men's issues because men experience inequality in the realms of beauty and sexual power. On a personal level each man internalizes this inequality in his own way. On a societal level the ramifications are profound. We may perceive "patriarchy" in a whole new light when we visualize a hierarchy of men created out of fierce competition with each other in their efforts to have and to be what the matrisensus is sexually/emotionally empowered to demand of them.

Reality Check:

As stated, the preceding Issues Download was written from a masculist perspective. Gender politics is essentially the politics of gender complaint. Feminism presents the rhetoric of female complaint. Masculism presents the rhetoric of male complaint. In its presentation of the male experience, masculist rhetoric is negative in its slant and victim-oriented because that is the mirror-opposite of feminism, and that is the nature of a *politicized* perspective. Masculism leads men (and women) toward a view of the world that focuses exclusively on the positives inherent in the female experience and the negatives inherent in the male experience. This is a *politicized* perspective in that it generates the emotional fuel (anger) required in order to bring about a political movement—the masculist movement.

As David Thomas said, I do not spend my whole time feeling miserable about being male. That is not the point. The point is that gender politics is a battle of rhetoric and if men chose to enter that battle, they'd find themselves well armed. In an effort to get men to "show up" for the Battle of the Sexes, masculism attempts the seemingly *impossible* task of goading men into mobilizing on their own behalf—enough, at least, so that *if* there should ever be something like an equalist movement, there would be masculist-savvy men enough to occupy the other side of the negotiation table.

Feminism is not simply the female perspective; it is the female perspective *politicized*. Polls indicate that the majority of women do not self-identify as feminists. Many women do not experience the world as feminism describes it. Likewise, many men do not experience the world as masculism describes it. Feminism and masculism are equally valid and equally flawed. Because they are equally flawed, they are equally vulnerable to counterargument and dismissal. Yet both feminism and masculism have *important* truths to offer.

To keep this masculism conscious, allow me now to remove my masculist "hat" and reflect on the meaning of all this. Rhetoric is the *art* of argument. There is no final proof. Yet rhetoric is also prose designed to persuade and so, like feminist rhetoric, masculist rhetoric attempts to assemble argument that is as unassailable as possible.

Therefore, I have tended to present these issues as less nebulous than they truly are. All gender issues are controversial. The sexual issues are *amazingly* hazy. And as soon as I get through venting about the vastly greater resources devoted to breast cancer as compared with prostate cancer, I read Cathy Young arguing that at least *some* of that extra emphasis is justified by the fact that breast cancer generally claims its victims at a younger age. And so it goes. There is *always* another fact, another truth, another angle—and thus these issues stretch on ad infinitum.

I have no problem with the open-endedness of gender politics because I do not enter gender politics with the goal of "wining." I'm not trying to tell the reader what the world *is*; only what the world *looks like* from the politicized male perspective. I present the truths of Issues Download to prove that masculist rhetoric can do whatever feminist rhetoric can do and thus invite the reader to join me in taking a leap of faith. There is only one conclusion that satisfies; there is only one bottom line that takes into account *all* the truths, *all* the facts, *all* the angles—It All Balances Out!

Do I lack sympathy toward women? I happen to think that women are *drowning* in sympathy, that *super*-sympathizing with women is an underlying *cause* of women's issues (more on that coming up). In any case, I present a vast litany of male complaint and conclude with It All Balances Out because I truly believe that Woman, in her own way, suffers her version of the human condition *equally*. I *do* sympathize with women; I just don't sympathize with women *exclusively*.

Nevertheless, if this male complaint should seem exaggerated and one-sided, or feel gratingly negative and shrill with self-pity, let it hold up a mirror to the equal-opposite rhetoric of female complaint that currently saturates our world. And bear in mind that within feminist rhetoric there are no reality checks. Feminism doesn't admit that its rhetoric is flawed and incomplete. Within female-ism there are no humble reminders of its limitations and no efforts to take in a bigger picture that would include female power, complicity, or accountability.

Summary:

We have only skimmed eight of the major men's issues—each worthy of book-length treatment. Other men's issues include: anti-male bias within social services, shelters, charities, and throughout the criminal justice system. Also, juvenile homes and imprisonment as *causes* of male criminality (teaching, instilling, and promoting violent, antisocial, and criminal attitudes in the approximately *two million* men currently incarcerated within the U.S.).[458] Also, the vast majority of those falsely arrested, imprisoned, and executed are male.

There are also numerous but vague issues regarding women's evident freedom to roam at will throughout the realms and roles of both masculinity and femininity while men remain relatively constrained. For example, "They were textbook tomboys. Now Pink, Avril Lavigne and Alicia Keys talk about their flip side." Pop star Alecia Moore, better known as Pink, says it best:

> I enjoy being a girl. . . . I'm a woman and I like to be cute. I love to wear dresses. But I'm still a tomboy. I like to go dirt-bike riding. . . . I grew up climbing trees with my brother. It's who I am. I'm both a tomboy and a woman. . . . On my wedding day my friends and family were shocked I was in a pretty white dress. I loved it! I loved feeling like a princess. It's so fun to feel sexy and it's so fun being a girl.[459]

A man can't imagine roaming from one gender realm into the other with comparable ease and freedom. Any little girl can don a baseball cap, T-shirt, jeans, and sneakers—the exact same outfit the boys are wearing—and join their opposite sex out on the playing field. By contrast, a little boy who dons a dress and joins his opposite sex to play with dolls risks a trip to the nearest psychiatrist. No male can proudly declare himself a "janegirl" and do so without diminishment to his masculine identity the way any female can proudly declare herself a tomboy at no cost to her feminine identity.

"In almost every realm of life, from clothing to jobs, it's considered perfectly fine for girls and women to do male things," comments Jean Twenge, a psychology professor at San Diego State University, "but it's not considered fine for males to do female things."[460]

According to fact-based reality, in *countless* ways, women have the power and men are the victims.

Perhaps the single most important point to be made here is this: whatever Woman's claim to owning victimhood and powerlessness may be, whatever grip upon the human psyche it may have, *it is based on something other than logic*. It is based on something primal and instinctual and erotic and mythopoetic and chivalrous and sentimental and emotional and *irrational*. And this is why logic proves so ineffectual against it. The logical case that turns feminism upside down has *long* been available to thinking men. In his book *The Fraud of Feminism* (1913), E. Balfort Bax made the case a century ago and expressed the exasperation masculists have been expressing ever since:

> It is rarely that anyone takes the trouble to refute the legend in general, or any specific case adduced as an illustration of it. When, however, the bluff is exposed, when the real facts of the case are laid bare to public notice, and woman is shown, not only as not oppressed but as privileged, up to the top of her bent, then the apostles of feminism, male and female, being unable to make even a plausible case out in reply, with one consent resort to the boycott, and by ignoring what they cannot answer, seek to stop the spread of the unpleasant truth so dangerous to their cause.[461]

To be sure, Woman has a long list of complaints. But . . . so what? Man, should he issue them, has a long list of complaints as well.

By what "reasoning" then is the MP/FV gender belief system maintained? It would seem that the traditional, foundational, irrational, unexamined network of assumptions that float so hazily in the mind add up something like this:

Men enjoy a patriarchal paradise of male power and privilege; therefore, when it comes to considerations of victimization, men become invisible. Since men occupy "paradise," any and all female suffering is received as *proof* that women suffer more—actual *comparisons*, unnecessary. Should the "privileged" sex have the temerity to complain, the assumption that men have *the* power and are therefore autonomous beings *solely* responsible for their self-inflicted miseries, negates empathy toward men. Besides, it is unseemly for big, strong, "tough as nails" men to complain in any case.

On the other hand, women, being "powerless," rate *only* empathy/*no* accountability for their miseries because *their* miseries are "forced" upon them by "patriarchy." Moreover, Woman's complaints prove that Man's not doing his job. If Man was *really* doing his job, he would so perfectly protect and provide for her—solve her problems, carry her burdens—that Woman should be left with *no* complaints. Besides, women, being essentially "angels," should never be made to suffer anything in any case.

Later in the book I'll address the value of sentimentality, the emotional richness sentiment adds to human life. But for now I wish only to suggest that the above "reasoning" may be sentimentally resonant and emotionally compelling, but *logically*, it is *bankrupt*.

The light side of Man's indulgence of Woman's cosmic complaint is a sincere love of Woman and a sincere desire to protect and please her and gain her admiration. The shadow side of Man's indulgence is a deep fear of Woman and a desire to enable Woman's flight from accountability that he may keep the gift of accountability all to himself. In this way Man maintains relative ownership of responsibility and adulthood, and Woman remains safely ensconced within an angelic group of humanity known collectively as *innocent* "women&children." Thus the myths of Male Power and Female Victimization dominate the belief system century after *century*.

But in *this* century, the game has truly changed. Having added a great deal of male power to her arsenal, her war against Man is wreaking havoc and both sexes are racking up war wounds. Do damage to Man and Woman does damage to her partner for love, for life, and for childrearing. All of society suffers the consequences. Do damage to masculinity and Woman does damage to her sons—so much so that the parents of an astonishing one-in-five boys has been worried enough about their sons to seek professional help for them![462]

The cost of maintaining the feminist fable has become *too high*. We desperately need the rational to overcome the primitive instinctual so we can finally see *both* sides of gender reality.

We are absolutely *sure* that the battle between Woman and Man is a battle between David and Goliath with Woman cast as little David, the underdog, hopelessly outmatched and in need of extra help, extra empathy, extra empowerment. But this parable has something to teach us. Let us not forget that in the end David defeated Goliath because David, sling in hand, ultimately possessed *the superior weaponry*.

"Arrows" #4: The Donner Party

Because logic by itself has never proven effective against the MP/FV paradigm, I have added these "arrows" essays as a means of adding a purely emotional component.

Many years ago I watched a documentary on the Donner Party, an ill-fated group of pioneers headed across country to settle in the old west. The historian David McCullough narrates with his usual mesmerizing ease. But when the camera focused upon him, there was a recurring theme to his commentary.[463] It was an "arrow" that pierced me over and over again.

Of the 81 members comprising the Donner Party—15 women, 25 men and 41 children—22 of the men perished while all but 5 of the women endured. In relaying these facts—and in what I regarded to be a rather smug, self-satisfied manner—McCullough invited the viewer to join with him in admiring the greater apparent strength and resilience of the women who managed to survive as compared with the apparently weak and relatively frail men who, under identical conditions, mostly all died off. If those are the facts of the matter, then why didn't I take my medicine like a man? Because, contained within the documentary itself, was evidence enough to suggest that the men had essentially sacrificed themselves so that the women and children could live. For additional background, among other sources, I read George R. Stewart's classic, *Ordeal By Hunger*.[464]

The ordeal began in May of 1846 with the endless trek across the Great Plains. The men walked plying the whips that kept the oxen moving. "Driving oxen was man's work. The women sat in the front seats of the wagons knitting."[465] What Stewart's book makes clear is that *all* the work, all the physically arduous *work*, was man's work.

With no road to travel on, the men had to build their own. "It was exhausting . . . the unceasing labor rapidly wore them down both in body and in temper."[466] Both the book and the documentary describe endless campaigns through intractable stretches of wilderness: "they struggled as if still in the nightmare, to open about six miles of road, cutting timber and hacking through brush, digging down side-hill, rolling out boulders, and leveling for creek-crossings."[467] And from the documentary: "Time and again the hostile terrain brought them to a standstill while the men cursed and toiled and hacked a road through the dense undergrowth." They hacked their way through dense thickets, pulled wagons sunk up to their axles in mud, hauled heavily laden wagons up embankments with block and tackle and cut down trees with axes; this they did hour after hour, day after day, week after week for *months* on end.

Men cut timber to mend the wagons and replace broken axles. On one such occasion, "a chisel slipped, and the blood spurted from a long gash across the back of 62-year-old George Donner's hand. It was bound up, and he made light of it; there were other things, he said, more to be worried about than a cut hand."[468] We don't know the half of men's sufferings because men make "light" of them and keep their vulnerability hidden. All bravado notwithstanding, before the advent of antibiotics, cuts of this kind frequently led to infections that resulted in amputation and/or death.

By October, six of the Donner Party had died. Not surprisingly, all but one was male. The 81 remaining travelers made it as far as the foothills of the Sierra Nevada Mountains when they were trapped by record snowfall. With hands numbed by the cold, men labored for hours to cut firewood, suffering frostbite, while women and children stayed warm burning the firewood inside their makeshift camp.

It was *men* who undertook the nearly hopeless efforts to cross the snow-covered mountains on foot in order to seek and bring back help. Many died in the effort while others, thwarted by impossible conditions, hobbled back to camp nine-tenths dead. For the rare man who made it all the way to California and safety, "Honor, no less than love, demanded his return, for no man could have held up his head in the West of those days who had left his wife and child and was not ready to risk his life to bring them out."[469] And this they did. Men are, and have always been, honor *bound*. The bindings of honor are, in their own way, as real as bindings of rope. In not complaining but making light of his pain and suffering, a man is effectively bound and gagged.

Because his family was starving, William Eddy was given a little coffee. "This he prepared in a hot spring and gave to Eleanor and the children, stubbornly refusing to keep any of the scanty supply for himself. It was sufficient joy to see the children revive."[470] Later: "Eddy had not eaten for forty-eight hours. Eleanor was almost as badly off, and even the babies had had nothing but the sugar and some coffee since leaving the sink."[471] If they shared food equally, then why was his wife Eleanor *almost* as badly off?

In life and death situations, the children come first. Whatever's left goes to the women, and *if* there's anything left after that, it goes to the men. Just as the men of the Titanic sacrificed themselves so that most of the women and children could survive, evidence suggests that the same basic principle held sway within the equally mortal dangers faced by the Donner Party.

Nevertheless, reverence for the women reverberates throughout the documentary. "Somehow, Margaret Reid had managed to keep all her children alive. So had Peggy Breen and Tamsen Donner." Somehow? I don't believe in magic. Pure female superiority alone could not keep children from starving. Consumption of calories must have had something to do with it. And why no such reverence toward the men who had miraculously kept the women and children alive? How about the two men who had earlier rode on ahead, crossed the mountains and returned with other men and seven mules bearing food?

Only when conditions became utterly desperate did women join with men in attempting to cross the mountains on foot. The "Forlorn Hope," as they called themselves, consisted of nine men, one boy of 12 and five women. In the aftermath, "Only 2 of the 10 men had made it through. All five women had survived." In this way the viewer is led over and over again to conclude that the women were stronger than the men. But didn't this documentary just get through making it clear that the women survived by eating the men who died? A little later we're told that: "Two thirds of the women and children made it through. Two thirds of the men perished."

The documentary is relentless on the matter, and, without further explanation, what else can the viewer conclude but that the women survived out of superior female strength while the men died owing to inferior male weakness? I guess we are to believe that even children are stronger than men.

But what *really* happened?

A more recent (2003) Discovery Channel documentary[472] shed light on the matter by exposing two men to the same conditions that the Donner Party had endured. To glean more detailed information, the men had scientific instruments attached to them, and their exertion, heat loss, and calories burned were measured. "And from that [data] we can estimate how long they would have until they starved."[473]

The Discovery Channel documentary makes *no mention* of the ratio of dying men/surviving women with which McCullough seems obsessed. How could it? Having established the connection between exposure/exertion/calorie burn and starvation, mention of the much higher male mortality rate would have made the male sacrifice much too obvious to pass the gates of political correctness.

If the Donner men even allowed themselves an *equal* portion of food throughout the ordeal (rather than chivalrously refusing even that much), then with their larger size and muscle mass, the men would, of course, tend to starve faster than the women. Additionally, men's bodies burned precious extra calories to stave off the freezing cold they were more often subjected to. And men exhausted their fuel burning countless thousands of calories in grueling unceasing labor.

There is no mystery why more men than women died of injury, exposure, and starvation. Even in dying, the men's bodies provided sustenance the women and children could feed upon. Despite McCullough's insinuations, the men did not die of male inadequacy. They died of heroism. The women did not survive out of female superiority. They survived out of chivalry.

In arguing that It All Balances Out, there are more than just facts to consider. There is also the *emotional* component. Whatever monopoly feminists may presume to have on feelings of moral outrage, I can assure you that aware men can match those feelings note for note.

As I watched, I felt like reaching right through the TV screen and choking that smug feminist male to death. With what that historian knew of the whole story, how *dare* he cast women in the light of strong heroic survivors and men in the light of inadequate, dying weaklings?

But my rage extends beyond the neutered academics who champion the FEMale chauvINIST party line. I admit to being angry with the feminists themselves. Their self-righteous rhetoric is omnipresent in our world and is, after all, the *source* of the misandry that surrounds us. It is feminist ideology that has created a cultural environment where the knee-jerk impulse to flatter the female and shame the male is expressed *automatically*. I very much doubt that McCullough and company harbored any anti-male agenda. Nevertheless, whatever their intentions may have been, media injustice like this is *torture* to endure, and it is everywhere!

I can't begin to convey the wounding of such staggering injustice toward my kind. It disgusts me. It is *evil*. Even when men are taking on the very worst of it, even when they are shielding women to the point of sacrificing their very *lives*, it is *still* against some absolute *law* of political correctness to say anything positive about males, *ever*.

Disparaging male toughness, strength, and courage cuts men to their core. It was to maintain their masculine image that those men took on *extra* hazards and hardships. In return, men ask only for fair acknowledgment, but we will *not* give it to them.

To add further insult to injury, there is the wound that comes of fighting an uphill battle against those (both female *and male*) who would suppress this very writing. It is all well and good for a man to writhe in agony over the cruelty of such injustice, but god forbid a woman should suffer the slight upset that may come from reading about it. To be an aware male is to suffer outrage upon outrage!

One of the reasons we so concern ourselves with women's vulnerable emotions is that women make no effort to hide those vulnerable emotions. Upsetting a woman results in an emotional outburst, tears and tirades that leave men puddles of shame. One of the reasons we concern ourselves so little with men's vulnerable emotions is that we don't fully embrace the truth that men *have* such emotions. And that's largely because men make *every* effort to hide those emotions. Part of the point of these "Arrows" interludes is simply to reveal my own male vulnerability. I cannot ask men to show their vulnerability if I'm not willing to risk the same ridicule.

I am a logical man. I do not vent just to be self-indulgent. Everything is written to make a point. And the point, ultimately, is always the same: It All Balances Out. Men are loath to express the kinds of feelings I'm expressing. While emotional reveal of this kind is everywhere expressed within the feminist literature, the male equivalent is largely missing. The illusion is thus maintained that *only women* suffer this kind of sexist torment. That's wrong. But the only way to prove it wrong is for men to *express* their true hurt and pain.

The Battle of Rhetoric

In our world today the greatest enemy men face is the belief that men have *the* power and women are *the* victims. This MP/FV paradigm is not only false, it is **poisonous**. Feminism is Man's enemy to the exact degree that it teaches, enforces, and exploits the MP/FV belief system.

Not only does a belief in MP/FV lead inexorably to the Man-Bad/WomanGood (MB/WG) paradigm, additionally, it is the MP/FV paradigm that allows feminists (Woman's self-appointed spokespersons) to come to the bargaining table saying in effect: "We women have *nothing*, you men have *everything*; just *give* us half of what you've got because that would only be fair." In his gender-political ignorance, his chivalry, and his blindness to the feminine shadow, Man sees no flaw in Woman's demand; so his honor and his integrity compel him to pour from his glass half "full" into Woman's glass half "empty" because that is only "fair."

Gender politics is essentially a battle of rhetoric and Man is losing this battle even to the point of abject absurdity.

Clearly, the assumption that men have *the* power leads to the assumption that justice is served by taking power away from men and giving it to women. If women are *the* victims, "fairness" dictates that women must be compensated with extra empathy plus special female-only attentions, efforts, advantages, and protections (feminism, affirmative action, quotas, Title IX, The Violence Against Women Act, women-only shelters, Offices of Women's Health (federal and state), President Obama's new White House Council on Women and Girls, over a thousand female-centric organizations of all kinds, plus *massive* federal funding to support women—emotionally, parentally, financially, educationally, domestically—and to advance women—in business, science, academia, government, military—and so on). Moreover, if women are *the* victims then men are *the* victimizers and should be punished accordingly. The costs to men (male-only conscription and battlefields, restraining orders, "beatdead dads," mass imprisonment, "sexual harassment" lawsuits, vulnerability to false accusations, permanent stigmatization) are, again, plain to see.

In short, the MP/FV paradigm is an absolute ***disaster*** for men and, ultimately, *all* of Man's gender-political woes and rapid decline can be traced to its ubiquitous and subversive influence.

And yet, ironically, the farther men sink, the more they cling to the MP/FV paradigm as if it were a life raft. In the preface to the 25th anniversary edition of *The Manipulated Man*, author Esther Vilar explains it best. In recounting the costs she has incurred for daring question the MP/FV paradigm, she acknowledges the expected feminist hostility—"violent threats have not ceased to this date."

> However, I had also underestimated men's fear of re-evaluating their position. Yet . . . the more that increasing unemployment forces them to adopt obsequious behaviour towards customers and superiors - then the more they have to be afraid of a recognition of their predicament. And the more essential it becomes to maintain their illusion that it is not they who are the slaves but those on whose behalf they subject themselves to such an existence.
>
> As absurd as it may sound, today's men need feminism much more than their wives do. Feminists are the last ones who still describe men the way they like to see themselves: as egocentric, power-obsessed, ruthless and without inhibitions when it comes to satisfying their instincts. Therefore the most aggressive Women's Libbers find themselves in the strange predicament of doing more to maintain the status quo than anyone else. Without arrogant accusations, the macho man would no longer exist, except perhaps in the movies.[474]

Since emotional reality is what you make of it, men cling to the increasingly unsupportable notions of male power and privilege in an effort to cling to the fine feelings that accompany those illusions. But, for men, clinging to the MP/FV paradigm to keep from drowning is like clinging to an *anchor* to keep from drowning.

A specific example: In 1985 Lenore Weitzman, Ph.D., published a book claiming that in the aftermath of divorce women and children suffer an average 73 percent drop in their standard of living while men enjoy an average *increase* in their standard of living by 42 percent.[475] Largely in response, Sanford Braver (with Diane O'Connell) wrote *Divorced Dads: Shattering the Myths.*

"If ever anyone needed any evidence to fuel their outrage against divorced fathers," says Braver, "to contribute to their bad divorced dad beliefs . . . this was what they were waiting for."[476] With the voracious manner in which the media and academia and divorce judges devoured Weitzman's MP/FV stats, says Braver, "It would probably be fair to say that Weitzman's findings are the most widely known and influential social science results of the last twenty years."[477] But how did Weitzman find a 73 percent drop where other researchers, including Braver, had found a 27 percent drop? Evidently, she did the number crunching that revealed divorced women *retaining* 73 percent of their former standard of living and mistook it for a *73 percent decrease* in standard of living.

Seven years after publication, Weitzman finally admitted her original figures were wrong. "Weitzman apparently accepted the erroneous finding at face value because it fit with the woman-as-victim stereotype she preferred to believe," asserts Braver. "And it caught the popular imagination for the same reasons. It 'proved' what we wanted to believe: Divorced moms suffer, while bad divorced dads profit."[478] The findings were embraced and disseminated sans skepticism because, like other Ms-information, these figures appeared to affirm deeply internalized MP/FV and MB/WG paradigms.

Angered by the gross injustice contained within Weitzman's grossly inaccurate stats, Braver took a deeper look at the situation—this time unconstrained by chivalry—and discovered mitigating factors he'd previously ignored. For example, there are a number of tax breaks accorded divorced mothers owing to their more common status as homeowners and heads of households with dependents as compared with divorced fathers more often taxed as renters and singles without dependents. Braver also added into the equation extra expenses many noncustodial fathers paid above and beyond childpayments (medical/dental insurance, gifts, food, clothing, etc.). In addition, many divorced fathers bore the extra cost of starting from scratch, having to purchase everything from linen to silverware, curtains to furniture.

Taking these and other factors under consideration, Braver concludes that, at the time of Weitzman's study, divorced mothers and fathers actually experience *the same* short-term 3 to 5 percent drop in economic standard of living. But, over the long-term, women tend to improve their economic situation through increased dedication to schooling/career, then improve their situation further by marrying a new breadwinner (while continuing to receive childpayments from her old breadwinner). Meanwhile, divorced fathers tend to marry into new financial *obligations*.[479] But these truths, not so widely embraced, have had little effect upon the MP/FV/MB/WG fallout that came in the wake of Weitzman's erroneous findings.

According to the best available fact-based *reality*, men fare *worse* in the aftermath of divorce, both economically *and* emotionally. Men are far more likely to forgive and go on loving and pining after their former spouse. Divorced husbands are far more likely to suffer parental alienation plus greater levels of depression and social isolation, more often seek psychiatric help, more often lose their jobs, and commit suicide.[480] Given these truths, it's not surprising that men initiate only a fraction of all divorce actions. According to MP/FV, however, Bad men, having *the* power, enjoying the "fruits" of divorce, abandon their families; while, Good women, *the* victims, suffering divorce, struggle vainly to establish and maintain committed relationships. The "solution"? Legislate extra punishments that would dissuade feckless, over privileged men from abandoning their families.

Let Bruce Walker, executive coordinator at the District Attorney's Council in Oklahoma City, paint a picture of what the MP/FV/MB/WG fallout actually looks like:

> Deadbeat dads are the special targets of politicians hungry for the perfect scapegoat. Child-support enforcement must be tougher and tougher until all of these deadbeat dads are made to feel the lash, and all will be well. I have put hundreds of these deadbeat dads in jail, and I have collected child support from tens of thousands of them. I was the primary or only trial attorney in three child-support enforcement offices for eight years, and then I ran the Oklahoma child-support enforcement program for three years. . . . Many deadbeat dads are homeless, and an even greater percentage are poor. Because the calculation of a woman's income excludes many of the social welfare benefits she receives, the statistical picture of women in poverty is highly misleading. Not only are many deadbeat dads destitute, it is often their failures as providers which led their ex-wives to divorce them. I prosecuted one deadbeat dad who had been hospitalized for malnutrition and another who lived in the bed of a pick-up truck. Many times I prosecuted impoverished men on behalf of ex-wives who had remarried successful men and were living in comfortable conditions.[481]

Beat-dead dads (men) are scapegoated, targeted, alienated, hounded, impoverished and imprisoned all under the pernicious falsehood that men have *the* power/women are *the* victims.

MP/FV-inspired divorce "reforms" include: alimony and child-payments set higher, often higher than men facing a "he-cession" can afford; increased aggression in hounding and/or imprisoning fathers for failure to pay what they are unable to pay; and "mandatory withholding of child support from all fathers' paychecks by the employer" (applicable in all 50 states).[482]

No longer do divorced fathers enjoy the solace of giving *directly* to their former families. Fathers pay the state and suffer the humiliation of being *presumed* "deadbeat" at the outset. All this, and mothers more often retain the children plus the family home and property, while men more often suffer paltry unenforced "visitation" rights, parental alienation, restraining orders, ex parte proceedings, false accusations, and going broke from legal fees attempting to overturn those false accusations.

Despite feminist indoctrination, by their *own* surveyed admission, "women actually reported feeling *more control* over the divorce settlement process than men . . . more 'empowered' than men. If any party feels he or she lacks empowerment, it is the fathers."[483] A subsequent survey found not one father who believed the system favored him in any way, but "*three times as many mothers thought it favored mothers as thought it favored fathers.* Indeed the newer reforms appear to have further tilted an already uneven playing field."[484] [Emphasis in the original] Even so, feminists "have unceasingly called for reforms that would, as law professor Kathleen Mahoney calls it, 'level the playing field for women.'"[485]

Even if Man's cup should be ¼ full while Woman's cup is ¾ full, feminists will demand that Man pour from his cup into hers to "level the playing field for women" (e.g., Emma Watson's "HeForShe" campaign). The MP/FV paradigm is Man's greatest enemy because belief in it leads to the widespread desire to take from and punish men. The degree to which Man embraces and reinforces belief in MP/FV is the degree to which Man foolishly draws unwarranted hostility in on himself. Man is thus manipulated into contributing to the anti-male prejudice that undermines him.

Fem-stats like Weitzman's seem to offer the world proof of MP/FV/MB/WG, yet the *phenomenon* of fem-stats actually indicate the opposite. The outraged male reaction that demands greater giving to women/taking from men is indicative of ManGood. The feminist glut of self-serving stats and the *seven years* it took this feminist author to admit her error, are indicative of WomanBad. Ignoring mitigating factors within the male experience is indicative of MaleVictimization through the withholding of empathy toward men. And the degree to which feminist findings are unquestioningly embraced, circulated, and acted upon is indicative of FemalePower.

Newly confronted with masculist research and the undeniable facts of MaleVictimization, feminism typically responds with: "Patriarchy" victimizes *both* sexes! Thus, men *remain **solely*** responsible for outcomes. But gender issues cannot be properly addressed so long as half the force of influence begetting those issues continues to be protected from accountability. More than this, in directing full societal blame and hostility at "Patriarchy," feminism seeks to "win" the Battle by destroying Patriarchy while Matrisensus keeps right on going. But, in the Battle of the Sexes, the only *win* position is a *draw*.

It's time to replace feminism with equalism.

Woman's demand to be given half of Man's power—while giving nothing in return—wreaks havoc because feminism's "equality" is *false*. An analogy may help us picture this more clearly.

Suppose Man and Woman each has a pound of rice. He has a pound of white rice; she has a pound of brown rice. Imagine they exist within some beige environment in which his white rice stands out clearly while her brown rice tends to blend into the background. Woman, working the situation, says: "You have *all* the rice; I have none. If you were a Real Man, you'd give me half your rice because that would be fair."

Now if Man—irrationally clinging to the MP/FV paradigm—gives Woman half his "rice," leaving himself with one-quarter and she with three-quarters, is he being honorable, or is he only having his masculine obligation for honor used against him?

In coming to understand that the traditional gender system was a deeply flawed yet essentially balanced system, we come to understand that women rising/men sinking leads not toward, but *away* from *true* gender equality. For this reason, *true* gender equality must be *negotiated*, not *manipulated*.

The MP/FV paradigm is a *disaster* for men. Rather than foolishly embracing it, men must repudiate it. It is false and, in a sense, it is killing us! By extension, it is a disaster for women as well. Diminish men and you diminish fathers, husbands, brothers, and sons. Daughters, wives, sisters, and mothers suffer accordingly.

Additionally, Woman will not rate authentic respect until she is prepared to come to the bargaining table speaking honest truth. "If," concurs Esther Vilar, "someone should want to change the destiny of our sex—a wish I had then as I have today—then that someone should attempt to do so with more honesty."[486] Imagine Woman coming to the bargaining table in *all* honesty.

Woman says to Man: You have power, *I* have power; I experience victimization, *you* experience victimization—let's *negotiate*. At that point Woman shows up as a high-integrity *adult* to be respected and bargained with. When it comes to loving men and respecting women—out to the truest and fullest extent—the MP/FV paradigm is that which stands in the way and It All Balances Out is that which clears the path.

So long as women are encouraged to view themselves as *the* victim sex and view men as the sex with *the* power, a battle (now escalated to a war?) between the sexes is inevitable. The "oppressed" sex will rail against their "oppressors" and their "oppressors" will, as always, run and duck for cover. The future "ceasefire" in the Battle of the Sexes in favor of a cooperative era of Peace, Love, and Understanding between the sexes is the reward; and it is attainable, but there is a deep psychic hurdle to jump.

Delving into the realms at the other end of the balance beam—realms from which both sexes tend to recoil—that is the hurdle to jump if we are to reach the perception of balance needed to bring about that ceasefire. We must dare recognize female power/accountability no matter how un-chivalrous it may *feel*. We must find the courage to recognize male victimization/vulnerability no matter how disconcerting it may *feel*.

However much it may disturb our collective image of the Marlboro Man, we must resist the impulse to dismiss male complaint (but *only male* complaint) as "whining." The three actors who played the part of the Marlboro Man—Wayne McLaren, David McLean, and Dick Hammer—*all* died of lung cancer![487] Like it or not, male vulnerability is *real*.

Despite their validity, men's issues remain virtually unknown. It is said that women are powerless, but what greater power can there be than control over what is thought, what is said, and what is believed?

The vast majority of us, female *or male*, are incredulous that men could possibly have issues as women do. So it's widely but falsely assumed that masculism must have something to do with "maintaining male supremacy." That damning assumption keeps masculism from gaining credibility, which keeps men's issues unknown. Nevertheless, if feminism at its best is about women seeking a fair shake in this world, then masculism at its best is nothing more sinister than men seeking the exact same thing for themselves.

Deeper Into the Duality Principle

Remember the two shoe store scenarios, the first occurring within our feminist reality and the second occurring within an imaginary masculist reality? While browsing a shoe store, I experienced the first scenario practically verbatim when a feminist friend went off on that very same rant.

For many years I was socially dependent upon a group of feminist women. I shared holidays, meals, and birthdays with them. I loved and needed them yet I often felt "beat up" by their rhetoric. Being male, I felt their judgment of men reflecting on *me*, as if I was somehow personally responsible. I rarely stood my ground though, because they were gender-political *experts*. They obsessed over feminist matters among themselves, studied feminism in school, and had an entire library-full of feminist rhetoric to quote from.

My shoe-store feminist friend wielded her vast knowledge of MalePower and FemaleVictimization like Ginsu knives. By pointing out the female victimization in all things, she effectively drew all empathy away from men. There was nothing wrong with *her;* she was a wonderful person. But there was something very wrong with the one-sided ideology she'd internalized. It led her to believe she was being righteous when she was being self-righteous.

I had no idea what to say when confronted with feminist anger and accusation. How was I to respond to the expectation that I should feel guilt-ridden and apologetic for being male and, to atone, I really ought to be out there championing the feminist cause? Ignorance of my own sexual-political perspectives left me *defenseless*.

I now know the facts of male victimization. That doesn't mean I've internalized "victim," it means I have knowledge, and knowledge is power. I now possess sexual-political weaponry with which to *stop* playing the victim. I still honor feminist validity, but I have ceased to be a doormat for feminism. I've armed myself to become a fairness- and peace-seeking warrior in The Battle of the Sexes.

So, in answer to the question "If women experience themselves as victims and men do not, doesn't that speak for itself?"—I say, yes and no. Yes, it speaks volumes about how men and women perceive the world. And no, it says nothing about which sex is *the* victim.

That Woman perceives herself *the* victim, and Man does not, tells us only that the politicized female perspective saturates our world while its mirror-opposite suffers invisibility. Yes, women more readily perceive themselves as victims, but it could not be otherwise. Victim perception is all but culturally *forced* upon women.

Note that without raised awareness, the shoe-store complaints of both the man *and* the woman would probably *never occur to them*. Friedan's *The Feminine Mystique* (1963) was revolutionary because it taught women (and men) a *new* way of looking at the world. The feminist perspective isn't something women arrive at automatically (fifty years ago, it barely existed). It is a *politicized* perspective—a *learned* perspective resulting from feminist "consciousness-raising."

While issuing her complaints, my shoe-store feminist friend made reference to an article she had read on the subject. Her complaints, you see, were not really her own. They originated in an article she had read in a women's magazine, *then* she experienced them at the shoe store (ideology leading perception).

According to Myrna Blyth, author of *Spin Sisters: How the Women of the Media Sell Unhappiness and Liberalism to the Women of America*, there is a cabal of female media elite who make it their business to keep women perceiving themselves as victims.

> I know as an editor it became the style to tell women over and over they had lots of reasons to worry and complain. So much so that talking about personal responsibility or making tough choices and living with them seemed downright harsh. Av Westin, the television executive who created the news magazine *20/20*, which became the template for so many of the magazine shows that followed, told me, "We started every story with a victim. That's what we said. 'We need a victim. Find me the victim.'" In magazines, we also got into the destructive, demeaning habit of looking at the world of women victim-first. Of course, this made us—the editors, producers, and news magazine anchors, Spin Sisters all—seem *so* understanding and caring about women. As if the only thing women deserved was sympathy.[488]

The Duality Principle guarantees that, like any gift, the gift of sympathy comes at a cost. Feminists seem to think that if only women's issues would receive stratospheric levels of sympathy, all of women's complaints would be addressed and neutralized. I believe the opposite is true. Women are *not* children, but I would go so far as to say that protecting them and sympathizing with them as if they *were* is a root *cause* of feminist issues. At excessive levels sympathy becomes toxic.

New York Times columnist Anna Quindlen is a Pulitzer Prize-winning "Spin Sister." According to Cathy Young, the title of Quindlen's 1990 column:

> "The Glass Half Empty," sums up the drift of many reports on women's lot. Women's magazines run stories on "The Schoolgirl Scandal," "Unequal Justice," and "Why Doctors Mistreat Women." Much of the *New Yorker's* special "women's issue" in 1996 was a catalog of wom-

en's wrongs, with artwork featuring such nuggets as, "The average salary of a black female college graduate is less than that of a white male high school dropout" (in fact, it's 80 percent higher). A 1994 *U.S. News and World Report* cover story, "The War Against Women," counts the ways in which women everywhere are victims of everything.[489]

Viewing the glass as half full or half empty is a choice we *all* make on a moment-to-moment basis. Teaching women to view the glass as half empty only teaches women what Camille Paglia has dubbed "women's victim-centered view of the universe." By seeking and obtaining ever more protection for women and ever more sympathy toward women, feminism further infantilizes women—in the eyes of society, and in the eyes of women themselves.

Ace men's work facilitator Bill Flynn teaches his techniques during weekend workshops. His students, myself included, practice facilitating processes that help men grow, enlighten, and empower themselves with personal accountability. "When do you give a man sympathy?" he asks rhetorically. "*Never*," he answers. "Sympathy is dreadfully disempowering." Sympathy reinforces our inner "victim."

The "women are victims" rhetoric reaches its zenith in the Women's Studies classroom. Given the severe negativity they encounter therein, it's not surprising that "students are apt to become depressed."

> At the end of one recent semester, Women's Studies faculty on the Women's Studies e-mail list engaged in a long discussion of what to do about students' sagging morale. Had they overdone their emphasis on the atrocities perpetrated against women? Had students concluded that the situation was hopeless? Had they just given up? Sustaining anger, it turns out, is exhausting.[490]

Victimhood, depression, blaming, negativity—these are hardly the cornerstones of personal success. Super-sympathizing inculcates a victim-dictum that is *self-fulfilling*.

Feminism instills in women the very *antithesis* of what any expert on personal success recommends. Jack (*The Success Principles*) Canfield: "If you want to be successful, you have to take 100% responsibility for everything that you experience in your life."[491] But how can a feminist take 100% responsibility for everything she experiences in her life when she believes that "patriarchy" is to blame for *everything* bad? "In fact, most of us have been conditioned to blame something outside of ourselves for the parts of our life we don't like," says Canfield. "We never want to look at where the real problem is—ourselves."[492] As is true of each of us as individuals, so it is that each sex is its own worst enemy!

Canfield's chapter headings say it all: "You have to give up blaming": "You have to give up complaining." Accountability is like medicine—it tastes bad, but it's good for us. The positive side of the zero-empathy-toward-men rule (yes, there's a positive side to *everything*) is that it effectively forces men to be accountable. Where there is no empathy, there can be no excuses.

Daphne Patai: "The most important goal of any Women's Studies course, as is widely taken for granted, is to convert students to feminism."[493] In place of tens of thousands of Women's Studies classrooms inculcating feminist rage, victimhood, and blame/hostility toward men, our world would be better served by tens of thousands of Equalist classrooms inculcating a "click" experience whereby young women and men come to see a world wherein it all balances out—a world Woman and Man fashioned in equal partnership.

"This is the best of times for American women," asserts Myrna Blyth. But large numbers of American women perceive themselves as victims. Why? Because, while women are doing better than men in virtually every measure of wellbeing and "Every statistic proves it. Yet you are being sold, day after day and month after month in soppy TV movies and scary TV news-magazines and on the slick pages of colorful magazines, the most negative interpretation of your lives."[494]

Feminism's victim-dictum is ideology (an article from a women's magazine) leading perception (the observation that women's shoes do indeed cost more) leading emotional reality (women are *the* victims). It is carefully selected bits of reality—the negative bits of the female experience and the positive bits of the male experience—presented as if they constituted gender reality in its entirety.

The man and woman in the *second* shoe-store scenario, however, live in an imaginary world where masculism is the dominant ideology and feminism barely exists. So, in the second scenario, when the woman goes to the store, she takes no ideological baggage with her. She loves shoes—she loves shoes that match her dress—she loves shopping—where's the problem? But, when *he* goes to the store, he brings what masculism has taught him. From his male perspective *politicized*, women have *the* power and men are *the* victims.

A Message to Masculists

Not all, but more than a few Men's Rights Activists frame their reality in the manner suggested by the second shoe-store scenario. They have deeply internalized the politicized male perspective. They've had their "click" experience.

They believe that Woman is the Giantess who ultimately pulls the strings and Man is but her sexual puppet. Woman controls the whole show in how she socializes humanity during infancy and childhood. Man earns the money; Woman spends it. Woman holds the majority vote; Man fights and dies on battlefields defending her right to vote. Man fights Woman's wars and picks up her garbage and works himself into an early grave keeping her in the safety and luxury she demands.

Men suffer comparison with women in virtually every measure of wellbeing. So, understandably, masculists conclude that it does *not* all balance out—women have *the* power and men are *the* victims. But what if it does balance out **except** for one thing, we don't believe it? What if the dreadful stats masculists see result from actions society has taken to advantage women in response to believing instead that men have *the* power and women are *the* victims? What if the one imbalance in the gender system is the imbalanced gender *belief* system? Declaring the gender system balanced—and believing it—may be *all* that's necessary in order to bring about balance because, in balancing the gender belief system, we balance out the one *overarching* imbalance from which other imbalances derive (more on this later).

Otherwise, who can say with certainty which sex has the greater inner experience of powerlessness and victimization? A masculist always knows when *he* is the target of a cultural "arrow," but how can a masculist be sure that he always knows when *she* is the target of a cultural arrow? How can a masculist be sure that his FP/MV conclusion isn't based on his own male bias?

These same questions apply to women in general and feminists in particular. How do you *know* that the "slings and arrows" pierce you more deeply and painfully? How do you know but in seeing the vastly greater amount of female complaint, you are only seeing the vastly greater latitude women are granted to complain? What if the cultural focus on female victimization is only indicative of a greater cultural caring, concern, and compassion toward women?

To masculists I say: we can see the damage feminism's victim-dictum has done womankind, how internalizing "victim" as an identity becomes self-fulfilling. Why would we want that for ourselves?

Besides, what good can come of two intractable ideologies doing battle? Is it not a Herculean enough task to drag the profoundly entrenched MP/FV belief system into the middle without trying to drag it all the way to the opposite extreme? Will we oust Woman from victimhood's center seat just so Man can sit there instead?

It All Balances Out has blunt power as a sound bite and rallying cry. It is a stand the major media—the only media that informs our *official* belief system—just *might* be willing to hear. It is a stand that could potentially unify masculism and keep masculism on a healthy path while it performs its primary task of balancing the belief system and is then phased out in favor of equalism.

I urge my masculist brethren to let a perception of balance be victory enough. In fact, given the feminist ideological dictatorship, would it not be a miraculous and ecstatic victory for men? In stating that It All Balances Out, you'll be asked to defend that position. In arguing balance, the door opens for presenting the truths of FP/MV—the truths that go on the *other* end of the balance beam. At that point the masculist truths are brought out, and once they're out, they're out!

Under a Balanced gender belief system, the one-sidedness of female-ism will be exposed. Policies, laws, and courts of law that currently favor women under the assumption that women need extra compensations within "patriarchy" will be reevaluated. Everything masculists hope for can be brought about within an It All Balances Out belief system (*much* more on all this at the book's conclusion).

The Global Victim

It is overwhelming enough to try and grasp gender reality here in our own culture without presuming to understand gender reality within foreign cultures that are alien to us. Convincing the reader that it all balances out in our western industrial culture would be victory enough for my purposes. But, for reasons I'll soon delve into, it's necessary to take a moment to argue balance globally.

In brief, my research keeps telling me that brutal cultures are brutal to both sexes. Cultures in which women are raped arbitrarily are cultures in which men are shot dead arbitrarily.

A case in point is provided in an editorial by Nicholas D. Kristof, published June 5, 2005 in the *New York Times* under the heading, "A Policy of Rape." Says Kristof, "More than two years after the genocide in Darfur began, the women of Kalma Camp—a teeming squatter's camp of 110,000 people driven from their burned villages—still face the risk of gang rape every single day as they go out looking for firewood." Now, of course, this is an abomination that demands attention. It is also an abomination that *receives* attention. My concern with this article comes from what's *missing*—at least up until the very end. "I'm still chilled by the matter-of-fact explanation I received as to why it is women who collect firewood, even though they're the ones who are raped," says Kristof. "'It's simple,' one woman here explained. 'When the men go out, they're killed. The women are only raped.'"

Well, that new information changes things a bit, doesn't it? So why then could this editorial not be titled "A Policy of *Murder*"? Why is all its emphasis on the rape of women and none of its emphasis on the murder of men? Why is this revelation thrown away as a tagline at the end of the article and offered only as "an indication of how utterly we are failing the people of Darfur" rather than as an indication of how utterly we are failing to direct equal compassion and attention toward atrocities inflicted upon men?

Says Kristof, "this policy of rape flourishes only because it is ignored." But it is *not* ignored, as the article itself makes clear. What's ignored is the "Policy of Murder," something to which the article doesn't even give a name. It's standard practice for books, editorials, articles, talk shows, news shows and newspapers to shout aloud how this or that female issue is being ignored. But if women's issues were being ignored, they wouldn't be the subject of all those books, editorials, articles, talk shows, news shows and newspapers in the first place. Meanwhile, you rarely hear about men's issues being ignored, exactly because *men's issues are in fact ignored*.

Media bias will tend to focus more on the rapes and other female miseries while focusing less on the executions, the worked-to-death laborers, the tortured prisoners, the nine-year-old boy soldiers trained to kill and be killed. We don't hear as much about male brutalization because we don't *care* as much about male brutalization. It is just one of innumerable examples of what men's activist Jerry Boggs[495] has dubbed "The Gender Compassion Gap."

Adam Jones, author/editor of *Gendercide and Genocide* (2004), has studied these issues in depth. Genocide may be defined as the attempt to exterminate a given population. Gendercide is the selective mass killing of one gender. As Jones makes clear, the gender of choice for extermination is nearly always the *male* gender. In part, males are selected because males are more easily assumed to pose a threat, but also because males may be slaughtered without over-burdening the slaughterers with guilt and trauma. Moreover, you can slaughter males and provoke only minimal world outrage. In fact, the media will focus mainly on hardships faced by the women deprived of men.

Jones takes a close look at such an instance of gendercide occurring in Rwanda in 1994. He cites The African Rights report *Death, Despair, and Defiance* describing the aftermath: "Within days, entire communities were without their men; tens of thousands of women were widowed."[496] Says Jones, "Many of these men and boys were killed in classic gendercidal massacres, such as the one in the parish of Mibilizi, Cyangugu prefecture, beginning on 20 April. *African Rights* describes hundreds of interahamwe militia arriving at the church, where they 'began the macabre 'favourite' game of the killers, selecting Tutsi men and boys for the slaughterhouse.'"[497]

Eyewitness Catherine Kanyundo describes what followed:

They took all the men and boys, everyone masculine from about the age of two. Any boy who could walk was taken. They put them on one side. They were particularly interested in men who looked like students, civil servants, in short any man who looked as if he had education or money. They left only very poor men, those who were already wounded and tiny babies. Not even the very old were spared. They were all killed with machetes, spears and swords.[498]

"One of the best indicators of the special vulnerability of men and boys is the frequency with which relatives and friends sought to disguise them in women's clothing," asserts Jones. "The *African Rights* report 'Death, Despair and Defiance' cites a number of examples of such procedures, which are reminiscent of similar practices followed in the Bosnian and Kosovan conflicts of the 1990s."[499] Clearly, if females were specially targeted, males would not be donning female clothing. Yet, as the media reaction to Rwandan atrocities makes plain, women will be presented as *the* victims almost no matter what the truth. Jones continues:

> The clear evidence of a gendercidal targeting of males casts into severe disrepute the many subsequent attempts to rewrite history and depict women as the principal targets of the genocide. Leading the way in this regard was the UN special rapporteur on Rwanda, Rene Degni-Segui, who stated in January 1996 that women "may even be regarded as the main victims of the massacres, with good reason, since they were raped and massacred and subjected to other brutalities."
>
> Here the "good reason" for passing an untenable comparative judgment is the fact that women suffered enormously; there is no serious attempt to evaluate the scale of their suffering compared to men. Christopher Taylor, in his important work *Sacrifice As Terror,* goes so far as to claim that "Tutsi women were killed during the 1994 genocide in numbers equal to, if not exceeding, those of men."
>
> Aloysia Inyumba, in her analysis "Women and Genocide in Rwanda," offers up a truly spectacular self-contradiction, in consecutive sentences no less: She claims that "The genocide in Rwanda is a far-reaching tragedy that has taken *a particularly hard toll on women.* They now comprise 70 percent of the population, since *the genocide chiefly exterminated the male population."* Such comments typify the general trend in discussions of "gender" and human rights, which tend to take women's disproportionate victimization as a guiding assumption, indeed as a virtual article of faith.[500] [Emphasis in the original]

Feminist rhetoric can afford to be so self-indulgent because it enjoys such protection and is subject to so little official challenge.

A full treatment of the Rwandan holocaust in all its complexity is beyond the scope of this book. Nevertheless, certain basic gender principles are revealed. The suffering of women stands alone. There is *never* a "serious attempt to evaluate the scale of their suffering by comparison with men." Rape, torture, and murder have visited womankind in Rwanda as in all other brutal environments. If, however, for the purposes of gender politics we must make the *comparison* then, by a *wide margin*, the total violence inflicted upon the person of Man nearly always exceeds the total violence inflicted upon the person of Woman.

In all things along the respect axis, women tend to suffer worse than men. But, in all things along the love axis, men tend to suffer worse than women. It is the relative loveless indifference toward men that renders them easier targets of violence and death. It is this same loveless indifference toward men that accounts for the shift in focus from male suffering to female suffering, which in turn explains why women's disproportionate victimization is "a virtual article of faith" in *all* contexts—so much so that bemused masculists joke of a headline blaring: "Aliens Destroy the Earth: Women Suffer Most."

The belief that men are *the source* of evil and women are but innocent victims who, by all rights, should never suffer *anything*, psychologically justifies the shift in focus away from male and toward female suffering. This is why the need for side-by-side comparisons *feels* unnecessary.

We will explore this ManBad/WomanGood assumption throughout the third section of this book. For now I will point out that the Rwandan civil war not only provides an example of men specially selected for slaughter, it also provides a prime example of what happens when patriarchal insulation between women and the dark side of the world and human nature is lifted.

Information regarding women's direct involvement derives largely from the *African Rights* report: "Rwanda—Not So Innocent: When Women Become Killers."

> The Organization—bravely, it must be said—countered the standard trend of portraying women as inherently or automatically the 'main' victims of the genocide. This stereotype, it claimed, had contributed to 'obscuring the role of women as aggressors.' . . . 'When it came to mass murder, there were a lot of women who needed no encouragement.' Indeed, one can speculate that *a greater proportion of women than men participated voluntarily in the killings*, since it was men, almost exclusively, who were forcibly conscripted into the 'work' of the roadblock killings, and who were exposed to suspicion or violent retribution if they did not take part.[501] [Emphasis in the original]

Jones describes the antics of Pauline Nyiramasuhuko, Rose Karushara, Odette Nyirabagenzi, Athanasie Mukabatana, and Sister Julienne Kizito, five of the "female architects of the genocide" who took part both in selecting Tutsi men to be killed (by the hundreds and the thousands) and in delivering death personally. Yet:

> These cases of female leaders represent only a small part of the story of women's participation in the genocide. At the grassroots, "very often, groups of women ululated their men into the 'action' that would result in the death of thousands of innocent men, women and children, many of them their own neighbours." Their role was dominant in the post-massacre looting and stripping of bodies, which often involved climbing over corpses (and those still alive and moaning in agony) piled thigh-high in the confined spaces in which many Tutsis met their end. Frequently these women assisted in administering the coup de grâce to those clinging to life.[502]

Women's direct, and perhaps most significantly, women's *indirect* involvement in the dark side of the world and human nature, is far more pervasive than generally recognized.

While the victimization of men is routinely downplayed, the victimization of women is as routinely overplayed. The issue of "white slavery," exposed here by Steve Moxon, author of *The Woman Racket*, provides an overwhelming example:

> It's not that there are no 'trafficked' women at all, but that the numbers are tiny. The World Cup in Germany was heralded as a magnet for 'trafficking' women, and huge resources were deployed to combat it. Just five 'trafficked' women were found. Even the Global Alliance Against Trafficking in Women, in a major report (GAATW, 1994) that trawled indirectly for all known 'victims' through their support organizations—which had a vested interest in inflating the picture—had to conclude that abduction in connection with 'trafficking' was actually very rare.[503]

Moxon argues that the vast majority of immigrant women who engage in prostitution do so by choice. Laura María Agustín concurs. A review of her recent book, *Sex at the Margins: Migration, Labour Markets and the Rescue Industry*, states that:

> Most migrant women, including those in the sex industry, have made a clear decision, says a new study, to leave home and take their chances abroad. They are not "passive victims" in need of "saving" or sending back by western campaigners. Rather, frequently, they are headstrong and ambitious women who migrate in order to escape "small-town prejudices, dead-end jobs, dangerous streets and suffocating families". Shocking as it might seem to the feminist social workers, caring police people and campaigning journalists who make up what Agustín refers to as the "rescue industry", she has discovered that some poor migrant women "like the idea of being found beautiful or exotic abroad, exciting desire in others."[504]

Needless to say, the "rescue industry" exists solely to rescue *women*.

Says Lisa Rende Taylor of the Asia Foundation: "It is important to get away from unhelpful stereotypes of passive trafficked victims." I happen to think that's pretty good advice regarding our perception of women in general. Taylor continues:

> Many northern Thai girls regard prostitution as a "bearable choice," according to Rende Taylor, because they feel obligated to repay their parents for past sacrifices and to improve the family's financial standing . . . In a setting devoid of any other well-paying job opportunities, the oldest profession represents the only way for a girl to make enough money to maintain or enhance her family's property and status in the village.[505]

In a setting devoid of any other well-paying job opportunities, her "*only*" way" to make a lot of money can only be better than her brother's *no* way. And, as compared with a worked-to-death laborer, at least she *has* a bearable choice.

"Most former prostitutes that Rende Taylor's team spoke to said that they had worked short hours and had had the freedom to choose or reject clients. The women generally didn't regret what they had done."[506] Nevertheless, the official feminist position insists that such testimony is drawn from "false consciousness." It is this sort of matronizing attitude toward those women who don't share their victim-dictum that has caused many strong women to reject feminism.

Steve Moxon reminds us: "To get at the true reality of the sex worker, you have to compare her with the male alternative."[507] Though gender *comparison* is the foundation of gender *fairness* and a matter of first principle, where gender issues are concerned, it is often the first principle neglected. In this case, however, there are so few male prostitutes that their numbers are negligible. So what *is* the comparison? Let's deal with first things first. Why are there so few male prostitutes?

The plain truth is men do not become prostitutes simply because few males and virtually no females show a willingness to pay and pay well for a male sexual partner. As a boy on his own living out on the streets, author Aaron Kipnis survived by selling his body to gay men for 10 to 20 dollars a "trick." "It wasn't until years later, when a friend's sister told me she made $500 a night hooking, that I realized my innocence was so cheaply sold." Why did the heterosexual Kipnis sell himself to men? "[S]ince few women seek male prostitutes, street boys, gay or straight, work the gay clientele."[508] Prostitution is primarily a female-only option because, sexually, male bodies have little market value.

Nevertheless, many sources contend that, for use in hard labor, males are vastly *more* trafficked than females. For example, Carey

Roberts quotes a recent United Nations report, Trafficking in Persons: Global Patterns: "it is men especially who might be expected to be trafficked for forced labor purposes." And yet it is the sex that is more loved that receives the greater empathy and protection.

> That became apparent in 2000 when the United Nations passed its Protocol to Prevent, Suppress, and Punish Trafficking in Persons, Especially Women and Children. What about men? That bias is also found in the legislation of many countries. According to the Trafficking in Persons report, "In many countries, the laws relevant to human trafficking are restricted in their application solely to women . . . In addition, many service providers limit their support and protection only to female and child victims.[509]

Doubtless males are more trafficked, in part, because trafficking the generally less protected male is often legal while trafficking the generally more protected female is always illegal. So, having little sexual value, what use *is* made of trafficked males? Steve Moxon:

> In China, India, Egypt and many other countries, boys are used by others as beggars; often deliberately mutilated so as to attract sympathy money. Bleach is injected into a joint which then become gangrenous, forcing amputation by hospital casualty staff. Alternatively, limbs are repeatedly broken, or twisted by the constant use of tourniquets. Other boys are forced by modern day Fagans to rob. In Africa, the age-old problem of slavery is a mass phenomenon mainly afflicting males. In India, there are estimated to be tens of millions of child slave labourers, the vast majority of whom are boys, some as young as six.[510]

This issue again demonstrates how Woman is declared *the* victim by drawing *no comparison* with her male counterparts. This deception, it would seem, is played out within the feminist analysis of cultures worldwide. Thus the Rescue Industry is female-*only*.

"The West is focused on the extreme cases of oppression against Muslim women," says Lorraine Ali, "but there's another world out there." Indeed, there is more in heaven and earth than is dreamed of in feminist philosophy. There is a whole other world of truth out there if only we could see past the feminist and chivalrous smoke and mirrors that bias our information and our perceptions. Says Ms. Ali:

> If I'd never known a Muslim woman, I'd probably pity any female born into Islam. In America we've come to see these women as timid creatures, covered from head to toe, who scurry rather than walk. They have no voices, no rights and no place outside the home. But . . . I've watched them argue politics with men at the dinner table in Baghdad, slap husbands on the back of the head for telling off-color jokes in Egypt and, at a recent Arab Women's Media Conference in Amman, fiercely debate their notions of democracy from under higabs and J.

Lo-inspired hairdos. The west's exposure to Muslim women is largely based on Islam's most extreme cases of oppression: Taliban-dominated Afghanistan, Wahhabi-ruled Saudi Arabia and postrevolutionary Iran. . . . In Egypt, female cops patrol the streets. In Jordan, women account for the majority of students in medical school. And in Syria, courtrooms are filled with female lawyers.[511]

If information questioning the victimization of women is kept out of the mass media, how then did the above make it into *Newsweek*? As will be made more clear when further quoted below, whatever else it may be, the above is still primarily an expression of *female complaint*. Women remain *the* victims even when women are being "victimized" by *false claims* of victimization! Lorraine Ali continues:

> Still, Muslim women are feeling like pawns in a political game: jihadists portray them as ignorant lambs who need to be protected from outside forces, while the United States considers them helpless victims of a backward society to be saved through military intervention. . . . Scholars such as Khaled Abou El Fadl, an expert on Islamic law and author of "The Great Theft: Wrestling Islam From the Extremists," says that this is an age-old problem. "Historically the West has used the women's issue as a spear against Islam," he says. "It was raised in the time of the Crusades, used consistently in colonialism and is being used now."[512]

Owing to its group-survival value, like other mammalian species, I believe that a "protect the females" imperative has been written directly into the human genetic code (see "Two Tribes," page 326). For this reason, the primal goal of every power and every faction and every political force is the same: Protect Women. The "age-old problem" is that the various powers, factions, and political forces can't agree on the best *way* to protect women and so they argue and do battle over it. The duality principle guarantees that the battle over the "perfect" way to protect women—the way to protect women at *no cost* to women—can only be an endless battle.

In the current political scene, women in general and Muslim women in particular may *feel* like pawns in this game, but they are *not* pawns; they are *participants*. It is Woman's own feminism—exploiting chivalry—that is calling the shots. "The United States considers them helpless victims"? No. *Female*-ism generates the rhetoric *demanding* that females be seen, responded to, and protected as "helpless victims." And in the U.S., feminism rules the belief system upon which the relevant U.S. policies are based. In this instance, feminism is the modern name for an ancient impulse. The game of protecting women and Woman's participation in that game are both as old as the hills.

What would be new and revolutionary and an immeasurable aid in Woman's escape from a category of humanity known collectively as "innocent-women-and-children" would be to hold Woman to adult standards of accountability for her power, her influence, and her co-equal partnership. Sadly, however, I see scant evidence that humanity is yet prepared to love men enough to empathize with them or respect women enough to hold them accountable.

The entire catalogue of real or alleged female victimizations worldwide is vast. Counter-arguing and/or pointing out the equal-opposite MaleVictimization for each instance is very doable, but beyond the scope of this book. A more thorough debunking will have to wait for book 3, *Love and Respect in the Present*.

It is ambition enough in this book to argue that It All Balances Out in the industrialized west. I would be content with that ambition except that conditions for women worldwide seem to act as a kind of MP/FV ideological sanctuary. As soon as it becomes clear that I have a comeback for every female complaint here in our culture, the question becomes: "How about conditions for women in the Islamic world?"

If the question conceded balance in our culture, I'd be content with that. But the question concedes nothing. It is brought forth to shame and stifle. Given the underlying assumption (the monumental victimization of women as compared with the patriarchal paradise of male power and privilege that men are presumed to enjoy in third world societies), the question is really asking: "How can you *be* such an insensitive *bastard?*"

"Well, you've absolutely *got* to admit FemaleVictimization in *Bosnia*, or *Arabia*, or *China*, or whatever, right?" People look at me then as if to say: Either he admits MP/FV or his credibility is *totally* shot. Well, I could be wrong but the best evidence I know of does not support the MP/FV paradigm *anywhere at all*. My research indicates that matrisensus influence is always a match for patriarchal influence, and brutal places are brutal to *both* sexes. China? Over a ten-year period, 59,543 men and *no women* died in coal mining accidents alone![513] Male slaves trafficked into China find prosecuting their slavemasters particularly difficult because Chinese law only protects *women* from being trafficked in as slaves.[514]

You can go to a brutal place, catalogue *only* the brutality toward women, and on that basis conclude that women are *the* victims, but if you don't research conditions for men, if you don't *compare* the female victimization against male victimization, your conclusion is logically *bankrupt*. Even worse, our perceptions of gender reality are further distorted when the only comparison that *is* regularly made is the comparison between conditions experienced by the *average* woman vs. conditions experienced by the *elite* male.

Now *obviously* I'm not saying that horrors never visit Womankind. They do. But I *am* saying that feminism, in league with chivalry, fabricates, inspires, and enforces so much MalePower and Female-Victimization bias in the media, that information regarding MP/FV is information that *cannot be trusted*. It's a matter of "The Boy Who Cried Wolf." Feminists' constant and hyperbolic cries of "victim" have eroded much of their credibility with me. When I see the saturation levels of female-as-victim stories pouring forth from every media worldwide, what *I* see is the incredible focus of empathy directed exclusively toward females.

The victim-dictum of feminism fails because it only understands female victimization within a hermetically sealed ideological bubble that shuts female power, accountability, complicity and culpability out of the equation. Worse, that same hermetic seal also shuts male victimization and male perspectives out of the equation, further distorting feminist conclusions. Worst of all, it tries to tell us that in addition to all things along the respect axis, women suffer all things along the love axis as well. And that's where the phony fem-stats regarding "Violence Against Women," under-valuing *mother*hood, discriminating against *women* in healthcare and education, being the primary victims of war and other female-only "brutalization" come into play.

In this way feminists would appropriate the victimization of men, claim it as their own and thus suck up *all* empathy. And it is there where feminism sinks to its most selfish, self-absorbed, self-serving, self-indulgent, self-righteous, self-proclaimed victimhood. It is there where female-ism becomes both false and *contemptible*.

It is important to come right out and *say* that because both sexes must be held accountable for the part they play in the love/respect dynamic. Both sexes are treated unfairly. Both sexes get "set up." Both sexes are faced with double binds. Both sexes suffer bias and stereotyping. And, *both* sexes are complicit in bringing it upon themselves!

Given the suffering of *both* sexes, what is to be admired, revered, and respected in Woman's self-proclaimed ownership of "victim"?

If I suggest that men are less loved because men are less lovable, I will expect no outraged outcry. If, however, I dare suggest that women are less respected because women are less respectable, I can expect a *firestorm* of protest. Even so, we must explore the possibility that certain male attitudes and behaviors contribute to men being less loved. *And* we must explore the possibility that certain female attitudes and behaviors contribute to women being less respected.

Empathy Power in Summation:

The old saying: "If Mamma isn't happy, no one is happy (If Dad's unhappy, no one cares)" received some clinical confirmation recently. According to a growing number of studies, it would seem that a mother's depression can substantially increase the likelihood of depression in her teenage children. But, "A depressed father does not increase the risk of depression in adopted or non-adopted teens."[515] To empathize is to stand in another's place and feel what they feel. Whatever *women* are feeling, it goes all through us.

Perhaps you'll agree that we seem to take more delight in a woman's joy than we would in the joy of her male equivalent. Don't we make greater efforts to keep women happy? Isn't that largely what feminism is all about? We're forever asking: What do women want? How often do we ask: What do *men* want?

In any case, when we empathize, it seems we generally empathize with another's fear, pain, and sorrow. We rarely talk of feeling *empathy* toward another's happiness. Is this why our extra empathy toward women has us tending to focus on the more negative, painful, vulnerable aspects of the female experience?

Perhaps the day will come when we look back and say, Feminism was favoritism—favoritism toward the sex both sexes like and love more. Of course, in matters along the respect axis, favoritism has always been shown men, but that's the purview of feminists to complain about, and they've got that base well covered.

*Feminism is all about Woman making full political use of her greater **power** to elicit empathy.* As humanity's admiration for itself is and has always been directed primarily at men (the sex that both sexes *respect* more), so humanity's empathy for itself has always been directed primarily at women (the sex that both sexes *love* more). Women in general and feminists in particular have utilized Empathy Power to float a political movement. *If* we're living in an age of Woman's ascendance over Man, we are seeing the power of being more loved supersede the power of being more respected.

Throughout the ages, complaining and plying "victim" have, for women, been effective adaptive behaviors. Tugging at heart strings has always been an effective way for women to get what they want and has helped individual women select from among those men who seemed most willing to "come to her rescue" (and weed out those who did not). These behaviors have been adaptive in that they were adaptations women made in response to overall circumstances. In short, Woman made full use of powers she had to compensate for powers she did not have (of course, Man has done the same for the same reason).

Woman still has this power; she still uses it and it continues to be highly effective. Over the course of human evolutionary psychology, the attitudes and behaviors involved in wielding empathy power have, perhaps, inculcated certain instinctual elements. Finally, the media and the mythos have, throughout history, cemented our MP/FV perceptions accordingly. Therefore, to understand the world as seen through the eyes of a masculist is apt to require nothing less than a paradigm shift in one's entire belief-system with regard to the relative positions of Man and Woman, Woman and Man.

How the MP/FV Paradigm Begets the MB/WG Paradigm

It works like this: if women are *truly* powerless then women *are* truly blameless.[a] Believing that all power is male, we will believe that all responsibility, fault, and blame is male—a path that leads to the perception of ManBad. If women are the victims we will, of course, direct our empathy toward women, which leads to empathy interpretations of female attitudes and behaviors, which leads to a perception of WomanGood.

If women are *the* victims, it follows that men—the ones with *the* power, the ones who bear responsibility, fault, and blame—must be *the* victimizers. Thus, ManBad.

Finally, though not logical, it is emotionally compelling to confer upon the victim an innate moral superiority over the victimizer. This assumption that the victims are morally superior is standard within storytelling of all kinds.[b] Within the confines of the MP/FV paradigm, to "blame" women is to "blame the victim," something that we all know to be wrong. Thus, Man is *solely* to blame as the Bad victimizer and Woman, the "*innocent* victim," is Good.

In this way, a belief in the MalePower/FemaleVictimization paradigm leads inexorably to the ManBad/WomanGood paradigm. And so, having completed our exploration of MP/FV and having found it wanting, we now focus our attention upon MB/WG.

Now we get to the fun part!

---

[a] To illustrate: imagine someone quadriplegic placed behind the wheel of a car and sent hurtling into a crowd of people. Being *truly powerless* to influence the situation, that someone cannot be held responsible for the outcome. Thus the truly powerless *are* truly blameless.

[b] The film *Avatar* is a prime example of such story telling. But there is no *innate* difference between the oppressed and the oppressors. As history has demonstrated time and again, given a shift in circumstances, the oppressed and the oppressor may readily exchange roles.

Part Three

Male Mea Culpa

"My Fault, My Fault, My Grievous Male Fault"

> If only it were all so simple! If only there were evil people somewhere insidiously committing evil deeds, and it were necessary only to separate them from the rest of us and destroy them. But the line dividing good and evil cuts through the heart of every human being. And who is willing to destroy a piece of his own heart? - Alexander Solzhenitsyn[516]

In the previous section, **The Duality Principle**, we took a hard look at the MalePower/FemaleVictimization (MP/FV) paradigm and found it wanting. We also found MP/FV assumptions leading to all manner of gender injustice—not least of which is the inexorable way that belief in MP/FV leads to a belief in ManBad/WomanGood (MB/WG). In this section we will challenge the MB/WG paradigm in the same way that we challenged the MP/FV paradigm. As always our ultimate aim is to demonstrate that It All Balances Out.

This third and last section of the book, **Male Mea Culpa**, is divided into three chapters. We begin by shedding light on the full range of The Female Shadow (from gray to black). We follow that with Protected Innocence, where we explore the many and varied ways in which the patriarchy acts as partial insulation between women and the dark side of the world and human nature. Finally, in a chapter called Man Demonized, we explore the costs associated with the MB/WG paradigm—the costs to men, to women, and to society in general.

Introduction

If the female emotional legacy is fear—fear of walking the streets at night, fear of rape, fear of incompetence in "a man's world," fear of powerful men—then the male emotional legacy is shame—shame for perpetrating violence and war, shame for crude "Neanderthal" sensibilities, shame for "pornographic" carnal desires, shame for manifesting human evil. *If demonizing men has led to excessive fear in women, then angelizing women has led to excessive shame in men.*

We know well the case for Man as *the* source of violence and criminality. We know the shadow side of Man well enough to support a culture-wide presumption that the shadow side of Man is the shadow side of humanity. Therefore, to show that it all balances out, to show that ManGood/WomanBad (MG/WB) is a match for MB/WG, we must again delve deep into realms that test our resolve.

To be convincing, we must expose Woman's dark side in depth, breadth, and detail. Let's be clear that the goal is not to denigrate Woman but rather to exonerate Man as moral inferior and *sole source* of evil. The goal is to elevate Woman to the status of equal partner—for good and for bad. We're here to show that It *All* Balances Out.

If arguing that Woman is as "bad" as Man will be received as denigrating Woman, what does that say about gender bias?

In daring to explore the dark side of Woman, we have at least two major psychological hurdles to overcome:

First, there is the chivalry factor. Like women themselves, the "angelic" image of women is protected. In fact, I believe this protection *itself* largely accounts for why we experience women as morally superior in the first place. Women and men alike will want to protect the "gentle sex" from the penetrating gaze. But protection carries costs. Let us lift the veil of protection and see the concealed reality behind it. Let us look beyond the flattering yet infantilizing image of Woman as harmlessly angelic and see her for the multi-dimensional adult and equal partner she truly is.

Second, being relatively bereft of acclaim for her intellect, competence, prestige; toughness, strength, and courage, how can we suffer Woman to give up her moral superiority? Our extra empathy toward women will make it extra difficult to ask Woman to suffer loss. But consider: knowing that Man is relatively bereft of acclaim for his beauty, grace, goodness; home, family, and parenting contributions has not stayed us from culture wide ridicule and denial of *his* traditionally perceived areas of superiority. Males are routinely referred to as the "weaker sex" (Google search "weaker sex;" see for yourself). Revisionist feminist history will tell you that Albert Einstein's wife supplied the genius while he merely stole the credit (seriously). Christopher Columbus has been transformed from hero to exploiter. And, in the world of film, when a man and woman square off in combat, we've come to know that the man doesn't stand a chance.

As Dan Abrams' new book *Man Down: Proof Beyond a Reasonable Doubt That Women Are Better Cops, Drivers, Gamblers, Spies, World Leaders, Beer Tasters, Hedge Fund Managers, and Just About Everything Else* (2011) makes clear, we've learned to take a very hard look at "male superiority." Let's dare take an equally hard look at "female superiority."

I'll not be coy about this. The research I will present makes it clear that female misbehavior has always been far more common and far darker than we care to know. "According to an extensive body of research on love, sex, and friendship, men and women do not behave as differently as we tend to think," asserts Kate Fillion, author of *Lip Service* (1996); "women are not mythic creatures of sweetness and light, but flesh-and-blood mortals who are capable of all the negative feelings and behavior we currently associate with masculinity."[517]

Patricia Pearson, author of *When She Was Bad: How and why women get away with murder* (1998), has done exhaustive research on the subject of female darkness and female violence.

> Women commit the majority of child homicides in the United States, a greater share of physical child abuse, an equal rate of sibling violence and assaults on the elderly, about a quarter of child sexual abuse, an overwhelming share of the killings of newborns, and a fair preponderance of spousal assaults. The question is how do we come to *perceive* what girls and women do? Violence is still universally considered to be the province of the male. Violence is masculine. Men are the cause of it, and women and children the ones who suffer. The sole explanation offered up by criminologists for violence committed by a woman is that it is involuntary, the rare result of provocation or mental illness, as if half the population of the globe consisted of saintly stoics who never succumbed to fury, frustration, or greed. Though the evidence may contradict the statement, the consensus runs deep. Women from all walks of life, at all levels of power—corporate, political, or familial, women in combat and on police forces—have no part in violence. It is one of the most abiding myths of our time.[518]

Within the literature on the subject there is a little-known body of informed opinion that assesses women's participation in evil in ways many will find disturbing. Women committing a *preponderance* of spousal assaults? Can such assertions be true? And we will ask: What is the point of reframing the feminine legacy from a civilizing force for goodness and refinement to equal partner in crime?

We will find that such assertions can indeed be true. In part, we go down this road in search of those truths. Harold Schechter begins his book *Fatal: The Poisonous Life of a Female Serial Killer* with America's crowning Aileen Wuornos "the first woman serial killer in our nation's history."[519]

> There is, however, a serious problem with this label. It's completely untrue. In spite of the popular belief that sociopathic violence is a strictly male phenomenon, the fact is that women have always accounted for a sizable proportion of humanity's most prolific and reprehensible multiple-murderers.[520]

A gender belief system built on falsehoods *is* a serious problem. In seeking after truth we must acknowledge *all* truths, not just those truths that comfortably fit with sentiment. Pursuant to those truths that do not fit with sentiment, Peter Vronsky, author of *Female Serial Killers: How and Why Women Become Monsters* (2007), offers his take on the matter:

> History, of course, is full of instrumentally violent women: Valeria Messalina, Queen Boadicea, Agrippina the Younger, Lucrezia Borgia,

Catherine the Great, Elizabeth the First, Madame Mao, Golda Meir, Margaret Thatcher. Some of these women can be characterized as serial killers; many had on numerous occasions killed and tortured serially, or ordered it to be done in the name of political power, patriotism, vengeance, or material greed and lust—and they did it as ruthlessly and obsessively as their male contemporaries—and sometimes more so.[521]

Some of the women Vronsky names could indeed be characterized as serial killers; it depends on how we choose to define the term. Others, like Margaret Thatcher, acted the way men in power normally do. But in acknowledging this, we acknowledge that women in power behave from no greater average moral high ground than their male counterparts. Still, if you're like me, you'll find such evidence . . . disconcerting.

Feminism has done much to disparage the protean image of Man. Nonetheless, we remain deeply invested in the image of women as "innocent," even "angelic" (I know I do). Women may not be "mythic creatures of sweetness and light," but in many ways, they *seem* to be (at least from the perspective of the average starry-eyed male).

It begins in childhood. Harry Stein, author of *One of the Guys*, expresses the feeling with élan:

> From the outset, there is the evidence of our eyes and ears and hearts—and as a species, girls strike many of us not merely as different from ourselves but, in important ways, as *better*. Instinctively subtle where we are obvious, reflective in contrast to our loutish impulsiveness, fine where we tend to be so terribly crude, they seem, in many cases, to have been touched by something approaching the divine.[522]

Indeed, charms women possess make it easy to experience a woman's feminine beauty extending to the depths of her feminine soul. No wonder Angel is such a common name and nickname for women.

Lately, I see an effort to make it official. Citing a wealth of research that reveals a near universal experience of women as being more likable/lovable then men, Alice Eagly has made a name for herself proffering what she calls the "Women Are Wonderful" (WAW) effect. "Both men and women hold much more favorable views of women than of men," comments Professor Roy F. Baumeister. "Almost everybody likes women better than men. I certainly do."[523]

I too could wax rhapsodic over the feminine. Of *course* both sexes seek out girlfriends for their deepest intimacies. Of *course* women are more loved and more deeply emotionally depended upon. Women possess the magic that makes life worthwhile. I am as mushy around femininity as anyone. And we mustn't forget that there is great beauty in sentimentality, the perspective of our hearts.

Exploration of the feminine shadow provokes considerable ambivalence. So, before proceeding further down this road, let us pause to set more ground rules. Let us begin with some foundational thinking we have yet to attend to.

Generally Speaking

"Boys will be boys and girls will be girls." If there were absolutely *no* truth to generalizations, there would be no basis for making them. Yet we've all heard someone correct another by saying: "That's a generalization" or "You mustn't generalize," as if to generalize was simply to act in error. But, in speaking of men and women, populations each in excess of three billion individuals, there can be no alternative to speaking in generalities.

Statistics are, in essence, generalizations formalized and rendered mathematically precise. If something is true *on average*, then it is true *in general*. Trends and tendencies, averages and bell-curves are all components of statistics and generalizing. They are also the basis for much of economics, biology, psychology, and sexual politics. Generalizations are indispensable tools for discussing the large-scale societal mechanisms that make the human world what it is. And generalizations are harmless so long as they remain within their large-scale sociological and theoretical realms.

The danger comes when a generalization is either perniciously exaggerated or taken from this macro realm and applied to individuals. A generalization applied to an individual becomes a stereotype. Stereotypes are objectionable because they set judgments and limits on people whom we know only or mainly by the "type" they represent. When stereotypes suggest the assumption that *all* members of a group either share or lack a given characteristic, they create unequal access and unequal opportunity. In short, they create injustice.

In this section of the book, we will explore the many ways that Man's vastly exaggerated reputation for evil, creates disadvantages and prejudices against individual men on the job, on the streets, in the courts, in the home, and in war.

Generalizing suffers guilt by association with stereotyping, but they are two distinctly different things. In sexual politics, generalizations may be distinguished from stereotypes in that generalizations deal with broad statistical averages and overviews which say a lot about men and women in general, but make no claims at all about individual men and women.

For example, in this section I will assert (supported by a variety of evidence) that women tend to work their aggression and mischief strategies *in*directly. Doubtless, as a generalization, this assertion has merit. But that doesn't mean that an individual woman is fairly accused without evidence about her as an individual.

Likewise, it is frequently asserted that men are more "lecherous" than women. As a generalization, this assertion too has merit. But, when the FBI warned law-enforcement agencies that the new Video Barbie could be used to make kiddie porn, the media responded by "telling parents that any man nice enough to play dolls with their daughters could really be videotaping 'under their little skirts!'"[524] When a father is presumed pedophile just because he happens to be the *male* parent, this is misandry. It is prejudice leading to injustice.

If you were to choose a man and a woman at random, the woman would sometimes be taller than the man, and yet the statement "Men are taller than women" is regarded as true because it is *generally* true (more true than false). That's all I claim for any gender generalization. Aside from a little reproductive biology, all differences between women and men (and most issues between women and men) exist only as *a matter of degree*.

But here's the thing; if you can't even say that men are taller than women without generalizing, then you can't say *anything* about men and women without generalizing. But we *must* be open to discussing gender issues and the large-scale trends and tendencies, the bell curves and averages, the aptitudes and proclivities that drive the large-scale cultural machinery—and therefore we *must* generalize.

Nature/Nurture

Variation between the genders need not be vast to be of great social significance. Men and women differ in height by about 8 percent—that's all. Yet that is more than enough to establish that difference as a social norm upon which *tremendous* significance is placed.

Men and women diverge only slightly, like the 8 percent divergence in height. The other 92 percent is overlap. Men are from earth and women are from earth. But the specialized realm of gender politics only exists to point out, ponder, and protest the differences. And, subtle though they may be, the differences between Man and Woman gain significance through the way they generalize out into the vast human population.

Moreover, out at the edges of the bell curves, these divergences show themselves clearly. For example, out at the very edge of human height, as we approach eight feet in height and there are very few men left, we can expect to find no women at all. Harmony between the sexes will come when we focus upon the vast commonality between women and men, while accepting and celebrating the mystifying differences for what they are. After all, if the sexes were identical there would be little point in having two of them.

The nature/nurture debate has been ongoing for thousands of years and remains a realm rich in philosophic paradox, depth, mystery, and contradiction. The evidence that demonstrates culture's influence upon gender is certainly unassailable. But the evidence demonstrating biology's influence is *likewise* far too vast to be dismissed.

Few, if any, deny the influence of culture. But, because many deny the significance of biology, the nature side of the nature/nurture debate requires defending. "The sexes are different because their brains are different," asserts brain scientist Anne Moir. "The brain, the chief administrative and emotional organ of life, is differently constructed in men and in women; it processes information in a different way, which results in different perceptions, priorities and behavior."[525] Neuroscience has established that there are two distinctly different types of human brain—female and male. And male and female brains differ *substantially*—structurally, morphologically, and neurochemically.

So, men and women are innately different where it counts most—the brain. Nevertheless, we are left to ponder the question . . . so what? So women and men are different; now what have we got? What, if anything, does that *mean?* What, if anything, does it portend for the future? What, if anything, does this truth impose upon us?

Also, it's clear to me that both nature and nurture exert influence, each in their own way; but we don't yet understand the complex synergistic relationship between the two. How do they interact? Which one usurps the other, and under what circumstances? Science tells us much, yet nature/nurture retains an air of mystery.

Much of the aversion to allowing for *innate* gender difference may come down to an aversion to complexity. If Woman and Man were identical, gender issues would be easy. But in some mysterious way men and women are the same . . . *but different*. And the *different* part won't go away just because it complicates matters.

All right, now comes the sticky part as it relates to a word that lies deep at the heart of this third and last section of the book—goodness. For millennia humanity has attributed its intellect, competence, prestige; toughness, strength, and courage to Man. This is Man's glass half "full" (if he *chooses* to perceive it so). Humanity has attributed its beauty, grace, *goodness*; home, family, and parenting to Woman—her glass half "empty" (if she *chooses* to perceive it so). Though each sex has sacrificed much in their efforts to *earn* them, clearly, these attributions have been grossly exaggerated. It is *not* clear, however, that these attributions have been *entirely* socially constructed. Many gender scientists make a strong case for *biology's* influence upon varying gender proclivities and aptitudes.

So, let's entertain this notion by supposing that Woman is innately "8 percent" superior in terms of what we'll agree to call "wonderfulness" and Man is innately "8 percent" superior in terms of, oh, let's call it "masterfulness." Is any harm done? Admittedly, that's no easy question to ponder. But if there *is* a kernel of truth within such generalizations, does it serve us to deny this truth?

So long we are generous enough to give Man credit where credit is due, I have no problem giving Woman credit where credit is due. That said, this final section of the book is dedicated, in large part, to arguing that while Woman may well deserve credit for an extra "8 percent" of innate goodness, that about covers it. As we'll soon see, the perception of woman as *vastly* morally superior does not hold up to scrutiny. If the sexes diverge in goodness by 8 percent, then the other 92 percent is overlap and in terms of good and bad, women and men diverge only a little.

Because feminism teaches women the most negative interpretation of their lives and legacy, Woman tends to perceive herself as *the* victim and Man does not. But what might account for Woman's evident receptivity to the same victimhood that Man so adamantly rejects? In addition to the nurture side, could there be a nature side to all this?

It is commonly asserted that high levels of testosterone result in high levels of energy and self-confidence and overall feelings of wellbeing. One female-to-male transsexual described the effects of testosterone injections thus:

> I felt [the effects of the testosterone injections] within the first three to four hours ... It was an intense experience. The next day, when I woke up, I had so much energy, I couldn't believe how much energy I had! I was like, "Oh my God!" I went walking down the street, and I was thinking, "Is this how men feel?" I felt like I could run around the block ninety times! It was like rock and roll injected into my body![526]
> [The words in brackets added in the original]

Clearly, *regardless* of the fact-based reality of his situation, this particular man will *not* be receptive to a victim outlook.

If antidepressants and other psychotropic chemicals can so dramatically alter an individual's outlook on life, why not naturally occurring neurochemicals? Camille Paglia has theorized that the "loss of voice" that allegedly afflicts girls as they enter puberty might be attributable not to "patriarchal dominance," but rather to the second wave of hormones that in adolescence finish the job of biologically differentiating female and male begun in the womb.

I think it likely that differing neurochemistry exerts some measure of influence in these matters. More studies are needed. But where *are* the studies that would either corroborate or contradict such theories?

"Researchers who study sex differences seem convinced that it is hard to get this work funded and the results published," asserts Steven Rhoads.[527] Rather than limit ourselves to feminist "patriarchy" theories, we owe it to ourselves to gather and discover and assimilate as much truth about gender as we can. Theories rise or fall according to scientific inquiry. Given the current cultural climate, however, the study of such possibilities is apt to be a career killer.

In fact, according to feminists, gender is strictly a social construct with no basis in biology. Note how gender is defined in the average American classroom:

> Gender – created through cultural and social ideas. These ideas establish a difference between males and females by suggesting that each sex is either masculine or feminine. Gender and sex are often confused and used as the same thing. Sex relates to the biological, physical characteristics such as genitals or chromosomes that make a person male or female at birth. Gender is not biological but based on perceptions associated with members of each sex.[528]

So a person's "sex" is nothing more than a few bits of superficial reproductive biology. Gender is not biological, but perceptual—"created through cultural and social ideas." In schools across the nation this feminist definition of gender is taught as *fact*, not opinion. What happens if you question this definition?

During an informal gathering Harvard University President Larry Summers was asked his opinion regarding men's continued dominance in the fields of math and science. Along with explanations including ongoing bias, discrimination, and sexism; Summers had the temerity to suggest that biological factors *might* be involved. It was enough to do him in.[529] Says Marcella Bombardieri, writing for the *Boston Globe*:

> The president of Harvard University, Lawrence H. Summers, sparked an uproar at an academic conference Friday when he said that innate differences between men and women might be one reason fewer women succeed in science and math careers. Summers also questioned how much of a role discrimination plays in the dearth of female professors in science and engineering at elite universities. Nancy Hopkins, a biologist at Massachusetts Institute of Technology, walked out on Summers' talk, saying later that if she hadn't left, "I would've either blacked out or thrown up."[530]

If Woman is properly credited with an extra "8 percent" of goodness, is Man properly credited with an extra "8 percent" of analytic ability? The gender science may be complex but the operative gender principle remains simple: IABO.

Here's another angle on the matter: perhaps it's not so much in terms of *ability* that men and women differ, but in *motivation*. Perhaps the sexes behave, perform, and excel differently *only* because their desires, interests, and obsessions tend to differ.

Here's yet another angle: there are more males than females at the low end of intelligence *and* men and women's *average* intelligence measures the same. These facts are well supported. The corollary fact may be politically incorrect, but it is no less substantiated: there are also more males than females at the *high* end of intelligence. Thus: more male imbeciles *and* more male geniuses.

Some of the most thorough research into the matter is presented in Roy Baumeister's book, *Is There Anything Good About Men?* As his title suggests, at present, the world seems not very amenable to notions of extra male genius. Nevertheless, "If the oversupply of retarded boys is not the result of men defending patriarchy, then quite likely the oversupply of genius boys isn't either."[531] And, if there are more male than female geniuses, more males than females will perform at the *very* top end of math and science.

Actually, males tend to occupy *both* extremes of *many* bell curves. As previously quoted, "Males are a breeding experiment run by females—a proving ground from which females can cull winning genes."[532] Many assert that, in part, it is the male's relative expendability (see "Two Tribes," p. 326) that accounts for why nature tends to do its "genetic experimenting" upon males, which, in turn, accounts for why males lean toward the extremes—good and bad.

We may have to wait for future generations, not so blinded by gender *illusion*, to gain a deeper grasp of gender *reality*. These issues are complex and perhaps, as yet, only poorly understood.

Even so, many gender scientists speak with an air of certainty: "the nature and cause of brain differences are now known beyond speculation, beyond prejudice, and beyond reasonable doubt," Says Anne Moir.[533] "Boys will generally outperform girls in areas of mathematics involving abstract concepts of space, relationships, and theory. At the very highest level of mathematical excellence, according to the biggest survey ever conducted, the very best boys totally eclipse the very best girls."[534]

Moir presents evidence that males excel in advanced math for a number of quantifiable reasons, including the assertion that male brains possess an area dedicated solely to abstract spatial reasoning, female brains do not.[535] She cites studies that chart female mathematical ability at various points during the female menstrual cycle. Apparently, these studies show that mathematical ability is at its lowest when estrogen levels are at their highest.[536]

Steven Rhodes, Simon Baron-Cohen, and many other authors on the subject are just as adamant. Out of my own research into these matters, I suspect that their adamancy may not be *entirely* justified. But, even if they are a little over-certain of their conclusions, the point is this: if the evidence many gender scientists are seeing is extensive enough and convincing enough to inspire such commitment to biology's influence on gender, how is it that a university president is powerless to include biology even as a *possible contributing factor?*

Adds Moir: "now, just at the very moment when science can tell us what the differences are, and where they spring from, we are asked to banish the assumption of difference as if it were a guilty thought."[537] Indeed, for failing to banish the assumption of difference, Summers was deemed guilty and in 2005 he was forced to resign.[538] At the risk of career suicide, who in the top ranks of academia will dare assert the nature side of the nature/nurture debate?

"Can you imagine," asks Kathleen Parker, "a man bolting from the room with light head and upset tummy if a woman college president suggested that genetic differences might account for males lagging behind females in reading and writing?"[539]

So, how many gender truths will we suppress because feminists are apt to "black out or throw up" upon hearing them? If freedom of speech and freedom of inquiry will not be supported even within our nation's universities, what becomes of intellectual freedom?

The Larry Summers incident is emblematic of feminism's shift in focus from an effort to *enlighten* to an effort to *control*. When feminism acts as a kind of ideological dictatorship, it sets limits on our thoughts, our explorations, and our theories. We *all* suffer the incomplete and distorted understanding that such limits impose.

The Female Shadow: From Gray to Black

It's true; women *are* wonderful. Saying so is only giving credit where credit is due. The "Women Are Wonderful" effect is now taught in Women's Studies classrooms across the country. So it's official. We happily credit women with extra wonderfulness (more evolved, nuanced, refined sensibilities and interpersonal skills). And why not? Why not be generous?

But what of a mirror-opposite effect? What would the reaction be if I were to assert a "Men Are Masterful" effect? Sadly, though 99 percent of firefighters are men, we are no longer permitted to call them fire*men*. Where men are concerned, political correctness enforces a kind of zero-tolerance policy regarding any form of extra praise or credit where credit is due. Feminists will happily take ownership of extra female facility in empathy and morality and relationship skills. But try suggesting that men might have the edge in math and science and feminists are apt to "blackout" or "throw up."

Feminism's ungenerous attitude toward men has become *society's* ungenerous attitude toward men.

In response, we may be justified in taking an equally ungenerous stand toward women. But we continue down our chosen path of uncovering the female shadow in pursuit of higher purposes. Not only is it important to absolve Man as *the* source of all things bad, it is equally important to offer Woman the gift of accountability.

Duality guarantees that with every loss there is gain. In losing her exaggerated ownership of goodness, Woman will gain the centeredness, the forthrightness, the honesty, the trustworthiness, the respectability, and the personal empowerment that comes of taking accountable ownership of the shadow side of her basic human nature.

The human shadow—that which we hide, repress, and deny—the dark side—the part of us that hates and rages and covets and envies and wants what we want when we want it—is an invaluable source of human strength and aggression and ambition and obsession.

In owning our shadow we fill our gas tanks with its fuel but in bringing the shadow to consciousness we keep it from getting its hands on the steering wheel. The shadow is selfish, resentful, and infantile. There is energy in it, but we don't want it driving the bus. If we don't own our shadow and keep it out in front of us where we can keep an eye on it, our shadow will control us unconsciously. It will trip us up and sabotage our efforts with its perversity and narcissism.

Is there reason to believe that Woman has a shadow and a dark side to rival Man's?

A First Look at the Evidence

According to *Newsweek,* "[s]ome gangs have recently included young women as members, and some cities report a growing number of all-female gangs. Some female gangs are reported to be every bit as ruthless as the male gangs."[540] Chicago Police Officer and veteran "gang specialist" George Figueroa asserts that, when it comes to gang life, "the girls are no different from the guys—the mentality is, it's better to be the toughest girl on the block than the smartest."

Girl gangs demonstrate that, under the right circumstances, women can become as ego-invested in toughness, strength, and courage as men. Once so invested, women can fall into the same traps with the same consequences that men have always endured.

> Despite her troubles, [Antoinette "Toni" Vazquez] speaks loyally of the gang and boasts about dodging sexist cops who don't suspect her because she's a woman. Chicago Police Officer Rose Gordon says it's common for girls to act as setup artists for their gangs. "They know they have that advantage over men," says Gordon, a gang specialist who studies girls. Vazquez herself says that she and her sister have helped pull what they call "tumbes" for their gang, luring male victims so the guys can rob them. "What do we do?" she says with a sly smile. "Nothin' nice."[541]

Note that women's presumed innocence is framed as "sexism"—a gender-neutral term nonetheless understood to mean bias that adversely affects women. Her talk of "dodging sexist cops" implies that she is the victim of this sexism, yet it is a sexism acknowledged as being an "advantage over men"! So are we to believe that women are *the* victims of sexism owing to higher expectations of them?

Surely the more serious sexist *dis*advantage is inherent in the male's presumed *guil*t, not the female's presumed innocence. Also, note that we now have both male and female perpetrators, but the article specifies only males as being lured in as victims.

You may recall a notorious series of social psychology experiments designed to test ordinary people's willingness to obey an authority figure even when asked to carry out actions in conflict with the subjects' moral guidelines. Conducted by psychologist Stanley Milgram in the early 1960's, the experiment was carried out utilizing three people: two participants—a "teacher" and a "learner"—plus the experimenter. In actuality, only one of the two "participants" was genuine. Only the "teacher" had responded to an advert for taking part in a "learning" experiment. The "learner" was actually an actor.

Dressed in a white lab coat to augment his authoritative image, the experimenter ordered the test subject to press a button administering an electric "shock" each time the "learner" answered a question incorrectly. To everyone's amazement, the *majority* of test subjects, though they protested, nevertheless administered what they believed to be ever increasing, very painful, even potentially "fatal" voltages when verbally pressured to do so.

The "learner," sequestered in a separate room, could be heard over a loud speaker. Starting at "45 volts" and ending at "450 volts," the test subjects administering the "electric shock's" could hear the "learner's" pre-recorded agitation escalate to screaming and pleading for the experiment to stop, yet about 64 percent bowed to "authority" all the way to administering the "450 volt" final "shock." Owing to ethical concerns, only recently has legal permission been given to duplicate Milgram's experiment. Sadly, it would seem that little has changed since the early 60s.

> In ABC News' version of the Milgram experiment, we tested 18 men, and found that 65 percent of them agreed to administer increasingly painful electric shocks when ordered by an authority figure. 22 women signed up for our experiment. Even though most people said that women would be less likely to inflict pain on the learner, a surprising 73 percent yielded to the orders of the experimenter.[542]

Doubtless, some study results will indicate MB/WG while other results (like these) indicate MG/WB. But what interest us here are the assumptions and the reported "surprise."

If assumptions are guided by stereotypes, why didn't the experimenters assume that women's stereotypical passivity would cause them to be more easily controlled? How is it that only male-negative stereotypes hold sway, guide thinking, and create assumptions? Why did the experimenters assume that men are bad and women are good? Why is it "surprising" when results indicate otherwise? And why do results like these consistently fail to diffuse into the culture and create change in MB/WG assumptions?

No less an authority than Margaret Mead wrote: "When women disengage completely from their traditional role, they become more ruthless and savage than men."[543] Maybe so.

"In a Princeton study using video games, men dropped significantly more bombs than women as long as their identity was known," reports Ellen Goodman for *The Boston Globe*. "But when promised anonymity -- when 'nobody was watching' -- women dropped more bombs than men. When the social constraints are off -- surely when women are rewarded for violence -- they can mimic the worst behavior of men. So, in Iraq, two of those 'female prisoners' were 'Dr. Germ' and 'Mrs. Anthrax,' Saddam Hussein's hench-women."[544]

This is an interesting example of Woman owning and disowning the feminine shadow simultaneously. Ostensibly Ms. Goodman is blowing the whistle on Woman's shadow side. Yet, by stating that women behaving badly are merely *mimicking* "the worst behavior of men," Ms. Goodman implies that men remain ultimately the *source* of evil. "The worst behavior" remains "the worst behavior *of men*" even when the behavior is enacted by women!

Perhaps, when they thought they were being observed, when they thought they had an audience, the men were "imitating" male behavior by dropping more bombs and the women were "imitating" female behavior by dropping fewer bombs. But, "when promised anonymity" and the "social constraints are off," isn't *that* when men and women would display their truest natures?

Women's Gray Side

Like the male shadow, the female shadow extends from the realm of misdemeanors to heinous acts of evil—from gray to black. And, like the male shadow, the female shadow involves the abuse of power. And so, we will not properly perceive and understand the female shadow until we have come to perceive and understand FemalePower—how it differs, how it works, and why it is relatively invisible.

Domination vs. Manipulation

> "The weakness of men is the facade of strength:
> the strength of women is the facade of weakness." – Warren Farrell

The Deal—the gender system that comes down to us from time immemorial—was set up, ratified, and maintained within a wheel of complicity enacted by two equally powerful sexes, each with equal influence over the world and over each other. The Deal owes its misty origins to a sensible and practical reaction to basic biology. In living out The Deal, each sex has enjoyed and suffered its part. There's no one to blame and no cause for rancor or resentment.

History will be the province of the next book, *Love and Respect in the Past*. But, because the dynamics surrounding domination vs. manipulation, love vs. respect, hero vs. victim, and credit vs. blame are timeless dynamics, I'll offer my take on them rendered within a brief historic context. I'll begin by quoting the results of a recent study conducted by Kurt Gray and Daniel Wegner:

> Great works and praiseworthy behavior may bring respect and admiration, but these won't help us to escape blame when we do something wrong . . . To do that, the researchers say, one needs to be a victim not

a hero! In the study, participants responded to a number of scenarios that mirrored real-life moral transgressions, from stealing money to harming someone. Results revealed that, no matter how many previous good deeds someone had done, they received just as much blame—if not more—than someone with a less heroic background. . . . "[P]eople ignore heroic pasts—or even count them against you—when assigning blame. . . . Psychologically, the perceived distance between a hero and a villain is quite small, whereas there's a wide gap between a villain and a victim. This means that heroes are easily recast as evil doers, whereas it's very hard to turn a victim into a villain."[545]

These results, I believe, bolster the following theories . . .

The Deal set men up as the "heroic" sex, which set men up to be vulnerable to and controllable by the sharp applications of blame and shame. Setting men up as the "elite" sex effectively blocks Man from fully perceiving facts/truths pertaining to the victim side of his reality. Setting men up to be the "tougher" sex effectively blocks Man from perceiving his own fear, pain, and vulnerability—turning many males into mules with lives "nasty, brutish and short." In playing the "hero," Man is more respected at the cost of being less loved.

For millennia women have done their best to affect an angelic, chaste, sweet, weak, pure and demure persona because this is the female persona that maximizes the male response to love, protect and provide. Woman's status as "victim" makes it very hard to reframe her in the role of villain. Thus Woman's shadow side becomes very hard to perceive. In playing the "*innocent* victim," Woman holds the moral high ground and is more loved at the cost of being less respected.

Women's tears tend to melt men's hearts. Woman has feigned weakness and victim status to evade blame and further her power to manipulate. The cost of appearing weak/victimized has been high, but the brutal nature of the world of the past induced women to pay the price willingly in return for some measure of insulation from that brutal world. Only in recent history, when the struggle merely to survive has been largely replaced with the struggle to self-actualize, has protection lost its value to the point where it can now be reframed as "oppression." If women have adopted what feminists perceive as submissive and passive personae, they've done so partly in response to men, but mostly to serve their own matrisensus purposes.

The Deal set Woman up to be dominated by Man and set Man up to be manipulated by Woman. When Woman manipulates, she plies influence by pulling strings that can't easily be traced back to her. In so doing, she sacrifices credit in order to avoid blame. Woman is as ego-invested in beauty/grace/goodness as Man is ego-invested in toughness/strength/courage. Thus blame is anathema to Woman. Blame accuses a woman of lacking goodness, which is equivalent to accusing a man of lacking courage. For this reason Woman has been willing to forgo credit for the sake of evading the blame she so abhors.

Women will tend to deny it and feel insulted when accused of working manipulation because, again, to accuse women of being manipulative is to cast aspersion upon their goodness. Patricia Pearson says it best: "Female aggressive strategies are never valorous, for they are by necessity underhanded, and partly because of that, they run completely counter to the way women want to view themselves."[546] These never-valorous but always-underhanded strategies do not inspire respect. However, such strategies may be employed without sacrificing lovability. No matter how she may have schemed and manipulated husband Ricky, *I Love Lucy*, and so do you. Applied right, manipulative strategies can be quite beguiling and charming.

Gazing into the mirror-opposite, we see that, like Woman, Man has also affected a persona. In large part, men feign strength and courage to further their power to dominate. In so doing Man seizes credit at the cost of absorbing blame. The Boss, the one with The Power, is referred to as The Man—an epithet rarely applied with affection. Domination strategies sacrifice lovability but, in compensation, those same strategies may well inspire respect. Men have adopted their tough, commanding, and confident personae, partly in response to women, but mostly to serve their own patriarchal purposes.

We are conditioned to rail automatically against the "sexism" of using the word "manipulative" to describe women. But, is it any more derogatory to accuse women of being manipulative than it is to accuse men of being domineering? If to dominate is to impose one's will over another through greater force, then domination is ethically indefensible. Male domination and female manipulation may be judged equally negative behaviors, make for equally pejorative aspersions and are about equally representative of reality.

The *true* sexism is found in the unequal protection women receive, from criticism, from accountability—protection even from those truths women would rather not hear. When we readily accept the idea that men are domineering, but recoil at the characterization of women as manipulative, we are only demonstrating our heightened sensitivity to anything that even *hints* at criticism of women.

Criticism of women is "sexism." Criticism of women is "male chauvinism." Criticism of women is "misogyny." Criticism of *women* is *forbidden*. This virtually universal stance is itself highly sexist.

What would happen if we dared take motherhood power seriously? "I reaffirm and celebrate woman's ancient mystery and glamour. I see the mother as an overwhelming force,"[547] says Camille Paglia, and I agree. Historically, what might Mother have done in service to Woman's purposes? How might she have worked her influence and to what end?

Says Esther Vilar, author of *The Manipulated Man*:

> She takes care that man is directly trained for a particular purpose: he must work and put the fruits of his labor at her disposal. Woman has had this aim in view throughout the upbringing of her child, and she engenders in him a series of conditioned reflexes which cause him to produce everything to satisfy her material needs. She does this by manipulating him from his first year of life. Consequently, by the time his education is complete, man will judge his own value by woman's estimation of his usefulness. He will be happy only when he has won her praise and produced something of value to her.[548]

I admit to only slight exaggeration when I claim that everything Man is, everything Man does, is—consciously or unconsciously—motivated by a desire to impress women, win female approval, and gain sexual/emotional access. What is Mother's role in this? What has Woman's overall force of influence been and how has she worked this influence? A vast body of evidence suggests that up until fairly recently in human history, average parenting was characterized by *extreme* levels of neglect, abuse and brutality toward children. In my next book, I'll argue that the evolution of human mothering is the evolution of human empathy and mental health—an evolution of profound import equal to the evolution of human technology.

It can fairly be said that Man has dominated virtually every culture, in every time period. But that is not so meaningful a statement as it first appears. If we open our minds to the many modes of Female-Power, we may come to the realization that Woman has manipulated every culture in equal measure.

At the outset, women will probably understand this better than men. Like Vilar, Patricia Pearson has an intuitive understanding of female power. "The history of Western women," says Pearson, "is a history of subterranean narratives. Through the centuries, we have fulfilled our ambitions and expressed our bids for power in a manner concealed from men."[549] Through the centuries, Woman has pulled strings that cannot easily be traced back to her. And of this Man has generally been only *partially* clueless.

> In peasant societies where men monopolize all positions of public power, anthropologist Susan Rogers observes that women have a great deal of *informal* influence. Indeed, neither men nor women in these communities believe that men actually rule women. Rogers concludes that men and women sustain a rough balance of power, and that male dominance is a myth.[550] [Emphasis in the original]

If men monopolize all positions of public power, then male dominance is no myth. The *myth* is that Man's dominance stands *alone*. The *reality* is that Man's dominance is *matched* by Woman's "informal" matrisensus influence. Marion Kranichfeld demonstrates how this matrisensus power may be better understood:

> It is evident from a comprehensive reading of any body of literature dealing with power that women are rarely portrayed as having power, *except where and to the extent that they hold the types of power that men generally wield*, in other words, economic, religious, or political power. Power appears to be automatically defined as whatever rights men have that women generally do not, and by this definition, women are indeed powerless. When power is viewed from a different perspective, however, it can be seen that women in fact have a great deal of power, of a very fundamental and pervasive nature; so pervasive, in fact, that it is easily overlooked.[551] [Emphasis in the original]

Yes, males wield more *Male*Power (MP) than females do. And, *equally*, females wield more *Female*Power (FP) than males do.

"In fact, women do not just change the behavior of others," asserts Kranichfeld, "they shape whole generations of families. This power to mold the lives of those around her exists over much of a woman's life, from early parenthood, in raising and shaping her children; to parenthood with adolescents, when she serves as a bridge between the generations above and below her."[552] As compared with monolithic, overt, objective MP; FP is like snow flurries; the ubiquitous, pervasive, covert subjectivity of which allows this "*informal* influence" to slip by "overlooked."

If *we* will not overlook FemalePower, yet another analogy is in order. If power is compared with butter, then Man's "butter" is drawn toward the middle of his "toast" while Woman's "butter" is spread thinner but wider. Examining her "toast" for signs of FP, we find only a thin and seemingly unimpressive layer everywhere we look. By contrast, in the form of a centralized lump of "butter," MP appears monolithic. But the *least* powerful *men* on earth (soldiers, prisoners, laborers) tend to be the least powerful *people* on earth. Man and Woman have power in equal shares but MP is largely confined to the male elite, while FP is more evenly distributed among women in general.

Because they are both effective, both sexes make use of *both* manipulative and dominance strategies to get what they want (ordinarily, men and women work these strategies subtly and harmlessly). Woman generally prefers not to work her power to achieve domination, in part to avoid the many and severe costs that go with domination (blame, corruption, incarceration, assassination, etc.), but also because domination isn't usually Woman's most effective *modus operandi* for wielding power. Men and women generally wield power in different ways because men and women generally possess different *kinds* of power.

In part, men have leaned more heavily on domination because the less evenly distributed kinds of power men tend to possess (physical strength, wealth, titles, status, prestige, etc.) best lend themselves to domination. And women have leaned more heavily on manipulation because the more evenly distributed powers women tend to possess (sexual leverage power; the power that comes of granting or denying men's only access to physical/emotional intimacy, home, family, and parenting; the power of presumed innocence; the primal power of motherhood; the power accorded under the influence of chivalry; the greater power to elicit empathy and inflict shame; verbal/emotional acuity, moral authority, etc.) best lend themselves to the strategies of manipulation.

Woman wields power "in a manner concealed from men," because her manipulative strategies work best when plied covertly.

If a woman subtly intimates that doing her bidding is apt to be rewarded with "sexual favors," a man is apt to do anything she wants him to do. But imagine a woman stating outright: "See these breasts? If you want 'em you'll do as I tell you!" Not an approach that's apt to work very well, is it? To be maximally effective, the man must get the hint that doing the woman's bidding may be rewarded with "sexual favors," but then he must be encouraged to think that doing what the woman wants is *his* idea. Again, "Do what I tell you or I'll withdraw my motherly love" is not an approach that's apt to go over well. But if he *fears* the loss of his mother's love, the male may do what he believes his mother wants him to do, yet believe that he does so out of his own volition.

Thus the male ego is used upon the male, *and* the male ego is preserved so that it can be used upon him again later. The male ego investment in toughness, strength, and courage can only be preserved if it goes unchallenged by *direct* assault. If a woman achieves domination over a man, the man's ego crushed, he becomes passive and less subject to shaming.

Male power, in contrast, is not diminished by the direct approach. "Do what I tell you or I'll put my fist in your face" is apt to work quite well. "Do what I tell you or I'll fire you . . . I'll bust you down to private . . . I'll arrest you;" the direct approach imposes *many* costs, but it *works* for men. The direct approach doesn't work so well for female modes of power. "Do what I tell you or I'll devastate you with an accusation of cowardice"? If a woman is forthright about it, her power is diminished.

No wonder we know so little about female power. It only works to its fullest when kept relatively invisible.

But, in keeping female power invisible to men, to a large extent, female power has been kept invisible to women also. These perceptual distortions lead to a paradox: even as Woman manipulates the system, plies power over Man, and gets what she wants, often times she *feels* powerless just the same. Even if she wraps her man around her little finger, a woman is apt to feel that she does what she does exactly *because* she has "no power." In her rage at having "no power" she may destroy a man with her weaponry and *still* insist that she has "no power."

It is as author Jack Kammer has observed: "It's tough to trust a person who holds a club behind her back and says, 'A club? What club? I don't have a club.'"[553]

A woman may tell herself, "This is what I must do because I'm powerless" (men, of course, have sought to dominate women out of a similar inner sense of powerlessness). In truth, without power, manipulation cannot be worked effectively. Vast throngs of slaves, convicts, prisoners of war—the *truly* powerless—cannot ply manipulation to get their wants and needs met. Manipulation is the recourse of those with *covert* powers—powers that may be more subjective and deniable in nature but are no less *real* for that. Without their many and varied modes of covert female power, women would not now nor would they have ever had the underlying power needed to work manipulation.

Of course, not *all* women experience themselves as powerless. Some are *very* conscious of the power that underlies manipulation. Herb Goldberg quotes such a woman:

> "Men are easy to manipulate," Sue Ellen, a Texas "blond beauty" told me matter-of-factly. "Most men are starving for a woman to feed their ego, making him feel like he's the best. Successful men are so vulnerable and easy to get to and control that it's hard to understand why some women think men are so difficult. The problem those women have is that they take men too seriously. They're mechanical, love-starved, defensive little boys. If you remember that, act accordingly, and limit your expectations, you can get next to almost any man."[554]

Note the woman quoted is a "blond beauty." This woman's power to manipulate is supported by sexual *power*, not powerlessness.

She sees men for the highly vulnerable and controllable people they are and plies her covert powers with full awareness. Sadly, however, she does not take *responsibility* for her power. Perhaps that's because she has conscious awareness of female power within a cultural landscape lacking that same awareness. She doesn't take responsibility for her power because *her* power has no *official* existence.

As women increasingly add male modes of power to their power base, some women, fearless of consequences, are becoming more forthright. Model Nickie Yager presents herself as a prime example. The words in italics are the words of the interviewer:

> I like having sexual power over powerful men. I love knowing that I can tease them and that they want me so bad. When you know that someone desires you sexually you can get away with a lot. . . . Yeah, I know when I'm driving someone crazy, and I enjoy it. I know it's so vicious and wrong but it's one of my biggest turn-ons. *What if they really beg?* You've got to turn them down if they beg for it. When a man breaks down enough to beg you know you can take advantage of that poor fool, so why bother? *Have men fought over you?* Yeah, they have. When I was a teenager, my new boyfriend and his friends manhandled my ex-boyfriend. I didn't see the actual fight, just the aftereffects. I felt sorry for my ex because he got beat up but I also felt he was asking for it because I had terminated the relationship and he wasn't accepting it."[555]

Might some women be a bit lacking in sexual *humility?*

One of masculism's greatest challenges is to bring FemalePower to common consciousness in both men and women. Only when "the jig is up" and Woman's power is *officially* revealed, studied, taught within academia and discussed forthrightly throughout the most respected sources of news and information; the home, the schools, and the government, will Woman come to *own* her power and accept accountability. Until then, Woman's shadow will freely abuse her power and men and women will suffer accordingly.

The Domestic Realm

In my experience facilitating personal growth work, I've been privy to the intimate stories of dozens of men and women. On a weekend we call Path to Spirit, a process called Life Review begins with the individual's experience of Mother and Father in childhood. I commented once to a fellow facilitator: "It seems like about 70 percent grew up in homes where the mother ran the show and the father hid behind his newspaper." He looked at me like I was crazy. "It's more like 90 percent," he said.

Female domestic power is enormous. In an interview with Bert Hoff, Robert Johnson (Jungian analyst and author of the books *He, She,* and *We* about masculine and feminine archetypes) said, "[Women] are stepping into [power] roles as men are retreating and becoming wimpish. I grew up in a family like that. My mother ruled, and my father said 'yes'. That's very common—almost a stereotype for post-World War II marriages."[556] Guy Garcia quotes thirty-two-year-old television producer Kevin Morra:

> What appalls him most is the knowledge that so many swaggering he-men can be reduced to cowering lapdogs by a woman's disapproving glance. "I do feel that men are losing their backbone," he says. "Nowadays I find men so easily contained and leashed by women. They no longer just do things they want to do. They ask permission.[557]

But what does this *mean*, "men are *becoming* wimpish" . . . "Men are *losing* their backbone"? Evolution hasn't hyper-accelerated in the last few decades, has it? Men haven't evolved into something "wimpish" or "spineless." *Men* haven't changed. The balance of gender *power* has changed and male *behaviors* have changed accordingly.

But the male ego may be preserved even so. Phyllis Schlafly illustrates with this anecdote:

> The story is told about the husband who proudly told his friends: "When my wife and I were married, we agreed that I would make all the major decisions, and she would make the minor ones. I decide what legislation Congress should pass, what treaties the president should sign, and whether the United States should stay in the United Nations. My wife makes the minor decisions—such as how we spend our money, whether I should change my job, where we should live, and where we go on our vacations."[558]

As Esther Vilar pointed out, the more powerless men become, the more irrationally and desperately men cling to their illusions of power. But the MP/FV paradigm is not a lifeline that would save men; it is the anchor that would sink them. Believing men have *the* power is *the* reason power is taken from men and given to women. Marjorie Campbell, attorney and speaker on social issues, knows female power:

> My mother-in-law once asked me disapprovingly, "Why are you so direct and confrontational with your husband? You should know by now he doesn't like it. It's no way to get what you want." She added with a twinkle in her eye, "You know, dear, I have everything I always wanted in life, but I always made sure it was my husband's idea!" I laughed a troubled laugh, wondering which of us followed the better path, reluctantly noting her long, successful marriage of more than 55 years.[559]

Say what you will, the old *balance* of power was functional.

Being an attorney, Ms. Campbell has "male" dominance power aplenty to get what she wants using the direct approach. Has she sacrificed "female" manipulative power? Hardly:

> I know many faithful women who steer, lure and outwit the men in their lives regularly. It's a strategy that seems to come naturally to my gender, married or single, and traces of it appear at startlingly young

ages. And, much to my own chagrin, I've caught myself in the same act. Indeed, it was not my intention to teach my only daughter how to manipulate her father, but it came so naturally – the lessons were done and mastered before I realized the subject.[560]

The direct approach, "Do as I tell you and, in return, I'll stroke your male ego," might not be the best approach for traditional modes of female power but, "Do as I tell you or I'll lay waste to you in divorce court" is apt to work extremely well.

What happens when women can control their men *indirectly* through manipulation *and* control their men *directly* through domination? If "so many swaggering he-men can be reduced to cowering lapdogs by a woman's disapproving glance," it can *only* be because these men know perfectly well that the women in their lives wield *more power* than they.

"Which do you prefer," Marjorie Campbell asked her husband, "being tricked and beguiled as your mother does your father, or my direct, to-the-point style?" After considerable thought, "I suppose," he finally concludes, "that I don't mind your manipulating me, as long as your objective is good and I don't know about it."[561]

Permit me, if you will, to expand upon Mr. Campbell's answer: "I suppose, given the choice between being controlled both directly *and* indirectly, I would prefer only being controlled indirectly. It wouldn't be the true *balance* of power my parents have enjoyed so successfully for so many years but, at least, it would preserve a *semblance* of balanced power. At least I might retain my illusions."

Woman Right/Man Wrong

Here's a story that may help illustrate female power as it commonly manifested within a traditional domestic setting. Author Harry Stein recounts a tale told by his father regarding his mother.

> "When we had a fight, she used to go into a dark room and smoke cigarette after cigarette, thinking all kinds of black thoughts. It used to drive me crazy."
>
> I laughed. "I remember. She'd be in the living room. Only I didn't know you were fighting."
>
> He nodded. "I thought she was so miserable, I'd keep apologizing just to get it over with. Not that the apologies necessarily worked. She usually had to go through at least a short period of being self-righteous."
>
> "Why'd you apologize if you didn't think you were wrong?"
>
> He laughed. "Who says I wasn't wrong?"[562]

Well, *I* do for one. I say that being male does not mean being "wrong;" even if—all too often—it does mean being *made* "wrong."

Author/researcher Richard Driscoll, Ph.D., asserts that "Women dominate in marital arguments about twice as often as men dominate."[563] I submit that Stein Sr. had two choices. He could admit either to being perpetually overpowered or perpetually "wrong." Being perpetually over-powered equals being a "wimp." Being perpetually "wrong" equals being a "bastard." Given the choice, men will choose "bastard" over "wimp" simply because a "bastard" is potent and "masculine," and attractive, but a "wimp" is a "sissy."

In every domestic conflict there are two perspectives, hers and his. Each perspective is based on judgment. When the judgments of one consistently prevail over the other, it's less likely to be because one is more "right" than the other and more likely to be because one is more *powerful* than the other. Man isn't "wrong" because he's morally inferior. Man is "wrong" because, within the domestic setting, he isn't empowered enough to stand firm within his own male perspective.

Dr. Driscoll has dedicated himself to the study of these matters. He tells us that "in those totally lopsided arguments in which only one argues, *by a ratio of 6 to 1,* it is the women who demand and scold and the men who are being scolded."[564] [Emphasis in the original] "At home, men routinely sit through harangues that demonstrate women's greater verbal skills and emotional agility," says Daphne Patai. Anyone, "hearing one woman say heatedly to another, '. . . stood there like a tree and said not a word!' knows that a man is being described."[565]

Those who've attended New Warrior Training Adventure weekends are known as "warriors." Within the New Warrior community it is customary to raise one's hand when one resonates with what another is saying. In groups of New Warriors I have often stated aloud: "Many men feel as though they've never won an argument with a woman ever in their lives." Invariably, the men smile and giggle—and raise their hands. "If a man says something in the forest and there's no woman there to hear him, is he still wrong?" Men make a joke of it because that's how men cope ("*He laughed.* 'Who says I wasn't wrong?'").

But what if men set glibness aside for a moment and expressed their politicized perspective *vulnerably?* "Society begins to emotionally disable men from the moment they are born," says Mike Adams, "and by the time they are grown they are practically helpless against emotion used by women as a manipulative tool."[566] Through the use of verbal/emotional, domestic, parental, and sexual power, Mrs. Stein *overpowered* Mr. Stein—but he could only make a "joke" of it.

It's not just women who are in denial of female power. Indeed, all of humanity appears to recoil at the very notion.

When a man displays bravado to cover his fear, we call that "macho posturing." I submit that Mrs. Stein's "period of being self-righteous" is an example of "femisa posturing," where "femisa" is a made-up word to mirror the word "macho." If the word "macho" refers to inauthentic, exaggerated, or otherwise negative attitudes and behaviors attributable to men, then the word "femisa" refers to inauthentic, exaggerated, or otherwise negative attitudes and behaviors attributable to women. If Mr. Stein's posturing protected his "fragile male ego," then Mrs. Stein's posturing protected her "fragile female pride."

Because women are every bit as ego-invested in holding the moral high ground as men are in holding their ground in the face of danger, it's as difficult for a woman to admit that she was "bad" as it is for a man to admit that he was "weak."

"Off the Couch and Back in the Bedroom in One Easy Step," intones a print ad. "Don't just *tell* her you're sorry, *show* her with the Stauer Apology Stone Ring." Why is it in the husband's best interest to apologize? "I only have two kinds of guy friends: those who know how to apologize and those who got divorced," the ad explains.

> Whoever said "True love means never having to say you're sorry" has obviously never been married. Nobody's perfect. Everybody makes mistakes. Change that . . . *you* make mistakes. That's just human nature. Unfortunately, as men, our "husband nature" forces us to make mistakes more often. Believe me, we've all been there.[567]

Remember that print ad from AT&T consisting of a photo of a payphone and a caption that read: "You were wrong; call her"? John (*Men Are From Mars, Women Are From Venus*) Gray's phenomenally popular books on gender instruct men in the art of apologizing to women through the use of "nadjectives" (negative adjectives): "I'm sorry, I was *rude*." "I'm sorry, I was *selfish*," and so on.[568] [Emphasis in the original] Needless to say, the notion of *women* apologizing is never broached.

Men may be doing most of the groveling, but it is not the "mistakes" that are out of balance—it is the *judgment* of those mistakes that's out of balance. It's not that wives are more "right" than husbands; it's that wives are more *powerful*, which is why wives banish their husbands to the couch or the "doghouse," not the other way around. So husbands either accept their wives' judgment and apologize accordingly or face the specter of divorce court. The ad copy and advice are out to sell something and operate from a shrewd knowledge of this basic gender reality—a gender reality confirmed by some serious research.

In 1998 a team of researchers headed by renowned University of Washington psychologist John Gottman studied factors that best predict marriages that fail vs. stable lasting marriages:

To their surprise, the authors found that men "should forget all that psychobabble about active listening and validation. If you want your marriage to last for a long time . . . just do what your wife says. Go ahead, give in to her. . . . The marriages that did work all had one thing in common—the husband was willing to give in to the wife." The researchers also appear to believe that this fact is a fairly recent development in marriage dynamics, coinciding with "the loss of power [in marriage] that men have experienced in the last 40 years."[569]

Within the world of women, Woman has *always* had more power than Man. But, within the world of men, Man always had more power than Woman—resulting in a functional *balance* of power. As that overall balance of power continues to shift, Man is evermore diminished in *every* realm, including the domestic realm.

The Toilet Seat issue is a highly symbolic and representative example of the WomanRight/ManWrong assumption. We *could* judge Woman's insistence that the toilet seat be kept down an example of Woman's femisa attitude. We could judge it a prim and prissy desire to avoid the gritty reality of the human animal's need to excrete as compared with Man's more straightforward, no-nonsense acknowledgment of reality—whether that reality is "pretty" or not. *Judgments are just judgments;* they *feel* important, but usually they're just . . . *judgments.*

Having adjusted the driver's seat forward to accommodate her shorter legs and lesser reach, what wife will readjust the seat back to her husband's specifications after each use of the car they share? What husband is empowered to insist upon such a thing? She who is *with* power is "right;" he who is with*out* power is "wrong." So, in accordance with *her* convenience and *her* sensibilities, the toilet seat is kept down and men who fail to abide buy gifts with which they hope to buy their way out of the "doghouse."

Domestic Sexual Power

Joan Sewell's book, *I'd Rather Eat Chocolate: Learning to Love My Low Libido,* offers an in-depth look at the dynamics within a contemporary marriage. Here, Joan describes her title-affirming inner experience of sex with husband Kip:

> It certainly isn't the case that Kip's not a sensitive lover. Kip knows what makes women tick sexually. . . . And there he is down there, licking my thighs, kissing my breasts, and giving me proficient, thorough tongue—again, not my thing, but maybe I could just get used to it. Again, there were times I'd have a twinge here and there, and sometimes I would come, but even then I just wanted him to get it *over* with. . . . I didn't care about having an orgasm—just get off of me.[570]
> [Emphasis in the original]

Erotic heat cannot be conjured through reasoning. Eroticism is a neurochemical *illusion* conjured by hormones, an illusion that Prozac can cause to vanish. It is not logical, but biological. One feels it or one does not. Lacking libido, the fiery ecstasy and erotic romantic *passions* of sex are incomprehensible. Instead, sex is apt to be experienced as an awkward, or repugnant, or perhaps even humiliating chore.

One day, Joan discovers husband Kip's hidden box of pornography: "was he trying to stab me in the back for not giving him enough sex?"

> There were soft-core magazines like *Playboy* . . . there wasn't *Hustler* or *Genesis* or something worse in the box. Indeed, the thought that it could've been worse didn't even enter my mind. This was bad enough. It was worse than bad. I lost it."[571]

Sewell's immediate reaction is to call it quits. She wants her unrepentant husband out! Kip melts into tears and tries to explain:

> He didn't really need the porn—he just used it to ride out the empty spans in our sex life. "So, what're you telling me? If I had sex with you every day, you wouldn't need porn? I'm driving you to it, right?" "No—well, sex every day—yeah, I probably would need porn a lot less." Thanks. My fault.[572]

No, not Joan's "fault"—no need for the judgment that makes her "wrong"—but, rather than framing reality solely in terms of being a victim "stabbed in the back," how would it be if she owned her share of accountability as equal partner in this dynamic?

"I said I'd throw them out. Okay?" says Kip. "Why? You ain't staying here. You're going, remember?" replies Joan. "He looked at me and said with grave sincerity in his voice, 'I don't want to go.'"[573]

According to Anne Moir's research, "women end romantic attachments more often than men."[574] All other things being equal, if the woman severs relations, it would seem the man is probably at fault in some way. If the man still clings, then the woman must be the one doing things right. On that basis it will appear that she is more often "right" and he is more often "wrong."

> "Kip," I said, smiling and shaking my head as if he were a little boy. "Kip. I don't need your apology, I need you to understand." I was hoping to get my moral authority back.[575]

Moral Authority is an important aspect of female power. Still, that authority is eroded somewhat when Joan is forced to admit that, prior to marriage, "I guess I led you to think I liked sex more than I did."

> "Well, even so, we were already in love with each other." He looked at me hopefully. "At least, I'm in love with you." It was hard not to be touched by that.[576]

Sewell is a good person. She reveals herself courageously. She soul searches. She feels guilty, relents, and allows Kip to stay.

To Joan, *Playboys* are no minor infraction. Among other things, they are emblematic of women being objectified and victimized—but her perspective being *valid*, does that make it *righteous?* Consider an alternate perspective: "If you get teary-eyed about exploited pornography workers," says author and free-speech advocate Laura Kipnis, "and haven't thought much about international garment workers, or poultry workers—to name just two of the countless and quotidian examples of those with less than wonderful working conditions—then maybe your analysis needs some work."[577]

Given that men, working the harshest most hazardous labor, are 16 times more likely to die on the job than women, perhaps Sewell could afford to let go of a little victim and shift a little empathy?

One of the many relationship-straining byproducts of feminism is the "righteousness" ("femisa" attitude) it tends to instill. But, on the human level, there's no such thing as "righteousness." Under equalism, women like Joan would still fight pornography (a *worthy* cause, not a *righteous* cause), but they'd do so with a little more humility.

In *every* Women's Issue they'd recognize the following two elements missing from feminist analysis: 1) For every female complaint there is an equal-opposite male complaint. 2) For every female complaint there is female complicity (i.e., women *choosing* to work in the sex industry because they find *being* desired powerful and erotic, plus the path is relatively quick, easy, and lucrative).

Feminism doesn't make women righteous; it makes women *self-righteous* and self-righteousness places a tremendous strain on the long-term stability and viability of any relationship. Joan seethes at every sexualized image of women they encounter then pounds Kip with feminist rhetoric. And, "I have to agree with you or you just go berserk."[578] But it's not her going "berserk" that Kip fears most.

On the basis of lessons learned, Kip lives in fear that either he agrees or it's "over." It's what I call the Tyranny of Indifference. Who is "right" and who is "wrong" have little to do with it. All other things are *not* equal. The blunt truth of the matter appears to be this: women end romantic attachments more often than men because, on average, women love/need/desire men less than men love/need/desire women.

It's not that lacking libido renders a woman loveless, but look at it this way: if a man experiences the woman he's with as a source of erotic bliss and rapture, he will want to cling to her through thick and thin. If, on the other hand, the woman he's with inspires no such flames of ecstasy, he will put up with less and be quicker to end the relationship. Surely this self-evident truth holds for both sexes.

Apparently, only about one-third of women are both hetero and *sexual* enough to view sex as a *valuable* erotic gift a man has to offer. For the other two-thirds, sex is experienced as a merely pleasant diversion at best or . . . at worst? "I love him. But sometimes I can't stand it," says a woman quoted by Sewell. "Sometimes, I'll be lying there and tears are coming down my face. . . . I think of leaving him, but then I can't. I just can't."[579] "Compare victims' reports of rape with women's reports of sex," comments University of Michigan law professor Catharine MacKinnon. "They look a lot alike."[580]

Far from providing an ecstasy that would bind a woman to a man, for some women the sex men offer is only a misery that would induce them to want out.

Author of *Divorced Dads*, Sanford Braver, Ph.D. cites Constance Ahrons' findings as corroborative of his own: "She found that no matter how it was measured, whether it was who made the decision, who actually filed for divorce, who brought up the suggestion of separation, or who made the first visit to a lawyer, it was the woman who most often was the initiator."[581] Moreover, "It is well accepted," states Braver, "that women are better at seeking and maintaining social support from friends, family, and associates than men, who generally have far less skill in building such networks."[582]

The facts of the matter are well known. "After a breakup," says columnist Michael Hendricks, "men have higher suicide rates, they're more likely to get fired from their job, and they're more likely to need counseling or therapy."[583] But his interpretation of the facts—"The reason for that is that most breakups are female initiated"—is derailed by the need to evade hard truth. Men don't suffer breakups so because they are female initiated. If Hendricks is right and, following the breakup, "we men hurt deeper and longer than you women would ever believe possible," then men hurt deeper because men love women that much more deeply and the breakups are female initiated because women love men that much less.

According to the standard antipathy interpretation, men are said to be more "emotionally dependent" upon women than the reverse. Consider: if a mother loses a child and is rendered inconsolable, suicidal, and dysfunctional with grief, will we honor her for the depth of her love or will we mock her for her "emotional dependence"? When a man loses the woman in his life and the man is rendered inconsolable, suicidal, and dysfunctional with grief, will we honor him for the depth of his love or will we mock him for his "emotional dependence"?

Surveys tell us that while 77 percent of married men, if they had it to do over, would marry the same woman; only 50 percent of married women would choose to marry the same man.[584] Collectively, we're able to wrap our minds around women respecting men more than men respect women but we recoil at the equal opposite truth: men love women more than women love men.[a]

Reality Check: Of course, every aspect of this dynamic also exists in reverse. Some women are extremely sexually desirous, *more* libidinous than some men (just as some women are taller than some men). Some women are more emotionally dependent upon their men than the reverse and may be induced to grovel under the threat of abandonment. But I'm here making the assertion, backed by corroborative evidence, that the Tyranny of Indifference impacts men *more* than women and generalizes out as a significant source of female interpersonal power.

While the average imbalance in emotional dependency (love) is primary, the average imbalance in sexual desire is a related contributing factor. *In general*, ending romantic attachments will come a little easier for large numbers of women—women who fake their orgasms—women who would "rather eat chocolate"[b] than have sex with a man.

Eroticism may be only one, but it is one of the more *potent* ties that bind—it adds sacredness to lovemaking—it is the difference in feeling toward sister vs. wife. To whatever extent love and sex overlap and intertwine, it stands to reason that men, with their greater average sexual need/desire, will tend to love/need that much more deeply and passionately.

Kip tries to explain how the culture bombards him with erotic imagery and he can't *help* but respond to it. "All that testosterone drives the 'Man Trance,'" says neuropsychologist Dr. Louann Brizendine, "that glazed-eye look a man gets when he sees breasts. As a woman who was among the ranks of the early feminists, I wish I could say that men can stop themselves from entering this trance. But the truth is, they can't."[585] Clearly, the male's flesh-lust is alien to most women.

---

[a] The archetype of Man looms as large within the psyche of Woman as the archetype of Woman within the psyche of Man. On that level It All Balances Out. But this truth opens onto territory that will have to wait till book 3, *Love and Respect in the Present*.

[b] According to a survey published in *Redbook* magazine (February 2007, p. 21), 70 percent of women said they would rather have chocolate than sex. Similarly, Ann Landers famously asked women, "Would you be content to be held close and treated tenderly, and forget about 'the act'?" "Yes" was the answer given by seventy-two percent of the over ninety thousand women who responded. [From her column dated January 15, 1984. See, *Time* magazine, January 28, 1985, p. 76] Incidentally, these assertions (exaggerated but not false) are *very painful* even *frightening* to men, which is why men reject them.

For women, who feel nothing comparable, a sexual starvation, drive, and *vulnerability* that would compel a male to drop a hard-earned week's wage at a Gentleman's Club, just to gawk at breasts, is quite incomprehensible. So feminists like Joan project nefarious ulterior motives: phone sex, pornography, prostitution—they *must* be all about "degrading and subjugating women"!

I believe that this non-comprehension of male sexuality underlies all manner of male-female misunderstandings within myriad settings.

Well, says Joan, "He might enjoy his truckload of vicarious thrills, but I thought he should have a nice dose of guilt to go with it. Because I'm just that kind of woman."[586] Could that be a femisa attitude I'm hearing? Throughout her book Sewell expresses outrage for being made to feel guilty or inadequate for lacking desire, yet Kip should feel guilty and inadequate for *possessing* desire?

"Wouldn't it be wonderful," muses Joan, "if men were urged to fall in line with women's sex drive rather than vice versa?"[587] Indeed, wouldn't it be wonderful if the world were made perfect for women without regard for men? Neither sex enjoys being judged and found wanting. Low libido should not be regarded a "defect" but the consensus is not irrationally targeting Sewell out of misogynist hostility.

Anyone and *everyone,* male *or female,* who has ever experienced sexual ecstasy, will want more, not less of it. Of *course* the doctors, therapists, and "sexperts" focus on raising Joan's libido. The cultural consensus is only being *reasonable* when it expresses a preference for Joan to join with Kip in passionate erotic union rather than for Kip to join with Joan in, what . . . sexless indifference?

The *preference* is reasonable, but the underlying *assumption*—that a woman's low sex drive may be increased psychologically—is generally *not* reasonable. Even so, the "sexperts" all insist that Joan's low libido has its origins in some event, some trauma from Joan's past. For curiosity's sake, Joan asks Kip the same probing questions she's been asked. It turns out Kip has a past *filled* with sex drive inhibitors. He went through a religious phase accompanied by fervent prayers for release from sexual desire and the resultant damnation he feared. He went through an acne phase that left him feeling ugly and shunned. Kip suffered every trauma believed to dampen female libido, yet Kip has oodles of libido. Joan suffered no such traumas, yet Joan has almost no libido. How can this be? Simple: Kip is male, Joan is female.

Yet, "Never shall we admit that women have much lower sex drives than men," fumes Joan. "Never."[588] And, so long as we never admit that women have lower average sex drives, we will never officially accept this reality as the source of an officially acknowledged female Sexual Power.

Women's lower average libido is outside women's control and should be accepted for what it is (and the larger implications culturally acknowledged and reckoned with). *And*, that same cultural acceptance should be extended to both sexes.

Actually, from Captain Kirk to Bill Clinton ("womanizers" who can't "keep it in their pants"), the male libido is the target of vast cultural contempt and ridicule. In fact, "The impulse on the part of radical feminists in trying to censor pornography is based at least in part on their fear of and their desire to dehumanize male sexuality," says Cathy Young. "Male sexuality is seen as evil."[589] By comparison, consider how emphasized is the "virgin" in the *Virgin* Mary (i.e., the Blessed *Virgin*). From Glinda to Gandhi, the ultimate in moral perfection (an angel) is *never* lustful but always assumed "chaste" and "pure."

Contrast *that* with the presumption levied upon Mirko Fischer. Seated next to his pregnant wife on an airplane awaiting takeoff, he's ordered to change seats owing to his being seated next to a 12-year-old boy. "This policy is branding all men as perverts for no reason . . . I was made to feel like a criminal in front of other passengers. It was totally humiliating,"[590] Given the standard airline policy of reseating men seated next to unaccompanied children, I'd say the "monstrous male libido" has been pathologized quite a lot, actually.

Could it be that Joan is a bit more aware of the "arrows" aimed at women than the "arrows" aimed at men? How might Sewell have developed such a profound perception of female powerless victimization without developing a perception of *male* powerless victimization? "I changed a lot after taking some consciousness-raising women's studies courses in college," says Sewell, "traditional feminism had become my creed."[591] Along with the feminist consciousness-raising, might there have been a little self-righteousness-raising?

How does Kip experience Joan's religious adherence to feminist ideology? "You're just . . . *controlling*, is all," says Kip.

> "Telling me what I should think. How I should think about women and society and how I should react. . . . You have to make political statements each and every time. It wears on me. . . . Your nonstop complaining during a Victoria's Secret bra commercial or because there are women jiggling on TV. Or any show or movie with sex in it. I can't even watch a movie with you anymore."[592]

"That's because the women are always the sex interest," says Joan.

According to feminist ideology, Woman's supremacy in beauty and innate desirability is strictly a matter of FemaleVictimization. And Kip had better adhere to the feminist "creed" . . . or else! But what of Kip's *male* perspective? What of the insult to the psyche that comes of deprivation/invalidation of one's *own* true inner perspective? In arguing their personal differences, Joan has a library-full of feminism to quote from while Kip has only what he can come up with off the top of his head—she wins; he loses. But what if Kip had undergone masculist consciousness-raising within Male Studies courses?

Let's imagine one possible outcome.

What if Kip went over to the bookshelf, pulled out a romance novel and said, "What about *your* pornography?" We imagine Joan saying, "*That's* not pornography, that's 'romance.' It's not obscene and it doesn't exploit men." But Kip, his consciousness raised, is armed with rhetoric of his own: "A look through the full range of men's pornography reveals that while young and beautiful are preferred, women of *all* ages and body types are well represented.[a] But in Men's Studies I learned that even an exhaustive search through Romance Novels cannot be expected to find a love interest described as anything less than an Alpha Male, a "billionaire Fabio." *Your* pornography shuts out 99.5 percent of men; I find *that* obscene. Another thing Romance Novels have in common is a heroine who feels innately *entitled* to take from rich men *far* more than she gives. It's also obscene how often the word "rape" is found in the title (followed by an exclamation point). Not for nothing are these novels also known as "bodice rippers." Rapists are "hot;" Nice Guys need not apply. Even worse is how often Romance Novels employ the formula: brother, husband, father dies; sister, wife, daughter takes instant possession of the man's hard-won economic empire. Women catapulted to wealth and political power through the fantasy of a man's convenient death: I judge that obscene and, in spirit, highly exploitive of men," says Kip.

While we cannot know what Joan's reaction will be, the primary *fear* is that she'll respond with something like, "Fine, now pack your bags and get out." If I exaggerate, I do so to make an important point: I believe that men's aversion to masculism derives in large part out of men's vague yet deep *fear* of being placed in ideological conflict with the women in their lives. It seems likely that Kip can only remain in

---

[a] See *Over 50* (over50.com) and *Plumpers* (plumpersandbw.com), magazines that doubtless sell as well to men as *Playgirl* sells to women. Note also the popularity of "amateur" porn, "milfs" "gilfs" and so on. Unlike the impossible standards imposed on romance novel Alphas, average porn starlet standards are hardly superhuman. A friend who prefers porn featuring "ordinary" looking women explained to me that he experiences beautiful women as too far out of reach. Emblematic of male sexual humility, "ordinary" looking women, being more credible, often fuel a more potent carnal fantasy. The nonexistent reverse would be women who preferred Romance Novels featuring men who are shoe salesmen, house painters, or middle management.

relationship with Joan if he conforms to the politicized *female* perspective. And he can only do that to the extent that he remains ignorant of his *own* politicized perspective.

The Tyranny of Indifference typically manifests as a game of brinksmanship. "Women are more willing to initiate conflict, more willing to escalate conflict," writes Richard Driscoll, while men "tend to placate, concede, or withdraw."[593] This is so partly because men tend to be emotionally/verbally outmatched, but also because men tend to fear the relationship's loss more deeply. In the minds of men, a woman's rapidly escalating emotionalism (going "berserk"), often carries an implicit threat: placate, concede, withdraw—or it's *over*.

In her mind's eye Joan conjures two images that even she responds to: "Mel Gibson as Mad Max. Yeah, when he was wearing tight black leather and had sidearms strapped to his thighs." And, "A Native American man in a sleeveless, ribbed T-shirt, with long, long black hair."[594] Powerful, wild, impulsive, dangerous, *masculine;* the exact antithesis of Kip, the neutered post-feminist male.

Finally, Kip and Joan come to an agreement. Sex will be under Joan's complete control. Brief intercourse will end the moment Joan wants it to end. Joan will "tease" (*being* desired is the one aspect of sex Joan truly enjoys) to whatever extent pleases her and Kip will provide his own orgasms. Given Joan's dislike of sex, that's about the best she can do. Some sex is better than none, so Kip is agreeable. But, as feminism has taught us, the acid test for revealing sexism in any scenario is simply to reverse genders.

If Kip were counting out 30 strokes and declaring "that's all you get," would we not see MalePower/FemaleVictimization? If Kip viewed sex as a gift he parcels out to his grateful wife, would we not see male arrogance, female powerlessness, and sexism?

> "I know you like to be in control," he said. "No, you're making it sound like I like to be in control of you. That's not it. I just want to be in control over what happens during sex. There's a difference." I was frustrated by my own inability to get the finer aspects of my point across. "Don't make this into a personal power issue."[595]

Given feminism's exclusive adherence to the truths of MP/FV, now is most definitely *not* the time to bring up the issue of personal power.

Sexual power might not be the *kind* of power feminists choose to *define* as power, but it is a power men must contend with; it is a power toward which men are *extremely* vulnerable; it is a power that has bent the will of many a man. If, in their relations with women, men are not even empowered enough to think and speak out of their own male perspectives, then men are *not* the sex with *the* power.

Sewell controls the relationship sexually. She determines what is and what is not "true" in matters of gender ideology and ethics. She is entitled to Moral Authority. In addition to his share of breadwinning, Kip also does almost all the cleaning.[596] All this and Sewell has yet to add motherhood power to her arsenal.

This is not about "Man Right/Woman Wrong." The problem lies neither within Joan nor Kip, but within a feminist gender belief system that indoctrinates MP/FV and responds by taking from men much of their desirability. As a result, heterosexual relations are tending to become less equal, workable, and sustainable.

"Arrows" #5: Tiger Woods – The Endless Grovel

I happened to be visiting a friend in the hospital and, catching sight of the image on the TV, I asked that the sound be turned up. I kept it to myself but, I confess to you the reader, what I saw and heard was an "arrow" that triggered me no end.

The following is an edited transcript of the speech delivered by Tiger Woods and broadcast globally February 19, 2010. Please note that I do not approve of adultery. At the outset, for the sake of this argument, I ask the reader to set aside Tiger Woods' guilt or innocence and simply bear witness to an endless, *endless* grovel:

> I want to say to each of you, simply, and directly, I am deeply sorry for my irresponsible and selfish behavior I engaged in. I know people want to find out how I could be so selfish and so foolish. People want to know how I could have done these things to my wife, Elin, . . . Elin and I have started the process of discussing the damage caused by my behavior. As she pointed out to me, my real apology to her will not come in the form of words. It will come from my behavior over time. . . . . I am also aware of the pain my behavior has caused to those of you in this room. I have let you down. I have let down my fans. For many of you, especially my friends, my behavior has been a personal disappointment. . . . For all that I have done, I am so sorry. I have a lot to atone for. . . . Some people have speculated that Elin somehow hurt or attacked me on Thanksgiving night. It angers me that people would fabricate a story like that. . . . Elin has shown enormous grace and poise throughout this ordeal. Elin deserves praise, not blame. The issue involved here was my repeated irresponsible behavior. I was unfaithful. I had affairs. I cheated. What I did is not acceptable. And I am the only person to blame. I stopped living by the core values that I was taught to believe in. . . . I felt that I had worked hard my entire life and deserved to enjoy all the temptations around me. I felt I was entitled. Thanks to money and fame, I didn't have to go far to find them. I was wrong. I was foolish. I don't get to play by different rules. The same boundaries that apply to everyone apply to me. I brought this shame on

myself. I hurt my wife, my kids, my mother, my wife's family, my friends, my foundation, and kids all around the world who admired me. . . . Achievements on the golf course are only part of setting an example. Character and decency are what really count. Parents used to point to me as a role model for their kids. I owe all of those families a special apology. I want to say to them that I am truly sorry. . . . I recognize I have brought this on myself. And I know above all I am the one who needs to change. I owe it to my family to become a better person. I owe it to those closest to me to become a better man. . . . I have a lot of work to do. And I intend to dedicate myself to doing it. . . . Starting tomorrow, I will leave for more treatment and more therapy. . . . I need to regain my balance and be centered so I can save the things that are most important to me: my marriage and my children. . . . I do plan to return to golf one day. I just don't know when that day will be. . . . I ask you to find room in your hearts to one day believe in me again. Thank you.

To express my gut reactions to the above, I'll present the speech as I, wearing my masculist "hat," heard it. This—infused as it is with sarcasm—is my emotional (angry) take on the *essence* of what I heard Tiger Woods broadcast to the world:

> I want to stand here tonight before the entire world and abjectly apologize over and over and over again for being male. I feel the need to express *nothing* other than *endless* mealy-mouthed groveling to atone for my maleness (My Fault, My Fault; My Grievous Male Fault). I (the male) am absolutely wrong; she (the female) is absolutely right. I don't deserve to breathe the same air as my "better half." Rumor has it that she was in some way complicit, responsible, or flawed. But I take Full Responsibility. I was dirt. I was trash. She is only to be worshiped as a perfected being and I am only to be reviled as loathsome. As part of the intensive therapy to fix my maleness I'll be castrated, after which I know I'll be a much better person. All that matters lies within the world of women. Perhaps if I grovel abjectly enough, I'll regain access to the only world that matters. Thank you.

Why was I so angry? While watching, I felt myself and my kind attacked and condemned by yet *another* dose of ManBad/WomanGood, WomanRight/ManWrong—assumptions that have reached truly prejudicial levels.

Everywhere I turn, it's flatter the female/shame the male; I just can't stand it anymore. Suicide is already the seventh leading cause of death among men.[597] How much more shamed are men supposed to be? If lustfulness is akin to sinfulness, what is the reflected verdict on men and masculinity? But the most galling aspect of all this is the degree to which Woods acquiesces to female perspective while owning no part of his own *male* perspective.

In witnessing one of masculinity's finest brought so low as to practically crawl upon his belly while flagellating himself, I believe many men had an emotional reaction not altogether dissimilar to mine: if even Tiger Woods can be brought so low for fear of losing the tenuous connection to his children (his children under his wife's ownership), what chance would *I* have? I use these "arrows" essays to vent *emotion*—my own and what I imagine to be the emotions of other men. In the big picture, it all balances out between men and women, but there remains one rage-worthy aspect of gender that does *not* balance out and that is the profoundly one-sided belief system.

So let's present the speech once again, this time infused with the *male* point of view missing from the real speech. Is Woods so irredeemable as to be bereft of a valid perspective? I'm in no position to judge Tiger Woods the man. I've never met him. I don't claim to know what The Truth is. Supported by various media quotes (see notes section), with tongue in cheek, here's my fantasy of what Tiger might have said had he stood as resolutely within his male perspective as a feminist stands resolutely within her female perspective:

> I learned early on that success was the key to gaining dating equality with women. In my youth I garnered little female attention.[598] And beautiful women were *way* out of reach. Even now, if I came to their door delivering a pizza I wouldn't rate a second glance. Truth is, the *power* of female beauty *scares me to death!* I have *no* such power. To compensate, while you were all out living life, I spent my youth hitting golf balls—ten hours a day, seven days a week. At considerable sacrifice to all other aspects of my life, I managed to rise up and gain success-appeal enough to even the playing field, even with beautiful women. *Sex! Wow!* I went crazy. I was like a kid in a candy store! But I'd become a super-*golfer*, not a Superman. To all the men who so piously judge me, here's what's true: it's easy to stay faithful when the women you want most are hard to get. But when women who make you ache with lust are all over you—and I'm not talking about some ambiguous flirting that may or may not be real, may or may not pan out—I'm talking about insanely *gorgeous* women *clearly* giving themselves to you; you'd cave just as I did! Those women are not powerless victimized children in need of protection; they are powerful adults in need of accountability. They pursued me with full knowledge of my marital status. In their eroticism they plied an *enormous* force of influence. And, for their time, they were *well* compensated. I was so overawed by my future wife, so nervous about asking her out, that I had a friend do it for me.[599] Though she was only a smalltime model, a clerk in a clothing store, and a nanny; her status as self-assured beauty was *so* powerful that, even in possession of extraordinary fame and fortune, I still didn't really feel equal to her. Indeed, for a year, she

rejected my advances as I stood in line behind any number of men all gaga over her.[600] I owe her nothing for the success I had already achieved before we ever met. Being neither naïve nor foolish, she knew when she married me, a world-class success object, that fidelity was not to be among the *expected* rewards. I have, however, secured for her and for her children a future guaranteed of vast wealth and status. Through me, she has gained access to the social environs of the world's most famous elite. That's why she married me (with the likes of Michael Jordan, Oprah Winfrey, and Bill Gates in attendance) and that's what I delivered. How can her take in the marriage bargain be regarded inadequate? Additionally, I've showered her and our children with love and kindness. For giving so little she has received so much. I see no monumental basis for her complaining and playing the victim. Am I a "sex addict"?[601] I'm a *male*, a male hetero*sexual*. Like other men, I'm torn by a profound ambivalence. I'm as steeped in the sentiments of loyalty and monogamy as anyone. *And* I experience sex with resplendent women as the single most exquisite ecstasy this earthly reality has to offer. I'm vulnerable to women who freely offer what I crave. There's good and bad about everything. The same testosterone-driven male lust that drove me to the pinnacle also caused me to seek additional sexual outlets. *And* it was that same male lust that supported the marriage bargain whereby my wife (plus nothing) equaled myself (plus stratospheric skill, accomplishment, fame and fortune). While drunk in lust I took the vow, as every husband must. But *I'd* risen high enough to escape the fate of sexual starvation that is the true if unspoken norm among men. Under the circumstances, I refused to accept solely what sex my wife squeezes from an eyedropper. For being a genetic celebrity my wife gained access to extravagant wealth and she cashed in. For being an *earned* celebrity I gained access to a wide variety of sexual ecstasy and *I* cashed in. That's *fairness,* as I see it standing resolutely within *my* point of view. I live in *here*. I look out at the world through *these* eyes, and this is what *I* see, what *I* feel, and what *I* experience. Thank you.

The above perspective is *mascul*-ist, not *femin*-ist. Shocking, isn't it?

Even in certain instances such as this where common wisdom would have us believe that the male is simply irredeemable and could have *nothing* to say, a non-righteous yet valid/vulnerable male perspective may well exist if only men were enlightened enough, empowered enough, and courageous enough to speak it. For good reason, some readers will be appalled; but others will throw a fist in the air, elated at long last to hear something from the other side of the coin.

Perhaps, read side by side, the sharp contrast between them will cast Tiger's actual speech in a new light?

As I experience it, we're currently enveloped within a matrisensus, feminist gender belief system wherein it's all too easy to antipathy interpret men and masculinity as "wrong," "guilty," "at fault," "culpable," and "punishable." I'll illustrate by imagining a mirror-opposite scenario played out within a mirror-opposite belief system.

What if Elin had grown up in a world in which it was femininity—not masculinity—that was subject to ruthless accountability sans compassion? What if Elin was obligated for honor and had that honor used against her to make *her* feel "wrong," "guilty," "at fault," "culpable," and "punishable"? In the grand scheme of things, neither Tiger nor Elin matter much where gender issues are concerned. I don't know them. I don't know The Truth about them. I'm *using* them as famous examples with which to explore gender truths in the Big Picture.

Supported by various media quotes, what follows is my masculist fantasy of what *Elin's* grovel might look like:

> I want to say to each of you, simply, and directly, I am deeply sorry for my irresponsible and selfish behavior I engaged in. I owe a special apology to a certain young man (you know who you are). You and I were equivalent in education, status, charm, resources, beauty—equivalent in every way. That equivalence bonded us in true love *and loyalty*. Together we could have built a lasting marriage. But I did not prioritize love and loyalty. I was weak. I was foolish. When presented with a ring holding a diamond as big around as my finger, I caved in to temptation. I *rejected* you, my male equivalent, because *I* could do "better." Exploiting my female beauty power/his male sexual vulnerability, I "married up" to a man of *far* greater wealth and status. Why should you weep for me being cheated upon? From your point of view, I got just what I deserved. In betting on a man who had already crossed the finish line and won the race without me, I sacrificed righteous entitlement. Yet I shamelessly cried "victim." In my arrogance, I thought being female entitled me to anything and everything a man could *ever* give me. I divorced that man and took him for at least one hundred *million* dollars.[602] In so doing I set an example to Womankind: Don't seek after well-earned respect. Forgo honor and just use "victim" power to get what you want. Of course I was awarded full custody.[603] I'll be taking our children with me to Sweden.[604] I want to apologize in advance for the self-righteous and vindictive parental alienation I intend. I want to apologize for being a very poor role model for women in *many* ways. In giving up my personal ambition to become a child psychiatrist,[605] I helped encourage yet another generation of women to become the "victims of a (sexual) trust fund." Through my example I sent the message: Be like me; don't put yourself through many grueling years of hard work and study in the mere *hope* of fulfilling high ambition, not when you can more easily use female wiles to simply *marry* hard-working risk-taking ambition! Though there's "never an excuse to hit a woman," I thought being female entitled me to break the rules and boundaries that apply to everyone.[606] I'm sorry the

women of Sweden[607] and certain feminists[608] acclaim me as their avenging hero. No cheated-upon husband who went after his wife with a golf club would ever be regarded a "hero" by either sex. I'm sorry my example was used to send the message: If you're female, it's OK to resort to violence. Thank you.

Hold Woman under the same high-power judgment microscope, hold her equally accountable, and *her* grovel might be as endless as *his*. With Woman and Man, it's not the Good and Bad that are so out of balance, it's the accountability and compassion. Apply accountability and compassion evenly, and the Good and the Bad come out even.

Even so, while Tiger's grovel was everywhere regarded as appropriate, in the world as we know it, *Elin's* grovel is *inconceivable*. Tiger acted poorly. Tiger's grovel was so painful to witness, not because he was so blameless, but because "Tiger's" grovel (i.e., *Man's* grovel) is so *omnipresent* in my world while "Elin's" grovel (i.e., *Woman's* grovel) is so *nonexistent*.

"I don't get to play by different rules," says Tiger. "The same boundaries that apply to everyone apply to me." Perhaps, but before we declare the subject closed, let's dare take a closer look at those Rules and Boundaries. Recently, it can seem as though the entire male elite might be brought down in a maelstrom of sex-scandal shaming. The cover of *Time* (May 30, 2011) asks: "What Makes Powerful Men Act Like Pigs." *I* ask: How is the MB/WG illusion sustained?

Staying within the Rules and Boundaries, the woman married to an elite male—reading her *Better Homes and Gardens*—gets what she wants most: financial security, leisure, luxuries, maids and nannies. With minimal effort, she claims primacy within her domestic and parental realms. But the elite male—hiding his stash of *Playboys*—does not get what he wants most. Year after year, the elite husband must forgo relatively easy access to what is likely to be his one most obsessive, gnawing desire. He falters *one* time, and he's a "pig."

By contrast, *if* two-thirds of women "would rather have chocolate than sex," then the majority of women require no great moral superiority to stay sexually faithful. *If* women more often abide within the marital Rules and Boundaries—one of many ways the MB/WG illusion is sustained—it's because limiting sex to the monogamous confines of marriage has been a Rule and Boundary of female design that women profit from more and suffer less than men.

As it stands, even if a man should rise to the level of President of the United States (e.g., Bill Clinton), he's *still* not allowed a blow job. Unlike the man, the Rules and Boundaries are unimpeachable. What does that tell us about FemalePower?

Who can doubt that if Woods had uttered the defiant words I gave him, the repercussions would have been brutal. If he were not actually stoned to death right on the spot, at the very least, he would have been reviled, disowned, outcast—the loss of his endorsements and his children a foregone conclusion. Even so, it may have been worth it. For, "What shall it profit a man to gain the whole world and lose his soul?"

Men . . . speak your truth! As is the case with female perspectives, male perspectives needn't be "righteous" to be valid. Because male truths are the truths that are *missing*, if Tiger had offered even a *few* well spoken truths—culled from his own inner *male* perspective, the defiance might have been remembered as courageous, perhaps even heroic—paving the way for other men to stand strong. In choosing instead to express *nothing,* other than groveling apology, Woods threw away an opportunity for a different kind of greatness.

The vast span of difference between what Tiger actually said and what he *might* have said is representative of the vast gulf between men's perceived, internalized *powerlessness* to stand firm within their male perspectives, as compared with the *power* women wield to own and to speak out of their imperfect feminist perspectives—on any and all matters of gender—and be rewarded, not punished, for it.

As always, Woman is accountable for her ideological dictatorship and Man is accountable for acquiescing to it.

"Henpecked"

Feminist ideology depends heavily on how reality is *defined*. Accordingly, Domestic Violence (to be addressed shortly) is defined as a male-on-female violence through which "patriarchy" "subjugates" women. There are, however, alternate perspectives. Camille Paglia:

> As a feminist, I detest the rhetorical diminution of woman into passive punching bag, which is the basic premise of the "battered woman syndrome." Men strike women for quite another reason: because physical superiority is their only weapon against a being far more powerful than they.[609]

During her experience masquerading as a man, Norah Vincent came to much the same conclusion:

> Sex is most powerful in the mind, and to men, in the mind, women have a lot of power, not only to arouse, but to give worth, self-worth, meaning, initiation, sustenance, everything. Seeing this more clearly through my experience, I began to wonder whether the most extreme men resort to violence with women because they think that's all they have, their one pathetic advantage over all she seems to hold above them.[610]

Perhaps physical size/strength *is* Man's only *innate* power advantage over Woman. Historically, muscle power lent Man enormous innate power—especially as seen from Woman's perspective (arguably, it was in response to male muscle power that Woman developed such formidable verbal/emotional weaponry). Within a modern context, however, it is indeed a rather pathetic advantage.

Upon physically overpowering her, his brief experience of power may cost him weeks or months of abject apologizing. Should police arrive at his door, his extra size and strength will only add to his presumed guilt. Once the legal machinery has entered the picture, the costs levied in exchange for a moment's triumph may now stretch on for a lifetime. Within intimate relations, Woman is innately *more powerful* than Man.

Her manipulative powers are *so* great, she has rigged the whole game in her favor. Yet Woman looks upon Man in decline and she is incredulous. *Manning Up: How the Rise of Women Has Turned Men into Boys*, responds Kay Hymowitz with evident derision. Here we are poised to elect a woman President of the United States, yet only men must Man Up and be accountable for their effect in the world?

In any case, men have not changed; cultural conditions have changed. They've changed because Woman has changed them.

The notion of men "becoming wimpish" or "spineless" is an illogical evasion of a far more unacceptable reality: men are *overpowered*—overpowered by *women*. It is exactly because this truth is so *repulsive* that we have yet to come to grips with it. Richard Driscoll cuts through gender illusion to reveal the missing half of gender reality:

> Men ordinarily hide their weaknesses and present themselves as in charge, wanting to seem strong even when they typically lose the arguments or withdraw to avoid losing. Women find it hard to respect men who fold in arguments. And women who see themselves as mistreated underdogs, fighting for a fair break, do not want to acknowledge that they usually defeat their opposites in personal confrontations. So as men and women, *we collude to conceal how we are and to show ourselves instead as we wish to be seen.* We hide behind social masks and create agreeable myths about ourselves. And we are taken in by our own fabrications, mistaking our myths for reality.... How far we will go to see men as more powerful![611] [Emphasis in the original]

To men everywhere I say this: incredible as it may seem, *there is no shame in being overpowered by a woman.* In addition to newly acquired economic/status power, Woman's arsenal includes: the ideological power of feminism (in the absence of masculism); the powers of presumed innocence and moral authority; closing ranks with *her* children against the husband/father; manipulative applications of shame; threatening false accusations, restraining orders, and divorce court; summoning the police . . . truth be told, wives have access to a vast weaponry few husbands can match.

Additionally, a woman's superior powers of sexual, emotional, and verbal manipulation will often leave a man putty in her hands. The phrases "pussy-whipped" and "henpecked" acknowledge this female power even as they trivialize it, thus dismissing it from official consideration. These phrases ply the standard trick of ridiculing male weakness to deflect attention away from FemalePower.

A man will be shamed out of all contact with fact-based reality by the unbearable thought of being overpowered by a harmless little "hen." The fact-based reality he's lost contact with, however, is this: within the *matri*sensus realm of *matri*mony, even the strongest men may be over-powered by a woman—"a being far more powerful than they."

We're told, "Behind every great man, there's a great woman." But we turn a blind eye to the many implications. Women have not always been governors and senators, but women have always been wives and mothers of governors and senators. It rarely occurs to us that the woman behind the man might have power over the man and thus, to varying degrees, his power might actually be *her* power.

Indeed, some unknown percentage of the MalePower in various leadership positions is and has always been FemalePower.

John Lennon

By now the reader is familiar with the vast realities of female power and male victimization. Even so, feminists would have you believe that "*Woman Is **the** Nigger of the World.*"[612] "We make her paint her face and *daaance*" screams Lennon in a paroxysm of male self-recrimination. It is particularly interesting that this should be a John Lennon song (co-credited to Yoko Ono) since, in the world John grew up in, the five Stanley sisters—his mother and four aunts—ran the whole show. The men handed over their paychecks and tried not to get in the way. Julia Baird, John's half-sister and author of *John Lennon, My Brother,* provides a look into Lennon's world.

Because his mother Julia wasn't up to it, John's Aunt Mimi raised him. According to Ms. Baird:

> Mimi, as the eldest, was always the family spokeswoman. After her mother died she had become the matriarch. As in many other country families, the women were the backbone of our family. They took all the decisions.[613]

Country families, city families, what's the difference? Says author and educator Elizabeth Herron, "if we look at who runs families, who runs the emotional life of families, who has the power when it comes to decision-making around the children, it's women, by and large."[614]

John's Aunt Mimi provides a case in point: "She put her foot down the minute she and George got married," says Baird. "'I am not going to have any children,' she announced. And she didn't."[615] And what say did her husband George have regarding a decision with such profound import upon himself and all his future life?—no say at all. Ditto the decision to adopt young John.

"Our uncles were always like that. They were never the domineering heads of the house who laid down the law. The Stanley girls were too strong-minded to put up with that kind of treatment."[616] Did this, in itself, give them the right to deal out that kind of treatment?

> And because of their particular personalities, almost the only role for the husbands was that of provider. [John's cousin] Leila explains: "The primary function of the men was to produce the money. Quite truthfully, the women were only as nice to them as they had to be for the bills to be paid. There were no rows or shouting. The men just weren't very important. It was such a very large family with all the kids about needing so much attention, these men just didn't feature."[617]

Joke: Though only *three* years older, why did Uncle George die *thirty-six* years before Aunt Mimi? . . . Because he wanted to.

Born in 1940, the world Lennon grew up in is what we call the "traditional" "patriarchal" world. Yet women ruled within the world of women. Harry Stein also grew up in "patriarchal" times, yet his father was nothing like a domineering head of the house who laid down the law. I see no compelling evidence that male rule *ever* extended into the homeplace.[618] In their efforts to cope within the *matri*sensus realm, perhaps those husbands and fathers who worked dominance strategies were just struggling to have a voice? I for one cannot condemn those traditional husbands/fathers who yelled and slammed their fists down in an effort to escape the humiliating invisibility too many of their less aggressive counterparts endured.

It's as Esther Vilar has said, "man hardly exists in a woman's world"[619] "The men were invisible," Lennon himself concurs. "I was always with the women. I always heard them talk about men and talk about life, and they always knew what was going on. The men never ever knew. That was my first feminist education."[620] Really?

So growing up in a world where men were shut out, unimportant, even invisible minions who laid down their paychecks in households ruled by women—that was where Lennon first learned that "Woman Is *the* Nigger of the World" uniquely in need of empowerment?

Too bad Lennon's early experience failed to be his first *masculist* education. But then again, maybe it was. The couple's friends report overhearing John and Yoko arguing over this very matter. Owing to his early experiences, John was *not* easily convinced of the righteousness behind women's ownership of powerless victimhood. But he relented nonetheless.

Advanced gender thinker Carol Iannone knows this dynamic well:

> The women in my family wielded enormous domestic power (too much as far as I was concerned), and even in later moments of utmost ideological fatuity, I could not pretend that they wielded this power out of frustration in not having careers. And in the family of a factory worker who labored long and hard to keep his wife at home with the children, it was difficult to make a case for the exploitation of women. Then too, if I often professed to be disappointed when men resisted feminism, I secretly found it even more disappointing when they succumbed to it.[621]

The male feminist might not be quite as impressive to women as he thinks he is.

There have always been women who wielded power within the world of men, but they have been the exception, not the rule. There have always been men who wielded power within the world of women, but they too have been the *exception*, not the rule.

Speaking like a victim, "The world of men *is* the world," says feminist author Natalie Angier.[622] But it is equally true that the world of women *is* the world. Our friend Harry Stein describes his emotional reaction to a particularly poignant John Lennon quote:

> Momentarily, I set aside the page to regain my professional bearing. No good; the concluding words of the passage were a blur, read through damp eyes; "... If I can't deal with a child, I can't deal with anything. No matter what artistic gains I may get, or how many gold records, if I can't make a success of the relationship with the people I supposedly love, everything else is bull shit."[623]

From the masculist perspective, the world of love, intimate connection, vulnerable emotion, home, family, and parenting—the world of women—*is* the world and "everything else is bull shit."

Even at the summit, at its most *freakishly* rarely rewarded, the male role enacted within the world of men is lacking certain *essentials*. While John was fulfilling the demands and obligations of being a Beatle, his son Julian grew up without his father and Lennon entered maturity without his son. Guilt and regret gnawed at Lennon for the rest of his life. Feminism victim-interprets the role of primary caregiver, but in many ways it is a powerful and enviable role. Wealth, fame, gold records, and screaming fans were a poor substitute for the love and intimacy of parenting. Doubtless, this is why Lennon chose to give it all up to stay home and raise his second child, Sean, full time.

While Yoko Ono grew up observing women shut out or rendered less-than within the world of men (the Glass Ceiling), John Lennon grew up observing men shut out or rendered less-than within the world of women (the Glass Wall). As his sister says, "John must have been very aware of this attitude toward the menfolk as he grew up."[624] Indeed, Lennon himself said that in the world he grew up in, "The men didn't count for *nothing*."

Lennon was a strong, dominant personality, always the leader of the gang. Yet, in singing "*Woman Is the Nigger of the World*," Lennon betrayed his own truth and sang Yoko Ono's truth instead. It was a case of a more powerful being (a female) bending the will of a less powerful being (a male).

In the public sphere John was far *more* powerful than Yoko. John's words were heeded; Yoko's words were dismissed. In this case, however, John's words were not *his* words. The power struggle that resulted in Lennon singing her truth instead of his own took place within the interpersonal sphere. John had his male physical size and strength power, economic power, fame power, and so on. But, in this instance, Yoko trumped all with her Emotional Intimacy power. Also, when it came to matters of "right" and "wrong," John deferred to Yoko's Moral Authority power. When Lennon sang Ono's words it was a case of *female* power channeled through a male mouthpiece.

"If I were a Jewish girl in Hitler's day," said Yoko, "I would approach him and become his girlfriend. After 10 days in bed, he would come to my way of thinking."[625] Ono's statement may be naïve, even foolish—but it is also highly revealing. It makes clear Yoko's own understanding of her special power as a woman. Yoko approached John, become his girlfriend, and after 10 days in bed, she molded him to her way of thinking.

It's like the old joke: How are men like floor tiles? Lay them right the first time and you can walk all over them for years. Lennon became an outspoken advocate of feminism till the day he died.

"We make them paint their face and *dance*," screams Lennon. Yes, men *are* complicit; *both* sexes ply a force of influence in *every* gender issue. But, in his impulse to take *Full* Responsibility, Man enables Woman's flight from accountability for her own *chosen* actions and inactions. Woman blames "Patriarchy" for the fact that her gifts come with burdens attached, but it is not "Patriarchy" that imposes the toll; it is the basic physics of human reality. In augmenting and working her feminine wiles Woman gains great power over Man. *And*, plying power over others, of *any kind*, comes only at a cost.

It's too bad Yoko Ono and other feminists haven't honor or integrity enough to admit that their bid for power is in reality a bid for *more* power.[626] One can only wonder how many male potentates all over the world, all through history, have set aside their own truths in favor of enacting oratory, policies, and legislation on behalf of the truths of their female intimates.

These are the kinds of truths that can only be dug out of the historical record by applied scholarship. But there can be no scholars, no historians devoted to searching out the evidence and the particulars of FemalePower until it is first acknowledged to exist!

To sum up: To conclude that women are just as "bad" as men is not to demonize women; it is to humanize women. Both sexes have plied their respective *modus operandi* in order to best utilize powers they've got in an effort to compensate for powers they haven't got. Dominating and manipulating may be deemed equally negative behaviors, but through their respective use, men have gained credit at the cost of being blamed while women have evaded blame at the cost of losing credit. Men have had overt power, but women have had covert power. When a woman prodded her husband into doing something right, she got neither the credit nor the prestige. But when she prodded her husband into doing something wrong, she took neither the blame nor the prison sentence.

Yes, every culture has been male dominated . . . *and* every culture has been female manipulated. It All Balances Out.

Investment in Illusion

One difficulty in revealing women's dark side is that both sexes are deeply invested in the notion that women don't possess a dark side, or even a gray side for that matter. Both sexes long to believe in female moral/ethical superiority over males.

Meet Mark Starr, former girls' soccer team coach and *Newsweek* columnist. News of the Northwestern women's soccer team's drunken hijinks has come to his attention and he is crestfallen. He begins his column waxing nostalgic over the initial feminist promise of women doing everything men do but, being superior, doing everything better and more virtuously. "The conceit was that they would imbue all they touched with a women's sensibility, which would be more nuanced, more empathetic and, ultimately, more humane," says Starr. "I confess that I more or less subscribed to that notion."

> Still, trust me on this: by virtually any standard other than sports trivia, Scrabble and the ability to grill medium rare, I don't measure up to any

of the following people—my mother, my wife, my daughter. But while I am certain I am right about those afore-mentioned individuals, the ascension of women hasn't produced anything remotely as glorious as the feminists or I once contemplated. It turns out that power corrupts with no apparent regard for gender, that ambition can be indiscriminately corrosive, that competitiveness brings out the best in both men and women—and, apparently, the worst. There is plenty of evidence now that women at the helm of a nation are every bit as tough and bloody-minded as their male counterparts, that female soldiers can also defile their honor codes, that women corporate bosses can be petty tyrants and that women athletes will resort to steroids and abuse their bodies to excel in sports.[627]

Well, Mark . . . I do *not* trust you. I for one do *not* accept as an article of faith that you are simply inferior to the women in your life. Nor am I inclined to believe that your passionately held assumptions of inferiority do your mother, your wife, or your daughter any service. Must men be such "Uncle Toms" where women are concerned?

What we have here is a guy who seems positively crushed to discover that his much-cherished inferiority to women might not be all he had hoped. Starr epitomizes the sentimental longing for female moral/ethical superiority that I suggest is virtually universal. I feel it too. But I feel no sentimental longing for female superiority in *all* things. That sentiment is something new in our world.

When Starr asks, "Why are women athletes in college choosing to mimic the worst behaviors of their male counterparts?" we see that his sentimental attachment to female superiority may have taken a hit, but it still lives. Women, having no "badness" within themselves to draw upon, can only behave badly by "mimicking" men? These women athletes weren't mimicking, they were *being*. They were acting out of the shadow side of their *own* human nature.

> To try and make sense of all this, I turned to my friend Kate, who is like a daughter to me and almost a dozen years ago was captain of her volleyball team, and who points out I might appear a little less naive had I read some of the "mean girls" and "queen bee" literature.[628]

Says Kate: "Women haven't been playing sports for quite as long and haven't had a chance to reach their full meanness. But they are going to be mean, just as men are."[629]

Lately, leaking out between the cracks, we are hearing more about "mean girls" and the sub-culture of girls bullying girls. Books like, Phyllis Chesler's *Woman's Inhumanity to Woman* (2001) and Hayley DiMarco's *Mean Girls All Grown Up: Surviving catty and conniving women* (2005), tell harrowing tales of female shadow. In her book,

Odd Girl Out: The Hidden Culture of Aggression in Girls, Rachel Simmons tells us:

> There is a hidden culture of girls' aggression in which bullying is epidemic, distinctive, and destructive. It is not marked by the direct physical and verbal behavior that is primarily the province of boys. Our culture refuses girls access to open conflict, and it forces their aggression into nonphysical, in-direct, and covert forms. Girls use back-biting, exclusion, rumors, name-calling, and manipulation to inflict psychological pain on targeted victims.[630]

We must love women enough to empathize with *why* they do what they do ("our culture" "refuses" and "forces") *and* we must respect women enough to hold them *accountable* for what they do *just the same*.

Being hidden, manipulative, indirect, and covert allows the female shadow to go relatively undetected, but it doesn't make it any less *real*. In fact, denying the human shadow only sets it free to control the individual and work its mischief through unconscious channels in the human psyche. Cathy Young supplies an example of self-righteous femisa attitude controlled by the female shadow:

> In a 1996 article in the campus paper the Daily Bruin, UCLA student Jessica Morgan calls it "creative feminism." Women, she asserts, should employ "a combination of feminist ideals and the advantages that come with being female" to achieve their ends: fall back on feminism if they feel sexually harassed but on femininity if they need to use sex appeal to get their way; refuse to defer to men but rely on them to do manly things like squash bugs. "So men are confused, and I say 'good,'" adds Morgan. "The more confused the men of this country are, the easier they are to manipulate. . . . The more easily they are manipulated, the more likely it is that we'll get what we want—whatever it is that we want."[631]

As Young herself comments: "Such frankness may be rare. But a having-it-both-ways philosophy is characteristic of much modern feminism."[632] While some espouse feminism out of a sincere if naïve belief that women truly are *the* powerless victim sex, others espouse feminism out of a conscious desire to manipulate the system, exact revenge on men, maximize female power, and get what they want—whatever it is that they want.

When we come to an understanding of masculist truths—the truths that are missing—we realize that whether conscious or unconscious, female-ism itself is a manipulative extension of the female shadow. When feminism comes to the bargaining table saying: You men have *everything*; we women have *nothing*; give us half of what you've got because that would be "fair," Woman is controlling her world through manipulation.

Battle of the Sexes

When we consider the straightforward nature of male warfare—fought with tanks and bombs and guns and missiles—the feminist allegation that Man is waging war upon Woman appears rather unsupported. Consider, however, women's indirect, covert strategies for plying aggression. Combine that with what we know of feminist efforts to infuse our world with false, defaming statistics designed to denigrate and undermine men and masculinity—tactics reminiscent of "back-biting, exclusion, rumors, name-calling, and manipulation."

Consider also efforts to infuse our world with what Daphne Patai has dubbed "heterophobia." What better way is there for Woman to attack Man than to drive a wedge that separates Man from the female emotional support he so profoundly needs? Feminist author Shere Hite paints the picture:

> Some women (sometimes called "feminist separatists") call on women to boycott men, that is, stop having relationships with men, remove their emotional support from men who haven't changed—in other words, remove their energies from men entirely, stop supporting the "male" system in all areas, including emotionally—in work, in love and any other way possible. This is a tactic that could clearly have a profound effect if large numbers of women did it. In fact, while most women would not think of themselves as "separatists," the high divorce rate, with most of those divorces being initiated by women, and women's emotional "leaving" of many marriages, even if staying physically in them, does resemble this actual position.[633]

Indeed, feminism has inflicted untold damage upon male-female relations on all levels. But, I suspect that it is the men who *have* changed (men like Kip), that run the greater risk of rejection.

Here again, notice the implicit assumption that men are so much more emotionally and sexually dependent upon women than women are on men, that it ultimately gives women the power to bring men to their knees. If women have such power, and I believe they do, then isn't the feminist's effort to make all *other* things equal an effort by these women to gain the upper hand? And is gaining the upper hand not the very essence of warfare?

Owing largely to feminist pressures, for the first time in history anywhere in the world, single-mother "families" are to be regarded as complete and equal to two-parent families in every way. What more devastating damage could Woman inflict upon Man than to disparage and minimize and marginalize his importance in parenting?

Certain female factions seek to drive a wedge between men and women, between men and children, and men and family—*and* fill the world with anti-male propaganda that blames and defames the character of Man. Taken all together, the masculist allegation that Woman is waging war against Man appears rather well supported.

It is often proffered that Man can't complain about Woman's ascension and should just accept it good-naturedly because, after all, it's just a case of Woman beating Man at his own game . . . right? Wrong—woman isn't beating Man at Man's own game; Woman is beating Man at *Woman's* own game—a game of character assassination, deception, victim mongering, rejection, exclusion, indirect aggression, verbal trickery, and manipulation.

"Somewhere in the back of the Matriarchal Feminist mind," says Nancy Friday, "there is the suspicion that if we allow men a humanity as vulnerable as our own, we women will become the brutes."[634] Nevertheless, "The assumption that women must defend themselves against an enemy who is waging an undeclared war against them," says Christina Hoff Sommers, "has by now achieved the status of conventional feminist wisdom."[635] And the best defense is a good offense?

Could it be that this alleged "war against women" has been fabricated to justify and motivate a for-real war against men? Could this supposed "war against women" be nothing more than a projection of Woman's own hostilities and ambitions? Says Sommers, "To the extent one can speak at all of a gender war, it is the New Feminists themselves who are waging it."[636]

Now . . . why does the notion of *women* "waging war" seem *so* unlikely, *so* incongruous?

The "Halo Effect"

For many years I got my hair cut by a young lady so lovely, she might have been mistaken for an angel. One day, while walking through a back alley, she chanced upon her cat chewing on a dead rat. So grossed-out was she that she had nothing further to do with that cat.

I was shocked. She *seemed* like such a "nice girl." Who'd have thought such a "nice girl" could harbor such a callous attitude? Yet, in abandoning her pet for nothing more than acting upon its nature, this young lady proved nothing like the angel she appeared to be.

Moreover, it seems to me that this young woman's "niceness" *itself* contributed to her inability to cope with that which is not "nice." As protected and coddled as she certainly appeared to be, apparently, she could not accept a non-sanitized reality. The shadow side of her human nature, a shadow she was in no way encouraged to own, snuck up from behind and acted out upon an innocent creature that failed to be "nice." Beware the shadow *not* owned!

Herb Goldberg quotes a man who has grown weary and wary of "niceness":

> "I like women better and I trust them more," said one man, "if they are direct and 'not nice.' 'Nice' women always make me feel guilty and inadequate, which makes me feel manipulated. I want to shake 'nice' women and say 'stop it! This is boring and dead and unreal. One day you'll turn on me and give it to me with both barrels and you'll say it's my fault because I didn't know how to be nice.'"[637]

Through femisa posturing Woman would disown her human shadow, but to no avail. Woman must *inevitably* possess and express her human shadow—all the *more* so if she does not own it.

As Woman is ever more called upon to *do*, *act*, and *take charge*; Woman's shadow is revealed in the same way and for the same reasons Man's shadow is revealed.

As women take on the same rush-hour stress, "women are also increasingly displaying the more aggressive driving tactics common among men."[638] The more women commute to work, the more women act out their "road rage." The more women handle company funds, the more women embezzle those funds. Exposed to the same circumstances, women fall prey to the same temptations.

> You couldn't help but like Doris Kearns Goodwin. . . . she was always charming and articulate. . . . but new revelations about the scope of Goodwin's plagiarism have made liking her a bit more difficult, and defending her impossible. On Friday, Goodwin announced that her copying from at least three other books in her 1987 book "The Fitzgeralds and the Kennedys" was far more pervasive than she first acknowledged. Her publisher, Simon & Schuster, will destroy remaining copies of the book and publish a new version, she told *The New York Times*; the new one will give proper credit to the sources from which Goodwin drew a far more vast portion of the book than she originally stated. Her excuse: She took notes and wrote the book in longhand, sometimes mixing up material from other books with her own.[639]

Though spared the pressures of supporting "a wife and children," nevertheless, the more women do what men do, the more women do what men do. They lie and cheat, steal and plagiarize.

Certain emotional/behavioral adaptations that women have made to their lover/nurturer role do indeed make women more lovable and likeable (the Women-Are-Wonderful effect). We want women to be the "innocent children" and "angels" they physically and vocally resemble (the "halo effect"), and so we protect that image. In fact, we protect it even while taking such women to task—if the plagiarizer had been a man, would we be given his "excuses"?

Dr. Farrell reminds us that women's gray side also manifests within the traditional realms of female power, albeit not in ways that are currently prosecutable. Here Farrell quotes Thomas Kiernan, author of *Citizen Murdoch,* reporting in the *New Jersey Law Journal* of his experiences while attending four different seminars for wives contemplating divorce.

> He reported that in *all* four cases, a female lawyer conducted the seminar and "recommended, with knowing winks and smirks, the 'advantages' of 'establishing' or 'creating' a 'record' of spousal violence, *whether true or not,* prior to the filing of a divorce complaint."
>
> What upset Kiernan was that a law designed to prevent domestic violence (the Prevention of Domestic Violence Act) was openly being used to falsely accuse men of spouse abuse. . . . But this is what most astonished Kiernan: "The number of women attending the seminars who smugly—indeed boastfully—announced that they had already sworn out false or grossly exaggerated domestic-violence complaints against their hapless husbands, and that the device worked! To add amazement to my astonishment, the lawyer-lectures invariably congratulated the self-confessed miscreants."
>
> Unsubstantiated and false accusations of spouse abuse or child abuse ruin a man's reputation even if he is ultimately found to be innocent. Why are men so damaged by "reputation ruining"? Men's ability to earn leads to their ability to gain love. Destroying earning potential means destroying love potential. Observe how frequently a man will die from a heart attack or cancer—or just commit suicide—shortly after his reputation is ruined. Yet these deaths are recorded as heart attacks, not husband abuse. And not murder.[640] [Emphasis in the original]

In the gender dance, *in relation to one another*: Man rejects victim /embraces shame; Woman rejects shame/embraces victim.

Because Man is deeply invested in personal honor/integrity, Man is deeply vulnerable to the applications, punishments, and invectives of shame. Man is obligated for manly standards of honor in his conduct—*especially* toward Woman. A Real Man must Man Up, says Woman. Thus, shame makes for a powerful weapon with which women can coerce, control, and punish men. Man cannot as effectively wield shaming as a weapon against Woman because in relation to Man, Woman—presuming to hold the moral high ground—rejects shame as vehemently as Man—presuming relative invulnerability—rejects victim.

I read the above and I see what comes of respect deprivation. I see the female victim within the female victimizer. I see women rendered children, acting out with all the unconscious glee of children getting the upper hand over their parents who "oppress" them.

Author Midge Decter sees this dynamic clearly:

> A husband's kindnesses and attentions to his wife, along with his concern that she be well housed and well fed and sexually gratified, are, that is to say (according to the feminist interpretation), only the plans from which he means to construct a towering edifice to his own vanity. . . . They are not, indeed, attentions to *her* at all but just a deceptive means for eroding her individual freedom. . . . This mode of standing the marital transaction exactly on its head, of repaying, as it were, kindness with the imputation of evil motive, is no everyday form of complaint. In fact, it resembles nothing so much as the tantrum of a young child who, unable to claim that he has received no parental indulgence, screams all the louder that such indulgence was meant in the first place to dismiss him and that thus his need is even greater than before.[641]

This is what comes of the infantilizing effect of directing excessive sympathy upon women while withholding accountability. As a result, Woman sets her weaponry at lethal maximum under the assumption that she is little underdog David in battle against the giant Goliath.

Meanwhile "Goliath" suffers antipathy interpretations, divorce court, heartbreak and heart attack. Woman does not comprehend herself as wielding powerful weapons against a highly vulnerable opposite sex because she has never been *asked* to comprehend gender reality in such terms. Her power has never been made *official*. Too much sympathy and not enough accountability: here we see the *true* victimization of women.

Toward the victim inside the male victimizer we must direct due compassion because compassion is what he is largely deprived of. Toward the victim inside the female victimizer we must direct accountability because accountability is what she is largely deprived of. To whatever extent men are less loved because male attitudes and behaviors render men less lovable, women are less respected because female attitudes and behaviors render women less respectable.

Does ruining a man's reputation do a man any less psychic damage than raping a woman? At least a rapist is respected enough to be held accountable for his effect in the world.

Once the accusations are made, it's easy for a wife/mother to take sole custody and with a restraining order further estrange the husband/father (now "alleged abuser") from his children. After the ex-husband/father has been falsely accused, abused, and ruined, the false accuser may indeed need a restraining order to protect her from his legitimate rage. In this way the law empowers women to destroy men, then protects them from retribution.

The shadow side of feminism has not only made it easier for women to devastate men, it has created a social-services infrastructure that often indoctrinates, encourages, even *pressures* women to rain devastation upon men. Says Barbara Dority, cofounder and cochair of the Northwest Feminist Anti-Censorship Taskforce, "The system encourages divorcing women to be vindictive."[642]

Let activist Marion Winters tell us *how* vindictive:

> When I decided to leave my marriage (I was bored) I went to three different lawyers for advice. I was asked by all three of them if I was ever abused by my husband. My answer was, never in any way shape or form was my husband abusive towards me. To my utter disbelief, all of them told me the same thing. Unless I accused my husband of abuse, I would not gain sole custody of my children. They also told me that by making these allegations against him, that I would get *everything* and more. When I asked them how we would prove the allegations, I was told that the courts don't require proof, and to go to a women's shelter, and that they would help me, and that it would support my allegations of abuse. . . . Reluctantly I took my children to a women's shelter.
>
> I couldn't believe what I was seeing. On the outside, it appears as they want the public and their funders to see it. This is, however, far from the truth. This place was a form of a cult, for lack of a better term. Male bashing was a top priority, and the administration was very adamant about recruiting yet another woman (me) to join this man-haters club. . . . By following their simple plan step-by-step, I would not only get sole custody of my children, but also the car, house and land, plus finances for the rest of my life. However, if I did not follow their game plan, but if I played fairly, I would lose everything, and I would be endangering the lives of other women, and would jeopardize any funding for them. The administration must have noticed that their brain washing techniques were not working as fast as they wanted, so I was 'thrown' at the other women staying there. Terms such as 'sperm donors', and that all men were abusive and must die, were used on a daily basis. They were very convincing, and not wanting to jeopardize my fellow housemates, I went along with their game plan.
>
> I saw the man that I was once married to destroyed emotionally, financially and physically. I was granted sole custody of our children, and because of a restraining order, I gained the house and car, so that our children wouldn't lose everything that they were used to. Not only was there a restraining order against him, he was charged with assault.
>
> The man who had equally created our children, helped raise them, and who loves them dearly, was ordered to stay away from them and to pay me (more than I ever needed) support for them. . . . My brother is now going through a custody battle, where my former sister-in-law is playing exactly the same game that was taught to me by a women's shelter, and my brother is in the same shoes that I once put my ex in. Knowing how I destroyed my ex, and seeing the wrong that I had committed, I have made it my personal endeavor to help my brother with his fight.[643]

Despite what she did, I'm grateful to Marion Winters for making it her personal endeavor to help her brother with his fight. God knows there are scarcely any men at all who make it their personal endeavor to help their brethren in the fight.

In summation: Here's the situation as I see it. Woman came to the bargaining table demanding to be given half of Man's power while giving nothing in return. As white and brown rice are just different kinds of rice, so male and female power are just different *kinds* of power. Even so, even now, Man is in the process of giving Woman half his "rice," leaving himself with one quarter and she with three quarters. We can see the results unfolding all around us. I see women who may feel threatened by men cracking the Glass Wall, empowered by social custom and societal machinery to slap those men down, put them back in their place, keep them shut out and/or less than in the world of women, and, through maternal gatekeeping and parental alienation (plied subtly or not so subtly) keep men loved *second* best.

I see high status women "owning" beauty, grace, goodness; home, family, and parenting as securely as they always have. In addition, I see higher status women taking *at least* equal ownership of intellect, competence, prestige and a sizable portion of the toughness, strength, and courage to boot. Such women leave their lower status husbands with little or nothing to call their own. I see these women divorcing those men as "inadequate." And I see men backing away in a pre-emptive effort to reject the all-but-inevitable rejection.

Toward women who are both beautiful and wealthy a man can only feel *staggering* desire. If men regard such women as unapproachable, it's because they've been given *no* reason to believe they have anything such women will *staggeringly* desire in return. It is not the beautiful/wealthy woman that is rejected; it is the hopelessly unequal *situation* that men back away from. In obeisance to the All Fault Is Male rule, men are said to be "commitment phobic." Marion Winters makes clear, however, that when it comes to marriage, men have much more than "commitment" to fear.

Men who back away from women more successful than themselves are *accused* of feeling "threatened." The word "threatened," when used against men, is a rather pitiless bit of emotional blackmail. When applied to men, the word implies unprovoked cowardice in the face of that which poses no *real* threat. Given this implication, men—highly ego-invested in courage—are compelled to deny feeling threatened, even toward that which *does* in fact *threaten* them. Once he has denied *feeling* threatened, he is unable to *act* upon that which does in fact threaten him.

Men are feeling threatened because they *are* threatened—threatened with perceived inferiority in all things on all levels; threatened with blame for all things on all levels; threatened with "obsolescence," threatened with rejection, threatened with divorce court, accusations, and restraining orders. It would seem that within the average marital situation the man is essentially at the woman's mercy. If the woman is merciful, things will probably work out just fine. If not . . .

Throughout the entire process of destroying her husband, Marion Winters may well have felt like a "powerless female." Like Man's feeling of power, Woman's feeling of powerlessness is culturally inculcated. Thanks to Myrna Blith's Spin Sisters, MP/FV bias is everywhere in the news and newspapers; it's a constant throughout women's magazines, books, talk shows, movies; it's *everywhere* in the cultural messages sent.

Only after seeing what she had done mirrored in her brother did Marion Winters finally wipe the feminist clouds from her eyes, come to *see* her weaponry clearly, and choose to take responsibility. Female Power will not be experienced as fully real until the media *makes* it real by *officially* acknowledging it. Until then, in the name of empowering the "powerless" female, the system will continue to cater to women without regard for *true* equality.

The Matrisensus in Action

For example, the Violence Against Women Act (VAWA) has within it provisions providing generous funding to what are, too often, feminist-indoctrination centers. VAWA is federally funded with taxpayer, which is to say largely male-generated, money. "At a minimum," asserts Cathy Young, "taxpayer money allocated for domestic violence should not go *exclusively* or *primarily* to organizations that espouse a view of battering as patriarchal oppression, and these organizations should not be permitted to dictate policy."[644] [Emphasis in the original] At present, however, they do both. Phyllis Schlafly:

> Advocates of the Violence Against Women Act assert that domestic violence is a crime, yet family courts often adjudicate domestic violence as a civil (not a criminal) matter. This enables courts to deny the accused all Bill of Rights and due process protections that are granted to even the most heinous of criminals. Specifically, the accused is *not* innocent until proven guilty but is presumed guilty, and he doesn't have to be convicted "beyond a reasonable doubt." Due process rights, such as trial by jury and the right of free counsel to poor defendants, are regularly denied, and false accusations are not covered by perjury law. The act provides funding for legal representation for accusers but not for defendants.[645]

In fact, the ex-husband is often required to pay for both his own attorney and hers as well! And all this is supported at the highest levels of government.

From the start, Vice President Joseph Biden has championed VAWA. Getting the legislation passed, renewed, and massively funded is, by his own public account, his single proudest achievement. "The Violence Against Women Act and related laws extract $1 billion from the federal purse and dispense the money to law enforcement agencies, legal aid programs, and abuse shelters," says Carey Roberts. So what's wrong with that? Critics allege that the act results in a veritable fountain of corruption, radical misandric feminist funding, and anti-male adjudication. In its very *name* the Violence Against *Women* Act stands in direct violation of the 14th Amendment's guarantee of equal protection under the law.

"While many rue the struggles of our nation's abuse shelters," asserts Roberts, "these pale in comparison to VAWA's effects on our nation's legal system."

> Forget everything you learned in your high school civics class about due process, innocent until proven guilty, and equal treatment under law. VAWA-inspired laws have carved out an Alice-in-Wonderland world in our legal system in which any partner disagreement qualifies as domestic "violence," in which persons never qualify "offender" with the word "alleged," and in which a person so accused can seldom restore his good name . . . This last year [Biden] introduced two new bills, the *International* Violence Against Women Act and the National Domestic Violence Volunteer Attorney Act. The second bill would farm out $55 million to the American Bar Association to sign up legal "volunteers" so they can chase more low-income dads away from their children . . . welcome to the wacky and wonderful world of VAWA, where a woman's word is proof enough.[646]

We will take a closer look at the issue of Domestic Violence shortly, but the real kicker is this: Biden himself, by his own testimony,[647] is a victim of family violence at the hands of his older sister Valerie. Carey Roberts quotes Biden:

> "In my house, being raised with a sister and three brothers, there was an absolute—it was a nuclear sanction, if under any circumstances, for any reason, no matter how justified, even self-defense—if you ever touched your sister, not figuratively, literally. My sister, who is my best friend, my campaign manager, my confidante, grew up with absolute impunity in our household." And this was Sen. Biden's bell-ringer: *"And I have the bruises to prove it. I mean that sincerely. I am not exaggerating when I say that."* I won't pretend to fathom the psychology of a man who was severely abused by his older sister, and

then later went on to champion an unconstitutional law designed, by name, to protect only women.[648] [Emphasis in the original]

What more clear-cut example could there be of female power channeled through a male mouthpiece?

Thanks in part to their tireless efforts, the rules within the home Joseph Biden and his sister Valerie grew up in are, or are becoming, the law of the land. Clearly, it is Valerie Biden's intention to extend the "absolute impunity" she grew up with to *all* women. And she has recruited the brother she beat up with impunity to make it happen!

Woman may abuse Man to any extent imaginable, but Man must not, "under any circumstances, for any reason, no matter how justified, even self-defense," take action on his own behalf.

President Barack Obama is a powerful man. But when it comes to *gender* politics, he too is largely a mouthpiece for female power.

In January 2009 he was pictured on the cover of a special issue of *Ms. Magazine*. There stands Obama in an iconic Superman pose ready to come to the rescue of women everywhere. But opening his shirt and jacket to reveal his chest, he is not Superman, but rather "Super-Feminist." The editor of *Ms.* Magazine explains: "When the chair of the Feminist Board, Peg Yorkin, and I met with Barack Obama, he immediately offered, 'I am a feminist.' And better yet, he ran on the strongest platform for women's rights of any major party in American history."[649]

From his 2008 Father's Day speech: "Too many fathers... are missing," Obama said, "missing from too many lives and too many homes. They have abandoned their responsibilities, acting like boys instead of men. And the foundations of our families are weaker because of it."[650] Too many fathers are missing, that much is certain. But, are men *solely* responsible? Again on Father's Day 2009 Obama proclaims, "I had a heroic mom," but:

> Growing up without a father left a hole in his heart, President Barack Obama told boys at the White House Friday in a remarkably personal Father's Day weekend message. He implored fathers everywhere - and the kids when they're older - to be involved in the lives of their own children . . . "Just because your own father wasn't there for you, that's not an excuse for you to be absent also. It's all the more reason for you to be present," Obama told the young men in his audience.[651]

Abandonment by his father may have left a hole in his heart, but only where men and fathers are concerned.

I for one have learned not to automatically accept the female interpretation of events. I want to hear Obama Senior's side of the story before passing judgment. Does Obama see his father through his own eyes, or, like countless other men, does he only see his father through the eyes of his mother? Obama tells us he got a basketball from his father and little else.[652] Is that why he's so misandric?

What if Obama were not a devotee of the all-fault-is-male and zero-empathy-toward-men rules? What if Obama loved men enough to lend them some empathy and respected women enough to hold them accountable?

"There's this assumption people make that if dad's not there it's because dad doesn't want to be there, and sometimes that's true, but sometimes dad's not there because mom doesn't want him to be there," says Glenn Sacks. "The vast majority of divorces are initiated by women, particularly the ones that have kids involved . . . and then once the marriage breaks up, if she doesn't want him to continue to see the children, a lot of times it's very difficult for him to have a meaningful role in their lives."[653] In *theory*, divorce law prohibits parental alienation. In *practice* . . .

> "I called my ex-wife Thursday to see what time I could pick my daughter up for the weekend," said Ben. "She laughed and hung up." Robert nodded knowingly. "My wife took my kids to Florida in April," he said. "I'm not even sure where they are." "I know where my son is," said Tom. "He lives with his mother not more than five minutes from my house. I haven't had any time with him in almost a year. I took him to a ball game just after he turned seven. We had a great time. A couple of days later, my ex convinced a judge that the kid didn't want to see me anymore. My lawyer and I have been to court I don't know how many times trying to get a judge to let me see my son or at least talk to him. We keep getting turned down." Tom's voice cracked. "She's teaching the kid to hate me," he said. "And I don't even know why."[654]

Consider also widespread damage to fatherhood inflicted upon low-income communities in the wake of past welfare program policies. Kathleen Parker explains: "Through welfare programs such as Aid to Families with Dependent Children, begun in 1935 as part of the New Deal and predicated on a no-man-in-the-house policy, the U.S. government inadvertently made unwed motherhood profitable and father abandonment predictable."[655]

Prior to reforms initiated in 1996, if a social worker found so much as a man's trousers hanging in the closet, a mother and her children could lose eligibility for welfare payments. The government reasoned that if there was a man nearby, then he ought to be the one paying expenses. But welfare checks could be substantial (especially to single mothers with multiple children) and many men, especially discriminated-against black men, simply could not earn enough to match them (and still have at least a *little* something left over for themselves). Some left; others were jettisoned.

Kate O'Beirne models for us what it'd be like to hold feminism accountable for its not-always-benevolent intentions. In her book:

> [R]eaders will meet the influential women who argued children don't need fathers, who argued that the full time attention of mothers is actually harmful to children, who argue that married women who report that they are happily so must be, "slightly mentally ill," because marriage is such an oppressive institution. I quote these women -- not marginal figures -- influential, and look at their handiwork -- given the attitudes they hold and the agenda they push -- on the current state of the American family. A third of our children born out of wedlock and half of our children will spend time during their childhood in a home without a father. It used to be that the majority of young adults believed, 20 years ago, that you should be married before you have children. Now only 40% of young women hold that view. I do attribute the weakening of the family in part to the activism of these kinds of women who are so hostile to marriage, family obligations, and the traditional roles of fathers and mothers.[656]

The legacy of welfare and tax systems that effectively discriminated against low-income fathers, feminist efforts to undermine marriage and father rights, disparagement of fathers together with the sanctification of single-mother "families," female initiated divorce, mothers blocking father involvement (before and after divorce), mothers badmouthing fathers, and women choosing single motherhood from the outset—these are among the mitigating truths as seen from the male perspective, but they will not be among the truths feminist mouthpieces are wont to utter.

At http://vimeo.com/4483467, there is footage of Obama speaking at a rally: "My daughters, and all of your daughters, will forever know that there is no barrier to who they are and what they can be in the United States of America. They can take for granted that women can do anything the boys can do and do it better." During a White House interview: "When I think about policy, I'm constantly thinking about how can we strengthen families... so that women can thrive," said Obama. "Because I think if women are thriving, then everybody is thriving."[657] But Obama's policies only strengthen *single-mother* families. When one sex "wins," both sexes lose. Women can only thrive in a world in which *both* sexes are thriving.

Unlike women—who are less powerful in some ways, more powerful in other ways; more victimized in some ways, less victimized in other ways—by *every* measure blacks comprise a truly oppressed sector of America. Yet Obama could not *begin* to express pro-black/anti-white sentiments equal to the pro-female/anti-male sentiments he expresses with impunity. Somehow, all as one, we've decided that it is all but *impossible* to be too pro-female/anti-male.

Mark Silva reports on the Obama household:

> President Barack Obama acknowledges that, in his own marriage, he and his wife, Michelle, have faced some sensitive "negotiations" in the past as to who does what, and why - the woman or the man? He also says that men tend to be "obtuse" about these matters - and "need to be knocked across the head once in a while." He "absolutely" had to learn to be more sensitive . . . "Five years ago, six years ago, we were having a lot of negotiations... because Michelle was trying to figure out, OK, if the kids get sick, why is it that she is the one who has to take time off from her job to go pick them up from school, as opposed to me. What I've tried to do is to learn to be thoughtful enough and introspective enough that I wasn't always having to be told that things were unfair," Obama said.[658]

Like John Lennon and other powerful men, does Obama reflexively bow to the woman's presumed Moral Authority? Does he automatically look to a woman to be told when things are "unfair"? In a world where *both* sexes have heads filled with feminism, while masculism remains a word rarely found in the dictionary, could it be in the realm of *men's* issues and *men's* perspectives that *both* sexes tend to be a little "obtuse"?

Could it be that Michelle isn't more righteous as much as she is, within the intimate realm, simply more powerful? What if in response to the question: "why is it that she is the one who has to take time off from her job to go pick them up from school, as opposed to me," Barack had said, "Because that's how you *earn* the parental primacy that you as the children's mother insist upon." Could we imagine *any* man enlightened enough and empowered enough to stand so resolutely within his own male perspective—and withstand the "righteously" enraged rebuke that follows? Is being "knocked across the head" all that men need? Or would a little compassion be in order?

"I'm surrounded," says Obama regarding his wife and two daughters. Could it be that when it comes to gender issues, Obama is a mouthpiece for the women who surround him and, in this regard, his male power is only female power in disguise?

The House of Representatives regular basketball game was invited to the White House—all players were male. "Some people might look at that, interviewer Savannah Guthrie told the president, and say, 'Gosh, there's the old boys club again.'"[659] Apparently, even a "super-feminist" must constantly reaffirm his feminist credentials.

It is not my intention to disparage Barack Obama. I appreciate what he has done to improve global goodwill toward the U.S. I respect his intellect, statesmanship, and leadership. I realize of course that there are *many* issues outside of men's issues for a president to address.

That said, given the extreme prejudice shown black men, given the upward assent of the black female vs. the downward spiral of the black man, it is *particularly* disappointing that a black man should succumb so utterly to feminist mythology. Statistics assert that "more African-American men are in jail than in college."[660] Black men have sunk far below black women in virtually *every* measure of wellbeing. Yet Obama offers black *men* no support, no encouragement.

In his role as super-feminist, President Obama created the White House Council on Women and Girls (needless to say, there is no White House Council on Men and Boys). From the official White House website: "The mission of the Council will be to provide a coordinated federal response to the challenges confronted by women and girls" (men and boys be damned?).

> "The purpose of this Council is to ensure that American women and girls are treated fairly in all matters of public policy," said President Obama. "My Administration has already made important progress toward that goal. I am proud that the first bill I signed into law was the Lilly Ledbetter Fair Pay Restoration Act."[661]

So, a male-only basketball game is an outrage but official, federal, permanent female-only offices and agencies go unprotested? What if yet another "Fair" Pay Act only serves to widen the *reverse* pay gap? How is that fair?

American men and boys are not treated fairly in all matters of public policy—far from it. Hyper-medicated, corporally punished boys taught using methods that favor girls, taught under a 90 percent female teaching staff, without even a recess period to work off their extra energy, are not treated fairly. Boys singled out to register for the draft are not treated fairly. But a male female-ist does not concern himself with such matters. He is a male proudly channeling *fe*male power.

We have a president and a vice president both of whom are avid, self-proclaimed *femin*ists. What sort of "*patri*archy" is that?

Nancy Friday: "When I write about the coming Matriarchy, I see its most obvious roots in the female-dominated homes today where a man's absence isn't questioned. It is, in fact, preferred."[662] Arguably, the coming matriarchy (as women add ever more hierarchical power to their arsenal, the term "matri*archy*" becomes ever more apt) is already upon us. Given that the words "men's issues" have yet to pass through the lips of any major politician, it is perfectly reasonable to view our world as a matrisensus—a matrisensus still largely administered by men—but a matrisensus nonetheless.

The significance of men administering our world is *huge* and should not be discounted, of course. But neither should this truth be allowed to supersede all other truths. Let's not forget that women majority-vote the "Patriarchy" into office, decade after decade. Let's bear in mind also that men are extra-motivated toward aggressively vying for the top slots in their efforts to achieve the status that women, especially beautiful women, are apt to hold out for—both sexually and matrimonially.

Remember the story Phyllis Schlafly told?—"When my wife and I were married, we agreed that I would make all the major decisions, and she would make the minor ones." Man makes major decisions such as, "what legislation Congress should pass, what treaties the president should sign, and whether the United States should stay in the United Nations," but an *individual* man makes no such decisions. Such decisions are made inside a realm far outside ordinary experience. Woman may make only minor decisions, "such as how we spend our money, whether I should change my job, where we should live, and where we go on our vacations." But in so doing, the average woman rules in realms wherein we actually *live out our private lives!*

And let's not forget that those major decisions are often *agonizing* decisions. Admiral Elmo Zumwalt was a powerful man. He opposed the Vietnam War but, like all military men, he had to *follow* orders. With little information to go on he was *ordered* to decide whether or not the U.S. military would use Agent Orange to defoliate Vietnamese battle zones. The result? His own son, exposed to Agent Orange while fighting in those jungles, contracted fatal cancer and his grandson was born with multiple birth defects.[663]

Even the most powerful man responsible for making the most agonizing decisions (and living with the consequences) may experience himself as but a powerless cog in the wheel.

Note also that the vast majority of male administration has nothing to do with *gender*. The major decision whether or not the U.S. stays in the U.N. is a gender-*neutral* decision. It is a decision having little effect upon the average man's or the average woman's experience of power. I'm male; what power do *I* derive out of the fact that the International Monetary Fund is largely administered by men? Isn't administration merely a task to be performed? The top administrator may get a big paycheck, but how much of that paycheck is spent by his wife and/or ex-wife?

Whenever gender *does* enter the picture, however, decision makers, be they female or male, self-identify as *fem*inists and take action to further *fem*inist goals. When it comes to what legislation Congress should pass, Obama proudly prioritizes the Lilly Ledbetter Fair Pay Restoration Act.[664] The decision to pass that legislation was a gender-*related* decision with a direct effect upon the average man's and woman's experience of power.

An average woman may decide that she deserves the same pay as her male equivalent even though she took four years off work to raise children (and ensure her parental primacy) while her male equivalent kept his nose to the grindstone. "Fair" Pay legislation empowers an *average* woman, within an average environment, to either "have it all" or sue to get it.

The men who administer the matrisensus are powerful but, for the most part, it's not precisely *Male*Power that they're wielding. These feminist men have never even *heard* of masculism. They know misogyny to be an evil in our world to be fought and never tolerated. But they know nothing of misandry.

They do not concern themselves with the *reverse* pay gap, or the compassion gap, or the sexual power gap, or the intrinsic-value gap, or the generosity gap, or the consumer spending gap, or the college graduation gap, or the majority-vote gap, or the capital-punishment gap, or the gender-related healthcare spending gap, or the life expectancy gap, or the suicide gap. There is only *one* gap that concerns politicians and that's the imaginary "pay gap." They do not concern themselves with male bashing, or male rates of work-related injury/fatality, homelessness, imprisonment, battlefield death, or men having their children taken from them. They've never heard of the Glass Wall or the Glass Floor (the Glass Floor is coming up soon).

Just because the truths of FemalePower and MaleVictimization are rejected as revolting to our sensibilities and illusions doesn't render these truths any less true. Our revulsion toward the truths of FP/MV only manages to render these truths shut out. Most of the top politicians may be male but their *gender-related focus* is directed toward the concerns, the issues, the rights, and the empowerment of women.

It is from this angle that we see the men high up in government as analogous to "chauffeurs." These men, in fancy uniforms, their hands on the wheel, appear to be controlling the machine. But, as Jack Kammer puts it, "The men in government drive Miss Daisy wherever she wants to go."[665] Wherever gender enters the picture, these administrators serve female purposes and wield *female* power—female power channeled through men. We know it's not MalePower they're wielding because *Male*Power does not seek a world made perfect for *fe*males, with *no* regard for males!

Could the domestic realm *ever* be too anti-male for the likes of Biden/Obama? As we know, mothers often smear fathers with false accusations of abuse, *especially* when those fathers seek child custody. On that basis: "In 1994, lawyers were informed by their leadership that 'Studies show that abusive fathers are far more likely than nonabusive parents to fight for child custody.'"[666] To the degree such feminist studies are believed, men who seek custody will not get custody because fighting for custody, wanting to be a real father with a real relationship with his children, has now been reframed as an indicator that the father is an abuser of his children!

Obama is dedicated to a world of fairness toward women within a world of injustice toward men. He admonishes America's young men "to be involved in the lives of their own children." He might follow that by saying: And I'll back you up. I'll champion joint custody, clear legal obstacles from your path, and bolster fathers' legal rights. But instead, in effect, he tells boys: This is what I demand of you, but I'll do *nothing* to help you. I don't care about the biases, injustices, and hurdles you face in your lives, your homes, or the legal system. My energies are devoted to empowering your sisters and backing the very feminism that has undermined fatherhood in the first place. You boys are on your own.

"We need fathers to step up," says the President, "to realize that their job does not end at conception; that what makes you a man is not the ability to have a child but the courage to raise one."[667] Imagine the father who knocks on the door of his former home only to hear his ex-wife giggling behind the door but not opening the door. What is the "courageous" father to do? Visitation is *rarely* legally enforced. The story has been told of courageous fathers who courageously force open the door, courageously *demand* their visitation rights, and bundle the kids up for a trip to the zoo as promised. The story ends hours later when these men are arrested. Their children watch as their Dad is handcuffed and dragged off to jail on "kidnapping" charges—a federal offense. Fathers don't lack courage; fathers lack *rights*.

Fathers lack rights because the men at the top are channeling *Female*Power. Blind to the degree to which the men "in charge" are ardent feminists obsessed with *Women's* Rights, men fix their gaze upon the very tip of the success pyramid, see that it is still primarily male-occupied, and foolishly reassure themselves that they are still on the side that's "winning." Seeing no need for a politicized men's movement; no need to confront Woman's ever escalating power; no need to stand firm in their own male perspective (or even learn what their male perspective *is*); seeing no need to risk ideological conflict with the women in their lives (a *terrifying* prospect); and seeing no need to come to the aid of their less fortunate brethren, men heave a great sigh of relief and plant their heads back firmly in the sand.

If Obama "ran on the strongest platform for women's rights of any major party in American history," it's because feminism's increasing stronghold keeps upping the ante required of each new president's commitment to feminism. Each new president must top the previous president's female-ist zeal or he won't get female-majority-voted into office. Thus Obama's current budget proposal includes "significant funding increases for women's programs"[668] at a time when virtually all other funding is either frozen or cut.[a]

We may soon see a time when no man could *ever* be feminist enough and the men on top will be replaced by women ("the coming matriarchy"). What we think of as "Patriarchy" is really equal parts patriarchy and matrisensus. How would men fare in a world in which The Matrisensus isn't even male-administered? What is Matrisensus/Matriarchy in the absence of an equal-opposite Patriarchy but Absolute Matriarchy—a world in which women rule not only the world of women but *every* sphere of human life?

Should the day come when high-status men are too few in number to steal focus, when (movie/sports imagery aside) just about the *only* realities cultural observation can statistically equate with maleness are things like truancy, delinquency, gangs, incarceration, war, "deadbeat" dads, rape, suicide, hard/hazardous labor, violence, pathology, Columbine, criminality, terrorism, social isolation, and homelessness; the day may have come when men are definitively, even *officially* understood as inferior to women in every meaningful way. Men, is that really the world you want to leave as legacy to your sons?

I bring all this up in an effort to sharpen our *thinking* on these matters. The point is this: *True* gender justice must be *negotiated*, not *manipulated*. And true gender justice must be negotiated under equalism, not female-ism.

It's not that Obama is without honor—just the opposite. It is exactly because Obama is so deeply invested in manly honor that he is so particularly susceptible to having his honor used against him. It's all that manly honor that turns Obama, and other honorable men, into chivalry puppets—so easily controlled, indoctrinated, and manipulated by feminism. Obama is *exactly* the kind of man to take Full Responsibility and come to women's rescue (even though it is *men* who are floundering in nearly every measure of wellbeing).

---

[a] For a thorough analysis, see Diana Furchtgott-Roth's *How Obama's Gender Policies Undermine America* (New York: Encounter Books, 2010).

He automatically looks to a woman to be told when things are "unfair." He is honor bound to give Woman half of Man's "rice" because Woman tells him that is only "fair." He is far too *manly* to ask for anything in return. Like other chivalrous men in power, he doesn't care how much MalePower he gives away so long as it doesn't affect him personally. Obama worships female superiority *and* he is male chauvinist. He doesn't respect women enough to recognize their power or their adult accountability. It is women who largely call the shots in the sexual/domestic/parental arena, yet Obama holds the respected sex *solely* responsible for all outcomes.

Marion Winters (quoted above) can afford to publicly expose her actions. Chivalrous feminists like our president and vice-president are dedicated to protecting women from retribution "under any circumstances, for any reason, no matter how justified, even self-defense." Thanks to the efforts of Joe/Valerie Biden et al., the female false accuser enjoys "absolute impunity." If it seems as if women stand above and beyond the law, this is not surprising when you consider the degree to which the law was written by chivalrous feminists.

"I'm going to marry a really rich guy, then divorce him," explains a young woman to a Toronto newspaper. "But first I'm going to have his kids, so I get child support." [669] Even the most heinous bunko artist can't steal someone's children, yet this woman's evil intention is at no risk of prosecution because the chivalrous feminists who administer the matrisensus do not define her actions as criminal. False accusations, using paternity fraud to trick a man into paying for a child not his own, fleecing a man with false promises of sex/love, or marrying a man with the preconceived plan of divorcing the man and keeping his home, his children, and his salary; because women have so many ways of wreaking devastation upon men—without legal/criminal consequences—much of the evil women inflict is over-looked when official abuse statistics are compiled.

Clearly, this relative immunity to consequences does little to encourage women to act out of "the better angels" of their natures. To whatever degree that Woman is absolved of accountability, Woman's shadow can be expected to expand along with her power. Our profound attachment to overlooking or excusing Woman's dark side means that she gets away with much that we would officially recognize and penalize if done by Man, which means that men look much worse in comparison, which reinforces our perception of women's moral superiority, which infuses a presumption of male guilt into courts of law, which increases male rates of conviction/incarceration, which results in damning crime statistics, which distorts and exaggerates perceptions of male guilt, which . . .

Women's Dark Side

We've looked at Woman's crimes and misdemeanors, but we've yet to reveal the female shadow all the way from gray to *black*.

Domestic Violence

We'll now examine the single most volatile and counterintuitive of all masculist assertions. Though it is almost universally believed that domestic violence (DV) is something initiated and perpetrated by men against women, masculists insist that DV is in reality a two-way street. Moreover, to support this claim, there is a wealth of evidence to draw upon—evidence compiled by both male *and female* researchers.

It's time now to substantiate Patricia Pearson's claim that "Women commit . . . a fair *preponderance* of spousal assaults."[670] "When the first scientific nationwide sample was conducted in 1975—by Suzanne Steinmetz, Murray Straus, and Richard Gelles—the researchers could hardly believe their results," says Warren Farrell. "The sexes appeared to batter each other about equally."[671] Not surprisingly, there followed numerous surveys, many conducted by feminists determined to prove these findings false.

> To their credit, despite their assumptions that men were the abusers, *every* domestic violence survey done of both sexes over the next quarter century in the United States, Canada, England, New Zealand, and Australia, found one of two things: **Women and men batter each other about *equally*, *or* women batter men more. In addition, almost all studies found women were more likely to *initiate* violence and much more likely to inflict the *severe* violence. Women themselves acknowledged they are more likely to be violent and to be the initiators of violence. Finally, women were more likely to engage in severe violence that was not reciprocated.**[672] [Emphasis in the original]

Though the Steinmetz/Straus/Gelles surveys indicated approximately equal male-female patterns of abuse, the media focused exclusively on the violence against women results and ignored the violence against men results. Feminists then made famous the statistic that in the United States a woman is beaten every 15 seconds. That the same number crunching from the same Steinmetz/Straus/Gelles data reveals that in the United States a man is beaten every *14* seconds went unreported.

Methodology has improved and "More precise and balanced results from the most recent National Family Violence Survey reveal a woman being severely assaulted every 17.5 seconds and a man being severely assaulted every 15.7 seconds," says Philip Cook author of *Abused Men*. "The data on male spousal abuse are generally not cited."[673] As we found in cases of FemaleVictimization reported worldwide, here again we see the illusion of women as *the* victims created and supported simply by omitting the comparison with men.

On October 24, 1999 *The Sunday Times* (UK), under the headline "Deadlier Than the Male," featured an excerpt from Melanie Phillips' book *The Sex Change Society: Feminised Britain and the Neutered Male*. The article provides an excellent distillation of the issues.

"Feminism has become the unchallengeable orthodoxy in even the most apparently conservative institutions," says Phillips. "And that 'orthodoxy' is this—'men oppress women.'"

> Buried within this doctrine, though, is an even deeper assumption. Male oppression of women is only made possible by the fact that men are intrinsically predatory and violent, threatening both women and children with rape or assault. Men are therefore the enemy - not just of women but of humanity, the proper objects of fear and scorn. This assumption runs through feminist thinking as a given. "Most violence, most crime . . . is not committed by human beings in general. It is committed by men," wrote Jill Tweedie.[674]

It is testament to the malevolent power of radical feminism that *men,* in vast numbers, have internalized this defamation of character and the self-contempt that goes with it. Phillips continues:

> According to Gloria Steinem, "patriarchy requires violence or the subliminal threat of violence in order to maintain itself . . . The most dangerous situation for a woman is not an unknown man in the street, or even the enemy in wartime, but a husband or lover in the isolation of their own home". All this has been enough to turn the stomachs of some feminists, particularly those who love husbands or sons. Novelist Maggie Gee said she once thought the sex war was exciting, but had now concluded it went too far. "Women are giving up on their relationships too quickly. Living with a man I love very much, I keep thinking that all the generalizations about men just aren't true." These generalizations, however, are now the stuff of public policy. Male violence against women, said the government in June 1999, was no longer going to be "swept under the carpet". Virtually nobody questioned the premise that men were invariably victimizers and women always their victims.[675]

Despite Steinem's misandry, women are, of course, at their *safest* within marriage. "Marriage is a strong safety factor for women," says Phillips—a point Phillips develops throughout her book. If I could I would say to Gloria ("A woman without a man is like a fish without a bicycle") Steinem a paraphrase of the words that finally brought down Senator Joseph McCarthy: "Have you no sense of decency, madam, at long last? Have you left no sense of decency?"

It is to Ms. Phillips' immense credit that she disavows these themes embraced almost everywhere else. Let it be here acknowledged that some women reject the anti-male rhetoric and hold to account those feminists who spread it. In feminist circles such women are reviled as "traitors." Those who defy feminism stand little to gain but much to lose. In *my* book, that makes these women heroic defenders of what is true and just. Throughout this book I quote *many* women, women like Melanie Phillips who model for us the kind of women that men can both love *and respect*. Says Phillips:

> There are now dozens of studies which show that women are as violent towards their partners, if not more so, than men. Unlike most feminist research, these studies ask men as well as women whether they have ever been on the receiving end of violence from their partners. They are therefore not only more balanced than studies which only ask about violence against women, but are more reliable indicators than official statistics which can be distorted by factors affecting the reporting rate - women using claims of violence as a weapon in custody cases, for example, or men who are too ashamed or embarrassed to reveal they have been abused.[676]

When the media tells you that 94 percent of domestic violence is perpetrated by men against women, I can find no evidence at all that corroborates that claim. When the media tells you that about two thirds of domestic violence is perpetrated by men against women, it is relying on Justice Department statistics showing that about two thirds of those *reported, arrested, prosecuted,* and *punished* for domestic violence are men. Melanie Phillips draws upon survey evidence that measures DV both reported *and unreported:*

> A 1994 British study by Michelle Carrado and others, for example, interviewed 1,800 men and women with heterosexual partners. Some 11% of the men but only 5% of the women said their current partner had committed acts of violence towards them, ranging from pushing, through hitting, to stabbing. Five per cent of married or cohabiting men reported two or more acts of violence against them in a current relationship, compared with only 1% of women. A further 10% of men but 11% of women said they had committed one of these violent acts. Study after study shows women are not merely violent in self defense but strike the first blow in about half of all disputes. . . . Moreover, there is now considerable evidence that women initiate severe violence more frequently than men. A survey of 1,037 young adults born between 1972 and 1973 in Dunedin, New Zealand, found that 18.6% of young women said they had perpetrated severe physical violence against their partners, compared with 5.7% of young men. Three times more women than men said they had kicked or bitten their partners, or hit them with their fists or with an object.[677]

If, within the domestic realm, women are actually inflicting more physical damage on men than the reverse, a likely explanation is that while men more often use their hands to inflict hurt, women are about 70 percent more likely to use weapons against men than men are to use weapons against women.[678]

Admittedly, the picture of domestic violence painted here is hard to swallow. I've had my own skepticism to work through. But then, beyond what the media tells us, what can any of us know of what goes on in "average" homes all across the country? Facts that fail to support the MP/FV, MB/WG paradigms receive less publicity than facts that do. Such information exists in the literature, but it's obscure. Neither *Time* nor *Newsweek* nor any other official couriers of mass information are apt to touch it, let alone shout it from their covers.

If we do some digging, however, such information can be found. The book *Legalizing Misandry*, by Paul Nathanson and Katherine K. Young, for example, quotes studies on lesbian violence.

> ...[R]ates of abuse were higher among lesbians in their prior relationships with women than in their prior relationships with men: 56% had been subjected to sexual aggression by their female lovers, 45% to physical aggression, and 64.5% to emotional aggression. Another study found that levels of violence were higher among lesbians than among gay men: 55% of gay women reported physical violence but only 44% of gay men. Yet another study found that 47.5% of gay women reported violence in their relationships but only 22% of gay men. Moreover, 38% of the women reported using violence against their partners but only 22% of the men.[679]

After decades of feminist ideology we're used to seeing the myths of masculinity turned upside down. We've become quite acclimated to the idea that Man may be the weaker sex, but the idea that Woman may be as capable of intimate violence as Man remains anathema. The myths of female moral superiority remain cherished and protected, both informally in the social sphere and formally in laws and policies.

"Women who murder violent husbands may be treated leniently because they were provoked;" says Philips, "yet men who are violent against women are never granted the same understanding. Provocation, it appears, is a feminist issue."[680] It is also a legal issue. The biases Ms. Philips exposes are infused throughout all phases of suspicion, arraignment, arrest, probation, bail, trial, and punishment.

Feminists would have women disown their own dark side and project evil onto "patriarchy." In so doing women are encouraged to see themselves as "pure," "innocent" "victims" of *the* source of evil: Man. The women I quote cut through the feminist flattery of women as "angels," seeing instead a feminist condescension, an infantilizing ideology dictated by "Big Sister." The women I admire would have Woman own her power and live up to the standards of an autonomous responsible *adult*.

Joe Biden may be the poster child, but nearly *every* man who grew up with sisters remembers being told, "Never hit your sister." She could hit her brother, but he was forbidden to hit her back. A man's "never hit a woman" conditioning (learned helplessness?) may leave him defenseless against the violence of an angrier, more aggressive woman. In fact, men may be rendered helpless against female aggression in *many* ways. A recent study helps paint the picture.

Set up in a public place, passersby were witness to a woman screaming abuse at a man. "At times her rage boils over to physical abuse: she pulls the young man's hair, slaps the side of his head, and beats him with a rolled-up newspaper."[681]

> Fortunately, the troubling scene isn't real. The abusive woman and her boyfriend are actors, hired by *Primetime* for a hidden camera experiment. On previous shows, *Primetime* has staged scenes of abuse in which the man is the aggressor, and the woman is the victim. And in these situations, passersby — men and women — often stepped up and intervened. So producers were curious. What would happen if the tables were turned, and the man was suddenly the victim? Would people be just as willing to come to his defense?
>
> This staged scenario happens more often in real life than you may think. According to Colgate University psychology professor Carrie Keating, women abusing, even assaulting their male partners "is a big problem in this country. There are some data that suggest that women actually hit more than men do," says Keating.[682]

How did passersby react to a woman emotionally and physically abusing a man?

> One after another, passersby witnessed the abusive scene... and kept right on going. Mathilda was one of those bystanders. She says she didn't think the man was in any physical danger, and could probably take care of himself.
>
> "I didn't immediately think to protect the man at all," she said. "It didn't look like any harm was being done."
>
> The reaction of another woman, Lynda, was stunning. As our actress continued to heap abuse on her make-believe boyfriend, she walked by the scene and pumped her fist in a show of sisterly solidarity. "Good for you. You Go, Girl!" is how Lynda recalls her reaction. "I was thinking he probably did something really bad," she said. "Maybe she caught him cheating or something like that...and [it] made her lose it and slap him in the face. I reacted like, 'Yes. Woman power.'"

This type of reaction didn't come as a surprise to Keating. Observers often excuse their "own lack of response by denigrating the victim and making up stories that he really deserved the punishment he was receiving," Keating says.[683]

The reaction of "Lynda" and other passersby is all too indicative of the zero-empathy-toward-men and all-fault-is-male rules infusing themselves into ordinary people's attitudes and perceptions. Suppose we transplant the scenario into a court of law and those passersby comprise the jury. What hope for justice would the man have?

The reactions of one couple strolling by are even more telling, given that the man happened to be a police officer.

> "What they were havin' there...[they were] just havin' a little tiff. They'll be all right," said the man, a police officer in a nearby community. His wife told *Primetime* that she would have found it "more upsetting if [the young man] had put his hands on the young woman."
>
> "Oh, without a doubt," her husband readily agreed, acknowledging the double standard. "Call it old-fashioned views. If you're raised the way I was raised, you don't put your hands on a woman, right?"

Keating says that holding those kinds of values and beliefs "is going to give them a very different lens through which they see the behavior of the actress, the aggressiveness of the woman against the man. They under-value the potency of her responses."[684]

It is particularly troubling when such "old-fashioned" views are held by a police officer. One wonders if calling 911 would do any good. Suppose that particular officer (or another with similar bias) had been called to the scene. Would the man have any hope for justice? If the woman simply claimed that the man was the one abusing her, wouldn't such an officer probably arrest the man rather than help him? Mightn't the police arrest the man in any case?

In fact, all too often, that is exactly what happens. Glenn Sacks refers his readers to domestic violence researcher Denise Hines:

> Denise Hines of Clark University found that when an abused man calls the police, the police were more likely to arrest him than to arrest his abusive female partner. This is partly the result of laws such as Maryland's primary aggressor law. Primary aggressor laws encourage police to discount who initiated and committed the violence but instead look at other factors (such as size and strength) that make them more likely to arrest men. When the men in Ms. Hines' study tried calling domestic violence hot lines, 64 percent were told that they only helped women, and more than half were referred to programs for male DV perpetrators.[685]

Men have few advocates. Over a two-day period 163 people were filmed walking right past the scene without any attempt to intervene on the man's behalf. If anything, men are probably even less likely to come to the aid of a man than women are. The *sole* effort on behalf of the man was offered by a group of four women. "I was concerned for both their safety," said one of the four while another actually approached the couple and a third called 911.

In the English language there have been over fifty studies done on domestic violence as it affects both women *and men*. All, without exception, indicate that women (by the respondents own free admission) are initiating and inflicting violence upon men, *at every level of violence*, to a degree equal to or *greater* than the violence of men toward women.[686] In fact, "The larger and better designed the study," says Warren Farrell, "the more likely the finding that women were significantly more violent."[687]

Researcher Tom James, author of *Domestic Violence*, concurs:

> The Dunedin longitudinal study is one of only a small number of studies I have come across that makes an intelligent and responsible effort to control for extraneous variables such as lying. It also happens to be one of the studies that comes to the conclusion that a man is more likely to be abused by a woman than a woman is to be abused by a man, and that men are more likely to be victims of severe abuse than women are. The Dunedin study was unusual because it demonstrated a high probability of accuracy based on statistical correlates, by virtue of the fact that *both* members of a couple were interviewed and were interviewed separately, at the same time but in different rooms, neither one knowing what the other said.[688]

Despite all evidence to the contrary, feminism paints a domestic picture of innocent women bullied and beaten by evil dominant men. According to their heterophobic belief system, male-female intimacy is only a precursor to male-on-female abuse. Cathy Young:

> Indeed, the very concept of privacy becomes suspect, merely a smokescreen for, in [Catherine] MacKinnon's words, "the right of men 'to be let alone' to oppress women one at a time." The evil that women do—to children, other women, men—must be erased. The same people who choke with indignation if someone suggest that women lack the "killer instinct" in the workplace or the military will sneer at the idea that women might be aggressors in domestic violence.[689]

In his book, *Domestic Violence: The 12 Things You Aren't Supposed to Know*, Tom James stands all common knowledge about domestic violence upside down. Direct from the table of contents, those 12 things are:

1) Most victims are male
2) Violence against men is just as severe as violence against women

3) Women who abuse are not normally acting in self-defense
4) Most child abuse victims are male
5) Violence against males is on the rise
6) Violence against females is decreasing
7) Violence by males is decreasing
8) Violence by females is on the rise
9) Domestic violence against men is the most under-reported crime
10) It is not impossible for a woman to lie about being a victim of violence
11) Many domestic violence researchers are gender bigots
12) Males are the primary targets of gender bias in the American legal system[690]

Knowing that these assertions lack credibility within our belief system, the book is an astonishing compendium of sources, references, and documentation. Echoing what Christina Hoff Sommers already told us of what those who fail to toe the feminist party line face, says James:

> Whenever researchers discover numbers suggesting that women may be violent, all of the basic tenets of responsible research are suddenly suspended. Instead of conducting additional controlled research to test hypotheses and isolate causes, the response among most researchers appears to be to do everything possible to rush to the defense of these women, at whatever cost. "Well, yes," the researchers will say, "We did find that women are at least as violent as men, but they only do it in self-defense or to defend their children; it's still only the men who are the real aggressors." Then, when that argument is proven incapable of holding water any longer, the researchers will say, "Well, all right, maybe it's not always self-defense, but when it's not, well, it's not like it really hurts the guy or nothin'." Then, when some smart-aleck points out that it often does hurt the guy—severely—the name-calling starts: the smart-aleck must be an anti-feminist, a misogynist, a warrior against women, a backlasher, or perhaps even a closeted woman-batterer himself. And these are just the tactics that government officials and educated social scientists use. At the other extreme are the radical feminists who threaten to bomb, injure and kill anyone who dares reveal any fact about domestic violence that might tend to call the "patriarchy" model into question.[691]

Nevertheless, the only real arbiter in a domestic feud lies in which partner is willing to take aggression to the higher level. If she's willing to use a knife and he is not, then he will fall prey. So long as he is unwilling to take violence up to her level, he's at her mercy.

At the outset we had only two facts to go on: Lorena Bobbitt cut off her husband's penis with a kitchen knife, and did so as he lay helplessly asleep. With no other facts to go on, the nearly universal assumption (myself included) held that he *must* have had it coming. Christina Hoff Sommers: "The personal tragedy of this unhappy couple has been appropriated as a symbol of righteous feminist revenge. The in-joke among Lorena's feminist admirers is that Lorena has since been greeting John by saying, '*Now* do you get it?'"[692] "Rather than being appalled by Mrs. Bobbitt's actions," notes Kathleen Parker, "a startling number of women embraced news of John Wayne's comeuppance as gratifying and overdue."[693] Indeed, women's near-universal jubilation was something *I'll* never forget.

Overnight Lorena became (in the words of Camille Paglia) a "feminist folk hero" and women everywhere held up two fingers in a "V" for victory salute complete with snipping scissor action. No wonder the word misandry is unknown. To slap man-hating with a negative label, man-hating must first register as a negative thing.

Being female, Lorena had only to *allege* prior abuse for us all to assume that she was no doubt blameless. The courts operated under the same assumption and let her go without so much as a rap on the knuckles (she wasn't even placed on a sex offenders list).

> The immediate problem created by the Bobbitt verdict was not vigilantism, however—millions of women were not ready to copy Lorena by castrating men physically—but they were ready to exploit her by castrating men psychologically. . . . According to Jamie Lee Evans, a rape crisis counselor in San Francisco, we "don't need a judge or jury to tell us whether or not Lorena's telling the truth. Lorena came forward herself, said this man was battering her, this man was raping her. That's all we need to know to know that Lorena's telling the truth."[694]

Does such certainty hold up knowing that a few years later Lorena Bobbitt was arrested for violently assaulting her own mother?[695]

In her new role as *advocate for DV victims* (!), Lorena was recently interviewed by CNN reporter Alina Cho. "I have to ask you this; as you well know, there was a time when joking about the Bobbitts was a national pastime. I wonder after all these years – are you finally able to laugh about it?" "I finally am," replies Lorena.[696] Of course, *we* were all able to laugh about it from the start.

Even a cursory investigation into Lorena and John Bobbitt reveals two mutually abusive people. Of the two, Lorena was simply the one willing to take violence to the higher level. It would be naive to assume that other women wouldn't do the same.

Within a domestic setting, a man's greater size and strength won't help him while he's reading on the couch or sleeping in bed (ask John Bobbitt, remember Phil Hartman). It's just a matter of time before inattentiveness renders a man defenseless against even the tiniest woman who comes up from behind, heavy iron skillet in hand.

What does a man's size do for him against poison or hired killer or if she simply has a gun? There are all kinds of ways a wife might kill or injure her husband; many don't involve direct confrontation. Yet, a man's claim of being attacked or threatened by his wife has so little credibility he's apt to be met only with utmost impatience at the police station and he stands a good chance of being laughed out of court. What's going to happen when his wife takes the witness stand wearing a frilly pink dress?

Furthermore, he'll find no men's shelter to go to, no "violence-against-men" hotline to call, no "Violence Against Men Act," no "Violence Against Men" task force. His wife's violent intentions may place him in grave danger. But, as a victim, his low credibility in the eyes of society may well seal his fate.

It is clear the average woman will feel less embarrassed to report being beaten by a man than a man would to report being beaten by a woman. She will feel more comfortable asking for help while he's apt to suspect that his cries for help will not be heeded and may even be turned against him. When *she* gets hit over the head, she knows she's the victim of a *crime*. The phrases "domestic violence" and "violence against women" have been imprinted upon her consciousness. When she tells her friends, her emotional pain will show and her friends will react in horror and insist that she report the man to the police and leave him immediately. *If* her male equivalent chooses to tell his friends at all, he is apt to show them the bump on his head as if it were a joke. He might as well. His friends are apt to laugh as if it were a joke whether he intends it that way or not.

Taking in the above, it's no wonder surveys reveal female domestic violence to a degree that crime statistics do not. At this point we begin to see VAWA in a new light. Rather than view it as righteously protecting the "powerless" sex from the "violent" sex, we may assess the no Violence Against Women (while violence against men keeps right on going) Act as perhaps the single most sexist doctrine in America today.

For forty-odd years the media have demonstrated a pronounced tendency to flatter women and shame men. A woman's magazines, her female friends, and the anti-male culture in general make it all too easy for her to feel self-righteously justified in laying blame and hostility on the man in her life.

She may believe, in accordance with common knowledge, that female violence toward men is rare and most likely justified while male violence toward women is commonplace, brutal, unprovoked, Patriarchal Domination that can *never* be justified. So, should she lash out, it will be all too easy for her to feel like a lone avenger striking a blow for women everywhere suffering under "male oppression."

Indeed, the phenomenally successful movie *Thelma and Louise,* among others, celebrates female-on-male violence, even murder, as "justified." Trudy Schuett recalls *The Burning Bed*, a movie that "helped establish a framework for dozens of later theatrical and TV movies that depict men as dangerous, violent abusers and women as saintly victims with nowhere to turn for help."

> Even after 25 years, this story of a single extraordinary case, exaggerated for effect, has become omnipresent. The male character is generally accepted as typical, and murder is sanctioned if not openly encouraged as a solution to the problem. Later films, such as *Sleeping With the Enemy* starring Julia Roberts, built on the myth and added the aspect of relentless stalking, also unusual in the real world. Other movies added more, and there is now a whole TV network devoted to almost nothing but the theme of awful, despicable men vs. glamorous female victims.[697]

"When Lenore Walker created the 'Battered Woman Syndrome' around the same time as the release of the movie," says Schuett, "it was accepted as gospel and formed the basis for public policies and laws that eventually would attempt to hold women blameless for a wide range of crimes, from shoplifting to 1st degree murder."[698] And what might be the fallout of directing more blame and guilt upon men?

"Men are far more apt to kill themselves in the aftermath of family violence," writes Patricia Pearson, author of *When She Was Bad: How and Why Women Get Away With Murder*. "An extraordinarily high number of Chicago men turn guns and knives on themselves after killing their mates; more than 25 percent of white men, about 29 percent of Latino men (who otherwise have a low suicide rate), and 10 percent of black men. Less than 2 percent of women in all race categories do."[699] Michael Newton, author of *Bad Girls Do It: An Encyclopedia of Female Murderers*, agrees: "Suicide is not uncommon in the wake of murder, especially where family slayings are concerned, but female killers bear up fairly well." And do so, even though "When it comes to choosing victims, 45% of our collected female multicides preyed on family members."[700]

The image of the "homicidal maniac" out killing strangers may seem more terrifying and make for scarier horror movie fodder, but I would point out that, as compared with killing strangers, killing "loved ones" is arguably even *more* evil.

Feeling, on average, greater righteousness and lesser guilt, a murderous wife is apt to take extra precautions against being caught lest she be punished for doing what was, after all, the "right" thing to do. Meanwhile, her male equivalent's greater average guilt feelings more often compel him to act rashly, turn himself in, or turn the murder weapon against himself. At the crime scene, his suicide renders his guilt crystal clear. Crime statistics are affected accordingly.

Finally, that defense attorneys often advise female defendants to play up their femininity in dress and in manner is common knowledge. Meanwhile, it would be pure absurdity for a defense attorney to advise a male defendant to play up his masculinity. Pro-feminine, anti-masculine bias in the legal system is far from subtle.

If a woman has behaved badly, a jury may all too easily be convinced that a man led her astray. A prosecuting attorney, who aggressively cross-examines a *woman*, may lose even an open-and-shut case should the jury come to see him as a "bully." For *many* reasons, it is far more difficult to prosecute women than it is to prosecute men. In a chapter entitled "Women Who Kill Too Much and the Courts That Free Them,"[701] Dr. Farrell lists twelve female-only defenses including "the PMS defense," "the 'learned helplessness' defense," "the 'postnatal depression' defense," and "the 'children need their mother' defense." Comparable male-only defenses could exist, but don't.

From myriad angles, we can see why crime statistics are *not* reliable measures of domestic violence. Also, to whatever extent a woman figures that her femininity may shield her from legal consequences is the extent to which she may be further emboldened to act out violently.

Reality Check: We cannot see inside millions of homes all across America. The Truth with regard to Domestic Violence is unknown. Where gender is concerned bias is omnipresent. You can survey, but there's no guarantee the responses will be both honest and accurate. Men may be getting the worst of it or women may be getting the worst of it; there's no real certainty.

But the evidence is strong enough to know this much: the assertion that DV is nothing more than men beating up women is *false*. We can't know what all the "traffic patterns" are, but we do know that domestic violence is a two-way street.

Lady Madonna

The dark picture we have of men would lead us to believe that most child abuse is male-inflicted. In fact, "Women commit a greater share of physical child abuse," says Patricia Pearson, and "an overwhelming share of the killings of newborns."[702] Kathleen Parker: "A 1999 federal report found that 70.3 percent of perpetrators of child abuse were women. Of those resulting in death, 31.5 percent were committed by a female parent only, three times the number of those committed by a male parent only."[703] Of course, all this is connected with women performing the majority of childcare. Nevertheless, our assumption that men are the primary perpetrators against children is emblematic of our attachment to MB/WG.

We would hate to think that there's anything less than a Madonna in the nursery, but the facts don't always paint an "angelic" picture. And if we dare look more deeply, in the shadows lurks a picture of motherhood darker than any we care to know.

Before embarking down this road it is important to remind ourselves why. Why reveal the darkest corners of the maternal psyche? I will answer that question with another. "Why do dads kill?," asks the front-page headline of the June 25, 2007 *Chicago Sun-Times*. The answer, also from the front page: "In family-murder cases, a clear pattern emerges, experts say. The father wipes out his family simply because he's tired of dealing with them." As simple as that? Also on the cover is a narrow-cropped photo of Christopher Vaughn, alleged to have killed his wife and three kids. With his eyes staring out, he looks a lot like Satan. So, here on the front page of a major metropolitan newspaper we are told that dads kill their families simply because they grow weary of them. Message sent: men are evil, violent scum; don't marry a man—he'll kill you and your children the moment he grows tired of dealing with you.

So why delve deeply into the darkest corners of the maternal psyche? Because, in failing to do so, we are left with only a demonizing of men and an angelizing of women—we are left with ManBad/WomanGood. We are left with a distorted, false-to-fact image of the world that leads us to unfair judgments and wrong decisions in our personal lives and ineffective or counter-effective laws and policies in the intersocial world.

When Andrea Yates drowned her children in the bathtub—all five of them, one after another—it made the cover of *Newsweek*.[704] The headline? "'I Killed My Children': What Made Andrea Yates Snap?" Note how *Newsweek* treats Andrea Yates and what she did as unique. By contrast, in dealing with Christopher Vaughn and what he allegedly did, the *Chicago Sun-Times* asks why *dads* kill, as if to implicate all dads. Not some dads kill, or this particular dad killed, but just: "Why do dads kill?" A headline that asked "Why do moms kill?," would rightly be protested (even though infanticide is overwhelmingly a maternal crime).

The *Newsweek* cover quotes Andrea's reply when a police officer asked, "Do you realize what you have done?" Her reply, "I killed my children," could be taken either as cold-blooded or as an expression of horror and remorse. What follows nudges us toward the latter interpretation: "What made Andrea Yates snap?" Isn't that really asking: What was Andrea Yates' excuse? Also on the cover: "Understanding Postpartum Depression" and "Anna Quindlen on Every Mother's Secret." Yes, Anna ("It's not that I don't like men; women are just better"[705]) Quindlen is asked to give her unbiased opinion on the matter. So now we know what made Yates "snap" and we are nudged toward an empathy interpretation of her actions.

Many will merely glance at the covers. The verdict will be obvious. Look with awareness and you'll find the MB/WG paradigm insinuating itself into our media/cultural products with a pervasiveness comparable to the way food additives are included in the products we buy at the grocery store. Comparing the two covers, the greater empathy shown a woman could not be more apparent. Let's delve deeper into each article, starting with *The Chicago Sun-Times*.

According to Minneapolis criminal profiler Pat Brown, men who commit "familicide" fall into one of two categories. "Some men decide to commit suicide because they are heavily in debt, have failed in their jobs or are otherwise falling apart. In a supremely selfish act, they decide to take their families with them. Those who don't kill themselves are more likely to just want to be free, Brown said."[706]

When a father kills we don't ask what made him "snap." We don't care to know what his excuse was. He may well have been provoked in the worst way imaginable, but we're too intent upon vilifying him to seek out that which might mitigate his guilt. We are not invited to consider his "depression" or his "stress." In fact what we're told explicitly precludes *any* possibility of redemption or empathy: "They are manipulators. They're narcissistic, filled with grandiose thoughts. And they're pathologic liars who blame everyone but themselves for their problems. . . . But they're usually not insane . . . they know right from wrong."[707] So, when it comes to *fathers* who kill, it's *all* about accountability; there can be no empathy and there can be *no possibility* of an "excuse."

When the article shifts its attention to their female equivalents, however, the tone shifts dramatically. According to John Philipin, psychologist, crime profiler, and author of true-crime books, "By contrast, many mothers who kill their families suffer from depression, depressive psychosis, schizophrenia and other mental illnesses."[708] Perhaps female killers are merely more often *diagnosed* with these illnesses? Women who kill are said to *suffer* from these illnesses, implying that even women murderers remain *the* victims.

The *Newsweek* article begins: "Andrea Yates was the ultimate caregiver—until depression and the strains of raising five children drove her to an unspeakable crime."[709] Note the air of incredulity that accompanies a heinous act when committed by a woman. "How could a mother commit such an act against nature and all morality, ending the lives she had so recently borne and nurtured. And kill them so methodically, one by one, holding them under the bath water (imagine eyes staring back) and laying them out on the bed wrapped in sheets like little Christian martyrs."[710]

"Sometimes moms blame the Devil. Or they think they are saving their children from a hellish life by sending them to heaven. The psychologists call these 'altruistic killings.' Andrea Yates was apparently suffering from a specific, diagnosable—and treatable—condition called postpartum psychosis."[711] And it was on the basis of that diagnosis that Yates was eventually found not guilty by reason of insanity. "Yates' attorneys never disputed that she drowned 6-month-old Mary, 2-year-old Luke, 3-year-old Paul, 5-year-old John and 7-year-old Noah in their Houston-area home in June 2001. But they said she suffered from severe postpartum psychosis and, in a delusional state, believed Satan was inside her and was trying to save them from hell."[712] It seems Yates committed five of those "*altruistic* killings."

Patricia Pearson, author of *When She Was Bad*, comments:

> By contrast, when a sample of men convicted of infanticide were surveyed in Brixton Prison in Great Britain, those who offered altruistic motivations were scoffed at. Wrote their interviewer: "The statement 'that it was best for the children' . . . is an expression of the fact that the perpetrator himself thought that the infanticide was the best way out—that is to say, the act was egosyntonic."[713]

No matter the circumstances, a father who drowned his five children one at a time couldn't possibly be received so empathically as to be called "the ultimate caregiver" and have his actions labeled "altruistic."

Newsweek quotes Andrea's mother, the one person we would expect to love Andrea most unconditionally—"She was the most compassionate of my children. Always thinking of other people, never herself. She was always trying to care for everybody."[714]—and follows that with a pitiful image of Andrea Yates caring for her Alzheimer's-stricken father while pregnant. "Between caring for her father and her children, it is hard to think that Andrea ever had time for herself."[715] Between working/commuting 70 hours a week plus domestic and other chores expected of him, many a husband/father similarly has no time for himself.

According to the *Newsweek* article, most multicide killers are coldly psychopathic. "Andrea was the opposite; if anything, she apparently cared too much. She may have felt she could never do enough for her demanding husband. In a horribly twisted way, she may have tried to be too good a mother."[716] Even as we're excusing (if not actually canonizing) the female killer, note how we begin blaming the nearest male, her "demanding" husband.

Not even Rusty Yates, the devastated father of those five murdered children, blames Andrea. "One side of me blames her because, you know, she did it. But the other side of me says, 'Well, she didn't, because that wasn't her.'"[717] Spoken like a truly chivalrous and infinitely magnanimous male.

Houston police officer Frank Stumpo: "'Do you realize what you have done?' he asked her. She looked right at him and said, 'Yes, I do.' She told the police, 'I killed my children.' Stumpo looked around. The house was a mess, he thought, dirty and unkempt."[718] At this point Rusty had returned home but was kept out of the house, presumably to protect Andrea. Asked if he wanted a glass of water, Rusty "doubted anyone would find a clean glass in the house. Stumpo looked anyway, and couldn't find one—until Andrea calmly pointed him to the china cabinet."[719] Obviously, any man who did what Andrea did then, in the aftermath, spoke and behaved as Andrea did could only be condemned in the worst ways imaginable.

Being male, Rusty Yates was subject to harsh judgment merely for the "crime" of not "allowing" his wife to work and bring in a second income. Yet, simultaneously, Rusty Yates was harshly judged "demanding." Well, if he didn't demand housekeeping, and he didn't demand help with the financial burdens, then perhaps he wasn't all *that* demanding. Many a wife is "demanding": demanding toughness, strength, and courage of her husband; demanding of competence, demanding of domestic chores, demanding of career success, and demanding financially. Even so, if a husband/father did what Andrea Yates did, who would ever think to pin the blame on his "demanding" wife? Yet the media made every effort to vilify Rusty Yates and hold *him* responsible for the murders committed by his wife.

In a follow-up article, *Newsweek* describes Rusty's tireless campaign on behalf of Andrea. He defended her on every show from *The Today Show* to *Larry King* to *Oprah*. His chivalrous efforts even put him at risk of contempt of court charges for violating a gag order. But that's only the beginning; "as he crisscrossed the nation, simmering questions about his own accountability have boiled over."[720]

> Andrea's mother and siblings told reporters that Rusty, a controlling husband who often downplayed his wife's mental illness and shut them out, bears some responsibility for the tragedy. Andrea's best friend, Deborah Holmes, did the same. On radio call-in shows, Internet chat rooms and newspaper editorial pages, the questions continue. . . . Rusty is "innocent of any criminal offense," says his lawyer, Ed

Mallet. Some legal experts, however, think that even if Yates escapes criminal charges (including contempt of court) he may have a tough time defending himself in civil court where a jury could find him partly responsible.[721]

More than just "questions" circulated on the Internet. "Andrea went to prison, but many people believed that she was not the only one who was culpable in this tragedy. Rusty had been warned not to leave her alone with the children and a doctor had taken her off medication while apparently believing that she could be a danger to herself or others. Many people believed that they shared in the blame."[722]

In fact, some expressed more hostility and blame toward Rusty than toward Andrea. A typical sentiment was voiced by Barbara Robinson: "Rusty Yates is Culpable, Too: Father's Bizarre, Domineering Actions Played a Role in Children's Deaths"[723] Robinson goes so far as to suggest that "her husband should have been on trial instead of Andrea."

"I couldn't understand," says Robinson, "how a man could repeatedly impregnate a mentally ill wife and force or allow her to homeschool their children." Surely Rusty and Andrea were equal partners in creating those pregnancies, and there's a world of difference between "force" and "allow." Rusty claimed that he and Andrea made all major decisions jointly. Was Andrea an adult woman accountable for her actions, or a child? Was Rusty her husband or her father?

The formula is inviolable: toward men, accountability sans compassion; toward women, compassion sans accountability.

Is Rusty Yates implicated? Of course he is. He's in it; he was involved; he plied a force of influence in the overall situation. But the same can be said of *any* wife whose husband "snapped" and did what she did. To whatever degree husbands may be judged "domineering," wives may be judged "manipulative" in equal measure.

But not *everyone* assessed Andrea Yates so lightly. According to CBS News, Dr. Park Dietz, the state's expert witness, "testified that Yates' thoughts about harming her children were an obsession and a symptom of severe depression, not psychosis." Additionally there was "the state's key expert witness, Dr. Michael Welner, a forensic psychiatrist who evaluated Yates in May. He testified that she did not kill her children to save them from hell as she claims, but because she was overwhelmed and felt inadequate as a mother."[724] Damning opinion regarding Andrea Yates exists, but you have to dig to find it. Where male killers are concerned, the opposite prevails.

Back to the *Chicago Sun-Times* article: "Police aren't saying why Christopher Vaughn allegedly shot his wife Kimberly, and three kids in the family's red SUV on June 14. But in other family-murder cases, a clear pattern emerges, experts say. Fathers often wipe out their families simply because they're tired of them. They want to be free again, without going through the hassles and obligations of divorce and child support."[725] We don't know why Vaughn allegedly shot his wife and children, but even so, we'll just lump him in with the rest of his presumed inferior gender as an article of faith.

Compare antipathy like that with the extra empathy shown Andrea Yates. Following the *Today Show* report on the Yates tragedy, Katie "Couric provided an address where viewers could send contributions for Yates's defense fund"![726]

If anyone got in close enough to the Yates tragedy to hold an informed opinion, it was journalist Suzanne O'Malley. She "covered this trial for numerous publications and had unique access to Andrea and Rusty Yates. As the author of *ARE YOU THERE ALONE?: The Unspeakable Crime of Andrea Yates,* O'Malley talked with Bookreporter.com's Diana Keough."[727]

Says O'Malley, "Sure, spending time with Rusty Yates changed my thinking about him. But the 2,000 pages of Andrea Yates's medical records affected me more. Before I read them, I felt Rusty Yates was a monster."[728] Perhaps, like everyone else, O'Malley simply *presumed* the worst guilt upon the nearest male?

Such would seem to be case with Diana Keough, O'Malley's interviewer. Keough even expresses suspicion with regard to Rusty's forgiveness of Andrea. O'Malley responds to her with: "How I explain it is that Rusty Yates understands his wife is mentally ill. For him, the crime of killing their five children never required forgiveness—the deaths were a tragedy from which to seek future safeguards, not blame."[729] *Wow!* It never ceases to amaze me how forgiving Man is where Woman is concerned.

The interview continues:

> Q: Characterize Rusty Yates for us. He seems like a man who things happen to. The world seems to circle around him with him not really taking grasp of any issue except as a topline thought. He knew Andrea was ill, but never hired an attorney or other advocate to help him get her the care she desperately needed. He knew she was ill, but still left the children with her that morning. Andrea's attorney was hired by her three brothers without Rusty even being consulted. This does not seem like a man "in charge." Are these sentiments on target?
>
> SOM (Suzanne O'Malley): No.[730]

Indeed, these sentiments are *not* on target. With one breath we condemn Man for being "controlling" and "demanding." With the next breath we hold him in contempt for not being "in charge." In an effort to avoid being regarded a "wimp" (i.e., "a man whom things happen to"), a man tries his best to take charge only to suffer being regarded a "patriarchal oppressor." Where is the win position? But, whether "wimp" or "oppressor," either way, we'll go to extraordinary lengths to hold the nearest male *solely* responsible.

Fortunately, O'Malley dug deeply enough into this tragedy, the people involved, and all surrounding factors to see things more clearly. Says she:

> 1) Read the book excerpts from the 2,000 pages of Andrea Yates's medical records. If there's one thing Rusty Yates is, it's an advocate. When psychiatrists are unable to diagnose an illness after years of family effort, I wonder how a family, a lawyer, or any layman can succeed.
>
> 2) Hindsight is 20/20. Andrea Yates was left alone with the children for an hour that Wednesday morning when Rusty Yates left for work. Andrea and the children were watching television and Rusty's mother was on her way over to look after them. When Andrea had been ill the first time (in 1999, after the birth of her 4th child), she had twice tried to kill herself. The family's focus was on making sure she didn't try to kill herself again. They never thought she would harm the children.
>
> 3) Andrea Yates' attorney was hired by her then 72-year-old mother two days after the murders (with the consultation of her three brothers). Prior to that Friday morning, Rusty Yates was identifying the dead bodies of his children at the coroner's office, selecting their coffins, making funeral arrangements, seeing a NASA grief counselor, ferrying relatives to and from the airport, giving the Assistant District Attorney a tour of the crime scene, and seeking advice from a friend who is an attorney. Rusty Yates had also scheduled a meeting that Friday afternoon with noted defense attorney Mike Ramsay (who recently won the Robert Durst murder and dismemberment case in Galveston, Texas). Ramsay had been recommended to Yates by the office of NBC's Katie Couric. So had the attorney Andrea's mother had selected. Rusty Yates agreed with his in-law's choice of George Parnham.[731]

But interviewer Diana Keough is *still* not satisfied.

> Q: In his grief, just about everything Rusty did—from creating a website in his children's memory to the way he methodically cleaned out the bathtub and removed the bed the children were placed on after they died—seems like the actions of someone rather emotionally detached from the situation at hand. Did you feel this way about Rusty?
>
> SOM: First, let me say that it was Randy Yates—Rusty's brother—who cleaned the bathtub. Relatives had begun to arrive for the funeral and some were staying at the house. Rusty says he himself was never able to set foot in that tub. He had it removed and smashed to pieces

with a sledgehammer. Rusty Yates is a career NASA engineer. His job is safety systems for the space shuttle program. It is fair to say he is methodical.[732]

Given the merciless blame and judgment aimed his way, one can only hope Rusty was emotionally detached. Sadly, however, as the sledge-hammered tub bears testament, a Dad's grief at the loss of all five of his children could only be *monumental*—especially when that grief is accorded so little compassion.

At such a distance I cannot judge the hearts of either Christopher Vaughn or Andrea Yates. I cannot know what The Truth is regarding either the depth of their guilt or innocence. What I *do* know is that there's a staggering difference in the empathy accorded each. Even after killing all five of her children, a woman is *still* accorded an empathy interpretation of her actions. Even after losing all five of his children, a man is *still* accorded only an antipathy interpretation. What I know is that irrespective of the circumstances, women are presumed innocent while men are presumed guilty.

It is ubiquitous misandry like this, at saturation levels, shouted aloud from the most official and respected sources of news and opinion that forces my hand. I could just give up. I could sit by while my sex is utterly denigrated. I could, like virtually all other men, watch passively as misandry and feminism conspire to turn men into second-class humans. Instead, I choose to fight back. I fight back the only way I know how.

I tell the other side of the story.

"In Houston, residents recently discovered that they had an epidemic on their hands: Over a 10-month period, 13 different new-born babies were found in trash cans, on front porches, by the side of the road. Three of them were dead. It got so bad that the city had to put up billboards telling women not to chuck their babies." A photo of one such billboard accompanies the article. "DON'T ABANDON YOUR BABY!" the sign pleads in great block letters printed in red.

Could this "epidemic" be spreading? No one can say for sure because "most states have no official records of baby dumping. And even if someone had been keeping track, because of the secretive nature of the act, there's no way of knowing the number of babies that were just never found—or why the mothers ditched their newborns in the first place"[733]

We can neither study nor understand the feminine shadow until we first allow that it exists. Still, "As long as patriarchs and feminists alike covet the notion that women are gentle," says Patricia Pearson, "they will not look for the facts that dispute it."[734]

So, how has society responded to this "epidemic" of women dumping their living babies? Have we increased the penalties, or demanded that young mothers be taught their responsibilities toward the children they bring into this world? Hardly. According to the National Abandoned Infants Assistance Resource Center website:

> In response to highly publicized media reports of infants discarded in public places and left to die, since 1999 most states have passed legislation that offers a safe, anonymous, and lawful means to relinquish a newborn. . . . The intent of these statutes is to encourage mothers, who might otherwise discard their children, to go to an emergency room or other safe place to drop off their infants.[735]

Whatever the intent, whatever the "legal abandonment" laws and "Safe Haven" centers may contribute to the greater good, they are also indicative of the lengths society will go to protect females and absolve them of accountability for the consequences of their actions.

Society has invented many ways of absolving women of accountability. Patricia Pearson:

> According to Dr. John Emery . . . the term sudden infant death syndrome was coined at the turn of the century in the state of Washington. "As deaths due to what you might call classic disease such as pneumonia disappeared," Emery explained, "relatively larger numbers of children died unexpectedly . . . at home instead of at hospital." . . . A group of Seattle doctors "said let us, as it were, invent a term which could be used to describe babies that are found unexpectedly dead, and we will say that this is a natural cause of death so these parents shall not be harassed. Eventually they called it sudden infant death syndrome, and this had a very fine effect."[736]

And what is the "very fine effect" of this fabricated term? "We will *say* that this is a natural cause of death," even though we suspect otherwise. This invented syndrome *intentionally* offered parents (actually, *mothers*) an easy out, a way to kill their children without being "harassed" by legal consequences. It has in many instances given mothers license to kill their children with impunity.

Michael Newton offers the example of Debra Sue Tuggle and the five children she murdered. William and Thomas were the first to go.

> Physicians in Debra's home town of Little Rock, Arkansas, were sympathetic to the grieving mother's plight. In the absence of physical symptoms, they blamed William's death on pneumonia, listing Thomas as a victim of Sudden Infant Death Syndrome (SIDS). A third son, Ronald Johnson, was nine months old when he suddenly stopped breathing, in 1976. Again, Debra's public display of grief was convincing; once again, SIDS was blamed for the death.[737]

Terranz Tuggle was next. "As far as Malvern's finest could determine, it was one more SIDS-related death."[738] The fifth child Tuggle murdered, Tomekia Paxton, was the daughter of paramour George Paxton.

> In custody, Tuggle admitted pressing a pillow over Tomekia's face to "stop her crying" while Debra watched television. She held the pillow in place for some two minutes, with the desired result, but claimed she still "didn't think Tomekia was dead." Only later—presumably when her program was finished—did the murderess realize her "mistake." . . . It was stretching credibility to blame SIDS for the passing of a child Tomekia's age, but stranger things have happened in the world of pediatric medicine.[739]

Perhaps strangest of all is the pediatric medical community's conscious and deliberate creation of SIDS—at least in part—to provide an easy out for mothers who kill their children.

Why do *mothers* kill? Two motives stand out. Historically, many of the mothers who killed their children have done so for the life insurance money. For example, in addition to at least one other child, Diana Lumbrera killed all six of her children, one by one, over the course of *fourteen years.* Ranging from a few months old to four years old, each child had been insured for amounts between $3,000 and $5,000.[740] Incredibly, another primary motive is craving attention!

There exists a little-known aberration called Munchausen Syndrome By Proxy (MSBP). Those with Munchausen syndrome affect illness for the payoff they get from all the attention they receive. Those with Munchausen syndrome *by proxy* afflict their children for the same payoff. Women comprise the vast majority of those exhibiting these two syndromes. Patricia Pearson:

> The psychiatrists Herbert Schreier and Judith Libow describe MSBP as "a 'career' pursued by ostensibly wonderful mothers who repeatedly offer their children's bodies to entice and simultaneously control their powerful, professional victims." Their victims—the targets of their power plays—are doctors. Their children are pawns. Although some of them kill their children (the death rate ranges from 10 to 30 percent), most keep them alive through careful dosing, tossing them with stunning cruelty into constant states of peril. . . . Though there is still no accurate tally in the United States of how common this phenomenon is (estimates run to about 500 new cases a year) "we can safely say that the disorder is far from rare, and that it is frequently missed."[741]

Pearson offers the specific case of Marybeth Tinning. In 1972, when her daughter Jennifer succumbed to meningitis only days after birth, Tinning discovered the consoling attention that grieving mothers receive upon the death of a child. She also discovered that she couldn't get enough of it.

> Within a matter of weeks, Tinning burst through the doors of Saint Claire's emergency room with Joe Jr. in her arms, the toddler gasping for breath as his mother screamed for help. Joe was admitted and recovered immediately . . . A few days later he was back. This time, the oxygen deprivation had gone on too long. By daybreak he was dead. Two months went by . . . Tinning arrived at the emergency room with five-year-old Barbara in convulsions . . . She, too, was stabilized by hospital specialists. She, too, went home to recover and came back in the same state. By March, she, too, was dead. . . . Tinning suffocated her infant daughter because power was more important to her than love; ego gratification more compelling than toil. She was a predator. Had she been a man she might have been a particularly ruthless entrepreneur, an organized criminal, a serial rapist. But she was a woman, and she located her well-spring of power in maternity.[742]

Tinning so enjoyed the attention dying children garnered that the mysterious death of this third child was followed by the mysterious deaths of child #4, child #5, child #6, child #7, child #8, and child #9. Barbara and Joseph and Timothy and Nathan and Michael and Mary Frances and Jonathan and Tami Lynne were officially pronounced victims variously of SIDS or pneumonia or Reye's syndrome but, in fact, they had all been smothered.[743]

The wellspring of power Tinning located in maternity is a power toward which men are extremely vulnerable. "Several nurses at Saint Clare were suspicious and called the child abuse hotline at various times, to no avail; Tinning's pediatricians were stalwart in their support of her."[744] Of course they were. No surprise there. But women aren't nearly so blinded by the feminine and maternal mystiques as men are.

In the words of corrections officer Toby Wong:

> "Women's view of women differs substantially from men's," says Lieutenant Wong. "Women know when women are lying. Men can get twisted around. Female officers will arrest and cite twice as many women as men do."[745]

Patriarchy protects women in many ways. In this case, it *long* protected Tinning from undergoing official suspicion or investigation. "Still, one wonders if any serious investigating would have taken place," muses Pearson. "The culturally celebrated mother at the center of tragedy is one of our most potent symbols."[746] Which is why it is so tempting to view the homicidal mother as the *sufferer* or *victim* of an illness.

According to Michael D. and C. L. Kelleher, authors of *Murder Most Rare*:

Mothers who suffer from MSBP will usually fabricate disorders in their children by such means as suffocation, induced seizures, induced bleeding, chronic poisoning with drugs such as ipecac (which leads to vomiting) or phenolphthalein (which induces diarrhea), or the injection of excrement in order to induce other severe physical symptoms. MSBP sufferers who attack their children are often trying to communicate their own anxiety, depression, extreme need for attention, and inability to care for their children. They are crying out for help and may be attempting to compensate for traumatic losses in their own early life. It is not uncommon to learn that individuals who suffer from MSBP have experienced a childhood dominated by discord, domestic violence, and abuse.[747]

Obviously, male serial killers also experienced childhoods dominated by discord, domestic violence, and abuse. In addition, violent males more often than violent females became pathological owing to abuse and trauma suffered in juvenile homes, prisons, and battlefields. Even so, can you imagine fathers who torture their children described as "suffering," "trying to communicate their own anxiety," "compensating for traumatic losses," and "crying out for help"?

Patricia Pearson:

> The name Munchausen syndrome by proxy was coined in 1977, around the same time as battered woman syndrome. The label is hugely misleading, insofar as it implies a treatable illness from which someone suffers, presumably without control, without the ability to make moral and rational choices. Many MSBP mothers suffered as children from neglect or abuse, but by the time they are adults, they are no more treatable than a serial killer like Paul Bernardo. Indeed, the psychiatrists Schreier and Libow contend that MSBP "may be a gender related form of psychopathy." In moral context, we might simply call it evil.[748]

Indeed, MSBP, the Kellehers state, "is a disorder that is rarely treated with any significant degree of success."[749] That's because it is not a "disorder;" it is a psychopathology. This is the female sociopath and she is both as rare and as commonplace as the male sociopath.

The male equivalent of a female "suffering" from MSBP is known to one and all as a "psycho." He's not a "victim" "suffering" a "disorder" that might be treated and cured. He's not given the excuse of an illness. We don't conjure up the equivalent of "postpartum psychosis," there is no "battered man syndrome," no "learned helplessness;" *no* excuses are offered to mitigate his guilt. He, being a *he,* is seen simply as evil and there an end to it.

Perhaps, in the case of Andrea Yates, we have a sympathetic person enacting evil while in the case of Christopher Vaughn we have an unsympathetic person enacting evil. In that event we must balance our media message. The stories of Ted Bundy, Ed Gein, and John Wayne Gacy, et al, have received their just deserts in feature films. So where's the Marybeth Tinning story?

If the Andrea Yates case involves a sympathetic person whose story deserves to be told sympathetically, then there is a mirror-opposite story to be told. To my knowledge the story of a sympathetic man who kills his family doesn't exist in the literature. Nevertheless, out there somewhere there's the true story of a man whose wife beats him. She cruelly abuses the children as well. In desperation the man calls the police but, in accordance with their feminist training, the police arrest *him*. After enduring court-ordered "anger management" sessions that do *not* end until he has accepted *sole* responsibility for all Domestic Violence, he returns home to an enraged wife who has beaten the children as never before. For having dared call the police, he too receives his worst beating ever. And, having witnessed her own legal immunity, she is now emboldened to wield violence unconstrained by fear of legal consequences. Like Marion Winters, quoted earlier, she checks into a Women's Shelter where she receives legal support plus feminist divorce-court strategy and training.

Having become legally defined as the "abuser," the man is removed from his home with a restraining order. Following divorce court, he's reduced to wage slave, paying for a home and family that a GPS transponder affixed to his ankle prevents even *approaching*. Stressed, exhausted, he falters in his career. He knows his ex-wife squanders the money he sends, but there's nothing he can do about it; he either keeps up with the payments, or he goes to jail.

He is by nature a kind and caring man who still loves his wife and dotes on his children—children suffering untold physical/emotional abuse at the hands of a cruel and violent mother. The sights and sounds, the terrified faces, the screams of his children, haunt his dreams and memories. Yet he cannot be there to offer even partial protection or emotional support. He searches for but finds no men's shelters, organizations, or legal assistance. Everywhere he goes his story is met only with disbelief and derision.

In his agony and powerless despair he "snaps," and, in a fit of madness, he shoots his wife and children.

Fortunately, a pair of fair and impartial profilers is called in to do a fair and impartial analysis. We know their verdict will be gender neutral because one feminist profiler is female and the other feminist profiler is male. Their conclusion? "After a thorough, in-depth, and balanced investigation we conclude that the man shot and killed his wife and children simply because he was tired of them and didn't want to have to pay child support."

We are not seeing headlines that ask: "Why Do Moms Kill?" We are not seeing front pages telling us that "In family-murder cases, a clear pattern emerges, experts say. The mother wipes out her family simply because she craves attention," or, "simply because she wants the life insurance money." The protest would be deafening.

For every evil man there is an evil woman. In part, we don't know that, because evil women so often go unsuspected let alone arrested, prosecuted, and convicted. If Tinning had simply run out of children at child #8, it's unlikely she would ever have been found out, which leaves one to wonder how many women have killed two or three or four children and never raised suspicion.

Woman's dark side equals Man's, but *her* dark side is culturally sympathized with, hidden, ignored, disbelieved, obscured, forgotten, skipped over, excused, denied, reframed, and minimized until an iron-clad illusion is created, leading virtually all to believe that Woman's dark side is only a tiny fraction of Man's.

Reality Check: What could be more fun than this!

Yeah, I'm angry; sure I am. Men's issues run deep and inspire appropriate *passion* in me. *And*, men's issues are matched by women's issues. So, the only element in these matters that inspires *rage* in me is the cruelly imbalanced belief system. The truths of male powerless victimization and female culpability "trigger" me so, *only* because they are set against the backdrop of a belief system that so unfairly refuses their existence. It's knowing what I know and seeing *none* of it reflected back from media, movie and TV screens.

Genghis Khan, Joseph Stalin, Adolf Hitler—clearly, masculinity has produced much that is evil. Not *all* of the feminist indictment of Man is unfair. Granted, Man has no claim to the moral high ground. Nevertheless, if Woman has a fair claim to an extra "8 percent" of *innate* goodness, I suppose that about covers it. The other 92 percent is overlap. Our focus here is on that "92 percent."

Protected Innocence

If the female shadow is a match for the male shadow, why then do we not perceive it so? Why is it that **ManBad/WomanGood** stands out in bold while ManGood/WomanBad is something we must strain to see? This chapter will focus on the various factors biasing our perceptions. We begin with the one factor that stands above all others: *protection*.

Men protect women's innocence in so many ways. Both sexes love to see burgers, chops and steaks on the dinner table, but only one sex does the dirty work of slaughtering the animals. The other sex is free to feel that she could "never do such an awful thing." What does it do to those men who spend their days working at a slaughterhouse, violently taking the lives of hundreds of animals, each one an aware living creature?

Since the Stone Age, Man has been assigned the role of hunter. Whalers are men who hunt and kill whales. With the decline of whale and other wildlife populations there comes the guilt of Man the exterminator of species. But what the hunter does, he does for the benefit of the entire community. Both sexes used whale oil in their lamps and whale oil had always been a key component in women's cosmetics, but these facts are indirect and do little to transfer guilt to Woman. The whaler's paycheck supports a wife and family. But that doesn't change our perception of him as a violent killer. Images of men wielding enormous scythes slicing whale abdomens—the guts spilling out onto the deck—linger in the mind. To support his family, a whaler endures one of *the* harshest, most hazardous, grueling, disgusting roles imaginable. But who would sympathize with a "killer"?

We've all seen footage of men clubbing baby seals (clubs are used because they are safer than guns and less likely to damage the valuable pelt). What do such images do to our collective image of Man? Those pitiable men aren't clubbing seals for sadistic thrills. They're earning a family-supporting wage in what is, perhaps, the only manner available to them. And let us not be so quick to forget that most of those sealskins become *women's* apparel.

Many a housewife isn't forced to confront the depth of *her* dark side even to the extent of killing a bug in her bathroom. While her husband is flushing the crawly thing down the toilet, his wife is free to believe she "wouldn't hurt a fly." She's not asked to darken her soul clubbing baby seals for the paycheck needed to support a husband and family. Down through the millennia the greatest protection Woman has received has been protection from the need to confront and/or act out the dark side of her human nature. In all areas of life, Man gives Woman the gift of feeling "angelic." In return Woman has given Man the gift of feeling "masterful." The gender system has always been an imperfect but *balanced* system.

There are many biases influencing our perception of women as morally superior. One of the more pervasive influences involves biases in the definition, the reporting, and the sentencing of crime. Crime statistics have always lent an air of objectivity to our condemnation of men as the Bad sex—the "criminal sex." They still do.

One way to study the effects of protected innocence is to study what happens as that veil of protection is slowly lifted.

Publicized Crime

As of 1993, no woman in the U.S. had been executed—for killing only men—since 1954.[750] Seven years later in year 2000 we had 49 women on death row. It is likely that many or perhaps most of them have been or will be executed—and not without cause.

We have, for example, the now famous Aileen Wuornos, age 43, who shot seven men dead. "Her motive for the killings was her hatred of men," said an investigator with the Marion County Sheriff's Office. "She worked as a prostitute just to lead the men to their deaths." And then there's Keny Lynn Dalton, age 40, who was not at all "ladylike" in her treatment of 23-year-old Irene May. Believing that the younger woman had stolen from her, she "beat her, shocked her with electricity and injected her with flesh eating battery acid before stabbing her to death with a screwdriver." She was easy to catch for her crime because she couldn't stop bragging about it. Mary Samuels, age 51, hired her own daughter's fiancé, James Bernstein, to kill her husband Robert so she could inherit her husband's $500,000 fortune. The new widow then tidied up the loose ends by having another hit man kill Bernstein. "Samuels celebrated her new wealth by throwing a big bash after treating herself to a new Porsche." Jacqueline Williams, age 33, killed a nine-months pregnant woman of her acquaintance, then sliced the woman open and stole the still-living fetus. Her crime was so premeditated that soon after thinking of it, "Williams began telling her friends she was pregnant and even had a baby shower."

The above stories are quoted from *The Globe*.[751] The same facts may be found in more respected sources. So, why quote a "tabloid?" Because, as compared with respected journals, the tabloid screaming its headlines at us while we wait in the checkout line is massively more effective in bringing these facts to public attention. These stories, and many more like them, are making the news more and more frequently.

The more women hear about the base things other women have done, the more *imaginable* such behavior becomes.

A segment of *The Twentieth Century* with Mike Wallace produced these next two opinions referring to the above dynamic as it relates to school-age kids. Dr. James Alan Fox, author and professor of criminal justice from Northeastern University: "The more it has happened in our century, the more schoolyard snipers that we've seen the more likely it is to happen again because of a contagion or copycat effect."[752] Forensic psychologist Dr. Charles Ewing, of State University of New York, agrees: "I think it's not that 'I want to be like the young man who was in the newspaper yesterday who killed somebody,' but 'I *could* be like him. He did it. I could do it.' The very fact that someone else has done it gives me, a disturbed child, the idea that I could do it."[753] Disturbed children and adults come in both sexes. Lately, a few of the female variety must be thinking, "I could be like *her*. *She* did it. *I* could do it."

Historically, most young women were brought up to think that being female precluded being truly violent. If being violent meant being less "ladylike," then gender pride and pressure would further inhibit such behavior (as it has, for example, always inhibited men's tears). But today's girls are being brought around to the thought that "just because I'm female doesn't mean I can't be violent."

Some members of urban girl-gangs are turning this very thought into lethal behavior. In an article for *Rolling Stone*, Léon Bing, author of *Do or Die*, "a book about rival L.A. gangs the Crips and the Bloods," quotes one such gang member.

> "Well, if we gonna rob somebody, we wear 'puttin' in work clothes—sweats, T-shirts, All-Stars, like that - but if we goin' in to do a payback, we'll dress like girls—little tennis shoes without socks, tank tops, shorts or a dress. We get out there like that and niggas'll try to talk to us, like they would to any girl walkin' down the street." She pauses. "And then we pull heat and bust on 'em." I interrupt to ask if that means to shoot. "Shoot, yeah. Bust a cap."[754]

This is as good an opportunity as any to point out a stray but important truth. Make note of it yourself and see if it isn't so. Whether in standup comedy or a movie or a book or whatever the media, whenever anyone refers to a "nigger," there is about a 95 percent chance he or she is referring to a black *male*, not female. Consciously, we think of men in terms of occupying the top, but unconsciously we also think of men as occupying the bottom.

By placing this story on its cover, *Rolling Stone* magazine is helping to publicize violent behaviors perpetrated by young female gang members roaming the streets of Los Angeles. Along with whatever good the reporting may do, whatever insights may be revealed, the publicizing of violence begets more violence, which begets more publicity and so on.

The pro-censorship position, argued since the days of Plato's *Republic*,[755] is reasoned something like this: Publicized accounts of aberrant behavior make such behavior more imaginable and thus more doable. There may always be those who harbor aberrant *thoughts*, but a societally enforced naiveté that would leave the public unaware of anyone ever *acting out* such thoughts should, theoretically, provide an effective inhibitor of aberrant *behavior*.

To a degree far more than we know, women have always behaved badly. But society has maintained a general naiveté with regard to this behavior, and has done so in much the same manner as Plato recommended it be maintained for *both* sexes. The rule has been to consider women essentially innocent of such things and to dismiss female acts of violence as rare aberrations, most likely justified and best kept quiet.

Lizzie Borden

> "Lizzie Borden took an ax, gave her father 40 whacks.
> When she saw what she had done, gave her mother 41."

If the rule has been to protect women and protect the angelic image of women, then the case of Lizzie Borden (1893) is both a prime example and striking exception.

Her case is an exception to the rule in that she and what she allegedly did became famous. She is a prime example of the rule in action in that, despite ample evidence against her and a prime motive (inheriting her father's wealth), Lizzie Borden was never at any appreciable risk of prosecution for murder—primarily because the contemporary populace were of the firm opinion that "A woman is not capable of such a thing."[756]

"Hosea Knowlton was a reluctant prosecutor, forced into the role by the politically timid Arthur Pillsbury, Attorney General of Massachusetts, who should have been the principal attorney for the prosecution. As Lizzie's trial date approached, Pillsbury felt the pressure building from Lizzie's supporters, particularly women's groups and religious organizations."[757]

Naturally, Knowlton was reluctant to prosecute a member of the presumed-innocent sex; consider the magnitude of the societal forces that mobilized in her defense. "Major newspapers, feminists groups such as 'The Bloomer Girls,' the Women's Christian Temperance Union and clergy criticized her arrest."[758] Well, of *course* they protested a *woman's* arrest. How *dare* the legal system fail to recognize the sanctity of a woman?! Then as now, the sisterhood (backed by chivalry) rose up to protect one of its own.

In his closing remarks, the chivalrous judge himself spoke as advocate for her "and even discredited certain points the prosecution had made."[759] Following the closing arguments from both the defense and the prosecution, "Justice Dewey, who had been appointed to the Superior Court bench by then Governor Robinson, then delivered his charge to the jury, which was, in effect, a second summation of the case for the defense, remarkable in its bias."[760] No more remarkable than the bias shown throughout.

> One of her defense lawyers, an ex-governor of the State, summed up the argument for the defense: "Gentlemen, to find Lizzie Borden guilty you must believe that she is a fiend. Does she look it? The prisoner at the bar is a woman, and a Christian woman, the equal of your wife and mine." The jury was out for an hour and a half. The verdict was unanimously for acquittal. Lizzie Borden, who had become somewhat of a symbol of women's rights, was tearfully embraced by throngs of well-wishers.[761]

Here we see the "halo effect" in action. Because women appear more like "angels," they are presumed to be more angelic.

The power of The Governor is impressive, but it is a power distributed only to a few *elite* men. By contrast, Ms. Borden's impressive female power was/is distributed among women *in general.*

Let's clear the haze here. Was Borden really a symbol of "women's *rights*"? No one doubted the legality of her trial, so what do "women's *rights*" have to do with it (unless of course by *women's* rights we mean a special, altogether higher class of rights)? Or, were women's groups rushing to her defense because her potential conviction was seen as a potential threat to women's presumed moral and ethical superiority? Church organizations also rushed to her aid yet, following the trial, "Lizzie found it impossible to attend church because of her ostracism."[762] Did throngs of well-wishers embrace her because they truly believed in her innocence (from then on, she was also immediately and permanently ostracized by the people of her town[763]) or were they rushing to protect a woman (innocent or guilty) and thus protect the myth (true or false) that "A woman is not capable of such a thing"?

Normally, once acquitted, such women and the deeds they had done fall into obscurity and do not sully the image of womankind. In her case though, what Lizzie had allegedly done with her ax when she gave her father's and her stepmother's faces "forty whacks" was so shocking, it became a rare example of female violence rendered immortal. Because it was believed to be so rare, even an extreme case like hers did little to change the public's conviction that "A woman is not capable of such a thing." Besides, she was *not* convicted.

"By her own admission, she had attempted to purchase hydrocyanic acid at a local pharmacy, to 'clean a sealskin coat.' The substance, several professionals testified, is fatal in small doses, absorbed readily into the nervous system, and leaves no post-mortem symptoms. It is not used as a cleaning agent." Furthermore, "The day before her imprisonment, Lizzie was observed by a friend burning a dress similar to the one she had on the day of the murders."[764] An ax with freshly broken handle and a blade that fit the wounds perfectly was found in the basement. It had recently been cleaned with ashes.

The attacks on both the father and stepmother had focused specifically on their faces. The father got ten whacks, the stepmother nineteen. Half of the father's face had been sliced clean off. On an intuitive level, we suspect that the attacker *must* have been profoundly emotionally invested in the victims to harbor the kind of deep personal rage that would target their *faces* in this manner. Thus the notion that some passing stranger had done the deed seems highly unlikely. "The prosecution presented an overwhelming case of circumstantial evidence; Lizzie's jury of twelve men acquitted her. Some think Lizzie's verdict was 'jury nullification' - when the jury ignores evidence. It was said the jury didn't believe a Christian young woman could have killed."[765]

It makes little difference whether Ms. Borden was, in fact, guilty or innocent. The point is, despite damning evidence, she was *never* seriously threatened with prosecution. Those twelve chivalrous men found her "innocent" after deliberating for little more than *one* hour. It was a case of a woman protected from sinking to the bottom of a jail cell—a woman walking upon her Glass Floor.

The Glass Floor

Throughout history, whenever Woman looked up, she perceived what we now call the Glass Ceiling, a sort of semi-permeable membrane composed of social conditioning, gender roles, tradition, bias, and various legal and sociopolitical structures. In looking down, however, she might have noticed that she was walking on a kind of Glass Floor composed of all the same stuff.

As the Glass Ceiling, in myriad ways both nebulous and concrete, has always tended to thwart Woman's rise to the top, so the Glass Floor, in myriad ways both nebulous and concrete, has always tended to safeguard her from sinking to the extreme bottom.

Throughout history, the Glass Floor has protected women from sinking to the bottoms of mine shafts, prison cells, and foxholes. The

Glass Floor has acted as partial insulation between women and the dark side of the world and human nature as well as insulation between women and most of life on earth's most *deeply* brutal, filthy, arduous, corrupting, and hazardous realities.

Through the Glass Ceiling a woman could view the tip of the success pyramid and see that it was mostly male occupied. In looking down through the Glass Floor, however, she could view the vast base of the pyramid and see that it too has been occupied mostly by men—men who were trained to kill in order to protect being killed or maimed by the thousands and the millions on battlefields (many tortured mercilessly in prisoner-of-war camps for months or years).

Many of these men end up on the streets to join the 85 percent male street homeless. Others end up imprisoned. Less than a third of men are veterans, yet more than half of the imprisoned are veterans. Thus veterans too often join other men—protector/providers corrupted in the pursuit of money (the root of all evil)—to be suffocated and tortured by the thousands and the millions in the penal system.

Consider also men obligated for toughness, strength, and courage who, throughout history, have been killed or maimed by the thousands and the millions through hard labor, the use of heavy machinery, and countless other at-work hazards. In recent decades women have comprised 45 percent of the workforce but a mere 6 percent of all work-related fatalities.[766] In keeping with being more loved, women are better *protected*.

Moreover, one woman's floor is another man's ceiling. A hefty proportion of men have always felt trapped *beneath* the Glass Floor down at the *base* of the human pyramid. When stigmatized prisoners, war-torn soldiers, and disabled laborers look up, the Glass Ceiling *they* experience is the Glass Floor women walk upon. Men have always occupied *both* extremes, the most *and* the least enviable positions on earth—the latter in far greater numbers than the former. Meanwhile, women have largely occupied the middle ground. In my view, that is neither "oppression" nor "victimization;" that is an even deal.

If we don't see it that way it's because conditions for women are not normally compared against conditions suffered by men occupying the true bottom rung. These "garbage men" and their sufferings have little presence in our minds and in our hearts.

The opposite of love isn't hate; it is *indifference.* As Woman has been given reason to feel intellectually invisible, Man has been given reason to feel invisible with regard to caring, concern, and compassion. Only those men who perform, achieve, and succeed rise to respect and visibility. Thus, only the elite male is present enough in our minds to compare against. Naturally, if we only compare conditions for the *average* woman against conditions for the *elite* male, women will seem to be *the* powerless victims every time. But this conclusion is the standard conclusion only because it sustains a beloved illusion.

Presumed Innocence

All Fault Is Male. That's the rule. It all balances out though because, by corollary, All Credit Is Male as well.

Michael Newton, author of *Bad Girls Do It!*, "the *only* book on female multiple murderers ever assembled," writes: "Feminists complain, and rightly so, that women's contributions have been largely overlooked and undervalued in the annals of American—and world—history. . . . Ironically, a venue typically ignored is also one where modern females demonstrate a strong determination to succeed. That field is crime."[767]

Again and again Newton expresses amazement at the murderess's astonishing immunity to suspicion, and tells the stories of many a "Black Widow" who made a *career* of killing one husband after another enabled by that immunity. As is true of MP/FV, our belief in MB/WG is based on something more powerful than logic. No matter how many times the myth is exploded it always reforms. Cultural amnesia takes place, and Aileen Wuornos is declared the "first-ever" female serial killer. Michael and C. L. Kelleher:

> Judging by the limited information about female serial murderers that has been made public in this country, the very concept of such a criminal seems to have been turned aside by a strong cultural bias that denies her existence. . . . In view of this social bias, it is no wonder that she is often able to go on killing for many years before she is finally apprehended. Whereas names such as Dahmer, Gacy, DeSalvo, and Ted Bundy are instantly recognized for their heinous exploits, few Americans have heard of Genene Jones, Bobbie Sue Terrell, or Jane Toppan. However, Jones, Terrell, and Toppan . . . may have been responsible for as many as 128 deaths. Clearly, these three women were killers whose stature in crime was equal or beyond that of Dahmer, Gacy, DeSalvo, and Bundy. However, to most Americans, these women bear unfamiliar names and their crimes have been largely ignored or forgotten.[768]

According to a law enforcement study, police officers are known to identify female law-breakers "with their mother, sisters, or daughters." Naturally they feel "reluctant" to arrest them. "Women of all races are the least likely offenders to be processed beyond the arrest stage."[769] The Glass Floor still holds. In many, perhaps the vast majority of instances throughout history, women who behaved badly, being women, were never suspected. Some were suspected but never arrested. Others were arrested but, being female, were all but immune to prosecution. Allowing memory to fade with regard to those statistically few women who were suspected *and* arrested *and* prosecuted *and* convicted has led to an exaggerated perception of female innocence.

From the masculist perspective, crime statistics only measure two things: female legal immunity and the zeal with which society exposes, targets, blames, and punishes men. Yet crime statistics are *damning*, seeming to condemn Man and exonerate Woman beyond any doubt. This culturally enforced naiveté of the female shadow has, at least to some extent, been self-fulfilling. But, of course, it has been in effect only where women are concerned.

Unlike the potential female killer, he knew that many had come before him, and had become famous to boot, but if Jeffery Dahmer had truly believed that taking action on the thoughts in his head meant doing things no man had ever done before, it's quite possible he wouldn't have done them either. For millennia a woman with depraved thoughts in her head was specially inhibited from acting out because she so firmly believed that women did not do such things.

Of late, however, a woman can scarcely believe that such behavior, coming from a woman, is anything like unprecedented. Despite media bias, women behaving badly *are* making the six o'clock news. And in the realms of popular fiction we're seeing increasing numbers of women acting out in increasingly cruel, belligerent, and brutally violent ways. Like men before them, women are having their naiveté and innocence taken from them. As in all things, the consequences are both good and *bad*.

Women who do what men do become what men are. And, as the veil of protection slowly lifts, Woman's shadow is revealed.

Abu Ghraib

A heavily publicized example is the prisoner-abuse scandal in Iraq. Though media-supplied rationalizations abound, this time, even certain feminists have been forced to admit that the behavior of certain female soldiers toward Iraqi prisoners cannot easily be dismissed.

Says Kathleen Parker:

> The American women of Abu Ghraib have put to eternal rest any notion that girls are made of sugar 'n' spice and prompted a flurry of possible answers to the question: How could women have done such things? . . . Some feminists have expressed deep disappointment to discover that women can be just as bad as men. Barbara Ehrenreich wrote that a certain kind of feminism - a feminist naiveté - died in Abu

Ghraib. No longer could men be viewed as perpetual perpetrators and women as perpetual victims. Activists in the men's movement - some of them victims of domestic violence - expressed no surprise. "What happened in Abu Ghraib is no isolated incident, no aberration," wrote Ray Blumhorst for MensNewsDaily.com. "I have little doubt that all of the females implicated at Abu Ghraib will have little trouble finding jobs in the multibillion-dollar VAWA (Violence Against Women Act) domestic violence industry, just as soon as 'American, gender feminist justice' rationalizes away all their misbehavior."[770]

What if "some masculists" had "expressed deep disappointment to discover that men can be just as dumb as women"? *Now* do we see the sexism?

The shock contained in the question "How could *women* have done such things?" is scarcely any different from the Victorian conviction "A woman is not capable of such a thing"—a conviction that sheltered Lizzie Borden over a century ago.

The feminist naiveté is humanity's naiveté with regard to the dark side of Woman's human nature. And that naiveté most definitely did *not* die in Abu Ghraib. National Coalition For Men (NCFM) member Ray Blumhorst is right of course; the culture will enlist "experts" to perform whatever ideological sleight of hand necessary to protect the myth of female moral superiority.

Mary Jo Malone for the St. Petersburg Times:

> I can't get that picture of [Lynndie] England out of my head because this is not how women are expected to behave. Feminism taught me 30 years ago that not only had women gotten a raw deal from men, we were morally superior to them. When it came to distinguishing right from wrong, the needle of our compass always pointed to true north. Our thinking was hardly radical. Victorian was more like it: Men were competitive and dangerous, women cooperative and comforting. Men were brutish, women gentle.[771]

No, this is *not* how women are expected to behave, certainly not within a culture as female chauvinist as is the feminist culture. But what of *male* chauvinism?

Larry Summers, then president of Harvard University, had only to suggest that biological factors *might* constitute *one* of the reasons for Man's ongoing dominance in math and science, and it was enough to take him down. Any notion of *male* superiority is attacked with a vengeance. Meanwhile, as the "How could *women* have done such things?" reaction to Abu Ghraib makes clear, feminists have felt scant challenge to assumptions of *female* superiority.

I observe the positive stereotypes regarding men (intellect, competence, prestige; toughness, strength, courage) plummet while the positive stereotypes of women (beauty, grace, goodness; home, family, parenting) diminish only a little. Moreover, I'm seeing women's presumed innocence diminish more within the false reality of the movie screen (in which fictional characters face no *real* consequences), than in the true reality of a court of law.

Sally Pipes, president and CEO of the Pacific Research Institute, quotes more of Ehrenreich's musings in the wake of Abu Ghraib:

> Feminist strategy Ehrenreich wrote, "rested on the assumption, implicit or stated outright, that women were morally superior to men. We had a lot of debates over whether it was biology or conditioning that gave women the moral edge -- or simply the experience of being a woman in a sexist culture. But the assumption of superiority, or at least a lesser inclination toward cruelty and violence, was more or less beyond debate." That assumption made strategy easy. Given the moral superiority of women, one simply puts as many women as possible into positions of power and, by some strange invisible female hand, we will have a better society than the version offered by morally inferior, inherently violent men.[772]

Men are assumed to be more inclined toward "cruelty," and "morally inferior" and "inherently violent" yet it is also assumed that "the experience of being a woman in a sexist culture" stands alone as a *uniquely* female experience?

Should the *sexist* myth of female moral superiority ever *really* fade away, it will come as part of a massive gender paradigm shift that; apparently, we're still not ready for. Truth be told, the goings on at Abu Ghraib have *already* faded from memory. Even so, I assume the MB/WG myth is destined to diminish over time. As the veil of protection lifts, the true *human* nature of Woman is revealed. And, as women climb ever higher up various success ladders, the need for female accountability rises apace.

Indira Gandhi, Golda Meir, Margaret Thatcher—the more women leaders there are, the more women we have sending men off to war in the usual numbers. But shouldn't female leaders be sending *females* off to war? Charges of "draft evasion" have plagued many candidates, including presidential candidate Bill Clinton. But aren't *all* female candidates "draft evaders"? We denigrate men for being "warlike," then turn around and imprison men for "draft dodging." We denigrate soldiers as the violent cause of war, then execute those same men for "cowardice" should they run *away* from violence.

Is it feminism's intention to change over to women leaders while men remain the cannon fodder? Is that arrangement justified because men really do have less human value? Are men really just no damn good?

ManGood

It is telling that, even with me, the case for ManGood comes as something of an afterthought. The Goodness of Man is far too easily rejected from the mind. No matter how many women behave badly, WomanBad continues to register as the exception. No matter how many men behave with honor, integrity, compassion, sensitivity, and high moral purpose, ManGood continues to register as the exception. Women say that "A good man is hard to find," and we accept the accusation without protest.

Granted, men like Jesus Christ, Mahatma Gandhi, Abraham Lincoln, John F. Kennedy, and Martin Luther King are universally accepted as Good. But it would seem that men can achieve that status only if they're martyred.

Remember Tiananmen Square, 1989, and the young Chinese man who stood in front of a line of advancing tanks? No matter how the lead tank swerved this way and that, the young man ran and stood directly in its path, daring the tank to run him over. With the whole world watching, the tank commander was unwilling to do so. Thus the young man thwarted, however temporarily, governmental use of force and violence. Known only as "The Tank Man," we don't know the man's name or what became of him. Though the names of dozens of violent men come readily to mind, the name of this warrior for peace is lost to us. Historically, there have been thousands of anonymous men who protested war and violence. But they have more often been labeled "draft-dodgers" and "cowards" than heroes.

We often hear of a man saved by the love of a good woman. But hasn't a woman still living in her parents' home been saved by the love of a good *man* who provides her with a home of her own? Aren't there millions of good men fighting fires and rescuing others at the risk or cost of their lives? Stories of men risking or sacrificing their lives to protect the lives of women are daily fare in newspapers all over the world. Says Warren Farrell, "Although I've asked over a million people (on TV and radio) to send me a story of a woman risking her life to save an *adult* man, so far, no stories."[773]

But then the role of rescuer is not a role women are expected to take. So much of what men and women are comes down the roles men and women are assigned to play.

"Good Cop/Bad Cop"

Interrogators regularly employ a technique known as "good-cop/bad-cop." In this "game," one cop plays the role of hard, cruel "bastard," while the other plays the role of soft, sympathetic "friend." Most often, either cop is fully capable of playing either role. And so, even if just for the sake of variety, the partners often switch roles when going from one case to the next. In this same way, women and men could also "switch roles." But, so long as men fulfill the role of Bad Cop, women are free to play Good Cop and appear relatively elevated above and beyond the dark side of the world and human nature.

In order to effect the unpleasant but necessary task of extracting a confession, one of the two partners must assume the unpleasant but necessary role of Bad Cop. Those assigned any one of countless unpleasant but necessary tasks must delve into the dark side of the world and human nature including, perhaps, the dark side of their *own* human nature. Traditionally, such tasks are assigned to men.

American women didn't respond to the Cuban Missile Crisis by taking up arms, but is that indication of female moral superiority or female confidence that American men would take the role of Bad Cop and deal with it? Had American men remained pacifist even as arms continued to build up, or even as an invasion force continued to build up, are we sure American women would have been entirely happy about that? Would women have praised their men for being so re-strained, so nonviolent, so Good? Or would women have screamed bloody murder at men for being such cowards?

In Britain during WWI, groups of feminists, including suffragettes Emmeline and Christabel Pankhurst, used public humiliation to coerce men into enlisting. They, and many other women, presented white feathers, symbols of cowardice, to men who had not enlisted.

"One young woman remembers her father, Robert Smith, being given a feather on his way home from work: 'That night he came home and cried his heart out. My father was no coward, but had been reluctant to leave his family. He was thirty-four and my mother, who had two young children, had been suffering from a serious illness. Soon after this incident my father joined the army.'"[774] Even as they bitterly campaigned for the right to vote, these women goaded only men into fighting and dying to defend their right to vote against fascist incursion. Suffragettes felt powerlessness, but the men handed white feathers also felt powerless—powerless to lift from themselves conflicting obligations in all directions (how was a man to defend his country *and* protect his family?).

Historically, British men had fought and died in *huge* numbers to replace aristocracy with democracy and win *their* right to vote. The election of 1910 was the *first* in which a majority of men (21 and over) qualified for suffrage.[775] Eight years later, without shedding a drop of blood, British women were given the right to vote. Yet, to this day, no women anywhere are saddled with the conscripted *obligation* to defend their right to vote out on the battlefield.

Do women abuse power? "Although he was a serving soldier, the writer, Compton Mackenzie, complained about the activities of the Order of the White Feather. He argued that these 'idiotic young women were using white feathers to get rid of boyfriends of whom they were tired'."[776] Is this not the power to shame raised even to the power to arbitrarily send a man to his death?

Women have always done their part in goading men into war. They haven't always done it quite so overtly as through the use of white feathers, but then, they haven't had to. One of the many reasons we don't see female power is that femininity is *so* powerful, it coerces even when plied with extreme subtlety. A mere look, a mere gesture, a sigh, a tear can be enough to compel male action. Back in 1962, it was taking all this for granted that allowed Woman to react passively to the threat of Soviet nuclear weapons placed a mere 90 miles off-shore. American women had nothing to worry about. American men reacted to the Soviet threat, *and* managed to avoid armed conflict.

We all rely on those men who get their hands dirty to keep the whole American enterprise going. Women have the same vested interest in these matters as men. And women's influence is not entirely passive. "Throughout history," says Martin Van Creveld, author of *Men, Women and War*, "there have been countless occasions when women actively and deliberately incited their menfolk to war. To adapt a reported saying of Karl Marx: 'it is impossible to overestimate the historical role played by women. When [war] comes they are swept along.'"[777]

The ramifications of consumerism insinuate themselves among the causes of war, and women's spending dominates almost every consumer category. Surely some of the greed that fuels war derives from women's "shop-aholism." And, arguably, women are far more into luxury and materialism than men.[778] It is legitimate to ask: how much of the impetus for war derives from women's insatiable consumerism? But we're very reluctant to ask questions that might upset women. Why are we so afraid to upset the "powerless" sex?

Could it be that Man's greatest material aspirations are motivated solely by the allure status-symbol possessions have upon Woman? (Any boat enthusiast will readily observe that the bigger the yacht, the more beautiful the women on board.) As Aristotle Onassis famously said: "If women did not exist, all the money in the world to me would have no meaning."[779] From the *masculist* perspective, fortunes are amassed and wars are fought for the sake of women.

Are only a rare few women causally involved in war and violence? "Not really," says Patricia Pearson. "Ordinary women have proven to be just as militaristic, supporting the continuance of war, shaming men who would dodge the draft, screaming for blood in a mob, fighting alongside their brothers and sons when they could, acting as snipers, as fighter pilots, as guerrilla soldiers and terrorists."[780]

Neither sex wants long lines at the gas station. Polls taken at the time made it clear that both sexes were in favor of the Gulf War because *both* sexes rely on the free flow of affordable oil and the steady economy that goes with it. Preaching "national security" is a universal vote getter. When women vote for those politicians who support the manufacture and use of armaments, they provide their 56 percent of the voting force that backs them.

Clearly, both sexes are subject to the potential violence of The Enemy, so both sexes are wary. Presumably, most of the populace, be they male or female, are levelheaded and peaceful. Even so, it only takes a few troublemakers to initiate a conflict that may rapidly spin out of control. Are there female "trouble makers" out there? Robert Winston, author of *Human Instinct*, believes so.

> In general, many women have shown themselves to be just as warlike as their male counterparts, and if they don't fight themselves, women can be the cheerleaders for warlike activity, even when the men aren't so eager. One eighteenth-century anthropologist described how women of the Ba-Huana tribe of the Congo used to make fun of their men if they didn't retaliate after an attack by a rival tribe. 'You are afraid,' they would say, 'and we will have no more intercourse with you.' The men, then, had little choice but to go out and fight.[781]

Not only is this an example of female "troublemakers," it is also indicative of female power: sexual power, power to shame, and the power to use men's honor against them.

We look at the women we know and the thought of them waging war certainly does seem absurd. But, if we take an unbiased look at the men we know, doesn't the thought of these men waging war seem very nearly as absurd? Within a well-established military structure, it only takes a few men well suited to the warrior ideal to shame the rest into following suit. Many of these "warriors" excel at nothing else. They "love" war because without it they go from being a "colonel" to being a "janitor" (and, in the eyes of women, they go from being a "catch" to being a "barrel scraping"). Few men truly become "warriors," and then only after *extensive* conditioning and training.

If women are so peace-loving, "what are we to make of the women who have hunted and fought battles—with no less ferocity than men—in societies throughout history: in, for example, Libya, Anatolia,

Bulgaria, Greece, Armenia, Russia, Celtic England, and northern Scotland? That Western historians have exhibited an almost universal tendency to ignore such women does not, in itself, render them freaks of nature."[782] Mainstream culture may presume female innocence but Interpol's anti-terrorist squads are advised to "shoot the women first," because female terrorists are widely regarded as more dangerous than their male counterparts.[783]

Both sexes have a causal influence on war. In fact, arguably, women are equal partners with men in plying the primal forces that lead to war. But, in keeping with Woman's preference for plying influence indirectly, manipulatively, and covertly, Woman is tarnished with almost none of the guilt for war.

Given the tricky, unstable emotional and psychological potentials, it doesn't take much for The Other, so strange and mysterious, to become The Enemy. Both sexes fear The Enemy. Only one sex, however, is forcibly recruited to risk nightmarish suffering and death to protect us from what both sexes fear. Both sexes stand to gain from "the spoils of war" but only the lives of men will be sacrificed in the process.

Why is that? The obvious answer would seem to be that men are the ones chosen to protect because men are larger, stronger, more physically aggressive. If we dig deeper though, we may discover some even more fundamental biology involved.

Two Tribes: Let's simplify matters. Let's imagine two tribes; we'll call them Tribe A and Tribe B. And let's sidestep the issue of size and strength by imagining that the men and women of these two tribes are the same in terms of size, strength, aggression, and so on. Finally, let's add that both tribes are comprised of exactly fifty men and fifty women (plus assorted children). War is declared! Tribe A sends its males off to do battle; Tribe B sends its females. When the dust settles, we see that ten men and ten women are left standing. The survivors on each side call it a draw and limp home to their respective tribes.

Both tribes now assess their situation.

The ten remaining men in Tribe A can easily impregnate all fifty of the women who stayed safely at home. So Tribe A can expect the same number of offspring in its next generation as if they had lost no men at all. With so few men Tribe A must endure hardship but, with luck, Tribe A will soon replenish its numbers and regain its former strength. Tribe B, on the other hand, now has only one fifth as many women as before and can expect only about one fifth as many offspring in its next generation. Further, many of the forty women who died will leave behind infant children (some not yet weaned) who will be left at risk without their mothers to feed and care for them. Also, in losing any pregnant women in battle, Tribe B lost not only the women, but also the unborn children. Tribe B will have to eke out survival for many generations before it slowly regains its former numbers.

Less than twenty years later Tribe A is ready for a rematch; Tribe B is not.

When left with only ten men, Tribe A is left with a strong chance for survival. When left with only ten women, Tribe B is left with only a slim chance for survival. The lesson? Send males off to do battle because, in military lingo, males are "expendable." (In fact, arguably, proto-humans—frail, neither fleet of foot nor well defended—survived and flourished, in large part, as a result of raising the protection of women and children up from instinct to *conscious* priority.)

Any hunter will tell you that it makes better sense to hunt males than females. Hunting males allows for a continuing population to hunt. Hunting females, on the other hand, is more likely to lead to extermination. A game reserve's quotas and penalties are set accordingly. For this reason, any species in which the females protected the males would be a species disadvantaged in the long-term fight for evolutionary survival, which is why few if any such species exist.

Increasing the size, strength, and aggression of the female relative to the male doesn't change the fact that females are the limiting factor in reproduction (the number of females, not the number of males, determines the number of offspring). Therefore, even if we imagine females larger and more aggressive than males, basic group survival strategy dictates that the females must still be the ones protected. Over time, simple Darwinism will evolve fighting males who grow larger, stronger, and more aggressive while protected females become smaller, weaker, and less physically aggressive.

I will offer the following three conclusions: 1) The chivalric instinct to protect females is *hardwired*. A "protect the females" imperative is written directly into the human genetic code. 2) The male's greater size, strength, and aggression are not the *reason* males protect females. Males protect females because female survival is more crucial to group survival. The relative expendability of the male is the true underlying reason why males are given extra weaponry (horns, antlers) and assigned the task of protecting the herd. 3) The male's greater size, strength, and aggression are not the *cause* of war. They are *adaptations* which allow the male of the species to better perform and survive the role (Bad Cop) to which biological fate has assigned him.

Author John Moore has reached similar conclusions:

> The requirement that he should develop strength and skill to procure more effectively became compounded by the increasing need for that prowess to be used for fighting and killing other human beings as well

as animals. . . . in a situation where there was no commonly recognized right of land ownership, defense and attack were more or less synonymous. Group survival thus much depended on a social conditioning which endorsed the male's instinct to be competitive. . . . Yet again, it has to be said that this conditioning was primarily instigated in the interests of group survival. The current feminist charge that the male is willfully aggressive seems conveniently to overlook the fact that for millennia the female must have condoned his being so . . . for her own matriarchal interests depended on it.[784]

Human communities no longer struggle to maintain numbers large enough to ensure long-term survival. The instinctual impetus for protecting females no longer applies in the human realm. But the deeply rooted sentiments and evolutionary psychology remain. And so, despite the 14th Amendment's guarantee of equal protection under the law, to this day only 18-year-old *males* are required, under *severe* penalty of law, to sign up at the draft board.

Additionally, size, strength, and aggression are often deciding factors when males fight each other for the dominance that will determine their breeding status. Mary Batten, author of *Sexual Strategies: How Females Choose Their Mates,* explains:

> "In preliterate societies competition over women probably is the single most important cause of violence," says anthropologist Donald Symons. Even among people known to be peaceable, such as the Bushmen of the Kalahari Desert, most murders are committed by men in argument over women. . . . The Yanomamo Indians of Venezuela and Brazil . . . wage bloody wars that usually begin over sexual issues such as infidelity or suspicion of infidelity, jealousy, attempts to seduce another man's wife, seizure of a married woman or a woman from a visiting group, and failure to give up a girl promised in marriage.
>
> The fighting can be so intense that villages split up. When this happens, each warring group becomes a new village and often an enemy of the other. . . . In an international study, sociobiologists Martin Daly and Margo Wilson found that the overwhelming proportion of homicides are committed by men against men, as opposed to murders of women by men or of men by women. In some North American cities, men kill other men at rates as high as 93 to 99 percent. Male-male murders are also concentrated among *young* men, from late adolescence through early adulthood—the period of life when they are most likely to be competing for the status and resources that attract mates.[785]

This is the kind of information/perspective that has masculists seeing a world controlled *entirely* by women. As Jerry Seinfeld once quipped: If women preferred men who went about on pogo sticks, overnight, all men would go about on pogo sticks. As they say: "Men rule the world, penises rule the men, and women rule the penises."

But I'm not suggesting that violence between men is caused solely by women. I'm simply saying that women are, and have always been, *involved*. They have a powerful effect on the men around them—*not always benevolent*.

Women are, for example, responsible for sexual choices that tend to reward the most aggressive "successful" male behaviors. Bad Boys are "hot;" Good Boys, not so hot. Upon release from prison, conscientious objectors are rarely mobbed by women with hearts aflutter, but everyone knows "women love a man in uniform." Women play a part in stimulating competition that pits one male against another (sometimes just to choose the winner and reject the loser).

To the degree one can argue, if there were no men there'd be no war, with equal validity one can argue, if there were no *women* there would be no war!

Dad plays Bad Cop, enforces the family rules, and administers punishment. Mom plays Good Cop and tends to the children's tears. But when the children misbehave she warns, "Wait till your father gets home!" Man plays Bad Cop; Woman plays Good Cop. Man plays the role of warrior and fights wars; Woman plays the role of lover/nurturer and stays home. Largely on the basis of the roles we play, Man is perceived as Bad and Woman is perceived as Good.

Corruption

Every boy who grows up to be a policeman, businessman, lawyer, politician . . . is subject to powerful forces of temptation and coercion that would corrupt or perhaps even destroy him. That's part of the risk he takes and the cost he pays for whatever prestige he earns. No housewives were involved in either torturing or humiliating the prisoners held at Abu Ghraib. The woman who stays home experiences many downsides in her role, but not ones that would lead to her moral corruption.

What corruption is a woman apt to encounter in her kitchen? What funds will she embezzle? Her policeman husband may have to decide what to do when faced with a paper bag containing two months' salary in bribe money. Whether he takes the money or not, either choice may destroy him. What comparable moral dilemma is his stay-at-home wife faced with? How much trouble is she going to get into during her trips to and from the grocery store? How much violence will she encounter in her cooperative world of women as compared with the violence a man may encounter fighting his way up the success ladder in his competitive world of men?

Now that women are entering the world of men and subjected to the same pressures and temptations as men, are these women behaving any better than men? Many think not: "there is simply no evidence," states Cathy Young, "that women in office are more compassionate or more ethical than men."

> In fact, Carol Moseley Braun, who was elected to the Senate as part of this wave of new women, is reported to have some really big ethical problems. I'm not saying that she's unique in this, because certainly a lot of male congressmen have ethical problems. All I'm saying is she's certainly no better in that respect. . . . I might add that in states where women are represented in large numbers in the legislatures, they have been every bit as likely as men to be involved in corruption scandals. There was a case in Arizona recently where a large number of legislators were caught in a sting operation involving bribery and organized crime. Several of the major culprits in that incident were women.[786]

When immersed in the world of money, "the root of all evil," and immersed in political power, the absolute of which "corrupts absolutely," women fall prey to the dark side as readily as men always have. The recent rise in female arrest and imprisonment statistics show that women are starting to pay the steep price men have always paid.

What else can we conclude but that the dark side of human nature was never male, it was always male *burden*.

The key to maintaining one's innocence is neither a will of iron nor a heart of gold. The surest route to remaining uncorrupted is avoidance of that which would corrupt you, and in this women are and always have been *hugely* advantaged. From time immemorial, Woman has been protected—not just from nature and not just from men. The single most all-pervasive protection Woman has experienced is protection from being confronted with, and from acting out on, *the shadow side of her own human nature.*

Woman's perceived innocence has been staunchly protected, but at what cost? What, for example, has Woman's successful evasion of blame cost her in gaining the respect and credit she deserves as equal partner in our world? What does Man's presumed moral inferiority cost him? And what price does society in general pay in exchange for its steadfast faith in the false MB/WG paradigm? These are the questions that concern us in the next chapter.

Man Demonized - The *Human* Cost

"The automatic and virtually universal assumption is that the source of evil is male."[787] – Lionel Tiger

We have looked at The Female Shadow: From Gray to Black and concluded that the female shadow is a match for the male shadow. We have looked at women's Protected Innocence and concluded that patriarchy has always provided partial insulation between Woman and the dark side of the world and human nature. In this third and last chapter of Male Mea Culpa, we turn our attention to the costs men, women, and society pay for strict adherence to the ManBad/Woman-Good (MB/WG) paradigm—a false paradigm.

Taken together, the Female Shadow and Protected Innocence came to the conclusion that the dark side of the world and human nature is not male, but rather male burden. Clearly, however, the world doesn't see it that way. Such condemnation has been heaped upon men as to lead many to question the value of masculinity in our world. "Could it be that men are determined to be greedy, aggressive, and brutish?" asks Sam Keen, author of *Fire in the Belly: On Being a Man*. "Does some selfish gene, some territorial imperative drive us blindly into hostile action?"[788] If so, what do we *do* with this evil, obdurate half of humanity?

Says author Andrew Kimbrell, "a little-known defective mythology about masculinity has been indelibly encoded into our social structures and psyches. Men live and breathe this myth on a daily basis. It is the basis for many of their dysfunctional daydreams and most of their nightmares. It has now led society into a dangerous 'misandry,' a belief that masculinity itself is responsible for most of the world's woes."[789] It is time now to catalogue the many destructive byproducts of this defective mythology.

Many costs have already been examined. We've looked at cultural misandry in education and the media. We know presumed guilt costs men a severe bias in courts of law that leads to longer average sentences in less well-funded prisons together with near exclusive subjection to capital punishment. We have also looked at the abuses men suffer in divorce court and ex parte proceedings within civil courts. The MB/WG assumption lies at the heart of society's demonization of "deadbeat" dads and leads also to the devaluing of fathers which leads to the deeply held impulse to award child custody to mothers. We've seen the evidence suggesting that lack of father energy is the single most virulent root cause of all the escalating social pathologies that concern us most. MB/WG assumptions also account for the lack of caring, concern, and compassion toward men that accounts for male levels of work-related fatality, homelessness, imprisonment, and suicide. And we've looked at the ways in which undermining men has left many women with the burden of single parenting.

In this chapter we will delve into the costs men pay within and throughout the entire military experience. We will also conjecture as to the damage MP/FV assumptions are having upon the military itself. In addition, we will look at current trends and what they portend. Finally, we will look at the costs women pay in conjunction with disowning their own human shadow.

Men, Women, and War

It would seem that women conditioned in feminism can find their victimhood in *anything*. In an issue of *Glamour Magazine* I find an article asking indignantly and in bold letters: **"When will women be allowed to go into combat?"**[790] *"Allowed"*? So, when will women be *allowed* to join men in hell? When will women be *allowed* in on the male-only "privilege" of being tortured in a prisoner-of-war camp, or mutilated by a land mine, or ordered to kill civilians, or look on helplessly as friends die, or . . . When will women no longer be "deprived" of such male "power" and "privilege"? From the masculist perspective, the feminist thinking regarding women and war is *incredibly* distorted.

Feminists, including feminist Hillary Clinton, will tell you that "Women have always been the primary victims of war. Women lose their husbands, their fathers, their sons in combat. Women often have to flee from the only homes they have ever known. Women are often the refugees from conflict and sometimes, more frequently in today's warfare, victims. Women are often left with the responsibility, alone, of raising the children."[791]

This sort of talk makes me wish I could fill a stadium with wartorn men and force feminists one at a time to step up to the podium and explain to these blinded, amputated, paralyzed, traumatized, disfigured, and otherwise physically/emotionally maimed men why women are the primary victims of war (especially upper-class American women like Hillary Clinton).

How about explaining women's ownership of victimhood to soldiers exposed to mustard gas?

> Mustard gas did not need to be inhaled to be effective — any contact with skin was sufficient. Exposure to 0.1 ppm was enough to cause massive blisters. Higher concentrations could burn flesh to the bone.

> It was particularly effective against the soft skin of the face and genitals. . . . A British nurse treating mustard gas cases recorded: "They cannot be bandaged or touched. We cover them with a tent of propped-up sheets. Gas burns must be agonizing because usually the other cases do not complain even with the worst wounds but gas cases are invariably beyond endurance and they cannot help crying out."[792]

Usually men keep *any* amount of pain invisible. It makes male pain so easy to ignore and dismiss. Even men can't keep *that* much pain invisible—but the men themselves can be hidden away in asylums, veteran's hospitals, prisons, and halfway houses across the nation.

Yet *women* have always been the primary victims of war? Perhaps we could drag these same feminists over to Arlington Cemetery so they can explain to dead husbands, fathers, and sons why they should pity those whose lives kept on going. With hearts as hard toward men as this, what hope for Man is there within "the coming matriarchy"? No matter how *hideously* men may suffer, the top female politicians of today find only their own gender's victimhood in *all* things—*even war*.

Fortunately, not all women see the battlefield on such naive terms. Author Patricia Pearson tells it like it is when she writes:

> In the First and Second World Wars, men in combat shit their pants with fear. They vomited and cried like babies, because, as one wrote, "Loud and violent death is screaming down from the sky and pounding the earth around you, smashing and pulping everything in the search for you." Men went into the world wars without hope of getting out—they died, went mad, or the war got won. In large part, the atrocities of war are committed as a response to the fear men feel. Terror and humiliation are the combustible fuels of rage. They are striking out blindly against their own predicament.[793]

The building of the Thailand/Burma railway during WWII witnessed the starvation and torture of over a *quarter million* Allied POWs resulting in the deaths of over *one hundred thousand* of these men. Cut through some of the harshest jungle on earth, the 250-mile railway (along with about a hundred bridges) was constructed by beaten, dying, disease-ravaged men. Though victimizers, the Japanese and Korean soldiers who administered the torture and death were themselves victims. "The Japanese soldier was trained in a world of cruelty. Brutality became a way of life."[794] "Recruits being knocked physically unconscious was . . . a routine part of the Japanese training."[795]

The Japanese soldiers suffered brutalization and in turn treated the Korean soldiers under their command like vermin, dealing savage beatings on a whim. In turn, the Korean soldiers took out their rage and humiliation upon the POWs. British POW Tom Collins forgot to bow to a Korean guard. "They hung me up by my fingers above my head," says Collins. "I was there about ten hours. And every time a Korean guard went by, you got kicked or shoved or punched."

One POW who fought back was punished to the extent of being chained upright with a heavy weight hung round his neck.

> They chained this poor devil and they just left him there. You could hear him crying at night. It went into hysteria. And he was living his life all over again. And the whole camp was as silent as a grave. It was terrible listening to him. We couldn't help him, couldn't do anything to help him. We couldn't go near him. And so he died.[796]

It is a terribly difficult concept to wrap our minds around, but the truth is, *all* these men, the Japanese, the Koreans, the Allied soldiers, *all* were victims. And *all* deserve our sympathies. Even the ones driven to unspeakable acts of cruelty deserve our empathy. *None* of these men entered the world with the intention of becoming monsters. They were *made* into monsters. When we fail to see the victim inside the male victimizer, we close our hearts to men (*boys,* actually) who are *the most* pitiful sort of victim.

Turning young innocents into killers must be among the most evil fates this earthly reality can inflict. Society has done some awful things to women, but human society has never dragged women en masse into boot camps and turned them into people who kill other people. Once men are made into victimizers their status as victims is unduly nullified and these men suffer further victimization in the withdrawal of empathy. Deprived of empathy, these men are left with no hope and *nowhere to go.* Moreover, when the world withdraws all empathy from these men, these men withdraw all empathy from themselves and only pure hard, cold bitterness remains.

The most vicious vicious-cycle I know is the one where society assumes the worst of men, therefore inflicts the worst on men, then accepts its initial assumption as "proven true" when those men subjected to the worst, act out in the worst ways!

We don't enter male pain into the larger gender equation, in part, out of the impulse to dismiss male pain saying: Man suffers, but it's his own fault; he does it to himself (of course, with enough courage, we could say the same of Woman). The dodge here is that "Patriarchy victimizes both sexes." But, not only is this accountability sans compassion, there is also the wheel of complicity to consider. Patriarchy does *nothing* in isolation. Matrisensus has a hand in everything.

In prior chapters we've explored the *many* ways in which Woman is involved and plies a force of influence in war and every other instance of men victimizing men. Men, driven to succeed their way into having what women are empowered to demand of them, form the male hierarchy. A hierarchy, by its very nature, takes the shape of a pyramid—the tip of which can only exist if supported by its middle and its base. The wealthy factory owner can only become so wealthy by exploiting the workers (i.e., men) at the base of the pyramid. If he distributed the profits to these men, he'd not be wealthy and he would not make the most "eligible" bachelors list. The beautiful women he desires most will turn their attentions to the more dominant, exploitive, successful, wealthy men. Males may exploit and victimize other males, but they do not do so in isolation. Women are *involved*.

Another particularly potent reason why male pain and suffering of this magnitude aren't entered into the larger male-female equation is that pain and suffering of this magnitude are quite simply *unimaginable* (thus, *one* soldier dying is a tragedy; one *million* soldiers dying is a "statistic"). We can empathize with the sufferings of women working in sweatshops, but how do we empathize with men ordered to charge a machinegun nest when such a horror doesn't even fit in the civilized mind? Moreover, who *wants* to empathize, that is, who *wants* to put oneself in another's place to feel what they feel when the other has been hung up by his fingers and beaten for *ten hours?* Who among us can truly imagine the agony of being hung by their fingers for ten minutes? In part, we don't empathize with the worst that men suffer—in war, in prison, and in hard/hazardous labor—because to do so would no doubt overwhelm us.

In keeping with the zero-empathy-toward-men rule, one impulse will be to dismiss the extreme victimizations of men with the rationalization that such extremes have been inflicted only on a small percentage of men. So let's take a closer look at that assertion.

First off, the percentages are not all *that* small. For every one CEO there have been *many* POWs. In the 1990s, almost a third of U.S. adult men were veterans. Consider also the extreme horrors that can and sometimes do inflict men in the form of hard/hazardous laborers. Add to that the extreme horrors that can and often do inflict men in the form of prisoners. Taken all together, the child born male is born with a true apparition on his roulette wheel—a dark mark that may fate him to truly evil cruelties.

For example, consider the fate of the men exposed to an exploding boiler in the bowels of the steamship Great Eastern (1859):

> Since they could walk, at first it was hoped that their injuries were not life threatening. But they had met the full force of the pressurized steam; they had effectively been boiled alive. One man was quite oblivious to the fact that deep holes had been burned into the flesh of

his thighs. A member of the crew went to assist another of the injured and, catching him by the arm, watched the skin peel off like an old glove ... They were nearly all stokers and firemen, whose faces were black with their work, and one man who was brought in had patches of red raw flesh on his dark, agonized face, like dabs of red paint, and the skin of his arms was hanging from his hands like a pair of tattered mittens.[797]

It was being *male* that exposed these men to the dangerous conditions that resulted in premature agonizing death.

Yes, even with their dying breaths, each of these traditionally "macho" men would doubtless thank God he hadn't been born a woman. But what is revealed in this absurdity except the extreme and irrational levels to which men are gender indoctrinated?

While female miseries are identified specifically as *female* miseries, the miseries that target *men* tend to be identified as the miseries of "grunts," "workers," "laborers," "prisoners," "soldiers," and "stokers." That these miseries are specifically *male* is evaded and never contrasted against the corresponding female privilege of being kept safe, kept clean, kept innocent. In the absence of a politicized male perspective, various gender sentimentalities eclipse reason and our thinking is driven out of all contact with fact-based gender *reality*.

Nonetheless, the wheel turned and for these men, and countless others, the dark mark came up. Surely *nothing* within the female experience (prostitution, *not* withstanding) matches the worst fates that go with being male. How does this reality factor into the larger gender equation? Admittedly, that's not an easy question to answer. But, as I see it, even a *little* of having your face eaten by mustard gas goes a *long* way. Woman's existential sufferings may be more generalized throughout womankind, but the vast majority of *the* most evil horrors that human reality can inflict have been inflicted upon men.

Assigning men to disproportionate exposure to danger is one of the not inconsiderable costs men have disproportionately paid under the assumption that men are Bad and women are Good. Let us admit, at the very least, a *logical* assessment of gender reality does *not* support the feminist assumption that the gender system has existed solely to advantage and serve males.

Today's coddled American has no idea how hideous battlefield conditions were in past wars. Christina Hoff Sommers tells this anecdote:

> The historian Stephen Ambrose, who has spent half his career listening to the stories of soldiers, tells of a course on the Second World War he gave at the University of Wisconsin ... "They were dumbstruck by descriptions of what it was like to be on the front lines. They were even

more amazed by the responsibilities carried by junior officers ... who were as young as they ... they wondered how anyone could have done it." Ambrose tried to explain to them what had brought so many men and women to such feats of courage, such levels of excellence.[798]

"At the core," says Ambrose, "the American citizen soldiers knew the difference between right and wrong, and they didn't want to live in a world in which wrong prevailed. So they fought, and won, and we all of us, living and yet to be born, must be forever profoundly grateful."[799] Indeed, and let gratitude give credit where credit is due.

If we're going to valorize the soldiers of WWII, let's get one thing straight. Four hundred thousand American men and *sixteen* American women died fighting that war. Not *one* American woman was tortured in a prisoner-of-war camp. So let's not talk of "what had brought so many men *and women* to such feats of courage" as if women and men had fought side by side. There is injustice enough—and I'm talking injustice toward *men*—in women not being "allowed" into combat without women taking half the credit for fighting and dying in combat.

Yet ever since a comparatively paltry few women have been exposed to one-third the risk of their male counterparts in a few recent U.S. military cakewalks, commentators have felt obliged to speak of our "brave men *and women* in uniform" as if women shared the dangers and costs equally—and not just in recent skirmishes, but throughout the whole of American military history!

The first occurrence I know of took place in 1998 during a pre-Memorial Day story on the Civil War when Peter Jennings had the politically correct gall to tell us that, "More than 600,000 men and women died before the war was over."[800] Even some of the *women* who heard it were appalled. "That would be true," comments Kathleen Parker. "But how many of the six hundred thousand were women? About sixty."[801] Many of those 600,000 "men" were *boys* as young as 14! And the mere *60* women who died, pretty much died by *accident*. Yet, if we are to cater to women to the degree feminism demands, we must give women equal credit without regard for truth.

It is an outrage that has repeated itself many times since.

"Everyone has their own personal Vietnam," wrote Kim Kozlowski, staff writer for the *Detroit News*. "It wasn't just the men and women who traipsed through the Vietnamese jungles, rifles strapped on their shoulders, fear racing through their minds."[802] Right, it was just the *men* and *no* women who traipsed through the Vietnamese jungle. About 58,000 American men died in the Vietnam War vs. *eight* women. Yet those eight names appearing on the Vietnam War Memorial isn't enough. In addition, those eight women have their own separate monument.

Historically, The Deal society offered Man read something like this: You risk and absorb all the very worst of it; occupy the dark side of the world and human nature and take on all that is most profoundly harsh and hazardous; in exchange, society will compensate you with extra credit and prestige and sex appeal. Under feminism, the New Deal offered Man now reads: You continue to risk and absorb all the very worst of it; occupy the dark side of the world and human nature and take on all that is most profoundly harsh and hazardous; in exchange, society will compensate you with *nothing*.

This New Deal doesn't lead to greater fairness or justice. This is no step closer to "equality." Men are in no way ennobled supporting efforts that aspire to a world made perfect for women, men be damned.

One of the more burdensome elements of the Masculine Mystique is the expectation that men are, or ought to be, invulnerable. Andrew Kimbrell, author of *The Masculine Mystique,* explains:

> In World War I those who showed extreme psychological distress after battle were called cowards; some were even shot. Later their condition was diagnosed as "shell shock." By 1939 over 130,000 World War I British vets were on disability based on psychological trauma experienced in the war. In World War II and Korea it was called battle fatigue. Often as many as 20 percent of U.S. troops were evacuated from battle sites in these wars as "psychological casualties."
>
> After Vietnam—too long after, it took almost a decade—a new term was coined for it: post-traumatic stress disorder. . . . Despite the increasing number of reports on trauma symptoms of Vietnam vets, experts remained divided on whether the veterans' symptoms were related to their war experience. As a result for years after the war there was no consistent diagnosis or treatment of stress disorders associated with service in Vietnam. . . . Subsequently the psychiatric profession joined the government in acknowledging what they should have known for a long time—that if an individual, even a supposedly invulnerable trained "killing machine," undergoes sufficient trauma, sees enough horror, he can suffer disabling psychological damage.[803]

The Feminine Mystique has had its downsides to be sure, but they have not included death by firing squad for acts of "cowardice":

> In World War One, the executions of 306 British and Commonwealth soldiers took place. Such executions, for crimes such as desertion and cowardice, remain a source of controversy with some believing that many of those executed should be pardoned as they were suffering from what is now called shell shock. The horrors that men from all sides endured while on the front line can only be imagined.[804]

Execution for "cowardice": is this not the *ultimate* in ruthless accountability sans compassion?

British soldier Victor Silvester: "As we were moving up to our sector along the communication trenches, a shell burst ahead of me and one of my platoon dropped. He was the first man I ever saw killed. Both his legs were blown off and the whole of his body and face was peppered with shrapnel. The sight turned my stomach. I was sick and terrified but even more frightened of showing it." [805]

Soldiers are men who've been gender indoctrinated even to the extent of valuing their masculinity more than they value their lives. Men can be marched off to certain doom because fear of shame outweighs fear of death.

"With no obvious end to such experiences and with the whole issue of trench life being such a drain on morale, it is no wonder that some men cracked under the strain of constant artillery fire." Even so:

> The accused did not have access to a formal legal representative who could defend him. Some got a 'prisoner's friend' while many did not even have this. Legally, every court martial should have had a 'judge advocate' present but very few did . . . On January 13th 1915, General Routine Order 585 was issued which basically reversed the belief of being innocent until found guilty. Under 585, a soldier was guilty until sufficient evidence could be provided to prove his innocence.[806]

Sounds a lot like the men in divorce courts and ex parte proceedings facing female accusations.

Once enclosed within the military system, men don't even have the right to *life*, let alone "the pursuit of happiness." We think of men in uniform as "powerful," but what is power without even the most basic civil rights and liberties?

> Some of those in firing squads were under the age of sixteen, as were some of those who were shot for 'cowardice'. James Crozier from Belfast was shot at dawn for desertion – he was just sixteen. Before his execution, Crozier was given so much rum that he passed out. He had to be carried, semi-conscious, to the place of execution. Officers at the execution later claimed that there was a very real fear that the men in the firing squad would disobey the order to shoot. Private Abe Bevistein, aged sixteen, was also shot by firing squad at Labourse, near Calais. As with so many others cases, he had been found guilty of deserting his post. Just before his court martial, Bevistein wrote home to his mother: "We were in the trenches. I was so cold I went out (and took shelter in a farm house). They took me to prison so I will have to go in front of the court. I will try my best to get out of it, so don't worry." [807]

We don't normally regard people under the age of seventeen to have reached the age of consent, yet these fifteen- and sixteen-year-old boys were held responsible as "men." That's one hell of a price some boys pay for the "privilege" of premature adulthood. Their sisters at home babysitting suffered the indignity of being called "girls," but their respect deprivation was duly compensated in the vastly greater love accorded them.

I'm not sure which is worse, executing boys for "cowardice" or forcing other boys to be their executioners. Deeper even than the omnipresent fear of death that soldiers face in battle is the fear and dread of killing others. Warren Farrell explains:

> A friend of mine wrote, "My ex-father-in-law, who strafed and bombed a train full of Nazi troops, woke up in a cold sweat and in terror night after night for years after having to kill." As one military historian put it, "The fear of killing rather than the fear of being killed was the most common cause of battle fatigue in World War II." [808]

Consider, if you will, the ensuing nightmares of those boys ordered to shoot and kill their peers in cold blood for the "crime" of running away from unimaginable horrors.

Of course in the modern West they no longer execute "cowards." The world of today is nowhere *near* as brutal as it once was. It's no coincidence that Woman only recently found the solidarity to demand and achieve "equality." In the far harsher world of WWI, it may be assumed that the majority of women would have wanted no part of "equality" with the disposable sex.

You know all about the small coterie of suffragettes who fought for women's right to vote. Did you know about the ordinary women across America who *opposed* giving women the vote? In plain truth, most women were perfectly happy to leave a world in which you could be shot dead for "cowardice" *exclusively* to men, thank you very much.

Prior to the advent of domestic and reproductive technologies, processed foods, the service industries, and daycare, women in general were fully absorbed into the world of women, a world with many downsides to be sure, but those downsides did not include Bataan death marches, or prisoner-of-war camps, or going down with the ship, or being mutilated by heavy machinery, or boiled alive, or worked to death on railway construction, or dying of black lung after working in coal mines. The assumption that womankind has always pined to join with men in the world of men is a *false* assumption.

Aside from those few women exceptionally well suited to the world of men—even the world of men at its darkest—the general throng of womanhood was never foolish enough to want any deep part in Man's more bestial world. "Before there were technological advancements and legal protections to make factories, railroads, mines and other workplaces safer," asserts Tom James, "women consented to the notion that the workplace should be the exclusive domain of men."[809] Until recently, only a small but vocal minority of women had any desire to join with men in what had always been the far harder, harsher, and more hazardous world of men.

Feminists resent the hell out of boys being called men, and receiving the extra respect that goes with it, but isn't that truly the very *least* society could offer males in compensation for their disposability? The Old Deal was bad enough. The New Deal would deprive men of any compensation at all.

The Duality Principle extends even into war and military service. There are no negatives without positives attached. And that makes it *possible* to talk of war and soldiering as something from which women have always been "excluded." But how did "exclusion" become the *preferred* term? The "historical record shows that women are capable of performing successfully in war," notes Joshua Goldstein, author of *War and Gender*. "Thus, the near-total *exclusion* of women from combat roles does not seem to be explained by women's inherent lack of ability."[810] [Emphasis added]

I'll never forget my older brother sweating it out. Would he be drafted into the Vietnam War? He did not shake and moan and wring his hands for fear of being "excluded." When the danger passed and he was no longer subject to the draft, it was the happiest day of his life. Over-representation of blacks on the battlefield is understood for the anti-black prejudice it is. No one speaks of whites being relatively "excluded" from the frontlines.

If there was ever an example of negatives outweighing positives, forced conscription into battle has to be the ultimate. The positives of a fancy uniform, prestige, a medal, job skills, and some excitement do add up and are substantial, but in no way approach, let alone equal, the negatives of torture, blindness, paralysis, disfigurement, dismemberment, imprisonment, court-martials, firing squads, innumerable physical and moral agonies and torments of all kinds, permanent mental trauma, and death before the age of twenty.

Putting it plainly, to speak of the battlefield solely as something to which women have been deprived and/or excluded is nothing less than *obscene*.

That women have always been barred from battle is, of late, a truth put forward to obscure and supersede a truth that dwarfs it by a hundred orders of magnitude—and that truth is this: *women have always been **exempt** from battle*. Women may go all righteous when asking: "When will women be *allowed* to go into combat?" Funny though how the question wasn't phrased: When will women be *obligated* to go into combat?

More and more often, more and more explicitly, popular entertainment capitulates to the feminist party line. If you've seen the wonderful *Lord of the Rings* film trilogy, then consider the "plight" of Eowyn, the King's niece (featured in the second and third installments). Eowyn (Miranda Otto) is given *numerous* (one might even say *endless*) speeches decrying the injustice of being a woman barred from battle.

Within the world of the film, the field of battle is only and exclusively a place of glory, and being "excluded" from it is deprivation of the *worst* kind. In fact, Eowyn suffers her lack of participation in blood sports so terribly the film would have us weep for her. We are to believe that to be female is to be a victim through and through even as the women are kept safe while the men are slaughtered. Not for an instant are we invited to consider the possibility that to be female is to be *spared* the horror of being hacked away at or, perhaps even worse, the horror of hacking away at another.

But an even more important point is this: even if I had the power to go in and "fix" *The Lord of the Rings* movie trilogy, there's not much I could do. Maybe I'd trim a few of Eowyn's more gratuitously righteous speeches and find some way of sneaking in the truth that battle is more about male burden than privilege, but that's about it. I'd change so little because there is simply *no way* of entering masculism into a mythopoetic setting.

To picture Aragorn, our hero, kicking the ground while bitterly complaining how he and the other men are forced into battle while those "lucky bitches" are protected is to picture the hopeless absurdity of entering masculist rhetoric into that setting. Truths of FemalePower and MaleVictimization have no place within the poetry of knights and princesses, chivalry and romance. But, as the film itself makes plain, feminist perspectives and rhetoric fit right in. Being in alignment with the myths and the mythos is part of what has made feminism appear unassailable. It's just another reason why there is feminism on the one hand and on the other hand there is nothing.

Recently, I watched *The Searchers* (1956), directed by John Ford and staring the great John Wayne. In his toughness, strength, and courage, in his confidence, independence, and Masculine Mystique, he is simply *magnificent!* I *totally* get the allure of the manly image men cling to. I would not ask men to give it up. At the same time, however, I would not have men lose sight of the costs. The 1945 war classic *They Were Expendable,* also directed by John Ford and starring John Wayne, manages to romanticize and attach tremendous pride, nobility, even *privilege* to being part of a sacrificial group of men sent on a suicide mission. Though less romantic the film's title could be changed to "*They Were Disposable*" with no loss of accuracy.

Men need to awaken from their romanticized vision of themselves. To reframe male expendability into male power and privilege is to romanticize male gender reality to the point of abject absurdity. Times have changed. Women are rising up in all arenas. The arena of gender politics has become much too deep, too powerful, and too far-reaching in its influence for men to ignore and remain ignorant of.

The masculine mystique is a dream, a magnificent dream, but a *dream* nonetheless (for further thoughts on that, see "Gender Sentiment," p. 382). While there was a time when that mystique was richly rewarded, under the New Deal, that time has largely come and gone. I get that vulnerable complaint coming from a John Wayne persona is more than a little incongruous. But, in adhering to John Wayne stoicism, Man allows female complaint to be the *only* complaint. Trapped within his mystique, Man continues to be exactly what feminism wants him to be: "strong and *silent*."

Thus, gender politics, gender understanding, and gender issues remain the *exclusive* province of female-ism, and the manipulated male plays the role of unconscious enabler.

In Summary: It's not enough that Woman might be equal partner in generating the forces that lead to war yet suffers lesser consequences and none of the blame. Within the dictates of the feminist belief system, we are *not* to regard Woman as gifted with exemption from war. Woman is not asked to be grateful, only resentful. Under the New Deal, no longer is Man credited with possessing extra honor and courage for taking the blows so she might be spared. When we frame Woman's exemption as *exclusion*, Woman has it all.

She is kept safe at no cost to her honor or perceived courage or willingness or ability to fight alongside men. Woman, walking upon her Glass Floor, can be credited with every quality of manliness; all she lacks is the "privilege" of equal access.

To speak this lesser truth as if it were The Truth may flatter Woman and absolve her of guilt when her brother is sent home in a body bag while she plans her future. It may cater to her addiction to feelings of righteous victimization in *all* things. But it does so at the not inconsiderable cost of cutting the hearts out of men.

Imagine the man with no face, no legs, twenty years have come and gone since he stepped on that landmine yet he can feel the shrapnel still lodged in his spine. Still in pain, forever reliving his nightmare, he's medicated and isolated in some halfway house or veterans' hospital somewhere. Nevertheless, the message reaches him that his profound sacrifice is to be regarded as privileged "inclusion" as compared with women's victimized "exclusion." And, on TV, he hears a feminist go uncontested when saying that *women* are the primary sufferers of war! That's not just heartless; that's *evil*.

Whether men verbalize it or not, that's the kind of rancor and resentment the feminist belief system generates. Meanwhile, each sex divesting itself of rancor and resentment toward the other is what an understanding of Balance is all about. In part, I generate the rhetoric of male heartache, resentment, despair, and victimhood to prove that I can. If masculists can match or exceed any of even the most passionate feminist rhetoric, then what aside from chivalrous sentimentality has the feminist perspective truly got in its favor?

However much it may seem as if I do, in point of fact, I do *not* begrudge women their exemption from the battlefield. I don't begrudge women any of their many exemptions, advantages, powers, and privileges because I understand that what women have comes only at great cost.

Unfortunately, our system of sexual politics ("female-ism") isn't balanced enough to allow us to understand that men's many exemptions, advantages, powers, and privileges also come only at great cost—a cost *equal* to that paid by women. Nor does it allow us to understand that women are and have always been equally powerful and equally responsible for creating and maintaining the gender system through which each sex has enjoyed and suffered its part.

I'm not angry because of the ways men have suffered. I know that in different ways for different reasons women have suffered equally. I am angry because male suffering isn't properly credited, empathized with, and entered into the larger sexual-political equation—or worse, is reframed into male privilege! I am angry because the denial of male suffering and denial of female power and denial of female complicity in the system allows women to go about gaining the upper hand through the guise of demanding their "equality," when equality between the sexes already is and has always been so.

I am angry with Woman for perpetrating a clever, manipulative ideological hoax, and I am angry with Man for falling for it hook, line, and sinker.

You want to know what's real? Well here it is: men and women have *always* been equal. For their brand of self-sacrifice, men have received the lion's share of the respect. For their brand of self-sacrifice, women have received the lion's share of the love. The power has balanced out. The victimization has balanced out. The culpability, the suffering, the gifts, the burdens, the injustices, the privileges: It has *all* balanced out!

Everything else is feminism and chivalry . . . smoke and mirrors.

Women in the Military

It All Balances Out—except, of course, for the belief system. And it is this gross imbalance in our cultural ideology that is the target of my wrath, not women. It may be assumed that I'm in favor of female conscription and female participation on the front line. But I'm not, not really. Being a product of male evolutionary psychology, role, and conditioning; the thought of women at war suffering what men suffer is anathema to me just as it is to most other men.

One man, Mike Strobel, columnist for the *Toronto Sun*, writes about the death of Capt. Nichola Goddard.

> Capt. Goddard served and died, aged 26, for her country. She did it willingly and bravely. Nothing can diminish that. But do not tell me your reaction to her face on our front page was the same as it was to the faces of the 16 brave Canadian men killed over there. If you are human, you had an extra catch in your throat. You were uneasy, disbelieving. Then, Len Fortune, a colleague and air force vet, shows me a page of photographs. They are of American women killed in action in Iraq. The youngest is 19, the oldest 43. They are moms, wives, girlfriends, sisters, daughters. . . . It would be terrible if those faces were of young men. I'm sorry, but it is even worse that they are of young women. True, they are little more than 2% of the U.S. toll in Iraq. But, I am surprised to learn, American women aren't even supposed to be in direct land combat roles. Their deaths have come in mortar attacks on camps and ambushes of supply convoys. Not what they call "combat arms" roles, though, of course, dead is dead.[811]

Most of us are surprised to discover that female American soldiers are spared the front lines (though, at the time writing, the situation is changing). We've been so inundated by the hype. We all saw the woman on the cover of *Newsweek*[812] looking tough as nails in her mirror sunglasses, rifle slung over her shoulder, leading her troops and a caption that proclaimed: "Women Warriors: Sharing the Danger." Little did we realize that this G.I. Jane was approaching nothing more dangerous than an unguarded dog kennel.[813]

An amazing number of the men I've talked with don't even realize that, to this day, only 18-year-old males, *not* 18-year-old females, are legally required to sign up for Selective Service. Should the need arise, the National Guard and Reserve units can place 100,000 boys in boot camps in four weeks.[814] If the draft is reinstated, it will be a male-only draft. How can the average American male not know that?

Feminist ideological dominance has rendered Strobel's position so politically incorrect as to inspire a storm of protest letters. "Writes Julie Kimmette, of Frankford, Ontario: 'To take away a woman's right to choose to serve her country is disrespectful and arrogant of men. . . .

We have the right to choose. That is what women's lib is all about.'" She's only right. Women-only liberation is indeed all about female-only rights and female-only options. For men, talk of rights is replaced with talk of responsibilities and for conscripted males, *choice* doesn't enter into it. For men the ethic is: "Ours is not to reason why; ours is but to do and die."[815] Military and draft-board policies guarantee that "a woman's right to *choose*" remains a female-*only* "right."

All protests *not*withstanding, Strobel's point is well taken. I am human. And, right or wrong, I too feel from deep within this same instinctual impulse to protect women. If, however, men alone are to bear the brunt of the darkest dark side, it is *imperative* that men get properly credited for their enormous sacrifice and women get properly contrite for their equally enormous exemption.

Rather than frame this exemption strictly in terms of "victimization," our culture might understand female exemption as indicative of female *power* and *privilege*. Women might receive the gift with humility and perhaps even with gratitude. And the full understanding of this power and privilege might stay women's tongues as they are about to proclaim themselves *the* victims.

What I would like to see is a balanced (as opposed to female-ist) society that is willing to place the male-only battlefield, the prisons, the hard/hazardous labor, et al., alongside the male elite, observe Woman largely occupying the middle ground, and take it as indication of male-female equality *already achieved*. That seems logical to me, but in today's gynocentric sexual-political climate such an understanding seems, to say the least, highly unlikely.

The solution, as many masculists see it, is to thrust women into the thick of combat ("There, take *that!*"). But aside from my own conditioning in chivalry, there are other factors that leave me unenthused with this "solution." To begin with, I believe the comeuppance masculists expect Woman to suffer in the military will *not happen*. And here's why:

Wherever women go they bring their *innate* powers with them. For reasons I will soon make clear, we can confidently predict that primal, instinctual, and sexual forces will compel men to die protecting women. In every way they can, men will carry the women's burdens as best they can. At a fraction of the cost in lives lost and bodies mutilated, Woman will be awarded as many medals and take equal credit for the military protection of this country, yet be smeared with none of the blame for war. Even now we've gone from "The brave *men* who fought and died in" WWI, WWII, Vietnam, etc., to the newly politically correct phrase: "The brave men *and women* who fought and died."

If the media blitz concerning Private Jessica Lynch taught us anything it taught us just how extraordinarily hungry the media is to seek out, honor, and exalt female military heroes—even when they're nothing of the kind. Author Thomas Ellis:

> We all heard how the aspiring kindergarten teacher emptied her weapon during the ambush, killing at least four Iraqis before being shot and taken prisoner. We learned how she was tortured in captivity. The Bambi-like private was beaten, stabbed, and the bastards even broke her legs. I confess, I bought into it. Hey, it was carried by all the major news outlets—even the Washington Post. It had to be true. I was ready to admit I may have been wrong on some fundamental levels. Maybe I was the one with the problem. I always thought women in dangerous situations would look to men for protection, and men would assume the risk for them. It's just how we work. Here was dramatic proof that a woman suddenly thrown into combat can respond with valor equal to that of men. . . . A few days later the real story was brought to light. No dramatic last stand, no torture, no gunshot or stab wounds. Jessica's broken bones were from an accident during the ambush. She didn't fire her weapon at all. In fact, she sought shelter between two male soldiers who took on the traditional male protective role, firing their weapons and accepting the risk for her.[816]

We take our reality off the media (what other information is there to go on?). The media blitz guaranteed that *everyone* heard about Private Lynch the hero. In this case the falsehood was such—and Jessica Lynch herself so adamantly refused to go along with it—that the debunking of this myth was more than usually thorough.

Kathleen Parker tells the revised story of Pvt. Lynch:

> Even though real male heroes emerged the day of Lynch's ordeal, they were largely ignored so that the girl from Palestine could be elevated and the image of woman-warrior burnished. . . The truth was something else. First, Lynch was never supposed to be exposed to combat. She was part of the 507th Maintenance Company, a convoy of thirty-three vehicles filed with cooks, clerks, and mechanics, including her boyfriend, Ruben, who promised to take care of her. . . When Lynch tried to "lock and load" her weapon on command, it jammed. . . While the men in the vehicle returned fire, Lynch sat with her arms wrapped around her shoulders, her head lowered to her knees, eyes closed, according to her own account.[817]

"'They were killing us,' she said."[818] That, of course, is what happens in war. But Lynch never expected to be subjected to military slaughter. Why would she? What was true for Lynch is true for female soldiers in general; they are "never supposed to be exposed to combat." The convoy she was on went off course and so, like other female soldiers exposed to battlefield conditions, she was exposed to battlefield conditions by *accident*. In contrast, male soldiers ordered to charge a machinegun nest die by *design*, not by accident.

I believe that, at the heart of the masculist agenda here, there is a longing to see women suffer what men have suffered (on some levels, it's understandable really). So it's tempting to argue that it's only the *novelty* of women in the military that accounts for the excessive acclaim heaped upon Lynch, and, as that novelty wears off, gender neutrality will increase. Fair enough, but humans can only be gender neutral to a *degree*. We are not a unisex species.

"The issues facing *women* warriors have *always* been - and *will always be* - a *top* priority for IAVA, and are a big part of our 2010 Legislative Agenda," writes chivalrous Tim Ebree, legislative associate of Iraq and Afghanistan Veterans of America.[819] [Emphasis added] On what basis would we assume that the underlying psychological forces and innate female power granting "*top* priority" to *women* warriors will disappear anytime soon?

According to Kathleen Parker, the media message could be summed up: "Our girl Jessica could do anything a man could do, and apparently, she could do it even better."[820] Indeed, that would seem to sum up the media message in all walks of life.

In the event of an authentic female war hero the media hullabaloo promises to be deafening. How long can it be before the media begins touting female "superiority" on the battlefield? If the present offers any indication of the future, then just as the story of the Donner Party has become the story of strong surviving females and weak dying males, we'll start hearing the same in battlefield scenarios; the part about men dying to protect the women will get buried. Already, military women are vilifying military men as "sexist" "harassers" and the courts and the media are eating it up.

Masculist fantasies envision women getting their just deserts in the military. But let's look at the *reality* of women in the military. Let me begin by introducing you to Sandra Rippey, a commander in the U.S. Navy (In the Navy a commander is one step down from captain, which is one step down from admiral). The following derives from an interview conducted by Jack Kammer and published in Kammer's seminal book, *Good Will Toward Men*.

> [O]ne of the more insidious things that's happening is that women officers junior to me will address the issue of sexual harassment as the first thing they want to talk about—how terrible the men are, how badly they've been treated, how they didn't get promoted, their assignments are no good. . . . The worst thing about it is that they will not consider evidence to the contrary. . . . These women all share a

loathing. There's no place in it for me, but they seem to almost feed on it. The men, for their part, see this gaggle of individuals who are sharply separated from them by these feelings.[821]

What do the women get out of all this hate, rancor, and resentment? What's the payoff to their "us-and-them" stance and cries of "discrimination" and "victim"?

> I hate to say this, but these women are looking for a vehicle to skip the steps. In other words, the men have to go through certain gradations to their Surface Warfare pin, or Submarine pin, or their Aviator wings. The women are looking for and being granted shortcuts only because they're women. This is wrong. There is resentment in the male community . . . because of the way these steps are "dumbed down" for the women, it degrades and makes less valuable the increased time that the men have to put in to acquire the same qualifications or promotions.[822]

As is true of the work environment, the military environment contains many obstacles and burdens that neither sex is over-eager to endure.

Men *know* that rank adds *far* more to a man's sexual/marital desirability than his personality ever could. Relatively lacking Woman's innate power, Man is more motivated to suffer what the work and military environs inflict because he is needier of the rewards of external sources of power (paycheck, rank, titles, etc.) that may come to those who demonstrate an ability and willingness to endure.

Thus men struggle and endure while women cry "discrimination." Efforts to eliminate this largely imaginary "discrimination" (affirmative action, female-only organizations, feminist pressures, and quota systems) inevitably result in true *reverse* discrimination.

> It takes the men probably a solid three or four months at sea with one liberty break, busting their butts with the books, taking their "qual" cards, going through all these different board levels up to their commanding officer to get their SWO—Surface Warfare Officer—pin. Women, on the other hand, have been known to be awarded the SWO pin in their spare time. . . . It's basically a quota thing. You've got to crank out so many women. And they're doing it in the most expeditious manner that they can find. If we're striving for equal pay for equal work, this is not it. And as a female, I don't want that. Make me do what they do. There should be no difference in the requirements. If you can't meet them, you're out. But I'm a lone voice crying in the wilderness here.[823]

As is true of the work environment, men in the military must endure compulsory humiliating "sexual harassment" trainings.

> The videotapes cast the typical male service member as basically this brutish predator who at all times would stare at, look at, suggest sex to any female in his vicinity. The man looked like a prowling tomcat,

which I didn't appreciate. The videos didn't apply to any situations that I've ever seen. And I thought that the level of sensitivity among the women was already so high that they were walking around like raw wounds waiting to be stuck.[824]

Needless to say, none of these "training" films ever depicts any negative behaviors coming from women. Nevertheless, if women are more sexually harassed it can only be because women are more sexually desired. Being more desired translates into an innate sexual power with which women can do considerable sexual harassing of their own. While the sexually powerless male must *act out* sexually subjecting his overtures to female judgment, and potential disciplinary actions, the sexually empowered female can work mischief with greater subtlety.

Besides, "sexual harassment" is defined as something women suffer at the hands of men. And so, in those instances when a woman sexually desires a man enough to take aggressive action, the man facing unwanted pressure to have sex will have difficulty getting anyone to believe him or see the problem.

"She keeps hounding me for sex!"

"Yeah, sure, buddy."

Notes Martin Van Creveld, author of *Men, Women & War*:

> On both sides of the Atlantic, scarcely a week goes by without some unfortunate male officer or soldier being accused of 'sexual harassment' and being hounded out to the services. This is likely to be his fate even if the alleged incident took place many years previously; even if it was the woman who made the initial advances and seduced him; even if his record of service is otherwise excellent; and often even if he is found innocent of the charges.[825]

"Virtually all media attention on a Pentagon report last week focused on an increase in service members' claims of sexual abuse, but unmentioned were statistics showing that a significant percentage of such actually investigated cases were baseless." From 2009 to 2012, sexual abuse reports rose by 4 percent while what the Pentagon calls "unfounded allegations" rose by 35 percent.[826]

What to do with a mess like this? Rippey quotes one young woman who had just watched one of those "training" films: "You know what training we really need? Women in the Navy need to be trained to be more sensitive to sexual harassment."[827] Hmm.

"I think," says Rippey, "the final issue that caused me just to shut down and say, 'Okay, that's it!' was when they were talking about feminist legal theorists and one of the women raised her hand to say, 'All sex is rape, even sex in marriage.'" Did anyone object? "I wish someone would have. I wish one of the guys would have stood up."[828] The guys, of course, remained seated.

According to top echelon feminist theorists such as University of Michigan law professor Catherine MacKinnon, "In a patriarchal society all heterosexual intercourse is rape because women, as a group, are not strong enough to give consent."[829] Though the notion that a man making love to his wife is raping his wife is an insult that would pierce the very heart and soul of men, in a "patriarchal" society, men, as a group, are not strong enough to protest. So:

> They just went blank. There's no avenue for the men to be able to counter this. That's why I'm not sitting still any longer. That's why I'll address every one of these issues, because no one can claim that I have an agenda because of my gender. If a man said the same things that I am saying, there would be an outcry.[830]

Not just the *servicemen*, but also male *officers* are powerless in relation to feminist-defined "sexism." Even an admiral must carefully monitor his words and actions to stay within strict P.C. guidelines lest some female junior officer use her "victim" power against him. And the situation can only worsen. "When these junior females come into positions of leadership," warns Rippey, "I can see where they will demand conformity, and any exceptions whatsoever will be noted somewhere in their fitness reports."[831]

> As soon as they address an issue, like women on ships, women in submarines, as soon as they address the issue, practically speaking, the hue and cry of sexism rears its ugly head and shuts them up.... To the extent that they cannot be honest with their counterparts, to the extent that they cannot fraternize with their own peers, men are shell-shocked in the military. They're spending so much time running and ducking for cover and looking over their shoulders waiting for the next incoming round that yes, it is demoralizing for them.[832]

The following is an unedited portion of Commander Rippey's interview. The words in italics belong to interviewer Jack Kammer.

What do you like about men?

I think men generally are very warm and caring individuals. What I have found, of late, particularly, is that when they find a woman like myself to whom they can address these issues and other personal issues, they're astonished.

Does it seem then that one of the reasons guys don't talk with women is not just that men have trouble talking, but that sometimes women have trouble listening?

Yes, absolutely. Because a woman hears from a man what she allows him to say. In other words, by her body language, by what she puts out, she's only going to hear what he reads and he sends back on the same frequency. If you're more open, and more accepting, and nonjudgmental, you'll hear the whole range of what this guy has to say. And it's quite diverse.

So you're talking about the ability of women to fairly thoroughly control what a guy will say.

Basically they do. Yes.

So where does this idea come from that women have no power?

Oh, that's the oldest, stupidest idea that's ever been conveyed. Women control what men say. Women control sex. Women control procreation. The whole idea is bogus.

It makes sense that women aren't going to stand up and say, "Hey, this idea that's been benefiting us is bogus."

That's right.

Why aren't men standing up and saying, "Hey, this idea that's hurting us is bogus!"?

Sexist!

If a guy were to say that, he would be accused of being a sexist?

Absolutely.

Does it disappoint you that men are taking this stuff?

Yeah. A little bit. But they've been so battered for the last ten years. I don't see that they have a choice at this point. Every time somebody does stand up, they get knocked down like a bowling pin. And there's just so much of that you can take. And I can see that there's a certain tired acquiescence on the part of men.

Not exactly an emotion we should want in our military, is it?

Tired acquiescence? Not if we ever want to win a war.[833]

Will feminism be *infinitely* indulged—even to the extent of compromising national security?

Reality Check: As always, in such matters, bias is omnipresent and it's hard to know who or what to trust. But I believe what we're seeing here reflects certain basic gender principles. Woman is as powerful as Man. Her power is largely innate. Man's relative *lack* of innate power and value force him to compensate by seeking extrinsic power and value. In these efforts many men fail, but some succeed and a few super-succeed, resulting in an overall *balance* of power.

Warren Farrell's research affirms Commander Rippey's assertions. Referring to the U.S. invasion of Panama plus the Persian Gulf practice operations and war, says Farrell:

For both wars combined, 27 men died for each woman; but since there are only 9 men in the armed services for each woman, then any given man's risk of dying was three times greater than any given woman's.... Women constitute 11.7 percent of the total military, but 12 percent of the officers. *Women receive more-than-equal promotions in the services despite less-than-equal time in the services* (the first females graduated from West Point in 1980).... Both sexes in the Persian Gulf received $110 per month extra combat pay... In brief, men get fewer promotions and, therefore, less pay for longer periods of service and a threefold greater risk of death, yet we read about discrimination against women, not discrimination against men.[834] [Emphasis in the original]

Basically, we hear what feminism will allow. We hear that which constitutes MP/FV; that which constitutes FP/MV gets suppressed. We hear about ManBad/WomanGood in the form of female accusations regarding male harassers. But WomanBad in the form of female soldiers getting pregnant in order to avoid deployment then aborting the fetus, *that* you don't hear so much about. Nevertheless, an Army physician stationed in Kuwait (who wisely prefers to remain anonymous) tells us:

> It isn't politically correct to even discuss this in the services, but ... a large percentage of women soldiers are electively aborting their fetuses after they've served their purpose of enabling them to avoid their tour of duty ... It is wrong to use a fetus to shirk the responsibility for which you have signed up, and then to kill that fetus.[835]

Even so, there is an obvious correlation between female military personnel receiving orders that would place them in harsh/hazardous conditions and those same female military personnel becoming pregnant. During workup for deployment it is not uncommon for 40 percent or more of a ship's female personnel to give themselves an easy out in this way.[836] Given the magnitude of the exemption accorded, I suppose if male soldiers could get out of harm's way by getting pregnant, many would do so. But they can't. They have no such power.

The ability to give birth confers all manner of innate power and privilege. Being female allows women to get away with a four-times-higher rate of reporting ill, thus rendering themselves "medically non-available."[837] While it has its downsides, the feminine mystique is not without its compensations.

Despite feminist fantasies, women are demonstrably and measurably physically weaker than men. "In fact, only 10 percent of women can meet the physical requirements of 75 percent of the jobs in the army."[838] Extra push-ups and pull-ups can only narrow the gap a little. Biology is no fantasy. Women cannot be expected to carry the wounded and the dying off the battlefield on their slender shoulders. But female aptitude is not the primary issue here. Of greater concern is women's ultimately demoralizing effect upon men.

Protecting the women at home is half the motivation that gets men to march off to war in the first place. John Eldredge:

> A man wants to be the hero to the beauty. Young men going off to war carry a photo of their sweetheart in their wallet. Men who fly combat missions will paint a beauty on the side of their aircraft; the crews of the WWII B-17 bomber gave those flying fortresses names like *Me and My Gal* or the *Memphis Belle*. What would Robin Hood or King Arthur be without the woman they love? Lonely men fighting lonely battles.... It's not enough to be a hero; it's that he is a hero *to someone* in particular, to the woman he loves.[839]

What happens when the women men are fighting for, are out fighting alongside them? How will men cope?

"It's already tough to lose any of your buddies," says Daniel, a present-day Israeli soldier quoted by Kathleen Parker, "but to see a girl get killed is just devastating. I don't think morale can survive. I don't think soldiers can continue to function after seeing something like that. We simply like women too much."[840] Accordingly, "The Israeli Army," says author Eileen MacDonald, "which once put women soldiers on the front line, eventually had to reverse its policy partly because the men got so upset when a woman was injured or killed."[841]

"It is not appropriate for women to engage in combat, to be captured or to be shot, as opposed to pushing a button someplace in a missile silo," said Supreme Court Justice Sandra Day O'Connor.[842] Is that *female* chauvinism I'm hearing? Truly, *both* sexes love women more than men.

What happens when men's filial (brotherly) love for each other—a soldier's most immediate motivation for fighting and dying—is disrupted by sexual jealousies and rivalries inevitable wherever men and women mix company? What happens to morale and combat readiness?

And it gets worse. Thomas Ellis observed:

> During the non-stop coverage of the Iraqi war in 2003 one of the news channels showed a tiny blonde female soldier trying to give orders to some looters with her Minnie Mouse voice. It wasn't working. How much more of this are we *not* seeing?[843]

I'm going to be blunt. I look at the situation and this is what I see: I see women—under-represented among the "grunts," over-represented among the officers—issuing/threatening accusations of "harassment" and "sexism;" subjecting men to humiliating "sexual harassment trainings;" controlling what men say and don't say; teasing; beguiling; stimulating reckless showoff behaviors; pitting men against each other in competition for their "sexual favors;" cashing in on their "sexual favors;" exempting themselves through pregnancy and "reporting ill," exempting themselves with a burst of tears; enjoying lesser demands and requirements for the same rewards while suffering far fewer risks and casualties yet receiving equal pay and equal credit and more than equal promotions and job training; getting away with all manner of manipulative mischief; vacillating between demands for equal respect and demands to be protected and coddled with feminine indulgences; already lording it over all these desperately desirous young men with their beauty/sexual power; already *hugely* advantaged and empowered, then ordering these men around, ordering them even to their deaths (with their Minnie Mouse voices no less). It all adds up to inestimable damage done the morale of men in our military. And, make no mistake about it, it is on the *men* in the military that our national security relies.

You see, if you strip away the perceptual distortions and faulty judgment that feminist political correctness constrains, what you end up with is a host of men all too ready to jump on the nearest landmine if that's the only way to put an end to such unendurable double standards, injustices, humiliations, and *falsehoods*.

Psychiatrist Theodore Dalrymple gets to the core of the matter:

> In my study of communist societies, I came to the conclusion that the purpose of communist propaganda was not to persuade or convince, nor to inform, but to humiliate; and therefore, the less it corresponded to reality the better. When people are forced to remain silent when they are being told the most obvious lies, or even worse when they are forced to repeat the lies themselves, they lose once and for all their sense of probity. . . . political correctness has the same effect.[844]

The King's New Clothes is the story of a clever tailor who drapes the King in "clothes" only the "enlightened" can see. Since everyone wants to be "enlightened," all outdo themselves gushing over the imaginary "clothes." Is feminist Political Correctness a case of The *Queen's* New Clothes? Is the Queen *so* powerful that all must applaud her "righteous" rhetoric even in those instances when her rhetoric is *nakedly* false? Forced to remain silent or worse, repeat the lies themselves, for aware men, it is indeed humiliating and demoralizing.

Martin Van Creveld takes in the big picture. In the world of war, the introduction of nuclear weapons changed everything:

> Since then, the armed forces of *no* developed country have fought a major war against a major opponent who was even remotely capable of putting its own national existence in danger; compared with the recent past, and with very few exceptions, all they have done was to engage in skirmishes. Even most of those were conducted in places hundreds if not thousands of miles away, against enemies who were often so small and weak they could hardly be located on a map.[845]

According to Van Creveld, "Women Warriors Sharing the Danger" is merely a feminist fantasy that Western society can presently afford to indulge only because national security is not seemingly or *foreseeably* threatened. So, under *current* circumstances, the purveyors of political correctness may treat the armed forces as "social laboratories for some feminist brave new world."

> This they do by compelling the forces to pretend, against all the evidence that soldiers and doctors can muster, that women are as fit for war as men: increase the proportion of women from near zero to as many as 10-13 per cent of the troops; turn training into a mockery and humiliation for those men who are involved in it alongside women; absorb the extra costs involved in paying for everything from separate toilets to pregnancy care and from special uniforms to post-natal leave of absence; deny or cover up any damage done and loss suffered; and ignore or silence or discharge anybody who objects. . . . If present trends are anything to go by, it will end only when the forces are no longer fit to fight at all.[846]

All must show their "enlightenment" by pretending that the Queen's (feminist) rhetoric is beyond critique.

Female military *competence* is the lesser part of this issue. At the *deepest* level, the problem is that women are so innately *powerful* they wreak havoc simply for being so desired, so adored, so indulged, so non-accountable, so protected. Because the military ethos operates off of *male powerlessness*—expendability; exposure to danger, hazing, and brutality; denial of vulnerability to pain and fear; ruthless accountability and absolute subservience—military functioning is undermined by the influx of such *innately* powerful beings.

Disposable males may be reduced to "maggots" and treated as cruelly as you please, but "That's no way to treat a lady." A male recruit might be forced to take hold of a bar and hang for minutes on end with a blade positioned directly under his scrotum, and even *this* level of brutality may go unpunished. Within the military such antics are understood as "hazing," the purpose of which is to determine the toughness and therefore the reliability of untested recruits *prior* to exposure to harrowing, killing-field conditions.

Soldiers *need* to know which recruits can be trusted to have their backs. Though their very lives depend upon it, soldiers can have *no way* of determining which female recruits can or cannot be trusted under combat conditions. The hazing of female recruits is renamed "harassment," with *severe* consequences to the perpetrators.

With supreme irony, these same women secure even *more* power by asserting their self-proclaimed "powerlessness" (a "powerlessness" that female *power* continues to protect from exposure as fraudulent).

Their 17, 18, 19-year-old man-child equivalents would also desire a softer, safer ride in the military and they would use complaint to get it. But they don't use complaint, simply because they are not em*power*ed to do so. *Male* complaint is met only with a General George Patton slap across the face.

But what happens when the slapped male observes his female equivalent's partial immunity to such treatment? It's one thing to endure an environment where *all* your peers are treated like vermin, but quite another to suffer such treatment in contrast to a special class of human that is relatively immune to such treatment.

When Mike Strobel pointed out the greater sense of emotional pain and loss accompanying the deaths of female soldiers as compared with male soldiers, he was merely pointing out the obvious. But in pointing out the obvious he was threatening the fantasy—the fantasy that women are engaged in a righteous battle for "equality" which will be achieved when women have their own perfect version of equality within the world of men (while men remain inferior within the world of women). So long as women constitute a mere 2 percent of the annual death toll[847] (the likes of which Vietnam produced on a weekly basis), the fantasy remains sustainable. Should the United States ever again go to *War*, however, the fantasy might not hold up so well.

Which brings us back to why conscripting women will *not* bring about the female comeuppance masculists pine for: the threat of conscripting women is nothing like the threat it once was.

Obviously, the U.S. military experience still includes hazards, horrors, and hardships, but it's a matter of degree. It's too late now to dump women out onto Omaha Beach to be mortared and machine-gunned by the *thousands*. If American women by the multi-tens of thousands *were* brutalized, shot dead, worked to death, and tortured the way WWII prisoners of the Japanese were tortured, and the survivors had microphones stuck in front of them and were asked, "Do you *still* want 'equality' with men?" masculists just might get the satisfaction they seek. But long gone are the days of mustard gas and the Bataan Death March. Horrors at the scale visited upon American men in the wars of the past may well be a thing of the past. In any case, the U.S. military hasn't seen the likes of "Hamburger Hill" in a long time.

But even if warfare should ever again become as brutal as it once was (brutal, I mean, for *U.S.* troops), who can doubt that Woman could reactivate her protection at will? However much masculists may revile it, the chivalric instinctual impulse to protect women is the product of millions of years of human (and mammalian) evolutionary psychology and it's not going to disappear any time soon.

Probably the best reasoning in favor of rendering women cannon fodder argues that *women* getting massacred might so traumatize nations as to lead to an end to war. Perhaps, but to achieve the desired result would require female death tolls at trauma-producing levels, and how would things ever get that far? At present, Woman isn't even subject to the draft! Are we to believe that Woman would *volunteer* for mass slaughter? If war ever again became the true *hell* of yesteryear, *long* before women were killed in anything like the millions, Woman would certainly bow out. After all, she'd be a fool not to.

Masculists *dream* of the day when battle-scarred Woman will say to Man: "I had no idea; I am so sorry for proclaiming myself *the* victim and hogging *all* empathy to myself. If I had known what you men have endured, I never would have complained the way I have. I'm so ashamed; can you ever forgive me?" Though such an apology *would* be quite appropriate, to those masculists who seek it I say, *dream on*.

At half the effort and a fraction of the danger, female soldiers will—and already do—receive full combat pay while riding the quota escalator to awards, pins, medals, prestige, fighter piloting, officer status, and job training. Given these realities, on what basis will military women be brought to their knees begging forgiveness?

If Woman were ever to return Man's apology with an apology of her own, it will be because she chooses to do so, not because she has been made to suffer what Man has suffered.

Balanced Equality

What might be the best approach to this conundrum is also the least likely to happen. In fact, it is *so* politically incorrect one is at risk to say it aloud. Nevertheless, what would be best all around, I suppose, is to keep the military the province of men. In that event Man remains the primary victim of the military experience, and he remains vilified as the sole cause of war, but at least he receives *some* compensation in being gifted with extra heroism and status and success-appeal.

When there are women in the military (beyond support positions), Man remains the primary victim of the military experience and remains vilified as the sole cause of war and is compensated with extra *nothing*.

If the battlefield remains the exclusive province of men then, *crucially*, this male inequality can be employed to justify female inequality in other realms. The inequalities men face in the world of women (sexually, domestically, parentally) are rather elusive. But the inequity men suffer in taking sole responsibility for the military defense of their country provides a clear-cut, objective male inequality which can be employed to expose the "You men have *everything*, we women have *nothing*; give us half of what you've got then things will be equal" manipulation. What's needed is an understanding of equality as a *balance* of power and victimization, not a *sameness* of power and victimization.

As it stands now, the situation is the most *un*just it can be. Even more unjust than exempting women altogether is privileging women with extra options that allow them to cherry-pick "equality." So if there is absolutely *no hope* of a culture-wide reframe allowing the male-only battlefield to be compensated by a male-majority political elite, if there is no hope for an understanding of equality as a *balance* of power then, for what it's worth, and to the degree possible, let women taste of *unisex* equality (exact *sameness* of equality in *every* way). Let them receive no extra protection, coddling, or immunity from horror.

But, again, I regard this latter option as a *very* poor substitute for the former. We need to see equality as something that already *is* and *has always been*. Unisex equality is better than cherry-picked "equality," but it is a very poor substitute for *balanced* equality. Essentially, "unisex equality" is so poor a substitute because *unisex* equality is, I believe, quite simply unachievable.

Consider just *one* issue from a purely practical standpoint. Given that there are more women than men, how can vote power be equalized? Even if we gave each man 1.1 votes, that may equalize vote power between Woman and Man, but the vote power between a woman and a man has been rendered unequal. So, what are you going to do?

But unisex equality is not just impracticable; it is untenable. In the real world as it *truly* is, efforts to achieve unisex equality can only result in further incursions down the road toward *female-only* "equality." "Women in the military" provides a prime example of what actually *happens* when you reach for unisex equality.

In *principle*, including women in the military achieves sameness of power and sameness of victimization. In *practice*, however, you end up expanding female-only power and male-only victimization. Women receive special options, exemptions, and coddling while men work harder just to endure the lion's share of the worst of it. Whatever the *intentions* of unisex equality may be, whatever the androgynous utopian aims may be, this is *what actually **happens***.

Within the objective, numeric, measurable world of men, laws can dictate that there must be an equal number of female senators as male senators (quotas of this type already exist in a number of countries[848]). Laws can dictate that men and women must be paid the same number of dollars, *regardless*. Quotas can dictate that an equal number of Pulitzer and Nobel Prizes *must* be accorded each sex.

As the example of the military makes clear, laws and policies, quotas and affirmative actions can Glass Escalator women to equal or better status at one-third the risk and half the effort. In this way, men's extra risks and extra efforts may all be neutralized. Even in the world of sports we're seeing female athletes gifted with head starts and other advantages that allow women to "win" the race.[a]

Within the more objective public world of men, extra efforts men make out of their need to compensate for being male can be undone by public laws and policies. But it would seem that the more private, subjective, interpersonal world of women and women's *innate* powers are out of reach of the law. No laws and policies, no quotas or affirmative actions imaginable could ever force men's equality to women.

I could be wrong but it seems to me that men will *never* give birth and breast feed. Fathers will never imprint themselves upon infants in a manner equal to mothers. Motherhood power will not bow to any conceivable laws. The hand that rocks the cradle will continue to rule the world. No law could ever force women to be as addicted to the bodies of men as men are addicted to the bodies of women. Men will never leverage sexual power to a degree anywhere close to equality with women. The law cannot transfer this power away from women and give it to men. The basic biology of female sexuality guarantees that Man's sex appeal will always be dependent upon his success appeal. No policy could ever bring about women's equal willingness to pay for sex and/or pay men's mortgages. Female sexual power is innate and inalienable. Men will *never* be beneficiaries of chivalry. The instinct to protect women is exclusive to women and cannot be undone. It is beyond the reach of the law. Women en masse will never lay down their lives to protect the lives of men. Women will *never* be subject to punitive, harsh, and hazardous conditions equal to what men are subject to. Women will never be shot dead for "cowardice."

In a book called, *The Bastard on the Couch: 27 Men Try Really Hard to Explain Their Feelings About Love, Loss, Fatherhood, and Freedom*, 27 men . . . well. Why must men try *really hard* to explain their feelings? Is it because men are stupid or because men have only rudimentary language skills? No. Men need to try really hard to explain their own perspectives on life because men have never been

---

[a] See, for example, Paula Radcliffe, 2008 New York City Marathon. She ranked 28th in terms of clock time, but, because she (like the other elite women runners) was given a 35-minute headstart, Radcliffe crossed the finish line first. Thus the media universally declared her the "winner" and she was awarded the full $130,000 first prize. There are *many* such examples making the news these days.

taught politicized male perspectives. Women, armed with a library-full of feminism, express themselves with righteous eloquence while men, with a head-full of feminism, express themselves with self-deprecation. In his contribution, an essay entitled, "I Am Man, Hear Me Bleat," Fred Leebron explains what the men of his generation typically do:

> We seek out and partner up with women who will have careers at approximately the same level as ours. But you know what men give up when they venture into this kind of so-called equality? They give up equality. Why? Because there is no such thing as equality. Because men have long recognized that women are their domestic superiors, and perhaps that's why we've so staunchly and unjustly guarded our castles of work.[849]

The problem isn't that men staunchly and unjustly held their ground—far from it. The problem is that men gave it away upon demand and asked for nothing in return. Kathleen Parker recalls the period unclouded by the male addiction to guilt and shame:

> All things considered, American males have been relatively patient, calm, and compliant . . . What angry feminism seems to forget or ignore is that women's elevated status in American society hasn't only been earned. It hasn't merely been allowed. Women's liberation from cultural restraint has been encouraged, supported, and codified by laws consciously designed primarily by men.[850]

Man, detecting no flaw in Woman's demands for female-*only* "equality," didn't merely *allow* Woman's rise in the world of men (while men remained less-than throughout the world of women). Men drafted and enforced laws and policies *forcing* female-only equality and punished those few men with the temerity to get in the way.

Considering the costs to men, including diminished attractiveness to women, loss of parental rights, becoming divorce fodder, encroaching "obsolescence;" "all things considered" I'd say men have been *incredibly* compliant. All it took was matrisensus solidarity (made possible in the wake of reproductive, domestic, and workplace technologies) and within a few decades (an historic blink of an eye) men were shoved aside, nary a drop of bloodshed—*that's* female *power!*

From the *masculist* perspective, the injustice wasn't in men guarding their castles; the injustice was in women taking without giving. As a result of decades of women taking without giving, men are feeling less than equal in their relationships with women because they *are* less than equal in their relationships with women. If men were enlightened to their own perspectives, they would not automatically interpret themselves as "unjust," they would not believe the unsupportable feminist accusation that men have staunchly guarded their territory.

Enlightened men need not characterize their legitimate complaints in terms of "bleating" like so many sheep. The vast throngs of "compliant" men who rolled over without a wisp of protest are the ones comprising male sheepdom. In truth, it is those freakishly rare men who speak up and complain that actually comprise the few *rams* among the sheep.

There *is* such thing as equality. It's called *balanced* equality, and it has been the norm throughout history. What there's no such thing as is *unisex* equality. Why? Because we're not a unisex species.

Fred Leebron expresses the dilemma faced by the modern man entering into the basic "all *other* things being equal" relationship. Fred observes his wife taking ownership of parenting and declares, "I can't compete with my wife in this arena. She can compete with me in the career arena, sure, but I can't compete with her in the parenting arena."[851] The fact of the matter is, women are biologically adapted to the role of parent—especially infant and child care—to a degree that men *in general* can never hope to compete with on a truly co-equal basis.

Actor Tim Allen breaks through millennia of male conditioning to express this truth with remarkable candor and vulnerability:

> The birth of a child—my wife's going, "Ohh"—I see them in love in a room, and my eyes are like I'm looking in Macy's at toys I'll never own. I'll never have that! And the two of them: "Ah"—these little coos. . . . And I was like, "Whooo!" I shrank down to this little man. So what I have to do is somehow—I have to get some reason for them to need me. . . . I have very little left. I have this little corner left.[852]

The father's experience of looking at the nursing mother/child nexus as if through a store window, what Tim Allen here describes, is something we've dubbed the Glass Wall.

Cultural wisdom tells us that women and children form single-parent families complete in themselves. So the man standing *outside* this mother/child nexus must find a way to get his wife and children to need him as he needs them (for emotional intimacy, love, family, and everything else that makes life worthwhile). The man who fails as protector/provider, the man who fails to compensate for being male, runs a particularly high risk of becoming superfluous.

Why is it that women can compete with men in the male arena of career? Because, by and large, modern careers are not particularly *male* in nature. Epochs of hunting and protecting lend males no adapted advantages in paper pushing, data entry, customer relations, middle management, and so on. As school and workplace grow ever more feminized, and societal pressures seek to ever more Empower Women, once again it is *men* who struggle to compete.

Now women can*not* compete with men on a truly co-equal basis within the military. Men *are* biologically better adapted to the role of soldier (how did men get so lucky?). But, as with other male environs, within the objective, public, controlled realm of the military, "equality" can be *forced* and all innate male advantage neutralized.

Men, within their traditional realms—whether in the workplace, the government, or the military—are expected to work under female superiors. Any men who feel threatened or resentful are ordered to get over it or get fired, demoted, disgraced. Women are not expected to invite men to take their place in the nursery and women are not pressured to initiate sexually or take second place to men in beauty or pay men's mortgages or "marry down." Within the average workaday world of men, men must accept being subordinate to female superiors. But, within the world of women, women are never expected to be subordinate to men.

As compared with historic norms, women in vast numbers are entering more deeply into men's workplace arena than ever before. Societal mechanisms designed to protect these women from resentful men are extensive. As compared with historic norms, those men not shut out entirely are, in relatively small numbers, entering more deeply into women's domestic/parental sphere than ever before. Societal mechanisms designed to protect these men from resentful women are nonexistent.

I told the story of Larry Summers, former president of Harvard University. There's an addendum to the story. In a desperate effort to save himself, Summers reportedly arranged for a massive endowment (*fifty million* dollars?) toward advancing women at Harvard.[853]

Now, I won't deny the pervasive and deeply rooted societal expectation of seeing mathematical genius *only* in men. It is a bias female mathematicians must face.

But then again, Professor Simon Baron-Cohen describes his academic environ of mathematicians, physicists, and engineers. "Chatting at lunch with my colleagues in these disciplines leads me to suspect that if anything, many of them hold the opposite bias: that if they catch a glimpse of a talented female applicant, they try extra hard to accept her into the course, to reverse centuries of discrimination."[854]

So, what if the sexism and bias women experience in math and science is either way overstated or already undone by countervailing societal forces such as, quotas, women's organizations, feminism, affirmative action, and prioritizing women out of the desire to act out of what feels like moral rectitude? What then does the fifty million actually end up *doing?* Like similar efforts and endowments throughout the American university system,[855] it seeks to *force* female equality in math and science. Stuart Taylor of *National Journal Magazine*:

> Administration officials and others are "promising to litigate, regulate, and legislate the nation's universities until women obtain half of all academic degrees in science and technology and hold half of the faculty positions in those areas," as my colleague Neil Munro detailed in the July 4 *National Journal*. . . The push for what some feminists call "Title-Nining" the sciences. . . . "The evidence of gender bias in math and science is weak at best, and the evidence that women are relatively disinclined to pursue those fields at the highest levels is serious."[856]

Women may relatively lack aptitude and inclination, but recruit them vigorously enough, advantage them, ease their path, and you can Glass Escalator women to the top regardless of aptitude and inclination. Meanwhile, what legal/institutional efforts and how many millions can we expect society to earmark toward *forcing* male equality in beauty, grace, goodness; home, family, and parenting?

We can imagine a world in which laws and policies have rendered women absolutely equal to men. It is a credible scenario. We can*not* imagine a world in which laws and policies have rendered men absolutely equal to women. It is *not* a credible scenario.

A system in which women are often more-than, but never less-than, is not a balanced system. If laws and policies dismantle patriarchy while matrisensus keeps right on going, the result is imbalance. A balanced system isn't the same as a perfect system, but, on balance, it's better than an imbalanced system. Where there's matrisensus on one end of the Balance beam, there must be patriarchy on the other.

The two ends of the Balance beam need not be identical to weigh the same.

Feminist Joshua Goldstein defined "masculinism" as "an ideology justifying, promoting, or advocating male domination." Have I left myself and, by association, masculism, open to that accusation? What if I were to invite Woman to share the "hot seat" with me? As I wrote at the beginning: directing equal caring, concern, and compassion toward men; equal accountability, responsibility, and respect toward women changes *everything*.

To feminists, "equality" means one thing and one thing *only*—female equality with men at the *top end* of the world of men. In the name of equality, feminism believes that Woman is entitled to half the Senate seats. By itself, Woman taking half the Senate is perfectly okay, *but*—what is she willing to give in return? How about giving Man equality in parenting? Or granting Man equal *intrinsic value*—in love making, in beauty, in marriage, and in parenting? How about paying his way and paying his mortgage as often as he pays hers? How about giving her life to protect his as often as he gives his life to protect hers?

Respecting Woman, holding her to the same adult standards of integrity and accountability that Man is held to, changes the entire game of gender politics. From Woman we may now demand fairness, *quid pro quo*, taking *and giving*. We may now demand that Woman come to the bargaining table prepared to *negotiate*.

Feminism would have us believe that "Woman Is *the* Nigger of the World" specially entitled to cultural reparations. But loving Man changes everything. It means recognizing men's fully human vulnerability to *male* inequality. But more than that, loving men allows us to *feel* why male inequality *matters*. Lending men our compassion we may ask, if *men* were to receive reparations for past inequities they've endured, what might that look like?

Given that about 3 million American men have died in wars, how about sending only women into battle until 3 million women have died—or replacing all the hard/hazardous laborers with women until that death toll evens out? How about bringing newborns directly to their fathers for some duration of bonding before allowing mothers into the picture; or awarding men child custody four times out of five; or obligating women to initiate sexually/romantically and pay for dates four times out of five? How about women required to make a family-supporting wage in order to be deemed "eligible" for a man's love?

Not very credible, you say? Clearly, feminist reparations are female-*only* reparations. Regarding men with warm affection, we may ask: are these female-only reparations responsible for a rise of women/decline of men so rapid, so all-encompassing it has an *Atlantic* magazine article predicting "The End of Men"? Author Hanna Rosin goes on about the worldwide push "to institute political quotas in about 100 countries, essentially forcing women into power."[857] Rosin, eagerly anticipating the coming matriarchy, asks, "For years, women's progress has been cast as a struggle for equality. But what if equality isn't the end point?"[858] Indeed, what if the feminist agenda is not yet *half* way to whatever its final female-ist conclusion might be?

What's at risk if we were to distract ourselves from the realities of female pain and powerlessness just long enough to take our first serious look at the *male* experience of pain and powerlessness? What's at risk if we were to distract ourselves from the realities of male power and influence just long enough to take our first serious look at female power and influence?

What's at risk? Our entire belief system with regard to the relative positions of Woman and Man in our world is at risk. What's at risk is gender's Grand Illusion.

Adding the politicized male perspective into our gender reality changes *everything*. It changes feminism into female-ism. It changes Woman's bid for power into a bid for *more* power. In view of Woman's extraordinary *power* to induce Man to pour from his cup half "full" into her cup half "empty," so-called Patriarchal Domination is revealed as nothing more than the mirror-opposite of Matrisensus Manipulation. Loving men and respecting women changes *everything*. Is society prepared to deal with those changes?

As promised, I won't try and tell you what the world is, only what the world *looks like* as seen from the politicized male perspective. Adding that perspective into the equation, the feminist future looks very much like matriarchy/matrisensus—an Absolute Matriarchy—a world in which women occupy at *least* as much of the tip of the pyramid while the base of the pyramid remains largely occupied by "unmarriageable" men—a world in which women are often more than but never less than—a world in which men are rendered clearly, perhaps even *officially*, second-class humans.

Taking none of the above under consideration, and with utmost indignation, the feminist demands to know: *When will women have equality with men within the world of men?* The equalist, observing many decades of feminist action in the absence of masculist action, throws the ball back in her court: That's up to *you*. Man cannot take Full Responsibility for gender equality. As equal partner equally responsible for outcomes it's *your* turn now to *give*, in order to *get* what you want. In short, under an equalist system, Woman will have her equality with men within the world of men only to the degree that she grants men equality with women within the world of women.

Culture-wide efforts *can* and *should* be employed to tweak and finesse the gender system. But it is not gender *equality* that must be bargained for (equality already *is* and has always been so). What we're bargaining for is gender *justice*. Keeping a watchful eye on equality of *opportunity*, the goals of the bargaining are twofold. The goal is a more *just* redistribution of Love and Respect (for life to be fulfilling men and women must be both loved and respected). And the goal is *balanced* gender ideology, leading to de-escalation in the Battle of the Sexes.

The goal: increase gender fairness/*maintain* gender equality!

A shift toward loving men, respecting women *is* the proper future of gender politics. But, after 40-plus years of feminism in the absence of masculism, future progress now depends upon Woman's willingness to come to the bargaining table prepared to *negotiate*. It will be the province of equalism to haggle out gender redistribution under an ongoing gender-neutral system of gender politics (wherein the Glass Wall and the Glass Floor receive equal weight with the Glass Ceiling).

Assuming negotiations of this sort ever take place, how far toward unisex equality can they take us? Will women *en masse* accept the truths of masculism as men en masse have accepted the truths of feminism? Will women die to protect men and *actively* bring men into equality in the nursery as men have *actively* brought women into equality in the workplace? Will Woman value and require and *equalize* husbands/fathers? Will women truly *lust* after men's *intrinsic* values as men lust after women's intrinsic values? Will successful attractive women in huge numbers marry *down* as successful attractive men in huge numbers have done for millennia? Only time will tell.

In the meantime, it is my belief that unless or until we are prepared to go in and directly tamper with the biology of gender itself, we must bear in mind that women will retain certain *innate, inalienable* female powers and privileges. For this reason, men must *not* be defeated in their efforts to compensate for being male. Take away the severe misandry, the scholastic sabotage, the Glass Escalator—take away the feminist ideological dictatorship—and men will do what they've always done. They'll do *whatever it takes* to perform, achieve, and succeed. They'll do this largely out of *extra* motivation imposed upon them by Woman's *extra* demands upon them.

A male elite born of extra male risks, sacrifices, and efforts is a just and equitable reaction to female power. These male elite balance out the "garbage men" at the true bottom of the human hierarchy. The result is patriarchy/matrisensus. The result is *balanced **equality***.

Until presented with compelling evidence to the contrary, masculists beware; unisex equality should be regarded with due skepticism. It would seem that the human animal is very flexible, but not *infinitely* flexible. The traditional balance of power between Woman and Man has been *functional* because it is in alignment with certain biological realities that may be nudged this way and that, but are outright dismissed only at great cost to gender relations in particular and society in general.

Taxing the "Criminal Gender"

True recompense for what a veteran of the battlefield has suffered would be incalculable. But society might at least *attempt* to compensate those men who have suffered combat action, especially prisoners of war, with, say, the promise of lifetime financial support.

But we so hate and blame men for "causing" wars that we close our hearts to the full magnitude of their suffering. Even when the male suffering is *caused by the society they're protecting* (as in the case of Agent Orange poisoning), society is nevertheless loath to offer these men any compensation at all.

Men generally have little awareness of how bad misandry has become. Nor do they seem to have a healthy apprehension regarding how much worse it could get. The MB/WG paradigm costs men empathy, but beyond that, believing men are Bad is an open invitation for society to *punish* the punished sex rather than *compensate* the punished sex. Warren Farrell:

> When *The Economist* evaluated men, it did so in an article titled "The Trouble with Men." A sample: "The next generation does not need the current crop of men to be carrying around their sperm all the time. A clean, well-run sperm bank, regularly topped off, would be just as good—and would dispense with men's unfortunate social side-effects." Although "men's unfortunate social side effects" include building the offices, computers, and presses by which *The Economist* is published, and disposing of every employee's bodily and office wastes, neither *The Economist* nor other books claiming an economic evaluation of men, such as Dr. June Stephenson's *Men are Not Cost-Effective*, acknowledge any of that. Rather, the conclusion of poor cost-effectiveness comes from evaluating what is described in its subtitle: *Male Crime in America*. As if men's only side effect was crime, and as if all men were criminals.[859]

The article "The Trouble with Men" positively reeks of hostility and contempt toward men. It would seem that the culture has declared "open season" for attacking and assassinating male character while simultaneously endeavoring to protect the feminine from even the mildest critique. If that weren't enough, says Nancy Friday:

> One Matriarchal Feminist's reaction to the growing violence among young men isn't to question why but to write that men should be charged a "user's fee" for the prisons and rehabilitation they monopolize. "Men are expensive," psychologist June Stephenson writes. "We cannot expect men to police their own, to take responsibility for their contribution to the violence in this country. . . . Men must pay for being men."[860]

In her book, *Men Are Not Cost Effective*, June Stephenson asserts: "An additional exemption on state and federal income-tax forms that allows a deduction for being female would serve two purposes. It would provide gender equity in taxation for crime, and it would so antagonize men as to make them take a second look at their responsibility."[861] "An *additional* exemption"? Women's exemptions from the dark side of the world and human nature together with most of life's most harsh and hazardous requirements aren't exemptions enough?

Effectively, a tax reduction for women is the same as an extra tax levied upon men. Stephenson herself now refers to a "Man Tax" and so will I. It more straightforwardly acknowledges the punitive intent. In Sweden the implementation of this tax is even now being considered. "Members of Sweden's Left Party have proposed a special tax on men to cover the 'social cost' of violence against women. 'We must have a discussion where men understand they as a group have a responsibility,' said party deputy Gudrun Schyman."[862] But Man can*not* take Full Responsibility. We've already explored the vast wealth of evidence suggesting that, within the domestic setting, women are just as violent toward men as the reverse.

I dive into this issue to illustrate three things: 1) The costs men pay under the MP/FV and MB/WG paradigms are escalating. 2) Before moving on to equalism, the feminist "common knowledge" that supports a Modest Proposal such as this must first be challenged. 3) Masculist facts and truths are the weaponry through which militant feminist self-righteousness may be exposed and curtailed.

Recently, Stephenson's Modest Proposal was given a veneer of respectability by a trio of economists. Alberto Alesina and Loukas Karabarounis of Harvard University and Andrea Ichino of the University of Bologna talk of "the Ramsey principle of optimal taxation" and "labor supply behavior" and "elasticity," but don't let the arcane economic jargon fool you; it's just the same old misandry.

> For historical and cultural reasons, the relative bargaining power of spouses is still such that men can get away with a lower share of unpleasant home duties. Hence, they can participate more in the market, exercise more effort and earn more than their spouses.[863]

What false feminist common knowledge are the authors exploiting here? *Why* do men feel the need to "exercise more effort" in the pursuit of money? And how is it fair to undermine those extra efforts by taxing away the extra income fairly earned?

> The avoidance of family chores allows men to engage in careers that offer "upside potential" in terms of wages and promotions. . . . Gender-based taxation induces a more balanced allocation of home duties because it increases the implicit bargaining power of women within the marriage by improving their outside option. Currently, women and men work exactly the same amount, but women more at home and men more in the market in all countries for which data are available.[864]

Having read this book, how would you counter-argue the above? What have we learned about the unpleasant duties *husbands* more often perform? What do *we* know of "the relative bargaining power of spouses"? Which spouse already enjoys the greater "outside option" in pursuit of full-time high-stress, high-wage work; fulltime low-stress, low-wage work; part-time work; emotionally fulfilling volunteer work; or fulltime parenting? What do *we* know of the *down*side potential of *the* worst and most hazardous jobs men more often endure in order to bring home that crucial family-supporting wage?

Truly, it is *outrageous* for a feminist to demand that men "take a *second* look at their responsibility" when women have yet to take a *first* look at their responsibility as equal partners—for good and for bad. "'Men are furious at the idea,' said Stephenson, who has floated it on radio and TV talk shows. 'They just get apoplectic.'"[865] Well, coming from the doormat sex, that's great news! Part of me hopes the proposal will come to fruition. Perhaps a male-only tax would "so antagonize men" they might finally pull their heads from the sand.

Where masculism doesn't exist, effective counterargument to Stephenson's proposal doesn't exist. Men may get "apoplectic," but they don't get very eloquent. Economist Raaj Sah of the Irving B. Harris Graduate School of Public Policy at the University of Chicago says: "It's an absurd argument. You do not seek retribution from a group of individuals for acts committed by specific individuals. There is no notion of social jurisprudence which supports such an approach."[866] Yeah, but that doesn't really convince, does it?

Sah's point is easily sidestepped by pointing out the precedence of unequal insurance premiums. "Not all boys cause car accidents, but all young men pay this," says Stephenson. "Nobody's telling the insurance company it's unconstitutional; they're simply covering their losses, and we should, too."[867] So long as we remain ideologically imprisoned by the feminist belief system, the true *outrage* of Stephenson's scheme will remain outside the reach of our thinking.

Men get apoplectic for good reason; they just don't fully grasp what that reason is. Stephenson's proposal amounts to society setting men up to bear the burden and suffer the consequences of the dark side of human nature (while women are protected from both), then forcing men to foot the bill for the punishments society inflicts!

Men can *feel* it, but they can't articulate it. Only someone with knowledge of men's issues is armed with what's needed to reveal the misandry, the unfounded feminist self-righteousness, and cruel gender injustice for what it is. An economist may get angry; he may label the proposal absurd, but he can offer only a rather technical, unsatisfying rebuttal. Raaj Sah has no knowledge of masculism. Few men do.

Especially in positions of political power, there are only feminists (e.g., our president and vice president). So maybe a special tax on men *will* be implemented. If you can tax the "criminal gender," what else can you do to them? If you can rape a boy then hit him up for child support payments, what other injustices can you inflict upon boys? If you can *assume* pedophilia of *any* male airline passenger, what other biased policies can you afflict males with? Perhaps one day men will get so "apoplectic" they may actually break through their bounds of chivalry and shame. In place of sexual-political ignorance, we might gain a population of men whose sexual-political savvy allows them to know and to speak their truths eloquently and with conviction—*in numbers too large to ignore!*

If the past is any indication, however, my fear is that men, *especially* influential men in high places, will dutifully accept *any* insult as their just deserts—only what the Bad sex deserves. Honor is, and has always been, a psychological obligation that can be twisted into a weapon used by Woman to manipulate Man.

The Honorable Man

When we believe that men have *the* power and women are *the* victims, we believe that men are Bad and women are Good. How will the Honorable Man cope within this MB/WG belief system?

The honorable man "knows" (has been taught that) masculinity is *the* source of sexism, oppression, criminality, violence, and all things bad. Yet the honorable man needs to experience himself as honorable. How then will he retain the sense of personal honor he *needs* to have when he "knows" himself to be a member of the Bad sex?

Well, by what other means *could* the honorable man distinguish himself from the vast sea of ignoble men except by aligning himself with the feminine? What other honorable choice is there but to fight for goodness and fairness *against* evil masculine forces that victimize and dominate, wage war and despoil the earth? In fighting "the good fight," the honorable man retrieves his personal honor out from the morass of evil masculinity.

In turning against his own kind the honorable man believes he is rejecting the low dictates of self-interest in favor of the higher cause of equality and justice—a highly honorable stance to take. While women dedicate themselves to the interests of sisterhood, honorable men disavow loyalty to their own kind, now decried under the umbrella term, "male chauvinism."

The honorable man does not shirk accountability. He "knows" (has been taught that) All Fault is Male and he is not about to evade his guilt. Because the honorable man owns his guilt and fault as a matter of pride, the honorable man rejects evidence that would mitigate his guilt and fault. It is through strict unflinching ownership of his guilt that the honorable man *earns* his honor. So he embraces the truths of feminism but rejects mirror-opposite truths as if such truths threatened to strip him of his honor.

The honorable man "knows" (has been taught that) powerful men pay powerless women 74 cents on the dollar just because they are women. Men who would present evidence to the contrary are assumed to be self-serving evaders of well-earned guilt. More contemptible even than those men who would exploit women are those men who would deny it! The honorable man "knows" (has been taught that) domestic violence equals evil men beating up innocent women. Men who would present a more balanced picture are judged in the worst way. The honorable man will leave it to lesser men, men who fail to take Full Responsibility, to hide behind "excuses." The honorable man *knows* masculinity to be the source of all things bad and believes it only proper that masculinity be shamed and punished accordingly.

The honorable man is a chivalrous man. His code of honor demands that he protect the "gentle sex," whom he assumes to be generally more virtuous than himself. He "knows" (has been taught that) feminism is the voice of women so he protects women/feminism as if they were one and the same. He will leave it to lesser men—weak, shameful, self-serving men—to critique the voice of women. The honorable man dutifully accepts the moral authority and admonitions of his moral superiors.

The honorable man is a masculine man. Who needs compassion when you're "tough as nails"? Men don't need empathy; men need what they *always* need—a good swift kick in the pants. The honorable man can't abide the complaints of men. Men who would protest are "whiners" to be regarded with contempt.

Toward men, the honorable man directs accountability without compassion, never realizing how ruthless that is. He respects his fellow man, but he is too invested in "toughening up" his fellow man to think in terms of *loving* his fellow man. Toward women he directs compassion without accountability, never realizing how infantilizing that is. He loves women, but the gift of accountability is something he keeps strictly for himself. Compelled and determined to take Full Responsibility, he's in denial of Woman's power and her half of the adult accountability that goes with it.

Neither the feminist nor the honorable man, want either Female-Power or MaleVictimization revealed. Neither the feminist nor the honorable man want to see women held accountable. Neither the feminist nor the honorable man can abide male complaint.

The honorable man is indeed honorable, but all too often he is something else as well. He is *the perfect* feminist patsy. He is the manipulated male personified. Cultural misandry has the honorable man experiencing himself as if he were the rare exceptional man but, in truth, he is the common man.

So long as he believes men have *the* power and women are *the* victims, he believes that men have no business protesting and women deserve every advantage they're given. Though the MP/FV paradigm leads Man down a path to diminishment, it simultaneously guilt-trips him into rejecting any truths that would refute it! Man passively watches his own decline without lifting a finger. His belief system renders him helpless against feminist machinations and precludes mobilizing on his own behalf even though he suffers comparison with Woman in nearly every measure of wellbeing.

Through feminism, Woman's shadow has constructed the perfect male conundrum and escape-proof ideological trap. Woman works her power to attack, take from, and disparage Man, all under the guise of having no power.

The New Warrior community is comprised of honorable men. They are particularly dedicated to personal accountability and the dictates of chivalry and political correctness. When it comes to truths from the politicized *male* perspective, their shields are at the ready. Masculist truths do not penetrate and the teachings of feminism are never questioned.[a] More than 45,000 men have been initiated into the New Warrior community. Only a fraction remain actively connected; nevertheless, New Warriors is, to my knowledge, the largest and strongest men's organization in the U.S.

The founders, sensing the decline and degradation of men, founded New Warriors with the mission to "Reclaim the sacred masculine in our time." But feminism has done its magic upon this community and thus far, all efforts to elicit support toward fulfillment of a politicized men's movement have failed.

No matter what ruin a drug wreaks, how will addicts respond to that which threatens to take their drug from them?

While Man rejects the victim that Woman grasps with both hands, Woman rejects the shame that Man grasps with both hands. I'm not surprised women and men tend to be hostile toward masculist truths. Introducing balance and fairness into gender ideology would deprive Woman of the victim to which she's addicted and it would deprive Man of the shame to which he's addicted.

---

a   In fact, I attended one workshop and know of others in which feminism was taught there in the Chicago New Warrior men's center. Needless to say, the organization has never heard of masculism.

A specific example: columnist George F. Will has said of men: "Nature blundered badly in designing males . . . because of neurochemical stuff like testosterone, males are not naturally suited to civilization."[868] In the moment he wrote it, in retrieving his personal honor out of the morass of evil masculinity, Mr. Will doubtless felt an internal rush of nobility and integrity.

I note that Mr. Will has subsequently become less enamored of misandry. Nonetheless, I submit that there could *never* be honor in gender bigotry. And yet, certain self-flagellating men in high places will, in the name of chivalry and self-righteous self-hate, eagerly endorse and masochistically embrace any new punishment for themselves and their kind. Sadly, it is likely that a male-only tax wouldn't anger men into taking action as much as it would further demoralize the "obsolete" male.

"Arrows" #6: "Dumb and Dumber": Glib and More Glib

Some of the more vicious "arrows" currently sent men's way revolve around the notion of male "redundancy," or "obsolescence."

In an essay entitled "Will science render men unnecessary?" author Brian Alexander, for example, comments on recent developments in reproductive technology:

> If a woman chose to do so, speculated tabloid journalists, she could make sperm from her own bone marrow, fertilize another woman's egg — and voila! "Men could be completely sidelined," according to Britain's Daily Mail. "Women to Self Create," blared the headline in Australia's Daily Telegraph. "Men beware!" began a story on one U.S. news Web site . . . the stories are reminiscent of some that were printed 10 years ago when the birth of Dolly the sheep, the first mammal cloned from an adult cell, was announced. We men were declared washed up then, too.[869]

A similar reaction greeted the theory that the "Y" chromosome is eroding with each generation and the male of the species must eventually become extinct. "As a headline in Britain's *Sunday Times* quipped: 'Bad news: Men Doomed. Good News: No Problem.'"[870]

In a chapter optimistically titled "The End of Men," the misandric Michael (*Stupid White Men*) Moore declares Man at fault and to blame for *all* the world's ills and glibly celebrates Man's imminent and "rightful" decline.

> As is our wont, we commenced work on a series of projects that stunk everything up and made a mess of our world. Women? They deserve none of the blame. They continued to bring life into this world; we continued to destroy it whenever we could. We can't pin any of this on

women . . . every bit of plunder and pillage, every attack on the environment, everything that has brought horror and destruction to all that was once pure and good has come from hands that, well, when they aren't busy bringing pleasure to one-self, are working overtime to wipe out this beautiful, wonderful home we were given.[871]

In honor of the new millennium, an issue of *Time* magazine offered essayists the opportunity to envision the future. Essayist Barbara Ehrenreich asks, "Will Women Still Need Men?" "We're only a few in vitro developments away from gender independence," intones Ehrenreich. "This could be the century when the sexes go their separate ways . . . And why not?"

Ehrenreich didn't title her essay Will the Sexes Still Need Each Other? No one doubts that men will still need women. "Obviously, women, with their built-in baby incubators, will have the advantage in a monosexual future," says Ehrenreich. "They just have to pack up a good supply of frozen semen, a truckload of turkey basters and go their own way." Leave it to a member of the "romantic" sex to anticipate a time when "the sexes go their separate ways" and with airy indifference ask "And why not?"[872]

"In the very near future women might be quite capable of dispensing with men altogether," agree preeminent science writers Jeremy Churfas and John Gribbin. "The technology of test-tube babies already exists, and if an adequately supported team were to put their minds to the problem it would be no time before women could do without men entirely."[873] Having perused some radical feminism from the likes of Sally ("The proportion of men must be reduced to and maintained at approximately 10 percent of the human race"[874]) Gearhart; Churfas and Gribbin know that "A small minority might like to do away with men completely. It is a theme that pervades the more extreme feminist propaganda." The authors take heart in the fact that radical feminists have not yet succeeded, "and we men are not yet completely useless."[875] Do the authors regard women who "might like to do away with men completely" as evil or insane? Hardly—they're described as "those women who see males for what they are, biological parasites on the parental care of females."[876]

Well, John Moore, author of *What About Men?*, has had it with all the male bashing. Behold the thunderous indignation of a man's furious response: "In view of the secondary yet demanding role assigned to the male in reproduction," rails Moore, "it seems rather unfair that some biologists should describe the male as 'parasitic.'"[877] Well, take *that*, Churfas and Gribbin; denigrate the male at your peril! Suggest that men are nothing more than parasites and a man is apt to become so enraged as to regard the accusation as something that "seems rather unfair." Gee, ya think? But hey, At least John Moore *protests*. That's more than can be said of other men.

Men are bashed so often because men are bashed for free.

Note that the invention of a biomechanical womb would most definitely *not* have us declaring women "obsolete." No one wants to be rid of women, least of all men. We would not so immediately concern ourselves with women's capacity to "dispense with men altogether" if women had not expressed sufficient hostility and sexual ambivalence toward men to render it a credible scenario.

All science aside, Brian Alexander gets to the true crux of the matter: "I just want to know why you women are in such a rush to get rid of us. Sci-fi and fantasy literature are full of all-female societies like Wonder Woman's home island."[878] Nineteenth century feminist Charlotte Perkins Gilman wrote of *Herland*, a female-only "utopia," "where women would lead placidly sexless lives and reproduce by parthenogenesis;" and Joanna Russ imagines *Whileaway*, a colony supported by the very same male high-technology that has rendered the male obsolete—a female-only world and therefore "a serene garden paradise."[879] Indeed, Wonder Woman's home island is called *Paradise* Island exactly because no men are allowed on it.

Brian Alexander's question is well put. But he proceeds to answer it with—what else—glib self-deprecating "humor."

> Being a man, I will assume that most women would prefer to give birth to female babies, girls being far more competent, intelligent and with less propensity to crash motorcycles. Two hundred years from now, a few isolated stag colonies are inhabited by men who have mutated to survive solely on Doritos. Male language has been reduced to a single word: "Wassup!"[880]

But this is no joke. Between 70 and 90 percent of couples seeking to adopt express a preference for girls.[881] Studies show that women do indeed prefer giving birth to girls and suffer, on average, worse levels of postnatal depression following the birth of a boy.[882] An article in *Vogue* magazine describes the severe disappointment women often experience upon being told the child they're carrying is a boy: "I cried on the ultrasound table."[883] Not to worry—a newly developed method allows mothers to *preselect* their child's gender!

How did Ronald Ericsson, the method's inventor, react to the news that his technology was primarily being used to select girls? He glibed of wanting a sex-change operation: "Women live longer than men. They do better in this economy. More of 'em graduate from college. They go into space and do everything men do, and sometimes they do it a whole lot better. I mean, hell, get out of the way—these females are going to leave us males in the dust."[884] All I hear is the sound of a sex prepared to go out without a whimper.

How will Man fare should Woman come to wield not just majority vote power but *vast*-majority vote power?

A new and improved method for pre-selecting a child's gender, called MicroSort, will soon be made available. "The girl requests for that method run at about 75 percent. . . . As [mothers] imagine the pride of watching a child grow and develop and succeed as an adult, it is more often a girl that they see in their mind's eye."[885] Medical science has enabled women to give birth only to the sex both sexes love more, the sex with the brighter future. Women can now be rid of males simply by choosing not to give birth to them.

In the meantime, women can simply shun men. "The next generation of young men may, in fact, be keener on marriage than their potential mates," says Cathy Young. "Seventy-three percent of teenage girls surveyed in 1994 but only 61 percent of boys thought they could have happy lives if they didn't marry; 60 percent of the boys and 77 percent of the girls said that they could be happy if they got divorced."[886] *The Janus Report* concurs: "We found a major role reversal in our interviews: a great many single men among our respondents disclosed that they and their male friends were looking, sometimes desperately, for commitments from women, and that the women wanted to play but not to commit."[887]

"Who Needs a Husband?" asks *Time* magazine's cover. "More women are saying no to marriage and embracing the single life." Nine and a half pages are devoted to how righteous women are to shun men and marriage and half a page is given to "One Man's Gripe." What does Walter Kirn offer in his precious opportunity to redress misandry? Why, self-deprecating humor of course. His "gripe"? Women have upped the ante! In times past: "To be considered promising husband material, a man didn't even have to be good-looking; he just had to have a job—and use deodorant."[888] Har, har, har.

Despite the rapier wit, Kirn's counterargument does not hold up too well. A letter to the editor responds: "Considering the old requisites Kirn listed ('get a good job and use deodorant'), we would have to be asinine not to demand more," says a woman sounding righteous as god.[889] Lesson *not* learned: glib self-hating stupidity is no way for men to stand up for themselves.

*Oh my **lord**,* how I long to read the words of a man who responds with genuine *feeling*—something like: "I take in the indictment and indifference Woman sends my way and it tears at my *heart!*" "From time immemorial Man has loved, cherished, protected Woman, done his damndest to be *everything* she wanted him to be, and the very *instant* Man's technology creates a world in which protector/providers cease to be a practical necessity, Woman tells Man she needs him the way a fish needs a bicycle?" "Man writes, sings, wails and moans an ocean of love songs and sonnets expressing his abject adoration and *this* is Woman's response?" "*We deserve better than this!*"

One of the many reasons Man stays out of sexual politics is that he figures the storm Woman has created is bad enough as it is, and adding his complaints and disputing Woman's complaints could only make matters even worse. So Man, hiding behind his "newspaper," means to keep the piece by stoically weathering Woman's cries and indictments without challenge.

In these matters, the logical, fair, and rational form only the tip of the iceberg. Roiling about in the undercurrents are powerful, instinctual, psycho/sexual elements. Drawing from these murky waters, what Woman wants, needs, and *demands* of Man is for him to be, well . . . *the man*. The *erotic* man, the *Real* Man, the *Alpha* Male found within her Romance Novels is the very antithesis of a glib self-deprecator who only rolls over, gives in, and panders.

"I often professed to be disappointed when men resisted feminism," but, Carol Iannone confesses, "I secretly found it even more disappointing when they succumbed to it." One faction of the female psyche truly believes she is *the* powerless victim and is disappointed when Man fails to cater to her every complaint. But, another faction of the female psyche looks around and sees no Real Men, and she is even *more* disappointed when Man turns out to be *so* easily manipulated.

Male feminists only address Woman's surface complaints, the complaints directed at Man the "oppressor." But, from deeper waters, I believe the more powerful psycho/sexual impulse driving Woman's rage is directed at Man the "wimp." It is toward the "wimp" in Man that Woman reserves a special contempt. "Man Up!" this part of Woman's psyche demands "or I'm done with you" (you're "obsolete"). It's a shadow demand drawn from instinctual waters and neither logic nor fairness are in charge.

Man would keep the Battle of the Sexes from escalating by not "showing up." It's a poor strategy. A primal aspect of Woman wants Man to stand up for himself, be capable of saying "no" to her, draw boundaries, "take charge," demand a sustainable fairness, and be a Man! This part of Woman will *never* be appeased by male female-ists, no matter *how* they may capitulate.

I suspect that Woman's demands will grow ever more strident until she either goads Man into the Manly response she's after, or she keeps taking until he's left without the proverbial pot to piss in.

So feminism stands *alone* as a movement of immense power and influence that advocates solely for females. Meanwhile, far too many *males* are undereducated, underemployed, shamed, timid, enervated, homeless, imprisoned, and otherwise "unmarriageable." Women are rising and men are in decline. It may appear then that women are "winning," but if that's so, then why are women so unhappy?

In the past, according to survey results, women worldwide consistently measured happier than men.[890] By "objective" measures, women are now doing better than ever—better than men. So, why is it that recently, and for the first time since such measures have been taken, women's happiness has sunk *below* men's?[891] And how do we account for the overwhelming correlation whereby the *most* feminist cultures produce the *least* happy women?[892]

Why do so many women still feel so powerless, so angry? What's missing here? How can Woman *truly* win?

The Shadow *Not* Owned

I co-lead a personal growth weekend called Path to Spirit. As far as we can figure it, Surrender, Acceptance, Forgiveness, and Thankfulness are the cornerstones of personal happiness. As *I* figure it, the feminist mindset tends to close a woman off to all four.

If the reader will indulge me a moment of Path to Spirit philosophizing, I will suggest that there are two ways of viewing emotional pain. There is the perspective that views pain as a violation or injustice inflicted upon us. Pain that is "*thrust* upon us" will be experienced and internalized as victimization. The "victim" will feel indignation, become guarded and angry, and will want to blame the situation and the people involved. Pain that leads to victim, indignation, defensiveness, and blaming is pain that leads to suffering.

There is an alternative. We can view pain not as something that has been done to us but rather as an *inevitable* part of life and really no one's fault. We can *accept* pain as just pain, something we all share and just one of an entire spectrum of human feelings. We can reframe the pain in our burdens by seeing the gifts in our burdens (the duality in all things). Viewing life from this high plane, we may conclude: Pain is inevitable, but suffering is optional. And "victim" may be re-understood as nothing more than a *chosen* mindset.

I imagine a feminist asserting: It's easy for *you* to reject victim. You're *not* a victim; you're a man—a member of the "favored" sex living within "Patriarchy." Needless to say, this entire book is a refutation of that assertion. It is *not* easy for me—or for anyone else—to give up "victim." Giving up "victim" is a lifelong endeavor.

But I do not endeavor to give up my personal "victim" under the assumption that life is perfectible. I seek to *Surrender* to what is and *Accept* and *Forgive* the world and be *Thankful* for my gifts even knowing that they come with burdens attached. Along with the light side, the dark side of the world and human nature will always be with us.

Throughout the feminist literature, however, I encounter the belief that the dark side of the world and human nature might be done away with, pain eliminated, and a peaceful perfect female utopia achieved. I regard this belief as the product of a certain feminine naiveté—which itself is a product of living life within a relatively sheltered world, the world of women. "What I call Betty Crocker feminism—a naively optimistic Pollyannaish or Panglossian view of reality—is behind much of this," asserts Camille Paglia. "Even the most morbid of the rape ranters have a childlike faith in the perfectibility of the universe, which they see as blighted solely by nasty men. They simplistically project outward onto a mythical 'patriarchy' their own inner conflicts and moral ambiguities."[893] And in so doing they fail to own the shadow side of their own human nature.

In his essay "The Dangers of Innocence," celebrated existential psychologist Rollo May warns us of the dark side not owned.

> The awareness that human existence is both joy and woe is prerequisite to accepting responsibility for the effect of one's intentions. My intentions will sometimes be evil—the dragon or the Sphinx in me will often be clamoring and will sometimes be expressed—but I ought to do my best to accept it as part of myself rather than to project it on you.[894]

Carolyn Baker, Ph.D., states the matter forthrightly: "we women need to look at the feminine shadow . . . and own that as a part of ourselves and stop projecting it onto males and onto the masculine."[895]

As Woman assumes leadership, she needs to look at the feminine shadow to better serve all humanity (including men), but also to serve her *own* purposes. In *dis*owning the shadow, women disown a substantive part of themselves that is energetic, forceful, ambitious. She who takes ownership of her human shadow stands solidly upon the bedrock of her *truth*—which, in turn, leads to being grounded, authentic, confident, and empowered through personal accountability.

When we consciously own our shadow we may utilize it constructively, *and* keep an eye on it (so it doesn't sneak around from behind, take hold of the wheel, and drive the bus). Only with "the awareness that human existence is both joy and woe" can pain be understood as an inevitable part of life that is really no one's fault. Duality, not "patriarchy," guarantees that positives *must* come with negatives. There can be no pain-free world for either sex.

Obviously, none of this is to say that peace, love, and understanding are not ideals to strive toward. But even if evil (war) could ever be done away with, is there reason to believe that women are the ones to make it happen? For me the gnawing question is this: what do naiveté and innocence transform into when challenged by conflicts, complexities, and realities that "innocence" and "niceness" cannot cope with? Rollo May continues:

> To admit frankly, our capacity for evil hinges on our breaking through our pseudo-innocence. So long as we preserve our one-dimensional thinking, we can cover up our deeds by pleading innocent. This antediluvian escape from conscience is no longer possible. We are responsible for the effect of our actions, and we are also responsible for becoming as aware as we can of these effects.[896]

The "innocent" may be ill equipped to suffer evil yet keep at least some part of their moral compass alive and functioning. According to the Bible, Lucifer (the Devil) was a fallen *angel*. I believe that, in part, this parable tells us that when purest innocence turns dark, it may turn all the way dark. If pure and perfect innocents have all their illusions shattered, what remains?

In short, I find Woman's claims of moral-ethical superiority, if not actual moral-ethical purity, more disturbing than reassuring. Just as it's hard to trust someone who beats you with their club while proclaiming: "Club, what club; I haven't got any club," it is equally hard to trust a leader who says: "Shadow, what shadow; I haven't got any shadow."

The veils of protection lifted, we could expect to see Woman's unowned shadow, her "victim," her blame projected outward, her shattered innocence, and her "righteous" *rage* prove violent, deadly. We can confidently make the prediction—we've explored plenty of corroborative evidence—but so long as men are relegated to deal with, embody, and succumb to the dark side of the world and human nature, women's capacity to do the same *still* remains largely untested.

Woman cannot have a "free lunch." Why? Because there's no such thing. Duality guarantees that efforts to make the world *perfect* for women cannot succeed. In fact, it would seem that the more Woman "wins," the more burdened and *un*happy she becomes.

The Battle of the Sexes is a battle neither sex can win. As Woman steps into official leadership, her true win position comes from owning her true shadow, her true power, and her responsibility toward *all* of humanity (not just the sisterhood). What's needed is a *rational* reassessment of gender "power" and "victim." What stands in the way of that happening?

Gender Sentiment

Humanity has yet to take an official, scientific, scholarly look at either *Female*Power or *Male*Victimization. What primarily constrains our thinking and our perception is an array of emotional/psychological factors (instinct, Eros, chivalry, etc.). If we were to boil these factors all down to one word, the word I'd choose is sentimentality. From a purely logical standpoint, sentiment is meaningless. But from a human standpoint, sentiment trumps logic.

> *"Boys are made of snips and snails and puppy dog tails.*
> *Girls are made of sugar and spice and everything nice."*

Though it is what stubbornly and primarily stands in the way of a rationally balanced view of gender, it won't do to simply dismiss sentiment. Though not logical, sentiment is powerful and important. I feel it too. I watch Clark Gable and John Wayne on the screen and I am far from immune to the masterful masculine personae they project. They thrill and galvanize and inspire me. And I know my female equivalent is far from immune to the sublime feminine personae as projected by the likes of Audrey Hepburn and Marilyn Monroe.

Nothing can bring me to tears like a deeply romantic depiction of love between a woman and a man, and such depictions show no sign of abating. What is romance without the ritual pleasantries of gender? As long as it's *mutual*, where's the harm in each sex showing the other a special deference? The imagery of "lords and ladies" (e.g., *The Lord of the Rings*) would not have such an ongoing grip upon the human psyche if this imagery didn't resonate at a deep level. Though illogical, humans maintain a sentiment-based gender "reality" and we do so for *deep* reasons.

So, if gender sentiment cannot and *should* not be done away with, then how can we keep the charm of gender sentiment without imprisoning ourselves to its falsehoods? How can we *feel* it without it distorting our *thinking*? We can no longer afford to look at the world limited by a chivalry/feminist blindfold that closes us off from a whole world of truth. Yet our world would be a far grayer place without the enriching poetry and beauty of gender sentiment.

To the degree that there is a "solution" to this conundrum, I think it's modeled for us in the way Great Britain has retained the sentiment of Kings and Queens, while divesting itself of the destructive by-products of "royalty." The English *love* their royalty, but the citizens of England long ago stopped believing that Kings and Queens rule by some kind of literal mandate from God. "Blue blood" is no longer regarded as real. The English enjoy the poetry, intrigue, pageantry, drama, and romance of Queens and Kings, Princes and Princesses without ever forgetting that these "royalty" are, in fact, only ordinary people. They compartmentalize. They feed off the dreams of royalty and then they shake their heads and come back to reality. In short, they don't take the whole thing too seriously.

Why can't we be like that where gender is concerned? We can have both logic *and* sentiment. We can enrich our lives with the poetry of gender, then shake our heads and come back to reality. Beautiful though it may be, we must not allow gender sentimentality to so thoroughly derail our *thinking*.

The prestigious *Oxford Companion to Philosophy* defines the word sexism thus:

> Sexism. Thought or practice which may permeate language and which assumes women's inferiority to men. The existence of sexism is acknowledged from a variety of ideological perspectives, and sexism may be conceived either as something one encounters instances of, or as a pervasive phenomenon endemic to society. Thus 'sexist' is applied pejoratively to individuals and to institutions . . .[897]

Sexism, as here defined, is indeed widely acknowledged and the word is applied pejoratively on a daily basis. The terms "male chauvinism" and "misogyny" are also commonly used to punish and censure anti-female prejudice and bias wherever found.

But, our understanding of "sexism" is itself stunningly sexist. No matter how denigrating the sentiment may be, it will not register as "sexism" unless it assumes *women's* inferiority. No matter how it may glorify women to men's detriment, no sentiment will register as "female chauvinism" because the term *female* chauvinism doesn't exist in common parlance. "I believe that women have a capacity for understanding and compassion which a man structurally does not have, does not have it because he cannot have it he's just incapable of it," said U.S. Congress-woman Barbara Jordan.[898] But this will not register as "misandry" because the word misandry is unknown to us.

The assumption that feminism—the sexual politics of females—sufficiently encompasses sexual politics in its *entirety* is the single most profoundly sexist assumption operating in our world today. There is more in heaven and earth than is dreamt of in the feminist philosophy. There is a whole other *world* of truth to explore.

Isn't it about time we replaced feminism with equalism—a sexual politics that would include the truths, realities, and politicized perspectives of *both* sexes?

Conclusion

Conclusion

We've described the problem. It's time to focus on the solution.

Let's begin by setting realistic expectations. History is littered with hyper-zealous movements based on the naïve notion that if only we altered our system or ourselves in some particular way, paradise would be ours. With "paradise" as the expected outcome, no feverish rhetoric, no manic action or emotion will be thought too extreme—and that's the problem. Feminism is a prime example of a zealous movement promising an end to war, violence, criminality and all things bad—a matriarchal paradise.[a]

But there is no "solution" to the human condition. Duality guarantees that all positives come with negatives. Pain is an inevitable part of life. Realistically, there will always be some degree of conflict between women and men, the fundamental human divide. Once we've grounded ourselves in realistic expectations we can look to the positive without succumbing to hyperemotionalism or naiveté.

There is no solution to the human condition but there are many ways to improve life on earth. All positives come with negatives, but positives can outweigh negatives, allowing for constructive change. Within ordinary human circumstances, pain is inevitable, but suffering is optional. There will always be conflict between men and women, but escalation of the age-old Battle of the Sexes into a war between the sexes is uncalled for.

Feminists look out at the world and see a male heaven and female hell. Masculists see a female heaven and male hell. The dominant impulse has been to take one side or the other. As a result, It All Balances Out is a truth that has been almost *entirely* overlooked. That is unfortunate because to the extent there is a "solution" to the escalating Battle of the Sexes, a culture-wide recognition of gender Balance is that solution.

In asking, "What is the solution," we are usually asking, "What are we to *do?*" I recommend a shift in focus from what is to be *done* to what is to be *understood*. As I see it, our level of understanding will determine the level of wisdom guiding our actions. I suggest, therefore, that a culture-wide perception and understanding of the true balance in

---

[a] For instance, the constitution of the National Women's Studies Association concludes: "Women's Studies, then, is equipping women to transform the world to one that will be free of all oppression . . . a force which furthers the realization of feminist aims." Cited in Adena Bargad and Janet Shibley Hyde, "Women's Studies: A Study of Feminist Identity Development in Women," *Psychology of Women Quarterly* 15 (1991): 181.

male-female power and victimization will, *all by itself*, effect enormous improvements in gender relations. Moreover, I believe that the ramifications of this higher and truer understanding will be felt in a positive way throughout society in general.

It All Balances Out *is* the solution: Instead of tens of thousands of Women's Studies classrooms leading tens of thousands of young women (and men) to a "click" experience where they come to see past and present composed solely of MalePower/FemaleVictimization (MP/FV) and ManBad/WomanGood (MB/WG), what we need are Equalist Studies classrooms leading tens of thousands to a "click" experience where they come to the realization that *it all balances out*. Indeed, the entire belief system is in need of such a "click." Not only is balance highest in both quantity and quality of truth, it is far and away the *healthiest* truth. Let's take a closer look at exactly *why* a realization of balance helps neutralize the emotional bile tending to poison love and respect between the sexes.

In part, the rage underlying the feminist view burns so intensely because feminism has been so hyper-validated that feminists are invited to feel absolute righteousness unconstrained by alternate truths granted *any* validity *at all*. The bearer of the belief stands mystified that their cause isn't universally recognized and astonished the world doesn't do back flips to remedy the situation *immediately*. The believer feels absolute *outrage* unmitigated by humility or doubt.

Meanwhile, because masculism is so bereft of validation, men are left to absorb "male bashing" and blame without a politicized perspective with which to defend themselves (from without and from within). Add to that there being few men's organizations or support systems, and each man in isolation will feel angry yet powerless to stand his ground. Lacking validation, doubt eats away at them ("Everyone *else* believes what feminists say. Is it *me*, am *I* crazy?"), Thus, in some men, awash in insecurity, impotent rage seethes even hotter.

Over the years I've read a roomful of books and articles in support of male perspectives by dozens of authors both male *and female*. The validation they offered set my mind at ease. Of course, one may rest easy, equally confident in the basic validity of the politicized female perspective. Feminists, however, drive themselves to hyper-emotionalism owing to their never-fully-successful efforts to convince themselves that the politicized female perspective encompasses gender reality in its *entirety*.

The reader will recall Christina Hoff Sommers describing feminist activists who "regularly whip themselves into an anti-male frenzy with their false statistics."[899] Well, how *else* can feminists fully commit to a one-sided, mythically resonant but logically bankrupt gender belief system, except to generate hyper-emotion and false facts with which to sustain it? When one opens to gender reality in the big picture, a belief in It All Balances Out requires no emotional gyrations to sustain. One of the many ways in which recognition of balance will improve gender relations is by providing deep truth both sexes may live in rationally and *peacefully*.

Both sexes are plagued with doubt that the feminist belief system might be missing something. This book and others like it offer the truths that are *missing*—truths that provide men with long overdue emotional validation and a safety valve for their emotional buildup—truths that help diffuse women's resentments by helping women to understand that they are *not* the only ones who suffer and that the world is *not* an anti-female conspiracy.

Our false gender assumptions (It's a man's world; women suffer all inequities of any consequence: men have *the* power; women are *the* victims) are assumptions that have never been seriously, *officially* questioned. We are long overdue for a paradigm shift on par with Copernicus' insight that the earth is not at the center of the universe. Should masculism ever penetrate the Lace Curtain, the mainstream media will, for the first time ever, present women with views that place their politicized perspective into perspective. For the first time, men will be presented with a gender-political position that is truly their own. The results promise to reduce inter-sex tensions in a big way.

Is it not foolish to hold a grudge against someone for what they did to you after you've come to realize what you did to *them* was every bit as bad? On what *legitimate* basis will you resent your opposite sex for the various powers, privileges, and exemptions it enjoys when you know your own sex enjoys powers, privileges, and exemptions in equal measure? How will you lay blame upon your opposite sex knowing that each sex is its own worst enemy primarily responsible for creating its own predicaments?

I've come to realize that feminism itself is co-created. Men have played their part in enabling, disseminating, and enforcing it. The wheel of complicity goes round and round. There is no legitimate basis for inter-sex envy and bitterness. The cost Woman pays for her privileges are equaled by the cost Man pays for his. For *both* sexes, a realization of balance is antidote to the emotional bile poisoning love and respect between the sexes. The realization of balance is compassionate, understanding, generous, mature, and wise.

For the problem of ever escalating inter-personal, inter-sex rage and resentment, victimhood and vengeance motives, understanding that It All Balances Out is the solution.

The same holds for inter-sex relations on a societal scale. Under an equalist system, gender politics may be reframed from Battle of the Sexes to a battle between gender-political conservatives (of both sexes) vs. gender-political liberals (of both sexes).

I will define conservatism as an effort to make the world a better place through a focus on *preserving* that which is judged to be of great and enduring value. I will define liberalism as an effort to make the world a better place through a focus on that which is judged to bring constructive *change*. Both conservatism and liberalism are fundamental perspectives to be respected.

Believing that men are *the* beneficiaries of the gender system, we'll believe that only men could be motivated to *preserve* the sexual-political status quo. Believing that women are *the* sufferers of the gender system, we'll believe that only women could be motivated to *change* the sexual-political status quo. It will appear, then, that sexual-political conservatives are comprised of men and sexual-political liberals are comprised of women. Thus it will seem that gender politics is a battle of one sex vs. the other.

With the understanding that It All Balances Out, however, the big picture shifts in a healthy way.

With the understanding that both sexes benefit and both sexes suffer under the traditional gender system comes the understanding that in changing the gender status quo *both* sexes have much to gain and much to lose. Therefore members of *both* sexes can be highly invested in changing the gender system and members of *both* sexes can be highly invested in maintaining the gender system. Should feminism's matrisensus demand for solidarity to the cause loosen its grip, we'll find that gender-political conservatives are comprised about equally of men *and women*. Should masculism enlighten men to the downsides of their lot in life, we'll find that gender-political liberals are comprised about equally of women *and men*.

Book 3, *Love and Respect in the Present*, will delve into this dynamic in greater detail, but already the potential is clear. Gender politics need *not* be viewed strictly as an inter-sex battleground of men's interests vs. women's interests. Under an equalist system, men's and women's interests and issues will be understood as intertwined and inseparable—leading to a *systemic* framework more effective at providing solutions to the issues of both sexes. Gender politics may then be viewed like any other politics—a battle between conservatives and liberals—*not* men vs. women.

For the problem of a dysfunctional and divisive gender politics that views the two sexes as perpetual adversaries, It All Balances Out is the solution.

The greatest enemy men face is the imbalanced and *poisonous* belief that men have *the* power and women are *the* victims. Not only does the MP/FV paradigm lead inexorably to the MB/WG paradigm, additionally, the narrow focus on MP/FV allows feminists (Woman's self-appointed spokespersons) to come to the bargaining table saying, in effect: "We women have *nothing*, you men have *everything*; so *give* us half of what you've got because that would only be fair."

In his gender-political ignorance, his chivalry, and his blindness to the feminine shadow, Man sees no flaw in Woman's demand; so his honor and his integrity compel him to pour from his glass half "full" into Woman's glass half "empty" because that is only "fair."

Clearly, the assumption that men have *the* power leads to the assumption that justice is served by taking power away from men and giving it to women. In his dedication to giving away half his power, among other things, Man dedicates himself to giving away half his attractiveness and long-term desirability. The costs to men (single motherhood by choice, sperm banks, 70 percent female-initiated divorce, the new "lesbian chic," estrangement from parenting, emotional isolation, and permanent bachelorhood) are plain to see.

Man in decline is diminishing in his role as protector/provider and, cultural evidence leaves little doubt that, in equal measure, Woman is experiencing Man as ever less desirable—sexually, romantically, matrimonially, and parentally. All this adds up to an unprecedented rise in the percentage of single adults and single mothers. Along with the disenfranchisement of fathers, we have seen a dramatic increase in the social pathologies (juvenile crime, drugs, violence, gangs, truancy, teenage pregnancy, etc.) that concern us most.

The above are just some of the ramifications that come of *not* perceiving the true *Balance* of power/victimization between the sexes. Woman's demand to be given half of Man's power is so problematic because feminism's "equality" is *false*.

Jack Kammer:

> Men have trouble putting their finger on women's strength and power. It's like Miss Piggy the Muppet saying "*Moi?*" There's no vocabulary for talking about women's power. It's easy to deny. We need a vocabulary for tagging, discussing and calling women's power into account.[900]

Nancy Friday:

> Until we design a new agreement between the sexes, which includes men's rights as well as women's, our men will grow ever angrier, and women will too, even as we edge toward economic parity while retaining the trump card, the ability to bear the human race and shape it without men.[901]

Camille Paglia:

Man has traditionally ruled the social sphere; feminism tells him to move over and share his power. But woman rules the sexual and emotional sphere, and there she has no rival. Victim ideology, a caricature of social history, blocks women from recognition of their dominance in the deepest, most important realm.[902]

Actor Tim Allen:

If you take the breeding power that you have, the reproductive strength that you have, child rearing . . . and you try to get what's left of us, you're going to get very angry men who will do very angry things to protect what little is left of their territory. . . . you really don't want me to exist. Well, fuck you—I exist. And not only that . . . I will build an army, and I will crush you! I mean, if you get me that way, I'll do it.[903]

As the above suggests, the Battle of the Sexes is escalating. Men, in growing numbers, are feeling increasingly pushed up against the wall and, sooner or later, something *very* bad may come of it.

Perhaps the Warren Farrell quote that helped open this book will ring more clearly now than it did when first read: "Fear of limiting the power of the sex with the greater spending power, the greater beauty power, the greater sexual power, the greater net worth among its heads of households, and the greater options in marriage, children, work, and life creates the corruptness of absolute power which will ultimately lead to a much bloodier battle between the sexes."[904]

Without an organized and politicized perspective to call his own, Man in decline is left with little more than impotent rage and amorphous fear. It is a potentially volatile combination.

It is as Fred Leebron observed regarding the new "egalitarian" domestic relationship. It is egalitarian in principle, "But you know what men give up when they venture into this kind of so-called equality? They give up equality."[905] Unlike the workaday world, which major sociopolitical forces have transformed into a realm as inviting to women as to men, the world of women remains the world of women and a man remains something of an interloper in that realm. We dubbed this reality the Glass Wall. Wives/mothers enjoy an innate inalienable advantage in parenting and they do so within an interpersonal realm that is beyond the reach of laws and policies.

Given that the world of women includes love, intimacy, vulnerable emotion, social fabric, home, family, and parenting; to be shut out or rendered less-than in the world of women carries consequences every bit as deep and painful as any experienced by Woman for being shut out or rendered less-than in the world of men. The degree to which large numbers of men may appear to be "crumbling" in our world today is the degree to which large numbers of men are getting shut out of the world of women and the emotional sustenance therein.

Meanwhile, if women are *the* victims, "fairness" dictates that women must be compensated with special empathy, attentions, efforts, and protections (feminism, affirmative action, quotas, Title IX, The Violence Against Women Act, women-only shelters, unique offices of women's health, Obama's White House Council on Women and Girls, over a thousand female-centric organizations of all kinds, and billions of extra federal funding toward supporting women—emotionally, parentally, financially, educationally, domestically—and advancing women—in business, science, academia, government, and military), all unavailable to "non-victimized" men. If women are *the* victims then men are *the* victimizers and should be punished accordingly. The costs to men (male-only conscription and battlefields, restraining orders, "beatdead dads," mass imprisonment, the Sexual Harassment Industry, excessive vulnerability to false accusations, permanent stigmatization) are, again, plain to see.

In short, the false MalePower/FemaleVictimization paradigm is a ***disaster*** for men and, by extension, it is a disaster for women as well. Diminish men and you diminish fathers, husbands, brothers, and sons. Daughters, wives, sisters, and mothers suffer accordingly. Additionally, Woman will not rate honest, authentic respect until she is prepared to come to the bargaining table saying: You have power, *I* have power; I experience victimization, *you* experience victimization; let's *negotiate*. Only then does Woman shows up as a high-integrity equal partner to be respected and bargained with.

When Woman is Glass Escalatored up as a handout, and without giving in return, she remains the "victim of a trust fund." She remains relatively unmotivated to perform, achieve, and succeed her way to greatness. Over sympathizing with women while withholding accountability: *this* is the *true* victimization of women.

It is a testament to the extraordinary level of feminist ideological dictatorship that gender politics is currently comprehensible only and exclusively in terms of taking from Man and giving to Woman. Though currently *inconceivable*, taking from Woman and giving to Man is the missing half of gender negotiation. Woman wants half the Senate seats, fine, that's okay; *but*—what is she willing to give in return? How about giving Man equality in parenting? Or granting Man equal *intrinsic value*—in love making, in beauty, in marriage, and in parenting? How about paying his way and paying his mortgage as often, or giving her life to protect his as often as he gives his life to protect hers? Whether we seek unisex or balanced equality, either way, the point is that gender politics must be re-invented as a system of *quid pro quo*, of reciprocity, of women taking *and giving*.

Man—more respected/less loved, Woman—more loved/less respected: to understand this Love/Respect dynamic is to know that, in the Big Picture, Woman and Man are, and have *always been*, equal (equally powerful, equally victimized). So the goals of equalism are:
1) bring balance to the imbalanced gender belief system,
2) increase gender *fairness* on the individual level, and
3) *maintain* gender equality on the macro level.

The days of "Let's make the world perfect for women without regard for men" must end. Woman *owns* beauty, grace, goodness; home, family, and parenting. When Woman wants to keep primacy in her realm and be *given* equality with Man in his, Woman wants to "have it all." But Woman can't have it *all*; she must share this world with Man and share it fairly. A gender system in which women are often more-than, but never less-than, is *not* a balanced system. *True* fairness and equality must be negotiated, not manipulated!

Nevertheless, feminists indignantly demand to know: *When* will women have equality with men within the top end of the world of men? The equalist responds: That's up to *you!* After 50 years of feminism, as equal partner in all this, it's time now for Woman to step up to the bargaining table prepared to *give* in order to *get* what she wants.

For the problem of Man pouring from his glass half "full" into Woman's glass half "empty," It All Balances Out is the solution. For the problem of marginalized fatherhood and concurrent rise in social pathologies, and for the problem of Woman infantilized and victim interpreted, It All Balances Out is the solution.

In addition to all the anti-male psychic forces that the MP/FV paradigm conjures, there is also the law and policy fallout.

In education, belief in MP/FV leads to anti-male biases in school rules, textbooks, curricula, and teaching methods together with a pervasive feminist presence and, in some instances, efforts to mold and medicate boys into girls. Out on the streets the assumptions of MP/FV lead to anti-male bias in shelters, charities, healthcare, social work and social services. In the workplace, MP/FV leads to affirmative action, quotas, fear of "pay gap" lawsuits, the Sexual Harassment Industry, and so on. In divorce courts, MP/FV leads to bias against husbands and fathers. The vast assumptions of MP/FV bias the laws that are drafted as well as the police, judges, and courts that enforce them.

Masculists exclaim, "What is to be *done* about all this anti-male bias?" There *is* much to be done (I'll explain shortly), but the *focus* should be on what is to be *understood*.

I'll assume that textbook writers know how to write textbooks, teachers know how to teach, social workers know how to do social work, policy writers know how to write policies, police know how to police, legislators know how to legislate, and judges know how to judge. My primary focus is not in telling these professionals how to do their jobs. The system is anti-male owing to their belief in a world made up exclusively of MalePower and FemaleVictimization. They've internalized feminism's sexist definition of sexism and their actions reflect this one-sided indoctrinated belief. Change that *belief* and you change what they *do*, without dictating anything.

We don't need another politically correct dictatorship. I would rather enlighten than control. Efforts to control are not to be trusted.

A passionate attempt to persuade Harvard President Larry Summers to change his views would have been a reasonable exercise of civil rights. But using hysterical emotionalism, lobbying, and political pressure to get Summers fired, and thus threaten other dissenters with the same, is using scare tactics to dictate and control. What happened at Harvard University was a shameful and all-too-characteristic abuse of feminist power. As Woman rises and Man declines, Woman's power continues to escalate, leading to the corruptness of absolute power. But that doesn't mean Woman is more respected; it only means Woman is ever more *feared*.

Masculism as well as feminism must stand up to challenge and scrutiny. But I would do *whatever it takes* to be *heard*. No one is harmed for being made aware of facts and truths from the male perspective politicized. No one need get fired just to *listen* to what gender-politically balanced men and women have to say. *Time* magazine has devoted countless pages to the politicized female perspective. No harm can come of devoting pages to the politicized male perspective. Yet masculism remains shut out of every large-scale, official, respected source of news, fact, and opinion. There is no excuse for censorship of this kind. Balance is benign. There is no way the concept can be malevolent. The politicized perspectives of men *must* be heard.

Under a MP/FV, MB/WG belief system, it seems "reasonable" to apply an extra tax upon the "criminal gender." Punishing the "bad" sex and rewarding the "good" sex, taking power/money away from the "patriarchy" sex and giving it to the "innocent victim" sex *feels* righteous. Men's Rights Activists seek to veto such proposals on the basis of legal technicalities. Such efforts are necessary, of course (especially to the degree that such efforts also raise awareness), but they are not the preferred *focus*. Not only do efforts to directly control the actions of others border on the dictatorial, under the current belief system, such efforts can only be *never ending*.

Yes, in the cosmic Big Picture It All Balances Out. But, as a society, *we don't know that*. And so IABO **except** for the belief system; but that's not a small thing, that's *huge!* It is the one imbalance from which other imbalances derive. So long as the imbalanced MP/FV paradigm continues to set off misandric "sparks" in all directions, MRAs will be putting out "brushfires" *forever*. We need to focus on the *source* of these brushfires. When there is no more MP/FV/MB/WG paradigm spewing misandric sparks, then anti-male laws and policies won't be inspired into existence in the first place. Thus a balanced gender belief system begets a balanced gender *reality*.

We don't need a new ideological dictatorship; we need only remove the current ideological dictatorship. We need only *allow* the other, *male* half of gender politics into the larger gender-political equation. Within a *balanced* belief system, professionals can be expected to do their jobs in a *balanced* way.

For the problem of anti-male bias in academia, in the media, in policies and in courts of law, It All Balances Out is the solution.

When we believe that men have *the* power and women are *the* victims, we believe that females have a special need for and entitlement to their own special "ism"—"female-ism." Because it absolutely relies on the MP/FV paradigm to justify itself, feminism will perpetrate whatever myths are required to sustain that paradigm. A bad statistic, says sociologist Joel Best, is "harder to kill than a vampire."[906] And, "among false statistics," says Christina Hoff Sommers, "the hardest of all to slay are those promoted by feminist professors."[907]

Recall, for example, the "Pay Gap" myth (evil men paying powerless women 74¢ on the dollar); the Super Bowl hoax (evil men beating up women for no other impetus than a ballgame); the March of Dimes defamation (evil men beating defenseless pregnant women resulting in more birth defects than all other causes combined). Recall outrageous feminist claims that nearly four million U.S. women are beaten to death per annum ("the leading cause of death among women") and anorexia as "gendercide" perpetrated by men.

To believe this Ms-information (a plethora of false, damning, anti-male aspersions) promoted by feminists, circulated throughout the media, and officially taught in Gender Studies classrooms across the nation is to believe that men are an irredeemable blight upon humanity to be indicted, imprisoned, hated and scorned. Man internalizes the condemnation and a heavy cloud of shame envelops him, saps him of vitality, and turns him against himself. Woman has no need for tanks and missiles to wage war against Man. She has other, *covert* methods of inflicting terrible damage.

So long as Woman views herself as powerless little David, engaged in a righteous battle for the righteous cause of taking down the giant "oppressor" Goliath, she will not hesitate to use her weaponry at full force to devastating effect. In defaming, shaming, and withdrawing emotional support, Woman threatens to devastate Man just as David (possessing the ultimately superior weaponry) slew Goliath.

We know that Man, his thumb poised over the buttons of mass destruction, has the power to devastate our world; we are not yet prepared to understand it, but Woman *also* has the power to devastate our world. It is my hope that in calling official attention to Woman's power, Woman may wield her power in a more responsible, less vengeful manner. If Woman better understood Man's vulnerability, if she understood that Man does *not* have *the* power, perhaps she'd deal with Man in a more conscientious and compassionate way. I hope that women who've read this book will develop new empathy toward the men in their lives, resulting in improved relations with those men.

With due respect for its many accomplishments, feminism cannot be "fixed." As a system of gender politics, by its very *name*, it is wrongheaded and biased to the core and must be replaced with a gender-neutral system of gender politics (what I'm calling "equalism"). Moreover, its many defamations and perpetrations are too great simply to be swept under the rug. To garner respect, and in the name of fairness, Woman must hold her feminism to account—anything less would be condescending.

Better that Woman confesses her manipulations and takes her "egg on the face" as an adult. This need not be any big deal. Man, it seems to me, is about infinitely forgiving where Woman is concerned. Besides, both sexes have shameful elements in their respective legacies, so in calling for Woman's confession I'm not asking Woman to suffer anything Man hasn't already suffered.

Woman has massive ego investment in holding the moral high ground. For Woman to admit the full extent of her selfish duplicity is akin to Man admitting the full extent of his weakness and cowardice. To what does author Guy Garcia attribute *The Decline of Man*? "Garcia's thesis: Men truly are the weaker sex."[908] What, you mean like *everyone* keeps saying? Despite his enormous ego investment in toughness, strength, and courage; Man has nevertheless become widely (if not *universally*) identified as "the weaker sex." If Man can take egg on the face, Woman can too. In the Big Picture, all Woman need ultimately confess to is her shared humanity.

With every change there is loss and there is gain. In giving up angel-status and victim power Woman gives up a lot. But, in owning rather than denying her power and the shadow side of her own human nature, Woman gains forthrightness, authenticity, respect, and adult status. In giving up the false projection of herself as *the* powerless innocent victim, Woman may enjoy the inestimable benefits that come of ceasing to live a lie.

Under an IABO belief system, feminism—bereft of the MP/FV paradigm that sustains it—will be phased out. The gender politics that carries on (equalism) would continue to address any and all women's issues; it just wouldn't address women's issues exclusively. Viewed *systemically*, no more will women's issues and perspectives be sealed within an ideological bubble that shuts out male issues and female complicity. No more women-*only* liberation. No more female-*only* "equality." Again, declaring the gender system balanced—and believing it—would go a *long* way toward bringing about Balance because, in balancing the gender belief system, we neutralize the one overarching imbalance from which other imbalances derive.

When asked, *How* does it all balance out?, the invitation is given to present the truths of FemalePower and MaleVictimization at the *other* end of the balance beam. Though conscious masculists teach the truths of FP/MV, so long as they lead with IABO, they cannot rightly be accused of victim mongering. It All Balances Out has a positive ring to it that inspires hope. It is an olive branch that promises to deescalate the Battle of the Sexes. Thus it is a message that just might be palatable enough to pass the gates of political correctness into the major media (if not immediately, then soon enough).

For the problems of feminism's ever-expanding power, ideological dictatorship, and exclusive ownership of gender politics, It All Balances Out is the solution. For the problem of Man stigmatized, defamed, and scapegoated, and for the problem of getting men's politicized perspectives into the mainstream media in a palatable, healthy, and constructive way, It All Balances Out is the solution.

When we believe that men have *the* power and women are *the* victims, we believe that men are Bad and women are Good. Honorable men internalize this belief system and become susceptible to crippling levels of shame.

The Honorable Man wouldn't be caught dead complaining. But at what point does a refusal to complain cease to be strength and turn into masochism and spineless acquiescence? "Because of the inner pressure to constantly affirm his dominance and masculinity," observed Herb Goldberg back in 1976, "he continues to act as if he can stand up under, fulfill, and even enjoy all the expectations placed on him no matter how contradictory and devitalizing they are. It's time to remove the disguises of privilege and reveal the male condition for what it is."[909]

But, nearly 40 years later, the honorable man *still* doesn't want his illusions shattered. He doesn't want his vulnerability or his victimization revealed to himself. When it comes to the politicized male perspective, he lives the principle, "Ignorance is bliss." There is a vague but real danger lurking in this scenario. Not *all* men are honorable. Right or wrong, many men have totally *had it* with female-ism.

If you've read this book then you know there's an ocean of masculist facts and truths from which a *massive* indictment of women in general and feminists in particular may be constructed. Websites such as *The Spearhead* and *A Voice For Men* spread this information. They are frequented by men, especially *young* men, in large and rapidly expanding numbers. Learning of feminism's many falsehoods, defamations, and manipulations, these young MRAs (Men's Rights Activists) grow enraged and it shows in their postings.

Defamed, undermined, raised by single mothers, matriculated in a female-centric school system that sabotaged them, underemployed, shunned as "unmarriageable" or reamed in Divorce Court, many of these fatherless men, never mentored in mature masculinity, are *justifiably angry!* The anger is *good*, but *some* of their MRA rhetoric suggests anger channeled not constructively but rather in ugly, frightening ways. With all the talk of male "obsolescence," what if men, even men in the *millions* started acting out of *desperation?* We can't throw them *all* in jail. The longer feminism's official exposure is delayed, the more massive the potential backlash becomes. That "much bloodier" battle of the sexes is becoming all too easily envisioned.

The Honorable Man has been manipulated into believing that in rejecting his own politicized male perspective, he is rejecting the low dictates of self-interest in favor of feminism's higher cause of "truth" and "justice." While honorable men are thus immobilized by their own honor used against them, will less honorable men finally break the bounds of chivalry, take action, and react in ways we don't even want to think about? I believe I can envision a *better* path.

It seems to me that Man has apologized over and over again—apologized for war, for violence, for being "macho," sexism, pollution, "raping the earth," criminality, science/technology gone wrong . . . on and on. Must only Man be big enough to apologize?

In my dreams, Woman says to Man: I accept your apology and in return I apologize for manipulating all those things that you dominated. In equal partnership, we created the dark side of the world and human nature. It has afflicted us in different ways but in equal measure. Sorry for projecting the evil onto you; sorry about a lot of things. The gender illusions we created together in unconscious collusion, blinded us *both*. Seeing beyond those illusions, it's clear that women are far more powerful and men far more vulnerable to victimization than our illusions permitted us to see. I accept the politicized male perspective as equal to the politicized female perspective, and I invite the Honorable Man to do likewise. Speak your piece with my blessing. Afterward, let's vent and laugh and cry and negotiate *together*.

Having taken the highroad, Woman garners well-earned *respect*. In approving the basic validity of the politicized male perspective, she gives the Honorable Man permission to speak his vulnerable truth. Such men in large numbers help balance the gender belief system. Feminism and masculism can now be phased out in favor of equalism. "War" is averted.

There is deep need for a *conscious* masculist men's movement paving the way to an equalist movement, and It All Balances Out is the mindset needed to keep it healthy. But "The men's movement has been in gestation for about twenty years," says Kathleen Parker, "and has yet to quicken, much less emerge to alter the gender ecosystem."[910] In fact, "The few male voices who have spoken up against anti-male feminists sound as lonely as moose calls;" says Nancy Friday, "a 'real man' just doesn't join in."[911]

The current president of NCFM (National Coalition For Men), Harry Crouch, quit his job and has exhausted his savings to fight for men's issues full-time. "NCFM has been an all-volunteer organization since inception in 1977 but not by choice," says Crouch. "Vast sums of private and public funds float organizations to support women's rights but none support men's rights. Why? Because 'real men' don't even stand up for *themselves,* let alone *other* men."

Perhaps all that stands between YOU and the loss/estrangement of your children is this ragtag, passionate handful of men's rights activists up against feminism's megalith. These men are doing battle against Ms-information that defames *you*. These men are laboring to help *your* sons gain a fair shake in the school system and laboring to help *you* gain a fair shake in courts of law. Why aren't YOU supporting them?

Men, in numbers too large to simply be dismissed, must apply the necessary pressure to get the *other* half of gender politics entered into the large-scale, official, sources of news, fact, and opinion—the media that, for better or worse, purveys our culture's *"official"* belief system. If large-scale activism *forced* the masculist message into the likes of *Time* magazine, with its credibility thus bolstered, honorable men ("real men") would read it and they would have their eyes opened.

Within a balanced belief system honorable men may find honor in extending *both* compassion and accountability to *both* sexes. Rather than coming exclusively to the rescue of women, the Warrior may *also* find his mission in coming to the rescue of his less fortunate brethren.

Within a balanced belief system, the Honorable Man will neither be warped by vengeance motives nor immobilized by shame.

For the problem of getting honorable men and women involved in the honorable cause of *true* gender fairness, It All Balances Out is the solution. For the problem of circumventing a potentially disastrous backlash movement, *a culture-wide perception and understanding* that It All Balances Out is the solution.

To the degree that there is a "solution" to the current Battle of the Sexes insanity wherein we now stand bewildered, proceeding from the *global* understanding that It All Balance Out *is* the solution!

On the human level, various injustices, biases and stereotypes will continue to afflict both sexes alike. As with any politic, there will be heated disagreements over what is fair and what is unfair. There will be haggling and deadlocks and all that goes with trying to work things out. It will be the ongoing purview of gender politics to address such matters in this imperfect world. No system of politics (sexual or otherwise) can be perfect, but equalism represents a mammoth improvement over feminism—for *both* sexes.

What Is to be *Done?*: what do we *do* in order to bring about Balanced understanding? Here's what I suggest:

» Do more reading on the subject (refer to the Notes section). Where gender politics and men's issues are concerned, become a well-informed force to be reckoned with.

» Go on line at www.ncfm.org, plug in, branch out, get involved.

» Men should discuss these matters among themselves, educate their friends, learn from each other, and bolster each other. Join or form men's groups. Encourage each other's activism.

» Speak out in public; take a stand. Write letters/emails to publications, authors, filmmakers, advertisers, politicians . . . protest misandry and sexism wherever you encounter it. File a lawsuit!

» Make some noise; issue complaints to your local schools, colleges, universities—demand that your sons and daughters be taught both sides—demand *masculist* Men's Studies classes or equalist classes to balance out feminist Gender Studies classes.

» If you're good at public speaking, organize a rally; speak at local schools, churches, libraries—anywhere that will have you. Pamphleteer. Seek to publicly debate feminists. Seek an audience with local or state government. If you are a leader, take a leadership position. Lead wisely; never lose empathy toward the politicized female perspective; never lose the principle, It All Balances Out!

» If you're a writer, write books and articles. If you're a filmmaker, tell the Marybeth Tinning story. Or tell the story of a migrant worker standing on a street corner at four in the morning hoping to get chosen for a grueling day in the fields. Follow him as he bends over until his back is permanently hunched over and his skin is ruined from absorbing the pesticides that eventually cause brain damage. Have the audacity to suggest that his is not the victimization of "workers" but rather the victimization of *men*. Drive home the point by following his paycheck all the way back to Mexico. Have the audacity to suggest that the woman receiving it enjoys female power and privilege. In short, use your chosen medium to tell the *other* half of gender reality!

Like anything else, gender politics may be viewed as a game. If we men, as *men*, invested in our own *male* point of view, are ever to enter the game—*and we must*—then men must learn the strategies and the jargon that go with it. If you want to be effective in the field of economics, archeology, computers, whatever, you have to know the associated lingo. Think of "victim" and "power" as gender-political lingo. To play the game, you have to know how to wield these two words that gender politics places above all others.

Psychotherapist Aaron Kipnis observes, "Men are often more resistant to discussing victimization of any kind than women."[912] Men reject the truths of female *power* and their own experience of powerlessness (victimization) in relation to women. In many ways, this is an honorable stance that has served men well.

In the realm of gender *politics*, however, it has been *disastrous*. In the "game" of gender politics, "victim" is the "ball." Woman, experiencing none of Man's aversion to "victim," grasps the "ball" with both hands and runs it up and down the field, scoring every point. Only women complaining creates the illusion that only women have anything to complain about. Hence: there is *fem*inism and there is . . . nothing. The "strong and silent" stance has sealed men and male perspectives out of gender politics (the politics of gender *complaint*).

There is a simple yet vital distinction to be made. On the one hand there is internalizing male victimization as a self-label or identity. This is the aspect of victim that men rightly shun. On the other hand there is coming to know the *facts* of male victimization and utilizing those facts as gender-political *weaponry* with which Man may *stop* playing the passive unconscious victim and start standing up for himself.

When feminists complain, they are telling the world that women are *the* victims (the *only* victims). In proclaiming themselves *the* victims, they take on victim status and demand that the world pour *extra* empathy upon them and take *extra* action on their behalf. Judge it as you will, this victim power has been effective enough to change the world (men could learn from this). If, however, when men complain they declare themselves "victims" *in equal measure*, this is not demanding *extra* empathy; this is demanding *equal* empathy, which is demanding justice. Men who demand justice are strong and worthy of respect. Men who do *not* demand justice are *doormats*. Ella Wheeler Wilcox: "To sin by silence when we should protest makes cowards out of men." Think about it.

Whether it is revulsion toward "victim," honor twisted into self-hate, feminist indoctrination, primal fear of women, fear of not getting laid, or some internalized defeatism that where Man is concerned the situation is simply "hopeless"—whatever stands against his entry into gender politics, Man had better work through it. The Battle of the Sexes has been dubbed a battle in which only one side showed up. For not showing up Man has only begun to pay the price.

Man *must* speak up! He owes it to himself; he owes it to his sons; he owes it to his daughters. But Man must fight back with words and reason and emotional truth, not self-righteous rage and hostility. The MP/FV paradigm is Man's enemy, not Woman.

Defeating feminism logically is the easy part. The question is: Will Man find the courage to risk his emotional lifeline in favor of expressing his truth? As it stands now it's unclear when, if ever, Man will find his voice. Woman's vast weaponry threatens to shame Man into an enervated, dysfunctional, self-hating, self-destructive *officially* second-rate human. But this doesn't mean that Woman "wins" the Battle of the Sexes. All it means is that Woman's shadow succeeds in wreaking terrible destruction upon our human world—a destruction from which *both* sexes ultimately suffer.

Men who learn the facts of male victimization need not *be* victims. In fact, men who become expert in their knowledge of masculism may be surprised and delighted to discover how *not* victimized, how *not* powerless they feel. Having read this book you now know everything a feminist knows plus an entire other world of truth from the politicized male perspective of which she knows little to nothing. No matter how red-faced she gets, no matter how entitled she feels, no matter how indignant she becomes, you do *not* have to grant her victimhood's center seat. You need not recognize her ownership of gender truth or her entitlement to seizing all empathy from the social environment. For every female complaint she hurls at you, you can have an equal-opposite male complaint at the ready.

There need be no tear in the eye or cry in the voice; men can state the *facts* of male victimization in a calm, logical, masculine way and still get their point across. Males comprise 85 percent of the street-homeless, 93 percent of all work-related fatalities, over 90 percent of the imprisoned, 80 percent of the suicides . . . the litany of masculist facts is *endless*. If men in huge numbers simply stood their ground and quoted these facts long enough and adamantly enough, this alone must eventually break feminism's stranglehold on gender politics.

And, for those men who've known real hardship for being male, I encourage the expression of authentic pain. If you got your arm chewed off working heavy machinery (the only family-supporting wage you could find), I invite you to let the world know how it *feels*. If your children were taken from you through the use of false accusations; if you were crippled playing college football; if you spent a year in a prisoner-of-war camp; if you were the victim of domestic violence and the police you summoned to the scene arrested *you*, not the woman beating on you, you owe it to your brethren to speak your truth and set the record straight. Simply stating the facts is sufficient. *And* expression of vulnerable emotion is particularly effective because breaking through the irrational, instinctual barriers is the *real* challenge.

The situation is *not* hopeless. What if a mere one percent of the 150 million men living in the U.S. got on board? *One* man "sounding as lonely as moose calls" may be powerless, but, imagine being one among a *multitude* of men all speaking their truth! So long as it remains conscious and temporary, the masculist cause is a *just* cause, and YOU can take part in it. It is up to *us, all* of us, to break the MP/FV paradigm that's maligning us.

The goal is for Man to oust Woman from victimhood's center seat—not so Man can sit there instead, but so that victimhood's center seat may go unoccupied. Internalizing victim status serves no one. For this reason, if Man should gather the knowledge and the courage needed to deny Woman her victim status, he would do her a great service. In fact, it might be the very *best* thing Man can do for Woman.

He might not expect a show of gratitude in the short run, but over the long run, I believe Woman will thank Man for respecting her enough to hold her accountable. So, if for some reason men are truly structurally *incapable* of mobilizing on their own behalf, then I invite men to do what they do best—come to women's rescue. Rescue women from their own self-fulfilling victim-dictum.

When it comes to loving men and respecting women—out to the truest and fullest extent—the MP/FV paradigm is that which stands in the way and It All Balances Out is that which clears the path.

The Future of Gender Politics: Loving Men, Respecting Women is the proper future of gender politics. We emphasize love toward men because it is *love* toward men that is relatively missing. We emphasize respect toward women because it is *respect* toward women that is relatively missing.

We may begin by doing our best to love men whether they are lovable or not and respect women whether they are respectable or not. We begin in this way because very often people do not behave in a respectable manner until they are respected and do not behave in a lovable manner until they are loved. "There is the great lesson of 'Beauty and the Beast;'" states acclaimed philosopher Gilbert K. Chesterton, "that a thing must be loved *before* it is lovable."[913]

This is the basic principle expressed by Johann Wolfgang von Goethe when he wrote: "Treat people as if they were what they ought to be and you help them to become what they are capable of being." We may love men by lending them compassion (while continuing to respect them enough to hold them accountable). We may respect women by holding them accountable (while continuing to love them enough to lend them our compassion).

Social pressures can impose a measure of obligation to love men and respect women, but ultimately men will be authentically loved only to the degree that they are lovable and women will be authentically respected only to the degree that they are respectable.

Loving men and respecting women are invitations. Society can hold a space open for them, but men and women must do the rest. Men must develop a language of sincerity that goes deeper than "glib." To be more lovable, men must develop their more lovable qualities, becoming more vulnerable, innocent, emotionally available, nurturing, and so on. From deep within, women must develop the hero that comes to the rescue rather than forever the "victim" to be rescued. To be more respectable, women must develop their more respectable qualities, becoming less complaining, more fair-minded, honorable, forthright, accountable, and so on.

And, for the invitation to be successful, it must be genuine. To invite men to feel their feelings just so feminist insults will hurt more, or invite men to soften just to be passed over in favor of men whose hardness results in higher levels of status/success-appeal, is to invite men into a trap. *Many* a man has fallen into the trap of househusband, only to discover that she doesn't really *want* or sexually *desire* a househusband. Women have experienced similar traps and feminism has spoken out about them. Each sex must be genuinely willing and able to celebrate and desire the resulting changes in their opposite sex. Change, however, is not always easily accepted.

Clearly, the sexes have depolarized considerably over recent history. I advocate shifting some love toward men and respect toward women under the assumption that, in the past, love and respect were artificially polarized in the same way that men and women were. As women and men depolarize becoming more who they truly are, loving men and respecting women becomes more truthful in equal measure.

Of late, however, it can be argued that certain factions of political correctness are pushing for androgyny and men trying to "get in touch with their feminine side" and women pressured to be aggressive breadwinners and soldiers may be symptomatic of that. In all this, biology exerts its mysterious influence and may set limits on how far the sexes can authentically depolarize. That's okay. The goal is not to force androgyny. In fact, the goal is not to *force* anything.

I see no reason to believe that human wisdom is sufficient to justify human control over such matters. In the non-dogmatic spirit of a general guideline, I believe in leaving the sexes alone to be whatever they are "naturally" inclined to be. The goal is to set the sexes free to seek equilibrium. Equilibrium is reached when the gender system is highest in truth. The goal is equality of *opportunity*—let the results fall where they may. The process will be slow and awkward and where it will lead, only time will tell.

As long as the result is steeped in both love and truth, untampered with by factions that would impose their own political agenda upon it, the result will be *okay*. If men are from Mars and women are from Venus, or, if men are from Earth and women are from Earth—if men and women are profoundly different or essentially the same—either way, whatever is *true* is fine just as it is. Again, in the spirit of a general guideline, I suggest that gender truth is what it is—leave it alone!

Final Thought: If you've read this book, then you've taken the "red pill." You've been awakened to gender reality. We haven't always agreed on the details, but the core validity of the politicized male perspective has been demonstrated beyond a reasonable doubt. Never again can you believe that gender reality is comprised *solely* of MalePower and FemaleVictimization.

Let us admit that no human mind can hold the entire female experience on one side of the brain, the entire male experience on the other, and claim to Know, *with certainty*, which side is lighter/which side is heavier; which is happier/which is sadder; more fulfilled/less fulfilled; freer/more constrained; which is "better"/which is "worse." The reality of the Big Picture is a reality that simply will not support any such *certainty*. In its place, what you end up with is mere opinion.

It All Balances Out is the one gender truth highest in both quantity and quality of truth. Nevertheless, the main objection to It All Balances Out is that it is not "true." In the *opinion* of masculists it isn't "true" because women have *the* power and men are *the* victims. In the *opinion* of feminists it isn't "true" because men have *the* power and women are *the* victims.

What will we do?—wait for the "right" time?—wait till *all* agree? Being a matter of opinion, the battle of MP/FV vs. FP/MV, feminism vs. masculism, can rage back and forth *ad nauseam!* What must we endure and for how long, before we set victim and vengeance aside and finally, *inevitably* call it a draw? It is exactly *because* there is no agreement and no certainly in these matters that we might as well be magnanimous about it. Why not take a leap of faith, demonstrate a little gender generosity, and simply call it even?

In so doing we put behind us an escalating intractable conflict and take the first crucial step toward a more evolved phase of gender relations. Let's deescalate a costly war that neither sex can "win," and go directly to an era of negotiated peace, love, and understanding!

It All Balances Out is the only mindset to replace rage and rancor with understanding and compassion leading to healthy negotiation and a healthy outlook from which to start anew. Whether present or distant, it is the inevitable future. What are we waiting for? There'll never be a "better" time to declare Balance. The *right* time is *now!* Let's make the decision and declare it aloud:

It All Balances Out!

Afterword

Was it as fun for you as it was for me?

This concludes book one of a four book series.

The next book in the series, *Love and Respect in the Past: The History of Gender Equality*, will begin at the beginning with a look at the biological origins of gender. In our exploration of FemalePower we will elevate Woman to her true status as equal partner in the molding of our world. We'll assert that the evolution of parenting (motherhood) is equally as important as the evolution of technology. We'll take a closer look at the Glass Floor that has always tended to safeguard Woman from sinking to the extreme bottom—and the extreme horrors therein. We'll make the case for It All Balances Out as a fundamental truth that has held true throughout history.

In *Love and Respect in the Present*, we will explore in more detail themes begun in this book. We'll take an in-depth look at the love/respect dynamic. We'll explore and define the words love and respect, and explore how these words play out in male-female romance and sexuality. We'll examine the double binds each sex faces, and what keeps men emotionally distant from each other and emotionally dependent upon women. We'll expand on the notion of Woman as the "victim of a trust fund." And we will also take a more extensive look at how the love/respect dynamic plays out in other parts of the world.

In *Love and Respect in the Future*, we will extrapolate on current trends and offer a portent of disastrous consequences should feminism's MP/FV paradigm continue to expand its influence. Is the "pay gap" (i.e., the extra income men earn through extra efforts, risks and sacrifices) all that stands against Man becoming Woman's *in*significant other? Are the high rates of male homelessness, imprisonment, unemployment, academic dropout, family/parenting disenfranchisement so plain to see in the black community a portent of things to come for all races of men? Conversely, we will also envision how things may be set *right* should It All Balances Out become the new guiding principle and default assumption.

In the meantime, for further thoughts, please check out my YouTube videos, or join me at:

https://www.facebook.com/lovingmenrespectingwomen
http://www.genderequalists.com/
https://www.facebook.com/wearegenderequalists?fref=ts

Or write to me at: tagoldich@hotmail.com

Notes

[1] WWII, Europe and North Africa, about 8.75 million allied POWs (Prisoners of War) taken by the Axis powers and 8.25 million German and Italian POWs taken by the Allies—in all, about 17 million soldiers, sailors, and airmen prisoners of war. This does not include the war in the Pacific, nor the Korean or Vietnam wars or any other armed conflicts worldwide. In comparing this number with the number of CEOs (Chief Executive Officers) up at the pinnacle of success, think of the "Fortune 500" companies. Multiply that number by as many as ten thousand and you still don't approach the total number of POWs [Source: Vance, Jonathan F (editor), *Encyclopedia of Prisoners of War and Internment* (Santa Barbara, CA: ABC-CLIO, Inc., 2000) p.341]

[2] Chesler, Phyllis, *Woman's Inhumanity to Woman* (New York: Thunder's Mouth Press/Nation Books, 2001) p.20.

[3] Sommers, Christina Hoff, *Who Stole Feminism?: How Women Have Betrayed Women* (New York: A Touchstone Book/Simon & Schuster, 1994) p.232.

[4] www.historylearningsite.co.uk/world_war_one_executions.htm, 10/20/06.

[5] Tucker, Todd, *The Great Starvation Experiment: Ancel Keys and the Men Who Starved for Science* (Minneapolis: University of Minnesota Press, 2007) p.5.

He splayed the fingers of his left hand across the flat top of the log and looked at them. Like everything else on his body, they looked alien to him now. His knuckles bulged on spidery, thin fingers. His pale skin was blue in the moonlight. . . . Number 20 pulled the ax down with a grunt and what remained of his strength. The blade came down straight and true. Before he passed out, Subject No. 20 watched with satisfaction as three of his fingers rolled off the log and into the neatly mown grass.

It was promised that July 29th 1945 would be the day the experiment would end and recovery begin, but Sam and seven others in the slowest recovery group received a mere 400 extra calories per day, a crushing disappointment. While his visiting sister ate her dinner, Sam had to go outside and chop wood until the meal was over. It was under these conditions that Sam temporarily lost his mind.

[6] Baskerville, Stephen, Ph.D., "Boy Victim of Statutory Rape Forced to Pay Child Support to Adult Woman Rapist," March 11, 2003, http://www.fact.on.ca/news/news0303/mnd030311.htm, "Children often pay child support to grown-ups. In California and Kansas, minor boys statutorily raped by adult women must pay child support to the criminals who raped him. In one case, the boy was drugged before sex."
See also: Jones, Ruth, "Inequality from Gender-Neutral Laws: Why Must Male Victims of Statutory Rape Pay Child Support for Children Resulting from Their Victimization?" https://litigation-essentials.lexisnexis.com/webcd/app?action=DocumentDisplay&crawlid=1&crawlid=1&doctype=cite&docid=36+Ga.+L.+Rev.+411&srctype=smi&srcid=3B15&key=740f075ecfed12a99ce6dd3dabf383c9

In County of San Luis Obispo v. Nathaniel J., a thirty-four-year-old woman had sex with a fifteen-year-old boy and became pregnant. The woman was convicted of unlawful sexual intercourse with a minor. . . . In holding Nathaniel J., a statutory rape victim, financially liable for child support, the California Court of Appeal joined other courts across the country that have held that a male victim of statutory rape can be forced to pay child support for a child resulting from his victimization. Without exception, appellate courts have held that while the criminal law deems minors incapable of consenting to sexual intercourse, family law can hold victims financially liable for children conceived during a criminal act. [Source: 36 Georgia Law Review, 411 (Winter 2002)].

[7] Clark, Andrew, "Airlines in hot seat over child policies," *The Sydney Morning Herald*, smh.com.au, November 30, 2005
Mr. Worsley, a shipping manager and father of two-year-old twins, had been allocated a seat next to a boy aged about eight. He was forced to change places with a woman who was reluctant to move because she was traveling with her husband. "Nobody wants to be pointed out as a possible pedophile," Mr. Worsley told the *Herald*. "It was humiliating. In the beginning, I was embarrassed. Later on, I was angry." . . . Other airlines contacted by the *Herald* said they had similar guidelines.

[8] Dychtwald, Maddy with Larson, Christine, *Influence: How Women's Soaring Economic Power Will Transform Our World for the Better* (New York: Voice/Hyperion, 2010) p.5. See also, Rosin, Hanna, July/August 2010, *Atlantic Magazine*, "The End of Men," http://www.theatlantic.com/magazine/archive/2010/07/the-end-of-men/8135/ "Earlier this year, women became the majority of the workforce for the first time in U.S. history. Most managers are now women too. And for every two men who get a college degree this year, three women will do the same. For years, women's progress has been cast as a struggle for equality. But what if equality isn't the end point?"

[9] Ibid., pp.10 & 6.

[10] Goldberg, Herb, *The Hazards of Being Male: Surviving the Myth of Masculine Privilege* (New York: Signet/Penguin, 1976) p.5.

[11] Farrell, Warren, Ph.D., *The Myth of Male Power: Why Men Are the Disposable Sex* (New York: Berkley Books, 1993) p.358.

[12] Angier, Natalie, *Woman: An Intimate Geography* (New York: Anchor Books/A Division of Random House, Inc., 2000) p.178.

[13] Bunzel, John H. (editor), *Political Passages: Journeys of Change Through Two Decades, 1968-1988* (New York: The Free Press: A Division of Macmillan, Inc., 1988). Quoted from Carol Iannone's essay, "The Wide and Crooked Path," p.318.

[14] Honderich, Ted (editor), *The Oxford Companion to Philosophy* (New York, Oxford University Press, 1995) p..528.

[15] Roiphe, Katie, *The Morning After: Sex, Fear, and Feminism* (New York: Little, Brown and Company, 1993) p.103.

[16] Ibid., p.103.

[17] Thomas, David, *Not Guilty: The Case in Defense of Men* (New York: William Morrow and Company, Inc., 1993) p.21.

[18] Goldstein, Joshua S., *War and Gender: How Gender Shapes the War System and Vice Versa* (Cambridge University Press, 2001) p.2.

[19] Pearson, Patricia, *When She Was Bad: How and Why Women Get Away with Murder* (New York: Penguin Books, 1998) p.24.

[20] Condrey, John and Condrey, Sandra, "Sex Differences: A Study in the Eye of the Beholder," *Child Development*, vol. 47. 1976, pp. 812-819. See also, Real, Terrence, *I Don't Want to Talk About It*, (New York, Simon & Schuster, 1997) pp.121-2.

[21] Farrell, Warren, Ph.D., *The Myth of Male Power: Why Men Are the Disposable Sex* (New York: Berkley Books, 1993) p.124. Original source: Susan Goldberg and Michael Lewis, "Play Behavior in the Year-Old Infant: Early Sex Differences," *Child Development*, vol. 40, no. 1, March 1969, p. 29.

[22] Kipnis, Aaron, *Angry Young Men: How Parents, Teachers, and Counselors Can Help "Bad Boys" Become Good Men* (San Francisco, CA: Jossey-Bass, 1999) p.40.

[23] Ibid., p.40.

[24] Ibid., p.38.

[25] Ibid., p.ix.

[26] James, Thomas B., *Domestic Violence: The 12 Things You Aren't Supposed to Know* (Chula Vista, CA: Aventine Press, 2003) p.43.

[27] Farrell, Warren, Ph.D., *Women Can't Hear What Men Don't Say: Destroying Myths, Creating Love* (New York: Tarcher/Putnam, 1999) p.139.
[28] Kimbrell, Andrew, *The Masculine Mystique: The Politics of Masculinity* (New York: Ballantine Books, 1995) p.8.
[29] Mulrine, Anna, "Are Boys the Weaker Sex?," *U.S. News & World Report*, www.usnews.com/usnews/issue/010730/ideas/boys.htm, July 02, 2001.
[30] Ibid.. See also, Marklein, Mary Beth, "College gender gap widens: 57% are women," *USA TODAY*, October 19, 2005, http://www.usatoday.com/news/education/2005-10-19-male-college-cover_x.htm
Last year for the first time, women earned more than half the degrees granted statewide in every category, be it associate, bachelor, master, doctoral or professional. . . . Not only do national statistics forecast a continued decline in the percentage of males on college campuses, but the drops are seen in all races, income groups and fields of study . . . There are more men than women ages 18-24 in the USA — 15 million vs. 14.2 million, according to a Census Bureau estimate last year. But nationally, the male/female ratio on campus today is 43/57.
[31] Kipnis, Aaron, *Angry Young Men: How Parents, Teachers, and Counselors Can Help "Bad Boys" Become Good Men* (San Francisco, CA: Jossey-Bass, 1999) p.41.
[32] Ibid, p.41.
[33] Kimbrell, Andrew, *The Masculine Mystique: The Politics of Masculinity* (New York: Ballantine Books, 1995) pp.7-8.
[34] Will, George, *Jewish World Review*, December 03, 1999. http://www.mapinc.org/drugnews/v99.n1323.a07.html.
[35] Ibid.
[36] Sommers, Christina Hoff, *Who Stole Feminism?: How Women Have Betrayed Women* (New York: A Touchstone Book/Simon & Schuster, 1994) p.61.
[37] Gurian, Michael, *Boys and Girls Learn Differently: A Guide for Teachers and Parents* (San Francisco: Jossey-Bass, 2001) p.126.
[38] See, for example, Parker, Kathleen, *Save the Males: Why Men Matter, Why Women Should Care* (New York: Random House, 2008) p.3. "Jackson Marlette was just fourteen when he summed up the anti-male zeitgeist for his father, political cartoonist and author Doug Marlette. They were in a North Carolina chicken joint awaiting their orders when the younger Marlette picked up a tabletop ad boasting boneless chicken and read aloud: 'Chicken good, bones bad.' Then, beaming with insight, Jackson made the analogous leap and proclaimed: Women good, *men* bad!"
[39] Farrell, Warren, Ph.D., *The Myth of Male Power: Why Men Are the Disposable Sex* (New York: Berkley Books, 1993) p391. The USDH & HS?NCHS, Center for Disease Control, Statistical Resources, *Vital Statistics of the United States* (Washington, D.C.: USGPO, 1991) vol. 2, part A, Mortality, p. 51, tables 1-9, "Death Rates for 72 Selected Causes by 5-Year Age Groups, Race, and Sex: U.S., 1988."
[40] Ibid., p.105. U.S. Department of Labor, Bureau of Labor Statistics (USBLS), *Employment and Earnings, 1988 Annual Averages*, January 1989, p. 187, table 22.
[41] Ibid., p.106. Men comprise 94% of all work-related fatalities due to on-the-job injury (disease-related deaths caused by on-the-job exposure are not included in this figure). U.S. Department of Health and Human Services, The National Institute for Occupational Safety and Health NIOSH, (Morgantown, West. Va.), on-line database titled "Basic Information on Workplace Safety and Health in the U.S."
[42] Ibid., p.109. See, the Associated Press description of the OSHA suit against John Morrell and Co. as reported in the *San Diego Union*, November 24, 1988. That almost 90% of meat packers in high-risk positions are male was revealed in an interview with Dan Haybes of NIOSH.

43 Ibid., pp.120-1. See, T. M. Schnorr, B. A. Grajewski, R. W. Nornung, M. J. Thun, G. M. Egeland, W. E. Murray, D. L. Conover, and W. E. Halperin, "Video Display Terminals and the Risk of Spontaneous Abortion," New *England Journal of Medicine*, March 14, 1991, pp. 727-33.

44 Ibid., p.106. According to OSHA there are 2,000 state and federal job safety inspectors. According to the Wildlife Management Institute in Washington, D.C. (*Basic Information*, ibid., p. 17, tables 3-5) there are 12,000 fish and wildlife inspectors. "Every workday hour . . ." See, A. V. Westin, executive producer, "Working in America: Hazardous Duty," ABC News, airdate April 20, 1989. (Transcript #Burn 6 from Journal Graphics, 267 Broadway, New York, NY 10007.)

45 Farrell, Warren, Ph.D., *Why Men Are the Way They Are: The Male-Female Dynamic* (New York: Berkley Books, 1986) p.12.

46 Kimbrell, Andrew, *The Masculine Mystique: The Politics of Masculinity* (New York: Ballantine Books, 1995) pp.8-9.

47 Ibid., p.9.

48 Barrett, Jacqueline K. (editor), *Encyclopedia of Women's Associations Worldwide: A Guide to Over 3,400 National and Multinational Nonprofit Women's and Women-related Organizations* (London: Gale Research International Ltd., 1993)

49 Farrell, Warren, Ph.D., *The Myth of Male Power: Why Men Are the Disposable Sex* (New York: Berkley Books, 1993) p.32. See, U.S. Department of Commerce, Bureau of the Census, *Statistical Abstracts of the US, 1989,* 109th edition, p. 459, table 747—"Household Net Worth—Median Value of Holdings: 1984."

50 Ibid., p.33. Source: the Internal Revenue Service. See the *Los Angeles Times*, August 23, 1990.

51 Dychtwald, Maddy with Larson, Christine, *Influence: How Women's Soaring Economic Power Will Transform Our World for the Better* (New York: Voice/Hyperion, 2010) p.6. "In the United States, women already control 51.3 percent of the nation's private wealth."

52 Farrell, Warren, Ph.D., *The Myth of Male Power: Why Men Are the Disposable Sex* (New York: Berkley Books, 1993) p.33. "Women dominate spending." See, Diane Crispell, "The Brave New World," *American Demographic*, January 1992, p. 38.

53 Kanner, Bernice, *Pocketbook Power: How to Reach the Hearts and Minds of Today's Most Coveted Consumers—Women* (NY: McGraw-Hill, 2004), back cover.

54 A.C. Nielsen ratings, 1984

55 Farrell, Warren, Ph.D., *Women Can't Hear What Men Don't Say: Destroying Myths, Creating Love* (New York: Tarcher/Putnam, 1999) p.234. Source: Gail Ann Schlachter, Directory of Financial Aids for Women, 1997-1999, biannual edition Directory of Financial Aids for Women, 1999-2001 (El Dorado Hills, CA: Reference Service Press, 1999).

56 Farrell, Warren, Ph.D., *The Myth of Male Power: Why Men Are the Disposable Sex* (New York: Berkley Books, 1993) p.181. See, U.S. Department of Health and Human Services, National Center for Health Statistics, Centers for Disease Control, *Monthly Vital Statistics Report,* vol. 38, no. 5, supplement, September 26, 1989, "Advance Report of Final Mortality Statistics, 1987," p. 6, table D, "Ratio of Age-Adjusted Death Rates for the 15 Leading Causes of Death by Sex and Race: United States, 1987."

57 Farrell, Warren, Ph.D., *Women Can't Hear What Men Don't Say: Destroying Myths, Creating Love* (New York: Tarcher/Putnam, 1999) p.66. See, Richard H. Ropers, "The Rise of the New Urban Homeless," *Public Affairs Report* (Berkeley: University of California/Berkeley, Institute of Governmental Studies, 1985), October-December 1985, Vol. 26, Nos. 5 and 6, p. 4, Table 1 "Comparisons of Homeless

Samples from Select Cities." Also, ½ the street homeless are veterans, ibid, p.239.

58   Farrell, Warren, Ph.D., *The Myth of Male Power: Why Men Are the Disposable Sex* (New York: Berkley Books, 1993) p.189. Source: Vivian W. Pinn, M.D., director of the Office of Research on Women's Health, National Institutes of Health.

59   Farrell, Warren, Ph.D., *Women Can't Hear What Men Don't Say: Destroying Myths, Creating Love* (New York: Tarcher/Putnam, 1999) pp.240-1. Source: AP, "Rate of Leading Types of Cancer," April 20, 1999, from AOL News. The incidence for prostate cancer is 135.7 per 100,000; for breast cancer, 110.7 per 100,000. "almost four times as much money . . ." Source: National Institute of Health data is from the National Cancer Institute's Budget Office. Department of Defense data is from the Medical Research Programs Office.

60   Farrell, Warren, Ph.D., *The Myth of Male Power: Why Men Are the Disposable Sex* (New York: Berkley Books, 1993) p.32. Among those over the age of 65, 2.7 women per 1,000 and 6.2 men per 1,000 are victims of criminal violence. For that and additional information see, U.S. Bureau of Justice Statistics, Office of Justice Programs, Bureau of Justice Statistics, *Criminal Victimization in the United States, 1988,* National Crime Survey Report NCJ-122024, December 1990, p. 18, table 5.

61   Ibid., p.36.

62   Ibid., pp.31, 197, 30. "Four to five times higher suicide rate." See, U.S. Bureau of Health and Human Services, National Center for Health Statistics (USBH & HS/NCHS), *Vital Statistics of the United States* (Washington, D.C.: USGPO, 1991), vol. 2, part A, "Mortality," p. 51, tables 1-9. "Three times higher incidence of alcoholism." Based on rates of hospitalization for alcoholism. Source: unpublished data, USDH & HS/NCHS, Centers for Disease Control, National Hospital Discharge Survey, op. cit. "Nearly 10 percent shorter life expectancy." National Center for Health Statistics, *Monthly Vital Statistics Report*, vol. 39, no. 13, August 28, 1991, p. 17. For the year 1990, female and male average life spans were 78.8 years and 72 years, respectively.

63   Ibid., p.198.

64   Kimbrell, Andrew, *The Masculine Mystique: The Politics of Masculinity* (New York: Ballantine Books, 1995) p.1.

65   Farrell, Warren, Ph.D., *The Myth of Male Power: Why Men Are the Disposable Sex* (New York: Berkley Books, 1993) p.146. Source: Louis Shagun, "VA Hospital Assailed on Care for Homeless Vets," *Los Angeles Times,* May 26, 1989.

66   Kimbrell, Andrew, *The Masculine Mystique: The Politics of Masculinity* (New York: Ballantine Books, 1995) p.255.

67   Ibid., p.10.

68   Ibid.

69   Ibid.

70   Ibid.

71   Farrell, Warren, Ph.D., *Women Can't Hear What Men Don't Say: Destroying Myths, Creating Love* (New York: Tarcher/Putnam, 1999) p.323.

72   Farrell, Warren, Ph.D., *The Myth of Male Power: Why Men Are the Disposable Sex* (New York: Berkley Books, 1993) p.241. Source: Dr David L. Fallen, research director, state of Washington, "Sentencing Practices under the Sentencing Reform Act: Fiscal Year 1991."

73   Ibid., p.241.

74   Farrell, Warren, Ph.D., *Women Can't Hear What Men Don't Say: Destroying Myths, Creating Love* (New York: Tarcher/Putnam, 1999) p.242.

75   Farrell, Warren, Ph.D., *The Myth of Male Power: Why Men Are the Disposable Sex* (New York: Berkley Books, 1993) p.240. See, U.S. Department of Justice, Bureau

of Justice Statistics (US-BJS), Profile of Felons convicted in State Courts, January 1990, publication #NCJ-120021 by Patrick A. Largan, Ph.D., and John M. Dawson (BJS statisticians), p. 9.

[76] Ibid., p.240 & 244. "1,900 homicides . . ." See USBJS, *Sourcebook of Criminal Justice Statistics*, 1991, p. 442, table 4.7. "No woman executed . . ." Source: Professor Victor L. Streib, *American Executions of Female Offenders: A Preliminary Inventory of Names, Dates, and Other Information*, 1988, Cleveland Marshall College of Law. "When women commit homicide . . ." Source: John T. Kirkpatrick and John A. Humpgrey, "Stress in the Lives of Female Criminal Homicide Offenders in North Carolina," *Human Stress: Current Selected Research*, vol. 3, ed. James H. Humphrey (New York: AMS Press, 1989).

[77] Ibid., p.245. See the *Summary of Distribution Per Capita Costs for the Year Ended June 30, 1989: Section E,* published by the Madison, Wisconsin, Department of Health and Social Services, Division of Correction, Office of Policy, Planning and Budget.

[78] Ibid., p.244. See USBJS, *Correctional Populations in the United States,* publication #NCJ-118762, December 1989, p. 105, table 5.17, "Deaths among Sentenced Prisoners Under State or Federal Jurisdiction, by Sex and Cause of Death, 1987."

[79] Ibid., p.170. "Vulnerable to accusations." See James, Thomas B., *Domestic Violence: The 12 Things You Aren't Supposed to Know* (Chula Vista, CA: Aventine Press, 2003) p.102.

[80] Ibid., p.169. Jack C. Smith, James A. Mercy, and Judith M. Conn, op. cit.

[81] Young, Cathy, *Ceasefire!: Why Women and Men Must Join Forces to Achieve True Equality* (New York: The Free Press, 1999) p.255.

[82] Etcoff, Nancy, *Survival of the Prettiest: The Science of Beauty* (New York: First Anchor Books Edition, 2000) p.9.

[83] Blyth, Myrna, *Spin Sisters: How the Women of the Media Sell Unhappiness and Liberalism to the Women of America* (New York: St. Martin's Press, 2004) p.6.

[84] Patai, Daphne, *Heterophobia: Sexual Harassment and the Future of Feminism* (New York: Rowman & Littlefield Publishers, Inc., 1998) p.8.

[85] Kammer, Jack, *Good Will Toward Men: Women Talk Candidly About the Balance of Power Between the Sexes* (New York: St. Martin's Press, 1994) p.79.

[86] Barrett, Jacqueline K. (editor), Encyclopedia of Women's Associations Worldwide: A Guide to Over 3,400 National and Multinational Nonprofit Women's and Women-related Organizations (London: Gale Research International Ltd., 1993)

[87] Ahrons, Constance, Ph.D., *The Good Divorce: Keeping Your Family Together When Your Marriage Comes Apart* (New York: HarperPerennial/HarperCollins, 1995) p.35. Some sources claim that women file *80 percent* or *more* of all divorces. See: Morrow, David C., *How Women Manipulate: Essays Toward Gynology* (West Conshohocken, PA: Infinity Publishing, 2004) p.60.

[88] http://en.wikipedia.org/wiki/He_Thinks_He'll_Keep_Her, retrieved 01/19/09.

[89] Ahrons, Constance, Ph.D., *The Good Divorce: Keeping Your Family Together When Your Marriage Comes Apart* (NY: HarperPerennial/HarperCollins, 1995) p.35.

[90] Strossen, Nadine, *Defending Pornography: Free Speech, Sex, and the Fight for Women's Rights* (New York: New York University Press, 2000) p.117.

[91] Friday, Nancy, *The Power Of Beauty: A Cultural Memoir of Beauty and Desire* (New York: HarperCollins, 1996) p.157.

[92] Tolle, Eckhart, *The Power of Now: A Guide to Spiritual Enlightenment* (Novato, CA: New World Library, 1999) p.24.

[93] Source: http://www.noogenesis.com/pineapple/Taoist_Farmer.html

94 Sommers, Christina Hoff, *Who Stole Feminism?: How Women Have Betrayed Women* (New York: A Touchstone Book/Simon & Schuster, 1994) p.42.
95 Patai, Daphne & Koertge, Noretta, *Professing Feminism: Education and Indoctrination in Women's Studies* Lnham (Maryland: Lexington Books, 2003) p.96.
96 "The Click Experience," *Ms. Magazine.* Cited by Sommers, Christina Hoff, *Who Stole Feminism?: How Women Have Betrayed Women* (New York: A Touchstone Book/Simon & Schuster, 1994) p.54.
97 Patai, Daphne & Koertge, Noretta, *Professing Feminism: Education and Indoctrination in Women's Studies* Lnham (Maryland: Lexington Books, 2003) pp.96-7.
98 Goldberg, Herb, *The New Male: From Macho to Sensitive But Still All Male* (New York: Signet/Penguin, 1980) p.15.
99 Ibid., pp15-6.
100 Kipnis, Aaron, *Angry Young Men: How Parents, Teachers, and Counselors Can Help "Bad Boys" Become Good Men* (San Francisco, CA: Jossey-Bass, 1999) p.77.
101 Goldberg, Herb, *The New Male: From Macho to Sensitive But Still All Male* (New York: Signet/Penguin, 1980) p.15.
102 Kipnis, Aaron, *Angry Young Men: How Parents, Teachers, and Counselors Can Help "Bad Boys" Become Good Men* (San Francisco, CA: Jossey-Bass, 1999) p.42.
103 McCullough, David, *The Path Between the Seas: The Creation of the Panama Canal 1870-1914* (New York: Simon & Schuster Paperbacks, 1977) p.610.
104 http://en.wikipedia.org/wiki/Health_measures_during_the_construction_of_the_Panama_Canal
105 Kipnis, Aaron, *Angry Young Men: How Parents, Teachers, and Counselors Can Help "Bad Boys" Become Good Men* (San Francisco, CA: Jossey-Bass, 1999) p.77.
106 Brady, Bill, *London Free Press*, April 14, 2005.
107 Alfano, Jennifer, *Harper's Bazaar*, February 2003.
108 For example, in 2009, Kelly Schatmeier et al., successfully sued Mastercuts (a California-based haircutting chain) for offering men $2.00 discount coupons good on Tuesdays. According to official court documents, Mastercuts faces a "Maximum Potential Payment" of $1,750,000.
109 Farrell, Warren, Ph.D., *The Myth of Male Power: Why Men Are the Disposable Sex* (New York: Berkley Books, 1993) p.174.
110 Ibid, p.175.
111 Kipnis, Aaron, *Angry Young Men: How Parents, Teachers, and Counselors Can Help "Bad Boys" Become Good Men* (San Francisco, CA: Jossey-Bass, 1999) p.201.
112 Bell, Dan, "The silent epidemic of male suicide," BBC News, http://news.bbc.co.uk/go/pr/fr/-/2/hi/uk_news/7219232.stm, February 04, 2008.
113 Pearson, Patricia, *When She Was Bad: How and Why Women Get Away with Murder* (New York: Penguin Books, 1998) p.23.
114 Kindlon, Dan Ph.D. and Thompson, Michael Ph.D., *Raising Cain: Protecting the Emotional Life of Boys* (New York: Ballantine Books/Living Planet Book, 2000) p.6.
115 Stein, Harry, *One of the Guys: The Wising Up of an American Man* (New York: Pocket Books, 1988) pp.18-19.
116 Kimbrell, Andrew, *The Masculine Mystique: The Politics of Masculinity* (New York: Ballantine Books, 1995) p.5.
117 Farrell, Warren, Ph.D., *The Myth of Male Power: Why Men Are the Disposable Sex* (New York: Berkley Books, 1993) p.181. Source: U.S. Department of Health and Human Services, National Center for Health Statistics (USCH&HS/NCHS), Centers for Disease Control, *Monthly Vital Statistics Report,* vol. 38, no. 5, supplement, September 26, 1989, "Advance Report of Final Mortality Statistics, 1987," p. 6, table

D, "Ratio of Age-adjusted Death Rates for the 15 Leading Causes of Death by Sex and Race: U.S., 1987."

[118] Driscoll, Richard, Ph.D., *The Stronger Sex: Understanding and Resolving the Eternal Power Struggles Between Men and Women* (Rocklin, CA: Prima Publishing, 1998) p.8. See also, J. Gottman, "Assessing the Role of Emotion in Marriage."

[119] Goldberg, Herb, *The New Male: From Macho to Sensitive But Still All Male* (New York: Signet/Penguin, 1980) pp.149-50.

[120] Stein, Harry, *One of the Guys: The Wising Up of an American Man* (New York: Pocket Books, 1988) p.19.

[121] *1988 Guinness Book of World Records,* Bantam Books, 1988, p.15.

[122] In 1920 in the USA male life expectancy was 53.6 years; female life expectancy was 54.6 years. National Center for Health Statistics, U.S. Department of Health and Human Services, *Life Tables: Vital Statistics of the United States* (Washington, D.C.: U.S. Government Printing Office), 1990, vol. 2, section 6.

[123] Farrell, Warren, Ph.D., *The Myth of Male Power: Why Men Are the Disposable Sex* (New York: Berkley Books, 1993) p.181. See U.S. Department of Commerce, Bureau of the Census, *Statistical Abstract of the United States: 1987,* 107th ed., p. 820, table 1439, "Urban Population, Growth, Birth, and Death Rates and Life Expectancy—Selected Countries;" p. 824, table 1445, "Gross National Product in Current and Constant (1982) Dollars and Per Capita: 1975 to 1983."

[124] Ibid., pp.182-4.

[125] Vincent, Norah, *Self-Made Man: One Woman's Journey into Manhood and Back Again* (New York: Viking/Penguin, 2006) p.38.

[126] Farrell, Warren, Ph.D., *The Myth of Male Power: Why Men Are the Disposable Sex* (New York: Berkley Books, 1993) p.350. Source: U.S. Department of Health and Human Services, Social Security Administration, Office of Research and Statistics, *Earnings and Employment Data for Wage and Salary Workers Covered Under Social Security by State and Country, 1985.*

[127] Ibid.

[128] Ibid., p.350.

[129] Young, Cathy, *Ceasefire!: Why Women and Men Must Join Forces to Achieve True Equality* (New York: The Free Press, 1999) p.7.

[130] Patai, Daphne & Koertge, Noretta, *Professing Feminism: Education and Indoctrination in Women's Studies* (New and Expanded Edition) (Maryland: Lexington Books, 2003) p.50.

[131] Farrell, Warren, Ph.D., *The Myth of Male Power: Why Men Are the Disposable Sex* (New York: Berkley Books, 1993) pp.188-9.

[132] Kipnis, Aaron, *Angry Young Men: How Parents, Teachers, and Counselors Can Help "Bad Boys" Become Good Men* (San Francisco, CA: Jossey-Bass, 1999) pp.186-7.

[133] Tucker, Todd, *The Great Starvation Experiment: Ancel Keys and the Men Who Starved for Science* (Minneapolis: University of Minnesota Press, 2007) p.197.

[134] Reese, Margaret, "Documents confirm soldiers were exposed to nuclear tests in Australia," 07/09/01, World Socialist Web Site, wsws.org, retrieved 08/06.

[135] Ibid.

[136] Farrell, Warren, Ph.D., *Women Can't Hear What Men Don't Say: Destroying Myths, Creating Love* (New York: Tarcher/Putnam, 1999) p.237.

[137] Farrell, Warren, Ph.D., *The Myth of Male Power: Why Men Are the Disposable Sex* (New York: Berkley Books, 1993) p.189.

[138] Ibid., p.192.

139 McElroy, Wendy, "The Anti-Male *New York Times*," June 10, 2003, www.ifeminists.com
140 Farrell, Warren, Ph.D., *The Myth of Male Power: Why Men Are the Disposable Sex* (New York: Berkley Books, 1993) p.190.
141 Farrell, Warren, Ph.D., *Women Can't Hear What Men Don't Say: Destroying Myths, Creating Love* (New York: Tarcher/Putnam, 1999) pp.240-1.
142 Ibid., p241.
143 "Prostate cancer treatment 'too costly,'" http://www.theaustralian.news.com.au/story/0,20867,20109192-1702,00.html, August 12, 2006.
144 Farrell, Warren, Ph.D., *Women Can't Hear What Men Don't Say: Destroying Myths, Creating Love* (New York: Tarcher/Putnam, 1999) p.238.
145 Moir, Anne and Moir, Bill, *Why Men Don't Iron: The Fascinating and Unalterable Differences Between Men and Women* (New York: CITADEL PRESS/Kensington Publishing Corp., 1999) pp.53-100.
146 Ibid., p.73.
147 Ibid., p.99.
148 Ibid., p.71.
149 Raloff, Janet and Harder, B., "Gender Measure: Pollutant appears to alter boys' genitals," *Science News*, June 04, 2005, Vol. 167, p.355.
150 http://www.newsweek.com/id/34310 (retrieved November 08, 2008)
151 Raloff, Janet, "Chemicals from plastics show effects in boys," *Science News*, December 19, 2009, p.10. "The greater a boy's fetal exposure to certain phthalates, the less often he tended to engage in typically masculine play."
152 Raloff, J., "Why Are Boys' Birth Rates Falling?", *Science News*, April 04, 1998, http://www.sciencenews.org/pages/sn_arc98/4_4_98/fob1.htm
153 Moore, Michael, *Stupid White Men . . . and Other Sorry Excuses for the State of the Nation!* (New York: Regan Books/HarperCollins, 2001), pp.144-5.
154 Farrell, Warren, Ph.D., *Women Can't Hear What Men Don't Say: Destroying Myths, Creating Love* (New York: Tarcher/Putnam, 1999), pp.239-40.
155 Crowley, Michael, "No Mercy, Kid!: In the name of 'zero tolerance,' our schools are treating innocent children (i.e. boys) like criminals," *Reader's Digest*, 05/2007, http://www.rd.com/content/printContent.do?contentId=37236
156 Tyre, Peg, The Trouble with Boys: A Surprising Report Card on Our Sons, Their Problems at School, and What Parents and Educators Must Do (New York: Three Rivers Press, 2008) p.55.
157 Moir, Anne and Jessel, David, *Brain Sex: The Real Difference Between Men and Women* (New York: Carol Publishing Group, 1991) p.65.
158 Will, George, JewishWorldReview.com, December 03, 1999. See also, http://www.mapinc.org/drugnews/v99.n1323.a07.html
159 Sommers, Christina Hoff, *The War Against Boys: How Misguided Feminism Is Harming Our Young Men* (New York: Simon & Schuster, 2000) pp.94-9.
160 Ibid., p.99.
161 Sommers, Christina Hoff, *The War Against Boys: How Misguided Feminism Is Harming Our Young Men* (New York: Simon & Schuster, 2000) p.120.
162 Ibid., p.121.
163 Ibid., p.19.
164 Kipnis, Aaron, *Angry Young Men: How Parents, Teachers, and Counselors Can Help "Bad Boys" Become Good Men* (San Francisco, CA: Jossey-Bass, 1999) p.40.
165 Sommers, Christina Hoff, *The War Against Boys: How Misguided Feminism Is Harming Our Young Men* (New York: Simon & Schuster, 2000) p.123.
166 Ibid., p.134.

[167] Tyre, Peg, *The Trouble with Boys: A Surprising Report Card on Our Sons, Their Problems at School, and What Parents and Educators Must Do* (New York: Three Rivers Press, 2008) pp.30-31.

[168] Moir, Anne and Jessel, David, *Brain Sex: The Real Difference Between Men and Women* (New York: Carol Publishing Group, 1991) p.62.

[169] Sommers, Christina Hoff, *Who Stole Feminism?: How Women Have Betrayed Women* (New York: A Touchstone Book/Simon & Schuster, 1994) p.61.

[170] Ibid., pp.59-61.

[171] Ibid.. p.62.

[172] Rhoads, Steven E., *Taking Sex Differences Seriously* (San Francisco: Encounter Books, 2004) p.40.

[173] For a detailed look at feminism's influence over textbooks, see Ravitch, Diane, *The Language Police: How Pressure Groups Restrict What Students Learn* (New York: Vintage Books/A Division of Random House, Inc., 2004). The book reveals the exhaustive and restrictive P.C. guidelines current school texts must adhere to. Not only do these restrictions foster dull texts void of vitality, conflict, or gritty reality; predictably, they also foster anti-male bias. For example, it is "appropriate to show women as strong and brave and men as weepy and emotional. Fairness might allow an equal distribution of these emotions, but the guidelines imply that women must not be shown as weepy and emotional and men must not be shown as brave and strong . . . The guidelines regulate what writers are permitted to say about specific groups in society, including women, the elderly, people with disabilities, and members of racial and ethnic minorities . . . All of these groups must be presented only in a positive light." Since only able bodied white men are unprotected, that leaves only white men to portray all human inadequacy. Feminism's hostility toward traditional family is also apparent: "men should not be portrayed as breadwinners; women should not be portrayed as wives and mothers." pp.26 & 34 & 27.

[174] Tiger, Lionel, *You've Got Male!*, Rutgers University, December 17, 2005, p.A10. The *Wall Street Journal*, http://online.wsj.com/article/SB113477972844425239.html.

[175] Vickers, Melana Zyla, "Where The Boys Aren't: The gender gap on college campuses," *The Weekly Standard*, weeklystandard.com, 01/02/06, Vol. 011, Issue 16.

[176] Tiger, Lionel, *You've Got Male!*, Rutgers University, December 17, 2005, p.A10. See the *Wall Street Journal* on line, http://online.wsj.com/article/SB113477972844425239.html.

[177] Kammer, Jack, *Good Will Toward Men: Women Talk Candidly About the Balance of Power Between the Sexes* (New York: St. Martin's Press, 1994) p.111.

[178] Ibid., p.111.

[179] Ibid., p.112.

[180] Ibid., pp.112-3.

[181] Ibid., p.113.

[182] Ibid., p.113.

[183] O'Beirne, Kate, *Women Who Make the World Worse: and How Their Radical Feminist Assault Is Ruining Our Families, Military, Schools, and Sports* (New York: Sentinel, 2006) pp.62-3.

[184] Grossman, Judith, "A Mother, a Feminist, Aghast: Unsubstantiated accusations against my son by a former girlfriend landed him before a nightmarish college tribunal." *The Wall Street Journal*, http://online.wsj.com/article/SB10001424127887324600704578405280211043510.html#articleTabs%3Darticle, April 16, 2013.

[185] *The Seattle Times*, "Feminist Art Students List All Males At University By

Name As 'Potential Rapists'", http://community.seattletimes.nwsource.com/archive/?date=19930508&slug=1700105, May 8, 1993. "The posters bore the heading 'Notice: These Men Are Potential Rapists.'"
[186] Hodges, Michael H., "Where are the boys? Women outnumber men on campuses," *The Detroit News*, detnews.com, December 4th, 2005.
[187] University of Michigan study cited by Tyre, Peg, *Newsweek*, January 30, 2006, p.46.
[188] Friday, Nancy, *The Power Of Beauty: A Cultural Memoir of Beauty and Desire* (New York: HarperCollins, 1996) pp.156-7.
[189] Ibid., p.278.
[190] Patai, Daphne, *Heterophobia: Sexual Harassment and the Future of Feminism* (New York: Rowman & Littlefield Publishers, Inc., 1998) p.146.
[191] See: Patai, Daphne & Koertge, Noretta, *Professing Feminism: Education and Indoctrination in Women's Studies* (New and Expanded Edition) (Maryland: Lexington Books, 2003) p18. The authors tell, for example, of two students in a Women's Studies class who were "treated unfairly because they were heterosexual women. They and the other heterosexuals had been asked to identify themselves at the beginning, with the suggestion that by the end of the term, if the course were successful, there would be no heterosexuals left. One of them had been asked to do extra papers. I actually went to the ombudsman about this, because a married woman with kids was being asked to do extra work as a kind of punishment, because she'd been stubborn about her sexual orientation."
[192] See Wikipedia: http://en.wikipedia.org/wiki/Lesbian_until_graduation. "The slang terms lesbian until graduation (LUG), gay until graduation (GUG), or bisexual until graduation (BUG), are terms used to describe women primarily of high-school or college age, who are assumed to be experimenting with or adopting a temporary lesbian or bisexual identity."
[193] Patai, Daphne, *Heterophobia: Sexual Harassment and the Future of Feminism* (New York: Rowman & Littlefield Publishers, Inc., 1998) p.158.
[194] Yan, Xiaochin Claire, "News & Comments on Women's Issues," *The Contrarian*, Vol. 8, No. 15, December 09, 2004.
[195] Elam, Paul, April 22, 2010, "Men's Studies Foremost Authority Opts for Castration, Literally," http://mensnewsdaily.com/2010/04/22/mens-studies-foremost-authority-opts-for-castration-literally/

Robert W. Connell is the premier authority in the world on masculinities. A native of Australia, his books have been ranked first, fourth, fifth and sixth of the top ten books considered to have a profound impact on sociological theory in that country. Connell's influence has reached global proportions, making his work required reading in men's studies programs internationally, earning him iconic status and widespread esteem. He is to men's studies what Darwin was to the study of evolution. And now, he is a she. . . . Robert Connell showed up at a 2008 Wake Forrest College meeting of the American Men's Studies Association (AMSA) as *Raewyn* Connell, a legally recognized female incarnation of the formerly male scholar. It was a startling change that must have stunned those attending, but not a word about it was formally spoken. One might think that the remarkable silence was a reflection of an enlightened collection of men and women, blind to the supposedly limiting constructs of gender, and practicing an acceptance so espoused by the causes they promote. But it is more likely that there was a different sort of silence in the audience that day; one of solemn concern about the implications of a masculinities expert who, in his sixth decade of life, had the masculinity cut from his body like a malignant tumor.

[196] Sommers, Christina Hoff, *Who Stole Feminism?: How Women Have Betrayed Women* (New York: A Touchstone Book/Simon & Schuster, 1994) p.50.
[197] Farrell, Warren, Ph.D., *Women Can't Hear What Men Don't Say: Destroying Myths, Creating Love* (New York: Tarcher/Putnam, 1999) p.244.
[198] Tyre, Peg, *Newsweek*, January 30, 2006, p.47.
[199] Ibid, p.46.
[200] Allen, Jodie, "Are Men Obsolete?," *U.S. News and World Report*, June 23, 2003, p.33.
[201] Farrell, Warren, Ph.D., *Why Men Are the Way They Are: The Male-Female Dynamic* (New York: Berkley Books, 1986) p.229.
[202] Yet another great Warren Farrell insight.
[203] "Foreign Women and Children Can Leave Iraq, Hussein Says," *Los Angeles Times*, August 29, 1990, cited by Farrell, Warren, Ph.D., *The Myth of Male Power: Why Men Are the Disposable Sex* (New York: Berkley Books, 1993) p.142.
[204] Ibid., p.230.
[205] Ibid., p.126.
[206] Schenk, Roy U., *The Other Side of the Coin: Causes and Consequences of Men's Oppression* (Madison, WI: Bioenergetics Press, 1982) p.37.
[207] Tucker, Todd, *The Great Starvation Experiment: Ancel Keys and the Men Who Starved for Science* (Minneapolis: University of Minnesota Press, 2007) p.46.
[208] Ibid., p.158.
[209] Ibid., p.158.
[210] Ibid., p.5.
[211] Ibid., p.171.
[212] Ibid., p.46.
[213] See the readily available video: *Atomic Cafe*.
[214] Sommers, Christina Hoff, *Who Stole Feminism?: How Women Have Betrayed Women* (New York: A Touchstone Book/Simon & Schuster, 1994) p.255.
[215] Friday, Nancy, *The Power Of Beauty: A Cultural Memoir of Beauty and Desire* (New York: HarperCollins, 1996) p.319.
[216] Parker, Kathleen, *Save the Males: Why Men Matter, Why Women Should Care* (New York: Random House, 2008) p.vi.
[217] Farrell, Warren, Ph.D., *The Myth of Male Power: Why Men Are the Disposable Sex* (New York: Berkley Books, 1993) p.210.
[218] Friday, Nancy, *The Power Of Beauty: A Cultural Memoir of Beauty and Desire* (New York: HarperCollins, 1996) p.327.
[219] Sommers, Christina Hoff, *Who Stole Feminism?: How Women Have Betrayed Women* (New York: A Touchstone Book/Simon & Schuster, 1994) p.35.
[220] Waldfogel, Joel, "Couch Entitlement: Surprise—Men Do Just as Much Work as Women Do," http://www.slate.com/id/2164268/, April 16, 2007.
[221] Farrell, Warren, Ph.D., *The Myth of Male Power: Why Men Are the Disposable Sex* (New York: Berkley Books, 1993) p.37. Source: F. Thomas Juster and Frank P. Stafford, "The Allocation of Time: Empirical Findings, Behavioral Modes, and Problems of Measurement," *Journal of Economic Literature*, vol. 29, June 1991, p. 477.
[222] Moir, Anne and Moir, Bill, *Why Men Don't Iron: The Fascinating and Unalterable Differences Between Men and Women* (New York: CITADEL PRESS/Kensington Publishing Corp., 1999) p.58
[223] Ahrons, Constance, Ph.D., *The Good Divorce: Keeping Your Family Together When Your Marriage Comes Apart* (N.Y.: HarperPerennial/HarperCollins, 1995) p.35.
[224] Farrell, Warren, Ph.D., *Why Men Earn More: The Startling Truth Behind the Pay Gap—and What Women Can Do About It* (N.Y.: AMACOM, 2005) pp.xv-xvii

225 Furchtgott-Roth, Diana and Stolba, Christine, *Women's Figures: An Illustrated Guide to the Economic Progress of Women in America* (Washington, D.C.: The AEI Press and Arlington, Virginia: Independent Women's Forum, 1999) p.4.
226 Ibid., pp.11-12.
227 Farrell, Warren, Ph.D., *Why Men Earn More: The Startling Truth Behind the Pay Gap—and What Women Can Do About It* (New York: AMACOM, 2005) p.74.
228 Ibid., p.75.
229 Ibid., p.79.
230 Sowell, Thomas, *Economic Facts and Fallacies* (New York: Basic Books A Member of the Perseus Books Group, 2008) p.70.
231 Furchtgott-Roth, Diana and Stolba, Christine, *Women's Figures: An Illustrated Guide to the Economic Progress of Women in America* (Washington, D.C.: The AEI Press and Arlington, Virginia: Independent Women's Forum, 1999) pp.11-21.
232 Stossel, John, "Is the Wage Gap Women's Choice? Research Suggests Career Decisions, Not Sex Bias, Are at Root of Pay Disparity," ABC News' *Give Me a Break*, May 27, 2005.
233 http://www.whitehouse.gov/the_press_office/President-Obama-Announces-White-House-Council-on-Women-and-Girls/ (retrieved 03/12/09)
234 Finley, Gordon E., Ph.D., "Gender pay gap myths and 2008," Op-Ed published in the Forum section of *The Washington Times* on Sunday November 18, 2007. http://www.washingtontimes.com/article/20071118/COMMENTARY/111180005/1012
235 Roberts, Sam, "Young women in big cities earn more," *Chicago Tribune*, August 03, 2007, http://www.chicagotribune.com/services/newspaper/premium/printedition/Friday/chi-pay_friaug03,0,3469147.story
236 Ibid.
237 Gavin, Robert, "Losing jobs in unequal numbers," *Boston Globe*, December 05, 2008. http://www.boston.com/business/articles/2008/12/05/losing_jobs_in_unequal_numbers/?page=full
238 Ibid.
239 Callahan, Maureen, "Men Worried They're Falling Behind in a 'He-cession'—They're Right," http://www.nypost.com/php/pfriendly/print.php?url=http://www.nypost.com/seven/07182009/postopinion/opedcolumnists/men_worry_theyre_falling_behind_in_a_he__179998.htm, July 18, 2009
240 Warner, Fara, *The Power of the Purse: How Smart Businesses Are Adapting to the World's Most Important Consumers—Women* (Upper Saddle River, New Jersey: Pearson/Prentice Hall, 2006) p.xx.
241 Kanner, Bernice, *Pocketbook Power: How to Reach the Hearts and Minds of Today's Most Coveted Consumers—Women* (New York: McGraw-Hill, 2004) p.1.
242 Ibid., p.5.
243 Ibid., pp.5-6.
244 Farrell, Warren, Ph.D., *Why Men Are the Way They Are: The Male-Female Dynamic* (New York: Berkley Books, 1986) p.57. Source: *Romantic Times*, New York Office estimate, February 12, 1985. This estimate is also the agreed-upon figure of the publishing industry in New York.
245 Kammer, Jack, *Good Will Toward Men: Women Talk Candidly About the Balance of Power Between the Sexes* (New York: St. Martin's Press, 1994) p.35.
246 Cose, Ellis, *Newsweek*, March 3, 2003, pp.48-49
247 Ibid., p.49.
248 Baskerville, Stephen, *Taken Into Custody: The War Against Fathers, Marriage, and the Family* (Nashville, TN: Cumberland House Publishing, Inc., 2007) p.11.
249 Ibid., p.11.

250 Popenoe, David, *Life Without Father: Compelling new evidence that fatherhood and marriage are indispensable for the good of children and society* (New York: Martin Kessler Books/The Free Press, 1996) p.26.
251 Warner, Fara, *The Power of the Purse: How Smart Businesses Are Adapting to the World's Most Important Consumers—Women* (Upper Saddle River, New Jersey: Pearson/Prentice Hall, 2006) p. 68 & p. 76.
252 Farrell, Warren, Ph.D., *Women Can't Hear What Men Don't Say: Destroying Myths, Creating Love* (New York: Tarcher/Putnam, 1999) pp.269-270.
253 Farrell, Warren Ph.D., "Men as Success Objects", *Utne Reader*, May/June 1991, p.81.
254 Moir, Anne and Jessel, David, *Brain Sex: The Real Difference Between Men and Women* (New York: Carol Publishing Group, 1991) p.85.
255 http://www.census.gov/Press-Release/www/releases/archives/facts_for_features_special_editions/002265.html, July 19, 2004.
256 "America's Families and Living Arrangements: 2007," http://www.census.gov/population/www/socdemo/hh-fam/cps2007.html, see table A1, "All Races."
257 National Center for Health Statistics, part of the Centers for Disease Control and Prevention, "Out-of-Wedlock Birthrates Are Soaring, U.S. Reports," The *New York Times*, http://www.nytimes.com/2009/05/13/health/13mothers.html?_r=19&ref=health
258 Buss, David M., *The Evolution of Desire: Strategies of Human Mating* (Revised Edition 4, Basic Books, 2003) p 178.
259 Ibid.
260 Friday, Nancy, *The Power Of Beauty: A Cultural Memoir of Beauty and Desire* (New York: HarperCollins, 1996) p.432.
261 Etcoff, Nancy, *Survival of the Prettiest: The Science of Beauty* (New York: First Anchor Books Edition, 2000) p.80.
262 Ibid., p.79.
263 Ibid., p.79.
264 Farrell, Warren, Ph.D., *Why Men Are the Way They Are: The Male-Female Dynamic* (New York: Berkley Books, 1986) p.27.
265 Buss, David M., *The Evolution of Desire: Strategies of Human Mating* (Revised Edition 4, Basic Books, 2003) p.21.
266 Roiphe, Katie, "The Independent Woman (and other lies)," *Esquire*, February 1997.
267 Farrell, Warren, Ph.D., *The Myth of Male Power: Why Men Are the Disposable Sex* (New York: Berkley Books, 1993) p.33.
268 Kanner, Bernice, *Pocketbook Power: How to Reach the Hearts and Minds of Today's Most Coveted Consumers—Women* (N.Y.: McGraw-Hill, 2004), back cover.
269 Farrell, Warren, Ph.D., *The Myth of Male Power: Why Men Are the Disposable Sex* (New York: Berkley Books, 1993) p.34. Source: U.S. Department of Education, Office of Educational Research and Improvement, National Center for Education Statistics, "IPEDS Completions Study," 1989, 1990.
270 Ibid., p.34. In the late 1980's, a female engineer's starting salary exceeded her male counterpart's by $571 per year. See the Engineering Manpower Commission's *Women in Engineering* (Washington, D.C.: American Association of Engineering Society, EMC Bulletin no. 99, December 1989, table 5.
271 Pipes, Sally, "There's No Glass Floor," *The Contrarian: News and Comments on Women's Issues*, Vol. 9, No. 3, March 07, 2005.
272 Ibid.
273 La Monica, Paul R., CNN/Money senior writer, "Fiorina out, HP stock soars," money.cnn.com, February 10, 2005.

[274] Pipes, Sally, "There's No Glass Floor," *The Contrarian: News and Comments on Women's Issues*, Vol. 9, No. 3, March 07, 2005.
[275] Ibid.
[276] Ingraham, Laura, *New York Times*, April 19, 1995, p.A23.
[277] Weissman, Jordan, "Sorry, Marriage Is a 'Luxury Good'", October 30th, 2013, http://www.theatlantic.com/business/archive/2013/10/sorry-marriage-is-a-luxury-good/281016/
[278] Buss, David M., *The Evolution of Desire: Strategies of Human Mating* (Revised Edition 4, Basic Books, 2003) p.27.
[279] James, Thomas B., *Domestic Violence: The 12 Things You Aren't Supposed to Know* (Chula Vista, CA: Aventine Press, 2003) pp.65-66.
[280] Kammer, Jack, Good Will Toward Men: Women Talk Candidly About the Balance of Power Between the Sexes (New York: St. Martin's Press, 1994) p.145.
[281] Kiley, Dan, Living Together, Feeling Alone: Healing Your Hidden Loneliness, (Pawcett Book Group, 1991), pp5-6 of the hardcover version. Cited from Farrell, Warren, Ph.D., *Women Can't Hear What Men Don't Say: Destroying myths, creating love* (New York: Tarcher/Putnam, 1999) p.183.
[282] Camille Paglia quoted from the back cover of, *Who Stole Feminism?*
[283] Sommers, Christina Hoff, *Who Stole Feminism?: How Women Have Betrayed Women* (New York: A Touchstone Book/Simon & Schuster, 1994) p.11, quoting Wolf, Naomi, *The Beauty Myth*, p.207.
[284] Ibid., pp.11-12.
[285] Ibid., p.12.
[286] *Cosmopolitan*, August 2004, p.111.
[287] Friday, Nancy, The Power Of Beauty: A Cultural Memoir of Beauty and Desire (New York: HarperCollins, 1996) p.198.
[288] *Elle* magazine, June 2002, p.112.
[289] Lawson, Nigella, *Harper's Bazaar*, August 2004, p.92.
[290] Garcia, Guy, *The Decline of Men: How the American Male Is Getting Axed, Giving up, and Flipping Off His Future* (New York: Harper Perennial, 2009) p.161.
[291] Ibid., p.160.
[292] Sommers, Christina Hoff, *Who Stole Feminism?: How Women Have Betrayed Women* (New York: A Touchstone Book/Simon & Schuster, 1994) p.13.
[293] Ibid., p.14.
[294] Ibid., p.13.
[295] Ibid., pp.14-15.
[296] Hise, Dr. Richard T., *The War Against Men: Why Women are Winning and What Men Must Do If America Is to Survive* (Oakland, Oregon: Red Anvil Press, 2004) p.171.
[297] Ibid., p.171.
[298] Sommers, Christina Hoff, *Who Stole Feminism?: How Women Have Betrayed Women* (New York: A Touchstone Book/Simon & Schuster, 1994) p.33.
[299] Ibid., p.15.
[300] Ibid., p.15.
[301] Garcia, Guy, *The Decline of Men: How the American Male Is Getting Axed, Giving up, and Flipping Off His Future* (New York: Harper Perennial, 2009) p.xv.
[302] Ibid., pp.xv.
[303] Ibid., pp.xv-xvi.
[304] Ibid., p.xvii.
[305] Ibid., pp.51-52.
[306] Parker, Kathleen, *Save the Males: Why Men Matter, Why Women Should Care*

(New York: Random House, 2008) p.viii.
[307] Ibid., p.17.
[308] Rosin, Hanna, July/August 2010, *Atlantic Magazine*, "The End of Men" http://www.theatlantic.com/magazine/archive/2010/07/the-end-of-men/8135/. Source: sociologist Pierre Bourdieu, *The Bachelors' Ball*, published in 2007.
[309] Kranichfeld, Marion L., "Rethinking Family Power," *Journal of Family Issues*, Vol. 8 no. 1, March 1987, pp.42-56 ©1987 Sage Publications, Inc.
[310] Sommers, Christina Hoff, *The War Against Boys: How Misguided Feminism Is Harming Our Young Men* (New York: Simon & Schuster, 2000) p.48.
[311] Ibid., p.49.
[312] Ibid., p.49.
[313] Ibid., p.49.
[314] Schwartz, Howard S., *The Revolt of the Primitive: An Inquiry into the Roots of Political Correctness* (New Brunswick, NJ: Transaction Publishers, 2003) p.15.
[315] Hise, Dr. Richard T., *The War Against Men: Why Women are Winning and What Men Must Do If America Is to Survive* (Oakland, OR: RedAnvil Press, 2004) pp.167-9.
[316] Bunzel, John H. (editor), *Political Passages: Journeys of Change Through Two Decades, 1968-1988* (New York: The Free Press: A Division of Macmillan, Inc., 1988). Quoted from Carol Iannone's essay, "The Wide and Crooked Path," p.318.
[317] Sommers, Christina Hoff, *Who Stole Feminism?: How Women Have Betrayed Women* (New York: A Touchstone Book/Simon & Schuster, 1994) p.201.
[318] Farrell, Warren, Ph.D., *The Myth of Male Power: Why Men Are the Disposable Sex* (New York: Berkley Books, 1993) p.15.
[319] Ibid, pp.14-15.
[320] Lyndon, Neil, *No More Sex War: The Failures of Feminism* (London, UK: Sinclair-Stevenson, 1992).
[321] Lyndon, Neil, "Return of the Heretic," *The Sunday Times* News Review, (London, UK), December 17, 2000.
[322] Hope, Jenny, "Drug rape myth exposed as study reveals binge drinking is to blame," http://www.dailymail.co.uk/news/article-436592/Drug-rape-myth-exposed-study-reveals-binge-drinking-blame.html, 02/16/07. See *Emergency Medicine Journal*, 2007;**24**:89-91 doi:10.1136/emj.2006.040360
[323] Nathanson, Paul and Young, Katherine, *Spreading Misandry: The Teaching of Contempt for Men in Popular Culture* (Canada: McGill-Queen's University Press, 2001) p.78.
[324] Nathanson, Paul and Young, Katherine, *Spreading Misandry: The Teaching of Contempt for Men in Popular Culture* (Canada: McGill-Queen's University Press, 2001) p.141.
[325] Ibid., p.13.
[326] Ibid.
[327] Ibid., p.14.
[328] Ibid., p.16.
[329] CommunityNet, http://www.cnet.ngo.net.au/index.php?option=content&task=view&id=20729, November 29, 2006.
[330] Nathanson, Paul and Young, Katherine, *Spreading Misandry: The Teaching of Contempt for Men in Popular Culture* (Canada: McGill-Queen's University Press, 2001) p.15.
[331] Young, Cathy, *Ceasefire!: Why Women and Men Must Join Forces to Achieve True Equality* (New York: The Free Press, 1999) p.5.
[332] Goldberg, Herb, *The Hazards of Being Male: Surviving the Myth of Masculine Privilege* (New York: Signet/Penguin, 1976) p5.

[333] Parker, Kathleen, *Save the Males: Why Men Matter, Why Women Should Care* (New York: Random House, 2008) p.x.
[334] Farrell, Warren, Ph.D., *The Myth of Male Power: Why Men Are the Disposable Sex* (New York: Berkley Books, 1993) p.36.
[335] "Decriminalization of the Abandonment of Newborns," National Abandoned Infants Assistance Resource Center website, aia.berkeley.edu, 2000.
[336] Kammer, Jack, *Good Will Toward Men: Women Talk Candidly About the Balance of Power Between the Sexes* (New York: St. Martin's Press, 1994) p.43.
[337] Farrell, Warren, Ph.D., *Father and Child Reunion: How to Bring the Dads We Need to the Children We Love* (New York: Penguin Putnam Inc., 2001) p.145.
[338] Hetherington, E. Mavis and Jodl, Kathleen M., "Stepfamilies as Settings for Child Development," in Alan Booth and Judy Dunn, eds., *Stepfamilies: Who Benefits? Who Does Not?* Hillsdale, N.J.: L Erlbaum, 1994.
[339] Friday, Nancy, *The Power Of Beauty: A Cultural Memoir of Beauty and Desire* (New York: HarperCollins, 1996) p.59.
[340] Farrell, Warren, Ph.D., *The Myth of Male Power: Why Men Are the Disposable Sex* (New York: Berkley Books, 1993) p.364.
[341] Kammer, Jack, *Good Will Toward Men: Women Talk Candidly About the Balance of Power Between the Sexes* (New York: St. Martin's Press, 1994) p.144.
[342] Friday, Nancy, *The Power Of Beauty: A Cultural Memoir of Beauty and Desire* (New York: HarperCollins, 1996) p.52.
[343] Excerpted from "The mama lion at the gate" by Cathy Young for Salon.com. The same material may be found in her book *Ceasefire!: Why Women and Men Must Join Forces to Achieve True Equality* (New York: The Free Press, 1999) pp.56-57.
[344] Schenk, Roy U. Ph.D., *Thoughts of Dr. Schenk on Sex and Gender* (Madison, WI: Bioenergetics Press, 1991) p.28.
[345] Glenn Sacks quoted from: Garcia, Guy, *The Decline of Men: How the American Male Is Getting Axed, Giving up, and Flipping Off His Future* (New York: Harper Perennial, 2009) p.134.
[346] Goldberg, Herb, *The New Male: From Macho to Sensitive But Still All Male* (New York: Signet/Penguin, 1980) p.146.
[347] Slater, Lauren, *Elle*, July 2001, pp.69-70.
[348] Farrell, Warren, Ph.D., *Father and Child Reunion: How to Bring the Dads We Need to the Children We Love* (New York: Penguin Putnam Inc., 2001) p.48.
[349] Braver, Sanford L., Ph.D., with O'Connell, Diane, *Divorced Dads: Shattering the Myths* (New York: Tarcher/Putnam, 1998) p.149.
[350] Ibid., p.150.
[351] Ibid.
[352] Tiger, Lionel, *You've Got Male!*, Rutgers University, December 17, 2005, p.A10. See the *Wall Street Journal* on line, http://online.wsj.com/article/SB113477972844425239.html.
[353] Pace, Gina, "Letterman Fights Restraining Order," CBS News, December 21, 2005, http://www.cbsnews.com/stories/2005/12/21/entertainment/main1156547.shtml
[354] Hession, Gregory A., J. D., "Restraining Orders Out of Control," August 4, 2008, http://thenewamerican.com/node/8647
[355] Huttner, Richard, quoted by Young, Jane, *New York* magazine, November 18, 1985.
[356] Schlafly, Phylis, "Domestic violence law abuses rights of men," May 12, 2006, *San Diego Union-Tribune*, signonsandiego.com

[357] Cose, Ellis, *A Man's World: How Real Is Male Privilege—and How High Is Its Price?* (New York: HarperCollins, 1995) p.21.
[358] "Geldof: My grief at losing my girls," by Churcher, Sharon, *Daily Mail*, 05/14/07, http://www.dailymail.co.uk/pages/live/articles/showbiz/showbiznews.html?in_article_id=454490&in_page_id=1773.
[359] US Census Bureau, Current Population Survey, Table 1, 04/98 as quoted by Kammer, Jack, *If Men Have All the Power, How Come Women Make the Rules?* (2nd Edition, Jack Kammer, 2002) p.106.
[360] Popenoe, David, *Life Without Father: Compelling new evidence that fatherhood and marriage are indispensable for the good of children and society* (New York: Martin Kessler Books/The Free Press, 1996) p.197.
[361] Baskerville, Stephen, *Taken Into Custody: The War Against Fathers, Marriage, and the Family* (Nashville, TN: Cumberland House Publishing, Inc., 2007) p.12.
[362] Sommers, Christina Hoff, *The War Against Boys: How Misguided Feminism Is Harming Our Young Men* (New York: Simon & Schuster, 2000) pp.129-130.
[363] Farrell, Warren, Ph.D., *Father and Child Reunion: How to Bring the Dads We Need to the Children We Love* (New York: Penguin Putnam Inc., 2001) p.36.
[364] "Mackenzie v. Miller Brewing Co.," http://www.courttv.com/archive/casefiles/verdicts/mackenzie.html, July 1997.
[365] Parloff, Roger, "Sued If You Do, Sued If You Don't," Manhattan Institute For Policy Research, 09/1997. http://www.manhattan-institute.org/html/_amerlawyer-sued_if_you_do.htm
[366] Spivak, Cary and Bice, Dan, truthinjustice.org, JS Online, *Milwaukee Journal Sentinel*, 06/07/03.
[367] Roiphe, Katie, *The Morning After: Sex, Fear, and Feminism* (New York: Little, Brown and Company, 1993) p.87.
[368] Fillion, Kate, *Lip Service: The Truth About Women's Darker Side in Love Sex, and Friendship* (Toronto Canada: HarperCollins, 1996) p.85.
[369] Roiphe, Katie, *The Morning After: Sex, Fear, and Feminism* (New York: Little, Brown and Company, 1993) pp.89-90.
[370] Patai, Daphne, *Heterophobia: Sexual Harassment and the Future of Feminism* (New York: Rowman & Littlefield Publishers, Inc., 1998) p.159.
[371] Paglia, Camille, *Vamps & Tramps* (New York: Vintage, 1994) p..49.
[372] Patai, Daphne, *Heterophobia: Sexual Harassment and the Future of Feminism* (New York: Rowman & Littlefield Publishers, Inc., 1998) pp.163-164 & 165.
[373] Ibid, p.166.
[374] Kammer, Jack, *Good Will Toward Men: Women Talk Candidly About the Balance of Power Between the Sexes* (New York: St. Martin's Press, 1994) p.29.
[375] James, Thomas B., *Domestic Violence: The 12 Things You Aren't Supposed to Know* (Chula Vista, CA: Aventine Press, 2003) p..86.
[376] Farrell, Warren, Ph.D., *Women Can't Hear What Men Don't Say: Destroying Myths, Creating Love* (New York: Tarcher/Putnam, 1999) p.241.
[377] Roberts, Carey, "The Legacy of Michael Nifong," July 25, 2007, http://www.theconservativevoice.com/article/26874.html
[378] *Stuff magazine*, August 2000, p.110.
[379] Paglia, Camille, *Vamps & Tramps* (New York: Vintage, 1994) p.48.
[380] Kammer, Jack, *Good Will Toward Men: Women Talk Candidly About the Balance of Power Between the Sexes* (New York: St. Martin's Press, 1994) p.45.
[381] Friday, Nancy, *The Power Of Beauty: A Cultural Memoir of Beauty and Desire* (New York: HarperCollins, 1996) p.256.

[382] Young, Cathy, *Ceasefire!: Why Women and Men Must Join Forces to Achieve True Equality* (New York: The Free Press, 1999) p.193.
[383] Wallechinsky, David, and Wallace, Irving, *The People's Almanac* (New York: Doubleday & Company, Inc., 1975) p.321.
[384] Fillion, Kate, *Lip Service: The Truth About Women's Darker Side in Love Sex, and Friendship* (Toronto Canada: HarperCollins, 1996) p.87.
[385] Ibid., p.119.
[386] Ibid., pp.104 & 118.
[387] Ibid., p.120.
[388] Ibid., p.126.
[389] Burns, David D. M.D., *Intimate Connections: The Clinically Proven Program for Making Close Friends and Finding a Loving Partner* (New York: Signet/Penguin, 1985) p.Xvi.
[390] Friday, Nancy, *The Power Of Beauty: A Cultural Memoir of Beauty and Desire* (New York: HarperCollins, 1996) p.264.
[391] Farrell, Warren, Ph.D., *Why Men Are the Way They Are: The Male-Female Dynamic* (New York: Berkley Books, 1986) p.83.
[392] Moir, Anne and Jessel, David, *Brain Sex: The Real Difference Between Men and Women* (New York: Carol Publishing Group, 1991) p.106. "Two magazines designed primarily for a female readership conducted an intriguing survey, after featuring nude, male centerfolds. *Playgirl* and *Viva* discovered that their women readers were not particularly interested in the centerfold. *Viva* dropped the feature. *Playgirl* continued it, its readership including a high proportion of homosexual men."
[393] Califia, Pat, "Dildo Envy and Other Phallic Adventures," an essay in Giles, Fiona (editor), *Dick For a Day: What Would You Do If You Had One?* (New York: Villard, 1997) p.97.
[394] Ellis, Thomas, *The Rantings of a Single Male: Losing Patience with Feminism, Political Correctness... and Basically Everything* (Austin, TX: Rannenberg Publishing, 2005) p.8.
[395] Park, Ken, *The World Almanac* (World Almanac, 2006) p.272.
[396] Quoted off the cover of the September 1984 issue of *Cosmopolitan*.
[397] Farrell, Warren, Ph.D., *Why Men Are the Way They Are: The Male-Female Dynamic* (New York: Berkley Books, 1986) p.13.
[398] Kammer, Jack, *If Men Have All the Power, How Come Women Make the Rules?* (2nd Edition, Jack Kammer, 2002) p.120.
[399] Maxim Online, retrieved April 2005.
[400] Batten, Mary, *Sexual Strategies: How Females Choose Their Mates* (New York: Tarcher/Putnam, 1992) p.4.
[401] Buss, David M., *The Evolution of Desire: Strategies of Human Mating* (Revised Edition 4, Basic Books, 2003) p.201.
[402] Baumeister, Roy F., *Is There Anything Good About Men?: How Cultures Flourish By Exploiting Men* (New York: Oxford University Press, Inc., 2010) p.63-64.
[403] See http://www.sciencedaily.com/releases/2004/09/040920063537.htm
[404] Roiphe, Katie, *Last Night in Paradise: Sex and Morals at the Century's End* (New York: Little, Brown and Company, 1997) p.77.
[405] Rhoads, Steven E., *Taking Sex Differences Seriously* (San Francisco: Encounter Books, 2004) p.64.
[406] "Wealthy men give women more orgasms," *The Sunday Times*, January 18, 2009, http://www.timesonline.co.uk/tol/news/uk/science/article5537017.ece, "Scientists have found that the pleasure women get from making love is directly linked to the size of their partner's bank balance."

[407] Ibid.

[408] See, for example, http://en.wikipedia.org/wiki/Natalie_Dylan
A recent women's studies graduate from Sacramento State, Dylan planned to use the money to finance a Master's degree in family and marriage therapy. Dylan was inspired by her sister Avia, 23, who financed her own degree course working as a prostitute in the Moonlite Bunnyranch for just three weeks . . . Dylan retained the right to choose the winner of the auction regardless of who is the highest bidder. . . . With the increasing interest, the highest bid had reached, as of January 15, 2009, $3.7 million . . . In late October 2009, she said that she would sell her virginity "in the next few days" to a single American man for $1,000,000. She also said she had a book deal and a movie coming up.

[409] Sewell, Joan, *I'd Rather Eat Chocolate: Learning to Love My Low Libido* (New York: Broadway Books, 2007) p.110. Quoting Dr. Jamie Turndorf, aka, "Dr. Love."

[410] Bonaventura, Dr. Michael, *Why Can't a Woman Be More Like a Man? – A Woman's Guide to Revitalizing Her Natural Sex Drive* (Texas: Summit Arlington, 1995)

[411] Brizendine, Louann, "Love, sex and the male brain," Special to CNN, March 25, 2010, http://www.cnn.com/2010/OPINION/03/23/brizendine.male.brain/index.html?iref=allsearch

[412] *Newsweek*, May 29, 2000, p.53.

[413] Sewell, Joan, *I'd Rather Eat Chocolate: Learning to Love My Low Libido* (New York: Broadway Books, 2007) p.115.

[414] Ibid., p.116.

[415] Ibid., p.200.

[416] Michael, Robert T., Gagnon, John H., Laumann, Edward O., and Kolata, Gina, *Sex in America: A Definitive Survey* (New York: Warner Books, 1994), p.145.

[417] Ibid., p.148.

[418] *MAXIM* magazine, November 2001, p.126.

[419] Actress Shannon Elizabeth, *Maxim* magazine, January, 2000.

[420] Rudder, Christian, "Your Looks and Your Inbox," November 17, 2009 http://blog.okcupid.com/index.php/your-looks-and-online-dating/

[421] Bullough, Bonnie, R.N., Ph.D., Bullough, Vern L., R.N., Ph.D., Fithian, Marilyn A., Ph.D., Hartman, William E., Ph.D., & Klein, Randy Sue, Ph.D., *Personal Stories of "How I Got Into Sex"*: Leading Researchers, Sex Therapists, Educators, Prostitutes, Sex Toy Designers, Sex Surrogates, Transsexuals, Criminologists, Clery, and more . . . (Amherst, NY: Prometheus Books, 1997) Griffin, Garry, quoted from his essay, "Penis Power," pp.194-5.

[422] Friday, Nancy, *The Power Of Beauty: A Cultural Memoir of Beauty and Desire* (New York: HarperCollins, 1996) p.270.

[423] Janus, Samuel S., and Janus Cynthia L., *The Janus Report on Sexual Behavior* (New York: John Wiley & Sons, Inc., 1993) p.94.

[424] *Chicago Sun-Times*, February 10, 1999, p.2.

[425] Michael, Robert T., Gagnon, John H., Laumann, Edward O., and Kolata, Gina, *Sex in America: A Definitive Survey* (New York: Warner Books, 1994), p.126.

[426] Bourret, Caprice, *British Maxim*, January 2002, p.130.

[427] Paglia, Camille, "No Law in the Arena," *Vamps & Tramps* (New York: Vintage, 1994) p.35.

[428] Ibid., pp.30-31, 35.

[429] Batten, Mary, *Sexual Strategies: How Females Choose Their Mates* (New York: Tarcher/Putnam, 1992) p.22.

430 Strossen, Nadine, *Defending Pornography: Free Speech, Sex, and the Fight for Women's Rights* (New York: New York University Press, 2000) p.151.
431 Friday, Nancy, *The Power Of Beauty: A Cultural Memoir of Beauty and Desire* (New York: HarperCollins, 1996) p.179.
432 Michael, Robert T., Gagnon, John H., Laumann, Edward O., and Kolata, Gina, *Sex in America: A Definitive Survey* (New York: Warner Books, 1994) p.100
433 Ibid., p.96.
434 Ibid., p.105.
435 Decter Midge, *The New Chastity* (New York: A Berkley Medallion Book/Berkley Publishing Corporation, 1973) p.92.
436 Friday, Nancy, *The Power Of Beauty: A Cultural Memoir of Beauty and Desire* (New York: HarperCollins, 1996) p.323.
437 Moir, Anne and Jessel, David, *Brain Sex: The Real Difference Between Men and Women* (New York: Carol Publishing Group, 1991) p.107-108.
438 Michael, Robert T., Gagnon, John H., Laumann, Edward O., and Kolata, Gina, *Sex in America: A Definitive Survey* (New York: Warner Books, 1994) pp.106, 114.
439 Kornheiser, Tony, "Someone Save My Life Tonight," *Washington Post*, December 28, 1997. http://www.highbeam.com/doc/1P2-754822.html,
440 Michael, Robert T., Gagnon, John H., Laumann, Edward O., and Kolata, Gina, *Sex in America: A Definitive Survey* (New York: Warner Books, 1994) p.119.
441 Ibid., pp.88-9.
442 Moxon, Steve, *The Woman Racket: The new science explaining how the sexes relate at work, at play and in society* (Charlottesville, VA: Imprint Academic Philosophy Documentation Center, 2008) p.51.
443 Ibid., p.54.
444 Michael, Robert T., Gagnon, John H., Laumann, Edward O., and Kolata, Gina, *Sex in America: A Definitive Survey* (New York: Warner Books, 1994) p.114.
445 Sewell, Joan, *I'd Rather Eat Chocolate: Learning to Love My Low Libido* (New York: Broadway Books, 2007) pp.113-4.
446 Buss, David M., *The Evolution of Desire: Strategies of Human Mating* (Revised Edition 4, Basic Books, 2003) p.187.
447 Full quote: "The pressures of sexual frustration in this life and the lure sexual as well as spiritual rewards in the next are exploited as part of a cynical spiel by jihadist recruiters looking for boys and men to be suicide bombers. Hizbullah in Lebanon, Hamas and Islamic jihad among the Palestinians, and the various incarnations of Al Qaeda have all played on Muslim teaching that promise 72 houris—virginal beings with black eyes and alabaster skin—to attend the martyr's desires in paradise." *Newsweek*, December 12, 2005, p. 31.
448 Ibid., p.34.
449 Vilar, Esther, *The Manipulated Man* (N.Y.: Farrar, Straus and Giroux, 1972) p.25.
450 Allen, Marvin, *In the Company of Men: A New Approach to Healing for Husbands, Fathers, and Friends* (New York: Random House, 1993) pp.97-98.
451 Smoron, Paige, "Planet Paige," "Private life best kept private", "Chat Room," "Showcase," *Chicago Sun-Times*, September 13, 2000, p.65.
452 Ibid., p.65.
453 Goldberg, Herb, *What Men Really Want* (NY: Signet/Penguin, 1991) p.13.
454 Dubner, Stephen J. and Levitt, Steven D., "Monkey Business," *New York Times Magazine*, June 05, 2005.
455 Wadhams, Nick, "Chimps Trade Meat for Sex -- And It Works," http://news.nationalgeographic.com/news/2009/04/090407-chimps-meat-sex.html, April 7, 2009

[456] Moore, John H., *But What About Men?: After Women's Lib* (Bath: Ashgrove Press, 1989) p.5.
[457] Paglia, Camille, *Sex, Art, and American Culture* (NY: Vintage, 1992) p.66.
[458] U.S. Department of Justice: Office of Justice Programs: Bureau of Justice Statistics, 2007, http://www.ojp.usdoj.gov/bjs/prisons.htm
[459] *People magazine*, May 08, 2006, p.180.
[460] Garcia, Guy, *The Decline of Men: How the American Male Is Getting Axed, Giving up, and Flipping Off His Future* (New York: Harper Perennial, 2009) p78.
[461] Bax, E. Balfort, *The Fraud of Feminism* (Grant Richards Ltd., 1913) p.1.
[462] Tyre, Peg, "Struggling School-Age Boys: A new study says parents are right to worry about their sons," *Newsweek*, September 08, 2008. http://www.newsweek.com/id/157898?GT1=43002
[463] The American Experience: The Donner Party, WGBG Educational Foundation, WNET/Thirteen and Steeplechase Films, (1992), Directed by Ric Burns, PBS Paramount, DVD video. Note: When I saw this Ric Burns documentary on TV, it was presented as an episode of *The American Experience*. As such, short sequences hosted by David McCullough were filmed to introduce the documentary and integrate it into the series. These added sequences increased the number of references to women characterized as strong survivors as compared to the weak dying men. These inserts are not included in the DVD version cited above.
[464] Stewart, George R., *Ordeal By Hunger: The Classic Story of the Donner Party* (New York: Pocket Book edition, 1971)
[465] Ibid., pp.8-9.
[466] Ibid., p.26.
[467] Ibid., p.29.
[468] Ibid., p.67.
[469] Ibid., p.77.
[470] Ibid., p.59.
[471] Ibid., p.61.
[472] Unsolved History: Donner Party. Produced by Termite Productions for the Discovery Channel, Discovery Communications, Inc., 2003.
[473] Ibid., Pottgen, Paul, a representative from LifeCheck Corp.
[474] See, http://www.theabsolute.net/misogyny/vilar.html.
[475] Braver, Sanford L., Ph.D., with O'Connell, Diane, *Divorced Dads: Shattering the Myths* (New York: Tarcher/Putnam, 1998) p.55.
[476] Ibid.
[477] Ibid., p.58.
[478] Ibid., p.62.
[479] Ibid., pp.84-85.
[480] Ibid., pp.111-119.
[481] Walker, Bruce, "Deadbeat Dads? Look Closer!" *Christian Science Monitor*, August 16, 1996, p.18.
[482] Braver, Sanford L., Ph.D., with O'Connell, Diane, *Divorced Dads: Shattering the Myths* (New York: Tarcher/Putnam, 1998) p.102.
[483] Ibid., p.101.
[484] Ibid., p.103.
[485] Ibid., p.94.
[486] See, http://www.theabsolute.net/misogyny/vilar.html.
[487] http://en.wikipedia.org/wiki/Marlboro_Man (retrieved 06/17/10)
[488] Blyth, Myrna, *Spin Sisters: How the Women of the Media Sell Unhappiness and Liberalism to the Women of America* (New York: St. Martin's Press, 2004) p.48.

[489] Young, Cathy, *Ceasefire!: Why Women and Men Must Join Forces to Achieve True Equality* (New York: The Free Press, 1999) p.62.
[490] Patai, Daphne & Koertge, Noretta, *Professing Feminism: Education and Indoctrination in Women's Studies* Lnham (Maryland: Lexington Books, 2003) p.97.
[491] Canfield, Jack, *The Success Principles: How to Get from Where You Are to Where You Want to Be* (NY: HarperCollins/First Collins paperback edition, 2005) p.3.
[492] Ibid.
[493] Patai, Daphne & Koertge, Noretta, *Professing Feminism: Education and Indoctrination in Women's Studies* Lnham (Maryland: Lexington Books, 2003) p.97.
[494] Blyth, Myrna, *Spin Sisters: How the Women of the Media Sell Unhappiness and Liberalism to the Women of America* (New York: St. Martin's Press, 2004) p.49.
[495] Male Matters, http://battlinbog.blog-city.com/
[496] Jones, Adam, (editor) *Gendercide and Genocide* (Nashville, TN: Vanderbilt University Press, 2004) p.107.
[497] Ibid.
[498] Ibid.
[499] Ibid., p.109.
[500] Ibid., pp.111-2.
[501] Ibid., p.121.
[502] Ibid., p.122.
[503] Moxon, Steve, *The Woman Racket: The new science explaining how the sexes relate at work, at play and in society* (Charlottesville, VA: Imprint Academic Philosophy Documentation Center, 2008) p.226.
[504] O'Neill, Brendan, "The myth of trafficking," http://www.newstatesman.com/200803270046, March 27, 2008.
[505] Rende Taylor, Lisa, *Science News*, September 24, 2005, Vol. 168, p.200.
[506] Ibid., p.201.
[507] Moxon, Steve, *The Woman Racket: The new science explaining how the sexes relate at work, at play and in society* (Charlottesville, VA: Imprint Academic Philosophy Documentation Center, 2008) p.227.
[508] Kipnis, Aaron, *Angry Young Men: How Parents, Teachers, and Counselors Can Help "Bad Boys" Become Good Men* (San Francisco, CA: Jossey-Bass, 1999) pp.74-5.
[509] Roberts, Carey, "Half-Truths About Human Trafficking," ifeminists.net, 07/11/06.
[510] Moxon, Steve, *The Woman Racket: The new science explaining how the sexes relate at work, at play and in society* (Charlottesville, VA: Imprint Academic Philosophy Documentation Center, 2008) p.216.
[511] Ali, Lorraine, *Newsweek*, December 12, 2005, p.33.
[512] Ibid., p. 33.
[513] "The inexorable slaughter of Chinese miners: An overview," February 02, 2005, http://www.asianews.it/view_p.php?l=en&art=2652
[514] See, Kang Yi, "Some human traffickers may walk away in 'slave' case," June 15, 2007, www.chinadaily.com.cn/china/2007-06/15/content_895414.htm. "'Those traffickers who lure migrant workers, mainly adult males, to do forced labor will not be convicted as the criminal code only covers those who traffic women and children,' Guan Zhongzhi, a lawyer with Zhonghuan Law Firm told chinadaily.com.cn. The legal loophole has put male victims in an awkward position when fighting against their traffickers in the court of law."
[515] Bower, Bruce, "Mom can increase her child's risk of depression via nurture alone," *Science News*, October 11, 2008, p.9.

[516] Solzhenitsyn, Alexander, *The Gulag Archipelago: 1918 – 1956* (Harper Perennial Modern Classics, 2002) p.75.
[517] Fillion, Kate, *Lip Service: The Truth About Women's Darker Side in Love Sex, and Friendship* (Toronto Canada: HarperCollins, 1996) p.xii.
[518] Pearson, Patricia, *When She Was Bad: How and Why Women Get Away with Murder* (New York: Penguin Books, 1998) p.7.
[519] Schechter, Harold, *Fatal: The Poisonous Life of a Female Serial Killer* (New York: Pocket Books/Simon & Schuster, Inc., 2003) p.xi.
[520] Ibid., p.xii.
[521] Vronsky, Peter, *Female Serial Killers: How and Why Women Become Monsters* (New York: Berkley Books, 2007) p.6.
[522] Stein, Harry, *One of the Guys: The Wising Up of an American Man* (New York: Pocket Books, 1988) p.42.
[523] Baumeister, Roy F., "Is There Anything Good About Men?," http://denisdutton.com/baumeister.htm
[524] http://online.wsj.com/article/SB10001424052748703779704576073752925629440.html, Skenazy, Lenore, "Eek! A Male!:Treating all men as potential predators doesn't make our kids safer," January 12, 2011

> Last week, the lieutenant governor of Massachusetts, Timothy Murray, noticed smoke coming out of a minivan in his hometown of Worcester. He raced over and pulled out two small children, moments before the van's tire exploded into flames. At which point, according to the AP account, the kids' grandmother, who had been driving, nearly punched our hero in the face. Why? Mr. Murray said she told him she thought he might be a kidnapper. And so it goes these days, when almost any man who has anything to do with a child can find himself suspected of being a creep. I call it "Worst-First" thinking: Gripped by pedophile panic, we jump to the very worst, even least likely, conclusion first.

[525] Moir, Anne and Jessel, David, *Brain Sex: The Real Difference Between Men and Women* (New York: Carol Publishing Group, 1991) p.5.
[526] Sewell, Joan, *I'd Rather Eat Chocolate: Learning to Love My Low Libido* (New York: Broadway Books, 2007) p.115.
[527] Rhoads, Steven E., *Taking Sex Differences Seriously* (San Francisco: Encounter Books, 2004) p.20.
[528] From a handout given to students at a local high school on "Gender Awareness Day," November 21, 2003.
[529] Larry Summers' speech may be read in its entirety at: http://www.president.harvard.edu/speeches/2005/nber.html
[530] Bombardieri, Marcella, "Summers' remarks on women draw fire," *Boston Globe*, January 17, 2005, http://www.boston.com/news/local/articles/2005/01/17/summers_remarks_on_women_draw_fire/
[531] Baumeister, Roy F., *Is There Anything Good About Men?: How Cultures Flourish By Exploiting Men* (New York: Oxford University Press, Inc., 2010) p.32. In addition to measures of intelligence, "Whether we are talking about kindness versus cruelty, curiosity versus closed-mindedness, wisdom versus immature pigheadedness, self-control versus self-indulgence, or humility versus narcissism, there are more men than women at both the good and the bad extremes." (p.33.)
[532] Batten, Mary, *Sexual Strategies: How Females Choose Their Mates* (New York: Tarcher/Putnam, 1992) p.22. Quoting evolutionary anthropologist John Hartung.
[533] Moir, Anne and Jessel, David, *Brain Sex: The Real Difference Between Men and Women* (New York: Carol Publishing Group, 1991) p.11.
[534] Ibid., p.16.

[535] Ibid., pp.42-48.
[536] Ibid., p.93.
[537] Ibid., pp.11-12.
[538] See Parker, Kathleen, "You can't say that – ever," September 23, 2007, http://www.detnews.com/apps/pbcs.dll/article?AID=/20070923/OPINION03/709230315
[539] Ibid.
[540] *Newsweek*, August 1993.
[541] *Chicago Tribune* Magazine, March 28, 1999.
[542] Borge, Caroline, "The Science of Evil," *ABC News* Primetime, http://abcnews.go.com/Primetime/story?id=2765416&page=1, 01/03/07.
[543] Mead, Dr. Margaret, quoted by Goldberg, Herb in *The New Male-Female Relationship* (Coventure, London, 1984), p.126.
[544] Goodman, Ellen, "*Tender Terrorists?*" *Boston Globe*, September 23, 2004.
[545] http://www.sciencedaily.com/releases/2011/02/110216132042.htm "To Escape Blame, Be a Victim, Not a Hero, New Study Finds," February 16, 2011. See also, Kurt Gray, Daniel M. Wegner, "To escape blame, don't be a hero -- Be a victim," *Journal of Experimental Social Psychology*, 2010; DOI: 10.1016/j.jesp.2010.12.012
[546] Pearson, Patricia, *When She Was Bad: How and Why Women Get Away with Murder* (New York: Penguin Books, 1998) p.21.
[547] http://womenshistory.about.com/od/quotes/a/camille_paglia_2.htm
[548] Vilar, Esther, *The Manipulated Man* (New York: Farrar, Straus and Giroux, 1972) p.52.
[549] Pearson, Patricia, *When She Was Bad: How and Why Women Get Away with Murder* (New York: Penguin Books, 1998) p.16.
[550] Driscoll, Richard, Ph.D., *The Stronger Sex: Understanding and Resolving the Eternal Power Struggles Between Men and Women* (Rocklin, CA: Prima Publishing, 1998) p.21.
[551] Kranichfeld, Marion L., "Rethinking Family Power," *Journal of Family Issues*, Vol. 8 no. 1, March 1987, pp.42-56 ©1987 Sage Publications, Inc.
[552] Ibid.
[553] Kammer, Jack, *If Men Have All the Power, How Come Women Make the Rules?* (2nd Edition, Jack Kammer, 2002) p.29.
[554] Goldberg, Herb, *What Men Really Want* (New York: Signet/Penguin, 1991) pp.106-107.
[555] *Perfect 10 Magazine*, Spring 2001, pp.36-37.
[556] Johnson, Robert A., "Male and Masculine: An Interview with Robert A Johnson" interview with Bert Hoff, *Men's Voices: A Quarterly Journal*, Vol 1 #3, Summer/Fall '98, The WhiteRock Alternative, Seattle, WA, p.23.
[557] Garcia, Guy, *The Decline of Men: How the American Male Is Getting Axed, Giving up, and Flipping Off His Future* (New York: Harper Perennial, 2009) p.222.
[558] Schlafly, Phyllis, *The Power of the Positive Woman* (New York: Arlington House, 1977) p.56.
[559] Campbell, Marjorie, "Managing Men," InsideCatholic.com, October 02, 2009, http://insidecatholic.com/Joomla/index.php?option=com_content&task=view&id=6972&Itemid=48.
[560] Ibid.
[561] Ibid.
[562] Stein, Harry, *One of the Guys: The Wising Up of an American Man* (New York: Pocket Books, 1988) p.243.

563 Driscoll, Richard, Ph.D., *The Stronger Sex: Understanding and Resolving the Eternal Power Struggles Between Men and Women* (Rocklin, CA: Prima Publishing, 1998) p.9.
564 Ibid., p.9.
565 Patai, Daphne, *Heterophobia: Sexual Harassment and the Future of Feminism* (New York: Rowman & Littlefield Publishers, Inc., 1998) pp.8-9.
566 Baumli, Francis, Ph.D., (editor), *Men Freeing Men: Exploding the Myth of the Traditional Male* (Jersey City, NJ: New Atlantis Press, 1985) p.81.
567 *Science News,* inside front cover, January 31, 2009.
568 Gray, John, Ph.D., *Mars and Venus on a Date: A Guide for Navigating the 5 Stages of Dating to Create a Loving and Lasting Relationship* (New York: HarperCollins, 1997) pp.121-3.
569 Braver, Sanford L., Ph.D., with O'Connell, Diane, *Divorced Dads: Shattering the Myths* (New York: Tarcher/Putnam, 1998) p.140. Source of quotes: *Los Angeles Times*, February 1998. See also, Gottman, J. M., Coan, J., Carrere, S., and Swanson, C. 1998. "Predicting marital happiness and stability from newlywed interactions," *Journal of Marriage and the Family* 60:5-22.
570 Sewell, Joan, *I'd Rather Eat Chocolate: Learning to Love My Low Libido* (New York: Broadway Books, 2007) pp.92-3.
571 Ibid., p.127.
572 Ibid., pp.129-30.
573 Ibid., p.130.
574 Moir, Anne and Jessel, David, *Brain Sex: The Real Difference Between Men and Women* (New York: Carol Publishing Group, 1991) p.110.
575 Sewell, Joan, *I'd Rather Eat Chocolate: Learning to Love My Low Libido* (New York: Broadway Books, 2007) p.131
576 Ibid.
577 Kipnis, Laura, *Bound and Gagged: Pornography and the Politics of Fantasy in America* (Durham, NC: Duke University Press, 1999) p.xi.
578 Sewell, Joan, *I'd Rather Eat Chocolate: Learning to Love My Low Libido* (New York: Broadway Books, 2007) p.135.
579 Ibid., p.111.
580 Strossen, Nadine, *Defending Pornography: Free Speech, Sex, and the Fight for Women's Rights* (New York: New York University Press, 2000) p.108.
581 Braver, Sanford L., Ph.D., with O'Connell, Diane, *Divorced Dads: Shattering the Myths* (New York: Tarcher/Putnam, 1998) p.113.
582 Ibid., p.115.
583 Hicks, Michael, "The Thing About Women," McCook Daily Gazette, http://www.mccookgazette.com/story/1181593.html, December 16, 2006.
584 Stein, Harry, *One of the Guys: The Wising Up of an American Man* (New York: Pocket Books, 1988) p.248. "There it was in cold black-and-white: of 2,301 married men polled, fully 77 percent said that if given the chance, they would again marry the same woman. What made the numbers especially revealing was that they stood in such marked contrast to those on a survey that had appeared just a month earlier in *Woman's Day*. Asked the same question, merely half of married women polled said they would choose to marry the same man."
585 Dr. Louann Brizendine, "Love, sex and the male brain," CNN, March 25, 2010, http://www.cnn.com/2010/OPINION/03/23/brizendine.male.brain/index.html?iref=allsearch]
586 Sewell, Joan, *I'd Rather Eat Chocolate: Learning to Love My Low Libido* (New York: Broadway Books, 2007) p.134.

587 Ibid., p.118.
588 Ibid., p.118.
589 Young, Cathy, *Ceasefire!: Why Women and Men Must Join Forces to Achieve True Equality* (New York: The Free Press, 1999) p.11.
590 http://www.themercury.com.au/article/2010/01/18/122301_travel.html, "Man sues over seating policy," Daily Telegraph, January 18, 2010, "In line with the policy, BA cabin crew patrol the aisles before take-off to check that youngsters travelling on their own or in a different row from their parents are not seated next to a male stranger. If they find a man next to a child or teenager they will ask older person to move, and the aircraft will not take off unless the passenger obeys." See also, "Airlines in hot seat over child policies," by Andrew Clark, *The Sydney Morning Herald*, smh.com.au, November 30, 2005. "Other airlines contacted by the *Herald* said they had similar guidelines."
591 Sewell, Joan, *I'd Rather Eat Chocolate: Learning to Love My Low Libido* (New York: Broadway Books, 2007) p.138.
592 Ibid., pp.134-35.
593 Driscoll, Richard, Ph.D., *The Stronger Sex: Understanding and Resolving the Eternal Power Struggles Between Men and Women* (Rocklin, CA: Prima Publishing, 1998) p8.
594 Sewell, Joan, *I'd Rather Eat Chocolate: Learning to Love My Low Libido* (New York: Broadway Books, 2007) p.67.
595 Ibid., p.183.
596 Ibid., p.32.
I'm seemingly alone in thinking that doing the dishes does not constitute foreplay. Around here, it's Kip, not me, who is the clean, tidy, organized one. I'm Oscar to his Felix. But watching him cleaning the house, doing the dishes, and paying the bills does not make me one bit hornier. Not a bit.
597 See, for example, http://www.actualcures.com/most-common-causes-of-death-degenerative-disease/
598 McNeil, Liz, http://www.people.com/people/article/0,,20349693,00.html, "Tiger Woods's College Girlfriend: He Deserves Another Chance," March 09, 2010,
By [Irene] Folstrom's account, Woods was anything but a ladies' man back in college. "He definitely was a dork," she recalls with a laugh. "He was kinda scrawny and wore thick glasses. He didn't really have a lot of female attention."
599 Bernstein, Jacob, "The Mysterious Mrs. Woods," http://www.thedailybeast.com/blogs-and-stories/2009-11-30/the-mysterious-mrs-woods/2/, retrieved 03/30/10):
At first, Nordegren was reportedly uninterested in Woods. As Mia Parnevik later noted, her thoroughly competent nanny displayed no interest whatsoever in the sport. She also had hopes of becoming a child psychiatrist and was concerned about appearing to be a "gold-digger." Further, the famously awkward Woods did not make a smooth approach. According to a close friend of the Parneviks who spoke to SI, Woods was so nervous about asking her out, he had a friend do it for him. "Her reaction was, 'What the hell was that?'" the magazine quotes a close source as saying. "She thought it was so weird and pathetic. Of course she said no." But Woods persisted, flooding the Parneviks with calls, and she relented.
600 http://en.wikipedia.org/wiki/Elin_Nordegren (retrieved 03/30/10)
Nordegren took a job in a Stockholm clothing store called Champagne, where she met Mia Parnevik, wife of Swedish golfer Jesper Parnevik, who hired Nordegren as the nanny to their children, a job that required her to move to the U.S. He introduced her to Woods during the 2001 British Open. Previously, Woods had asked for a year to be introduced to Nordegren, who was seeing someone else at

the time. "There was a big line of single golfers wanting to meet her. They were gaga over her."

601 Folstrom, Irene, "Tiger's college girlfriend speaks," March 3, 2010, http://www.golf.com/golf/tours_news/article/0,28136,1968826,00.html?xid=cnnbin&hpt=Sbin

Like everyone else, I was shocked by the revelations about his infidelities. The Tiger I knew was loyal, devoted and self-controlled. I'm not naive, but I can say with certainty that he was faithful during the time we dated. The speculation that he's being treated for sex addiction is surprising because we enjoyed a normal sexual relationship.

602 http://www.cbsnews.com/stories/2010/08/24/earlyshow/leisure/celebspot/main6800493.shtml, August 24, 2010

Celebrity divorce attorney Raoul Felder remarked on "The Early Show" Tuesday that Woods was in "Desperateville" when he was making deals with Nordegren's lawyers. "He probably overpaid," Felder said. "I would judge (the amount Woods agreed to hand over at) anywhere from $100 million to almost $500 million."

603 http://www.aolnews.com/2010/06/30/tiger-woods-elin-nordegren-divorce-reportedly-final/, June 30, 2010 "Nordegren will get complete custody of their children (3-year old daughter Sam and 1-year old son Charlie)."

604 http://www.people.com/people/article/0,,20414961,00.html, August 23, 2010, "Sources have said that the split and continuing news have taken an emotional toll on the former sports model, and that she may move back to her native Sweden in upcoming months."

605 Bernstein, Jacob, "The Mysterious Mrs. Woods," http://www.thedailybeast.com/blogs-and-stories/2009-11-30/the-mysterious-mrs-woods/2/, retrieved 03/30/10): Elin "had hopes of becoming a child psychiatrist and was concerned about appearing to be a 'gold-digger.'"

606 http://sports.espn.go.com/golf/news/story?id=4990305, "Woods ambulance crew had concerns," Associated Press, March 13, 2010. "The ambulance crew that responded after Tiger Woods crashed his SUV would not allow his wife to ride with him to the hospital because they suspected domestic violence, documents released Friday by the Florida Highway Patrol show."

607 Franklin, Robert, Esq., http://glennsacks.com/blog/?p=4467, "Swedish Women Call Elin Nordgren their 'Heroine,'" December 23, 2009.

Well, according to this piece, women in Sweden (Nordgren's home country) couldn't be prouder of their Elin (*Washington City Paper*, 12/15/09). It quotes several female journalists and commentators as follows: "Swing it again, Elin!" wrote Jan Helin, editor in chief of Aftonbladet, the country's biggest newspaper, on his personal blog. One of the paper's top reporters, Ann Söderlund, proclaimed, "Thank God for girls like Elin. Next time, I hope she uses a bigger club." Britta Svensson, a well-known columnist at the tabloid Expressen and a former U.S.-based correspondent, commented, "Our Swedish hearts are overwhelmed with pride, because our very own Elin didn't take any s—. Just like a tough Swedish girl shouldn't. Elin is our heroine."

608 Young Cathy, http://reason.com/archives/2009/12/04/tiger-woods-and-domestic-viole, "What the Tiger Woods controversy says about the state of gender politics," December 04, 2009.

Whether or not the assault actually took place, the truly remarkable thing is that some voices in the feminist corner of the media have rushed either to defend it or to excuse it. The *Daily Beast* website ran a piece by culture correspondent Rebecca Dana under the title "The Year of Women Fighting Back," asserting that if Elin Nordegren did attack her cheating husband with a golf club, she belongs in the company of other scorned or betrayed women who have stood up to their no-good men. On Slate.com and its soon-to-fold female-oriented offshoot, *DoubleX*, journalist Hannah Rosin does not go quite so far as to cheer an alleged perpetrator. However, she speculates that Woods may have lied about the incident to spare his wife the arrest she would have faced under gender-neutral domestic violence laws—God forbid that "the glamorous Elin would be led out of their mansion in handcuffs"—and then proceeds to decry the absurdity of the gender-neutral approach. Rosin readily concedes that if the roles were reversed and the rumors were about Woods assaulting his wife, even over a possible infidelity, "we would be a lot less ambivalent and complacent"—and if his wife had tried to cover up for him, we would be appalled. But in her view, "all of these gender-dependent reactions make some instinctive sense." Yet one person's common sense is another's noxious cultural stereotype.

[609] Paglia, Camille, *Vamps & Tramps* (New York: Vintage, 1994) p.43 & 46.
[610] Vincent, Norah, *Self-Made Man: One Woman's Journey into Manhood and Back Again* (New York: Viking/Penguin, 2006) p.127.
[611] Driscoll, Richard, Ph.D., *The Stronger Sex: Understanding and Resolving the Eternal Power Struggles Between Men and Women* (Rocklin, CA: Prima Publishing, 1998) pp.10&13.
[612] John Lennon/Yoko Ono, Apple Records, 1972.
[613] Baird, Julia, *John Lennon, My Brother* (New York: Jove Books, 1988) p.13.
[614] Kammer, Jack, *Good Will Toward Men: Women Talk Candidly About the Balance of Power Between the Sexes* (New York: St. Martin's Press, 1994) p.216.
[615] Baird, Julia, *John Lennon, My Brother* (New York: Jove Books, 1988) p.6.
[616] Ibid., p.29.
[617] Ibid.
[618] Driscoll, Richard, Ph.D., *The Stronger Sex: Understanding and Resolving the Eternal Power Struggles Between Men and Women* (Rocklin, CA: Prima Publishing, 1998) p.8. "And female combativeness is not merely a product of our current era. Some of the early social sciences research conducted in the mid-1930s showed a similar pattern, with women typically dominating in arguments and men withdrawing."
[619] Vilar, Esther, *The Manipulated Man* (New York.: Farrar, Straus and Giroux, 1972) p.20.
[620] The Beatles, *The Beatles Anthology*, (San Francisco: Chronicle Books, 2000) p.7.
[621] Bunzel, John H. (editor), *Political Passages: Journeys of Change Through Two Decades, 1968-1988* (New York: The Free Press: A Division of Macmillan, Inc., 1988). Quoted from Carol Iannone's essay, "The Wide and Crooked Path," p.315.
[622] Angier, Natalie, *Woman: An Intimate Geography* (New York: Anchor Books/A Division of Random House, Inc., 2000) p.269.
[623] Stein, Harry, *One of the Guys: The Wising Up of an American Man* (New York: Pocket Books, 1988) p.231.
[624] Baird, Julia, *John Lennon, My Brother* (New York: Jove Books, 1988) p.29.
[625] Trunka, Paul, ed., *The Beatles: 10 Years that Shook the World*, (Darling Kindersley Ltd., 2004) p.391.
[626] Baird, Julia, *John Lennon, My Brother* (New York: Jove Books, 1988) pp. 115-116. Julia Baird recounts this story told by John's Aunt Harriet ("Harrie"):
John was a well-built man, but when Harrie saw him she became very concerned. "He was incredibly thin," she told me later. "He's a mere skeleton of the boy we all knew." Harrie was a great cook and her pièce de résistance was her Sunday

dinners. She decided to give John and Yoko the full works. She went out of her way to produce a traditional celebration dinner in their honor with roast leg of lamb, gravy, garden-grown mint sauce, roast potatoes and vegetables, and home-made apple pie with cream for pudding. Just as delicious smells from the oven were beginning to waft through the house, Yoko announced that she and John weren't eating "that sort of thing" anymore. They now ate only a macrobiotic diet, she said. Harrie watched most disapprovingly as Yoko started to prepare a macrobiotic meal with diced fresh vegetables which she then steamed in Tamari sauce and served up to John with a lilliputian portion of organic brown rice. "Chopping up carrots when all John needed inside him was a good meal," commented Harrie. Roast lamb had always been John's favorite and he must have been sorely tempted. But, as Harrie observed, he was so devoted to Yoko he would have made any sacrifice for her.

Was Yoko acting as John's culinary conscience, overruling his unhealthy eating habits for his own good? Perhaps not. From the Health Issues Download, the reader will recall Anne Moir offering scientific evidence that men have different dietary needs than women—including an extra need for red meat.

[627] Starr, Mark, "Girls Gone Wild," *Newsweek*, http://www.msnbc.msn.com/id/12979743/site/newsweek/, May 25, 2006, retrieved 10/20/06.
[628] Ibid.
[629] Ibid.
[630] Simmons, Rachel, *Odd Girl Out: The Hidden Culture of Aggression in Girls* (New York: Harcourt, Inc., 2002) p.3.
[631] Young, Cathy, *Ceasefire!: Why Women and Men Must Join Forces to Achieve True Equality* (New York: The Free Press, 1999) p.7.
[632] Ibid., p.7.
[633] Hite, Shere, *Women as Revolutionary Agents of Change* (University of Wisconsin Press, 1994) p.402.
[634] Friday, Nancy, *The Power Of Beauty: A Cultural Memoir of Beauty and Desire* (New York: HarperCollins, 1996) p.412.
[635] Sommers, Christina Hoff, *Who Stole Feminism?: How Women Have Betrayed Women* (New York: A Touchstone Book/Simon & Schuster, 1994) p.232.
[636] Ibid., p.45.
[637] Goldberg, Herb, *What Men Really Want* (N.Y.: Signet/Penguin, 1991) p.98.
[638] *Prevention magazine*, issue 47, 1995. "During the last 15 years the number of fatal accidents involving women drivers has increased dramatically while men's risks have dropped."
[639] Keller, Julia, *Tribune* cultural critic, February 25, 2002.
[640] Farrell, Warren, Ph.D., *Women Can't Hear What Men Don't Say: Destroying myths, creating love* (New York: Tarcher/Putnam, 1999) pp.152-3.
[641] Decter Midge, *The New Chastity* (New York: A Berkley Medallion Book/Berkley Publishing Corporation, 1973) pp.27-28.
[642] Kammer, Jack, *Good Will Toward Men: Women Talk Candidly About the Balance of Power Between the Sexes* (New York: St. Martin's Press, 1994) p.66.
[643] Winters, Marion, "One Canadian Woman's Personal Story," March 06, 2000, Equal Justice Foundation, www.ejfi.org
[644] Young, Cathy, *Ceasefire!: Why Women and Men Must Join Forces to Achieve True Equality* (New York: The Free Press, 1999) p.268.
[645] Schlafly, Phyllis, "Domestic violence law abuses rights of men," *The San Diego Union-Tribune*, 05/12/06, signonsandiego.com

[646] Roberts, Carey. "Senator Biden's VAWA cover-up," 08/26/08, http://www.renewamerica.us/columns/roberts/080826
[647] Biden's testimony occurred during Senate hearings on December 11, 1990.
[648] Ibid.
[649] Knowles, David, http://news.aol.com/political-machine/2009/01/12/ms-magazine-posits-obama-as-super-feminist/, January 12, 2009.
[650] Stephney, Bill, "Black Fatherhood In The Age Of Obama," 02/11/09, http://newsone.blackplanet.com/celebrate-44/black-fatherhood-in-the-age-of-obama/
[651] Feller, Ben, "Obama to fathers: Be involved in your kids' lives," *Columbia Daily Tribune,* June 19, 2009, http://hosted.ap.org/dynamic/stories/U/US_OBAMA_FATHERHOOD?SITE=MOCOD&SECTION=HOME&TEMPLATE=DEFAULT
[652] See: http://www.washingtontimes.com/news/2009/jun/21/obama-urges-men-to-be-better-dads-than-his-was/?feat=home_headlines, June 21, 2009
[653] Glenn Sacks quoted from: Garcia, Guy, *The Decline of Men: How the American Male Is Getting Axed, Giving up, and Flipping Off His Future* (New York: Harper Perennial, 2009) pp.132-133.
[654] Leving, Jeffery M., *Fathers' Rights: Hard-hitting & Fair Advice for Every Father Involved in a Custody Dispute* (New York: BasicBooks/A division of HarperCollins Publishers, 1997) pp.xiii-xiv.
[655] Parker, Kathleen, *Save the Males: Why Men Matter, Why Women Should Care* (New York: Random House, 2008) p.66.
[656] http://www.rightwingnews.com/interviews/kateo.php, Hawkins, John, "An Interview With Kate O'Beirne," (retrieved 12/01/09).
[657] Mark Silva, "Obama: Marriage tension" http://www.chicagotribune.com/topic/politics/government/barack-obama-PEPLT007408.topic, Posted on The Swamp: Tribune's Washington Bureau, October 22, 2009, http://www.swamppolitics.com/news/politics/blog/2009/10/obama_marriage_tension_allmale.html
[658] Ibid.
[659] Ibid.
[660] Kimbrell, Andrew, *The Masculine Mystique: The Politics of Masculinity* (New York: Ballantine Books, 1995) p.10.
[661] http://www.whitehouse.gov/the_press_office/President-Obama-Announces-White-House-Council-on-Women-and-Girls/ (retrieved 03/12/09)
[662] Friday, Nancy, The Power Of Beauty: A Cultural Memoir of Beauty and Desire (New York: HarperCollins, 1996) p.168.
[663] Farrell, Warren, Ph.D., *The Myth of Male Power: Why Men Are the Disposable Sex* (New York: Berkley Books, 1993) p.149.
[664] Ibid.
[665] Kammer, Jack, *If Men Have All the Power, How Come Women Make the Rules?* (2nd Edition, Jack Kammer, 2002) p.22.
[666] James, Thomas B., *Domestic Violence: The 12 Things You Aren't Supposed to Know* (Chula Vista, CA: Aventine Press, 2003) p.102.
[667] Obama, Barack, "We need fathers to step up," *Parade* magazine, June 2009, http://www.parade.com/news/2009/06/barack-obama-we-need-fathers-to-step-up.html
[668] Rosen, James, "Obama's budget proposal includes increase for women's programs," February 01, 2010, http://www.miamiherald.com/news/nation/story/1456615.html?story_link=email_msg
With women's advocacy groups voicing growing unease with administration policy, President Barack Obama will propose a $3.8 trillion budget on Monday that would exempt programs for women and girls from spending restrictions he's proposed for other programs. Obama aides denied that political calculation was

behind the emphasis on programs for women and girls, detailed in a budget document obtained by McClatchy [News Service] entitled "Opportunity and Progress for Women and Girls." "'We're looking at a lot of significant funding increases for women's programs in a year when the president has ordered a three-year, non-security, discretionary spending freeze,'" said Kate Bedingfield, a White House spokesman.

[669] http://www.fact.on.ca/news/news0303/mnd030311.htm, March 11, 2003.

[670] Pearson, Patricia, *When She Was Bad: How and Why Women Get Away with Murder* (New York: Penguin Books, 1998) p.7.

[671] Farrell, Warren, Ph.D., *Women Can't Hear What Men Don't Say: Destroying myths, creating love* (New York: Tarcher/Putnam, 1999) p.129.

[672] Ibid., p.129.

[673] Cook, Philip W., *Abused Men: The Hidden Side of Domestic Violence* (Westport, CT: Praeger, 1997) p.8.

[674] Philips, Melanie, "Deadlier Than the Male," *The Sunday Times* (UK), October 24, 1999.

[675] Ibid.

[676] Ibid.

[677] Ibid.

[678] Farrell, Warren, Ph.D., *Women Can't Hear What Men Don't Say: Destroying myths, creating love* (New York: Tarcher/Putnam, 1999) p.129.

[679] Nathanson, Paul and Young, Katherine, *Legalizing Misandry: From Public Shame to Systemic Discrimination Against Men* (Canada: McGill-Queen's University Press, 2006) p.244.

[680] Philips, Melanie, "Deadlier Than the Male," *The Sunday Times* (UK), October 24, 1999.

[681] Taylor, Clem, "Turning the Tables: How Do People React When There's Abuse In Public, But The Gender Roles Are Reversed? How Would You React?", *ABC News*, 12/26/06, http://abcnews.go.com/Primetime/story?id=2741047&page=1

[682] Ibid.

[683] Ibid.

[684] Ibid.

[685] Ned Holstein and Glenn Sacks, "The Violence We Ignore," *The Baltimore Sun*, http://articles.baltimoresun.com/2009-07-16/news/0907150032_1_domestic-violence-violent-couples-violence-victims, July 16, 2009

[686] Following the first such survey from 1975, "*every* domestic violence survey done of both sexes over the next quarter century in the United States, Canada, England, New Zealand, and Australia—more than fifty of which are annotated in the Appendix—found one of two things: Women and men batter each other about equally, or women batter men more." Farrell, Warren, Ph.D., *Women Can't Hear What Men Don't Say: Destroying myths, creating love* (New York: Tarcher/Putnam, 1999) p.129.

[687] Ibid., p.129.

[688] James, Thomas B., *Domestic Violence: The 12 Things You Aren't Supposed to Know* (Chula Vista, CA: Aventine Press, 2003) p.101.

[689] Young, Cathy, *Ceasefire!: Why Women and Men Must Join Forces to Achieve True Equality* (New York: The Free Press, 1999) p.6.

[690] James, Thomas B., *Domestic Violence: The 12 Things You Aren't Supposed to Know* (Chula Vista, CA: Aventine Press, 2003), TOC.

[691] Ibid., p.58.

[692] Sommers, Christina Hoff, *Who Stole Feminism?: How Women Have Betrayed Women* (New York: A Touchstone Book/Simon & Schuster, 1994) p.45.

[693] Parker, Kathleen, *Save the Males: Why Men Matter, Why Women Should Care* (New York: Random House, 2008) p.91.
[694] Nathanson, Paul and Young, Katherine, *Legalizing Misandry: From Public Shame to Systemic Discrimination Against Men* (Canada: McGill-Queen's University Press, 2006) pp.25-6.
[695] "Bobbitt's Ex-Wife Charged in Assault," http://www.nytimes.com/1997/12/08/us/bobbitt-s-ex-wife-charged-in-assault.html?sec=health, December 08, 1997.
[696] http://nation.foxnews.com/justice/2010/12/29/cnn-reporter-gushes-lorena-bobbitt-are-you-finally-able-laugh-about-it, December 29, 2010.
[697] Schuett, Trudy, "Farrah Fawcett's 'Burning Bed' legacy," http://www.examiner.com/examiner/x-12866-Domestic-Violence-Examiner~y2009m6d27-Farrah-Fawcetts-Burning-Bed-legacy, June 27, 2009.
[698] Ibid.
[699] Pearson, Patricia, *When She Was Bad: How and Why Women Get Away with Murder* (New York: Penguin Books, 1998) p.44.
[700] Newton, Michael, *Bad Girls Do It!: An Encyclopedia of Female Murderers* (Port Townsend, WA: Loompanics Unlimited, 1993) p.iii.
[701] Farrell, Warren, Ph.D., *The Myth of Male Power: Why Men Are the Disposable Sex* (New York: Berkley Books, 1993) pp.254-283.
[702] Pearson, Patricia, *When She Was Bad: How and Why Women Get Away with Murder* (New York: Penguin Books, 1998) p.7.
[703] Parker, Kathleen, *Save the Males: Why Men Matter, Why Women Should Care* (New York: Random House, 2008) p.23.
[704] *Newsweek*, July 02, 2001.
[705] Anna Quindlen quoted from *Live with Regis and Kathie Lee*, CBS, April 15, 1993.
[706] Ritter, Jim, "Why do dads kill? To be 'free,' experts say," *Chicago Sun Times*, June 25, 2007, p.4.
[707] Ibid.
[708] Ibid.
[709] Ibid., p.20.
[710] *Newsweek*, July 02, 2001, p.20.
[711] Ibid.
[712] "Andrea Yates Found Not Guilty By Reason Of Insanity; Will Be Committed To State Mental Hospital," CBS News, July 26, 2006, http://www.cbsnews.com/stories/2006/07/26/national/main1837248.shtml
[713] Pearson, Patricia, *When She Was Bad: How and Why Women Get Away with Murder* (New York: Penguin Books, 1998) p.88.
[714] *Newsweek*, July 02, 2001, p.20.
[715] Ibid., p.21.
[716] Ibid., p.20.
[717] Ibid.
[718] Ibid., p.25.
[719] Ibid.
[720] *Newsweek*, April 01, 2002, p.6.
[721] Ibid.
[722] http://www.crimelibrary.com/notorious_murders/women/andrea_yates/13.html, retrieved 08/02/07.
[723] http://www.commondreams.org/views02/0322-02.htm, retrieved 08/02/07, published March 22, 2002 in the *Las Vegas Review-Journal*.
[724] http://www.cbsnews.com/stories/2006/07/26/national/main1837248.shtml

[725] Ritter, Jim, "Why do dads kill? To be 'free,' experts say," *Chicago Sun Times*, June 25, 2007, p.4.
[726] *TV Guide*, September 01, 2001, p.10.
[727] http://www.bookreporter.com/authors/au-omalley-suzanne.asp, 02/20/2004.
[728] Ibid.
[729] Ibid.
[730] Ibid.
[731] Ibid.
[732] Ibid.
[733] *Jane magazine*, April 2000, p.95.
[734] Pearson, Patricia, *When She Was Bad: How and Why Women Get Away with Murder* (New York: Penguin Books, 1998) p.11.
[735] "Decriminalization of the Abandonment of Newborns," 2000, http://aia.berkeley.edu/media/pdf/abandoned_infant_fact_sheet_2005.pdf
[736] Pearson, Patricia, *When She Was Bad: How and Why Women Get Away with Murder* (New York: Penguin Books, 1998) p.108. Source: Dr. John Emery testifying at Marybeth Tinning's trial.
[737] Newton, Michael, *Bad Girls Do It!: An Encyclopedia of Female Murderers* (Port Townsend, WA: Loompanics Unlimited, 1993) p.168.
[738] Ibid., p.168.
[739] Ibid., pp. 168-9.
[740] Ibid., p.112.
[741] Pearson, Patricia, *When She Was Bad: How and Why Women Get Away with Murder* (New York: Penguin Books, 1998) pp.94-5.
[742] Ibid., pp. 95-6.
[743] Ibid., p.96.
[744] Ibid.
[745] Ibid., p.220.
[746] Ibid., p.97.
[747] Kelleher, Michael D. and Kelleher, C. L., *Murder Most Rare: The Female Serial Killer* (Westport, CT: Dell Publishing, 1998) pp.290-1.
[748] Pearson, Patricia, *When She Was Bad: How and Why Women Get Away with Murder* (New York: Penguin Books, 1998) p.97.
[749] Kelleher, Michael D. and Kelleher, C. L., *Murder Most Rare: The Female Serial Killer* (Westport, CT: Dell Publishing, 1998) p.293.
[750] American Executions of Female Offenders: A Preliminary Inventory of Names, Dates, and Other Information, Cleveland State University.
[751] *The Globe*, April 18, 2000, pp.27-47.
[752] Fox, Dr. James Alan, quoted in *The Twentieth Century* with Mike Wallace.
[753] Ewing, Dr. Charles, quoted in *The Twentieth Century* with Mike Wallace.
[754] Bing, Leon, *Rolling Stone*, April 12, 2001, p.82.
[755] Plato, *The Republic of Plato,* see book III, part 1. "Censorship of Literature for School Use."
[756] "The Strange Case of Lizzie Borden," History Channel documentary, *History's Mysteries*: DVD, 2005.
[757] http://www.crimelibrary.com /notorious_murders/famous/borden/index_1.html
[758] http://www.karisable.com/lizborden.htm, KariSable.com, retrieved 03/15/07.
[759] "The Strange Case of Lizzie Borden," History Channel documentary, *History's Mysteries*: DVD, 2005.
[760] http://www.crimelibrary.com /notorious_murders/famous/borden/index_1.html, retrieved 03/16/07.

[761] Wallechinsky, David, and Wallace, Irving, *The People's Almanac* (New York: Doubleday & Company, Inc., 1975) p.577.
[762] http://www.crimelibrary.com /notorious_murders/famous/borden/index_1.html
[763] "The Strange Case of Lizzie Borden," History Channel documentary, *History's Mysteries*: DVD, 2005.
[764] Wallechinsky, David, and Wallace, Irving, *The People's Almanac* (New York: Doubleday & Company, Inc., 1975) p.577.
[765] http://www.karisable.com/lizborden.htm, retrieved 03/15/07.
[766] Farrell, Warren, Ph.D., *The Myth of Male Power: Why Men Are the Disposable Sex* (New York: Berkley Books, 1993) p.106. "6 percent of all work-related fatalities." Men comprise 94% of all work-related fatalities due to on-the-job injury (disease-related deaths caused by on-the-job exposure are not included in this figure). U.S. Department of Health and Human Services, The National Institute for Occupational Safety and Health NIOSH, (Morgantown, West. Va.), on-line database titled "Basic Information on Workplace Safety and Health in the U.S."
[767] Newton, Michael, *Bad Girls Do It!: An Encyclopedia of Female Murderers* (Port Townsend, WA: Loompanics Unlimited, 1993) p.I.
[768] Kelleher, Michael D. and Kelleher, C. L., *Murder Most Rare: The Female Serial Killer* (Westport, CT: Dell Publishing, 1998) pp.xii-xiii.
[769] Pearson, Patricia, *When She Was Bad: How and Why Women Get Away with Murder* (New York: Penguin Books, 1998) p.37.
[770] Parker, Kathleen, "Dying of political correctness," Townhall.com, May 29, 2004, see: http://www.jewishworldreview.com/kathleen/parker052804.asp
[771] Melone, Mary Jo, "We've Come a Long, and Wrong Way," *St. Petersburg Times*, May 7, 2004, http://www.sptimes.com/2004/05/07/Columns/We_ve_come_a_long__an.shtml
[772] Pipes, Sally, "Prison Scandal Sparks Feminist Confession," *The Contrarian: News & Comments on Women's Issues*, Vol. 8, No. 8, June 4, 2004. Sally Pipes is president and CEO at the California-based Pacific Research Institute for Public Policy.
[773] Farrell, Warren, Ph.D., *Women Can't Hear What Men Don't Say: Destroying myths, creating love* (New York: Tarcher/Putnam, 1999) p.101.
[774] The National Archives Learning Curve, www.spartacus.schoolnet.co.uk, November 2004.
[775] Moxon, Steve, *The Woman Racket: The new science explaining how the sexes relate at work, at play and in society* (Charlottesville, VA: Imprint Academic Philosophy Documentation Center, 2008) p.111.
[776] The National Archives Learning Curve, also; http://www.diggerhistory.info/pages-medals/white-feather.htm, retrieved April 2007.
[777] Van Creveld, Martin, *Men, Women and War: Do Women Belong in the Front Line?* (London: Cassell & Co., 2001) p.16.
[778] Gogoi, Pallavi, "Father's Unspectacular Day," June 14, 2005, http://www.businessweek.com/smallbiz/content/jun2005/sb20050615_7302_sb017.htm
"Dad tends to be more low-maintenance than mom," says Tracy Mullin, president and CEO of the National Retail Federation, a Washington (D.C.) trade association for retailers. "While moms love to receive luxury items such as jewelry or a trip to the spa, dads are happy with an afternoon barbecue or watching the ball game without distraction." . . . According to BIGresearch, women—who make the most purchases for either dads or husbands—tend to head to discount stores to find that perfect gift for dad.
[779] Onassis, Aristotle. See: http://www.hellenicomserve.com/quotethegreeks.html

780 Pearson, Patricia, *When She Was Bad: How and Why Women Get Away with Murder* (New York: Penguin Books, 1998) p.15.
781 Winston, Robert, *Human Instinct: How our primeval impulses shape our modern lives* (U.K.: Bantam Press a division of Transworld Publishers, 2002) p.232.
782 Pearson, Patricia, *When She Was Bad: How and Why Women Get Away with Murder* (New York: Penguin Books, 1998) p.15.
783 MacDonald, Eileen, *Shoot the Women First: The first book to tell why women are the most feared terrorists in the world* (London: Arrow Books/Random House, 1991). See p.4.
784 Moore, John H., *But What About Men?: After Women's Lib* (Bath: Ashgrove Press, 1989) p.27.
785 Batten, Mary, *Sexual Strategies: How Females Choose Their Mates* (New York: Tarcher/Putnam, 1992) pp.4-5.
786 Kammer, Jack, *Good Will Toward Men: Women Talk Candidly About the Balance of Power Between the Sexes* (New York: St. Martin's Press, 1994) pp.7-8.
787 Tiger, Lionel, *The Decline of Males: The First Look at an Unexpected New World for Men and Women* (New York: St. Martin's Griffin, 1999) p.2.
788 Keen, Sam, *Fire in the Belly: On Being a Man* (New York: Bantum Books, 1992) p.36.
789 Kimbrell, Andrew, *The Masculine Mystique: The Politics of Masculinity* (New York: Ballantine Books, 1995) p.xiv.
790 *Glamour* magazine, November 1999.
791 First Ladies' Conference on Domestic Violence in San Salvador, El Salvador, November 17, 1998.
792 Cook, Tim, *No Place to Run: The Canadian Corps and Gas Warfare in the First World War* (University of British Columbia Press, 2000) p. 153.
793 Pearson, Patricia, *When She Was Bad: How and Why Women Get Away with Murder* (New York: Penguin Books, 1998) p.53.
794 Narration (Edward Woodward) from a segment of "Time Machine," © 2000 A&E Television: "The True Story of the Bridge on the River Kwai," produced by Greystone Communications, inc. for The History Channel.
795 Ibid., Kinvig, Clifford, historian.
796 Ibid., Holtham, William, British POW.
797 Cadbury, Deborah, *Dreams of Iron and Steel* (New York: Fourth Estate/HarperCollins, 2004) p.27.
798 Sommers, Christina Hoff, *The War Against Boys: How Misguided Feminism Is Harming Our Young Men* (New York: Simon & Schuster, 2000) p.135.
799 Ibid., pp.135-6.
800 *ABC News,* May 22, 1998.
801 Parker, Kathleen, *Save the Males: Why Men Matter, Why Women Should Care* (New York: Random House, 2008) p.178.
802 *Detroit News,* April 30, 2000.
803 Kimbrell, Andrew, *The Masculine Mystique: The Politics of Masculinity* (New York: Ballantine Books, 1995) pp.253-4.
804 www.historylearningsite.co.uk/world_war_one_executions.htm, retrieved October 20, 2006.
805 Ibid.
806 Ibid.
807 Ibid.

808 Farrell, Warren, Ph.D., *The Myth of Male Power: Why Men Are the Disposable Sex* (New York: Berkley Books, 1993) p.147. Military historian: S. L. A. Marshall, cited in Jean Elshtain, *Women and War* (N.Y.: Harper & Row/Basic Books, 1987).
809 James, Thomas B., *Domestic Violence: The 12 Things You Aren't Supposed to Know* (Chula Vista, CA: Aventine Press, 2003) p.98.
810 Goldstein, Joshua S., *War and Gender: How Gender Shapes the War System and Vice Versa* (Cambridge University Press, 2001) p.5.
811 Strobel, Mike, "Are We Really Ready For This?", *Toronto Sun,* May 26, 2006.
812 *Newsweek*, September 10, 1990.
813 Farrell, Warren, Ph.D., *The Myth of Male Power: Why Men Are the Disposable Sex* (New York: Berkley Books, 1993) p.128. See: Michael Gordon, "Woman Leads GIs in Combat in Panama, in a 'First' for Army," *The New York Times,* January 4, 1990, front page.
814 Ibid., p.131. Source: Bob Secter, "The Draft: If There's a War, There's a Way," *Los Angeles Times,* January 3, 1991, pp. E-1 & E-5.
815 Famous paraphrase from "Charge of the Light Brigade," by Alfred, Lord Tennyson.
816 Ellis, Thomas, *The Rantings of a Single Male: Losing Patience with Feminism, Political Correctness... and Basically Everything* (Austin, TX: Rannenberg Publishing, 2005) pp.85-6.
817 Parker, Kathleen, *Save the Males: Why Men Matter, Why Women Should Care* (New York: Random House, 2008) p.163.
818 Ibid.
819 Quoted from an email sent May 06, 2010 from Tim Embree, IAVA [mailto:mail@iava.org], thanking the author for his contribution to Iraq and Afghanistan Veterans of America.
820 Ibid., p.164.
821 Kammer, Jack, *Good Will Toward Men: Women Talk Candidly About the Balance of Power Between the Sexes* (New York: St. Martin's Press, 1994) pp.203-4.
822 Ibid., p.204.
823 Ibid., pp. 210-11.
824 Ibid., p.205.
825 Van Creveld, Martin, *Men, Women and War: Do Women Belong in the Front Line?* (London: Cassell & Co., 2001) p.10.
826 Scarborough, Rowan, "False Reports Outpace Sex Assaults in the Military," http://www.washingtontimes.com/news/2013/may/12/false-reports-outpace-sex-assaults-in-the-military/#ixzz2W1eHpInn, The Washington Times, May 12, 2013.
827 Kammer, Jack, *Good Will Toward Men: Women Talk Candidly About the Balance of Power Between the Sexes* (New York: St. Martin's Press, 1994) p.205.
828 Ibid.
829 MacKinnon, Catharine, quoted by O'Beirne, Kate, *Women Who Make the World Worse: and How Their Radical Feminist Assault Is Ruining Our Families, Military, Schools, and Sports* (New York: Sentinel, 2006) p.61.
830 Kammer, Jack, *Good Will Toward Men: Women Talk Candidly About the Balance of Power Between the Sexes* (New York: St. Martin's Press, 1994) p.206.
831 Ibid., p.207.
832 Ibid., pp.207,9.
833 Ibid., pp.212-13.
834 Farrell, Warren, Ph.D., *The Myth of Male Power: Why Men Are the Disposable Sex* (New York: Berkley Books, 1993) pp.129-30.
835 Ibid., p.132.

836 Ibid.
837 Parker, Kathleen, *Save the Males: Why Men Matter, Why Women Should Care* (New York: Random House, 2008) p.174.
838 Ibid., p.173.
839 Eldredge, John, *Wild at Heart: Discovering the Secret of a Man's Soul* (Nashville, TN: Thomas Nelson Publishers, 2001) p.15.
840 Parker, Kathleen, *Save the Males: Why Men Matter, Why Women Should Care* (New York: Random House, 2008) pp181-2.
841 MacDonald, Eileen, *Shoot the Women First: The first book to tell why women are the most feared terrorists in the world* (London: Arrow Books/Random House, 1991) p.7.
842 U.S. Congress, Senate, Committee on the Judiciary United States Senate, *Nomination of Sandra Day O'Connor,* Report no. J-97-51, 97th Cong., 1st sess., 1982, p. 127-128.
843 Ellis, Thomas, *The Rantings of a Single Male: Losing Patience with Feminism, Political Correctness... and Basically Everything* (Austin, TX: Rannenberg Publishing, 2005) p.84.
844 Glazov, Jamie, interviewing Dr. Theodore Dalrymple, FrontPageMagazine.com, Wednesday, August 31, 2005
845 Van Creveld, Martin, *Men, Women and War: Do Women Belong in the Front Line?* (London: Cassell & Co., 2001) pp.10-11.
846 Ibid., p.11.
847 Baumeister, Roy F., *Is There Anything Good About Men?: How Cultures Flourish By Exploiting Men* (New York: Oxford University Press, Inc., 2010) p.19.
848 Dychtwald, Maddy with Larson, Christine, *Influence: How Women's Soaring Economic Power Will Transform Our World for the Better* (New York: Voice/Hyperion, 2010) pp.5, 24, 187-188.

> Equality Leapfrog: quotas requiring that women win a specific number of seats are a stunning example of how quickly change can happen. . . . "Quotas are one way to leapfrog ahead, but there are other mechanisms and systems that are friendlier to people who aren't historically in power," says Laura Liswood, secretary general of the Council of Women World Leaders. For instance, the prime minister of Spain promised that half his cabinet would be women.

849 Jones, Daniel, (editor) *The Bastard on the Couch: 27 Men Try Really Hard to Explain Their Feelings About Love, Loss, Fatherhood, and Freedom* (New York: William Morrow/An Imprint of HarperCollins Publishers, 2004). Fred Leebron quoted from the essay, "I Am Man, Hear Me Bleat," p.72.
850 Parker, Kathleen, *Save the Males: Why Men Matter, Why Women Should Care* (New York: Random House, 2008) p.194.
851 Jones, Daniel, (editor) *The Bastard on the Couch: 27 Men Try Really Hard to Explain Their Feelings About Love, Loss, Fatherhood, and Freedom* (New York: William Morrow/An Imprint of HarperCollins Publishers, 2004). Fred Leebron quoted from the essay, "I Am Man, Hear Me Bleat," p.72.
852 Paglia, Camille, "When Camille Met Tim," *Esquire*, February 1995, p. 70.
853 See for example the website Inside Higher Education and the comments by Jonathan Cohen, Professor of Mathematics at DePaul University: "In the storm that followed, Summers backtracked and sponsored a committee that announced it was devoting 50 million dollars basically to increase the number of women at Harvard. This clearly was not enough because within little more than a year he was forced to resign. His replacement is a women who directs an institute devoted to women and gender studies. Under the circumstances there is no way that this appointment will not

be seen in large measure as a public relations move aimed at lessening the perception that Harvard is unfriendly to women."
http://www.insidehighered.com/news/2007/02/12/harvard, February 12, 2007.

[854] Baron-Cohen, Simon, *The Essential Difference: The Truth About the Male and Female Brain* (NY: Basic Books/ A Member of the Perseus Books Group, 2003) p.71.

[855] See for example: Ray, Barry, "Grant aims to advance academic women in chemistry, engineering," In the amount of $600,000, "Five Florida universities, including The Florida State University, are partners on a professional-development project funded by the National Science Foundation (NSF) that seeks to increase the representation and promote the advancement of women educators in the fields of science, technology, engineering and mathematics."
http://www.fsu.edu/news/2009/11/17/nsf.grant/ (retrieved 12/01/09).

[856] Taylor, Stuart, "Gender-Equity Cops Are Pushing for Preferential Treatment for Females Over Males in the Sciences," National Journal Magazine, http://www.nationaljournal.com/njmagazine/openingargument.php, October 24, 2009.

[857] Rosin, Hanna, July/August 2010, *Atlantic Magazine*, "The End of Men" http://www.theatlantic.com/magazine/archive/2010/07/the-end-of-men/8135/

[858] Ibid.

[859] Farrell, Warren, Ph.D., *Women Can't Hear What Men Don't Say: Destroying Myths, Creating Love* (New York: Tarcher/Putnam, 1999) pp.187-188. See also, "The Trouble With Men," http://www.flatrock.org.nz/topics/men/trouble_with_men.htm

[860] Friday, Nancy, *The Power Of Beauty: A Cultural Memoir of Beauty and Desire* (New York: HarperCollins, 1996) p.426.

[861] Stephenson, June, *Men Are Not Cost Effective: Male Crime in America* (1995) pp.450-2.

[862] Schyman, Gudrun, quoted in *REASON* magazine, January 2005, p.12.

[863] Alesina, Alberto, Karabarounis, Loukas and Ichino, Andrea, "The Y chromosome tax policy," http://www.livemint.com/2008/01/10232012/The-Y-chromosome-tax-policy.html, January 10, 2008.

[864] Ibid.

[865] Brotman, Barbara, "Should Men Pay A Price For Being Men? -- Since They Commit Most Crimes, Let Them Foot The Bill, Some Women Say," *Chicago Tribune*, May 2, 1993, http://community.seattletimes.nwsource.com/archive/?date=19930502&slug=1698975

[866] Ibid.

[867] Ibid.

[868] Will, George F., "Nature and the Male Sex," *Newsweek*, June 17, 1991, p.70.

[869] Alexander, Brian, "Will science render men unnecessary?", http://www.msnbc.msn.com/id/17937813/, June 27, 2007.

[870] http://www.theage.com.au/articles/2003/10/12/1065917281078.html.

[871] Moore, Michael, *Stupid White Men . . . and Other Sorry Excuses for the State of the Nation!* (New York: Regan Books/HarperCollins, 2001) p.146.

[872] Ehrenreich, Barbara, "Will Women Still Need Men?", *Time Magazine*, February 21, 2000.

[873] Cherfas, Jeremy and Gribbin, John, *The Redundant Male: Is Sex Irrelevant in the Modern World?* (New York: Pantheon Books, 1984) p.177.

[874] Gearhart, Sally Miller, "The Future—If There Is One—Is Female," *Reweaving the Web of Life,* ed. Pam McAllister (Philadelphia: New Society Publishers, 1982) p. 271.

[875] Cherfas, Jeremy and Gribbin, John, *The Redundant Male: Is Sex Irrelevant in the Modern World?* (New York: Pantheon Books, 1984) p.178-9.

[876] Ibid., p.179.
[877] Moore, John H., *But What About Men?: After Women's Lib* (Bath: Ashgrove Press, 1989) pp.99.
[878] Alexander, Brian, "Will science render men unnecessary?", http://www.msnbc.msn.com/id/17937813/, June 27, 2007.
[879] *Time* magazine, February 21, 2000.
[880] Alexander, Brian, "Will science render men unnecessary?", http://www.msnbc.msn.com/id/17937813/, June 27, 2007.
[881] Gravois, John, "Bringing Up Babes: Why do adoptive parents prefer girls?" adoptachild.us, 2004.
[882] Smith, Rebecca, "Boys 'lead to more post-natal depression'", http://www.telegraph.co.uk/news/main.jhtml?xml=/news/2008/02/13/nboys11 3.xml, February 13, 2008. "Research carried out in France found three quarters of women who were diagnosed with severe post-natal depression had sons."
[883] Klass, Perri, "Gender Bias," *Vogue*, March 2001, p. 519.
[884] Rosin, Hanna, July/August 2010, *Atlantic Magazine*, "The End of Men" http://www.theatlantic.com/magazine/archive/2010/07/the-end-of-men/8135/
[885] Ibid.
[886] Young, Cathy, *Ceasefire!: Why Women and Men Must Join Forces to Achieve True Equality* (New York: The Free Press, 1999) p.255.
[887] Janus, Samuel S., and Janus Cynthia L., *The Janus Report on Sexual Behavior* (New York: John Wiley & Sons, Inc., 1993) p.143.
[888] *Time* magazine, September 11, 2000.
[889] *Time* magazine, September 18, 2000.
[890] "Global Gender Gaps: Women Like Their Lives Better," Pew Research Center, http://www.pewglobal.org/2003/10/29/global-gender-gaps/, October 29, 2003.
Women are somewhat happier than men with their lives overall, according to 38,000 interviews in 44 countries conducted by the Pew Research Center for the Pew Global Attitudes Survey . . . Women's greater satisfaction with life is pervasive in many of the less-developed regions of the world: in 7 of the 8 countries surveyed in Asia, 6 of the 8 nations in Latin America and all 5 nations in east and southern Africa. In particular, women are much happier than men in Japan, India, the Philippines, Pakistan and Argentina.
[891] Betsey Stevenson & Justin Wolfers, 2009. "The Paradox of Declining Female Happiness," American Economic Journal: Economic Policy, American Economic Association, vol. 1(2), pages 190-225, August.
By many objective measures the lives of women in the United States have improved over the past 35 years, yet we show that measures of subjective well-being indicate that women's happiness has declined both absolutely and relative to men. The paradox of women's declining relative well-being is found across various datasets, measures of subjective well-being, and is pervasive across demographic groups and industrialized countries. Relative declines in female happiness have eroded a gender gap in happiness in which women in the 1970s typically reported higher subjective well-being than did men.
[892] Ibid. See, also: "Liberated and Unhappy," Ross Douthat, May 25, 2009, http://www.nytimes.com/2009/05/26/opinion/26douthat.html?_r=2&em
On some fronts — graduation rates, life expectancy and even job security — men look increasingly like the second sex. But all the achievements of the feminist era may have delivered women to greater unhappiness. In the 1960s, when Betty Friedan diagnosed her fellow wives and daughters as the victims of "the problem with no name," American women reported themselves happier, on average, than

did men. . . . In postfeminist America, men are happier than women.

[893] Paglia, Camille, *Vamps & Tramps* (New York: Vintage, 1994) p.25.

[894] Zweig, Connie and Abrams, Jeremiah, (editors) *Meeting the Shadow: The Hidden Power of the Dark Side of Human Nature* (Los Angeles: Jeremy P. Tarcher, Inc., 1991) pp.173-4.

[895] Baker, Carolyn Ph.D., interviewed by Kammer, Jack, *Good Will Toward Men: Women Talk Candidly About the Balance of Power Between the Sexes* (New York: St. Martin's Press, 1994) p.163.

[896] Zweig, Connie and Abrams, Jeremiah, (editors) *Meeting the Shadow: The Hidden Power of the Dark Side of Human Nature* (Los Angeles: Jeremy P. Tarcher, Inc., 1991) p.175.

[897] Honderich, Ted (editor), *The Oxford Companion to Philosophy* (New York, Oxford University Press, 1995) p.824.

[898] From a speech given in Austin, Texas, *The Houston Chronicle*, Section: A Page: 1, September 28, 1991.

[899] Sommers, Christina Hoff, *The War Against Boys: How Misguided Feminism Is Harming Our Young Men* (New York: Simon & Schuster, 2000) p.49.

[900] Kammer, Jack, *Good Will Toward Men: Women Talk Candidly About the Balance of Power Between the Sexes* (New York: St. Martin's Press, 1994) p.21.

[901] Friday, Nancy, *The Power Of Beauty: A Cultural Memoir of Beauty and Desire* (New York: HarperCollins, 1996) p.120.

[902] Paglia, Camille, *Vamps & Tramps* (New York: Vintage, 1994). From the essay "No Law in the Arena," pp.30-31.

[903] Paglia, Camille, "When Camille Met Tim," *Esquire*, February 1995, pp.70-71.

[904] Farrell, Warren, Ph.D., *The Myth of Male Power: Why Men Are the Disposable Sex* (New York: Berkley Books, 1993) p.358.

[905] Jones, Daniel, (editor) *The Bastard on the Couch: 27 Men Try Really Hard to Explain Their Feelings About Love, Loss, Fatherhood, and Freedom* (New York: William Morrow/An Imprint of HarperCollins Publishers, 2004). Fred Leebron quoted from the essay, "I Am Man, Hear Me Bleat," p.72.

[906] Sommers, Christina Hoff, http://www.aei.org/article/100695, American Enterprise Institute for Public Policy Research, "Persistent Myths in Feminist Scholarship," Chronicle of Higher Education, June 29, 2009.

[907] Ibid.

[908] Callahan, Maureen, "Men Worried They're Falling Behind in a 'He-cession'—They're Right," http://www.nypost.com/php/pfriendly/print.php?url=http://www.nypost.com/seven/07182009/postopinion/opedcolumnists/men_worry_theyre_falling_behind_in_a_he__179998.htm, July 18, 2009

[909] Goldberg, Herb, *The Hazards of Being Male: Surviving the Myth of Masculine Privilege* (New York: Signet/Penguin, 1976) p.5.

[910] Parker, Kathleen, *Save the Males: Why Men Matter, Why Women Should Care* (New York: Random House, 2008) p

[911] Friday, Nancy, *The Power Of Beauty: A Cultural Memoir of Beauty and Desire* (New York: HarperCollins, 1996) p.62.

[912] Kipnis, Aaron, *Angry Young Men: How Parents, Teachers, and Counselors Can Help "Bad Boys" Become Good Men* (San Francisco, CA: Jossey-Bass, 1999) p.194.

[913] Chesterton, Gilbert K., *Orthodoxy* (NuVision Publications, LLC, paperback, 2007) p. 40 (Originally published 1908).

Index

Abraham, Jed H. 146
Abrams, Dan 217
Abu Ghraib 319-321, 329
abuse
    accusations of 42
    exaggerated claims of 129
    of legal proceedings 146
    of power 156
academia power 48
accountability 29, 31
affirmative action 54
Agent Orange 280, 368
Agustín, Laura Maria 207
Alexander, Brian 374
Ali, Lorraine 209-210
Allen, Jodie 89
Allen, Marvin 177
Allen, Nancy 69
Allen, Tim 362, 390, 397
All-Fault-Is-Male rule 14, 53, 110, 121, 232, 272, 318
American Association of University Women (AAUW) 81
American Institute of Stress 68
An, Liu 56
anger 69
    boy baby's cries seen as 36
    creation of in Women's Studies 58, 200
    fuel for political movement 12, 58, 182
    gender differences 69, 250
    women's toward men 119
Angier, Natalie 10, 108
anorexia 36, 119-120, 122
attention deficit/hyperactivity disorder (ADHD) 79
Australian Nuclear Veterans Association 73
Baber, Asa 92
baby seals, clubbing 311
Baird, Julia 259
Baker, Carolyn 380
Balanced Equality 358-367
Bardot, Bridget 45
Baron-Cohen, Simon 226, 363
Bartky, Sandra 58
Baskerville, Stephen 106, 146-147
Batten, Mary 170, 328
battle of rhetoric 22, 31, 182, 191

Battle of the Sexes ...... viii, 4-5, 18-19, 43, 182, 196, 198, 202, 266, 366, 378, 385, 388, 398, 401, 405
Baumeister, Roy F. 219, 225
Bax, E. Balfort 19, 184
Beatles, the 31, 261
beauty 58
    as burden 10, 57
    female ownership of 44, 88
    male 159
    men respond to 109, 165
    as seen by gay men 159
    power 161, 165-166
    products to enhance 66
    turns a woman into a celebrity 165
    valued by women 175
Bell, Dan 68
Berardinetti, Lorenzo 63-64
Best, Patricia 149
Beveridge, Andrew 102
Biden, Joseph 129, 274-275, 282, 284, 289, 437
blame vs. accountability 29
Blankenhorn, David 148
blonde jokes 25
Blumner, Robyn 122
Blyth, Myrna 46, 198, 200
Bobbitt, Lorena 292-293
Boggs, Jerry 204
Bogguss, Suzy 53
Bonaventura, Michael 166
Bonhomme, Jean 146
Borden, Lizzie 314-315, 320
boys
    alcohol and drug violations 36
    and sex 168, 180
    and sports 59
    as prostitutes 208
    as slave labourers 209
    Attention Deficit Disorder 36
    bad boys 26, 329
    corporal punishment of 36
    dislike school 86
    doing worse than girls 36, 82
    exuberance 79
    frogs 'n snails 382
    greater risk of suicide 37
    held responsible 153, 340
    lack of advocates for 80
    lagging in school 88

learning disabled......................... 36
majority of abuse victims 36
more frequently punished ... 36, 81
need for fathers 148
physically injured in sports....... 36
role and socialization................. 26
sabotaged by schools 37, 79, 81
slow response to cries of........... 36
socialized to be like girls 82
sports as disposability training . 60
sports injuries 36
steroid use by.................... 36, 121
suicide 37, 67-68
target of 78
trafficking in............................ 209
use of Ritalin by 37,79
Brady, Bill 63
Braver, Sanford............. 142, 192, 245
breast cancer
research and funding 40, 74
Brownmiller, Susan 48
Brumberg, Joan............................. 120
Bruyère, Jean de la.......................... 35
Buckingham, Steve 53
Buel, Sarah 121
Burns, David 158
Bush, George W. 146
Buss, David M. 112-113, 117, 163, 174
Caldwell, Doris............................. 105
Califia, Pat 160
Canfield, Jack 200
Carpenter, Mary Chapin 52
Center for Men and Young Men..... 86
Chesterton, Gilbert K..................... 403
chivalry 16, 42, 47, 50, 74, 80, 109, 125, 152, 189, 191, 193, 210-211, 217, 235, 283-284, 314, 342, 344, 346, 360, 371, 373-374, 382, 389, 398
Churchill, Winston.......................... 82
Cihra, Robert 116
Cinemonde 45
Civil War 83, 337
Civilian Public Service (CPS)......... 91
Clinton, Bill 102
Clinton, Hillary 102, 332
corporal punishment 36
Cose, Ellis............................. 106, 146
Costello, Tony 75
Crouch, Harry 398
Crowley, Michael 78
custody bias 42, 140, 144-146, 282

Dalrymple, Theodore.....................355
Darfur 203
date rape................................. 131-132
David and Goliath.......... 186, 270, 395
death penalty................................... 42
Decter, Midge 172, 269
DeLauro, Rosa 101-102
domestic violence surveys 41
Domestic Violence...... 257, 269, 274, 285- 296, 309,
Donaldson, Sam..................... 154-155
Driscoll, Richard..... 69, 240, 250, 258
Durbin, Karen 132
Eagly, Alice 219, 383
Ehrenreich, Barbara 319, 321, 375
Einstein, Albert......... 79, 83, 217, 378
Ellis, Thomas 161, 347, 354
England, Lynndie......................... 320
Ensler, Eve...................................... 54
equalism 11, 14, 22-23, 129, 200, 202, 244, 283, 366, 369, 392, 399
Ericsson, Ronald 376
Esquire magazine............................ 68
estrogen pollution 77
estrogenic chemicals....................... 76
Etcoff, Nancy.......................... 45, 112
Evans, Eddie 78
Fabio 164
Faludi, Susan 60
Farmer, Stephen.............................. 83
Farrell, Warren......v, vii, 9, 21-22, 35, 70, 72-74, 76, 87, 89, 94, 96-97, 100, 102, 108, 113-114, 119, 130-131, 136, 138, 140, 148, 152, 162, 230, 285, 291, 322, 340, 352, 368, 390, 397
Father's Day .... viii, xi, 50, 93, 442
fathers
barred from childbirth............. 143
deceived by mothers............... 137
importance in child development 147-148
lack of empathy for.....x, 145, 147, 275-277, 279, 282
legal injustices ... 42, 146, 276-277
love for their children 142-143, 146-147
loved second best.. x, 57, 141, 143
prejudice against............. 138, 145
respect for..............................ix, xi
unequal partners in parenting..viii, 135, 139-143, 259-262, 362
undervalued..... viii, x, 51, 93, 143

Fein, Ellen 160
female
    anger at men 119, 137, 266, 349
    beauty power 9, 44, 161
    chores 96
    domestic power 46, 237-263
    fragile ego 143, 241
    innocence power 45
    majority-vote power 4, 40, 45, 64, 201, 283, 377
    moral authority .. 45, 174, 243, 257
    power 44, 48-49
    power of accusation/lawsuit 47
    powerlessness 48, 54, 184, 236, 273, 356
    righteousness 52-53, 244, 378
    sexual power 44, 46, 151, 154, 157, 159, 163, 166, 169-170, 175-177, 179-180, 237, 250
    spending 39-40, 46, 104-105
    superiority ... 24, 26, 217, 263, 321
    trafficking 207
    verbal acuity 47, 240
female equivalent 28, 99, 153, 164, 298, 357
female-ism 10, 43
    selfishness 81
feminism 10, 16
    "click" experience 58
    a learned perspective 21
    aligned with culture 19, 54, 342
    antithetical to its stated goals .. 16, 30, 43, 140, 200
    arrogant 183
    blocks respect for women 14
    built on female discontent 12
    contemptible 74, 212
    critiques of 19
    definition 19
    disempowers women 30, 43
    equated with women 15
    filler feminism 82
    founded on emotion 49
    holds Man as the enemy 12, 58
    infantilizes women 199
    is anti-male ... 71, 76, 97, 119, 127, 129, 214
    is female-ism 10-11, 43, 71, 92
    keeps women victims ... 10, 43, 55, 200
    militant 76, 122, 266-267, 394
    one party system 53
    one-sided .. 10, 15, 23, 43, 212-213
    power 48, 96, 122, 130, 416
    protected from criticism 128
    scapegoats men 214
    sees gender nurture not nature .. 29
    sees Man as the enemy 5, 76, 86, 119, 127, 137
    sees only negatives for women 10, 43, 57-58, 96, 181
    sees only positives for men 10, 43, 96
    stands unopposed 53, 100-101, 128, 197
    supported by media 211
    supported by men 95
    the female perspective politicized 12, 200
    unaccountable 123
    unconscious 22-24, 183, 212
    victim power 48, 54-55, 212
femisa (attitude) 241-242, 244, 247, 265, 268
filler feminism 82
Fillion, Kate 150, 155-156, 217
Finley, Gordon E. 102
Fiorina, Carly 115
Fisher, Helen 151
Flynn, Bill 199
football injuries 36
Fremon, Celeste 79
Friday, Nancy 54, 86, 93, 95, 112, 120, 138-139, 154, 158, 171, 368, 389
Friedan, Betty 198
Furchtgott-Roth, Diana 39, 99, 283
Galston, William 148
Garcia, Guy 104, 123, 238, 395
Geldof, Bob 146
Gelles, Richard 129
gender
    balance 2, 4, 14-17, 43, 61, 233
    dual nature .... ix, 34
    injustice 43, 366
    politics 4, 11, 182
    reparations 365
    truth 31
Gender Compassion Gap 204
gender-based pricing 64-66
gendercide 127, 204
genocide 203-206
Geritol 51
gift of accountability, the .. 30-31, 176, 185, 227, 372

Gilligan, Carol 80-81
girls, sugar 'n spice 382
glass ceiling 99, 101, 115, 116
Glass Escalator 115-116, 118, 349, 360, 364, 367
Glass Floor.... 281, 316-318, 343, 367, 406
Glass Wall 135, 139, 142, 143, 148, 262, 272, 281, 362, 367, 390
Goldberg, Herb .. 9, 19, 35, 59, 60, 69, 135, 140, 178, 236, 268, 397
Goldstein, Joshua 23, 341, 364
Goodman, Ellen 129
Gottman, John 242
Great Eastern steamship 335
Great Starvation Experiment 6, 91
Gulf War 325, 352
gynocentrism 78, 255-256
Halo Effect, the 45, 267, 315
Hanson, Katherine 127
Harris, Emmylou 53
Harter, Susan 80
hazardous labor 7, 37, 61, 335-336
Hazelwood, Captain 94
health, cancer 68, 75
Healthy People 2010 76
Hendricks, Michael 245
Herron, Elizabeth 260
heterophobia. . 122-126, 132, 266, 291
Hill, Anita 54
Hise, Richard ..89, 122, 128, 141, 143, 147, 187
Hite, Shere 266
Hochschild, Arlie 95
homophobia 69
housework 96
Hussein, Saddam 90
Huttner, Richard 145
Iannone, Carol 13, 128, 261, 408
Independent Women's Forum 116
Ingraham, Laurie 116, 137, 154
Innocence Project 153
internalized oppression 91-92
Interpol 326
Intrinsic Value gap, the.... 55, 88, 124, 127, 364, 392
Isaac, Nancy 123
Izumi, Shigechiyo 70
Jack Armstrong 79
jail time 42
James, Tom 118, 152, 291, 340
Janus Report 168, 377

Jennings, John 53
job safety 38
Johnson, Magic 164
Johnstone, Rick 73
Jones, Adam 204
Jordan, Barbara 384
Kamarck, Elaine 148
Kammer, Jack 85, 105, 236, 281, 348, 351, 389
Kanner, Bernice 104
Keen, Sam 331
Kerry, John 102
Keys, Alicia 184
Keys, Dr. Amcel 91
Kiley, Dan 119
Kimbrell, Andrew 35, 41, 68, 331, 338
Kindlon, Dan 68
Kipnis, Aaron 36, 61, 67, 72, 208
Kirn, Walter 377
Kornheiser, Tony 172-173
Krainova, Simona 153
Kramden, Ralph 114
Kranichfeld, Marion 127, 234
Kristof, Nicholas D. 203
Lavigne, Avril 184
Lawson, Nigella 121
lawyer jokes 25
learned helplessness ... 91-92, 289, 296
Leebron, Fred 361-362, 390
Legg, Sam 6, 91, 407
Lennon, John 259-262, 278, 436
Letterman, David 144
Levine, Beth 139
libido gap 168
life expectancy 41, 70
Lilly Ledbetter Fair Pay Restoration Act 102, 281
Lincoln, Abraham 82
Lindbergh, Anne Morrow 82
Lindbergh, Charles 82
Lindgren, David 143
longevity 70
Lord of the Rings 342, 382
Louis Harris Associates 81
Loveless, Patty 53
Lynch, Jessica 347
Lyndon, Neil 130
Mackenzie, Jerold 149
MacKinnon, Catharine... 22, 245, 291, 351
Macnamara, Jim 133-134

male
- alcoholism ... 41
- bashing ... 3, 97, 119, 134
- beauty ... 45
- chores ... 96
- disposability ... 73, 89, 92
- drunk-driving ... 67
- feelings ... 50, 360
- life span ... 60
- pain ... 50
- power ... 48, 54, 258
- powerlessness ... 7, 48, 50, 68, 161, 257, 323, 351, 356
- prostitutes ... 208
- sexual pursuit ... 155
- sports ... 59-60
- strength ... 61, 258
- suicide 41-42, 67-68, 71, 127, 253
- superiority ... 24, 26

male equivalent ... 28, 37, 44, 255, 294, 308, 349, 356
Mamet, David ... 27
ManKind Project ... 24
Mann, Judy ... 129
Manolo Blahniks ... 65
Marlboro Man ... 50, 197
marriage ... 82, 105, 152
- commitment in ... 97
- controlled by women. 50, 139, 178
- erosion of ... 106, 109, 146, 172
- good for children and society. 107
- hours worked in ... 96
- polygyny ... 163
- attacked by feminism 82, 266, 277
- serial marriage ... 163
- sex within ... 173-174, 242-245
- victimization within ... 52, 286

masculism
- admires strong women ... 30
- built on male discontent ... 18, 182
- conscious ... 9, 21-22, 182
- critiques feminism ... 12, 19
- definition ... 19
- introduction to ... 9
- is male-ism ... 21
- masculinism - masculism as seen thru a feminist lens ... 23, 364
- mirror opposite of feminism ... 15, 19, 21-22, 24, 34, 197
- needed for gender equality. 11, 16
- politically invisible ... 19, 22-24, 95, 197, 278-281, 342, 370, 387, 393
- revolutionary ... 20, 387
- sees only negatives for men ... 18, 21, 59-63, 181-183, 201-202
- sees only positives for women. 18, 21, 182
- the male perspective politicized ... 11, 21-22, 201
- unconscious ... 21-22, 201
- will transform into equalism ... 15, 23, 202

maternal chauvinism ... 139
maternal gatekeeping ... 139, 141
matriarchy .. 28, 85, 112, 279, 333, 365
matrisensus ... 28, 53, 60, 66, 81, 84, 143, 170-171, 173, 178, 182, 190, 211, 231, 252, 255, 259-260, 280-281, 283, 361, 366-367, 379, 388
Mattea, Kathy ... 53
May, Rollo ... 380-381
McCamish, Ron ... 90
McDowell, Charles ... 152
McElroy, Wendy ... 74
McGuinness, Dianne ... 79
Mead, Margaret ... 229
medical research ... 72
men
- black ... 106-107, 118, 279, 406
- conscientious objectors 90-91, 329
- deadbeat dads ... 133, 145, 147, 194
- dietary needs ... 76
- executed for "cowardice" ... 338
- execution of ... 42
- fear of commitment ... 97, 130, 272
- feminized ... 37, 76
- feminizing chemicals ... 76
- forced labor ... 208
- hazardous labor ... 37, 61, 335-336
- health ... 40, 67
- higher insurance premiums ... 71
- househusband ... 71, 88, 139
- indifference towards .. 41, 132, 134
- jail time ... 42
- lack of empathy for ... 37
- obligation to pay ... 39, 162
- obligation to succeed ... 39
- physical size and strength power ... 258
- presumed guilty ... 85
- prison rape ... 41
- prostate cancer ... 40
- prostitutes ... 208
- respect for ... 26, 94

stereotyped as abusers 170, 282
street homeless 40
success appeal...62, 108, 111, 114, 164, 360
taking Full Responsibility....... ..31, 125, 252, 262, 283, 366, 369, 372
television viewership 40
trafficking in 208
men's studies 87
Milgram, Stanley 228
Millea, Holly................................ 120
misandry 3, 46, 50, 61, 81, 83, 116, 119, 126-127, 132, 134, 137, 142, 189, 221, 281, 293, 304, 331, 367-370, 373-374, 377-378, 384, 400
misogyny 3, 51, 134
Mitchell, Maria 83
Moir, Anne .76, 79, 96, 108, 172, 222, 225
Moore, Alecia (Pink) 184
Moore, John ... 179, 327, 375-376, 381
Moore, Michael 77, 374
Mother's Day...................... viii, xi, 92
motherhood.................................... 57
mothers
    love for ix
    power................. 46, 57, 233, 307
    single.....104, 106, 109-110, 148, 191, 277, 389
    surrogate 136
Moxon, Steve......................... 207-209
Ms. Magazine 58, 113
Nathanson, Paul 132, 288
National Black Men's Health Network 146
National Coalition For Men ... 24, 320, 398
National Institute of Health 40, 72
National Organization for Women. 22, 130, 140
Net worth power 46
Neufeld, Peter 153
Neuropsychiatric Institute, UCLA .. 69
New Warrior Training Adventure ... 25
New Warriors 25, 29-30, 143, 240, 373
Newton, Michael 295, 305, 318
Nixon, Richard.............................. 155
O'Beirne, Kate........................ 85, 277
O'Malley, Suzanne 302
Obama, Barack 102, 191, 275-279, 281-284, 391, 436

Office of Women's Health.............. 72
Oleana.. 27
Onassis, Aristotle.......................... 324
O'Neill, June 102
Ono, Yoko 259, 262-263, 435
Paglia, Camille..... 119, 150, 154, 170, 180, 199, 223, 233, 257, 293, 380, 390
Palmer, Laura................................ 90
Panama Canal 61
Parker, Kathleen ..... .35, 93, 125, 135, 226, 276, 293, 296, 319, 337, 347-348, 354, 361, 398
Patai, Daphne...... ..47, 58, 72, 86, 150-151, 200, 240, 266
Path To Spirit.................. 25, 237, 379
patriarchy 28, 99
Pearson, Patricia ...... .29, 68, 218, 232-233, 285, 295-296, 299, 304-308, 325, 333
Phillips, Melanie 35, 286-287
Pipes, Sally 115
Pipher, Mary 81
Plato's *Republic* 314
Playboy magazine 92, 113, 243-244
Playgirl magazine 159
Pollack, William S. 86
Pollet, Thomas 164
polygyny 163
Popenoe, David..................... 106, 147
power
    academia.................................. 48
    "butter" analogy..................... 234
    of feminism 48, 92, 96
    victim power....... 48, 54, 351, 401
    "white rice/brown rice" analogy 196, 272, 284
prison rape 41
prisoners
    drug testing on 73
    funding for................................ 42
    POWs 333-335, 407
prostate cancer funding.................. 75
prostitution......159, 165, 167, 207-208
Quindlen, Anna..................... 129, 199
Queen's New Cloths, the.........355-356
Raloff, Janet................................... 77
rape...7, 48, 83, 85, 131-132, 152-154, 203, 216, 245, 249, 286, 293, 350-351, 370, 380, 394, 407-408
Reagan, Ronald............................ 177
Rende Taylor, Laura 207-208
restraining orders 42, 143-146, 271

reverse discrimination ...102, 108, 349
reverse wage gap .. 102-103, 115, 118-119
Rhoads, Steven E. 82, 164, 224
Ringle, Ken 123
Rippey, Sandra 348, 350-352
Ritalin 37, 79
Roback Morse, Jennifer 122
Roberts, Carey 153, 208, 274
Roe vs. Wade 137
Rogers, Susan 233
Roiphe, Katie ... 22, 114, 149-150, 164
romance 82
romance novels 105, 164, 249
Rosch, Paul J. 68
Rosin, Hanna 365, 378
Rosy the Riveter 92
Rwanda 206
Ryan, Private 90
Schechter, Harold 218
Scheck, Barry 153
Schenk, Roy 90, 140
Schiffer, Claudia 45
Schlafly, Phyllis 146, 238, 273, 280
Schlitz, Don 53
Schneider, Sherrie 160
schools
    female-centric 37, 78, 80-87
    recess 37, 79-80, 279
Schroeder, Pat 129
Schuett, Trudy 295
Schwartz, Howard 127
Schwartz, Pepper 139
Seinfeld (TV Show) 149
Seneca Falls 95
Sewell, Joan 167, 242
sex object 22, 44
Sexual Cartel 171, 174
sexual harassment 20, 48, 54, 87, 149-152, 155-158, 192, 348, 350, 355
sexual revolution 171-172
Shalit, Ruth 84
shame 47
Slater, Lauren 141, 143, 145
Smith, Jan 155
Smoron, Paige 177-178
Social Security 71
soldiers
    drug testing on 73
Sommers, Christina Hoff 5, 35, 58, 79-82, 87, 92, 95, 119-123, 127-129, 131, 148, 267, 292-293, 336, 364, 387, 394
Sowell, Thomas 100
Spacek, Sissy 89
Spellings, Margaret 88
Spin Sisters 198-199, 273
Stalin, Joseph 82
Starr, Mark 263
Stein, Harry 68-69, 219, 239, 258, 260-261
Steinem, Gloria 55, 119, 132, 286
Steinmetz, Suzanne 129, 285
Stephenson, June 368
Stolba, Christine 39, 99, 101
stress-related illnesses 68, 71
Strobel, Mike 345, 357
Strossen, Nadine 54, 171
Sudden Infant Death Syndrome (SIDS) 305-306
suicide
    boys 67-68
    by police confrontation 67
    following death of spouse 42
    gap 67-68, 127
Sum, Andrew 103
Summers, Larry 224, 226, 320, 363, 393, 430, 444-445
testosterone .... .10, 77, 166-169, 177, 223, 247, 254, 374
Thatcher, Margaret 219, 321
The Deal 230-231, 338
The New Deal 338, 341
Thomas Yaccato, Joanne 63
Thomas, David 22, 35, 182
Tiananmen Square 322
Tiger, Lionel 83
Tillis, Pam 53
Tinning, Marybeth 306, 310, 400
Title IX 12, 48, 54, 83, 87-88, 191, 391
Tolle, Eckhart 55
Tosi, Char 47
Townsend, John Marshall 113
Tubman, Harriet 82
Tuggle, Debra Sue 305
Tyranny of Indifference . 244, 246, 250
Tyre, Peg 79, 88
unisex equality 359, 362, 367, 392
U.S. Department of Justice 40
Vagina Monologue 54
Van Creveld, Martin 324, 350, 355
Vaughn, Christopher 297, 304

Vera, Veronica............................. 171
veterans.............41, 73, 317, 338, 367
   imprisoned............................... 41
   suicide 41
Veterans Administration Center 41
Vickers, Melana............................. 83
victim power........48, 54, 76, 255, 351
victimhood........54, 88, 152, 184, 200, 212, 223, 332
Vietnam War........... 41, 280, 338, 341
Vilar, Esther..175, 192, 196, 233, 238, 260
Vincent, Norah...................... 70, 257
Violence Against Women Act . 40, 54, 146, 273-274, 294, 320, 437
visitation 42
Vitz, Paul 82
Vronsky, Peter 218
wage gap......39, 97, 99-103, 107-109, 115-119, 126, 279, 281, 392, 406, 419
Waldfrogel, Joel............................. 95
Walker, Bruce.............................. 194
Warner, Fara 104, 107
Wayne, John .. 293, 309, 342-343, 382
Weinberger, Casper 90
Weitzman, Lenore........................ 192
wheel of complicity 18, 230, 334, 387
white feathers......................... 323-324
White House Council on Women and Girls 191, 279, 391
white slavery................................ 207
Whitehead, Caroline 121
Wilder, Jason 164
Will, George F. 79, 374
Winfrey, Oprah 95
Winston, Robert............................ 325
Winters, Marion..... 271-273, 284, 309
Wolf, Naomi 57, 60, 119
Woman Within, Inc. 47
women
   anger at men ... 119, 137, 266, 349
   beauty power 9, 44-45, 161
   black 106
   child custody 42, 144-146, 282
   domestic power 46, 140
   empathy for 95
   exempted from violence 42
   false accusations..................... 152
   federal programs for 40, 279
   greater net worth.................. 39-40
   homicides by 42
   intrinsic value 88
   jail time.................................... 42
   love for 26, 382
   maternal chauvinism............... 139
   parental power 140
   responsibilities......... 110, 148, 304
   righteousness.......52-53, 244, 248, 378
   rights............................... 148, 315
   spending power 104, 114
   television viewership................ 40
   trafficking............................... 207
   valued more 90, 354
   verbal acuity 47, 240
   violence against 40
Women Are Wonderful effect 219, 227, 321, 383
women's studies ... .48, 58, 60, 70, 80, 87-88, 120, 151, 200
Woods, Elin 251, 433-435
Woods, Tiger 251, 433-435
world of men... 20, 27-28, 62, 70, 107, 141, 242, 252, 261-262, 330, 340, 357, 359, 360-361, 366, 391-392
world of women.... 20, 27-28, 62, 107, 112, 141, 143, 178, 199, 242, 252, 260-262, 272, 283, 330, 340, 357-358, 360-361, 366, 380, 390-392
Wuornos, Aileen........... 218, 312, 318
Yates, Andrea 297-304, 309, 439
Yates, Paula 147
Yearwood, Trisha 53
yin and yang.................................. 55
Young, Cathy....... .35, 44, 54, 72, 134, 139, 154, 183, 199, 248, 265, 273, 291, 330, 377, 423
Young, Jane 118, 138
Young, Katharine K..................... 132
Young, Leroy................................. 86
zero tolerance................................ 78
Zero-Empathy-Toward-Men rule... 14, 37, 53, 78, 95, 106, 145, 147, 200, 276, 290, 335
Zumwalt, Admiral Elmo 280

www.ingramcontent.com/pod-product-compliance
Lightning Source LLC
Chambersburg PA
CBHW031641170426
43195CB00035B/148